Studies in Hellenistic Religions

Studies in Hellenistic Religions

Luther H. Martin

Selected and Edited with an Introduction by
Panayotis Pachis

CASCADE *Books* · Eugene, Oregon

STUDIES IN HELLENISTIC RELIGIONS

Copyright © 2018 Luther H. Martin. All rights reserved. Except for brief quotations in critical publications or reviews, no part of this book may be reproduced in any manner without prior written permission from the publisher. Write: Permissions, Wipf and Stock Publishers, 199 W. 8th Ave., Suite 3, Eugene, OR 97401.

Cascade Books
An Imprint of Wipf and Stock Publishers
199 W. 8th Ave., Suite 3
Eugene, OR 97401

www.wipfandstock.com

PAPERBACK ISBN: 978-1-4982-8308-3
HARDCOVER ISBN: 978-1-4982-8310-6
EBOOK ISBN: 978-1-4982-8309-0

Cataloguing-in-Publication data:

Names: Martin, Luther H., 1937-, author | Pachis, Panayotis, editor.

Title: Studies in hellenistic religions / Luther H. Martin ; selected and edited with an introduction by Panayotis Pachis.

Description: Eugene, OR: | Includes bibliographical references and index.

Identifiers: ISBN: 978-1-4982-8308-3 (paperback) | ISBN: 978-1-4982-8310-6 (hardcover) | ISBN: 978-1-4982-8309-0 (ebook).

Subjects: LCSH: Religion—History | Hellenism | Mediterranean religion—History—To 476.

Classification: BL722 M335 (print) | BL722 (ebook).

Manufactured in the U.S.A.   FEBRUARY 22, 2018

Scripture quotations come from the Revised Standard Version of the Bible, copyright © 1946, 1952, and 1971 National Council of the Churches of Christ in the United States of America. Used by permission. All rights reserved worldwide.

Contents

Preface | vii
Acknowledgments | xiii
Abbreviations | xvi

Introduction: General Characteristics of the Hellenistic Era / Panayotis Pachis | 1

PART 1: THE GRAECO-ROMAN RELIGIOUS WORLD

1. Greek and Roman Philosophy and Religion | 35
2. The Very Idea of Globalization: The Case of Hellenistic Empire | 64
3. Fate, Futurity, and Historical Consciousness in Western Antiquity | 79
4. Why Cecropian Minerva? Hellenistic Religious Syncretism as System | 97
5. Kingship and the Consolidation of Religiopolitical Power during the Hellenistic Period | 113
6. Biology, Sociology, and the Study of Religion: Two Lectures | 124

PART 2: ORACULAR DREAMING

7. Religion and Dream Theory in Late Antiquity | 143
8. Prayer in Graeco-Roman Religions | 151
9. Petitionary Prayer in the Graeco-Roman World: Comparison, Consequences, Cognition, and a few Conclusions | 156

PART 3: GRAECO-ROMAN MYSTERIES

10. Imagistic Traditions in the Graeco-Roman World | 171
11. Those Elusive Eleusinian Mystery Shows | 181
12. Greek Goddesses and Grain: The Sicilian Connection | 196
13. History, Cognitive Science, and the Problematic Study of Folk Religions: The Case of the Eleusinian Mysteries of Demeter | 210

14. Mithras, *Milites* and Bovine Legs: A Response to Aleš Chalupa and Tomáš Glomb, "The Third Symbol of the *Miles* Grade on the Floor Mosaic of the Felicissimus Mithraeum in Ostia: A New Interpretation" | 230
15. "Star Talk": Native Competence; Initiatory Comprehension | 236
16. When Size Matters: Social Formations in the Graeco-Roman World | 246

PART 4: HELLENISTIC JUDAISM AND CHRISTIANITY

17. Josephus's use of Heimarmenē in the *Jewish Antiquities* 8.171–173 | 263
18. Gods or Ambassadors of God? Barnabas and Paul in Lystra | 274
19. The Hellenisation of Judaeo-Christian Faith or the Christianisation of Hellenic Thought? | 281
20. The *Encyclopedia Hellenistica* and Christian Origins | 299
21. Past Minds: Evolution, Cognition, and Biblical Studies | 309

PART 5: GNOSTICISM

22. Genealogy and Sociology in the *Apocalypse of Adam* | 323
23. Technologies of the Self and Self-Knowledge in the Syrian Thomas Tradition | 338
24. Self and Power in the Thought of Plotinus | 349

Index | 361

Preface

WHEN I BEGAN THE study of Hellenistic religions in the early 1980s, the heterogeneity of Mediterranean religions initially embraced by the expansive conquests of Alexander the Great was studied largely by New Testament scholars interested in the pagan background against which the inauguration of a new Christian era might be contrasted. Since then, there has been an explosion of interest by historians in these fascinating examples of religious formations and transformations in their own right. The year in which my book *Hellenistic Religions: An Introduction* was published (1987) alone saw the appearance of Walter Burkert's important study of the *Ancient Mystery Cults*,[1] an anthology of texts pertaining to these mysteries,[2] and Robin Lane Fox's magisterial study of *Pagans and Christians*.[3] I am gratified by any contribution that my studies may have made to this rekindled and still vibrant interest among historians of religion.

My approach to the often bewildering array of religious alternatives during the Hellenistic period of religious (in contrast to political) history, the period from Alexander (fourth century BCE) to the antipagan decrees of Emperor Theodosius (end of the fourth century CE), within which the early Christianities are included, was to map their permutations and their transformations, their similarities and their differences, by situating them in relation to the spatial architectures of the emerging Ptolemaic cosmology and that of imperial expanse they all shared and in terms of which their mythic and iconographic expressions more or less explicitly referenced. Although I would most certainly revise and refine any number of my descriptions and conclusions in light of the profusion of more recent research, I believe that the fundamental structure of my understandings of these religions in terms of the spatial representations of the Hellenistic era remains sound. Consequently, the contents of the studies in the present volume remain unchanged apart from the correction of typos and references. Rather than

1. Burkert, *Ancient Mystery Cults*.
2. Meyer, *Mysteries*.
3. Fox, *Pagans*.

altering or adding to the studies of Hellenistic religions that are collected in this volume, I should like to emphasize two additional levels of analysis in which I have suggested that the original spatial framework of my studies might benefit: the communal and the cognitive.

The spatial inferences characteristic of the Hellenistic era, like all representations of past cosmologies, are essentially artificial constructions that have subsequently been abstracted by scholars from the diverse inflections of and reflections by any number of groups and their traditions—schools of philosophers, guilds of astrologers/astronomers, practitioners of religion, all of which populated a stipulated geography over a specified period of time— upon sundry and intertwined issues and problems, differently perceived and variously addressed. Therefore, I began to explore the various kinds of social formations prominent during the Hellenistic era, and the kinds of perceived problems they addressed—whether social, political, economic, intellectual, or some combination of these. I discovered that sociopolitical—including religious—formations during this era could be modeled on the basis of two "ideal types" of social organization: "fictive kinship" (e.g., the community clubs and *collegia* that proliferated during the Hellenistic period) and kingship (the ambitions for the consolidations of power, whether political or religious, during this same period).[4] By identifying the formal structures of any religious system with its expressive productions, we come closer to understanding its diverse social, political, and economic aspects as well.

Despite formal practices of social formation (e.g., initiation rites, tokens of membership, rules of relationship, and so forth), the notion of a "discrete social group" is as much an academic abstraction as is "cosmology," for social groups are characterized by notoriously porous boundaries and exhibit among their distributed membership a diversity of interpretations of their rites and rules. Rather, it is more accurate to consider social groups as a stipulated aggregate of individual minds that share a more or less common set of ideas, beliefs, and practices. Such an approach opens a second complementary level of analysis that addresses questions about how human minds represent religious, social, and cosmological ideas in the first place, how they are transmitted from mind to mind, how and why just certain behaviors are associated with these ideas and representations, how these ideas and behaviors come to be related one to another among a population that shares a common environmental domain in order to constitute what might, in this sense, be termed a particular "culture," and how that "culture"

---

4. See Martin, "Kingship" (chapter 5, this volume); Martin, "Plotinus" (chapter 24, this volume).

is remembered and transmitted in ways that constitute enduring sociopolitical features.

Consequently, I have explored the relevance of the capacities and constraints of human cognition in representing, selecting for, and transmitting just those cosmological ideas and communal structure that we associate with Hellenistic religiosity.[5]

For any community, religious or otherwise, to be judged successful (i.e., to maintain itself transgenerationally), it must encode what it selects and holds to be significant values and knowledge in a way that is memorable, and it must effectively and efficiently transmit that information. The sociopolitical dynamics of any human association are determined, in other words, as much by universal biological and cognitive constraints as by its particularistic social and historical developments. I have recently attempted to illustrate these dimensions of religiosity from the example of the Roman cult of Mithras.[6] The ability comprehensively to outline those mental mechanisms whereby the cosmological and communal representations of the Hellenistic period and, consequently, of the religions of this, and of all eras, are produced and transmitted is a rapidly growing area of research.

The incongruous relationship between Greek assumptions about the ordered structure of the cosmos and widespread Hellenistic concerns with the capricious and unpredictable effects of luck during this same period might suffice to indicate the promises of a cognitive approach to the historiographical issues. If the diverse cultural—literary, philosophical, and religious—thought during the Hellenistic era referenced assumptions of a given, uncreated order expressed in the mathematically precise structures of Ptolemaic cosmology, why then did inhabitants of this era so often represent their existence as fortuitous—as subject to μοῖρα, τύχη, *fortuna*, and εἱμαρμένη?

Hellenistic religiosity is largely concerned with representing luck as a kind of intentional agent—an agentic representation that cognitive scientists of religion have since argued is a necessary (if insufficient) characteristic of social formations that might be deemed "religious".[7] Such representations suggest that the same cognitive templates that predisposed the Greeks and Romans to represent mundane occurrences as the intentional actions of gods and goddesses also predisposed them to personify luck. Such re-representations of nonagentic randomness as intentional agency, e.g., as Τύχη Ἀγαθή or, in the guise of traditional deities, as e.g., Ἶσις Τύχη Ἀγαθή,

5. See Martin, "Cognitive" (chapter 13, this volume).
6. Martin, *Mind*.
7. Boyer, *Religion Explained*.

allowed for an adoption of actions or rituals considered to influence, especially improve, their mundane fortune. This religious re-representation of capricious fortune as benevolent agent aligned the characteristic of luck as random with intellectual presumptions about the predictable character of cosmic order. The ready identification of intentional agency is a developmentally early bias of humans (and other species) that is itself a cognitive requisite for identifying events in the world on the basis of incomplete data and to infer causes from that data efficiently, both by-products of natural selection that would greatly enhance possibilities of survival in a complex world of predation and predators.[8]

The assumptions of the cognitive sciences—that there is no distinction between mind and brain, that the morphology of human brain and the general functions of that morphology have been shaped by evolutionary processes of natural selection and are common to the species *Homo sapiens*, both now and from the distant past—present the possibility that knowledge about the architecture of the human mind currently being researched might provide explanations for why humans have tended to organize themselves in terms of just the nonrandom types of sociopolitical organizations that they have and for why these groups have selected and transmitted just the ideas and behaviors they have, rather than others that were historically possible. Together, an integrated cosmological-communal-cognitive paradigm, such as I have suggested, can be sketched for Hellenistic culture, and presents a comprehensive paradigm by which historians (including historians of religion) might organize their often fragmentary data and draw their historiographical conclusions with greater precision and confidence than might otherwise be the case.

I would like to thank Professor Panayotis Pachis, the editor of this volume, my colleague, my collaborator, and my very good friend, for his continuing interest in my work, and for his invaluable editorial work in producing this volume. I dedicate this volume to him in recognition of his own many important contributions to the academic study of religion generally, and to the study of Graeco-Roman religions in particular, both within his native land of Greece and in the international community of scholars.

References

Boyer, Pascal. *Religion Explained: The Evolutionary Origins of Religious Thought.* New York: Basic Books, 2001.
Burkert, Walter. *Ancient Mystery Cults.* Cambridge: Harvard University Press, 1987.

8. Slone, "Luck Beliefs."

Fox, Robin Lane. *Pagans and Christians*. New York: Knopf, 1987.
Martin, Luther H. "Cognitive Science, Historiography and the Study of So-Called Folk Religions: The Case of the Eleusinian Mysteries of Demeter." *Temenos* 39/40 (2004) 81–100 (chapter 13, this volume).
———. "Kingship and the Consolidation of Religio-Political Power During the Hellenistic Period." *Religio: Revue pro Religionistiku* 8 (2000) 151–69 (chapter 5, this volume).
———. *The Mind of Mithraists: Historical and Cognitive Studies in The Roman Cult of Mithras*. Scientific Studies of Religion: Inquiry and Explanation. London: Bloomsbury, 2015.
———. "Self and Power in the Thought of Plotinus." In *Człowiek i Wartości*, edited by Antoni Komendera et al., 91–99. Kraków: Wydawnictwo Naukowe WSP, 1997 (chapter 24, this volume).
Meyer, Marvin W., ed. *The Ancient Mysteries: A Sourcebook. Sacred Texts of the Mystery Religions of the Ancient Mediterranean World*. New York: Harper & Row, 1987.
Slone, Jason. "Luck Beliefs: A Case of Theological Incorrectness." In *Religion as a Human Capacity: A Festschrift in Honor of E. Thomas Lawson*, edited by Timothy Light and Brian Wilson, 375–94. Studies in the History of Religions 99. Leiden: Brill, 2003.

Acknowledgments

THE AUTHOR AND EDITOR would like to express their gratitude to the publishers and academic journal editors for their permission to reprint the following chapters. Except for minor corrections and updating the references, these articles are reprinted in the original form.

"Greek and Roman Philosophy and Religion." In *The Early Christian World*, edited by Philip F. Esler, 1:53–79. 2 vols. London: Routledge, 2000; a slightly revised version of this article has now been published in the second edition of Esler, *The Early Christian World*, 2017: 48–72.

"The Very Idea of Globalization: The Case of Hellenistic Empire." In *Hellenisation, Empire and Globalisation: Lessons from Antiquity*, edited by Luther H. Martin and Panayotis Pachis, 123–39. Thessaloniki: Vanias, 2004.

"Fate, Futurity, and Historical Consciousness in Western Antiquity." *Historical Reflections/Réflexions Historique* 17/2 (1991) 151–69.

"Why Cecropian Minerva? Hellenistic Religious Syncretism as System." *Numen* 30 (1983) 131–45.

"Kingship and the Consolidation of Religio-Political Power During the Hellenistic Period." *Religio: Revue pro religionistiku* 8/2 (2000) 151–60.

"Biology, Sociology, and the Study of Religion: Two Lectures." *Religio: Revue pro religionistiku* 5/1 (1997) 21–35.

"Religion and Dream Theory in Late Antiquity." In *The Notion of "Religion" in Comparative Research*, edited by Ugo Bianchi, 369–74. Storia delle religioni 8. Rome: "L'erma" di Bretschneider, 1994.

"Prayer in Graeco-Roman Religions" (with Larry J. Alderink). In *Prayer from Alexander to Constantine: A Critical Anthology*, edited by Mark Kiley et al., 123–27. London: Routledge, 1997.

"Imagistic Traditions in the Graeco-Roman World." In *Imagistic Traditions in the Graeco-Roman World: A Cognitive Modeling of History of Religious Research*, edited by Luther H. Martin and Panayotis Pachis, 237–47. Thessaloniki: Vanias, 2009.

"Those Elusive Eleusinian Mystery Shows." *Helios* 13/1 (1986) 17–31.

"Greek Goddesses and Grain: The Sicilian Connection." *Helios* 17/2 (1990) 251–61.

"History, Cognitive Science, and the Problematic Study of Folk Religions: The Case of the Eleusinian Mysteries of Demeter." *Temenos: Nordic Journal of Comparative Religion* 39/40 (2003–2004) 81–99.

"Mithras, *Milites* and Bovine Legs. A Response to Aleš Chalupa and Tomáš Glomb, 'The Third Symbol of the *Miles* Grade on the Floor Mosaic of the Felicissimus Mithraeum in Ostia: A New Interpretation.'" *Religio: Revue pro religionistiku* 21/1 (2013) 49–55.

"'Star Talk': Native Competence; Initiatory Comprehension." *Pantheon: Religioinistický časopis/Journal for the Study of Religions* 7/1 (2012) 59–69.

"When Size Matters: Social Formations in the Graeco-Roman World." In *"The One Who Sows Bountifully": Essays in Honor of Stanley K. Stowers*, edited by Caroline Johnson Hodge et al., 229–41. Providence: Brown Judaic Studies, 2013.

"Josephus's Use of Heimarmenē in the *Jewish Antiquities* XIII, 171–173." *Numen* 28/2 (1981) 127–37.

"Gods or Ambassadors of God? Barnabas and Paul in Lystra." *New Testament Studies* 41/1 (1995) 152–56.

"The Hellenisation of Judaeo-Christian Faith or the Christianisation of Hellenic Thought?" *Religion & Theology* 12/1 (2005) 1–19.

"The *Encyclopedia Hellenistica* and Christian Origins." *Biblical Theology Bulletin* 20/3 (1990) 123–27.

"Past Minds: Evolution, Cognition, and Biblical Studies." In *Mind, Morality, and Magic: Cognitive Science Approaches in Biblical Studies*, edited by István Czachesz and Risto Uro, 15–23. Bible World. Durham: Acumen, 2013.

"Genealogy and Sociology in the Apocalypse of Adam." In *Gnosticism & the Early Christian World: In Honor of James M. Robinson*, edited by James E. Goehring et al., 25–36. Forum Fascicles 2. Sonoma, CA: Polebridge, 1990.

"Identity and Self-Knowledge in the Syrian Thomas Tradition." In *Technologies of the Self: A Seminar with Michel Foucault*, edited by Luther H. Martin et al., 50–63. Amherst: University of Massachusetts Press, 1988.

"Self and Power in the Thought of Plotinus" (Originally published in Polish). In *Czlowiek i Wartosci*, edited by Antoni Komendera et al., 91–99. Kraków: Wydawnictwo Naukowe WSP, 1997.

Unless otherwise noted, all classical sources in all chapters are cited from the editions of the Loeb Classical Library, London: Heinemann; or Cambridge: Harvard University Press.

Abbreviations

ANF	*The Anti-Nicene Fathers*, vol. 2. Fathers of the Second Century. A. Roberts and J. Donaldson, eds. Buffalo: The Christina Literature Company, 1885
CH	*Corpus Hermeneticum*
CIMRM	M. J. Vermaseren, *Corpus Inscriptionum et Monumentorum Religionis Mithriacae*. 2 vols. The Hague: Nijhoff, 1956–1960
EPRO	*Études préliminaires aux religions orientales dans l'Empire romain*
HCS	*Hellenistic Culture and Society*
LCL	Loeb Classical Library
RGRW	*Religions in the Graeco-Roman World*
RSV	Revised Standard Version
SHC	*Studies in Hellenistic Civilization*
SHR	*Studies in the History of Religions* (Numen Supplements)

Introduction

General Characteristics of the Hellenistic Era

Panayotis Pachis

THE HELLENISTIC PERIOD CONSTITUTED a radical era and perhaps a precursor—*mutatis mutandis*—of the modern age. To avoid any misunderstandings, I should mention at this point that this comparison between the two periods may be considered incompatible and misleading as it lacks the assurance of any historical confirmation. This claim is validated, though, if we take into account the variations that occur between a premodern and a modern society. Moreover, the use of the term *modern* in a preindustrial society may seem, according to data of modern sociological research, misplaced.

The term *Hellenistic period* is associated with both the political-economic and the religious system of the period after the death of Alexander the Great. According to J. G. Droysen, who was the first to use this term, and his proponents, the Hellenistic period started right after Alexander's death (323 BCE) and ended with Octavian Augustus. There followed the period of the Roman Empire and the Pax Romana. But according to modern research data, which is free from the partiality and prejudices of the past, this era ended with Theodosius (379–395 CE) and not with Augustus, as the final victory of Christianity marked a milestone for the end of a whole world. Augustus merely performed a political reshuffling of the world, initiating the imperial system, while the conquest of Egypt by Octavian (30 BCE) indicates the transition to a different form of political governance. Therefore, the Hellenistic period should be regarded as a political system that extended from the fourth century BCE to the fourth century CE.

One of the main problems caused by the above definition is that it specifies the exact time limits of this period. The starting point of the Hellenistic era is clear: it started with the death of the Greek commander. The main difficulty lies in determining its end. The opinions on this point differ. To reach a valid conclusion, free of generalizations that usually characterize such research efforts, we should consider the specific time period as a whole. The aforementioned examination method does not only apply to the study of this case, which happens to be a transitional and highly complex era, but also to the study of any historical period. As Luther H. Martin maintains, "historical periods are defined in terms that express all of the cultural values."

Martin's positions on the definition of the Hellenistic period, as well as the study of the phenomenon of syncretism, constitute key research proposals that marked the investigation of specific issues at the end of the twentieth century, although a large number of researchers still embrace the traditional positions. This does not diminish the value of his proposal; on the contrary, it integrates it in the overall spirit of the era, dominated by both tradition and modernity. Pluralism and multidimensionality, especially nowadays, form the most appropriate way worth characterizing any modern scientific research.

All the above can be well understood through Martin's studies, already published since the early 1980s, and especially his monograph *Hellenistic Religions: An Introduction* (1987). In the same year, Walter Burkert's book *Ancient Mystery Cults* was also published. These two books were intended, at least initially, for the North American public. The first was written as an introductory study of the religion and religiosity of the people in the Hellenistic world, while the second is based on four lectures given at Harvard University. Their presentation is made in a period dominated—mainly in Europe—by the methodology of the so-called Italian school, represented by Ugo Bianchi and his students. Their recommendations were based on the historical-comparative methodology and began to dominate the study of these cults from the early 1960s, gradually replacing the dominant positions of the *Religionsgeschichtliche Schule*. Moreover, one should mention here the particular contribution of the studies published in the series titled *Études Preliminaires aux Religions Orientales dans l'Empire Romain*, under the supervision of Maarten J. Vermaseren. Studies of leading scholars on the religions of the Graeco-Roman period have also been published in the series *Aufstieg und Niedergang der Römischen Welt*, while one should not overlook the research proposals in North America by Jonathan Z. Smith, the prominent historian of religions at the University of Chicago.

The innovation of the scientific work of L. H. Martin on the study of the Hellenistic period lies in his revolutionary and groundbreaking proposals based on the data of a sociohistorical methodology that approaches religion as part of a system. Maintaining that merely the research of literary and archaeological sources—the sine qua non for the study of the religions of the ancient world—does not suffice, he approaches this multifaceted era, in which a real transformation of the ancient world takes place, in a comprehensive manner. During this period, every aspect of life is subjected to constant change and transformation: scientific, ethical, and religious. The various parts compose a whole and construct a diverse picture that corresponds to the ecumenical and syncretistic character of the Hellenistic world.

This view is particularly understood in the studies presented in this volume, where emphasis is given to the broadening of the intellectual horizons of contemporary human beings through the constant exploration and curiosity about the discovery of the novel within the context of the universe. This is nicely articulated in Martin's characteristic view, when he argues that

> the designation *enkyklios paideia*—'instruction in the circle of knowledge'—was first used during the Hellenistic period by Pliny the Elder (23/24–79 CE) to describe his *Natural History* [*praef.* 14]. This first Western attempt to compile a complete system of knowledge was followed by other, more specialized, compilations of knowledge: the Egyptian compendia of magical formulae (from the second century BCE to the fifth century CE); the astronomical syllabus of Claudius Ptolemy (c. 140 CE); the religious propaganda of the various mystery traditions (e.g., the second-century-CE romance of Apuleius, popularly known as *The Golden Ass*); the oneiromantic taxonomy of Artemidorus of Ephesos (late second century CE); the second century CE Jewish anthology of Mishna, and that of the Christian Second Testament; the second and third century CE texts collected as the *Corpus Hermeticum*; the alchemical reflections of Zosimos of Panopolis (late third and early fourth century CE). This consolidation of knowledge that began with Pliny and intensified in a second century CE concentration was a characteristic trait of the Hellenistic period. Together these compilations gave expression to the Hellenistic 'circle of knowledge' and, collectively, may be termed the "Encyclopedia Hellenistica."[1]

Martin also mentions that the above correspond to

> Foucault's history of 'discourses,' those "verbal expressions of the mental structures through which man organizes his activities and classifies his perceptions of the world," is theoretically equivalent to the historian Lucien Febvre's inventory of "possibilities of thought" as they are delimited by the "mental horizons

---

1. Martin, "Encylopedia Hellenistica," 300 (Chapter 20, this volume).

of an age." It is these historically specific possibilities of thought that organize what is knowledge in a given age and make up its metaphorical "encyclopedia."[2]

The historical circumstances of that era brought about political and social changes, which allowed the communication between the traditional world of the Greek and Roman society and the world of the East, that is, the area of the unknown, the "Other." This created a new world, an *oecumene*, which was clearly differentiated from what it used to be in the past. As a result, the traditional way of thinking that dominated the Greek space during the classical period ceased to exist. The closed Hellenic-centric system of the city-state gave way to an open society of a cosmopolitan character and universal dimensions. The *Zeitgeist* gives the impression that within the vast empire the collective spirit and the cohesion of the city-state were pushed aside. The traditional social and religious values were partly challenged but not completely eliminated. The ecumenical character, that defined this era, definitely altered the Graeco-Roman world, but did not completely transform it. Its structures remained broadly unchanged until the final victory of Christianity.

The main characteristic of this era was the dissemination of Greek culture in the East, a phenomenon that not only occurred during the sovereignty of Alexander's Successors but continued during the imperial era, despite the fact that this period witnessed the formation of a new, completely novel situation when compared to the previous one. Nevertheless, the Greek culture still prevailed, especially during the second century CE, with the known "Second Sophistic," during which the Greek language became dominant again since its withdrawal a few years earlier. The Greek language and outlook were favored by intellectuals at the expense of the Latin language and Latin way of thinking. This continued after the domination of Christianity, a crucial development that introduced a new way of thinking as it marked the end of the transitional period of the Hellenistic era. In several areas, the new cultural climate prevailed until the seventh century CE. When the areas of the East fell into the hands of the Muslims, the achievements of Greek culture were disseminated to other cultures through their translation into Arabic, marking in this way the definitive end of late antiquity.

The new era brought about sociopolitical changes. The closed limits of the classical Greek city-states began to expand and heralded the Hellenistic cosmopolitanism, without, however, forgetting their cultural superiority over other peoples. Aristotle was the thinker whose teachings created the conditions for the beginning of the Hellenistic era. He is considered to be

2. Ibid., 299–300.

the precursor of all Hellenistic philosophers, who taught, as he did, in a foreign land, free from local prejudices. However, the real driving force of the upcoming new reality was Isocrates (436–338 BCE), who wished to create a new world in which people would live a more flexible life compared to the rigid and Hellenic-centric one of the classical times. All of his views seem to be tailored to the ideals and outlook of the emerging new era. His thinking is radically opposed to the parochial one of Demosthenes, who tenaciously refused to accept the end of an era and the beginning of a new one.

One of the innovations that took place at the beginning of the Hellenistic period was the establishment of new relations among peoples. It was during this era that any idea about the racial superiority of the Greeks against the barbarians—associated with the Hellenic-centric ideals of the classical period—was abolished. Isocrates's pioneering positions caused a real ideological earthquake in the fourth century BCE, as he was considering Greeks all those who partook of Greek education. The contrast between "us," the exponents of culture and harmony, and the "others," the exponents of barbarism and chaos, gave way to universal ideals. It continues, however, to exist during the entire Hellenistic era, especially during the imperial age. The characteristic feature of the "others" does not refer to the relations developed between the inhabitants of the *oecumene*, but to their contrast to the peoples living beyond its limits. The new reality found its ideal expression in the concept of "equality before the law," which dominated Stoic and Cynic thought.

An important factor in the creation of this cultural edifice was the Greek language. The common (*koinē*) Hellenistic language becomes the lingua franca of arts, letters, and trade. It was the language used by various ethnic groups within the boundaries of the *oecumene* in order to communicate with one another, and its use indicated that people shared the Greek ideals. Its importance was particularly evident in the urban centers. The rulers promoted it in various ways while trying to impose it. It was the means that differentiated Greeks from native inhabitants, even in the far Hellenistic East, and later it became the most suitable tool for their interactions. Those who refused to use it lived on the margins of the dominant sociopolitical and spiritual reality of that time. With the passage of time, its unquestionable value was more and more reinforced as it constituted an indispensable means of communication for people who were moving from place to place. Its significance soon became obvious in the field of religion as well, when the "eastern" cults started spreading first in the Greek and later throughout the Graeco-Roman world. The Greek language became a determinative factor for their acceptance by the Greek population.

One of the main effects of this period was the decline of the common and collective ideals of the Greeks, especially those of the Athenians during the classical times. At the beginning of the Hellenistic period, the spirit of individual prosperity and the indifference of citizens for the common had already dominated—which was entirely contrary to Aristotle's principle that man is a social being. The representatives of the various philosophical schools that dominated the intellectual life of the Hellenistic era played a decisive role in this change. However, despite the decline of the traditional way of thinking, especially during the fourth century BCE, many eminent men tried to restore the traditional ideals. Such efforts were made in the cities of mainland Greece—especially in Athens. There, adherence to the past coexisted with the perseverance for renewal. In contrast, the trend for renewal was mainly observed in the Hellenistic kingdoms, where a groundbreaking new reality was created that reflected the spirit and ideals of the time. It was in this environment where the ongoing transformation in the people's outlook was evident, as shown by the adoption of new types of power and the development of cosmopolitanism. The Hellenistic times should be considered a transitional period of continual transformation—a time of increasing knowledge of the physical environment and cosmological redefinition. The whole spirit of this era is epitomized by Ptolemaic cosmology, which began to appear in the second century CE, specifically because the cosmology brought about a reclassification of the dominant worldview.

Cosmopolitanism was another element that characterized the Hellenistic world, a multidimensional urban system associated with specific changes in the sociopolitical structure of the traditional city-state. As a political system, cosmopolitanism was the creation of the Stoics and Cynics and succeeded the policy of racial isolation. The term derives from Zeno of Citium; for a localized resident of Phoenicia, there was no difference between native and nongenuine Greeks. During the Hellenistic era, the limited action and perception of space in the traditional way of thinking gave way to an ecumenical worldview and governance. With the expeditions of Alexander the Great, the traditional Greek city-state was converted into a cosmopolitan city, thus breaking the narrow frames of the Greek sociopolitical reality. The communication between various regions of the *oecumene*, despite the incessant competitive wars of the Successors, became easier than in previous periods. This allowed the Cynic philosopher Telis, for example, who lived in the mid-third century BCE, to declare that, as he could move around without any difficulty, he felt that he was a citizen of an *oecumene* without borders. This new situation enabled more and more Greeks to immigrate to the East for various reasons, primarily economic, who thus mingled with the native populations of the East.

This is directly related with a major problem that has been of concern to scholars since the time of Droysen and refers to the shaping of the world during the Hellenistic period. Previous researchers had shared the views of the German scholar, influenced by the nineteenth-century worldview, that were based on a clear separation between the worlds of the East and West. On the contrary, contemporary research is mainly based on the concept of "acculturation." According to H.-J. Gehrke, there is no full reconciliation of the two worlds during this historical period but mere coexistence with interactions. This is more understandable in areas with a particular cultural tradition. The Greek culture, adapted of course to the times, dominated the East and especially some specific places in that area. A typical example is the city of Ai-Khanoum (Alexandria Oxeiana) in Afghanistan. In other cases, however, there were strong reactions to the new reality within the newly formed Hellenistic kingdoms. This situation became even more intense during Roman rule.

All the above allow us to understand that the barriers within the classical era ceased to exist and a new reality was established. Societies characterized by a "centrifugal"—as opposed to "centripetal"—character developed because of their potential and openness. People moved endlessly into the unknown, often ignoring the dangers and changes and aiming to reach the limits of the world. The world of the Hellenistic period was characterized by the constant movement of people, who did not feel bound to a particular place or have special links with their ancestral gods and the traditional sociopolitical environment. They literally renounced their old selves, fleeing their ancestral homes in order to give new meaning to their lives, which became increasingly difficult—especially from the end of the classical period. This created new conditions for the Greek population, which was historically used to moving to different areas around the ancient world. The special ability given to individuals of this time to travel from place to place, without the constraints of the past, further contributed to the intensification of this phenomenon. Foreigners were invading the cities of the Hellenistic period. For example, the important commercial center of Piraeus was a constant pole of attraction for all sorts of guests, which gave a cosmopolitan feel to the main Athenian seaport. Greek movement was related to commercial pursuits and colonial activities. The establishment of Greek colonies in the Hellenic period brought to the fore feelings of homesickness. However, this tie to the homeland appeared to become less important during the Hellenistic period. Although the new inhabitants of the Hellenistic East carried many ancestral habits to their new homes, they were nevertheless influenced by the political, social, cultural, legal, and religious characteristics of their new environment in the Hellenistic monarchies; they came to care more about their new homes than about their homeland. The second-generation colonial residents better understood this, and further underlined the principle of self-sufficiency that characterized the lives of people in this era. The only element reminiscent of their origin was the Greek language, common to all, as well as their identification as Greeks.

The ideal of fraternity among people was the second feature of the Hellenistic period, particularly highlighted by Alexander the Great. Authors of the time pointed to the Alexander's personal interest in values that would further strengthen ties between citizens of the new state. His principal concern was to create a state of universal dimensions, in which all people could coexist without the traditional prevailing discriminations. Plutarch, in *On Alexander's Fortune, or Virtue* (Περὶ τῆς Ἀλεξάνδρου τύχης ἢ ἀρετῆς), reported that Alexander issued a decree calling people to consider the whole world their homeland (I 329 C–D). These ideas are further reinforced by intermarriages between Macedonians and Asians. Additionally, Alexander was the first to set an example, marrying eastern princesses, thus further strengthening the ties between the two worlds. His ambitious unifying effort stopped immediately after his death, which was followed by a fierce competition among the Successors; this battle contributed to the prevalence of multilateralism, which replaced the unified form of the state. The heterogeneity of this age was also reflected in governance. Even then, however, universal and cosmopolitan ideals still remained. What Alexander the Great envisioned and realized, even for a short period, was finally established with the vast Roman Empire under Augustus and with the dominance of the Pax Romana.

Nonetheless, the harmonious coexistence of different peoples in the new states was disturbed in many occasions. Quite often the new monarchies that arose after the death of Alexander the Great demonstrated strong reactions to the presence of Greek settlers. This occurred mainly in places with great cultural heritage since the natives believed that the presence of Greek culture and institutions did not enhance their cultures but, on the contrary, constituted an insult to their long-established traditions. Their responses varied: sometimes they remained indifferent and thus cut off from the new reality whereas in other cases they reacted against the Greeks in various ways.

Such reactions were not observed in the large urban centers, where the heterogeneous populations coexisted harmoniously. Indigenous people, mainly the members of local aristocracy, embraced with great eagerness the spirit of Greek culture as well as the radical tendencies of the time. All those contributed to the development of a dialectical and oppositional relationship between the population in urban centers ("center") and rural areas ("periphery") in the Hellenistic kingdoms; this oppositional relationship constituted one of the dominant features of the era.

An equally important factor, which further enhanced the communication between peoples and shaped the cultural life of the era, was the establishment of new cities already from the early years of Alexander's expeditions. Alexandria, Ptolemais, and Antioch were founded during this period. Without underestimating the importance and value of other Hellenistic cities, it is worth mentioning at this point the special status of Alexandria, which was founded in 323 BCE by Alexander the Great and became the new capital of the state in 320/319 BCE under Ptolemy I, the Savior.

The development of urban centers gave greater impetus to the trends that characterized this period. New cities were built according to the traditional Greek models, and Greek settlers felt that they were living in a quite familiar environment. But despite their Greek background, it is clear that the structure of the Hellenistic cities was suited to the needs of the new era. Thus, during this period, new urban planning and design trends were developed, which enabled cities to accommodate many visitors. The buildings were distinguished by their enormous dimensions and had a totally different form from the traditional expression of moderation and harmony in the classical period. The same applies to sculpture and art, which in the Hellenistic era was characterized by an extreme sense of passion and a tendency towards the vast and the sophisticated.

In the meantime, another innovation arose with the establishment of new Hellenistic urban centers. Traditionally, cities had legitimized their social and political status with a hero whom they considered to be the founder of both the city and the whole community. Given the new global reality, however, this perception shifted. Beginning in the Hellenistic period, the establishment of an ecumenical polity could no longer be attributed to a local hero. Rather, local founders were supplanted by the mortal rulers of empires, who were eventually deified and who entered, thereby, the world of myth and the divine. Through the exercise of their political propaganda, these founders of ecumenical states came to offer salvation their residents. These rulers exercised power that allowed them to enter the world of myth and the divine realm through political propaganda.

The Successors cared for cultivating the arts and letters in their environment, thus the Hellenistic cities were developed into important cultural centers. Each one of them ensured their personal supremacy as a means of domination in the constant competition that developed among the rulers of the Hellenistic monarchies. Making impressions, especially at such times, was the best ally in the effort of those who sought by any means to increase their personal glory and, mainly, their power. Meanwhile, the ongoing support and interest of the leaders in the religious and artistic trends of the time may be attributed to the influence of the dominant philosophical perceptions of this period. According to the views of the Stoic philosophers, who followed the Platonic tradition, kings must have an inclination for spiritual pursuits. A ruler must be distinguished for his wisdom and care for the development of the cultural life of his city. In this way rulers enhanced their personal prestige while simultaneously legitimizing their power. For this reason, they promoted dissemination of arts and letters and provided for the creation of intellectual circles in the environment of their direct jurisdiction. Moreover, they knew that the views of authors bore great strength and constituted a means of influencing readers. Not only did knowledge contribute to the cultural rehabilitation of individuals, but knowledge was also a means that contributed to a ruler's social recognition and a power increase. Knowledge helped individuals achieve social development and recognition within their surroundings more easily. Many times this recognition as well as the successful exploitation of certain circumstances led to their participation in central decision-making, and they became actors who shaped daily life and activity. Besides, the leaders of this era needed their help to a great extent. All those created a network of relations that constituted another special feature of everyday life in Hellenistic kingdoms, and later on in the Roman Empire. A typical example of this may be Demetrius Falireas, especially during his stay in Alexandria, under the patronage of Ptolemy the Savior. His views affected the ruler of Egypt so much that during his reign the city developed culturally to a much greater degree than the rest of Ptolemaic Egypt. Other examples are the poets of the time of Octavian Augustus, who are the best-known exponents of the spirit of this new era.

The beginning of the Hellenistic period also saw the emergence of a new reality for traditional political status: the monarchy became the dominant political power system. "This type of social organization," according to Martin, "could be understood as extensions and variations of a 'kinship'." As he adds,

> whereas the πόλεις were highly centralized organizations of 'tribes' (φυλαί) and smaller kinship groups such as φρατρίες and δῆμοι, the ἔθνη preserved some measure of local autonomy and identity. Both of these types of socio-political organizations established a collective identity based upon an extended social homogeneity. [. . .] It is upon such claims to inclusive kinship that extra familiar policies were constructed and by which the early kinship organization became subordinated to larger political entities. Monarchs typically attempted to appropriate the

ideological values of kinship alliances in support of imperial allegiance and stability. Such values of universal kinship were attributed to Alexander himself.[3]

Its establishment as the dominant political system of the universal state, initially of the Successors and later of the Roman emperors, was directly linked to the sovereignty that characterized those in power. The same factors also shaped the nature of the sociopolitical reality of the whole Hellenistic era. The cult of rulers emerged within and came to dominate the Hellenistic world, introducing new habits that radically altered the expression and thinking of the Greek world in daily (and religious) life. The institution of deified rulers of the Hellenistic kingdoms found its perfect expression in the cult of the emperor in Rome of the imperial times, which became an integral part of state power and state organization. The practice of deification continued during late antiquity. In this new era of despotism, the emperor was the only recipient of divine values and the main subject of the worship events. All this eventually resulted in the absolute centralization of power in the figure of the emperor.

The individual efforts of people played an important role in Hellenistic societies. For the first time people felt released from traditional, local, and tribal predispositions. Individual initiative to explore the unknown reached its peak during this period, but not at no cost. The constant alternation of events and situations increased the feeling of uncertainty; everything was volatile and unpredictable. The measure and harmony of classical collective life gave way to the feeling of enormity and immensity that dominated all areas of the sociopolitical reality. From the organized social and religious life of the city-state, people entered into a world of limitless freedom, constant changes, and continuous wandering. The laws of the ancestral environment, which dictated living according to the rules of the tribe and the city-state, no longer played a decisive role. Thus, by escaping from the traditional way of life, Hellenistic people were faced with a constantly changing world whose main features were unlimited freedom and the continual blending of incessantly wandering people. Nevertheless, all these new quests and the travels into the unknown brought about feelings of uncertainty and despair. The corollary of all the above is found in texts of that time in which terms such as ἐπιθυμεῖν ("wish") στενάζειν ("moan"), and ποθεῖν ("desire") prevail. As a result of these changes, citizens no longer felt the confidence of the closed city-state, which led to their constant traveling, often without any particular destination. Additionally, they felt a crisis of freedom, and for this reason understood themselves as ἄπολις.

3. Martin, "Kingship," 116–17 (Chapter 5, this volume).

Although the Hellenistic era offered great potential for personal recognition, at the same time it became more than clear that control of the social-political situation did not lie with the individual. The citizen no longer had special power. Decisions were made by the few who rendered their absolute power immediately apparent. The people of this era were becoming increasingly passive with respect to participation in social and political affairs. Such a passive attitude pervaded every field of human activity in the Hellenistic period and brought people closer to religious perceptions, mainly of eastern origin.

The situation became even more tragic at the beginning of the imperial age. The imposition of the Pax Romana and the coexistence of many peoples under Roman authority, besides the positive effects that it brought about, actually aggravated people's lives to a greater extent. This was a time during which the individuals felt that they were part of the broader cosmic firmament that extended beyond the measures of worldly reality, and for this reason they felt that they were ruled by powerful and unpredictable forces. The bigger the size of the state, the more prevalent the above conceptions became, which were associated with the dominance of the demonic elements, especially in the provinces of the vast Roman Empire. Their inhabitants felt at the mercy of the unpredictable and ravenous moods of the local government officials and, above all, at the mercy of the imperial power. The final victory of the Romans and the imposition of the so-called Pax Romana decisively influenced the way of thinking and expression. Aelius Aristides gave us a clear picture of the new political reality when he stated that the entire empire now looks like one city. The vision of Alexander the Great finally found its perfect expression. Concepts such as Peace (Εἰρήνη) and Concord (Ὁμόνοια) were even more accentuated during this period. This contributed to the particular personification of abstract concepts, which were primarily intended to highlight the achievement of the ideal political situation. Furthermore, the whole reformation program of Augustus aimed at realizing a new society that emphasized traditional values (*mos maiorum*). The emperor was the ultimate carrier and exponent of all these trends during the Roman Empire.

Uncertainty about the future created the perception that everyday life was affected by eternal and incomprehensible forces. People reacted fatalistically and passively to such forces. Magic practices increasingly dominated the whole Hellenistic era. Wandering priests of various cults, mainly of eastern origin, and representatives of philosophical schools complemented the whole situation. The more novel the ideas, the more attractive they seemed, as they offered a wide range of options in order to overcome all daily problems. This period witnessed the formulation of a multitude of ideas and philosophical concepts that affected the spirit of the era, but that were also affected by it. The thought of Plato and Aristotle continued to dominate along with other philosophical worldviews. Among them, those of the Stoics, Epicureans, and Cynics held a dominant position.

The fundamental concepts that greatly affected the daily life and human relationships were friendship, gentleness, charity, and egalitarianism. Posidonius and Panaetius of Rhodes related charity to power, maintaining that only in this way may power find its ideal form of legitimacy. Egalitarian ideals decisively influenced critical thinking and ways of life. This influeence was evident mainly in a loss of interest in tackling mundane problems: the theoretical life prevailed against the practical. Posidonius and Panaetius thought that mundane activities contributed to a tarnishing of the ideal life that should be pursued by all. In this way, the individual was transformed into an ideal citizen. Moreover, the teachings of the Stoics (notably Zeno) about finding an ideal place without disputes and prejudices about coexistence were a key differentiating factor in the social thought of the time. This can be clearly seen in the widespread obsession to find an environment in which all these ideas would shape the daily routine and the established order. The search for a better world often turned into an unrealistic goal and permeated the dominating mentality. Many writers of the time contributed to this mentality; dominant among them was Euhemerus of Messene, who in his work described the search for the fictional island of Panchaea.

The Hellenistic world was distinguished by a "mental flexibility" that increasingly facilitated the conversion of people of the time to new cults and novel concepts. The more flexible the moods of people toward the divine world, the easier became the worship of abstract concepts, such as Wealth, Peace, Friendship, and Victory. The above trend contributed to the domination of the abstract concept of Fortune, which the Greeks deified as Σώτειρα Τύχη and the Romans as Fortuna. Everything was under the relentless power of the blind and uncontrollable goddess Tychē; contingencies and strange phenomena were an everyday routine. It was normal for everyone to believe that they were under the tyranny of Tychē. None of the traditional gods could protect them. Such perceptions were reinforced by the teachings of the authors of this period. Examples of those trends can be found in the work of Demetrius Phalireas *About Tychē* (Περὶ Τύχης). Often, Tychē simply constituted an acknowledgment of the uncertainties involved in human affairs. After the conquests of Alexander the Great and the ensuing changes at the geopolitical scene, the concept of the unforeseen Tychē became even broader, decisively influencing the people's lives; nothing was certain and stable anymore in this vast world. Tychē was always distinguished by her unpredictable intervention in the lives of people and the flow of history, and this was the reason she was characterized in the inscriptions as "blind Fortune." The people of the Hellenistic era had surrendered the social dimension of their identity while the lack of political and economic stability increasingly reinforced their uncertainty. The blasphemies against Tychē in many funerary inscriptions showed that, like Fate, she was often identified with the unpredictable and unavoidable death.

But alongside the negative aspect of Tychē, there was the positive one as well. People never stopped hoping that the bad and unpredictable moments in their lives would end and favorable ones would follow. For this reason, the goddess was also considered to have a well-intentioned and helpful character that complemented her ill-tempered nature. In this case she is characterized as ἀγαθή. Her positive side is connected with the worship of the protecting deities of Hellenistic cities (Τύχη Πόλεως). It is highly likely that this was a cult that intended to placate all the unpredictable effects of her alter ego. City leaders were well aware of the devastating effects that could arise for cities and their residents. She was usually depicted bearing a castellated crown and holding the cornucopia. Abundance, wealth, and happiness constituted the main gifts she offered to each city; therefore, this form of her was associated with the worship of the Agathodaimon.

Tychē held a leading role in the teachings of all philosophical schools of this period. What seemed to dominate were the views of the Stoics and Cynics who spoke of the overwhelming effects of Necessity and Fate (Εἱμαρμένη) in people's lives. As counterbalance to this situation, there developed, especially in the teachings of the Stoic philosophers, the concept of Providence. According to the law of cosmic sympathy, which prevailed in the Stoic teachings, a direct relationship existed between the macrocosm and the microcosm. Posidonius (ca. 135–50 BCE), loyal to the principles of the Stoics, argued that the volatility of human life was decidedly determined by the stars and by Εἱμαρμένη. Stoics also believed that the divine providence acted in a similar way and undoubtedly influenced the religious beliefs of this era. During late antiquity, the influence of Εἱμαρμένη constituted the dominant factor in the antisecular worldview of Gnosticism as well as the quintessential difference between Gnosticism and other cults of the Hellenistic period.

The original meaning of Tychē began to change in the environment of the new cults coming from the East. She was defined no longer by her usual ill-tempered nature but by benevolence, and as an ἐπήκοος (a hearing god). She was also called Πανθέα and was associated, just like most deities of this period (for example, Isis/S(e)arapis with the henotheism of imperial times. The importance of the unforeseeable goddess and the concept of Εἱμαρμένη found particular resonance in the area of the astrological concepts of this period.

Astrology was one of the dominant expressions of religiosity in the Hellenistic period. Tychē or Εἱμαρμένη contributed to its particular development in the third century BCE, especially in Egypt, and was directly related to the development of scientific cosmology during this era. The context of the Hellenistic world was described by the Ptolemaic cosmology, the first comprehensive scientific view of the world. Claudius Ptolemy based his theories on concepts expressed in previous times by the Babylonian, Persian, Egyptian, and Greek sages. The encounter and amalgamation of the two worlds created a new perception of the universe; the Ptolemaic cosmology described a geocentric system according to which seven successive globes or planets rotated around the earth. Although various theories about the order of the planets were proposed, the commonest one was the following: the moon (which according to the geocentric system was considered to be a planet); Mercury, Venus, the sun (like the moon also regarded as a planet), Mars, Jupiter, and Saturn. This system was based on the theories of Eudoxus of Cnidus (ca. 390–340 BCE), who described the motion of celestial bodies as concentric circles around different axes. This view is radically opposed to the static worldview of traditional ancient cosmology. People began to pay particular attention to the movement of the stars, which became particularly important in the context of popular religiosity. The stars, especially the coupling of planets, revealed the presence of great and prominent men on earth. The astral perceptions were put in the service of political interests of this period.

These sociopolitical rearrangements did not leave unaffected the religion of the Olympian pantheon, which constituted the main expression of the ancient Greek city-state. Due to the adverse social, political, and religious conditions, the third century BCE could be characterized as the period of the second great crisis of traditional ancient Greek religion. Many traditional forms were disputed and rejected, while chroniclers of the time attest that this reversal shook many fundamental values of religious faith in particular and ancient of Greek life in general. This caused a spirit of confusion among the people, who had lived until then in accordance with the norms of traditional religion. The principle of χρῆσθαι θεοίς κατὰ τὰ πάτρια (worshiping the gods according the ancestral customs), which was a regulatory factor of the traditional religious expression, was increasingly questioned.

Despite the difficulties of the time, ancestral gods persisted. Some, such as Demeter, enjoyed general acceptance among worshipers, even in times of crisis and doubt: this is demonstrated by the multitude of offerings and tributes in her honor. Oracles also ranked high in the preference of the faithful and so did the cults of some hearing gods. More specifically, from the fourth century BCE onward, a very important position among them was held by the cult of Asclepius. The habit of incubation (ἐγκοίμησις/*incubatio*) in the sanctuaries of the god flourished during the whole Hellenistic era.

Religion flourished at this time. The traditional religious expression, despite the attacks it accepted, continued to be the mainstay for a large part of the population and especially for those who continued to live in their ancestral homelands. Many times it functioned as a means for surpassing the current adverse situation and returning to past glory and grandeur. A typical example is the effort of Lycurgus, who, when he took the power in Athens (330 BCE), sought to address the disorderly situation in the city with reforms inspired by ancestral traditions. At the same time, however, there also appeared new religious cults especially from the East, which complemented the overall picture of people's religiosity. These cults were initially considered strange but over time became accepted and influenced people's lives. Their acceptance was distinguished by a particular ambiguity: these religious ideas were also influenced by the Greek way of approaching religious worship. Receptivity and adaptability played a decisive role for their establishment, originally in the Greek and later in the broader environment of the Graeco-Roman world.

Alongside traditional religion was an increasing domination of new cults in Greece and other parts of the wider *oecumene*. This period attests to the dissemination of many "cults of eastern origin," which were associated with the Greek language, the scientific and astronomical ecumenism, the political and ecumenical worldview of the Successors and later Roman emperors, and especially with the movement and constant migration of people from the one part of the world to the other. Those include the worship of Isis and S(e)arapis, Cybele and Attis, Adonis, and the Anatolian god Men. These cults, attractive and impressive compared to the traditional religion of the ancient Greek world, offered special experiences to the people of this era with luxurious rituals, ascetic trials, and complex rules of ritual purification. On many occasions, the new concepts were based on preexisting traditional views. In this direction, the influence of the so-called *interpretatio Graeca* played a vital role. The religions of the Mediterranean area, designated as "national," were known for their strict adherence to tradition, and therefore a foreign cult or an entire religious system could be accepted only after being purified through the filter of the *interpretatio*.

This became even more intense after the conquest of Egypt, the last bulwark against the Hellenistic world, in 31 BCE by Octavian Augustus. The beginning of the so-called imperial age and the prevalence of the Pax

Romana set new standards for the free movement of different groups, commercial goods, and also religious and cultural beliefs from one part of the vast empire to another. Augustus's main objective was to make the empire a single sociopolitical entity. The polymerization of the Hellenistic kingdoms gave way to the vast and unified space of the Roman Empire. Those moving around the most were people in the service of imperial power (soldiers, officials, state administrators of the Roman Empire), merchants, travelers (e.g., Pausanias), priests of various eastern cults (e.g., priests of the Great Mother, of the Syrian goddess), magicians, and philosophers (e.g., the Cynics).

Due to the great Roman conquests, from the second century BCE onwards, there was an increase in the movement of slaves, foreign citizens, teachers, philosophers, and traders within the vast Roman territory. All were moving—freely or against their will—incessantly in a state that was constantly transformed, likely feeling as prisoners of Fortune. Within this world of doubt, controversy, and discontent, all "eastern cults" found suitable ground for their dissemination. Of particular preference were the cults of Isis-S(e)arapis, Cybele-Attis, Mithras, and Jupiter Dolichenus. Propagation of such ideas started on the Italian peninsula and then in other places of the Roman Empire, mainly through the major ports, such as those of Ostia and Puteoli. Eastern cults became particularly popular in this area, since the suspicion of citizens gradually decreased mainly because the cults afforded a cosmopolitan character. The adherents of the so-called eastern cults came mainly from the ranks of slaves and freedmen, while one may observe at the inscriptions a lack of faithful among the members of the aristocracy, who maintained a particularly cautious attitude already from the beginning of the appearance of those foreign cults.

The surprise caused by the penetration of new cults and deities in the religious environment to Greeks, and later to conservative Romans, was succeeded by fear and hesitation. Official traditional religion (*religio*) was clearly distinguished from foreign religious perceptions (*superstitiones*). The latter were regarded dangerous for the harmony and greatness of the state, which was created by the victorious struggles against nations and with the full support and goodwill of the ancestral gods. The terms *sacra peregrina* and *sacra publica* constituted a crucial distinction in the devotional life of the Romans. But the initial resistance was gradually reduced during the first imperial period with the consolidation of Roman rule across the then-known world. From a simple urban center (*Urbs*), Rome was transformed into a global ruling city (*Orbis*).

During the imperial times, the agents of dissemination and propaganda of all foreign cults were not only the residents of the East who moved around in the Empire, but also the Roman soldiers, who during their stay in the East became acquainted with and eventually adhered to those cults. A typical example is the cult of Mithras, with the vast majority of followers found among the ranks of the Roman army. The prevalence of the Pax Romana and the domination of the common Hellenistic language throughout the empire were two additional factors that accommodated the spread of foreign cults.

From the early adoption stages, followers of most religious groups took special care to use the Greek and then the Latin language in their rituals. The complete adoption of the Greek language, particularly during late antiquity—in the so-called Second Sophistic period—was one of the most effective strategies to be followed by adherents of these cults. This virtually permitted a smooth movement and communication of people and ideas in an era characterized by a universal spirit.

The acceptance of a foreign cult was possible only if it provided the absolute assurance that it posed no risk to the destabilization of the city. This condition became even more imperative in Rome. This was the capital of the state and should therefore be protected against anything that could threaten its glory and grandeur. The same practice was followed later on, when the penetration and establishment of foreign cults in the Roman environment was easier. The followers of new cults were forced to show on a daily basis, during the performance of their religious duties, their submission to those practices that guaranteed the stability and happiness of the Roman state. Maintaining this attitude became even more imperative for the adherents of foreign cults in subsequent times (especially after the third century CE), when the idea that imperial authority was absolute and divine became even more prevalent. The same spirit of subordination and adaptation to the standards of the Roman state characterized the cult of Mithras, which according to R. Merkelbach, reveals the spirit of loyalty to the Roman state power.

Prescribing the connection of the state and the cult can be seen as a kind of defense, given the marginal position of the cults in relation to the official state religion. We should not of course overlook the fact that the usual practice of the members of these communities towards the representatives of the Roman power was one of conformism. It is worth mentioning here that modern research maintains that most of these cults were fully integrated over time in Roman society and actually became integral parts of the broader collective socioreligious life. On the contrary, the negative attitude of various groups of adherents toward Roman authorities—expressed primarily by rejecting the emperor's divinity—had negative repercussions on their living conditions and their acceptance into the imperial environment.

This was also the case with Christian, Gnostic, and Manichaean communities during late antiquity.

Most of the new cults were influenced by the Greek culture, thus developing a new form that was a product of syncretism. This is evident in the works of most scholars of this specific historical period, who characterize it as a "time of syncretism." This is a concept that causes—even nowadays—various reactions (both positive and negative) depending on the adopted viewpoints. The term *syncretism* was the creation of modern theoretical thought in order to address and describe—according to the data of a usually apologetic tactic—the conditions or trends of a particular era. Luther Martin's specific approach to syncretistic changes constitutes one of the most innovative aspects of his research. This specific approach to syncretism changes, particularly in Martin's work, constituting one of the most innovative aspects of his research. This is apparent in his view that "syncretism is the most characteristic phenomenon that prevails upon religions and cults of the Hellenistic era . . . Hellenistic religious syncretism may best point to coherent patterns of relationships that must be described in their systemic particulars, rather than a cultural mixture born of historical happenstance."[4] Syncretism develops whenever a society is going through historical periods characterized as "periods of crisis" because of certain circumstances and constant changes. When foreign cultures and traditions come into contact with each other, new religious phenomena arise. In the development of such new forms, the elements of the local tradition usually prevail. Any kind of comparison between deities from various cultures should always be based on analogy, and analogy on proportion. The concept of proportion, in accordance with the basic principles of historical-religious methodology, was based primarily on the principles of synchronic and diachronic comparison, and it is achieved when comparing two phenomena on the basis not only of their similarities but mainly of their differences. In this way, and by taking into consideration the specificity of the cultural environment from which the compared concepts are derived, we may obtain a more complete and comprehensive picture of the subject or ideas under study.

The syncretistic spirit of the time may find matches in the Ptolemaic worldview, which prevailed from the second century CE. The last book of Apuleius's *Metamorphoses* is the best example of syncretism in this time. The identification of Isis with other deities should be understood as a compilation of disparate concepts in the face of a special deity (that is, Isis), who is still depicted as dominating Tychē. For Plutarch, syncretism is considered to be a concrete system of relations, which is defined by similarities and

---

4. Martin, *Hellenistic Religions*, 10–11.

organized on the basis of a relation of sympathy (similarities) and nonsympathy (differences).

Of the cults invading the space of the Roman world, it is worth concentrating mainly on the "mystery cults." Initiation was the major difference in relation to the previous category of ceremonies—that is, Roman state cults. Through initiation ἐποπτεία was achieved, which led to mystic beatitude and, eventually, to both worldly and posthumous salvation. Thus, the adherent acquired a feeling of absolute security and bliss that made him different from the rest of the population. The Mysteries of Eleusis, the Kabeiroi on Samothtrace, and the cult of Mithras were considered to be typical mystery cults. The rites of Eleusis took place only at the Telesterion of Eleusis, which was regarded as the quintessential religious sanctuary. Even during the Hellenistic era, it preserved its ritual particularity, which was strictly linked to its local character. Conversely, the Mithraic worship, as a true creation of the ecumenical era, produced numerous temples (*Mithraia*) throughout the Roman Empire. The worship of Isis/S(e)arapis and Cybele/Attis took a different form, distinguished by their external and public rituals, which were shaped in the regions where their worship was spread during this period. After their dissemination in the Greek area, they were influenced by the rituals of the Eleusinian mysteries (between the first century BCE and the first century CE.

The initiation ceremonies of these cults contributed to the creation of a special affinity between the adherent and the celebrated gods. This practice found its ideal form of application in the legal practice of adoption. The devotees stopped having any contact with the traditional family and tribal environment, and created within the frame of these groups new family ties, which were radically different. The practice of "adoption" of a foreigner in order for them to enter the environment of a social group was commonplace in the ancient Greek and Roman law. Once again, the traditional notions of the Graeco-Roman world decisively influenced the formation of these peculiar social groups of this era. The concept of the founder of traditional societies of the time was conveyed into the environment of these groups. The ceremony of initiation, which constituted the culmination of all rituals, contributed to the great transformation of the followers and their transition into a new reality.

The trends of this transitional period led modern research into generalizations that rather obfuscated the particular character of the Hellenistic period than led to correct scientific conclusions. Main exponents of these trends were the researchers of the nineteenth century, who argued that the Hellenistic era was distinguished by its individualism. We need, however, to examine a historical period without biases, taking seriously into consideration all the data and elements pertaining to both space and time. In regard to the Hellenistic period, individualism was only one side of the coin; the other was a type of intense social life that attempted to overcome unsettling new conditions. Hellenistic times represented a radical era and perhaps a precursor—*mutatis mutandis*, of course—of the modern era. The people of that period continued to seek integration into a whole that would offer them, at any cost, the lost confidence created by belonging in a group.

Sociability was manifested in various groups known as θίασοι, ἔρανοι, and σύλλογοι, which appeared with striking frequency throughout the Hellenistic period. The environment of the Hellenistic cities of mainland Greece, as well as that of the Near East, was ideal for their activities. The same occurred later on throughout the Roman *Imperium*. Such groups had been well known in the Greek world since the ancient times—especially in Athens, after the reform imposed upon the city by Cleisthenes (507 BCE). The cosmopolitanism of the Hellenistic world, the great trade development, and the constant movement of people contributed to their flourishing: ports and commercial centers of the time became the epicenters of such activities. These groups were thought to provide the most amicable environments within the hostile and unfamiliar space of the ecumenical cities. Among them, individuals could find a safe haven and meet with people that came from the same place or faced the same problems, could talk with them, and so could feel more confident. The saying γνῶθι σαυτόν ("know thyself") was supplemented at this time by the saying γνῶθι τούς ἄλλους ("know others"), while Aristotle's position seems to prevail: κοινωνικόν ἄνθρωπος (ἐστὶ) ζῷον ("Man is by nature a social animal"). Their initial homogeneity eventually disappeared, as they admitted into their environments people of other ethnicities. All these communities were actually miniatures of the Greek system—with political, economic, and religious actors living harmoniously in their environment. Such communities could be likened to the imaginary isles developed in the urban environment in the form of utopian spaces, where people could find much-needed egalitarianism.

Within these environments, native kinship, which characterized traditional ancient social groups, took the shape of a fictive kinship. This was a typical characteristic of the so-called eastern cults of this period, as well as of the Christian, Gnostic, and Manichaean communities. The organization of festivals and feasts by the members, which included participation by "foreigners" (παρεπιδημοῦντες), was also typical during this period. Freedmen and slaves also took part in all these religious events. The spirit of brotherhood and equality that prevailed found its ideal expression within the context of such groups. By entering and integrating into these socioreligious groups, members were automatically separated from the rest of society.

Thenceforth, they interrupted all contact with their traditional family and tribal environment and created, within the frame of these groups, new family ties shared only among the group members. This paved the way for an innovation: the coexistence of the traditional and the novel. The plethora of new perceptions, literally invading the Greek space, caused confusion for the Greeks of this period, who were eventually trapped in a maze of problems and became prisoners of a "peculiar crisis that resulted from unrestricted choice" of perceptions that dominated the ideology of that period.

Salvation was directly related to a new adherent's entrance into an alternative religious environment in one of these groups. The believer ceased to be an individual who lived outside the social reality (*dividuus*), and was then accepted into the community (*individuus*) as a full member, with obligations but also expectations that made him different compared to the rest of the population. This created explicit social boundaries between those who belonged and those who did not belong in such a group, thus inevitably leading to discrimination.

The sense of uncertainty became even greater during late antiquity, when the borders of the vast empire were threatened by the emergence of barbarian tribes living beyond the "boundaries" of the world. The dualism between the world of light and order and the world of darkness and disorder was further broadened. Occultism and apocalyptic prognosis revealed a growing anxiety among contemporary people to find, by any means, much-needed salvation in the turbulent period they lived in. Experiencing this unprecedented situation, they reached the point of suffering from "cosmic paranoia." They believed that they were threatened by dangerous forces originating in the area of the unknown—more specifically, by the oppressive and tyrannical influence of Fate, that made their lives increasingly difficult and unpredictable. In their effort to move away from the traditional way of life, they resorted to a utopian state, which was located beyond the limits of the ecumenical world and knew nothing of the problems and uncertainties of this world. The real hero became the one who managed to escape the painful conditions of the everyday political-social reality. As such, people all the more felt the need to break away from this world's shackles, which were considered the main cause for their suffering—as well as a place of trial rather than salvation. Escape was achieved with their ritual ascension into the broader cosmic firmament, beyond the seven planets, which was considered to be the return to their ancestral homeland. It was a reverse movement, aimed at regaining the lost sociability and avoiding the oppressive effect of the seven planetary spheres. This was a time, as Jonathan Z. Smith has argued, when the individual felt as part of the wider cosmic firmament.

The value of this collection of Luther H. Martin's articles lies mainly in his proposed methodology as well as in his critical penetration into the complex world of the Hellenistic era. His tireless research does not cease there however, but continues with more fervor as he introduces us to the cognitive tendency that prevails in the modern study of religions. This groundbreaking initiative constitutes a transition that is also consistent with the transitional nature of this historical period. Martin's research initiatives have great value because they provide a more comprehensive picture of the religions of the Hellenistic period.

Martin's overall scientific approach is twofold: on the one hand, he offers proposals about the study of the religions and the cults of the Hellenistic world; and on the other hand, he lays out proposals in regard to issues related to the scientific study of religion. His scientific enterprise has been very successful due to his conscientious research, which can be compared with the investigations of a detective who patiently and insightfully is trying to find solutions to unresolved problems. Martin's detective tactics work in such a way that he always "goes behind the familiar metaphors, typologies or sets of concepts proposed on the modern historical assumptions" in order to achieve his goal.[5] His tools are principles of an explanatory approach for matters that lie at the core of current scientific study in order to achieve "a theoretical filling-in of the evidential gaps that is based upon testable hypotheses."[6]

In addition, Martin's research can be compared with the construction of a sophisticated mosaic in which one cannot completely represent the desired image unless every tessera is placed in the appropriate position. This is the only way to acquire the necessary basis for a complete and objective research. The modern scholar, especially of the scientific study of religion, should always keep in mind that the different testimonies which shape the framework of his study are a part of a system and must always be studied as such. Viewing religion as a social system, which is justified by the reference to a superhuman power, constitutes the sine qua non of current research. The interdisciplinary method of research is a necessary feature in the study of human religious events. If we do not take into consideration all the elements that shape the period in which a particular religious phenomenon takes place, we will inevitably end up with generalizations and shallow conclusions.

---

5. Martin, "Promise," 5.
6. Ibid.

Suggested Bibliography

(In addition to works cited, additional relevant bibliography is also referenced.)

Aalders, G. J. D. *Political Thought in Hellenistic Times.* Amsterdam: Hakkert, 1976.
Ager, Sheila L., and Riemer A. Faber, eds. *Belonging and Isolation in the Hellenistic World.* Phoenix Supplementary Volume 51. Toronto: University of Toronto Press, 2013.
Aleshire, Sara B. *Asklepios at Athens: Epigraphic and Prosopographic Essays on the Athenian Healing Cults.* Amsterdam: Gieben, 1991.
Amstrong, Arthur H., ed. *Classical Mediterranean Spirituality: Egyptian, Greek, Roman.* World Spirituality 15. New York: Crossroad, 1989.
Archibald, Zosia H., et al., eds. *The Economies of Hellenistic Societies, Third to First Centuries BC.* Oxford: Oxford University Press, 2011.
Ascough, Richard S., et al. *Associations in the Greco-Roman World: A Sourcebook.* Waco, TX: Baylor University Press, 2012.
Ashton, Sally-Ann. *The Last Queens of Egypt.* London: Pearson/Longman, 2003.
Athannassiadi, Polymnia, and Michael Frede, eds. *Pagan Monotheism in Late Antiquity.* Oxford: Oxford University Press, 1999.
Austin, M. M. *The Hellenistic World from Alexander to the Roman Conquest: A Selection of Ancient Sources in Translation.* 2nd ed. Cambridge: Cambridge University Press, 2006.
Barrett, Caitlin. *Egyptianizing Figurines from Delos: A Study in Hellenistic Delos.* Columbia Studies in the Classical Tradition 36. Leiden: Brill, 2011.
Baslez, Marie.-F. *Recherches sur la conditon de pénétration et de diffusion des religions orientales à Delos (IIe-Ier s. Avan notre ère).* Collection de l'École Normale Supérieure de Jeunes Filles 9. Paris: École normale supérieure de jeunes filles, 1977.
Beard, Mary, et al. *Religions of Rome.* Vol. 1, *A History.* Vol. 2, *A Sourcebook.* Cambridge: Cambridge University Press, 1998.
Beck, Roger L. *Beck on Mithraism: Collected Works, with New Essays.* Ashgate Contemporary Thinkers on Religion. Aldershot, UK: Ashgate, 2004.
———. *A Brief History of Ancient Astrology.* Brief Histories of the Ancient World. Malden, MA: Blackwell, 2007.
———. *Planetary Gods and Planetary Orders in the Mysteries of Mithras.* EPRO 109. Leiden: Brill, 1988.
———. *The Religion of Mithras Cult in the Roman Empire: Mysteries of the Unconquered Sun.* Oxford Scholarship Online. Oxford: Oxford University Press, 2006.
Berner, Ulrich. "Religio und Superstitio. Betrachtungen zur römischen Religionsgeschichte." In *Die Fremden wahrnehmen: Bausteine fur eine Xenologie,* edited by Th. Sundermeier, 45–64. Studien zum Verstehen fremder Religionen 5. Gütersloh: Mohn, 1992.
Bianchi, Ugo. *The Greek Mysteries.* Iconography of Religions, Section XVII, Greece and Rome, fasc. 3. Leiden: Brill, 1976.
———. "Initiation, Mystères, Gnose. Pour l' histoire de la mystique dans la paganisme gréco-oriental." In *Selected Essays on Gnosticism, Dualism, and Mysteriospophy,* 159–76. SHR 38. Leiden: Brill, 1978.
———. "Iside dea misterica. Quando?" In *Perennitas: Studi in onore di Angelo Brelich: Promossi di Cattedra du Religioni del mondo antico dell' Università degli Studi di Roma,* 9–36. Rome: Dell'ateneo, 1980.

———. *Mysteria Mithrae. Atti del Seminario Internazionale su "La specificità storico-religiosa dei Misteri di Mithra," con particolare riferimento alle fonti documentarie di Roma e Ostia', Roma e Ostia 28-31 Marzo 1978*. EPRO 80. Leiden: Brill, 1979.
Bianchi, Ugo, and Maarten J. Vermaseren, eds. *La sotetiologia dei culti orientali nell' impero Romano. Atti del colloquio internazionale su La Soteriologia dei culti orientali nell'impero Romano, Roma 24-28 Settembre 1979*. EPRO 92. Leiden: Brill, 1982.
Bilde, Per, et al., eds. *Aspects of Hellenistic Kingship*. SHC 7. Aarhus: Aarhus University Press, 1996.
———, eds. *Centre and Periphery in the Hellenistic World*. SHC 4. Aarhus: Aarhus University Press, 1996.
Bilde, Per, et al., eds. *Conventional Values of the Hellenistic Greeks*. SHC 8. Aarhus: Aarhus University Press, 1997.
Bøgh, Brirgitte S. *Conversion and Initiation in Antiquity: Shifting Identities, Creating Change*. Early Christianity in the Context of Antiquity 16. Frankfurt: Lang, 2014.
Bommas, Martin. *Heiligtum und Mysterium: Griechenland und seine ägyptische Gottheiten*. Zaberns Bildbände zur Archäologie. Sonderbände der Antiken Welt. Mainz: Von Zaubern, 2005.
Bonnet, Corinne, and André Motte, eds. *Les syncrétismes religieux dans le monde méditerranéen antique. Actes du Colloque Internatinal en l' honneur de Franz Cumont à l' occasion du cinquantième anniversaire de sa mort. Rome, Acdemia Belgica, 25-27 settembre 1997*. Études de philologie, d'archéologie et d'histoire anciennes = Studies over oude filologie, archeologie en geschiedenis 36. Brussels: Institut Historique Belge de Rome, 1999.
Bonnet, Corinne, and Laurent Bricault, eds. *Quand les dieux voyagent: Cultes et mythes en mouvement dans l' espace méditerranéen antique*. Histoire des religions. Geneva: Labor et Fides, 2016.
Bonnet, Corinne, and Sergio Ribichini, eds. *Religioni in contatto nel Mediterraneo antico. Modalità di diffusione e processi di interferenza: Atti del 30 colloquio su "le reliigoni orientali nel mondo Greco e romano." Loveno di Mennaggio (Como), 26-28 Maggio 2006*. Mediterranea 4. Pisa: Sera, 2008.
Bonnet, Corinne, et al., eds. *Religions orientales-culti misterici. Neue Perspektiven-nouvelles perspectives–perspective nuove*. Stuttgart: Steiner, 2006.
Bonnet, Corinne, et al., eds. *Les religions orientales dans le monde Grec et Romain: Cent ans après Cumont (1906-2006). Billan historique et historiographique, Colloque de Rome, 16-18 Novembre, 2006*. Études de philologie, d'archéologie et d'histoire anciennes 45. Brussels: Institut Historique Belge de Rome, 2009.
Bonnet, Corrinne-Haeperen Françoise van, avec la collaboration de Toune, Bastian, Franz Cumont, *Les religions orientales dans le monde romain*, Bibliotheca Cumontiana, Scripta Maiora,I. Torino: Aragno, 2009.
Borgeaud, Philippe. *La Mère des Dieux, de Cybéle à la Vierge Marie*. La Librairie du XXe siècle. Paris: Seuil, 1996.
Bowden, Hugh. *Mystery Cults of the Ancient World*. Princeton: Princeton University Press, 2010.
Braun, Willi, and Russell T. McCutcheon, eds. *Introducing Religion: Essays in Honor of Jonathan Z. Smith*. London: Equinox, 2008.
Bremmer, Jan N. *Greek Religion*. Greece & Rome: New Surveys in the Classics 24. Oxford: Oxford University Press, 1994.

———. *Initiation into the Mysteries of the Ancient World*. Münchner Vorlesungen zu antiken Welten 1. Berlin: de Gruyter, 2014.
Bricault, Laurent. *Atlas de la diffusion des cultes Isiaques (IV s. Av. J.-C.—IVe apr. J.-C.)*. Mémoires de l'académie des inscriptions et belles-lettres 23. Paris: Boccard, 2001.
———. *Bibliotheca Isiaca*, I. Bordeaux: Ausonius, 2008.
———. *Les Cultes Isiaques dans le monde Gréco-Romain: Documents réunis, traduits et commentés*. La roue à livres/Documents. Paris: Les Belles Lettre, 2013.
———. ed. *De Memphis à Rome: Actes du Ier Colloque International sur les études isiaques, Poitiers-Futuroscope, 8-10 avril 1999*. RGRW 140. Leiden: Brill, 2000.
———. ed. *Isis en Occident: Actes du IIéme Colloque International sur les études isiaques, Lyon III, 16-17 Mai 2002*. RGRW 151. Leiden: Brill, 2004.
———, et al., eds. *Nile into Tiber: Egypt in the Roman World; Proceedings of the IIIrd International Conference of Isis Studies, Leiden, May 11–14 2005*. RGRW 159. Leiden: Brill, 2007.
———. *Recueil des Inscriptions concernant les cultes Isiaques (RICIS), Vol. 1–2, Corpus*. Mémoires de l'Académie des Inscriptions et Belles-lettres n.s. 31. Paris: Boccard, 2005.
Bricault, Laurent et al. *Sylloge Numorum Religionis Isiacae et Sarapiacae (SNRIS)*. Paris: Boccard, 2008.
Bricault, Laurent, and Corinne Bonnet, eds. *Panthée: Religious Transformations in the Graeco-Roman Empire*. RGRW 177. Leiden: Brill, 2013.
Bricault, Laurent, and John M. Versluys, eds. *Isis on the Nile: Proceedings of the IVth International Conference of Isis Studies, Liège, November 27–29 2008*. RGRW 171. Leiden: Brill, 2010.
———, eds. *Power, Politics and the Cuts of Isis: Proceedings of the Vth International Conference of Isis Studies, Boulogne-sur-Mer, Ocrober 13–15, 2011*. RGRW 180. Leiden: Brill, 2014.
Bricault, Laurent, and Richard Veymiers. *Bibliotheca Isiaca*, II. Bordeaux: Ausonius, 2011.
———. *Bibliotheca Isiaca*, III. Bordeaux: Ausonius, 2014.
Brown, Peter. *The World of Late Antiquity, AD 150–750*. Library of European Civilization. London: Thames & Hudson, 1971.
Bugh, Glenn R., ed. *The Cambridge Companion to the Hellenistic World*. Cambridge: Cambridge University Press, 2006.
Bulloch, Anthony, et al., eds. *Images and Ideologies: Self-Definition in the Hellenistic World*. HCS 12. Berkeley: University of California Press, 1993.
Burkert, Walter. *Ancient Mystery Cults*. Cambridge: Harvard University Press, 1987.
Cameron, Alan. *The Last Pagans of Rome*. Oxford: Oxford University Press, 2011.
Cartledge, Paul, et al., eds. *Hellenistic Constructs: Essays in Culture, History, and Historiography*. HCS 26. Berkeley: University of California Press, 1997.
Chalupa, Aleš. "Paradigm Lost, Paradigm Found? Larger Theoretical Assumptions behind Roger Beck's *The Religion of the Mithras Cult*." *Pantheon* 7/1 (2012) 5–17.
Chamoux, François. *Hellenistic Civilization*. Translated by Michel Roussel. Malden, MA: Blackwell, 2003.
Chaniotis, Angelos. "Old Wine in a New Skin: Tradition and Innovation in the Cult Foundation of Alexander of Abounoteichos." In *Tradition and Innovation in the Ancient World*, edited by Edward Dabrowa, 67–85. Electrum 6. Krakow: Jagiellonian University Press, 2002.

———. *Unveiling Emotions: Sources and Methods for the Study of Emotions in the Greek World*. Stuttgart: Steiner, 2012.
———. *War in the Hellenistic World: A Social and Cultural History*. Ancient World at War. Malden, MA: Blackwell, 2005.
Clauss, Manfred. *Cultores Mithrae, Die Anhängerschaft des Mithras-Kulte*. Heidelberger althistorische Beiträge und epigraphische Studien 10. Stuttgart: Steiner, 1992.
———. *The Roman Cult of Mithras: The God and His Mysteries*. Translated by Richard Gordon. Edinburgh: Edinburgh University Press, 2000.
Clinton, Kevin. *Myth and Cult. The Iconography of the Eleusinian Mysteries*. The Martin P. Nilsson Lectures on Greek Religion delivered 19–21 November 1990 at the Swedish Institute at Athens. Acta Instituti Atheniensis Regni Sueciae, Series in 8o, XI. Stockholm: Paul Åströms, 1992.
Cole, Susan Guettel. *Theoi Megaloi: The Cult of the Great Gods at Samothrace*. EPRO 96. Leiden: Brill, 1984.
Collar, Anna. *Religious Networks in the Roman Empire: The Spread of New Ideas*. Cambridge: Cambridge University Press, 2013.
Cumont, Franz. *Astrology and Religion among the Greeks and Romans*. New York: Dover, 1960.
Dignas, Beate. *Economy of the Sacred in Hellenistic and Roman Asia Minor*. Oxford Classical Monographs. Oxford: Oxford University Press, 2002.
Dimitrova, Nora M. *Theoroi and Initiates in Samothrace: The Epigraphic Evidence*. Hesperia Supplements 37. Princeton, NJ: The American School at Athens, 2008.
Droysen, J. G. *Geschichte des Hellenismus*. Edited by Erich Bayer. 3 vols. Munich: Deutsche Taschenbuch, 1980 (1st ed.: 1836–1843; 2nd ed.: 1877).
Dunand, Françoise. *Le culte d'Isis dans le Bassin Oriental de la Méditerranée*. 3 vols. EPRO 26. Leiden: Brill, 1973.
———. "Cultes Égyptiens hors d' Égypte. Nouvelles voies d'approches et d' interpretation." In *Egypt and the Hellenistic World: Proceedings of the International Colloquium, Leuven 24–26 May 1982*, edited by Edmond van't Dack et al., 75–98. Studia Hellenistica 27. Leuven: Peeters, 1983.
Dunand, Françoise, and Christiane Zivie-Coche. *Gods and Men in Egypt, 3000 BCE to 395 CE*. Translated by David Lorton. Ithaca, NY: Cornell University Press, 2004.
Easterling, P. E., and J. V. Muir, eds. *Greek Religion and Society*. Cambridge: Cambridge University Press, 1985.
Eder, Walter, ed. *Die Athenische Demokratie im 4. Jahrhundert v. Chr. Vollendung oder Verfall einer Verfassungsform? Akten eines Symposiums, 3-7 August 1992, Bellagio*. Stuttgart: Steiner, 1995.
Egelhaaf-Gaiser, Ulrike. *Kulträume im römischen Alltag: das Isisbuch des Apuleius und der ort von Religion im kaiserzeitlichen Rom*. Potsdamer Altertumswissenschaftliche Beitrage 2. Stuttgart: Steiner, 2000.
Erskine Andrew, ed. *A Companion to the Hellenistic World*. Blackwell Companions to the Ancient World. Malden, MA: Blackwell, 2003.
Ezquerra, Jaime Alvar. *Romanising Oriental Gods: Myth, Salvation and Ethics in the Cults of Cybele, Isis and Mithras*. Translated and edited by Richard Gordon. RGRW 165. Leiden: Brill, 2008.
Ferguson, William S. *Hellenistic Athens: An Historical Essay*. 1911. Reprint, Chicago: Ares, 1974.

Fowden, Garth. *The Egyptian Hermes: A Historical Approach to the Late Pagan Mind.* Cambridge: Cambridge University Press, 1986.

Fox, Robin Lane. *Pagans and Christians: in the Mediterranean World from the Second Century AD to the Conversion of Constantine.* London: Lane, 1986.

Frangoulidis, Stavros. *Witches, Isis and Narrative: Approaches to Magic in Apuleius' "Metamorphoses."* Trends in Classics. Supplementary Volumes 2. Berlin: de Gryuter, 2008.

Frankfurter, David. *Religion in Roman Egypt: Assimilation and Resistence.* Princeton: Princeton University Press, 1998.

Fraser, Peter M. *Ptolemaic Alexandria.* 3 vols. Oxford: Clarendon, 1972.

Funck, Bernd, ed. *Hellenismus: Beiträge zur Erforschuing von Akkulturation und politischer Ordnung in den Staaten des hellenistischen Zeitalter. Akten des Internationalen Hellenismus–Kolloquiums, 9-14 März 1994 in Berlin.* Tübingen: Mohr/Siebeck, 1996.

Garland, Robert. *Introducing New Gods: The Politics of Athenian Religion.* London: Duckworth, 1992.

Gehrke, Hans.-J. *Geschichte des Hellenismus.* Munich: Oldenbourg, 1991.

Gordon, Richard. *Image and Value in the Graeco-Roman World: Studies in Mithraism and Religious Art.* Collected Studies Series. Aldershot: Variorum, 1996.

Graf, Fritz. "What Is Ancient Mediterranean Religion?" In *Religions of the Ancient World: A Guide*, edited by Sara Iles Jonston, 3–16. Harvard University Press Reference Library. Cambridge: Belknap, 2004.

Grandjean, Yves. *Une nouvelle Arétalogie d' Isis à Maronée.* EPRO 49. Leiden: Brill, 1975.

Green, Peter. *From Alexander to Actium: The Hellenistic Age.* London: Thames & Hudson, 1990.

———. *The Hellenistic Age: A Short History.* New York: Modern Library, 2008.

Griffith, Alison B. "Dead Religion, Live Minds: Memory and Recall of the Mithraic Bull-Slaying Scene." *Journal of Cognitive Historiography* 1/1 (2014) 72–89.

Griffiths, Gwyn J., ed. and trans. *Apuleius of Madauros: The Isis-Book (Metamorphoses, Book XI).* EPRO 39. Leiden: Brill, 1975.

———, ed. and trans. *Plutarch's "De Iside et Osiride," with and Introduction, Translation and Commentary.* Cardiff: Cardiff University Press, 1970.

Gruen, Erich S. *The Hellenistic World and the Coming of Rome.* 2 vols. Berkeley: University of California Press, 1984.

Harland, Philip A. *Associations, Synagogues, and Congregations: Claiming a Place in Ancient Mediterranean Society.* 2nd rev. ed. with links to the inscriptions. Kitchener, ON: Philip A. Harland, 2013.

———. *Greco-Roman Associations: Texts, Translations, and Commentary.* Vol. 2, *North Coast of the Black Sea, Asia Minor.* Berlin: de Gruyter, 2014.

Hazzard, R. A. *Imagination of a Monarchy: Studies in Ptolemaic Propaganda.* Toronto: Phoenix. Supplementary Volume 37. Univesrity of Toronto Press, 2000.

Henrichs, A. "The Sophists and Hellenistic Religions: Prodicus As the Spiritual Father of the Isis Aretalogies." *Harvard Studies in Classical Philology* 88 (1984) 139–58.

Hinnells, John R., ed. *Mithraic Studies: Proceedings of the First International Congress of Mithraic Studies.* 2 vols. Manchester: Manchester University Press, 1975.

———. ed. *Studies in Mithraism: Papers Associated with the Mithraic Panel Organized on the Occasion of the XVIth Congress of the International Association for the History of Religions, Rome 1990*. Storia delle religioni 9. Rome: L' Erma" di Bretschneider, 1994.

Hoffmann, Adolf, ed. *Ägyptische Kulte und ihre Heiligtümer im Osten des Römischen Reiches*. Byzas 1. Istanbul: Yyainlari, 2005.

Hölbl, Günther. *A History of the Ptolemaic Empire*. Translated by Tina Saavedra. London: Routledge, 2001.

Keulen, Wytse, and Ulrike Egelhaaf-Gaiser, eds. *Aspects of Apuleius' Golden Ass*. Vol. 3, *The Isis Book: A Collection of Original Papers*. Leiden: Brill, 2012.

Keulen, Wytse, et al. *Apuleius Madaurensis Metamorphoses, Book XI, The Isis Book: Text, Introduction and Commentary*. Groningen Commentaries on Apuleius. Leiden: Brill, 2015.

Kloppenborg, John S., and Richard S. Ascough. *Greco-Roman Associations: Texts, Translations, and Commentary*. Vol. 1, *Attica, Central Greece, Macedonia, Thrace*. Berlin: de Gruyter, 2011.

Kloppenborg, John S., and Stephen G. Wilson. *Voluntary Associations in the Graeco-Roman World*. London: Routledge, 1996.

Lane, Eugene N., ed. *Cybele, Attis and Related Cults: Essays in Memory of M. J. Vermaseren*. RGRW 131. Leiden: Brill, 1996.

Lincoln, Bruce. "Epilogue." In *Religions of the Ancient World: A Guide*, edited by Sara Iles Jonston, 657–67. Harvard University Press Reference Library. Cambridge: Belknap, 2004.

Long, A. A. *Hellenistic Philosophy: Stoics, Epicureans, Sceptics*. 2nd ed. Berkeley: University of California Press, 1986.

Malaise, Michel. *Les conditions de pénétration et de diffusion des cultes Égyptiens en Italie*. EPRO 22. Leiden: Brill, 1972.

———. *Inventaire préliminaire de pénétration et de diffusion des cultes Égyptiens en Italie*. EPRO 21. Leiden: Brill, 1972.

———. *Pour une terminologie et une analyse des cultes isiaques*. Mémoires de la Classe des lettres. Collection in-8o, 3rd ser., 35. Brussels: Acadèmie royale de Belgique, 2005.

Manning, J. G. *Land and Power in Ptolemaic Egypt: The Structure of Land Tenure*. Cambridge: Cambridge University Press, 2003.

Martin, Luther H. "The Anti-Individualistic Ideology of Hellenistic Culture." *Numen* 41/2 (1994) 117–40.

———. *Deep History, Secular Theory: Historical and Scientific Studies of Religion*. Religion and Reason 64. Boston: de Gruyter, 2014.

———. *Hellenistic Religions. An Introduction*. New York: Oxford University Press, 1987.

———. "Kingship and the Consolidation of Religio-Political Power during the Hellenistic Period." *Religio: Revue pro religionistiku* 8/2 (2000) 151–60 (chapter 5, this volume).

———. *The Mind of Mithraists: Historical and Cognitive Studies in the Roman Cult of Mithras*. Scientific Studies of Religion: Inquiry and Explanation. London: Bloomsbury, 2015.

———. "The Promise of Cognitive Science for the Historical Study of Religions, with Reference to the Study of Early Christianity." Lecture Held in Helsinki. on September 1, 2005. http://www.Helsinki.fi/collegium/events/Luther Martin.pdf, 1–35/.

Martin, Luther H., and Panayotis Pachis, eds. *Hellenization, Empire and Globalization: Lessons from Antiquity. Acts of the Panel Held during the 3rd Congress of the European Association for the Study of Religions, Bergen, Norway, 8-10 May 2003*. European Association for the Study of Religion. Thessaloniki: Vanias, 2004.

———, eds. *Imagistic Traditions in the Graeco-Roman World: A Cognitive Modeling of History of Religious Research: Acts of the Panel held during the XIX Congress of the International Association of History of Religions Tokyo, Japan, March 2005*. European Association for the Study of Religion. Thessaloniki: Vanias, 2009.

———, eds. *Theoretical Frameworks for the Study of Graeco-Roman Religions: Adjunct Proceedings of the XVIIIth Congress of the International Association for the History of Religions, Durban, South Africa, 2000*. Thessaloniki: Vanias, 2003.

Merkelbach, Reinhold. *Isis Regina–Zeus Sarapis: Die griechisch-ägyptische Religion nach den Quellendargestellt*. Stuttgart: Teubner, 1995.

Mikalson, Jon D. *Religion in Hellenistic Athens*. HCS 29. Berkeley: University of California Press, 1998.

Munne, Mark. *The Mother of Gods, Athens, and the Tyranny of Asia: A Study of Sovereignty in Ancient Religion; A Study of Sovereignty in Ancient Religion*. The Joan Palevsky Imprint in Classical Literature. Berkeley: University of California Press, 2006.

Mylonas, George E. *Eleusis and the Eleusinian Mysteries*. Princeton: Princeton University Press, 1961.

Nock, Arthur D. *Conversion: The Old and the New in Religion from Alexander the Great to Augustine of Hippo*. Oxford Paperbacks 30. Donnellan Lectures at Trinity College, Dublin 1931. Oxford: Oxford University Press, 1965.

North, John A., and Simon, R. F. Price. *The Religious History of the Roman Empire: Pagans, Jews, and Christians*. Oxford Readings in Classical Studies. Oxford: Oxford University Press, 2011.

Pachis, Panayotis. "Data from Dead Minds? Dream and Healing in the Isis/Sarapis Cult During the Graeco-Roman Age." *Journal of Cognitive Historiography* 1/1 (2014) 52–71.

———. "The Discourse of Myth: Diodorus Siculus and the Egyptian *theologoumena* During the Hellenistic Age." In *Chasing Down Religion: In the Sight of History and the Cognitive Sciences*, edited by Panayotis Pachis and Donald Wiebe, 303–36. Thessaloniki: Barbounakis, 2010.

———. "*Hominibus vagis vitam*: The Wandering of *Homo Hellenisticus* in an Age of Transformation." In *Introducing Religion: Essays in Honor of Jonathan Z. Smith*, edited by Willi Braun and Russell T. McCutcheon, 388–405. London: Equinox, 2008.

———. "Induction Into the Mystery of 'Star-Talk': The Case of Isis Cult during the Graeco-Roman Age." *Pantheon* 7/1 (2012) 79–118.

———. "'Manufacturing Religion': The Case of Demeter Carpophoros in Ephesus during the Graeco-Roman Age." In *Studioum Sapientiae: Atti dela Giornata di studio in Omore di Giulia Sfameni Gasparro, 28 gennaio 2011*, edited by Augusto Cosentino and Mariangela Monaca, 171–87. Catanzaro: Rubbettino, 2013.

———. *Religion and Politics in the Graeco-Roman World: Redescribing the Isis-Sarapis Cult*. Thessaloniki: Barbounakis, 2010.

———. "Sacra Publica-Sacra Peregrina: Επίσημη παραδοσιακή θρησκεία και ανατολικές λατρείες στη Ρώμη των ελληνορωμαϊκών χρόνων." *Επιστημονική Επετηρίς Θεολογικής Σχολής* (n.s.) 7 (1997) 223–51.

———. *Οι Ανατολικές λατρείες της ελληνορωμαϊκής εποχής: Συμβολή στην Ιστορία και τη Μεθοδολογία την Έρευνας*. Thessaloniki: Barbounakis, 2010.

———. *Ίσις Καρποτόκος. Vol. 1, Οικουμένη. Προλεγόμενα στον συγκρητισμό των ελληνιστικών χρόνων*. Thessaloniki: Vanias, 2003.

———. *Η λατρεία της Ίσιδας και του Σάραπι: Από την τοπική στην οικουμενική κοινωνία*. Thessaloniki: Barbounakis, 2010.

Pakkanen, Petra. *Interpreting Early Hellenistic Religion. A Study Based on the Mystery Cult of Demeter and the Cult of Isis*. Papers and Monographs of the Finnish Institute at Athens 3. Helsinki: Suomen Ateenan-instituutin säätiö, 1996.

Panagiotidou, Olympia. "The Asklepios Cult: Where Brains, Minds, and Bodies Interact With the World: Creating New Realities." *Journal of Cognitive Historiography* 1/1 (2014) 14–23.

———. "The Cognitive Route of 'Star-Talk': The Scene of the Tauroctony as a System of Signs." *Pantheon* 7/1 (2012) 70–78.

———, and Roger L. Beck. *The Roman Mithras Cult: A Cognitive Approach*. London: Bloomsbury, 2017.

Parker, Robert. *Athenian Religion: A History*. Oxford: Clarendon, 1996.

———. *Polytheism and Society at Athens*. Oxford: Oxford University Press, 2005.

Pitts, Martin, and Miguel John Versluys, eds. *Globalisation and the Roman World: World, History, Connectivity, and Material Culture*. Cambridge: Cambridge University Press, 2015.

Price, S. R. F. *Rituals and Power: The Roman Imperial Cult in Asia Minor*. Cambridge: Cambridge University Press, 1998.

Rauh, Nicholas K. *The Sacred Bonds of Commerce: Religion, Economy, and Trade Society at Hellenistic Roman Delos*. Amsterdam: Gieben, 1993.

Robinson, James M., ed. *The Nag Hammadi Library*. 3rd rev. ed. San Francisco: Harper & Row, 1988.

Roller, Lynn E. *In Search of God the Mother: The Cult of Anatolian Cybele*. Berkeley: University of California Press, 1999.

Roubekas, Nickolas P. *An Ancient Theory of Religion: Euhemerism from Antiquity to the Present*. Routledge Monographs in Classical Studies. Abingdon, UK: Routledge, 2017.

———, ed. *Theorizing 'Religion' in Antiquity*. Studies in Ancient Religion and Culture. Sheffield: Equinox, 2018.

Rudolph, Kurt. *Gnosis: The Nature and History of Gnosticism*. Translated and edited by Robert McLachlan Wilson. 2nd ed. San Francisco: Harper & Row, 1983.

Rüpke, Jörg, ed. *A Companion to Roman Religion*. Blackwell Companions to the Ancient World. Malden, MA: Blackwell, 2007.

———, ed. *The Individual in the Religions of the Ancient Mediterranean*. Oxford: Oxford University Press, 2014.

———. *Pantheon: A New History of Roman Religion*. Princeton: Princeton University Press, 2018.

———. *Pantheon: Geschichte der Antiken Religionen*. Historische Bibliothek der Gerda Henkel Stiftung. Munich: Beck, 2016.

Raja, Rubina, and Jörg Rüpke, eds. *A Companion to the Archaeology of Religion in the Ancient World*. Blackwell Companions to the Ancient World. Malden, MA: Wiley-Blackwell, 2015.

Rutherford, Ian, ed. *Greco-Egyptian Interactions: Literature, Translation, and Culture, 500 BCE–300 CE*. Oxford: Oxford University Press, 2016.

Scheidel, Walter, et al., eds. *The Cambridge Economic History of the Graeco-Roman World*. Cambridge: Cambridge University Press, 2007.

Sfameni Gasparro, Giulia. *Misteri e Teologie per la storia dei culti mistici e misterici nel mondo antico*. Hierá. Collana di studi storico-religiosi 5. Cosenza: Giordano, 2009.

Smith, Jonathan Z. *Drudgery Divine: On the Comparison of Early Christianities and the Religions of Late Antiquity*. Jordan Lectures in Comparative Religion 14. Chicago Studies in the History of Judaism. Chicago: University of Chicago Press, 1990.

———. "Hellenistic Religion." In *Encyclopædia Britannica*, 8:746–61. 15th ed. Chicago: University of Chicago Press, 1982.

———. "Here, There and Anywhere." In *Relating Religion: Essays in the Study of Religion*, 323–39. Chicago: University of Chicago Press, 2004.

———. *Map Is Not Territory: Studies in the History of Religions*. 1978. Reprint, Chicago: University of Chicago Press, 1993.

———. "Native Cults in the Hellenistic Period." *History of Religions* 11/2 (1971) 236–49.

———. *Relating Religion: Essays in the Study of Religion*. Chicago: University of Chicago Press, 2004.

Stephens, Susan A. *Seeing Double: Intercultural Poetics in Ptolemaic Alexandria*. HCS 37. Berkeley: University of California Press, 2003.

Steuernagel, Dirk. *Kult und Alltag in römischen Hafenstädten: Soziale Prozess in archäologischen Perspektive*. Geschichte. Stuttgart: Steiner, 2004.

Takâks, Sarolta A. *Isis and Sarapis in the Roman World*. RGRW 124. Leiden: Brill, 1995.

Turcan, Robert. *The Cults of Roman Empire*. Translated by Antonia Nevill. Oxford: Blackwell, 1996.

Versnel, Henk S. *Coping with the Gods: Wayward Readings in Greek Theology*. RGRW 173. Leiden: Brill, 2011.

———. *Inconsistencies in Greek and Roman Religion*. Vol. 1, *Ter Unus: Isis, Dionysus, Hermes; Three Studies in Henotheism*. Studies in Greek and Roman Religion 6. Leiden: Brill, 1990.

Walbank, F. W. *Die Hellenistische Welt*. Munich: Deutscher Taschenbuch, 1983.

Walbank F. W., et al., eds. *The Cambridge Ancient History*. Vol. 7.1, *The Hellenistic World*. 2nd ed. Cambridge: Cambridge University Press, 1984.

Weber, Gregor, ed. *Kulturgeschichte des Hellenismus von Alexander dem Grossen bis Kleopatra*. Stutttgart: Klett-Cotta, 2007.

Wickkiser, Bronwen L. *Asklepios, Mesicine and the Politics of Healing in Fifth-Century Greece: Between Craft and Cult*. Baltimore: Johns Hopkins University Press, 2008.

Williams, Michael Allen. *Rethinking "Gnosticism": An Argument for Dismantling a Dubious Category*. Princeton: Princeton University Press, 1996.

Whitehouse, Harvey, and Luther H. Martin, eds. *Theorizing Religions Past: Archaeology, History, and Cognition*. Cognitive Science of Religion Series. Walnut Creek, CA: AltaMira, 2004.

PART 1

The Graeco-Roman Religious World

1

Greek and Roman Philosophy and Religion

> Doctrines must take their beginnings from that of the matters of which they treat.
>
> GIAMBATTISTA VICO[1]

BEGINNINGS, IT HAS BEEN suggested, is a more useful category for the investigation of early Christianity than the more common notion of *origins*, an idea that implies an ahistorical view of religion as somehow sui generis. Commenting on the passage from Vico cited above, Edward Said has argued that *beginnings* acknowledges historical relationships of "continuity or antagonism or some mixture of both" between doctrines and institutions studied and their context.[2] In this sense, any historical investigation of early Christian beginnings must include their intellectual and religious alternatives in the Graeco-Roman world and the relationship of the early Christianities to these alternatives.

The Graeco-Roman, or Hellenistic, World

A change in the course of Western history was initiated by the conquests of Alexander the Great of Macedon (356–323 BCE) who successfully united the Greek peoples in opposition to Persian hegemony and, in the process, established a Graeco-Macedonian empire that extended from the Aegean in

---

1. Vico, *New Science*, par. 314.
2. Said, *Beginnings*, 3, 347–81.

the west to the Indus River in India and from the Black Sea in the north to Nubia and the Sahara in Africa.

Already, the second-century-CE Bithynian historian Arrian had written a seven-book history of Alexander, the *Anabasis of Alexander*, and a ten-book history of *Affairs after Alexander* (of which only fragments survive). It was not until the eighteenth century, however, that Alexander's imperial conquests became defined as initiating a discrete period of history with a conclusion in 30 BCE, the year Augustus annexed Egypt, the final autonomous kingdom of Alexander's former empire, into that of Rome.[3] The significance of this period of history, defined in political terms as extending from Alexander to Augustus, was initially dismissed by scholars as "of no interest in itself, and is only so far of value as it helps us to understand the preceding centuries," at least until "the absorption of Greece by the Romans." It was certainly considered to have no influence "on the destinies of the future world."[4] Only in the final quarter of the nineteenth century did this important and transformational period of history begin to attract scholarly attention.

Scholarly neglect of the historical period after Alexander until late in the nineteenth century had much to do with the prevailing assumption among scholars in Christian Europe that a new historical era had been inaugurated during the reign of Augustus with the birth of Jesus (Luke 2:1–7). The "pagan" world of the period immediately preceding this Christian "charter event" became relegated, thereby, to a theologically and thus historically diminished background against which the emergence of a new Christian period of Western history might be writ. A predominantly Christian culture was only realized historically and politically, however, in the final decades of the fourth century CE with the imperial decrees of the Christian emperor Theodosius that prohibited all non-Christian religious practices and established Christianity as the sole legitimate religion of the Roman empire. From this perspective, a Graeco-Roman period of cultural—in contrast to political—history may be defined as extending from the encounter of ideas and religious practices occasioned by the internationalism of the first *Western* empire in the late fourth century BCE to the establishment of the West as a *Christian culture* in the late fourth century CE; it includes the intellectual and religious histories, not only of the Greek empire established by Alexander and those of his successors, but also that of the Roman imperium as well. It is out of the world of this Graeco-Roman period with its

---

3. Gast, *History of Greece*; similarly, Gillies, *History of the World*.
4. Grote, *History of Greece*, x.

largely *Hellenistic* culture[5] that the early Christianities emerged and were given their shape.

Broadly understood, the predicate "Hellenistic" refers to the general diffusion of Greek culture among those peoples conquered by Alexander as a consequence of his Hellenizing policies, a cultural program actively pursued by his successors. It included the establishment of Greek as the international language of politics and commerce, the introduction of Greek cultural and civic institutions into those cities among the peoples Alexander had incorporated into his empire, and even the founding of new Greek cities, such as Alexandria in Egypt, and subsequent Greek emigration as well as non-Greek immigration with a consequent dissemination of Greek values and ideas. Despite interactions that occurred as a consequence of cultural contact among the diverse cultures included in Alexander's empire, especially in the area of religion, it was Greek values and ideas that dominated into late antiquity, even through the reign of Rome, and which defined a Hellenistic cultural world.

The category of *world* has reemerged in cultural studies to describe a boundaried set of social relationships together with its system of acquired knowledge. It differs from the earlier idea of *Weltanschauung* or "worldview" first used by Kant to describe the holistic comprehension of the phenomenal world.[6] In the nineteenth century, the notion was internalized to designate the subjective "meaning" of the world in terms of an individual's total experience of reality; its formulation was considered the proper function of culture, preeminently, of religion.

In contrast to its Enlightenment and Romantic predecessors, the current usage of *world* is as an analytic category employed to describe a particular religious system in terms of *cosmos* (κόσμος) and *nomos* (νόμος), coextensive scientific and sociopolitical categories of world formation and maintenance.[7] Whereas the scientific framework of Hellenistic culture has received some attention in connection with the relationship between cosmology and religion,[8] the nomic or social aspects of both Hellenistic philosophy and religion have received less. And the question concerning the relationship between these "vertical" and "horizontal" grids of world structure remains largely unaddressed.

---

5. Droysen, *Geschichte*.
6. Kant, *Critique*, 93.
7. Berger, *Sacred Canopy*, 24; see Paden, *Religious Worlds*.
8. Martin, *Hellenistic Religions*.

Hellenistic Cosmology

The scientific framework of the Hellenistic world is well exemplified by the Ptolemaic cosmology, the first comprehensively scientific view of the cosmos. Named after the second-century-CE Alexandrian astronomer and mathematician Claudius Ptolemy, who compiled and systematized contemporaneous astronomical knowledge in his thirteen-book *Almagest*, this cosmological model developed earlier Babylonian, Persian, Egyptian, and Greek astronomical and astrological observations into a mathematically precise system. Its descriptive and predictive efficacy endured until the sixteenth century, when the Copernican cosmological revolution established for modernity a view first proposed in the third century BCE by Aristarchus of Samos—the heliocentric model of the "solar system."

Most simply, the Ptolemaic cosmology described a geocentric system in which the earth, fixed in its position, was encompassed by seven successive spheres identified with the planets visible to the naked eye. Although alternative planetary orders were proposed, the most common was this: the moon (considered, from a geocentric perspective, a planet), Mercury, Venus, the sun (like the moon, considered a planet), Mars, Jupiter, and Saturn. The scientific basis for this system may be traced from the fourth-century-BCE astronomer Eudoxus of Cnidus, who described the motion of these heavenly bodies as concentric spheres moving around different axes, and devised a mathematical explanation for these motions. This entire planetary system was understood to be encompassed within a stationary "realm of the fixed stars." This image of the cosmos—though not all of its mathematical evidence—was dominant in Hellenistic culture from its beginnings.

In the second century BCE, the Bithynian astronomer Hipparchus discovered the precession of the equinoxes, the gradual movement of the plane of the earth's equator relative to the stars. This observation, explained in modern astronomy as a wobble in the earth's axis, could only be understood in terms of the static geocentricity of Hellenistic science as movement in the entire celestial structure, including the realm of the stars. Since the fixed and motionless character of the stars was seen as the most important source of and reference for regularity and stability in the universe, and provided the empirical reference for speculations concerning an "Absolute," Hipparchus's discovery challenged any view of existence modeled upon cosmic immutability.[9]

Following Hipparchus's discovery, philosophical and religious questions and reflections were increasingly modified or reformulated in

---

9. Ulansey, *Origins*, 76–82.

consonance with this revisionist scientific discovery. The natural order of things, for example, once acknowledged as the inviolate rule of *fate*, became relativized as the problematic of cosmic transitoriness now designated by the play of *chance* (personified as Τύχη or Fortuna). And the gods, once imagined as superhuman beings inhabiting high places and the celestial regions, had to be relocated from their now transitory terrestrial—and increasingly even from their celestial—loci to an atemporal, transcendental locus, and reimagined as supernatural and "otherworldly." This Hellenistic problematic was expressed by Pliny the Elder in the first century BCE:

> Everywhere in the whole world at every hour by all men's voices Fortune alone is invoked and named . . . and we are so much at the mercy of chance that Chance herself, by whom God is proved uncertain, takes the place of God. (*Naturalis historia* 2.5.22)

A few examples will suffice to illustrate that early Christians, too, were concerned with these cosmological transformations and referenced their problematic. The astrological character of the story in the Gospel of Matthew about "magi from the east" who followed a star to Bethlehem in order to pay homage to the "newborn King of the Jews" (Matt 2:1-12) has been well considered.[10] Less noticed are the astrological implications of the discrepancy between the Gospel according to Matthew and that according to Luke as to whether conception or birth was the most propitious moment from which to calculate the "starting point" of Jesus's life. The author of Matthew seems to attribute significance to the birth of Jesus (1:16, 18-24) while the author of Luke emphasizes his conception (1:30, 35). These different views concerning the beginning of life reflect a technical debate in astrological practice, as Ptolemy documented (*Tetrabiblos* 3.1).

Second, we might note that the Gospel according to Mark, which recounts stories neither of conception nor of birth, begins its account of Jesus's life with his baptism by John. On this occasion, the gospel reports, "the heavens opened . . . and a voice came from heaven, 'Thou art my beloved Son'" (Mark 1:10-11). The Greek verb for the opening of the heavens is σχίζω, "to tear" or "to rend asunder." The only other occurrence of this word in this gospel is at the conclusion of the life of Jesus when he "uttered a loud cry, and breathed his last." At that moment, the gospel notes that "the curtain of the [Jerusalem] temple *was torn* in two, from top to bottom" (Mark 15:37-38; emphasis added). This temple veil was described by Josephus as depicting a comprehensive representation of the heavens (Josephus, *Bellum*

---

10. E.g., Brown, *Birth of the Messiah*, 166-77.

Judaicum 5.214). Thus, the author of this gospel marks the end of Jesus's life as he marks the beginning—with reference to a "rending of the cosmos."[11]

Even as the Gospel of Mark seems to equate the life and death of Jesus with an alteration in the existing cosmic order, so Paul proclaims that Christians are liberated from an earlier view of the cosmos (Gal 4:3). Paul described the dominance of this earlier view in terms of an observance of "days, and months, and seasons, and years" (Gal 4:10), seemingly a reference to the biblical creation story, in which God creates the "lights [the sun, the moon and the stars] in the firmament of the heavens . . . for signs and for seasons and for days and for years" (Gen 1:14–15). However, this passage also references Hellenistic astrological concerns generally. The various early Christian groups, in other words, regularly referenced their scientific/cosmological context in their theological formulations.

The Sociopolitical Context of the Hellenistic World

More complex than the more or less commonly assumed cosmological framework of the Hellenistic world was its diverse sociopolitical structure. This complex structure can be typologized, however, in terms of two alternative kinds of social organization: kingship, on the one hand, a consolidation of power such as was claimed by the Hellenistic rulers; and kinship, on the other, a dispersion of power consequent upon the spread of numerous alternative social groupings typically organized on the basis of kin claims.

Power in the Graeco-Roman world was officially claimed, and often imposed, by the structures and functionaries of the imperium, whether that of Alexander, those of his diverse successors, or that reinstated by Rome. These imperial or kingship claims were reinforced by state cults, including, finally, the deification of the emperor. Already Alexander had encountered in Persia cult practices that attributed divine qualities to their king. In Egypt he found a formal cult of the king as god[12] and, in both places, the young king himself was so received. In 324 BCE, in response to Alexander's demand, Athens, followed by other Greek cities, voted Alexander to be Dionysus.[13] In later accounts, Alexander's virgin mother was impregnated by a lightning bolt; her son nevertheless claimed to be descended on his father's side from Heracles, the greatest of the Greek heroes, and on his mother's side from Achilles, the bravest of Homeric heroes.[14] Both heroes, according

11. Ulansey, "Heavenly Veil Torn."
12. Taylor, *Divinity*, 6.
13. Ibid., 21–23.
14. Plutarch, *Alexander* 2; Nilsson, *Cults, Myths, Oracles*, 108.

to Greek mythology, had ascended to divine status. By claiming "succession" from Alexander, the Hellenistic kings also made claim to heroic and divine descent.[15] Julius and Augustus were the real successors of Alexander, both in political terms as in that of the divine right to rule they claimed—a right subsequently claimed by monarchy in the West until the rise of the modern democratic state.

Alternative to the consolidation and centralization of political power exemplified by Alexander's empire and by the subsequent Hellenistic and Roman kingdoms, a legion of countercultural groups—clubs or *collegia*—proliferated during the Hellenistic period, claiming, by default, social power for themselves, whether that dispersion of power was expressed in political, religious, esoteric, or transcendental terms. Documented from the political context of classical Greece (Thucydides 3.82; 8.54, 65), the founding and spread of such associations was provoked by the new possibilities of commercial and mercenary activity occasioned by the international successes of empire itself. As inhabitants of once locally defined cultures ventured forth into the cosmopolitan context of the Hellenistic world, they understandably sought to retain something of their traditional ancestry and identity: their language, their dress, their cuisine, their religion. Consequently, these new immigrants often formed "social clubs" with their compatriots. They met together and drew up rules of association, they paid dues, they ate and drank together, they typically venerated one of their native deities as their patron, and they often assumed the traditional familial responsibility for the "proper" burial of their brethren in the alien lands they now inhabited. The ubiquitous characteristic of these Hellenistic associations was their sense of being a household or extended family, perhaps the most fundamental mode of human social organization. As one scholar summarizes the evidence concerning some twenty-four voluntary associations on Delos, they "reinforced a sense of kinship and national identity on an island where disparate nationalities and languages abounded."[16]

Greek society and state, like that of virtually all cultures, had been founded on the family—groups of men who claimed descent from a common ancestor. This ancestor gave his name to the family and the veneration of the ancestor gave religious sanction to these social entities.[17] If, for some reason, a common ancestor was absent, one might be invented, especially if a heroic or divine progenitor was desired. Whether ethnic or fictive, the sense of kinship was the most common characteristic of the Hellenistic

---

15. Taylor, *Divinity*, 25.
16. McLean, "Place of Cult," 189.
17. Nilsson, *Cults, Myths, Oracles*, 65.

associations.[18] The establishment of fictive kin ties by adoption was a common Graeco-Roman practice of kin recruitment that ensured legitimate descendants in the face of high mortality. And Hellenization, in the sense of assimilating non-Greeks to Greek culture, often involved inventing for colonized or conquered peoples eponyms that might be connected with figures from Greek myths who had similar names.[19] "Greekness" was a matter of kinship (Thucydides 1.95.1).

While the Hellenistic kinship groups or *clubs* seem to have limited membership to a particular ethnic group and/or to class or gender, some at least, experimented with values of inclusiveness and equality in the face of a largely segregated and hierarchical world—as did some early Christians. The association of Zeus in Philadelphia, for example, admitted "men and women, freeborn and slaves."[20] These alternative values may have derived from the private religious associations of classical Athens in which foreigners, women, and slaves all enjoyed equal rights with Athenian citizens.[21] Or, these values may have been championed for the Hellenistic world by the notion of "the brotherhood of mankind" attributed to the emperor Alexander.[22] Whether or not such a program was ever advanced by Alexander himself, Hellenistic romances about him clearly propagated this value in his name. Thus, the first-century-BCE historian Diodorus Siculus wrote that the bringing together of the largest continents through intermarriage and ties of kinship to a common harmony and family ties was among Alexander's "last plans" (Diodorus Siculus 18.4.4). Similarly, Plutarch averred that Alexander "instructed all men to consider the inhabited world to be their native land . . . being blended together by ties of blood and the bearing of children" (Plutarch, *De fortuna Alexandri* 1.329 C–D).

The claims to universal brotherhood and, thus, to centralized power inevitably established the political state in opposition to the dispersion of alternative social organizations with their local and limited criteria of kinship, no matter how egalitarian they may otherwise have been. It is this oppositional character inherent in the two differing types of sociopolitical organization and to their differing views of power that thrust Hellenistic efforts at imperial rule into conflict with the kinship associations. The dispersion of any such organized subgroups is typically viewed as a threat to

---

18. Kloppenborg and Wilson, *Voluntary Associations*, 13, 18, 112, 132, 134–35, 180, 189.

19. Nilsson, *Cults, Myths, Oracles*, 97–98, 105.

20. Kloppenborg, "Collegia and *Thiasoi*," 25; see Paul in 1 Cor 12:13.

21. Foucart, *Des Associations Religieuses*, 5–12.

22. See the prayer for the "unity of mankind" reported by Arrian, *Anabasis* 7.11.

the centralized authority and stability of political power unless a mutually accommodating relationship can be assured.

Classical Greek philosophy had always attempted to legitimate the dominant nondemocratic forms of rule. "Thales' (sixth-century BCE) *sophia* was an attempt to legitimate tyranny, whereas the *philosophia* of Pythagoras and of later thinkers was designed to provide a non-democratic alternative to post-tyrannical society."[23] And Greek religion was always supportive of the state. As the classical Greek view of a world ordered by laws of nature that man and polis sought to replicate and to which even the gods were subject became confounded by the sociopolitical conflict wrought by the warring successors to Alexander's empire, innovative and redefined philosophical schools and novel religious associations proliferated as alternatives to political order imposed by the Hellenistic kings.

Examples from both the philosophical and religious traditions were accepted by political power as supportive, or at least nonthreatening, while others, including the early Christianities, were viewed as subversive, or at least suspicious. The writing of a Christian "universal history" by the author of Luke–Acts, was an early Christian referencing of Roman international hegemony; the author even has a Roman centurion support the innocence of Jesus (Luke 23:47). However, this Lucan history, established by the later Christian world as "normative," was at the time of its writing only one of a wide spectrum of views held by various "Jesus people" and "Christ cults" making differing claims upon the name of Jesus.[24] Some of these groups— the group which produced "Q," the early Jesus *sayings source*, for example, and those who compiled Mark and the other *canonical* gospels, and, of course, the letters of Paul—would eventually be reconciled, harmonized, or synthesized into the Lucan-Roman model of a universalized theological history. Those "Christian" groups who would not or could not accept the Lucan standard were branded as heretical: the group that produced the *Gospel of Thomas*, for example, or those that composed other noncanonical gospels or "acts" of various apostles. When the Lucan view was accorded the authority of the "Great Church" in the fourth century, these alternative Christian groups were themselves banished or burned.

The problematics, then, referenced by the early Christian movements, mirrored those addressed by Greek and Roman philosophical and religious groups generally. They pursued similar cosmic and nomic questions with similar assumptions. They all offered explanations for their view of the world,

---

23. Frischer, *Sculpted World*, 16.

24. Smith, *Drudgery Divine*; Mack, *Myth of Innocence*; Mack, *Lost Gospel*; Mack, *Who Wrote*.

required a disciplined style of life with a clearly articulated goal, produced a tradition of exemplary predecessors—some of whom, like Socrates, were martyred—which culminated in a contemporaneous teacher, compiled an authoritative literature, and they all organized themselves in social groups defined by kinship terminology, membership in which required some type of formal conversion or initiatory rites.[25] And claims to superhuman power as the legitimating basis for their authority, the most minimal definition of a religious system, were as likely to be made by "philosophical" as by "religious" groups.

Of course, there were differences between groups within both traditions—for example, between those whose views were influenced by the supernaturalism of Platonic tradition and those which adhered to the more naturalistic tradition of Aristotle. And a major difference between Greek philosophical and religious systems generally was a different "division of labor" concerning ethics. Whereas Hellenistic religious groups had been concerned, for example, with venerating and propitiating the gods and with legitimating the social boundaries over which they presided, whether of kin or king, they were not, like those groups that identified with the biblical tradition, concerned with questions of ethics, relegating this issue to philosophy.

To map the differing philosophico-religious groups that populated the Graeco-Roman period, their goals and aspirations, their differences and similarities, is to map a central feature of the cultural world of Christian beginnings.

Hellenistic Philosophies

Although a classical period of Greek philosophy is generally concluded with the death of Aristotle in 322 BCE, the year following the death of his student, Alexander the Great, the naturalistic and empirical tradition of research exemplified by Aristotle's work continued throughout the Hellenistic period. This tradition was exemplified not only by the observations of such astronomers as Aristarchus (fl. mid-third century BCE) and Hipparchus (fl. second half of second century BCE) but also by the advances of such mathematicians as Euclid (c. 325–c. 250 BCE), Archimedes (c. 287–212 or 211 BCE), Apollonius of Perga (fl. 200 BCE), and Eratosthenes (c. 285–194 BCE), as well as by the work of the naturalist Theophrastus (372/1 or 371/2–288/7 or 287/6 BCE). Despite continuing progress in scientific knowledge, however, Hellenistic philosophy was primarily characterized by

---

25. Nock, *Conversion*, ch. 5.

"a critical synthesis of earlier philosophies about the world";[26] and life during this period was increasingly understood as subjected to irrational forces—to chance for example, or to powers beyond ordinary human control, which could only be dealt with by cult and magic.[27] This intellectual lapse, popularized in modern judgment as "a failure of nerve,"[28] was as evident in the philosophical traditions as in the religious alternatives of the period. The popular successes of the Hellenistic philosophies were bought, in other words, at the price of their separation from scientific research.[29] By the time Rome eventually restored an ordered world through its efficient administration of empire, the general investigation of nature and of the role of rational man in the ordered cosmos had been largely replaced by a practical concern with ethics, the rule and exercise of life that might offer a viable view of human identity in the face of both cosmological and sociopolitical transitoriness and transformation. Philosophical *theoria* (θεωρία) was replaced, in other words, by *praxis* (πρᾶξις). All of the Hellenistic philosophical schools emphasized the question first posed by Plato and Aristotle: "What is happiness or well-being and how does a man achieve it?"[30]

The increased focus upon practical ethics during the Hellenistic period established philosophers as exemplars and their philosophical "schools" as, ideally, groups of exemplary followers. These schools not only endeavored faithfully to transmit the teachings of their founder, whose thought, however, was in fact often elaborated and modified, but also to emulate his lifestyle. The first of the philosophical schools, established by Pythagoras in the sixth century BCE, was organized as quasi-religious associations that included rites of initiation, private teachings, a dietary regime, and provisions for burial.[31] In addition to the well-known contributions by the Pythagoreans to mathematics, music and astronomy, Pythagoreanism subsequently became a designation also for recondite religious movements. The establishment of the Pythagorean societies was followed in the fourth century by that of the Platonic Academy and the Aristotelian Peripatetics, both organized on the legal model of religious associations, and then in the early third century by the founding of the Epicurean Garden and of Stoicism.[32]

26. Frischer, *Sculpted World*, 34.
27. Samuel, *Promise of the West*, 169.
28. Murray, *Five Stages*.
29. Long, *Hellenistic Philosophy*, 12.
30. Ibid., 6.
31. Burkert, *Greek Religion*, 302–3.
32. Mason, "*Philosophiai*."

In his historical overview of philosophers from Thales to Epicurus, the third-century-CE writer Diogenes Laertius described these philosophical schools as "successions." He further organized these successions into two major traditions (1.13): an Ionian lineage, from the pre-Socratics, through Plato and Aristotle, culminating with the Stoics (1.22–27), and an Italian lineage, from Pythagoras to Epicurus (8–10). The Epicurean and Stoic traditions dominated philosophy in the early Hellenistic period along with a subsequent renaissance of Platonism from the late first century BCE.

The Epicureans

Epicurus (341–270 BCE), an Athenian citizen born on Samos, first met with some followers in the secluded garden of his home in Athens. His school, named after this original meeting place, soon spread throughout the Greek world and subsequently developed branches in Egypt, Asia, Mytilene, and Lampsacus. By the first century BCE, Epicureanism had been introduced to the Roman world by Lucretius (c. 94–55 or 51? BCE) through his magisterial poem *On the Nature of Things*. Therefore, the Epicurean schools—to which women were admitted as equals alongside men—epitomized the cosmopolitan and inclusivistic values of the larger Hellenistic world. Nevertheless, Epicurus and his followers rejected the allure of internationalization, opting instead for small alternative associations of philosophers bound by the ideal of friendship. The Epicureans recognized, however, the political reality of the civic world from which they sought to retire, and they attempted, consequently, to establish good relations with those in power in order that they might be left alone.[33]

Like students of Hellenistic philosophy generally, the Epicureans were not so concerned with abstractions such as Plato's Good or Aristotle's superlunar and superhuman cosmos; rather, they were concerned with the immediate human condition and the practical goal of a happy life. Although they did not deny the existence of the gods, the Epicureans—like the eighteenth-century deists—did reject any view of divine intervention in the affairs of this world. Rather, the deities, in their sublime and tranquil detachment, provided the model for human detachment from civic life. The Epicureans attributed value, consequently, only to this-worldly reality as defined by sense perception.

Adopting and adapting the atomic theory of the fifth-century-BCE philosopher Democritus, they understood the world as the consequence of an infinite number of atoms that might collide and, from time to time,

---

33. Frischer, *Sculpted World*, 40–41.

combine to form the phenomena of the sensible universe. Holding the cosmos to be a natural if accidental combination of atoms that would, at some point, decompose, they epitomized the Hellenistic attribution of existence to chance. Since, consequently, any phenomenon had value only in terms of its immediate practical advantage, pleasure was considered the highest good by Epicurus and his followers. By "pleasure," however, the Epicureans did not mean "the pleasures of the prodigal or the pleasures of sensuality," as many understood them in antiquity as today. Rather, as Epicurus wrote in a *Letter to Menoeceus* preserved by Diogenes Laertius: "By pleasure we mean the absence of pain in the body and of trouble in the soul... It is sober reasoning, searching out the grounds of every choice and avoidance, and banishing those beliefs through which the great tumults take possession of the soul" (Diogenes Laertius 10.122–35). For the Epicureans, in other words, pleasure referred to the ideal of a trouble-free existence in which the body was healthy and the mind undisturbed.

Despite a veneration of Epicurus to the point of divinity by his followers (Lucretius, *On the Nature of Things* 5.1–54), the Epicurean emphasis on withdrawal from the political world and the dismissal of any transcendent destiny had little appeal to Romans and their ideal of a just and good state guaranteed by the gods. Consequently, this thoroughly materialistic tradition was eclipsed by Stoicism in the philosophical imagination of the later Hellenistic period.

The Stoics

Stoicism was founded by Zeno of Citium (335–263 BCE), who had begun his career as a student of Crates (c. 368/365–288/285 BCE), a follower of the Cynic philosopher Diogenes of Sinope (c. 412/403–c. 324/321 BCE). In some ways similar to the Epicureans, the Cynics had taught that the wise man will reject what is conventional in order to follow a "natural" way of life based on action rather than thought. By natural, however, Diogenes meant "primitive," and the Cynics consequently not only withdrew from civic life, as did the Epicureans, but flouted as well all social convention as constructs contrary to their ascetic style of life. Although never institutionalized as a philosophical school, Cynicism continued to be influential throughout the Hellenistic period. Some have even noted a relationship between the simple lifestyle advocated by the Cynics, the aphoristic form of their teachings and their social critiques, with those of the earliest Jesus traditions.[34]

---

34. Mack, *Myth of Innocence*, 67–69; and Mack, *Lost Gospel*, 114–21.

When Zeno broke with Crates, he began to expound his own teachings in the marketplace of Athens among the colonnades (*stoa*, from which his school derived its name.) He essentially developed the Cynic way of life into an ethical system, which he integrated into a comprehensive philosophy. Zeno and his followers prided themselves on "the remarkable coherence of the[ir] system and the extraordinary orderliness of the subject-matter" (Cato, in Cicero, *On the Ends of Good and Evil* 3.74). Generally, the Stoics conceived of the cosmos as an organic whole, a pantheistic system of universal law. They owed much of their success to an ability to unify, by means of allegory, the various philosophical and popular expressions of cosmic law, whether this "many-named" cosmic law was imaged as fire, as taught by the fifth-century-BCE philosopher Heraclitus, or as fate, the natural order of things (εἱμαρμένη), or as the rational order of things (*logos*, Gk: λόγος). This law received "religious" expression by Zeno's successor, Cleanthes (331–232 BCE) in his *Hymn to Zeus*:

> Most glorious of immortals, Zeus
> The many-named, almighty evermore,
> Nature's great Sovereign, ruling all by law—
> [...]
> For thee this whole vast cosmos, wheeling round
> The earth, obeys, and where thou leadest
> It follows, ruled willingly by thee.[35]

Stoicism provided, thereby, a philosophical rationale for the increasing universalism that came to characterize the Hellenistic philosophical and religious traditions. Chrysippus (c. 280–207 BCE), the third head of the school after Cleanthes, refined the teachings of Zeno and consolidated them with various directions that were beginning to develop within Stoic teachings into what thereafter was considered throughout the Hellenistic period to be the orthodox or standard position. "Had there been no Chrysippus," the saying went, "there would have been no Stoa" (Diogenes Laertius 7.183).

Despite the Stoic's comprehensive integration of logic, physics and ethics, Stoicism attracted less interest in late antiquity as a philosophical system than as a way of life, as the ethical writings of Seneca the Younger (c. 4 BCE/1 CE–65 CE), Epictetus (c. 50—c. 150 CE), and Marcus Aurelius (121–180 CE) exemplify. Since cosmic law, in the Stoic view, governed moral order as well as the natural world, to live a life of virtue was to live a harmonious life in accord with nature. The primary characteristic of this natural law was rationality (λόγος), and reason, consequently, was the way

---

35. Grant, *Hellenistic Religions*, 152.

to knowledge of its universal truth.³⁶ To cultivate this rationality, both a human endowment and the essence of divinity, and to live in harmony with it, were to become "offshoots" of god (Epictetus, *Discourses* 1.14.6) and thus "kin" with deity (Marcus Aurelius, *Meditations* 10.6). The Stoics thus shared with Epicureans the goal of human perfectibility in this existence, but, in stark contrast to the Epicureans, the Stoic idea of a universal norm of virtue accorded more with the Platonic (and later Christian) view concerning the transcendental nature of truth.

Hellenistic Platonism

A middle Platonism may be traced from the reaction of Antiochus of Ascolon (c. 130–69/8 BCE) against the first-century-BCE emergence of philosophical skepticism, a position that, claiming the authority of Socrates, rejected all doctrine and questioned all positions on the ground that things are finally unknowable (Diogenes Laertius 1.16). Influenced by Stoicism, however, Antiochus had understood that the goal of life was to live in accordance with nature. During this same century, Eudorus of Alexandria challenged this Stoic view of nature with the Platonic ideal of living in accordance with the "likeness of god."³⁷ At about the same time, Nigidius Figulus, considered by Cicero to be the founder of Neoplatonism (Cicero, *Timaeus* 1), revised and revived Pythagoreanism in Rome. Pythagoras's teachings had been preserved by Plato and had influenced especially Plato's views of cosmology (*Timaeus*) and religion (*Phaedo*). The transcendentalism of Hellenistic Platonism constituted a reaction against the scientific traditions of the Hellenistic period as well as against the materialistic and empirical philosophies of the Epicureans and, in part, the Stoics. Platonists had always differentiated between the world of the senses and the world of ideas, insisting that sense perception is subject to deception. Consequently, early Hellenistic philosophical appeals to sensual reality became supplemented and, in late antiquity, even replaced by claims to a transcendental truth that blurred the distinction between philosophy and religion.

If Stoicism first provided a philosophical rationale for the universalism that came to characterize Hellenistic religions, middle Platonism reinforced that rationale with a hypercosmic transcendentalism appropriate to the Ptolemaic cosmological map. This commitment of Hellenistic Platonism to "a non-material, intelligible world beyond this one" together with "a

---

36. Samuel, *Promise of the West*, 203.
37. Plato, *Theaetetus* 176B; Dillon, *Middle Platonists*, 44.

transcendent supreme principle" was central to all variations of Hellenistic Platonism; it culminated in the Neoplatonism of Plotinus (205–69/70 CE).[38]

Plotinus understood that the true self or soul is a child of "God," the "Father," or the "One" (*Enneads* 2.9.16), and that those who are with the One are, consequently, "brothers" (5.18.12). The souls, in other words, are children of "their father, God," which are "brought up far away" not knowing "who they themselves or their parents are" (5.5.1). Those who know themselves—which is the command of God (4.3.1)—will know their genealogy and, consequently, their divine origins (6.9.7). For Plotinus, in other words, the human soul is kin by nature to the higher reality (1.6.2; 2.3.9; 2.9.18; 3.3.1; 3.5.1; 4.4.45). Recognition of this kinship with God is the beginning of the soul's return. Early philosophers had routinely claimed descent from the gods who gave sanction to the existing social and political order, or at least they claimed some analogy between themselves and divine characteristics.[39] Pythagoras, for example, had not only claimed descent from Hermes (Diogenes Laertius 8.4) but asserted also that "only god is wise" and that philosophy was "the love of wisdom" (1.12).[40] Modern differences assumed between at least some of the philosophical schools and religious traditions, both social alternatives which sought legitimation by claims to superhuman power, were not so sharp in antiquity; their claim of kinship with the gods by descent later became transformed into philosophical and theological claims of epistemological privilege concerning Truth.

Given Plotinus's emphasis on the kinship of realized souls, his vision of the ideal society would be constituted as a kinship group on the social model of those alternative communities that proliferated in the Hellenistic period generally. Plotinus actually petitioned the Emperor Gallienus to consign him a deserted city in Campania which he and his aristocratic companions might resettle according to his utopian ideals under the name of Platonopolis (Porphyry, *Vita Plotini* 12). Although Plotinus's request was rejected, his utopian vision was revived in Christian metaphor by Augustine's ideal of a transcendental City of God—a legitimating model for political hierarchy[41] and the "dream of many Christian centuries."[42]

---

38. Dillon, *Middle Platonists*, 51.
39. Frischer, *Sculpted World*, 18, 77–79.
40. Ibid., 20–21.
41. Williams, "Significance of St. Augustine," 9–10.
42. Hardy, "City of God," 257.

Hellenistic Religions

Whereas philosophy retained an essentially Hellenic character during the Graeco-Roman period and, consequently, was one of the factors that shaped Hellenistic culture, the history of religions was profoundly altered by the cultural contacts and interactions initiated by the conquests of Alexander. Native cults with their base in local populations, including native Greek cults such as those of Dionysus, for example,[43] or of the Eleusinian Demeter, found themselves increasingly situated in an international and multicultural context. The Hellenization of these previously local deities, the Egyptian Isis, for example, and of their cults, involved their adaptation and transformation to the newly established and increasingly dominant Greek language, to conditions of scientific/astronomical universalism, political internationalism, and consequences of military and commercial mobility and subsequent emigration.

Not all native religions wholeheartedly embraced Hellenization. Some, like the Hellenistic associations, resisted by attempting to preserve their traditional linguistic and cultural forms and, especially, the native character of their local deities; some even resisted Hellenization to the point of revolt against its political pressures and its military forces.[44] A series of Egyptian anti-Hellenistic revolts from 245 BCE provide one example, as do the Jewish revolts against Seleucid attempts to Hellenize Jerusalem in the second century BCE (see 1 and 2 Maccabees). Even Judaism, however, was strongly influenced by Hellenistic culture—especially in its diaspora—as the translation of the Hebrew Bible into Greek around the second century BCE indicates. Known as the Septuagint (LXX), after the alleged team of seventy-two translators, six from each of the twelve Israelite tribes, this translation, completed in exactly seventy-two days, was held to be as inspired and thus as authoritative for Greek-speaking Jews as was the Hebrew original (*Letter of Aristeas* 32, 307, 310–11). Those native cults that did not in some way adapt to the transformed conditions of the Hellenistic world survived only in poetic reference or political rhetoric, if at all.

Hellenistic Mysteries

The religious form generally considered most characteristic of Hellenistic religiosity is the *mystery cult*. The characterization is, however, elusive since *mystery* is both the self-designation of a wide range of Hellenistic social

---

43. Nilsson, *Dionysiac Mysteries*.
44. Eddy, *King Is Dead*; Rudolph, *Gnosis*, 286, 288.

groups, from small collegial associations to some well-established Hellenistic religions, as well as a modern categorization for a number of Hellenistic cults for which a certain "family resemblance" is proposed. As a self-designation, *mystery* indicated minimally an association in which membership required some formalized procedure or initiation (Gk. μυστήρια = Lat. *initia*), usually under the patronage of a particular deity. As a modern category, the Eleusinian Mysteries—also a self-designation—is most often presented as paradigmatic.

The Mysteries of Demeter

The Mysteries of Demeter, celebrated in the town of Eleusis, fourteen miles west of Athens, seemingly developed from a family cult that initially admitted only citizens of Eleusis and perhaps only members of certain noble families of that town. At least the prerequisite for the priestly administrators of the cult was membership in one of two Eleusinian hereditary "lineages" (*gens*).

According to a brief account of the origins of the Eleusinian Mysteries by the Athenian orator Isocrates (436–338 BCE), Demeter founded her cult in Eleusis out of gratitude for certain unspecified "services" extended her by the "ancestors" of Eleusis, and that initiation into the cult consisted, in part at least, of revealing to the initiates the nature of these services (*Panegyricus* 28). According to the *Homeric Hymn to Demeter*, one of the ancestors of Eleusis who had first shown Demeter hospitality and among those to whom she subsequently "showed the conduct of her rites and taught . . . all mysteries" was Eumolpus, a presumed son of Poseidon and one of the mythical rulers of Eleusis (*Homeric Hymn to Demeter* 184, 475). In any case, the Hierophant, or chief priest of the Eleusinian cult, was selected from the Eumolpidae, the family that claimed descent from this ancestor, as did the so-called Exegetes of the Eumolpidae. Similarly, the "Daduch," the second-highest administrator of the cult, and the offices of "Sacred Herald" and "Altar-priest" were selected from the Kerykes. Although the genealogy of this family is less clear, they claimed descent from the lineage of Keryx, the herald, who was a son either of Eumolpos (Pausanias 1.38.3) or of Hermes, the divine herald.[45]

Γεννῆται, members of a particular γένος (*genos*), were identified generally by their claims of descent from a common ancestor. Such γεννῆται were particularly concerned with the deity who was considered to be their ancestor or who had been the protector of the ancestors from whom they claimed

---

45. Clinton, *Sacred Officials*, 8; Mylonas, *Eleusis*, 234.

descent and who, consequently, had some responsibility in the cult of that deity.[46] In addition to those claiming descent from a common ancestor, a (fifth-century?) law defined γεννῆται as including also "foster-brothers" or "sisters" as well as members of religious associations (Philochorus, fr. 35). The implication is that membership in a particular γένος might also be conferred by adoption (or initiation)—even as a fictive ancestor might be adopted to give heroic or divine legitimacy to the γένος. Under Greek and Roman law, adoptees were fully received into the family of the adopter—and into the familial cult—and accorded full rights of inheritance, succession, and divine protection. Isocrates's account suggests, in other words, that a special relationship, claimed for the ancestral families of Eleusis and the deity Demeter, was ritually replicated in the instruction/initiation of the mysteries. In this way, initiation into the rites of Demeter established a fictive/adoptive relationship between the ancestral families of Eleusis and the initiate and, thereby, between Demeter and the initiate such as was claimed for the ancestors and the deity. At least one Hellenistic source indicates that claims to relationship with Demeter were even extended to kinship with the deity herself. According to the pseudo-Platonic dialogue *Axiochus*, dated in the second or first century BCE, Axiochus became "kin to the gods" as a consequence of his initiation into the Eleusinian mysteries (Pseudo-Plato, *Axiochus* 371D). Though there is little further documentation for this view, the notion of kinship with deity through adoption or ritual initiation might have had a basis in Homer's *Odyssey*, where Menelaos is promised an afterlife on the Elysian Plain as a consequence of his adoption into the family of the gods through his marriage to Helen (*Odyssey* 4.561–69). And, of course, Paul uses the juridical terms for adoption to describe those redeemed by God's son as themselves adopted sons of God (Rom 8:14, 23; Gal 4:4–5).

The ten-day initiation rite into the Mysteries of Eleusis was celebrated in the latter part of each September. The celebration began at the Eleusinion in Athens, where a branch of the Eleusinian cult had been established and "Lesser Mysteries" were celebrated each spring in recognition of Athenian political dominance; but then a procession in torchlight moved to Eleusis along the "Sacred Way." The institution of a procession from the ruling center to the cult place was a procedure typically followed in the spread of cults too closely identified with their locale to be fully disseminated.[47] After a day of rest and fasting, the pilgrims would enter the sacred precincts of Demeter and into the Telesterion or the "House of Initiation" therein for the initiation rite itself. This "night of mysteries" was followed again by rest

---

46. Foucart, *Mystères d' Éleusis*, 224–25.
47. Nilsson, *Cults, Myths, Oracles*, 16, 38.

and finally by the return of the new initiates from the religious center of the pan-Hellenic world to Athens, its cosmopolitan center.

The sole requirement for initiation throughout the history of the mysteries (apart from such practical necessities as sufficient funds to travel to Eleusis, per diem, and cultic expenses such as providing for the required sacrifices) was that the initiates not have taken human life and that they speak Greek—the latter being the same linguistic criterion that defined the social boundary between Greek and barbarian generally. Thus, initiatory admission into the Eleusinian community generally supported kin claims of *Greekness*. To this extent, the international popularity of the Eleusinian cult during the period following the conquests of Alexander furthered his program of Hellenization, and that of his successors. Whatever their attraction, the Eleusinian mysteries continued to expand at the beginning of the Hellenistic period and endured through the fourth century CE as an empirewide festival.

The Mysteries of Isis

Although the worship of Isis had been familiar to Greeks since the fifth century BCE when Herodotus had identified Demeter with the Egyptian deity (Herodotus 2.42, 48, 145), the worship of Isis outside of Egypt was initially limited to associations of expatriate Egyptians. In the fourth century BCE, for example, the veneration of a pre-Hellenistic Isis is documented among some Egyptian immigrants in Athens.[48] By the third century BCE, however, Hellenized cults of Isis are documented along the Greek coast and on some of the Greek islands.[49] In contrast to the Mysteries of Demeter, which retained the traditional cult center at Eleusis and to which initiates were required to travel if they desired to become initiates, a non-ethnically based Hellenized Mysteries of Isis finally spread, according to Diodorus Siculus, through "practically the entire inhabited world" (1.25.4)—not, however, without resistance from Rome. Given imperial suspicion of foreign-sounding associations, Rome attempted to suppress the cult in the first century BCE and again early in the first century CE. This popular cult nevertheless survived and flourished until the prohibition of paganism at the end of the fourth century CE.

The Hellenistic Mysteries of Isis shared some interesting features with the cult of Demeter. Whereas similarities between differing religious groups sharing a cultural context can often be accounted for by varying perspectives

---

48. Heyob, *Cult of Isis*, 6.
49. Ibid., 7.

on common cultural problematics, similarities between the Demeter and Isis cults, as among a number of Hellenized native cults and religious innovations during the period, may in part be accounted for by their overt modeling on the renowned Eleusinian rites. According to Plutarch, Timotheus, a Hierophant of the Eumolpid family, had been summoned from Eleusis by Ptolemy Soter of Egypt (367/6–282 BCE) to assist the king in propagating a new cult of S(e)arapis as Isis's consort (Plutarch, *De Iside et Osiride* 28). And, in Plutarch's account, there are a number of similarities between the Hellenized myth of Isis and the version of the Demeter myth preserved in the *Homeric Hymn to Demeter*: Isis, like Demeter, founded her own cult after a period of sorrowful wandering, during their wanderings both goddesses came to rest by a spring in silence until taken in by the local queen as a nurse for her infant child, and in a curious story common to both accounts, the two deities burned away the mortality of their adopted child by night. Despite such common motifs, apparently borrowed from the earlier myth of Demeter, the Hellenized Mysteries of Isis retained its Egyptian "aura" by employing Egyptian iconic motifs and by displaying sacred books purportedly written in Egyptian hieroglyphics, a language that, according to the second-century-CE writer and purported initiate Apuleius, was "impossible to be read" for noninitiates (*Metamorphoses* 11.22).

Since Hellenistic religious groups apparently recognized no official headquarters or authority (the Eleusinian cult being an exception) that might have sent out missionaries to propagate a particular doctrine or that might have ensured some measure of "orthodoxy," the question remains how to account for the widespread dissemination of such formerly native religious cults as that of Isis. It would seem that a number of formerly native religions might initially have developed from the Hellenistic proliferation of ethnic associations; there is no question that a religious (or idealistic) dimension was "embedded" in virtually all of these groups.[50] When the ethnic or familial rationale for these ethnic societies was no longer compelling, as in cases of assimilation, mobility, or demise of the first generation, new members could be recruited by conferring kinship status upon nonethnic petitioners through rites of initiation modeled on the juridical practice of adoption. Some of these fictive-kin societies, many of which already claimed the designation *mystery*, may have evolved into the famous mystery cults of the Hellenistic world in which formerly familial or native deities became universalized in order to provide patronage for their clientele in an internationalized context.

50. Kloppenborg, "Collegia and *Thiasoi*," 18; Cotter, "Collegia and Roman Law," 79.

The sole reason for anyone to be initiated into such a cult as that of the Egyptian Isis would be if he or she were in fact "non-Egyptian." Membership in the Hellenized (second-century-CE) Mysteries of Isis was no longer attainable, according to Apuleius's Isis novel *Metamorphoses*, by birth or by inheritance (11.15), but by an initiatory rebirth (11.16, 21), in which Isis became recognized as the initiate's spiritual mother and the presiding priest of Isis as his spiritual father (11.25). An earlier story in the novel proleptically confirms this view of initiation: Venus, who is subsequently identified with Isis (11.2), admonished her son for his disobedience and threatened to "produce another son much better than him" through "adoption" and bequeathing to this adopted son her divine legacy (5.29).

Whereas the Mysteries of Isis, like that of Demeter, retained its character of conferring fictive kinship, at least in its initiatory discourse, the Hellenized cult of Isis thoroughly redefined the character of its formerly Egyptian deity as a "universal queen of heaven" (11.2, 5). Unlike the local deities of an earlier period, Hellenistic deities like Isis came to be understood as playing a cosmic role. Thus, in contrast to the Hellenistic problematic of life governed by a cosmic rule of chance or fortune, Isis was portrayed as the beneficent "Good Fortune" that "is not blind, but can see" (11.15). Initiation into the Mysteries of Isis involved, in other words, not only adoption into the *ethnic* circle of the Hellenized Isis and the acquisition of her "Egyptian" wisdom but also her universalized cosmic protection.

The Mysteries of Glycon

The oracle and "mysteries" of Glycon, established in the second century CE by Alexander of Abonoteichos, offer a good example of Hellenistic religious innovation on the model of the Eleusinian mysteries. According to an exposé of Alexander by his contemporary Lucian of Samasota (*Alexander the False Prophet*), Alexander began his career as a teacher of spirituality in the tradition of Apollonius of Tyana, a first-century contemporary of Jesus and an itinerate neo-Pythagorean sage who healed the sick, exorcised demons and taught ascetic purity. Subsequently, Alexander teamed up with a certain Cocconas and the two devised an elaborate scheme to construct an oracle of "Glycon," who they claimed was a new manifestation of Asclepius, the physician deity who cured illness by giving oracular instructions through dreams and who was most often portrayed with a serpent coiled about his staff. Following the untimely death of Cocconas, Alexander successfully established his oracle in Abonoteichus. This oracle, which involved a serpent, a puppet head controlled by hidden strings and a speaking tube, amazed the growing crowds, which responded to extravagant reports that Alexander had planted throughout the empire (Lucian, *Alexander the False Prophet* 15, 26).

Eventually, Alexander established "a celebration of mysteries" over which he presided as hierophant accompanied by "a number of would-be Eumolpids and Kerykes" but that explicitly excluded such "atheists" as Epicureans and Christians. The rites of these mysteries included an initial proclamation "as at Athens," a reference to the Athenian proclamation that preceded the Eleusinian mysteries, and "torchlight ceremonies" as in the Eleusinian celebrations (Lucian, *Alexander the False Prophet* 38–40). The widespread popularity of this cult, which was given imperial recognition by Marcus Aurelius, is corroborated by a number of gems, coins, and inscriptions discovered from this period.[51]

The Mysteries of Mithras

The Mysteries of Mithras provide an example of religious innovation based on fictive claims to ethnicity. According to Plutarch, Romans were introduced to the cult of Mithras, originally an Indo-Persian deity, by Cilician pirates who had been transported to Italy following their defeat in 67 BCE by the Roman general Pompey (Plutarch, *Pompeius* 24). Whatever the historical origins of Roman Mithraism, it is clear that the Mysteries of Mithras were one of the *new* religions of the late Hellenistic period. Its widespread presence is documented from the second through the fourth century CE by archaeological finds of Mithraea or Mithraic temples. While Mithraic finds are distributed throughout the Roman world, they are clustered especially in Rome and its vicinity as well as along the borders of the empire, especially along Hadrian's Wall in England, along the Rhine and Danube, and Rome's Eastern frontier. This distribution of Mithraea along the boundaries of the empire but centering in Rome itself has led some to suggest that perhaps Mithraism was largely a Roman innovation rather than a cult transported from Persia. Although Persia itself was one of Rome's traditional enemies, this view capitalizes upon Mediterranean peoples' attraction to "wisdom from the East"—similar to the attraction of eastern wisdom in the modern West, an attraction that in antiquity dates from the attribution of universal wisdom to Pythagoras as the consequence of his purported travels in Egypt.

While dispersed throughout the empire, Mithraic organization was characterized by numerous small, apparently autonomous, groups. Inscriptions indicate that these Mithraic cells, similar to other religious groups of

51. Harmon, *Lucian 4*, 173.

the Hellenistic period, were organized as "brotherhoods" under the leadership of a "father," the highest of the seven grades of Mithraic initiation. Initiation into this brotherhood, consequently, must have had overtones of adoption into the Mithraic "family lineage," a fictive genealogy that originated with the "Persian" deity, Mithras, and, according to the name of the fifth stage of initiation, claimed Persians as ancestors. Consequently, all members of this *gens* (Gk. γένος) were in principle eligible to achieve the highest grade of initiation, the presiding *pater*—functionally equivalent to hierophant—and to minister to his own Mithraic cell, contributing thereby to the spread of the cult.

Although the Mithraic groups seem to have shared the similarity of kin organization, there seems to have been no unifying doctrine for the cult apart from the ubiquitous presence of the tauroctony or central cult image of Mithras slaying a bull. This image has been identified as a "star-map" with each of its component images (e.g., the dog, cup, scorpion, or bull) representing signs of the zodiac positioned with respect to the celestial equator.

The cult icon clearly indicates an astral orientation. Each Mithraeum, constructed in caves, or rooms made to resemble caves (with a spectacular example of the latter to be seen in the Baths of Caracalla and that beneath San Clemente in Rome), symbolized the cosmos; their arched ceilings were often decorated with planets, stars, or the signs of the zodiac.

When initiates, in rites held in these Mithraea, proceeded progressively through the seven grades of Mithraic initiation, they symbolically ascended a seven-runged, cosmic ladder of initiation. As a result, Mithraic initiates ritually transcended this-worldly existence with its cosmic and social problematics and symbolically entered into the eighth, hypercosmic heaven. Mithraism thus shared with Platonism of late antiquity a soteriological goal of cosmic transcendence.[52]

Gnostic and Hermetic Traditions

At the core of those positions that may be termed "gnostic" is a dualistic view of the cosmos, in which spirit and matter are understood to be sharply antithetical, together with the conviction that the true or spiritual self is consubstantial with a spiritual reality or deity that transcends the material cosmos. This consubstantiality with a transcendental or hypercosmic deity was based on gnostic claims to spiritual descent from and, therefore, kinship with the deity. The nature of this genealogical descent was spelled out

---

52. See the reports of the Neoplatonist Porphyry on Mithraism in Origen, *Contra Celsum* 6.22; and Porphyry, *De antro nympharum* 5–6, 15, 18, 20, 24.

in various mythologies of cosmogonic fall that offered an explanation for the gnostics' earthly existence in the flesh, governed by the senses. In a tractate representative of the "Sethian" gnostic tradition, we read, for example, that after the Invisible Spirit had placed Adam over the first aeon "with the mighty one, the Autogenes, the Christ,"

> he placed his son Seth over the second aeon. And in the third aeon the seed [descendants] of Seth was placed . . . And the souls of the saints were placed [there]. And in the fourth aeon the souls were placed of those who do not know the Pleroma and who did not repent at once, but who persisted for a while and repented afterwards.[53]

If a soteriological "restoration" was to be "realized," one's true origin and spiritual genealogy must be "known." In the famous words of Theodotus, a second-century Valentinian (one of the two major gnostic traditions alongside the Sethian), true knowledge is that "of who we were, and what we have become, where we were or where we were placed, whither we hasten, from what we are redeemed, what birth is and what rebirth."[54] Gnosticism explicitly represented, consequently, the kinship claims characteristic of Hellenistic social groups generally but now expressed cosmologically in terms of the revival of Platonic transcendentalism in the late Hellenistic period.

Some gnostics in third-century Rome, in fact, associated themselves with the Neoplatonic circle of Plotinus and even attended some of the philosopher's lectures (*Enneads* 2.9.10). Perhaps because of the closeness of this association, Plotinus wrote a treatise *Against the Gnostics*, attempting to distinguish his teachings from theirs (2.19). Whereas the gnostics rejected this material world and, consequently, its creator as evil and developed their teachings around the theme of a hypercosmic or transcendental goal, Plotinus maintained that this creation is good and beautiful—an argument that later led Augustine to break with the Manichaean-gnostic tradition with which he had earlier identified. And, according to the philosophers, the gnostics complained that "Plato had not penetrated to the depths of intelligible reality" and they appealed, consequently, to occult revelations by such figures as Zoroaster, Zostrianus, Nicotheus, Allogenes, Messos (Porphyry, *Vita Plotini* 16). This claim by the gnostics to an oral tradition of revelation allowed a degree of mythological imagination in these traditions that exceeded the rational speculations of even the most metaphysically inclined of the philosophers and was matched only in the hermetic tradition.

---

53. The *Apocryphon of John* 2.1.9.11–22; translated by Robinson, *Nag Hammadi Library*, 109–10.

54. *Excerpts of Theodotus* 78.2; in Casey, ed. and trans., *Excerpta ex Theodoro*.

Hermeticism was a philosophico-religious tradition similar in many ways to that of the gnostics, though the oral teaching to which the hermetists appealed was transmitted characteristically in the "succession" of Hermes, the Greek name for the Egyptian deity Thoth (Herodotus 2.67, 138). Like the Greek Hermes, Thoth was a guider of souls, a messenger of the gods and the lord of wisdom. In addition, the Hellenistic Hermes/Thoth was considered by some to be the ruler of the heavenly bodies and of their influence on individual destiny.[55] Whereas the hermetic traditions also assumed consubstantiality with deity, many of them assumed some sort of continuity rather than dualism between matter and spirit and employed, consequently, an "alchemical" strategy in which matter as well as spirit might be transformed.

Though there may have been organized gnostic and hermetic associations, little is known of their social organization; rather their transcendental views seem to have been interpretations of existing traditions such as Pythagoreanism, Platonism, Judaism, and especially Christianity. Thus, Valentinus, one of the more well-known of the Christian gnostics, claimed an interpretation of Christianity based upon direct revelation from the child *Logos*. And Theodotus wrote, with reference to typical Hellenistic cosmic imagery, that "a strange and new star arose doing away with the old astral decree, shining with a new unearthly light, which revolved on a new path of salvation, as the Lord himself, men's guide, who came down to earth to transfer from Fate to his providence those who believed in Christ" (*Excerpts of Theodotus* 74.2).

Adherents of these hierarchically structured interpretations understood themselves to possess an understanding superior to that held by non-gnostic, "orthodox" representatives of the various traditions to which they adhered, even as Plotinus understood his philosophical interpretations to be superior to those of traditional Platonism. Nevertheless, their claims to kinship with transcendental reality, which essentially divinized the human, represented a bold, humanistic challenge to the enduring materialistic traditions of Hellenistic philosophy, and came to dominate Western philosophy and religion until the modern rise of the empirical sciences.

Conclusions

Recent scholarship has redeemed the Graeco-Roman period and its Hellenistic culture from earlier judgments about its insignificance. In addition to their own intrinsic and enduring values, Hellenistic intellectual traditions

---

55. Fowden, *Egyptian Hermes*, 22–23.

and religious practices were the forces that produced and propelled those first experiments in thought and practice that later became known collectively as "Christian," as well as providing the foil against which the early Christianities defined their identity. These forces and foils, only a few of which have been proposed in the previous discussion, were diverse markers on the cultural map of the Graeco-Roman world. A complete philosophical cartography for the context of the Christian beginnings must include, in addition to further discussion of the Epicurean, Stoic, and Sceptic traditions,[56] a full discussion of the emergence and influence of Hellenistic Platonism[57]—and not only the ideas of these philosophical traditions but their style of expression and argumentation as well as their real practices—the development and use of Stoic technologies of the self in late antiquity, for example.[58] And, in addition to those religious options surveyed above, a complete cartography of religious options during the Graeco-Roman period would include discussions of the introduction into the West of Hellenized rites of such cults as those of the Syrian goddess Atargatis and of the Syrian Jupiter Dolichenus, the introduction into Rome of Asclepius and of the Phrygian "Great Mother of the Gods," and of the largely neglected influence of official Roman religious practices. And the web of "continuities and antagonisms" between all these philosophical, religious, and religiophilosophical alternatives and those of the early Christianities must be precisely traced. These relationships must include not only those of thought and practice but of mythology and social formation as well. The significance of philosophical claims to truth and those of religion to salvation and redemption, for example, is clear with reference to the cosmological architecture of the Hellenistic world,[59] but what were the social or political attractions of such claims?—as surely there must have been. Perhaps the previous overview provides some hint of the richness and complexity of that culture that has so determined the intellectual and religious views of subsequent Western civilization, both in its own right and through the Christian religion to which it gave birth.

---

56. For which, see Long, *Hellenistic Philosophy*.
57. Dillon, *Middle Platonists*.
58. Foucault, *History of Sexuality*, vol. 3, *Care of the Self*.
59. Martin, *Hellenistic Religions*, 134–37.

References

Berger, Peter. *The Sacred Canopy: Elements of a Sociological Theory of Religion*. Garden City, NY: Doubleday, 1967.

Brown, Raymond E. *The Birth of the Messiah: A Commentary of the Infancy Narratives in Matthew and Luke*. New York: Doubleday, 1977.

Burkert, Walter. *Greek Religion: Archaic and Classical*. Translated by John Raffan. Ancient World. Oxford: Blackwell, 1985.

Casey, Robert P., ed. and trans. *The Excerpta ex Theodoto of Clement of Alexandria*. Studies and Documents 1. London: Christophers, 1934.

Clinton, Kevin. *The Sacred Officials of the Eleusinian Mysteries*. Transactions of the American Philosophical Society n.s. 64, pt. 3 Philadelphia: American Philosophical Society, 1974.

Cotter, Wendy. "The Collegia and Roman Law: State Restrictions on Voluntary Associations, 64 BCE–200 CE." In *Voluntary Associations in the Graeco-Roman World*, edited by John S. Kloppenborg and Stephen G. Wilson, 74–89. London: Routledge, 1996.

Dillon, John. *The Middle Platonists: A Study of Platonism, 80 BC to AD 220*. London: Duckworth, 1977.

Droysen, Johann G. *Geschichte des Hellenismus*. Edited by Erich Bayer. 3 vols. Munich: Deutscher Taschenbuch, 1980 [1836–1843; 2nd ed. 1877].

Eddy, Samuel K. *The King Is Dead: Near Eastern Resistance to Hellenism, 334–31 BC*. Lincoln: University of Nebraska Press, 1961.

Foucart, Paul F. *Des Associations Religieuses chez les Grecs*. Paris: Klincksieck, 1873.

———. *Les Mystères d'Eleusis*. Paris: Picard, 1914.

Foucault, Michel. *The History of Sexuality*. Vol. 3, *The Care of the Self*. Translated by Robert Hurley. New York: Pantheon, 1986.

Fowden, Garth. *The Egyptian Hermes: A Historical Approach to the Late Pagan Mind*. Cambridge: Cambridge University Press, 1986.

Frischer, Bernard. *The Sculpted Word: Epicureanism and Philosophical Recruitment in Ancient Greece*. Berkeley: University of California Press, 1982.

Gast, John. *The History of Greece from the Accession of Alexander till its Final Subjection to the Roman Power*. London: Murray, 1782.

Gillies, John. *The History of the World from the Reign of Alexander to that of Augustus*. London: Strahan and Cadell and Davies, 1807.

Grant, Frederick C. *Hellenistic Religions: The Age of Syncretism*. Library of Liberal Arts. Indianapolis: Bobbs-Merrill, 1953.

Grote, George. *History of Greece*. New York: Harper, 1854.

Hardy, Edward R. "The City of God." In *A Companion to the Study of St. Augustine*, edited by Roy W. Battenhouse, 257–86. Oxford: Oxford University Press, 1955.

Harmon, A. M. *Lucian 4*. LCL. Cambridge: Harvard University Press, 1925.

Heyob, Sharon Kelly *The Cult of Isis among Women in the Graeco-Roman World*. EPRO 51. Leiden: Brill, 1975.

Kant, Immanuel. *Critique of Judgment*. Translated by J. H. Bernard. Hafner Library of Classics. New York: Hafner, 1951.

Kloppenborg, John S. "Collegia and *Thiasoi*: Issues in Function, Taxonomy and Membership." In *Voluntary Associations in the Graeco-Roman World*, edited by John S. Kloppenborg and Stephen G. Wilson, 16–30. London: Routledge, 1996.

Kloppenborg, John S., and Stephen G. Wilson, eds. *Voluntary Associations in the Graeco-Roman World*. London: Routledge, 1996.

Long, A. A. *Hellenistic Philosophy: Stoics, Epicureans, Sceptics.* 2nd ed. Berkeley: University of California Press, 1986.
Mack, Burton L. *The Lost Gospel: The Book of Q & Christian Origins.* San Francisco: HarperSanFrancisco, 1993.
———. *A Myth of Innocence: Mark and Christian Origins.* Philadelphia: Fortress, 1988.
———. *Who Wrote the New Testament? The Making of the Christian Myth.* San Fran-cisco: HarperSanFrancisco, 1995.
McLean, B. Hudson. 1996. "The Place of Cult in Voluntary Associations and Christian Churches on Delos." In *Voluntary Associations in the Graeco-Roman World,* edited by John S. Kloppenborg and Stephen G. Wilson, 186–225. London: Routledge, 1996.
Martin, Luther H. *Hellenistic Religions: An Introduction.* New York: Oxford University Press, 1987.
Mason, Steve. "*Philosophiai*: Graeco-Roman, Judean and Christian." In *Voluntary Associations in the Graeco-Roman World,* edited by John S. Kloppenborg and Stephen G. Wilson, 31–58. London: Routledge, 1996.
Murray, Gilbert. *Five Stages of Greek Religion.* Garden City, NY: Doubleday, 1955.
Mylonas, George E. *Eleusis and the Eleusinian Mysteries.* Princeton: Princeton University Press, 1961.
Nilsson, Martin P. *Cults, Myths, Oracles, and Politics in Ancient Greece.* Skrifter utg. av Svenska institutet i Athen 8/I. Lund: Gleerup, 1951.
———. *The Dionysiac Mysteries of the Hellenistic and the Roman Age.* Ancient Religion and Mythology. Svenska institutet i Athen. Skrifter. Acta, Series altera 5. New York: Arno, 1975.
Nock, Arthur D. *Conversion: The Old and the New in Religion from Alexander the Great to Augustine of Hippo.* Oxford: Oxford University Press, 1933.
Paden, William E. *Religious Worlds: The Comparative Study of Religion.* Boston: Beacon, 1994.
Robinson, James M., ed. *The Nag Hammadi Library.* 3rd rev. ed. San Francisco: Harper & Row, 1990.
Rudolph, Kurt. *Gnosis: The Nature and History of Gnosticism.* Translated and edited by Robert McLachlan Wilson. 2nd ed. San Francisco: Harper & Row, 1983.
Said, Edward W. *Beginnings: Intention and Method.* New York: Basic, 1975.
Samuel, Alan E. *The Promise of the West: The Greek World, Rome and Judaism.* London: Routledge, 1988.
Smith, Jonathan Z. *Drudgery Divine: On the Comparison of Early Christianities and the Religions of Late Antiquity.* Jordan Lectures in Comparative Religion 14. Chicago Studies in the History of Judaism. Chicago: University of Chicago Press, 1990.
Taylor, Lily R. *The Divinity of the Roman Emperor.* Philological Monographs 1. Middletown, CT: American Philological Association, 1931.
Ulansey, David. "The Heavenly Veil Torn: Mark's Cosmic Inclusio." *Journal of Biblical Literature* 110 (1991) 123–25.
———. *The Origins of the Mithraic Mysteries: Cosmology and Salvation in the Ancient World.* New York: Oxford University Press, 1989.
Vico, Giambattista. *The New Science of Giambattista Vico.* Translated by Thomas Goddard Bergin and Max Harold Fisch. Ithaca: Cornell University Press, 1970.
Williams, Daniel D. "The Significance of St. Augustine Today." In *A Companion to the Study of St. Augustine,* edited by Roy W. Battenhouse, 3–14. Oxford: Oxford University Press, 1955.

2

The Very Idea of Globalization: The Case of Hellenistic Empire

> **Reg** [leader of the Peoples' Front of Judea seeking to rally a group of his followers for a commando raid on Pilate's palace, smugly demands of them]: What have [the Roman Imperialists] ever given us . . . ?
> **Commandos**: The aqueduct [replies one of the Commandos brightly]. . . And the sanitation [offers another] . . . And [they continue, in turn,] roads . . . , irrigation . . . , medicine . . . , education . . . , health . . . , wine . . . , public baths . . . , public order . . . , [and, finally] peace.
> —THE LIFE OF BRIAN[1]

THIS COMEDIC INTERCHANGE FROM the film Monty Python's *The Life of Brian*, in which local activists ironically enumerate for their revolutionary leader the benefits introduced into the provinces by Roman conquest, well instantiates the shrewd observation by Michel Foucault that relationships of power represent "a complex strategical situation" that is not only prescribed by the dominators but that is also generally acquiesced to by the dominated.[2] "What makes power hold good, what makes it accepted," Foucault writes,

> is the fact that it doesn't only weigh on us as a force that says no, but that it traverses and produces things, it induces pleasure, forms knowledge, produces discourse. It needs to be considered as a productive network which runs through the whole social

---

1. Chapman et al., *Life of Brian*, 20.
2. Foucault, *History of Sexuality*, 1:93.

body, much more than as a negative instance whose function is repression.[3]

In the view of many commentators, contemporary shifts in the "organizing principles of social life and world order" termed *globalization* concerns precisely the ambiguous relationships of power described by Foucault.[4] But such shifting relationships of power can be located already in antiquity with, for example, the realization of the ecumenical ideals attributed to Alexander the Great by Roman rule, a universalizing organization of power that has inspired all subsequent Western political history.[5]

Analysts of globalization have tended to be concerned with describing correlative sets of sociopolitical factors and their positive or negative consequences (i.e., the "instrumentalities, configuration, distribution, and impacts" of power[6]) rather than offering any explanation for *how* globalization occurs and *why* it is so often tolerated—if, indeed, this is a valid assessment of globalization at all. The question, then, in other words, concerns the ways the pleasures, the forms of knowledge and the discourses produced by power relations are transmitted in such a way as to be generally accepted by those dominated. As the cognitive anthropologists Scott Atran and Ara Norenzayan have recently essayed:

> Many factors are important in determining the extent to which ideas achieve a cultural level of distribution. Some are ecological, including the rate of prior exposure to an idea in a population; physical, as well as social, facilitators and barriers to communication and imitation; and institutional structures that reinforce or suppress an idea. Other factors are psychological, including the cognitive and emotional ease with which an idea can be accommodated, represented, and remembered; the intrinsic interest that it evokes in people so that it is processed and rehearsed; and motivation and facility to communicate the idea to others.[7]

Whereas the ecological, physical, and institutional factors of imperial globalization in antiquity have been well addressed by historians, the psychological factor has been neglected. With an eye towards the contemporary

---

3. Foucault, *Power/Knowledge*, 119.
4. Held and McGrew, *Globalization*, 7.
5. Ternes, "Study of Roman Religion"; Gilhus, "Globalization and Religion."
6. Held and McGrew, *Globalization*, 8.
7. Atran and Norenzayan, "Religion's Evolutionary Landscape," 30.

situation, I venture an exploration of the psychological factors underlying the proximate successes of Alexander's Graeco-Roman empire.

I

Given the evolutionary and cognitive history of *Homo sapiens*, the development of anything like the "flows and patterns of social interaction" linking together "distant communities," that are currently termed 'globalization,'[8] are preternatural. As the cognitive psychologist Pascal Boyer has observed,

> our systems for social interaction did not evolve in the context of vast groups and abstract institutions . . . We evolved as small bands of foragers and that kind of existence is the context in which we developed the special features of our social mind. Sedentary settlements, large tribes, kingdoms and other such modern institutions are in terms of evolutionary time, a very recent development.[9]

The evolutionary basis for small-scale, face-to-face social organizations is found in the theory of "inclusive fitness"—the argument that altruism among kin exists in proportion to their relatedness in order to protect and propagate a shared genetic inheritance.[10] Biologically based kinship groups subsequently came to be mentally represented in terms of legitimate and legitimating social relationships, and extended to nonkin through juridical strategies such as adoption—a technique of kin recruitment, and marriage—the basis of kin alliances through systems of exchange, and finally, as the self-conscious formation of extended group membership as fictive kin societies.[11] In other words, when inclusive fitness was maximized in ways valued by its individual members over competitor groups, nepotism became replaced by reciprocity as the basis of human association.[12] Enhancements of inclusive fitness that become self-consciously manipulated for the perceived good of a particular association spawned hierarchical distributions of power (Aristotle, *Politica* 1.2),[13] which have been termed, since antiquity, "political" (1.1).

---

8. Held and McGrew, *Globalization*, 1.
9. Boyer, *Religion Explained*, 250.
10. Hamilton, "Genetical Evolution."
11. Martin, "Akin to the Gods"; Martin, "Biology, Sociology"; Martin, "Comparativism."
12. Alexander, *Darwinism*, 161.
13. Dunbar, "Coevolution," 687.

Boyer has noted that when large-scale political entities did develop, people nevertheless still tended to cluster in face-to-face "solidarity-based groups."[14] Even contemporary America is rife with what the nineteenth-century political writer Alexis de Tocqueville presciently described as "secondary associations."[15] As one more recent observer has noted, such subcultures arise and flourish most notably "in places that lack rootedness and a sense of space."[16] Such "special interest associations" often "fill the void left by the erosion of traditional social groupings" by self-consciously organizing as extended families.[17] It was a similar disintegration of the traditional locative definitions of social existence, consequent upon the expansive mercantile and military ventures characteristic of the Hellenistic period, that occasioned the proliferation of social clubs and religious cults, more often than not organized as fictive kin associations during this period, even as emigration and immigration in modernity occasioned the emergence of ethnic societies, and of their fictive expansions, in the new world.[18] The perseverance of such "solidarity-based groups," which Boyer reports tend always to be of "the same size and involve similar emotions, regardless of the country, language, size of the institution or town, and other differences,"[19] not only expresses the sociobiological basis for their production but suggests a cognitive constraint as well.[20]

It would seem, consequently, that local, small group formations represent a biocognitive optimum for sociopolitical organization by *Homo sapiens* and that it is the emergence even of the idea for large-scale anonymous communities among humans that requires explanation. As the cognitive anthropologist Harvey Whitehouse has argued, large-scale communities and their universalizing ideologies only make sense "once the capacity for conceptualizing [them] . . . ha[s] been established. Before something so abstract could be codified," he concludes, its "conceptual reality" must somehow be realized.[21]

14. Boyer, *Religion Explained*, 249.
15. Tocqueville, *Democracy*, II.2.5.
16. Sides, *Stomping Grounds*, 17–18.
17. Martin, "Anti-individualistic," 124.
18. Martin, Review of *Voluntary*.
19. Boyer, *Religion Explained*, 249.
20. Dunbar, "Coevolution," 681–87, 691–93.
21. Whitehouse, *Arguments and Icons*, 41; see Held and McGrew, *Globalization*, 27.

II

Historians and social scientists tend to ontologize abstractions of large-scale human associations—states, empires, societies, and so forth—and to assume that the presence of these "entities" requires no further explanation than a presumed historical development. But how did these historical developments take place in just the way they did given historical possibilities for alternative lines of development? And how did these diverse histories proceed independently one from another in ways that are nevertheless comparable and generalizable?

In the early 1970s, the anthropologist George Peter Murdock proposed that abstractions of "supraindividual concepts," such as "culture," "social system," and, we might add, "globalization," are "mere epiphenomena" and that human behavior might be more precisely studied as the outcome of "pluralities of individuals."[22] In the recent summary of this point of view by Atran, such large-scale entities

> are not ontologically distinct "superorganisms" or "independent variables" with precise contents or boundaries. They are no more things in and of themselves, or "natural kinds" with their own special laws, than are cloud or sand patterns.[23]

The task then, Atran concludes,

> is to scientifically explain [such abstractions] . . . in terms of material causes. [They] . . . exist, and are explained, to the extent that they reliably express structurally enduring relationships among mental states and behaviors and where these material relationships enable a given population of individuals to maintain itself in repeated social interactions with a range of ecological contexts.[24]

Even that indomitable genitor of sociological analysis, Émile Durkheim, had argued that "society exists and lives only in and through . . . individual minds . . . It is real only in so far as it has a place in human consciousness."[25] An explanation for the emergence of large-scale human interactions and communities might best begin, therefore, by thinking about them in the

---

22. Murdock, "Anthropology's Mythology," 19, cited in Alexander, *Darwinism*, 48, 141.
23. Atran, *In Gods We Trust*, 10.
24. Ibid., 10, 112; see Sperber, *Explaining Culture*.
25. Durkheim, *Elementary Forms*, 359.

way cognitive scientists think of "culture," that is, about how they are represented in the minds of individuals.

In his perceptive study of the rise and spread of nationalism in the second half of the twentieth century, Benedict Anderson has argued that "all communities larger than primordial villages of face-to-face contact ... are imagined" in that members "will never know most of their fellow-members, meet them, or even hear of them, yet in the minds of each lives the image of the communion."[26] Abstractions like "imagined community" are best understood, in other words, as more or less similar ideas, occupying an aggregate of individual brains, whether those ideas have been spread from mind to mind by conquest or by more benign forms of contact.[27] Such an "epidemiological" explanation for culture, based on an exploration of microprocesses, is not completely alien to historians. William McNeill, for example, has studied the effects of a series of microprocesses on world history—that of the spread of infectious diseases being perhaps the most well known.[28] Historians have, however, been generally reluctant to extend their explorations of microprocesses to the level of the human mind. The question remains, consequently, about why ideas are selected by some individuals but rejected by others, all of whom occupy the same context under the same conditions.

Contagion, in itself, does not explain contamination by an idea, the redundant assumption often employed in explanations of "syncretisms."[29] As the epidemiological analogy suggests, some minds might exhibit either an innate or an acquired immunity to certain ideological infections. This immunity might be based upon an intuitive rejection of ideologically possible but cognitively exceptional proposals, exploitation of close kin, for example, or representations of nonkin as benign. Or, an immunity to certain notions may have developed through exposure to indigenous ideas since birth—what Giambattista Vico termed "common sense"[30]—and/or through explicit indoctrination since early childhood about the inherent dangers of those perceived to be alien. The successful expression of either of these possibilities exploits sociobiological and biocognitive biases. Consequently, a discussion of the spread of a particular idea, or that of an aggregate of ideas (globalization, for example), must also include an explanation for how inva-

26. Anderson, *Imagined Communities*, 6.
27. Sperber, *Explaining Culture*, 1.
28. McNeill, *Plagues*. Also see McNeill, *Pursuit*; McNeill, *Keeping Together*; Gaddis, *Landscape of History*, 25–26.
29. See Martin, "To Use 'Syncretism'"; Pachis, "Manufacturing Religion."
30. Vico, *New Science*, II.xii.142.

sive ideas overcame local ones in the first place and how the palliative ones came to be lost. How in other words are ideas represented and selectively retained by, and transmitted among, human minds?

III

Certainly one idea central to any instance of human sociality is, as I have suggested above, that of kinship. And the universal kinship of mankind is precisely one *idea* that was successfully employed by Alexander the Great in the consolidation of his empire, or at least this was an idea attributed to his authority (Arrianus, *Anabasis* 7.11; Diodorus Siculus 18.4.4.; Plutarch, *De fortuna Alexandri* 1.329C–D).[31] Once an idea such as kinship is introduced into a population, it would resonate with the salient biocognitive proclivity of all humans for kin solidarity and tend to be selected for to the exclusion of alternative ideologies of association among nonkin.[32] And since kinship among *Homo sapiens* has functioned within recorded history as an ideal for sociopolitical formation and legitimation, its extension to that of large-scale imagined communities would fall upon receptive ears. "Regardless of the actual inequality and exploitation that may prevail," such an imagined sense of fraternity, Anderson concludes, makes the conception of large-scale communities possible.[33]

The origins of large-scale communities may, according to evolutionary biologists, have been motivated primarily by intergroup predation and aggression, and by the maintenance of a balance of power between them.[34] "Arguably the most dangerous and deceptive predator for the genus Homo over a substantial portion of the past few million years has been Homo itself,"[35] and "it appears that no other species or set of species could possibly fulfill the function of forcing the ever-larger groups that have developed during human history."[36] In Atran's summary of this argument, "this 'runaway social competition' led to larger groups of a non-kin sort that is absent from the rest of the animal world."[37] As genetic ties weakened among the members of such communities, however, such "large groups," Atran continues, "would also generate more and greater threats from defecting non-kin

31. Martin, "Comparativism," 300.
32. Alexander, *Darwinism*, 153.
33. Anderson, *Imagined Communities*, 7.
34. Alexander, *Darwinism*, 222, 232.
35. Atran, *In Gods We Trust*, 69.
36. Alexander, *Darwinism*, 232.
37. Atran, *In Gods We Trust*, 69.

within and prod competitors to form even larger groups that would threaten from without."[38] Certainly the successful rise to power of Alexander and his Graeco-Macedonian empire is seen in the context of Persian competition and predation.[39]

Defecting nonkin, on the other hand, would most likely also represent themselves in terms of kinship. A preeminent example of such resistance during the Hellenistic period was, of course, the Jewish resistance to Hellenization that led to the Maccabeean revolts—whether that resistance was to Hellenization imposed by Seleucid rule (1 and 2 Maccabees), to that advocated by a party of Hellenizing Jews themselves,[40] or to both. Ideas of Hellenization in this instance—as well as of globalization in the contemporary world—may, in other words, be understood as imposed by external power, as advanced by some within the dominated population itself, or as a contagious infection of individual minds across differing domains of a particular population which produced a range of similar symptoms.

Once established, dominant forms of power can explicitly operate to weaken or to suppress local domains of power.[41] An example of the assertion of such power at the expense of localized alliances with reference to kinship was Greek and Roman funerary legislations that distanced kin from their ancestors by requiring burials to be beyond the city walls (i.e., beyond "civilization") while encouraging at the same time obeisance to a divine sovereignty or to state-sanctioned universalized and universalizing deities that transcended and superseded any and all kin allegiances.[42]

IV

A second idea often associated with universalization is that of a common language, an idea identified by the Greeks with that of extended kinship (Herodotus 8.144). Language, it has been suggested, might actually have evolved as a consequence of increasing group size as the crucial bonding component for maintaining the stability, through social communication, of all human groupings that exceeded those maintained by face-to-face

---

38. Ibid., 69–70.

39. I have argued that the same dynamic of kinship-kingship is also to be found in China. See Martin, "Akin to the Gods."

40. Hornblower, "Hellenism," 678b.

41. Whitehouse, *Arguments and Icons*, 2.

42. Martin, "Comparativism," 300–301.

contact.⁴³ Whatever the merits of this argument for evolutionary history,⁴⁴ the idea of a common language as the basis for large-scale association is documented for the Greeks since at least the fourth century BCE (Thucydides 2.68)—even though nothing approaching the reality of a standard Greek language emerged until the κοινή of the Hellenistic period.⁴⁵

Like Alexander's invocation of kinship, that of a Greek κοινή was both widely accepted as well as resisted. This linguistic sense of "Hellenization" (Thucydides 2.68) provided a basis for the development of a pan-Hellenic nationalism—"the idea that what the Greeks have in common as Greeks, and what distinguishes them from barbarians, is more important that what divides them";⁴⁶ and, of course, competency in Greek was a requirement for initiation into what became the universal mysteries of Demeter celebrated at Eleusis.⁴⁷ But while Greek was spoken in the Persian Empire already in the fifth and fourth centuries BCE, even prior to the Hellenization associated with Alexander and in spite of Persian anti-Greek sentiments,⁴⁸ numerous localities retained or revived their traditional languages in the face of Hellenism; Jewish anti-Seleucid propaganda in Hebrew is a well-documented example.⁴⁹

V

Space precludes a full discussion of the role of economics in processes of "globalization." Fundamentally, economic processes are grounded in the human need for survival, or in perceptions of that need, when the requirements of a particular population are greater than available resources (e.g., when the Greek city-state was unable to provide sufficient domestically produced grain to feed its citizenry,⁵⁰ or when modern industrial states are unable to provide sufficient domestically produced resources to fuel their economic growth). Initially, systems of exchange, based in the bio-cognitive dynamics of mutual altruism, emerged to provide available goods among kin. Because of the competition for such resources between groups of nonkin inhabiting the same or proximate domains, networks of trade

43. Dunbar, "Coevolution," 687–93.
44. See "Peer Commentary" in Dunbar, "Coevolution," 694–720.
45. Davies, "Language," 653b–654a.
46. Rohde, "Panhellenism," 1106a.
47. Mylonas, *Eleusis*, 248.
48. Hornblower, "Hellenism," 678a.
49. Eddy, *King Is Dead*, 219, 242–43.
50. Martin, "Eleusinian Mysteries."

subsequently emerge along with a military to establish and maintain these networks. To be successful, systems of exchange between nonkin require that a shared currency or an acceptable metrics of exchange be established, whether through agreement or through imposition.[51] In the latter case, retention of traditional systems of exchange or the striking of a local currency function as resistance to large-scale economic interaction.

VI

Religious community as much as dynastic realm and economic well-being has provided taken-for-granted frames of reference for human sociopolitical organization[52] and has oft times proved to be the more stable through time. The spread of religions during premodern times not only confirms that globalization is a relatively early historical phenomenon[53] but indicates the historical and continuing role of religion in that process (e.g., the implications of Confucianism with the imperial rule of China, of Buddhism with the empire of Ashoka, of Christianity with that of Rome, of Manichaeism with that of Persia and later with the kingdom of the Uigars, of Islam with Arabic civilization, and the like).[54] In fact, the very idea of *kingship* derives its legitimacy, Anderson observes, "from divinity, [and] not from populations, who, after all, are subjects, not citizens."[55] In the context of Graeco-Roman history, one need only refer to the reception, however reticent, of the ruler cult into the strategy of Alexander's imperium and subsequently into Augustine's Pax Romana,[56] or to the invention of new "religions of loyalty" to the Roman state such as Mithraism,[57] to appreciate claims to divine authority as legitimation for nonlocal exercises of power. On the other hand, it has long been acknowledged that resistance to the Graeco-Roman imperium "was justified almost universally in religious terms,"[58] even as resistance to contemporary processes of globalization are also legitimated.

The universalizing propensity of some religious traditions is a characteristic of what Whitehouse has termed the doctrinal mode of religiosity.

51. For Rome, see Crawford, "Coinage."
52. Anderson, *Imagined Communities*, 12.
53. Held and McGrew, *Globalization*, 6, 25.
54. Durkheim, *Elementary Forms*, 244; Martin, "Manichaean Mission"; Benavides, "Buddhism, Manichaeism."
55. Anderson, *Imagined Communities*, 19.
56. Martin, "Kingship."
57. Merkelbach, *Mithras*, 153–88.
58. Eddy, *King Is Dead*, vii.

In short, this doctrinal modality is characterized by the establishment of a set of beliefs, narratively expressed and cogently argued, that can be widely transmitted by missionaries or by representatives of some stratified central authority that controls these beliefs through routinized repetition and frequent review, and which become, thereby, commonly held by the "imagined community." By contrast, localization might be maintained by what Whitehouse terms an imagistic mode of religiosity, in which the precepts and practices of the same universalizing religious tradition, or those of some traditional alternative, are transmitted through infrequently performed but emotionally salient rituals, such as initiation rites, the locally restrained exegeses of which ensure the solidarity of small-scale, face-to-face groups. Whitehouse explains the presence of both modalities cognitively, in terms of differential processes of human memory, the doctrinal mode being primarily a function of semantic or pedagogically encoded memory, the imagistic mode being primarily that of analogically encoded episodic or autobiographical memory.[59]

From a cognitive perspective, of course, the hierarchical representations of power that we term "political" and those that we term "religious" are both evolutionary by-products, shaped, however, by a common set of selective pressures and constrained by shared mental mechanisms. For that reason, we find that religious and political claims and practices are equally implicated one with one another, whether in manifestations of religiopolitical disseminations or in those of dissent.

Political ideas, in and of themselves, are not so infectious as are religious ideas, and even if they do take hold, they do not prove to be particularly tenacious—as the recent history of socialist states suggests. The counterintuitive ideas associated with religion have, on the other hand, been shown to be especially attention arresting and, thus, highly memorable and readily and widely transmissible.[60] Examples of such counterintuitive ideas include ordinary notions of intentional agency that are nevertheless represented as exhibiting some sort of superhuman trait. Re-representations of the superhuman as supernatural, a process which was characteristic of Hellenistic religiosity generally,[61] can espouse disembodied and abstract forms of power that can override or annihilate specific cultural and environmental attachments.[62]

---

59. Whitehouse, *Arguments, and Icons*; Whitehouse, "Modes of Religiosity."
60. Boyer, *Religion Explained*.
61. Martin, *Hellenistic Religions*.
62. Atran, *In Gods We Trust*, 9.

Conclusion

None of the ideas presented in this paper concerning peoplehood, language, economics, or religion during the Hellenistic period, whether expressive of ethnicity or of empire are, in and of themselves, particularly new. Nor is the argument new that these ideas are among those to which many people intuitively cling as local expressions of traditional identity; nor is the idea new that these ideas constitute for others, as for James Joyce's Stephen Dedalus, divisive and confining nets flung over a people, from which they must escape.[63] What is new, however, is the question of *why* just these particular ideas have proven to be so powerful, not only in the Graeco-Roman context but elsewhere. I have attempted to answer this question by presenting these ideas, together with the contrasting evaluations of them, in the framework of evolutionary, biological, and cognitive theories, the "conceptual integration" of which, in contrast to the descriptions of sociopolitical correlations by historians and social scientists, offers an explanatory account of why just these ideas and not others tend to be selected for.[64] To that extent, this presentation offers support for the biocognitive theories herein employed and confirms the utility of such theories for organizing historical data and for drawing nonarbitrary conclusions from that data.

While products of natural selection are not necessarily beneficial, as the continuing transmission and mutation of disease-causing viruses demonstrate, selection does present a model supplementary to—perhaps even alternative to—those of colonialism and imperialism for understanding processes of globalization. In face of the continuing tyranny of contemporized categorizations (in other words, biocognitive theorizing) may offer historians a common human foundation upon which to construct, with greater confidence, their historiographical conclusions, even when their historical data are incomplete or fragmentary—as is the case, of course, with most historical data. This approach is already proving to be of historiographical significance: for example, in recent research on the Hellenistic mystery religions, in which I and others are currently engaged.[65]

In the present case, such theorizing suggests that large-scale sociopolitical organization, instantiated in the West at least since Hellenic antiquity and termed "globalization" by modernity, is a powerful idea rooted in the very foundations of human sociality. Although the natural optimum of human social organization may well be small, face-to-face, local communities

---

63. Joyce, *Portrait of the Artist*, 203.
64. Cosmides et al., "Introduction."
65. E.g., Martin. "Ritual Competence"; Beck, "Four Men"; Gragg, "Old and New."

and their values will, consequently, inevitably continue to be robustly represented;[66] the very idea of "globalization" (that is, of increasingly broad, nonlocal webs of social interaction with their large-scale sociopolitical implications) has nevertheless repeatedly been selected for throughout human history, whatever its threat to local distributions of power.

References

Alexander, Richard D. *Darwinism and Human Affairs*. The Jessie and John Danz. Lectures Seattle: University of Washington Press, 1979.

Anderson, Benedict. *Imagined Communities: Reflections on the Origin and Spread of Nationalism*. Rev. and extended ed. London: Verso, 1991.

Atran, Scott. *In Gods We Trust: The Evolutionary Landscape of Religion*. Evolution and Cognition. Oxford: Oxford University Press, 2002.

Atran, Scott, and Ara Norenzayan. "Religion's Evolutionary Landscape: Counterintuition, Commitment, Compassion, Communion." *Behavioral and Brain Sciences* 27 (2004) 713–70.

Beck, Roger. "Four Men, Two Sticks, and a Whip: Image and Doctrine in a Mithraic Ritual." In *Theorizing Religions Past: Archaeological and Historical Evidence*, edited by Harvey Whitehouse and Luther H. Martin, 87–104. Cognitive Science of Religion Series. Walnut Creek, CA: AltaMira, 2004.

Benavides, Gustavo. "Buddhism, Manichaeism, Markets and Empires." In *Hellenisation, Empire and Globalisation: Lessons from Antiquity*, edited by Luther H. Martin and Panayotis Pachis, 21–40. Thessaloniki: Vanias, 2004.

Boyer, Pascal. *Religion Explained: The Evolutionary Origins of Religious Thought*. New York: Basic, 2001.

Chapman, Graham, et al. *Monty Python's The Life of Brian of Nazareth*. New York: Grosset & Dunlap, 1979.

Cosmides, Leda et al. "Introduction: Evolutionary Psychology and Conceptual Integration." In *The Adapted Mind: Evolutionary Psychology and the Generation of Culture*, edited by Jerome H. Barkow et al., 3–15. New York: Oxford University Press, 1992.

Crawford, Michael H. "Coinage, Roman." In *The Oxford Classical Dictionary*, edited by Simon Hornblower and Antony Spawforth, 358a–61a. 3rd ed. Oxford: Oxford University Press, 1996.

Davies, Anna Morpurgo. "Greek Language." In *The Oxford Classical Dictionary*, edited by Simon Hornblower and Antony Spawforth, 653a–56b. 3rd ed. Oxford: Oxford University Press, 1996.

Dunbar, R. I. M. "Coevolution of Neocortical Size, Group Size and Language in Humans." *Behavioral and Brain Sciences* 16/4 (1993) 681–735.

Durkheim, Emile. *The Elementary Forms of the Religious Life*. Translated by Joseph W. Swain. New York: Free Press, 1915.

Eddy, Samuel K. *The King Is Dead: Studies in the Near Eastern Resistance to Hellenism, 334–31 BC*. Lincoln: University of Nebraska Press, 1961.

Foucault, Michel. *The History of Sexuality*. Translated by Robert Hurley. 3 vols. New York: Pantheon, 1978.

66. Meyer-Dietrich, "City-God"; Lease, "Globalization for Religion."

———. *Power/Knowledge: Selected Interviews & Other Writings 1972-1977*. Edited and translated by Colin Gordon. New York: Pantheon, 1980.
Gaddis, John L. *The Landscape of History: How Historians Map the Past*. Oxford: Oxford University Press, 2002.
Gilhus, Ingvild Sælid. "Globalization and Religion in the Roman Empire." In *Hellenisation, Empire and Globalisation: Lessons from Antiquity*, edited by Luther H. Martin and Panayotis Pachis, 85-100. Thessaloniki: Vanias, 2004.
Gragg, Douglas L. "Old and New in Roman Religion: A Cognitive Account." In *Theorizing Religions Past: Archaeological and Historical Evidence*, edited by Harvey Whitehouse and Luther H. Martin, 69-86. Cognitive Science of Religion Series. Walnut Creek, CA: AltaMira, 2004.
Hamilton, W. D. "The Genetical Evolution of Social Behaviour, I-II." *Journal of Theoretical Biology* 7 (1964) 1-52.
Held, David, and Anthony McGrew. *Globalization, Anti-Globalization*. Cambridge: Polity, 2002.
Hornblower, Simon. "Hellenism, Hellenization." In *The Oxford Classical Dictionary*, edited by Simon Hornblower and Antony Spawforth, 677b-679a. 3rd ed. Oxford: Oxford University Press, 1996.
Joyce, James. *A Portrait of the Artist as a Young Man*. Compass Books. New York: Viking, 1956.
Lease, Gary. "What Constitutes Globalization for Religion? Hallmarks from Antiquity: Late Antiquity Egypt." In *Hellenisation, Empire and Globalisation: Lessons from Antiquity*, edited by Luther H. Martin and Panayotis Pachis, 101-22. Thessaloniki: Vanias, 2004.
Martin, Luther H. "Akin to the Gods or Simply One to Another: Comparisons with Respect to Religion in Antiquity." In *Vergleichen und Verstehen in der Religionswissenschaft*, edited by Hans-Joachim Klimkeit, 147-59. Studies in Oriental Religions 41. Wiesbaden: Harrassowitz, 1997.
———. "The Anti-individualistic Ideology of Hellenistic Culture." *Numen* 41 (1994) 117-40.
———. "Biology, Sociology and the Study of Religion." *Religio: Revue pro religionistiku* 5 (1997) 21-35 (chapter 6, this volume).
———. "Comparativism and Sociobiological Theory." *Numen* 48/3 (2001) 290-308.
———. "Those Elusive Eleusinian Mystery Shows." *Helios* 13/1 (1986) 17-31 (chapter 11, this volume).
———. *Hellenistic Religions: An Introduction*. New York: Oxford University Press, 1987.
———. "Kingship and the Consolidation of Religio-Political Power during the Hellenistic Period." *Religio: Revue pro religionistiku* 8/2 (2000) 151-60 (chapter 5, this volume).
———. "The Manichaean Mission: Systemic or Syncretistic." In *Religion & Modernization in China: Proceedings of the Regional Conference of the International Association for the History of Religions*, edited by Dai Kangsheng et al., 187-96. Cambridge: Roots & Branches, 1995.
———. "Performativity, Narrativity, and Cognition: 'Demythologizing' the Roman Cult of Mithras." In *Rhetoric and Reality in Early Christianities*, edited by Willi Braun, 187-217. Studies in Christianity and Judaism 16. Waterloo, ON: Wilfrid Laurier University Press, 2005.

———. Review of *Voluntary Association in the Graeco-Roman World*, edited by John S. Kloppenborg and Stephen G. Wilson. *Method & Theory in the Study of Religion* 11 (1999) 150–55.

———. "Ritual Competence and Mithraic Ritual." In *Religion as a Human Capacity: A Festschrift in Honor of E. Thomas Lawson*, edited by Timothy Light and Brian Wilson, 245–63. SHR 99. Leiden: Brill, 2003.

———. "To Use 'Syncretism' or Not to Use 'Syncretism': That is the Question." *Historical Reflections/Réflexions Historique* 27 (2001) 389–400.

McNeill, William H. *Keeping Together in Time: Dance and Drill in Human History*. Cambridge: Harvard University Press, 1995.

———. *Plagues and Peoples*. Garden City, NY: Doubleday, 1976.

———. *The Pursuit of Power: Technology, Armed Force, and Society Since A.D. 1000*. Chicago: University of Chicago Press, 1982.

Merkelbach, Reinhold. *Mithras*. Königstein: Hain, 1984.

Meyer-Dietrich, Erika. "The City-God: An Expression for Localization." In *Hellenisation, Empire and Globalisation: Lessons from Antiquity*, edited by Luther H. Martin and Panayotis Pachis, 140–62. Thessaloniki: Vanias, 2004.

Murdock, George P. "Anthropology's Mythology." *Proceedings of Royal Anthropological Institute of Great Britain and Ireland* (1972) 17–24.

Mylonas, George E. *Eleusis and the Eleusinian Mysteries*. Princeton: Princeton University Press, 1961.

Pachis, Panayotis. "'Manufacturing Religion' in the Hellenistic Age: The Case of the Isis-Demeter Cult." In *Hellenisation, Empire and Globalisation: Lessons from Antiquity*, edited by Luther H. Martin and Panayotis Pachis, 163–207. Thessaloniki: Vanias, 2004.

Rohde, P. J., "Panhellenism." In *The Oxford Classical Dictionary*, edited by Simon Hornblower and Anthony Spawforth, 1106a. 3rd ed. Oxford: Oxford University Press, 1996.

Sides, Hampton W. *Stomping Grounds: A Pilgrim's Progress through Eight American Subcultures*. New York: Morrow, 1992.

Sperber, Dan. *Explaining Culture: A Naturalistic Approach*. Oxford: Blackwell, 1996.

Ternes, Charles M. "The Study of Roman Religion after World War II." In *The Academic Study of Religion during the Cold War*, edited by Iva Doležalová et al., 3–17. Toronto Studies in Religion 27. New York: Lang, 2001.

Toqueville, Alexis de. *Democracy in America*. Translated by H. Reeve. London: Colonial, 1900.

Vico, Giambattista. *The New Science of Giambattista Vico*. Translated and edited by Thomas G. Bergin and Max H. Fisch. Ithaca: Cornell University Press, 1970.

Whitehouse, Harvey. *Arguments and Icons: Divergent Modes of Religiosity*. Oxford: Oxford University Press, 2000.

———. "Modes of Religiosity: Towards a Cognitive Explanation of the Sociopolitical Dynamics of Religion." *Method & Theory in the Study of Religion* 14.3/4 (2002) 293–315.

3

Fate, Futurity, and Historical Consciousness in Western Antiquity[1]

> Without Memory there can be no hope—the Present is a phantom known only by its pining, if it do not breathe the vital air of the Future: and what is the Future, but the Image projected on the mist of the Unknown, and seen with a glory round its head.
> —SAMUEL TAYLOR COLERIDGE[2]

I

THE PROXIMATE CATALYST FOR this essay was the dismay expressed by colleagues in history over my assertion that the ancient Greeks never fully developed a historical consciousness. My argument followed from my work on Hellenistic religions in which I had concluded that the *mentalité* of the Graeco-Roman world was structured primarily by a spatial or cosmic order of things, and articulated by a grammar of fate expressed in various formulations: from a given order of things to a designation for randomness to outright determinism.[3] The syntax of this grammar appeared to disallow any notion of temporality as a primary arena of meaning. "The father of history" seemed to confirm my suspicion when he affirmed the subjection of human

---

1. An earlier version of this paper was presented at The College of Holy Cross, March 1989 as part of the Boston Area Colloquium on Ancient Philosophy.
2. Coleridge, *Collected Letters* v: 266.
3. Martin, *Hellenistic Religions*.

and divine doings alike to fate. "None," Herodotus has the Delphic oracle proclaim, "may escape his destined lot, not even a god" (Herodotus 1.91).

No less an authority than Plato provides support for the idea that Greek consciousness was ahistorical. In a well-known passage from the *Timaeus*, Plato described Time as "a moving likeness of eternity," which is immobile and belongs to the unity of the intelligible world (37–38). Echoing Parmenides's pronouncement that the One Being "never nor ever will be, since it is now all at once" (frag. 8,5), Plato denied reality to the past and future, the changing forms of time, arguing that only the present describes eternal being—a position still enounced in the second century CE by Plutarch (*On the E at Delphi* 392E–F), and by later Neoplatonists.[4]

Time did not exist for Plato apart from the periodic motion of the Heavens, with which he understood Time to have come into being. This cyclical model for change, common among the Ionian thinkers with whom Herodotus is associated,[5] became widespread in Greek popular and philosophical conceptions, as Aristotle showed in his survey of the subject (*Physica* 5.218.11),[6] and was later elaborated by the Stoics (see especially Posidonius [Diodorus Siculus 1.1.3] and Livy 5.37.1; 44.30.3). And it clearly characterized the view of Greek historians in their descriptions of human events. Herodotus, for example, described a dynamics of history whereby "many states that were once great have now become small: and those that were great in my time were small formerly" (1.5),[7] a dynamics he characterized as a wheel or cycle (1.207).[8]

The convention of biblical studies that the Israelites were unique among the peoples of antiquity in developing a historical consciousness provided further support for my original contention.[9] According to this argument, the Western historical attitude is a Hebraic rather than Hellenic legacy—a secularization of the Jewish, and Christian, eschatological pattern.[10]

---

4. Conford, *Plato's Cosmology*, 97–105; Sambursky and Pines, *Concept of Time*.

5. How and Wells, *Commentary on Herodotus*, 1:55. The cultures of Halicarnassus, Herodotus's birthplace, and Samos, where he spent part of his early life, were Ionian: Athens, where Herodotus later lived was of Ionian origin, and Ionia had influence in Thurii where he died.

6. Conford, *Plato's Cosmology*, 103.

7. Fornara, *Nature of History*, 105.

8. Immerwahr, *Form and Thought*, 75, 80, 150, 189, 237. See also Thucydides 1.22.4; 2.64.3; and Cochrane, *Thucydides*, 161.

9. See, for example, Anderson, *Understanding*, 487.

10. Dobschütz, "Zeit und Raum." For a philosophical justification of this position, see Löwith, *Meaning*; Butterfield, *Origins*.

The now classical statement of this view is found in Thorleif Boman's comparison of Hebrew and Greek thought.[11] Boman argued, on lexical grounds, that the two expressed quite different ways of viewing reality, especially with respect to their understanding of time and space. He concluded that

> for the Hebrews who have their existence in the temporal, the content of time plays the same role as the content of space plays for the Greeks. As the Greeks gave attention to the peculiarity of things, so the Hebrews minded the peculiarity of events.[12]

Based on such conventions, I had concluded that when Western historiographers followed Cicero in understanding Herodotus as "the father of the history" (*De legibus* 1.1.5), they simply made a Hellenophilic error.

On the other hand, I later discovered that some scholars, especially James Barr, Arnaldo Momigliano, and John Van Seters have summarily challenged these historiographical conventions. According to Van Seters, these researchers agree that "no cyclical view of time is evident in the Greek histories, whatever the philosophers might say, and there is no eschatology in the Israelite histories, whatever prophet and apocalyptist might propose."[13]

Whatever their different views of history and historiography, many classicists and biblical scholars now agree on the importance of acknowledging the circle of knowledge that is shared by a text's author with his audience for any understanding of that text. As François Hartog argues in his recent "text-centered" study of Herodorus: "Between the narrator and his addressee there exists, as a precondition for communication, a whole collection of semantic, encyclopedic, and symbolic knowledge common to both sides."[14] David Halpern, who argues that history, including biblical history, is referential and that text-centered interpretation is meaningless when applied to such literature, nevertheless agrees with Hartog that authors work within a circle of knowledge shared by their readers. As he puts it more prosaically: "Greeks write for Greeks about Greeks . . . If mad dogs wrote history, they would write about mad dogs, and exhibit the biases of their breed." These shared biases, the common knowledge to which a historian

---

11. Boman, *Hebrew Thought*.

12. Ibid., 139.

13. Van Seters, *In Search of History*, 8–9; Barr, *Biblical Words*; Momigliano, "Time," 179–204.

14. Hartog, *Mirror*, 7.

is loyal and that provides the condition for the perception of patterns in events, is requisite to any writing of history.[15]

The issue that emerges from these recent discussions is not so much one of formally comparing kinds of writing, nor one of discovering who "invented" the idea of history.[16] Rather, the questions suggested by recent research concern the culturally constituted nature of collective mentality that allowed a comprehending audience for the ancient historians and that produced them. With reference to biblical tradition, what was the nature of the Israelites' historical awareness in which they located their deity? With reference to historiographical convention, to what extent is "the father of history" actually a "son of history"?[17] Or an exemplary of historiography at all, other than in name?[18]

To provide focus for these questions, I will compare the accounts given of a common person and event, Cyrus of Persia and his conquest of Babylon, by two approximate contemporaries, Deutero-Isaiah and Herodotus. Although commentaries on the one customarily refer to the accounts of the other, the two accounts have rarely been compared with respect to what they reveal about differences or similarities between the historical understandings of their respective audiences.[19]

The Colerige quotation opening this essay presents two themes central to the following investigation that I consider to be requisite to any historical consciousness: the past as it exists in memory, and a notion of the future as "a mist of the unknown."

II

Herodotus and Deutero-Isaiah both cast Cyrus as a pivotal figure in their historical dramas. For Herodotus, Cyrus was "the Great King" (1.188) and divine founder of the Persian empire.[20] For Deutero-Isaiah, Cyrus was "the Messiah of god" (Isa 45:1)—like only non-Isrelite so nominated in the Jewish Bible—who, like god, trampled kings underfoot (40:23—41:2).

---

15. Halpern, *Historians*, xvii, 11, 219, 227.

16. For an insightful discussion of the question of origins with respect to Herodotus, see Boedeker, *Herodotus*; with respect to the Deuteronomic historians, see Halpern, *Historians*.

17. Croce, *Theory*, 181–82.

18. Hartog, *Mirror*, xiii n26.

19. See, however, Smith, *Book of Isaiah*, 2:169–73.

20. Immerwahr, *Form and Thought*, 161.

Persian power began to emerge following the death in 631 BCE of Ashurbanipal, the last of the great Assyrian kings. Subsequently, the Babylonians, the Medes, the Egyptians and even the Israelites declared independence from Assyria. Under Nebuchadnezzar, Babylonia consolidated its power in 604, dividing the lands of the former Assyrian Empire with Medes. With Nebuchadnezzar's death in 562, however, his Neo-Babylonian empire went into decline while the Median Empire began to rise. In alliance with Nabonidus, last of the Neo-Babylonian kings (556–538), Cyrus, king of Elem, challenged Median dominance over his small Persian principality. In 550, he defeated the Median king, Astyages, to become sole ruler of the Medes and Persians. Cyrus then engaged and in 546 defeated Croesus and the Lydians; in 539, Babylon, an ally of Lydia fell to Cyrus as well. Although Cyrus's planned conquest of Egypt had to await the campaign in 525 of his son and successor Cambyses, Cyrus had joined the entire Semitic world into his Persian Empire.

Babylonian forces under Nebuchadnezzar had swept through Judea and exiled the Jewish to Babylon in 598 and again in 587. Deutero-Isaiah, a student or disciple of the preexilic Isaiah of Jerusalem, wrote from the midst of this exiled community towards the end of the Neo-Babylonian period. From his perspective, preserved in chapters 40–55 of the present canonical book of Isaiah, the anticipated fall of Babylon to Cyrus in 539 offered the promise of a Jewish return to Jerusalem and the reestablishment there of the temple. Cyrus in fact did restore to their homelands conquered peoples and the plunder from their sanctuaries. The extant "Cyrus Cylinder," a clay barrel commemorating the conquest of Babylon, is cited by Deutero-Isaiah (Isa 45:1–6) (and two other Hebrew historians [2 Chr 36:22–33; Ezra 1:2–4; 6:3–5]) in language close to that of the Cylinder, suggesting it as the historical source.[21]

For both Jews and Greeks the rise of the Persian Empire established new conditions for universal categories of culture and thought,[22] an ecumenical possibility rivaled only by Alexander's Graeco-Macedonian Empire two hundred years later, and again by the rise of imperial Rome. Although both Polybius (1.4.3) and Posidonius (Diodorus Siculus 1.1.3) criticized the Greek historians for the narrow scope of their subjects, most modern commentators have recognized a universal concern in Herodotus's history, as in that of Deutero-Isaiah.[23] In the case of Herodotus, according to Immerwahr,

21. Muilenburg, "Introduction" and "Exegesis," 398; Anderson, *Understanding*, 482. For the text of the Cyrus Cylinder, see Pritchard, *Ancient Near Eastern Texts*, 314–15.

22. Muilenburg, "Introduction" and "Exegesis," 393; Anderson, *Understanding*, 467–68, 485; Momigliano, "Time," 189.

23. Immerwahr, *Form and Thought*, 16; Fornara, *Nature of History*, 32; Muilenburg,

"man is part of the world as a whole and cannot be understood without inquiry into the world as it effects him,"[24] a perspective also evident in Deutero-Isaiah's location of contemporary historical and political events in the discursive context of creation (Isa 40:15, 17, 23–24; 42:5; 43:1–7; 54:15–16).

But an imposed universalism threatened the traditional identities of Jew and Greek alike. The destruction of the Jerusalem temple by the Babylonians in 586 (2 Kgs 25:8–17) had removed from the Israelites, whether in Babylonian exile or in Palestine residuum, their defining locus. From the midst of Cyrus's new global distribution of power, Deutero-Isaiah contemplated the implications of Jewish dislocation and possible relocation for their continued identity.

Similarly, the spread of Persian power from "Asia" into "Europe" threatened the locative precinct of Greek identity. Some hundred years after Deutero-Isaiah, Herodotus, who was from Halicarnassus, a city on Western Asia Minor situated at the boundary of Greek and Asian culture, reflected upon "the unification of Asia [by the Persians and] the attempted extension of empire beyond the borders of the continent."[25]

Hartog has argued that Herodotus's inquiry into the margins of his world and the customs of foreign people beyond perfected for the Greeks a representation of their world.[26] His global topography drew upon that developed by Anaximander and Hecataeus. A circular, flat earth was divided by rivers into three symmetrical parts: Africa, Asia, and Europe, the whole encircled by Ocean.[27] An east/west equator, drawn through the Mediterranean Sea, divided north from south, The Ister (or Danube) River in the north flowed from west to east through Europe, and then south into the Black Sea at Istria, dividing Europe from Asia. Correspondingly, the Nile in the south flowed west to east through Libya, and then north into the Mediterranean Sea, dividing Africa from Asia. Scythia in the north was the land between Europe and Asia, as Egypt in the south stood between Libya and Asia.[28] By mapping a distribution of others, by cataloging their existence and fixing their limits, Herodotus positioned the Greek speaker at the center of the world; to tell of "others" was a way of characterizing a Greek "us"

"Introduction" and "Exegesis," 402–3.

24. Immerwahr, *Form and Thought*, 315.

25. Ibid., 42.

26. Hartog, *Mirror*, 313.

27. Immerwahr, *Form and Thought*, 315–17; for bibliography on Herodotus's geography, see ibid., 316 n24.

28. Hartog, *Mirror*, 14–19.

"constituted on the basis of a Greek space of shared knowledge."[29] Herodotus indicates at the outset of his inquiries, for example, that he will report on the "great and wondrous deeds done by Greeks and foreigners" (1.1), but he actually attributes amazing things only to the "others."[30] "From ancient times," he opines, "Greeks have been distinguished from non-Greeks by their greater cleverness and . . . from [such] silly foolishness." (1.60). Herodotus's differentiation between Greek and non-Greek, Hartog continues, is political, and establishes a differentiation of Greek power from that of the uncivilized, nomadic Scythians on one hand and the tyranny of absolute monarchy on the other (5.92).[31]

As the "surveyor of otherness,"[32] Herodotus fits well the convention of Greek preoccupation with space and spatial paradigms in contrast to that of a supposed Hebraic preoccupation with temporality. Deutero-Isaiah, however, from the orientation of his Babylonian exile, provides as comprehensive a representation of the world as does Herodotus. To the north lies Assyria (Isa 41:25; see 14:31 and Jer 6:22), while to the south is Africa, divided into Egypt and Ethiopia on the one hand and Seba (or Arabia) on the other (Isa 43:3; 45:14). To the east are Persia (41:2, 25) and Kedar, the latter a distant place of nomads (42:11; 21:16; 60:7; Jer 49:28-29). To the west lie the Mediterranean lands (Isa 40:15; 41:1; 42:4, 10, 12; 49:1; 51:5) and Jerusalem (52:9-10). Deutero-Isaiah recognized in Cyrus the greatest political power of the day, and the return of Israel to Jerusalem was an event requiring political power.[33] Like Herodotus, Deutero-Isaiah constructed a cartography of power: a vertical axis extending from Egypt in the south to Assyria in the north positioned the historical (but not the present) oppressors of the Israelites (52:4); a historical axis of deliverance traced a line from Cyrus's Persia in the east (41:2-4) to the west, towards Jerusalem and redemption (45:6; 52:9-10).

By genealogical promise, Deutero-Isaiah also evoked the temporal schema conventionally associated with Hebrew thought. In the time of deliverance from foreign domination, according to Deutero-Isaiah, those to be gathered from the ends of the earth (41:8-9)—from the east and west and from north to south (43:5-6; 49:12)—will be the descendants of Abraham (51:1-3). But Herodotus also challenged a differing collective identity of Persians and Greeks based on descent. As Cambyses had inherited the kingship and the Egyptian campaign from his father, Cyrus, so Xerxes inherited

---

29. Ibid., 368.
30. Van Seters, *In Search of History*, 32.
31. Hartog, *Mirror*, 368.
32. Ibid., 371.
33. Smith, *The Book of Isaiah*, 2:169-70.

the empire by Cyrus and Cambyses from his father, Darius, along with the campaign against Greece. In contrast to the "other's" monarchic genealogy of tyranny, Herodotus emphasized a common Greek language, common religious practice, and customs based upon common descent (8.144). His contrast between the dynastic or structured society of Persians, in which birth determined rank, and Ionian egalitarianism, in which achievement established status, parallels Hebraic resistance to imperial domination on the basis of the prophetic view of equality before the law.[34]

Deutero-Isaiah and Herodotus both equated the dynamics of a past and the distribution of foreign countries with analogous effects.[35] They represent their world in both spatial and temporal discourses in which geography provided the spatial component of history, and history the temporal component of geography.[36] From their located perspectives, both defined a central and present "we" over against peripheral and transitory "others." Rather than coordinating objective events, their histories are better seen as coordinating relationships.[37]

III

As social awareness presupposes prior social existence, all societies preserve statements of some kind about events located in a past time, the awareness of which play some part in their present.[38] By remembering their past, both Jews and Greeks addressed the Persian threat to their collective identity. This identifying past, constructed on collective memory, served as an assurance against Persian domination and as the basis for a renewal of national loyalties.[39]

According to Maurich Halbwachs, the student of Durkheim who pioneered research into the relation of collective memory to collective mentality, the former operates generally by locating identity in particular images of both space and time.[40] The technique whereby collective memory becomes

34. Brown, *Hierarchy, History, and Human Nature*, 14 (on open and closed stratification); 151–52 (on Ionian egalitarianism); 137 (on egalitarianism in ancient Israel).

35. Hartog, *Mirror*, 313.

36. Smith, *To Take Place*, 32.

37. After Evans-Pritchard, *Nuer*, 108; cited by Pocock, "Origins of Study of the Past," 212.

38. Pocock, "Origins of Study of the Past," 211; Lowenthal, *Past*, 186.

39. Lowenthal, *Past*, 44.

40. Hutton, "Collective Memory." Although Halbwachs sharply differentiated the collective memory from his positivistic view of history, Hutton argues on the basis of Philippe Aries's contribution to historiography that Halbwachs's characterization of

localized, according to Halbwachs, is commemoration, the ritualized mnemonic practices that throw the paradigmatic designs of collective memory into bold relief. As Patrick Hutton has summarized, commemoration, "in its rites and rituals as in its monuments and shrines," externalizes memory "on a geographical plane where it may visually fix and affirm collective beliefs."[41]

For Deutero-Isaiah, collective memory was focused by the Jerusalem temple tradition, the restoration of which, Jonathan Z. Smith has shown, was imagined by Ezekiel, another exilic prophet, in terms of social mapping.[42] And for Deutero-Isaiah, Muilenburg concludes that Israel's

> sanctuaries are places where the tradition is remembered and transmitted; her rituals rehearse the ancient stories; her festivals re-enact and dramatize the holy events of the past; her prophets recall epochal moments . . . ; her priests recite and listen to the recitations of . . . instructions; her myths are transformed by the covenant acts and words."[43]

The acts and words of the covenant, the political and social basis for Hebrew alliance and distinctiveness, were remembered through ritual commemorations.

For Herodotus, too, Greek collectivity and identity were focused by practices associated with renowned sanctuaries. At Olympia, for example, Herodotus reported that only Greeks could participate in the games to the exclusion of foreign "others" (2.160; 5.22).[44] But for Herodotus, Delphi, whose authority ordered history (1.13) and whose oracles spoke to "all Greeks" (4.159) provides important symbol of Greek unity and identity, a significance this sanctuary retained throughout the Hellenistic period.[45] It is this local or "patriotic" concern with social or political identity that subsequent Greek historians considered central to Herodotus's work,[46] and that characterized almost solely the Latin historians' focus on the *res gestae populi Romani*.[47]

---

collective memory is, in fact, not opposed to the method of the historian.

41. Hutton, "Collective Memory," 315. The classic work on such externalization through commemoration is Halbwachs's study of the cultural geography of the Holy Land, *La Topographie légendaire*; see also Smith, *To Take Place*, 115–16.

42. Smith, *To Take Place*, 47–73.

43. Muilenburg, *"Introduction" and "Exegesis,"* 541.

44. Peters, *Harvest*, 34.

45. Immerwahr, *Form and Thought*, 235–36 and n137; Rostovtzeff, *Social and Economic History*, 1122; Peters, *Harvest*, 37–38.

46. Immerwahr, *Form and Thought*, 1.

47. Fornara, *Nature of History*, 41.

Collective memory thus unfolds within an enduring spatial framework in which a community distributes its richest ideas and images with respect to specific locations and sanctuaries. These areas of space, in which societies find both shelter and support for their traditions, are forbidden to others.[48]

Since time, as presented by Halbwachs and the Durkheimian tradition generally, is a social construct, the convention that views Herodotus and the Greek historians as assuming a cyclical view of time might be understood as concomitant to the structures of repetition characteristic of ritual commemoration. Thus Deutero-Isaiah, for whom no one suggests a cyclical view of time, understood his historical situation typologically, in terms of such repeated historical patterns. Babylonian exile replicated, for example, Egyptian captivity, which the prophet associated with Assyrian oppression (Isa 52:4). He remembered the Hebrews' deliverance from Egypt as a model for a return to Jerusalem following Cyrus's anticipated victory (35:1–10; 43:16–18; 48:20–21). And memory of the ancient covenant—that with Noah (54:9), then with Abraham (51:2–3), and finally the "everlasting" covenant with David (55:3–9)—structured the prophet's perception and understanding of both Israelite and world history.[49]

Against those who have argued that Herodotus's perception of repetition in history was grounded in some metaphysical view of time, Immerwahr argues that Herodotus perceived an order or pattern in the way any historian views individual events as part of an orderly process.[50] "Balance and separation, polarity and identity of opposites, permanence in change are found everywhere [in Herodotus's world]," Immerwahr concludes, "and serve to bind the world together in ever-recurring patterns"[51]—a socially constructed order in the midst of the transitoriness of existence that had so impressed the Greek mentality since the observations of Heraclitus.

Memory "is a complex and deceptive experience," Jonathan Z. Smith has written. "It appears to be preeminently a matter of the past, yet it is as much an affair of the present. It appears to be preeminently a matter of time, yet it is much an affair of space."[52]

In ritual practices of commemoration, society constitutes its collective memory—its identifying past—with reference to place as the dynamic of a present. This mnemonic construction of identity is clearly central to the writings of both Deutero-Isaiah and Herodotus.

48. Halbwach, *Collective Memory*, 139–40, 151, 156.
49. Anderson, "Exodus Typology."
50. Immerwahr, *Form and Thought*, 148.
51. Ibid., 342.
52. Smith, *To Take Place*, 25.

IV

Discussions of memory frequently slight the importance of "remembering to perform future actions."[53] Whereas historiography may concern the past, historical consciousness, the condition for writing history, is the social construction of temporality as a significant arena of meaning in all of its dimensions—past and future. Thus, amid Deutero-Isaiah's emphases on remembering, one finds his remonstrance to "remember not the former things, nor consider the things of old," for "behold, I am doing a new thing" (Isa 43:18–19). This juxtaposition of the past with a future is the key to the historical consciousness represented by Deutero-Isaiah. The meaning of the past is shaped and disclosed only in light of new things (42:9); the past is validated only by the impingement of a future.

For Plato, as we have seen, Time, whatever its significance or lack thereof, has two forms: a future as well as a past—a phenomenology of temporality affirmed by philosophers of history from Augustine to Heidegger. Awareness of a past is an acknowledgement of determinism—whether by nature of by nurture. Future, by contrast, signifies an infinite, and therefore unrealizable, possibility. The present is a collective identity localized in space and time in which the particularization of a remembered past is enlivened by an open future, and an indeterminate future becomes actualized by the limiting effect of a determining past.

Convention holds that the eschatological dimension of Hebrew thought balanced the emphasis on memory to constitute a fully developed historical consciousness, albeit expressed in mythological (or theological) discourse. This concern with the future, which may or may not be present in the Israelite historians, is nonetheless central to the prophetic tradition of which Deutero-Isaiah is a prime representative.[54] On the other hand, in the understated words of Momigliano, "the future did not loom large in the works of Greek historians."[55] As Thucydides put it, events will happen in a fashion identical or similar to the way they have already taken place (Thucydides 1.22.4). But this neglect of the future by Greek historians does not establish its absence from the popular Greek mentality. We might better, then, turn our attention to the popular concern in antiquity with πρόγνωσις, or divination.

Divination, in the Graeco-Roman antiquity, belonged to the widespread practices of piety (Gk. εὐσέβεια; Lt. *pietas*). These practices generally

---

53. Meacham and Leiman, "Remembering to Perform"; Lowenthal, *Past*, 193.
54. Muilenburg, *"Introduction"* and *"Exegesis,"* 399–400.
55. Momigliano, "Time," 193.

were techniques for establishing and maintaining "right relationships" between man and wife, or master and slave, or a general and his legions, and, by extension, between gods and mortals. In other words, they established and maintained the structure of society, whereby the "rightness" of the relationship was socially prescribed.

For the Greeks, piety presumed a cosmic order guaranteed by the gods, by whom, according to Herodotus, "all things and the due assignment thereof were... set in order" (2.52).[56] Given, as Herodotus noted, the "many clear proofs of the divine ordering of things" (9.100), it was considered prudent to consult the gods. Consultation took place through omens and auguries, practices later classified by Cicero as "natural divination," and through dreams and oracles, which Cicero described as "artificial divination" (*De divinatione* 1.18.34).

Divinatory techniques played an instrumental role in Herodotus's inquiries, and, apart from those he explicitly characterized as false, were recognized by him as true.[57] Herodotus writes, for example, that "I have no way of gainsaying the ... truth [of oracles], for they speak clearly, and I would not essay to overthrow them" (8.77). In his view, only non-Greeks ever questioned the integrity of oracles, or, what amounted to the same thing, consulted various oracles (1.46–47; 2.174; 8.133).[58]

The Greek practices of divination provided the link to a system of fate that signified the cosmic syntax of the natural order. Herodotus, for example, related two dreams of Astyages concerning Mandane, his daughter and Cyrus's mother. The first portrays her urinating over Atyages's city, and then over all Asia (1.107). In the second, a vine grows from her genitals and covers Asia (1.108). For Astyages's divines, these dreams meant that "his daughter's offspring [i.e., Cyrus] should rule in his place" (1.108). Despite Astyages's attempt to eliminate the potential usurper, Herodotus reports that Cyrus was fated to survive (1.121).

According to Quintus, Cicero's antagonist in his *De divinatione*, fate is "an orderly succession of causes wherein cause is linked to cause and each cause of itself produces an effect" (1.55.125). "He who knows the causes of future events," Quintus continues, "necessarily knows what every future event will be ... [for] the evolution of time is like the unwinding of a cable:

---

56. Immerwahr, *Form and Thought*, 15, 306, 311–12, 315.

57. For examples of omens and auguries in Herodotus, see 1.19; 6.29; of dreams, see 1.34, 107, 209; 2.14; 3.124, 149; 6.107; 7.14–20; on oracles, see 1.19; 7.6; 8.77. Kirchberg, *Die Funktion der Orakel*, 116.

58. On the place of oracles in Herodotus's inquiries and their role in distinguishing between Greek and non-Greeks, especially the Persians, see Kirchberg, *Die Funktion der Orakel*; Klees, *Eigenart*.

it creates nothing new and only unfolds each event in its order" (1.56.127). The Herodotean subjection of gods and nations to fate (Herodotus 1.91; 3.43; 9.16) belongs, therefore, to the shared Greek concern for rational and logical explanation,[59] and to Herodotus's intent, announced at the outset of his work, "to tell the cause" (1.1).[60]

Herodotus's temporalized view of fate as an inevitable chain of causality opposed Plato's ontologization of a present only. With the former the determinate nature of past and future alike accorded privilege to the past in relation to the present, thereby preempting any view of future as temporal possibility. It expressed, as it were, a past view of the future.[61] Divination accorded the possibility for clarifying human decision in light of the designs of fate, a possibility which constituted the basis for Herodotus's history.[62]

Deutero-Isaiah, by contrast, faithful to Jewish law which forbade any kind of divinatory practice (Deut 18:10–11), repudiated Babylonian divination. He railed against the Babylonians, that

> Your wisdom and your knowledge led you astray
> [..]
> stand fast in your enchantments and your many sorceries,
> with which you have labored from your youth;
> perhaps you may be able to succeed,
> perhaps you may inspire terror.
> You are wearied with your many counsels;
> let them stand forth and save you,
> those who divide the heavens, who gaze at the stars,
> who at the new moons predict what shall befall you.
>
> Behold they are like stubble,
> the fire consumes them. (Isa 47:10–4; see 44:24–25)

For Deutero-Isaiah such technicians of nature will be destroyed along with their exaggerated concern for a determinate future, since nations and nature alike are implicated with Israelite agency. This agency, expressed in the discourse of Israel's election and in Deutero-Isaiah's paeans to Israel as historical servant (42:1–4; 49:1–6; 50:4–9; 52:13—53:12),[63] takes priority

---

59. Fornara, *Nature of History*, 62.
60. On fate as a series of causes and effects, see Arnols, *Roman Stoicism*, 202–3.
61. See Heidegger, *Being and Time*, 388, 443–44.
62. Kirchberg, *Die Funktion der Orakel*, 120.
63. Burrows, "Ancient Israel," 123.

over and becomes the context for reflection upon creation itself (44:1–2). A future, including the course of nature, was not a necessary consequence of a determining past. The difference is between a Deutero-Isaiah, who anticipates even the encroachment of Cyrus in his world as a constructive agent of change belonging somehow to the future of a Jewish "us," and a Herodotus, who viewed the rise of Persian power as a fated change of fortune portended in signs and oracles. Historical agency, for Deutero-Isaiah, is contingent and therefore indeterminate; for Herodotus it remains presumptuous and blind.[64]

Some six hundred years after Deutero-Isaiah's challenge to the Babylonian divines and their reliance on cosmic powers, Paul rejected the deterministic "elementary powers of the cosmos" (στοιχεῖα τοῦ κόσμου) (Gal 4:1–13; see Col 2:8, 20).[65] With the Torah, these celestial forces represented to Paul and the nascent Pauline Christians, the determinate power of their past.[66] Paul's message of freedom from such temporally and spatially cast emblems of determinism confirmed for Western culture a view of history in which a past-structured future emerged from a creative but finally unknowable possibility.[67] The Hellenocentric bias that has characterized historical thinking since the Renaissance, however, has relegated perceptions of Hebraic influence on Western culture to the area of "religion," while attributing a rational legacy for historiography to the Greeks and Romans. It is as though the Hebrews never "thought" and the Greek and Romans had no religion—an assertion actually made of the Romans except in the sense of a politically motivated formality.[68]

---

64. Immerwahr, *Form and Thought*, 309.

65. In the intervening Jewish apocalyptic tradition that followed the restoration of the temple and that negates time, Daniel, located in the reigns of both Nebuchadnezzar and Cyrus (Dan 1:1–7; 6:28), is portrayed as a diviner who surpasses even the Babylonian "magicians and enchanters" in understanding dreams and visions (1.17–20). But Jubilees, dated with Daniel from the second century BCE, emphasizes the importance of both time and history. See Wintermute, "Jubilees."

66. On the equivalence of Torah, the "elementary powers of the cosmos," past, and fate in Paul's argument to the Galatians, see Betz, *Galatians*, 174–80, 204–5, 213–17.

67. The Pauline view of historical process became officially accepted only in the fourth century with Jerome's successful subjugation of Theodosius to episcopal authority, an event Jerome justified by the developmental authority of history in contrast to the traditional divinatory authority of place claimed by Rome. See Martin, "Roman Mithraism." The fourth-century Christian Latin poet Prudentius makes this same argument. See *Contra Symmachum* 1.283–89, 587–92; 2.583–85; *Peristephanon* 2.413–44.

68. See Philips, "The Sociology of Religious Knowledge," 2697–711.

V

Moses I. Finley has counseled that, "the first questions to be asked of any written source are, why was it written? Why was it published?" And specifically of Herodotus (and we might add, of Deutero-Isaiah), he asks, why select the subject of war?[69]

To Finley's questions we might respond that both Hebraic and Greek historical texts gave expression to the collective identities of their respective audiences, and that the theme of conflict most dramatically differentiated those identities. The occasion for the histories of both Deutero-Isaiah and Herodotus was the protracted Persian conquest of space that threatened, but also gave definition to, their "us," and for which Cyrus was the common "other." In contrast to the convention of metaphysical distinctions between a Greek preoccupation with space and a Jewish involvement with time, Deutero-Isaiah and Herodotus both mapped traditionally specified parameters of Jewish and Greek social identity as a spatial as well as temporal distribution of allegiance and antagonism.

Although both Deutero-Isaiah and Herodotus understood social identity to be the product of a remembered past, they represented their social world with reference to the shared knowledge of their respective cultures, a collective knowledge constituted by differing historical memories. The social identity of Greece, for example, was commemorated as its oracular shrines with their pan-Hellenic framework of cosmic fate and their practices of divination, a practice which continued to exemplify popular piety until the establishment of Christianity, and beyond.[70] Whereas collective memory is always relational, the practices of Greek piety structured relations independent of memory. The Greek framework of shared knowledge did articulate a set of Greek "past-relationships," or documents and institutions "inherited from a past state of society and used to regulate conduct in the present, and concepts of authority which they enjoyed."[71] But, as Jean-Pierre Vernant emphasizes, this Greek recollection of past-relationships did "not seek to situate events in a temporal framework but to reach the depths of being, to discover the original, the primordial reality from which the cosmos issued and which makes it possible to understand becoming as a whole."[72] It was the givenness of these structures that was remembered and not the process of structuring. To the extent that Greek popular practices of divination and

---

69. Finley, *History*, 105, 68; Fornara, *Nature of History*, 67.
70. Fornara, *Nature of History*, 77.
71. Pocock, "The Origins of Study of the Past," 225, 213.
72. Vernant, "Aspects mythiques," 7.

commemoration were concomitant to historiography as a social construct, I reclaim my assertion that the Greeks never developed a fully realized historical consciousness in the sense of collectively acknowledging the future as well as a past as the significant condition for historiographical meaning.

On the other hand, Hebrew prophetic commemoration, as focused by the temple tradition, did not seek to situate the shared past-relationships of Israel in nature but in a temporal framework, as its rejection of divination shows. This temporal framework included not only a constitutive memory of the changing historical fate of the preexilic temple but the promise of its postexile restoration through historical agency.

The two alternative views, represented by Deutero-Isaiah and Herodotus, of what counts as history may be exemplified by contrasting assumptions about time in two novels: H. G. Wells's *The Time Machine* and George Orwell's *1984*. Wells imagined, in the tradition from Greek antiquity to von Ranke,[73] a view of time in which one might, with the availability of appropriate technological competence, visit the past to "see how is actually was." And if the past might he visited for verification in this ontological world of time, so might one visit the future to know what actually will occur: what I have termed a past view of the future.

Orwell, in contrast, imagined a socially constructed view of time in which a future impinges upon the present in such a way that a remembered past might be continually reconstructed, not in terms of eliminating error by the marshaling of hitherto forgotten facts, but in terms of a shifting revaluation of agency—a view of human experience more readily documented by modern political and historical experience than that of Wells.

For those social scientists of the past who judge human deeds and events as belonging to a natural and finally knowable order of things, Herodotus remains the "father of history." For those commemorating the past who count human doings as collectively remembered images projected onto the mist of the unknown, the Hebraic legacy remains the condition for modern historiography.

---

73. The parallel between von Ranke's view of historical knowledge as a knowledge of "wie es eigentlich gewesen" and Thucydides's view (cf. 2.43.3) was drawn by von Ranke himself (see, Finley, *History*, 48 n5).

References

Anderson, Bernard, W. "Exodus Typology in Second Isaiah." In *Israel's Prophetic Heritage: Essays in Honor of James Muilenburg*, edited by Bernard W. Anderson and Walter Harrelson, 177–95. New York: Harper, 1962.
———. *Understanding the Old Testament*. 4th ed. Englewood Cliffs, NJ: Prentice-Hall, 1986.
Arnold, Edward V. *Roman Stoicism*. Cambridge: Cambridge University Press, 1911.
Barr, James. *Biblical Words for Time*. Studies in Biblical Theology 1/33. Naperville, IL: Allenson, 1961.
Betz, Hans D. *Galatians: A Commentary on Paul's Letter to the Churches in Galatia*. Hermeneia. Philadelphia: Fortress, 1979.
Boedeker, Deborah, ed. *Herodotus and the Invention of History*. Special volume of *Arethusa* 20.1/2 (1987).
Boman, Torlief. *Hebrew Thought Compared with Greek*. Translated by Jules L. Moreau. Library of History and Doctrine. Philadelphia: Westminster, 1960.
Burrows, Millar. "Ancient Israel." In *The Idea of History in the Ancient Near East*, edited by Robert C. Dentan, 101–31. Yale Oriental Series 38. New Haven: Yale University Press, 1955.
Brown, Donald E. *Hierarchy, History, and Human Nature: The Social Origins of Historical Consciousness*. Tucson: University of Arizona Press, 1988.
Butterfield, Herbert. *The Origins of History*. New York: Basic Books, 1981.
Cochrane, Charles N. *Thucydides and the Science of History*. Oxford: Oxford University Press, 1929.
Coleridge, Samuel Taylor. *Collected Letters of Samuel Taylor Coleridge*. Edited by E. L. Grigge. 6 vols. Oxford: Clarendon, 1956–1971.
Conford, Francis M., trans. and comm. *Plato's Cosmology: The Timaeus of Plato*. 1937. Reprint, New York: Liberal Arts Press, 1957.
Croce, Benedetto. *History: Its Theory and Practice*. Translated by Douglas Ainslie. New York: Russell & Russell, 1960.
Dobschütz, E. von. "Zeit und Raum im Denken des Urschristentums." *Journal of Biblical Literature* 11 (1922) 212–23.
Evans-Pritchard, E. E. *The Nuer*. Oxford: Clarendon, 1940.
Finley, Moses I. *Ancient History: Evidence and Models*. New York: Viking, 1986.
Fornara, Charles W. *The Nature of History in Ancient Greece and Rome*. Eidos. Berkeley: University of California Press, 1983.
Halbwach, Maurice. *The Collective Memory*. Translated by Francis J. Ditter Jr. and Vida Y. Ditter. Harper Colophon Books. New York: Harper & Row, 1980.
———. *La Topographie légendaire des évangiles en Terre Saint*. Bibliothèque de philosophie contemporaine. Paris: Presses Universitaires de France, 1941.
Halpern, Baruch. *The First Historians: The Hebrew Bible and History*. San Francisco: Harper & Row, 1988.
Hartog, François. *The Mirror of Herodotus: The Representation of the Other in the Writing of History*. Translated by Janet Lloyd. The New Historicism: Studies in Cultural Poetics 5. Berkeley: University of California Press, 1988.
Heidegger, Martin. *Being and Time*. Translated by John Macquarie and Edward Robinson. New York: Harper & Row, 1962.
How, Walter W., and Joseph Wells. *A Commentary on Herodotus*. Oxford: Clarendon, 1912.

Hutton, Patrick, H. "Collective Memory and Collective Mentalities: The Halbwachs-Aries Connection." *Historical Reflection/Réflexions Historiques* 15/2 (1988) 311–22.
Immerwahr, Henry, R. *Form and Thought in Herodotus*. Philological Monographs 23. Cleveland: Western Reserve University Press, 1966.
Kirschberg, Jutta. *Die Funktion der Orakel im Werke Herodots*. Hypomnemata 11. Göttingen: Vendenhoeck & Ruprecht, 1965.
Klees, Hand. *Die Eigenart des griechischen Glaubens an Orakel und Seher*. Tübinger Beiträge zur Altertumswissenschaft 43. Stuttgart: Kohlhammer, 1965.
Lowenthal, David. *The Past is a Foreign Country*. Cambridge: Cambridge University Press, 1985.
Löwith, Karl. *Meaning in History*. Chicago: University of Chicago Press, 1949.
Martin, Luther H., *Hellenistic Religions: An Introduction*. New York: Oxford University Press, 1987.
———. "Roman Mithraism and Christianity." *Numen* 36 (1989) 1–15.
Meacham, John A., and Burt Leiman. "Remembering to Perform Future Actions." In *Memory Observed: Remembering in Natural Contexts*, edited by Ulric Neisser, 327–36. San Francisco: Freeman, 1982.
Momigliano, Arnaldo. "Time in Ancient Historiography." In *Essays in Ancient and Modern Historiography*, 179–204. Middletown, CT: Wesleyan University Press, 1977.
Muilenburg, James. "Introduction" and "Exegesis": The Book of Isaiah, Chapters 40–66." In *The Interpreter's Bible*, edited by George A. Buttrick et al., 5:381–773. 12 vols. Nashville: Abingdon, 1956.
Peters, Francis E. *The Harvest of Hellenism: A History of the Near East from Alexander the Great to the Triumph of Christianity*. New York: Barnes & Noble, 1996.
Philips, C. Robert. "The Sociology of Religious Knowledge in the Roman Empire to AD 284." In *ANRW* II.16.3 (1986) 2677–773.
Pocock, John G. A. "The Origins of Study of the Past: A Comparative Approach." *Comparative Studies in Society and History* 4 (1962) 209–46.
Pritchard, James B., ed. *Ancient New Eastern Texts Relating to the Old Testament*. 2nd ed. Princeton: Princeton University Press, 1955.
Rostovtzeff, Michael. *The Social and Economic History of the Hellenistic World*. 3 vols. Oxford: Clarendon, 1941.
Sambursky, Samuel, and Schlomo Pines. *The Concept of Time in Late Neoplatonism*. Jerusalem: Israel Academy of Sciences and Humanities, 1971.
Smith, George A. *The Book of Isaiah*. 2 vols. Expositor's Bible 16. New York: Armstrong, 1905.
Smith, Jonathan Z. *To Take Place: Toward Theory in Ritual*. Chicago Studies in the History of Judaism. Chicago: University of Chicago Press, 1987.
Van Seters, John. *In Search of History: Historiography in the Ancient World and the Origins of Biblical History*. New Haven: Yale University Press, 1983.
Vernant, Jean-Pierre. "Aspects mythiques de la mémoire en Grèce." *Journal de Psychologie Normale et Pathologique* 56 (1959) 1–29.
Wintermute, O. S. "Jubilees: A New Translation and Introduction." In *The Old Testament Pseudepigrapha*, edited by James H. Charlesworth, 2:35–142. Garden City, NY: Doubleday, 1985.

4

Why Cecropian Minerva?
Hellenistic Religious Syncretism as System

> Up to the end of the sixteenth century, resemblance played a constructive role in the knowledge of Western culture ... it was resemblance that organized the play of symbols, made possible knowledge of things, visible and invisible, and controlled the art of representing them.
>
> MICHEL FOUCAULT[1]

I

THE IDENTIFICATION OF ISIS Regina in Apuleius's *Metamorphoses* 11.5 with Cecropian Minerva, and with nine other Mediterranean goddesses as well, illustrates the remarkable complexity and profusion of data that the study of Hellenistic religion surveys. While scholars recognize resemblances in such data from a common text or historical period, they have been embarrassed by their inability to formulate the data into any coherent totality. As Franz Cumont analogized in his pioneering study of *Oriental Religions in Roman Paganism*:

> Let us suppose that in modern Europe the faithful had deserted the Christian churches to worship Allah or Brahma, to follow the percepts of Confucius or Buddha, or to adopt the maxims of the Shinto; let us imagine a great confusion of all races of the world in which Arabian mullahs, Chinese scholars, Japanese bonzes, Tibetan lamas and Hindu pundits should all be

1. Foucault, *Order*, 17.

preaching fatalism and predestination, ancestor-worship and devotion to a deified sovereign, pessimism and deliverance through annihilation—a confusion in which all those priests should erect temples of exotic architecture in our cities and celebrate their disparate rites therein. Such a dream . . . would offer a pretty accurate picture of the religious chaos in which the ancient world was struggling before the reign of Constantine.[2]

In his introduction to Cumont's book, Grant Showerman summarized this problem as "the apparently chaotic condition of paganism when viewed as a system."[3]

Cumont's initial perception of the religious situation in imperial Rome as systemic confusion yielded, however, to his apprehension of a historical order:

As the religious history of the empire is studied more closely, the triumph of the church will, in our opinion, appear more and more as the culmination of a long evolution of beliefs.[4]

This evolutionary perspective from "the triumph of Christianity" disallowed Cumont any possibility of a systemic understanding of paganism and prescribed instead his historical inquiry into the "moral antecedents" of the Christian world.[5] As Showerman concluded: "M. Cumont is . . . a contributor to our appreciation of the continuity of history."[6] The view of Hellenistic religion as a historically ordered process has defined its study since the mid-nineteenth century.

II

A discrete period of Hellenistic history was first projected by J. G. Droysen in 1836: "The name Alexander marks the end of one world epoch, the beginning of a new."[7] Droysen's romantic attribution of epochal inauguration to the heroic exploits of Alexander gave currency to the now familiar account of the newly crowned young king, who, in his passion to unite the Greek race against Persian hegemony, conquered the known world by the time of his premature death thirteen years later. According to this view, the

2. Cumont, *Oriental Religions*, vii.
3. Ibid., vii.
4. Ibid., xi.
5. Ibid.
6. Ibid., xii.
7. Droysen, *Geschichte*, 1:3.

Hellenistic period had its beginnings with Alexander's rapid transformation of the world into his Graeco-Macedonian empire.

The rise of Roman power signaled for Droysen the end of his Hellenistic period.[8] Later historians anointed yet another heroic figure, Caesar Augustus, who finally had consolidated Roman power by his annexation of Egypt, to mark the end of the Hellenistic and the beginning of a Roman epoch.[9] Thus a Hellenistic period became accepted from Alexander's death in 323 BCE to Augustus's triumph in 31 BCE.[10]

Historical periodization does not represent fact, however, but the interpretative perspective of historical generalization.[11] Droysen's Hellenistic period presumes the so-called Great Man view of history, a generalization that claims that such men as Alexander are the key to an intelligible history.[12] Further, Droysen's periodization presumes the rise of empire, a political bias, as the criterion for bracketing his Hellenistic period.

Whatever the merits of Droysen's periodization, it must be asked if it is appropriate for the perspective of the religious historian to be organized according to the principles of political history. What is the relation between the Hellenistic political history and its religious counterpart?

Arguably, more significant for religious history than Alexander's conquests was the "Ptolemaic" cosmological revolution. This expanded cosmological image rivaled Alexander's concurrent political exploits in significance by exemplifying a widening of mental horizons.[13] Its new architecture of the world provided the occasion for the emergence of distinctive religious structures and confirms the beginnings of a period of a Hellenistic religious history contemporary with the beginning of a period of Hellenistic political history.[14]

---

8. Ibid., 2:442.

9. Bayer, "Nachwort," 475.

10. See, for example, Tarn, *Civilization*, ch. 1.

11. Carr, *What Is History?*, 76; Finley, "Generalizations," 23; and Gottschalk's summary (197) of Finley's position: "that assumptions about periodization in political history may impose an unexplained or unjustified organization of the subject matter to be presented and may bring in their wake other unexamined assumptions of generalizations."

12. Stover, "Great Man Theory."

13. To paraphrase E. R. Dodds's observation in *Greeks and the Irrational*, 237.

14. The importance of Ptolemaic cosmology for understanding Hellenistic religion in the face of its complexity and seeming contradictions is emphasized by Nilsson, *Geschichte*, 2:702–11. Nilsson also cites on this point (702 n1): Eisler, *Weltenmantel*, 631; and Burkitt, *Church*, 30ff. See also, Weiss, *Untersuchung*, 6. A helpful survey of Western cosmological theories is presented by Munitz, *Theories*.

Although *Hellenistic* has become a standard term to designate a period with is beginnings in the late fourth century BCE, there is less agreement, especially among religious historians, on where to end this period.[15] Droysen himself was somewhat more circumspect than his followers in fixing the terminus ante quem to his period. While recognizing that the consolidation of Roman power prescribed a conclusion to Hellenistic political history, he recognized also that religious history must include a consideration of the dominant influence of Hellenistic culture throughout the centuries of the empire.[16]

This discrepancy between *Hellenistic* as a political periodization and *Hellenistic* as a religious continuity extending beyond political limits has resulted in a confusing use of this term by historians of religion. Some scholars, accepting the political periodization established by Droysen's followers, limit a study of Hellenistic religion strictly to those religious texts and practices in the period between Alexander and Augustus; others, heeding Droysen's reservations about a politically determined terminus ad quem for religious history, or otherwise sensing some sort of apolitical continuity, speak rather of "Graeco-Roman" religions; and still others subsume *Graeco-Roman* to a generalized nominalization, *Hellenistic*.[17] Indeed, some scholars note the continuing influence of Hellenistic culture into Renaissance Europe.[18]

A suitable conclusion to Hellenistic religious history is well marked, as Cumont suggested, by the emergence of one of its constituent traditions to dominance in the imperial West. Theodosius's late fourth-century-CE religious legislation in favor of Christianity and outlawing paganism effectively signals this conclusion and affirms an antecedent period of Hellenistic religion enduring some 750 years from Alexander's empire to Christian catholicity.[19]

III

Historical periodization is not only a generalization based upon interpretative perspective, it is based also upon judgement about the essential

---

15. Finley, "Generalizations," 23.

16. Bayer, Nachwort," 474–75.

17. See, for example, the rather laborious discussion by Grant, *Hellenistic Religions*, xi–xiii.

18. Grant, "Hellenismus," 209. See also Seznec, *Survival*; Wind, *Pagan Mysteries*; Yates, *Giordano Bruno*.

19. Smith adopts also this dating in "Hellenistic Religion."

characteristics of that period.[20] When Droysen named his newly defined period Hellenistic, he also proposed its essential feature. He appropriated this adjective, which does not appear in ancient Greek, from the verbal and nominal forms signifying the acquisition of the Greek language and lifestyle by non-Greeks.[21] For Droysen, "Hellenistic" signified the "east-west mixture of people"[22] that occurred with Alexander's conquests, and that was dominated by the Greek language, and consequently, Greek lifestyle. Droysen seemed to waver, however, between two understandings of cultural mixture: *interpretatio graeca* and cultural fusion, both of which have been employed in subsequent interpretations of Hellenistic religion.

In the area of religion, *interpretatio graeca* signifies the identification of a foreign god by a Greek equivalent, a practice at least as ancient as Herodotus.[23] Droysen understood this interpretative reduction to have been justified by Alexander's own worship of foreign deities, and philosophically by Stoic pantheistic allegory.[24]

But for Droysen, "Hellenistic" also signified *Verschmelzung*,[25] a process of fusion resulting from the interaction between Greek civilization and those Oriental cultures incorporated by Alexander into his empire. It is this Hegelian notion[26] of the mutual influence of various cultures, and specifically of the eastern and the western, as constitutive of a "Hellenistic" culture that has dominated subsequent research, especially in the history of religions. Within a decade of the more influential second edition of Droysen's work,[27] religious studies had produced its technical tem for Droysen's Hegelian characterization of Hellenistic religious fusion: *syncretism*.[28]

As a modern generalization about "the main characteristic feature of Hellenistic religion,"[29] syncretism betrays modern theological and historiographical concerns. The term apparently was appropriated from the "Syncretists," a seventeenth-century Protestant movement that had attempted to harmonize the diverse sects of Protestantism in the face of Catholi-

20. Finley, "Generalizations," 24.

21. E.g., 2 Macc 4:13 speaks of "an extreme of Hellenization and increase in the adoption of foreign ways" (RSV).

22. Droysen, "Vorwort zur Zweiten Auflage," *Geschichte*, 1.

23. Solmsen, *Isis*, ch. 1, discusses Herodotus's interpretation.

24. Droysen, *Geschichte*, 3:18.

25. Ibid., 3:447.

26. Préaux, *Monde*, 7.

27. Droysen, *Geschichte*; Austin, *Hellenistic World*, preface.

28. Wendland, *Hellenistische-Römische*, 129 understood syncretism and Hellenization as virtually synonymous processes. See also Moffatt, "Syncretism."

29. Grant, *Hellenistic Religions*, xiii.

cism. Dogmatic and sectarian interests rejected these irenic overtures and thereafter this term was almost always used in a derogatory sense.³⁰

By 1853, the term was used as a generalization about pagan culture:

> Syncretism under every possible form—ethical, political, social, and theological—was the favorite policy of the Roman emperors. They would have all the varieties of mankind called in and restamped at the Caesarian mint.³¹

In 1886, Jean Réville used *syncretisme* as the central category for his historical study of Roman religion.³² Whereas Réville used this term in the service of historical description, it retained its theological overtones:

> And from the middle of all these gods, of all practices, of all these beliefs, emerges the idea that there are only, in the last analysis, diverse manifestations of the same divinity, diverse practices of the same cult, diverse conceptions of the same piety.³³

Almost immediately the term began to appear with this essentialist sense in studies of religion generally. Andrew Lang, for example, used it in 1887 to describe the historical process in Egypt whereby "various god-names and god-natures are mingled so as to unite the creeds of different names and provinces."³⁴ This "monotheistic tendency," as it came to be called became a common feature of syncretism as "historical" description.³⁵

---

30. Moffatt, "Syncretism."
31. Anonymous, "Octavius," 294.
32. Réville, *Religion*.
33. Ibid., 21.
34. Lang, *Myth, Ritual*, 2:94. The term is dropped from later editions. Apart from its use to designate Hellenistic religion, *syncretism* has been used most frequently as a description of Eastern religion: Baird, *Category*, 148. However, the tem often is used also in anthropological descriptions of tribal societies, e.g., Bennetta, *African Apostles*, 194; and even as a characterization of contemporary American cults by Ellwood, *Religious*, 29, 46. Baird, *Category*, 151 argues that "syncretism is a concept applied to a religion by those which stand outside its circle of faith and hence fail to see or experience its inner unity."
35. See already Réville, *Religion*, 116; also, for example, Usener, *Götternamen*, 340: "er [Synkretismus] war die Vorschule des glaubens an einen gott" [sic], 340; Usener, "Synkretismus," 1055: "Dei neue durch den Synkretismus aufgenommene Religiosität mit ihrer schwärmerischen Innigkeit, gestattete eine völlige Hingabe an Christus, ein Sichversenken in das Einzigartige seines Wesen, das schließlich seiner Religion zum Siege mußte"; Guthrie, *Orpheus*, 100: "it [syncretism] is the natural concomitant of a tendency towards monotheism." Cf. also ibid., 250; and Nilsson, *Geschichte*, 2:575: "so hat der Drang zum Monotheismus einen allumfassenden Synkretismus hervorgerufen."

The theological assumptions of syncretism began to be challenged by the end of the nineteenth century when the predominately German *religionsgeschichtliche Schule* placed Christianity itself in its context of Hellenistic religious history.[36] By 1903, Hermann Gunkel had clearly articulated a nontheological, historically formulated thesis that Christianity too was a syncretistic religion.[37]

Based upon its nineteenth-century usage, the oft-cited but incorrect etymology given for *syncretism* is the Greek verb συνκεράννυμι, "to mix or join together."[38] The liberal Latin translation of συγκρητισμός according to this etymology would be *confusio*. The acceptation implied in this etymology clearly influenced the work of such scholars as Cumont and Réville. Réville even spoke of the originality of syncretism as consisting "precisely in the confusion of its elements."[39] Yet, he betrayed the significance of his historical perspective when he admitted, indeed, lamented that this originality rested precisely upon his limits as a modern historian: "By its very nature a syncretism as complex and so confused defies complete analysis."[40]

Understanding syncretism in theological terms implied, of course, a regulatory belonging to the theological politics of orthodoxy.[41] It characterized a heterodox "they"—Roman Catholicism for the seventeenth-century Protestant Syncretists, paganism for Réville's and Cumont's Christianity—the existence and definition of which allowed for, in turn, an orthodox "we."[42] But the understanding of syncretism as historical process was no less problematic.[43] Such an understanding assumes some ideal antecedent or future time or state that is not syncretistic, or at least that is less so, by which the nature and extent of the syncretistic mixing process can be measured. In other words, syncretism defined as a cultural mixing implies already a norm, whether theological or historical, from which this fusion is viewed.

By contrast, syncretism in the ancient world signified a pattern of relationship rather than the monotheistic or essentialist tendency implied

36. Kümmel, *Neue Testament*, 310–11.

37. Gunkel, "Religio-Historical Interpretation," 455. Gunkel stated his overall thesis as "the religion of the New Testament, in important, and even in some vital, points can be interpreted only in the light of the influence of extraneous religions" (398).

38. Sergert, "Remarks."

39. Réville, *Religion*, 23.

40. Ibid.

41. On the theological or normative use of *syncretism* see also Baird, *Category*, 142–52.

42. For the anthropological basis of the we/they distinction, see Redfield, *Primitive World*, 92.

43. Baird, *Category*, 145–46.

by "mixing together." It was derived from συγκρητίζω, "to make two parties joined against a third,"⁴⁴ and was used first, and in the ancient world exclusively, by Plutarch to describe the reconciliation of the normally factious Cretans in the face of attack by a foreign foe.⁴⁵ In other words, Plutarch employed the term to signify a coherent system whereby resemblance structured the relations of its constituent parts. This system organized a play of sympathy and antipathy: antipathetic foes who resembled one another, Cretans, came into sympathetic relationship with one another only in antipathetical relationship with dissimilar foes, foreigners.⁴⁶

Syncretism in the Plutarchian sense suggests precisely the possibility of what Showerman and others had so disparaged: the perception of Hellenistic religious syncretism as a coherent system. Syncretism understood as a system specific to a Hellenistic period contravenes Robert Baird's objection that "no real purpose is served by applying" this term to describe a historical process that is "both inevitable and universal."⁴⁷ Syncretism so understood might better inform a modern generalization about Hellenistic religions by offering a systemic model for understanding how divine relations came into being in the Hellenistic period.

IV

The locus classicus for Hellenistic religious syncretism is book 11.5 of Apuleius's *Metamorphoses*. Its introductory self-description by Isis—"manifested alone under form of all gods and goddesses . . . my name, my divinity is adored throughout all the world, in diverse manners, in variable customs,

---

44. Sergert, "Remarks." Although not signified by the term συγκρητισμός, a process of religious "mixing together" is described by the first-century-CE popular philosopher Dio Chrysostom:
> Indeed, some do maintain that Apollo, Helius, and Dionysus are one and the same, and this is your view, and many people even go so far as to combine all the gods and make of them one single force and power, so that it makes no difference at all whether you are honoring this one or that one. (21.11; translated by Cohoon and Crosby)

Chrysostom's meaning has less to do with the signification of syncretism, however, than with Stoic allegory.

45 the Cretans . . . though they often quarreled with and warred against each other, made up their differences and united when outside enemies attacked; and thus it was which they called "syncretism." (*De fraterno amore* 19; translated by Helmbold)

46. See Foucault's discussion of pre-seventeenth-century thought (*Order*, 22–25), where he discusses resemblance as the play of sympathies; and Lloyd, *Polarity and Analogy*, especially part 1.

47. Baird, *Category*, 146.

and by many names"[48]—has been identified as "the syncretistic formula of union."[49] In commentary upon this passage, J. Gwyn Griffiths exemplifies the customary understanding for this example of syncretism by relating it to "universalism engendered by the widening political horizons in the Hellenistic era."[50] This explanation presumes the relation between political events and religious reaction that has characterized the study of Hellenistic religion since Droysen.

A systemic analysis of this passage, however, would not understand this example of syncretism in terms of politicohistorical cause, but in terms of religious discourse specific to Apuleius's Hellenistic novel. Like empire and cosmos, the *Metamorphoses* constitutes a finite field of inclusion. It contains a series of framed tales within framed tales, each mirroring the others; and its conclusion turns back upon the opening tale to render its meaning, and that of the entire novel, anew. In this way, the episodes in the novel are related to one another as part of an interconnected whole.[51] If the concluding episode of the *Metamorphoses* exemplifies Hellenistic religious syncretism, it is not because it profoundly culminates a bizarre collection of tales with a religious moral; it is because it provides an effective paradigm, both constitutive of and constituted by the entire novel.

In Apuleius's novel, the opening story of Aristomenes not only foreshadowed the plight of Lucius, the novel's hero, but suggests the plight of man in the Hellenistic world as a whole. Aristomenes tells Lucius of his chance meeting with a long-lost friend, Socrates, who had fallen onto bad luck and been reduced to a pale, thin beggar. Socrates had been attacked by bandits while on a business trip to Macedonia and finally escaped to an inn to fall under the power of a wicked sorceress, Meroe. Ultimately, however, Socrates blamed not Meroe but Fortune for his condition:

> O my friend Aristomenes, now perceive I well that you are ignorant of the whirling changes, the unstable forces, and slippery inconstancy of fortune. (*Metamorphoses* 1.6)

By the end of the story, Fortune had placed Aristomenes in the situation of Socrates at the beginning. Before long, Lucius too would know the buffetings of Fortune.

---

48. *Metamorphoses* 11.5 (translated by Adlington).
49. Griffiths, *Apuleius of Madauros*, 144.
50. Ibid.
51. See the provocative analysis of Apuleius's *Metamorphoses* by Merkelbach, *Roman und Mysterium*, 1–90.

Lucius became subject not only to the buffetings of an antipathetic blind fortune but also the recipient of the sympathetic benefits of Isis, who came to take pity on his fortune.[52] This beneficent aspect of Isis was known also as Ἀγαθὴ Τύχη, Good Fortune, a virtue commonly attributed to Isis.[53] As the priest of Isis said to Lucius at the time of his soteriological transformation,

> Let fortune go . . . for fortune hath no puissance against them which have devoted their lives to serve and honor the majesty of our goddess . . . Know thou that now thou are safe, and under the protection of that fortune that is not blind but can see, who by her clear light doth lighten the other gods. (11.15)

Isis, the antithesis of blind fortune, is "that fortune that is not blind but can see." Fortune's name (Gk: τύχη, Lt: Fortuna) means chance or luck, both good and ill. Her ambiguity, inconstant as the moon itself,[54] was her most characteristic trait.[55]

As a cosmological deity, Fortuna personified the universal but inclusive principle of resemblance with her contagious play of sympathy/antipathy. Considered by some the most important deity of the Hellenistic period,[56] Fortuna was the absolute sovereign of Lucius's world.[57] Personified in Apuleius's novel as Isis, she tells Lucius:

> I am she that is the natural mother of all things, mistress and governess of all the elements, the initial progeny of worlds, chief of the powers divine, queen of all that are in hell, the principal of them that dwell in heaven. (11.5)

---

52. *Metamorphoses* 11.5 (trans. Adlington).
53. Vanderlip, *Four Greek Hymns*, 31–32.
54. Isis/Fortuna is introduced to Lucius in lunar imagery: *Metamorphoses* 11.1.
55. So Pliny:
    [Fortuna is] alone accused, alone impeached, alone pondered, alone applauded, alone rebuked and visited with reproaches; deemed volatile and indeed by most men blind as well, inconstant, uncertain, fickle in her favours and favouring the unworthy. To her is decided all that is spent and credited, all that is received, she alone fills both pages in the whole of mortals account . . . (*Natural History* 2.22; translated by Rackham)
56. Pliny, for example, writes:
    Everywhere in the whole world at every hour by all men's voices Fortune alone is invoke and named . . . and we are so much at the mercy of chance that Chance herself, by whom is proved uncertain, takes the place of God. (*Natural History* 2.22)
57. Tatum, *Apuleius*, 73.

Lucius and the other characters of the novel are related to each other and to the goddess, both sympathetically and antipathetically, throughout. As the theriomorphic antipod of Isis,[58] Lucius is the emblem of the play of fortuitous antipathy; as the initiate into her cult, he is simultaneously the emblem of fortuitous sympathy. Similarly, the particular syncretistic configuration in book 11.5 of Apuleius's novel is best understood as a sympathetic assemblage of normally discrete goddesses,[59] representing good fortune in the face of an antipathetic relation to ill fortune.

To understand this Apuleian example of syncretism as a mixing together of rather obvious and overlapping divine attributes[60] "engendered by the widening political horizons in the Hellenistic era" tells us little. Why is Isis associated with just Cecropian Minerva and the nine other goddesses and not, for example, with the Syrian Goddess, Atargatis? This goddess also is one of the characters of the novel[61] and shares with them the Hellenistic political universe as her domain;[62] she shares also characteristics with other of the goddesses identified in book 11;[63] and she is identified with Isis in other contexts.[64] However, she is mocked in the *Metamorphoses*. Apparently, Atargatis is excluded from Apuleius's particular configuration of sympathetic relationships established with good fortune because of her association with Lucius's ill fortune.[65]

---

58. "Der Esel is nämlich die Verkörperung alles dessen, was der Isis feindlich ist. Er is das Tier des Seth, des Mörders des Osiris." Merkelbach, *Roman und Mysterium*, 1.

59. Nock, "Ruler-Worship," 557–58 has argued that the Hellenistic age is marked by the distinction of its religions, by individual deities, and individual initiation.

60. These shared characteristics include associations with fertility: Isis, Minerva (Athena), Venus (Aphrodite), Diana (Artemis), Ceres (Demeter), Juno, and Nemesis; with virginity: Minerva, Diana, and Proserpine; with the protection of cities: Minerva, Diana, and Juno; with wisdom: Minerva and Isis; with lunar characteristics: Diana, Juno, Hecate, and Isis; as mother goddesses: Minerva, Ceres, and Isis; with aid to women in childbirth: Diana, Juno, and Hecate; and with the underworld: Proserpine, Hecate, and Isis.

61. *Metamorphoses* 8.24–25 (translated by Adlington).

62. See Lucian, *De Dea Syria* (translated by Harmon), and the commentary on this text by Strong and Garstang, *Syrian Goddess*.

63. Especially the characteristic of fertility as a mother goddess.

64. Vanderlip, *Four Greek Hymns*, 28 n18.

65. The ass introduces the account of his purchase by and ritual service to Philebus, a priest of the Syrian Goddess with the observation:

> my evil fortune, which was ever so cruel against me, whom I, by travel of so many countries, could in no wise escape nor appease the envy thereof by all the woes I had undergone, did more and more cast its blind and evil eyes upon me, with the intervention of new means to afflict my poor body, in giving me another master very fit for my hard fate. (8.24)

V

Why just Cecropian Minerva?[66] Why not Atargatis? The example from Apuleius presents indeed the crux of Hellenistic religious syncretism. In any case of cultural contact, why and how does it occur? Why is just *a* borrowed from one culture rather than *b*? And why just *c* from the other rather than *d*? A systemic analysis of the problem offers an alternative to syncretism viewed as historical process. The word *system* is used here to signify that field shared by political, cosmological, and religious structures, and that governs the conditions of their possibility.

A systemic view of Hellenistic religious syncretism understands it as an enduring, finite field. This field is exemplified by the architecture of Ptolemaic cosmology, which endured from about the fourth century BCE until the Copernican revolution of Renaissance Europe. Historical shifts in both political and religious configurations occurred within this system. Thus, the Augustan empire signaled a first-century-BCE political reconfiguration within the Western succession of imperial embrace, while Theodocius signaled a fourth-century-CE reconfiguration in religious jurisdiction. An analytic of Hellenistic religious syncretism belongs to religious discourse specific to a period of religious history extending from the fourth century BCE to the fourth century CE.

As the example from Plutarch suggests and that from Apuleius illustrates, Hellenistic syncretism best signifies systemic relationships of resemblance construed in terms of sympathy and antipathy. These relationships were not understood in the Hellenistic period as a mixture of cultural particulars to be historically disentangled, but as patterns of relationships to be described in their particulars.

To be sure, there are instances of Hellenistic syncretism for which historical intention ostensibly accounts. For example, the well-known interpretation of the fabrication of the cult of S(e)arapis under the direction of Prolemy I Soter of Egypt has been understood as "a new religious concept to go with his own power."[67] While conforming to Droysen's political strategy, even this politicohistorical theory for the "artificial"[68] creation of a syncretistic deity suggests the systemic alternative. For the cult of S(e)arapis aspired to universal acceptance throughout the Hellenistic world. By achieving, to some degree this aspiration, the cult became more

---

66. Cecrops was the mythical first king of Athens. The adjective "Cecropian," then, is analogous to "Athenian." Thus, the title Cecropian Minerva is itself a syncretistic conflation.

67. Ferguson, *Religions*, 36.

68. Ibid.

attractive than would have some eclectic hodgepodge of already accessible deities. Consequently, its vitality must have drawn upon and been governed by an effective, existing system of religious structures.

Similarly, Gnosticism, long considered the most syncretistic of Hellenistic traditions, generally has been understood in its historical relationship to Christianity as a confusing and bizarre Christian heresy, or, in terms of its largely conjectural origins. A systemic approach shows Gnostic syncretism as yet another parallel configuration of Hellenistic resemblance, a relational system of sympathetic elements organized in terms of their antipathy to a cosmic εἱμαρμένη.[69]

Showerman's view of "the apparently chaotic condition of paganism when viewed as a system" exemplified the assumptions of Droysen's historical definition. Actually, however, it has been the attempt to understand syncretism as a historically continuing process, based upon fragmentary and confusing historical remains, which has proved to be chaotic. When its constituent elements are viewed as related parts of a system, however, Hellenistic syncretism discloses not chaos, but a relatively clear sympathetic/antithetic structure of resemblance.

---

69. This understanding of Gnosticism was already suggested in Anz, *Frage*, 13.

References

Anonymous. "The Octavius of Minucius Felix." *Frazer's Magazine for Town and Country* 47 (1853) 293–95.

Anz, Wilhlem. *Zur Frage nach dem Ursprung der Gnostcismus*. Texte und Untersuchungen zur Geschichte der altchristlichen Literatur 15/4. ATLA monograph preservation program ATLA fiche 1987-1624. Leipzig: Hinrich, 1897.

Apuleius. *The Golden Ass*. Translated by Robert Graves. New York: Noonday, 1951.

———. *Metamorphoses*. Translated by William Adlington. LCL. Cambridge: Harvard University Press, 1915.

Austin, Michel M. *The Hellenistic World from Alexander to the Roman Conquest: A Selection of Ancient Sources in Translation*. Cambridge: Cambridge University Press, 1981.

Baird, Robert D. *Category Formation and the History of Religions*. Religion and Reason 1. The Hague: Mouton, 1971.

Bayer, Erich. "Nachwort." In *Geschichte des Hellenismus*, by Johann G. Droysen. Edited by Erich Bayer, 3:435–95. 3 vols. Munich: Deutscher Taschenbuch, 1980.

Bennetta, Jules-Rosette. *African Apostles: Ritual and Conversion in the Church of John Maranke*. Symbol, Myth, and Ritual. Ithaca: Cornell University Press, 1975.

Burkitt, Francis C. *Church and Gnosis: A Study of Christian Thought and Speculation in the Second Century*. Cambridge: Cambridge University Press, 1932.

Carr, E. H. *What Is History?* New York: Vintage, 1961.

Cumont, Franz. *Oriental Religions in Roman Paganism*. With an introductory essay by Grant Showerman. 2nd ed. New York: Dover, 1956.

Dio Chrysostom. *Discourses. 31–36* Translated by James W. Cohoon and Henry L. Crosby. LCL 358. Cambridge: Harvard University Press, 1940.

Dodds, E. R. *The Greeks and the Irrational*. Berkeley: University of California Press, 1971.

Droysen, Johann G. *Geschichte des Hellenismus*. 3 vols. Edited by Erich Bayer. Munich: Deutscher Taschenbuch, 1980 [1st ed.: 1836–1843; 2nd ed.: 1877].

Eisler, Robert. *Weltenmantel und Himmelzeit: Religionsgeschichtliche Untersuchungen des antiken Weltbildes*. 2 vols. Munich: Beck, 1910.

Ellwood, Robert S, Jr. *Religious and Spiritual Groups in Modern America*. Englewood Cliffs, NJ: Prentice-Hall, 1973.

Ferguson, John. *The Religions of the Roman Empire*. Aspects of Greek and Roman Life. London: Thames & Hudson, 1970.

Finley, Moses I. "Generalizations in Ancient History." In *Generalization in the Writing of History*, edited by Louis Gottschalk, 19–35. Chicago: University of Chicago Press, 1963.

Foucault, Michel. *The Order of Things*. New York: Vintage, 1994.

Grant, Frederick C. "Hellenismus." In *Die Religion in Geschichte und Gegenwart*. 3: cols. 209–12. 3rd ed. Tübingen: Mohr/Siebeck, 1959.

———. *Hellenistic Religions: The Age of Syncretism*. The Library of Liberal Arts. Indianapolis: Bobbs-Merrill, 1953.

Griffiths, J. Gwyn, ed. *Apuleius of Madauros: The Isis-Book (Metamorphoses Book XI)*. EPRO 39. Leiden: Brill, 1975.

Gunkel, Hermann. "The Religio-Historical Interpretation of the New Testament." *Monist* 13/3 (1903) 398–455.

Guthrie, W. K. C. *Orpheus and Greek Religion.* New York: Norton, 1966.
Kümmel, Werner G. *Das Neue Testament: Geschichte der Erforschung Seiner Probleme.* Orbis academicus. Freiburg: Alber, 1958.
Lang, Andrew. *Myth, Ritual and Religion.* 2 vols. London: Longmans, Green, and Co., 1877.
Lloyd, G. E. R. *Polarity and Analogy: Two Types of Argumentation in Early Greek Thought.* Cambridge: Cambridge University Press, 1966.
Lucian. *De Dea Syria.* Translated by Austin M. Harmon. LCL. Cambridge: Harvard University Press, 1924.
———. *The Syrian Goddess: Being a Translation of Lucian's* De Dea Syria, *with a Life of Lucian.* Translated by Herbert Strong and John Garstang. London: Constable, 1913.
Merkelbach, Reinhold. *Roman und Mysterium in der Antike.* Munich: Beck, 1962.
Moffatt, James. "Syncretism." In *The Encyclopedia of Religion and Ethics,* edited by James Hastings, 12:155–57. New York: Scribner, 1922.
Munitz, Milton K., ed. *Theories of the Universe: From Babylonian Myth to Modern Science.* The Library of Scientific Thought. New York: Free Press, 1957.
Nilsson, Martin P. *Geschichte der Griechischen Religion.* 2 vols. 2nd ed. Handbuch der Altertumswissenschaft 2. Munich: Beck, 1961.
Nock, Arthur D. "Ruler-Worship and Syncretism." In *Arthur Darby Nock: Essays on Religion and the Ancient World,* edited by Zeph Stewart, 2:551–58. 2 vols. Cambridge: Harvard University Press, 1972.
Pliny. *Natural History.* Translated by Harris Rackham. LCL. Cambridge: Harvard University Press, 1949.
Plutarch, *De fraterno amore.* In *Moralia,* vol. 5. Translated by William C. Helmbold. LCL. Cambridge: Harvard University Press, 1939.
Préaux, Claire. *Le Monde Hellénistique.* 2 vols. Nouvelle Clio 6. Paris: Presses Universitaires de France, 1978.
Redfield, Robert. *The Primitive World and Its Transformations.* Cornell Paperbacks. Ithaca: Cornell University Press, 1953.
Réville, Jean. *La Religion à Rome sous les Sévères.* Paris: Leroux, 1886.
Segert, Stanislav. "Some Remarks Concerning Syncretism." In *Religious Syncretism in Antiquity: Essays in Conversation with Geo Widengren,* edited by Birger A. Pearson, 63–66. Series on Formative Contemporary Thinkers 1. Missoula: Scholars, 1975.
Seznec, Jean. *The Survival of the Pagan Gods: The Mytholological Tradition and Its Place in Renaissance Humanism and Art.* Translated by Barbara Sessions. Harper Torchbooks. The Bollingen Library. New York: Harper & Row, 1961.
Smith, Jonathan Z. "Hellenistic Religion." In *The Encyclopædia Britannica,* 8:746–61. 15th ed. Chicago: University of Chicago Press, 1982.
Solmsen, Friedrich. *Isis among the Greeks and Romans.* Martin Classical Lectures 25. Cambridge: Harvard University Press, 1979.
Stover, Robert. "Great Man Theory of History." In *The Encyclopedia of Philosophy,* edited by Paul Edwards, 3:378–82. Reprint ed. 8 vols. in 4. New York: Macmillan, 1972.
Tarn, W. W. *Hellenistic Civilization.* Rev. ed. by the author and G. T. Griffith. New York: World, 1952.
Tatum, James. *Apuleius and "The Golden Ass."* Ithaca, NY: Cornell University Press, 1979.

Usener, Hermann. *Götternamen: Versuch einer Lehre von der Religiösen Begriffsbildung.* 1896. Reprinted, Frankfurt: Schulte-Bulmke, 1948.

———. "Synkretismus." In *Lexikonreihe Die Religion in Geschichte und Gegenwart*, vol. 5, col. 1055. Tübingen: Mohr/Siebeck, 1913.

Vanderlip, Vera F. *The Four Greek Hymns of Isidorus and the Cult of Isis.* American Studies in Papyrology 12. Toronto: Hakkert, 1972.

Weiss, Hans-Friedrich. *Untersuchungen zur Kosmologie des hellenistischen und palästinischen Judentums.* Texte und Untersuchungen zur Geschichte der altchristlichen Literatur. Berlin: Akademie, 1966.

Wendland, Paul. *Die Hellenistische-Römische Kultur in ihren Beziehungen zu Judentum und Christentum.* Handbuch zum Neuen Testament 1. 2 vols. Tübingen: Mohr/Siebeck, 1912.

Wind, Edgar. *Pagan Mysteries in the Renaissance.* The Norton Library of Art and Architecture. New York: Norton, 1968.

Yates, Frances. *Giordano Bruno and the Hermetic Tradition.* Vintage Books. New York: Random House, 1969.

5

Kingship and the Consolidation of Religiopolitical Power during the Hellenistic Period[1]

Introduction

IN LECTURES I GAVE at Masaryk University in December 1996 on "Hellenistic Religious Communities,"[2] I argued that the multiplicity of Hellenistic communities, whether clubs, cults, philosophical schools, or the early Christianities, could be understood as extensions of and variations of a "kinship" type of social organization—in the Weberian sense of ideal types—and I sought to illustrate this model of social organization with the example of the so-called Hellenistic mystery cults. I also argued in these lectures for a second type of social organization that is antithetical to kinship, namely, kingship. Whereas kinship, in its original anthropological definition by William Robertson Smith, is a "natural" mode of social organization in which every human being becomes a member "simply in virtue of his birth and upbringing,"[3] kingship, in Smith's definition, refers to the tendency for "the primitive equality of the tribal system . . . to transform itself [over time] into an aristocracy of the more powerful kins, or of the more powerful families within one kin . . . [with the consequence that

---

1. This lecture, presented here in a revised form, was delivered on March 8, 2000, at the Masaryk University in Brno, Czech Republic. It was sponsored by the Czech Society for the Study of Religions and by the Institute for the Study of Religions, Masaryk University, Brno. My stay at the Masaryk University was realized thanks to the kind support of the Spencer Foundation, Chicago, USA.

2. Martin, "Biology."

3. Ibid., 41.

wealth] begins to be unequally distributed."[4] This human tendency towards the social organization of power may be more "natural" than that which Smith attributed to kinship, as the ubiquitous pecking order among chickens and the dominance of alpha males among most social animals suggest.[5] In addition to evolutionary adaptation in response to the vicissitudes of survival, it is likely that our ancestor also evolved adaptations in response to recurrent problems faced by emergent human societies which included, among other adaptive mechanisms, cognitive "capacities for representing social dominance."[6] This evolutionary basis for human dominance has given rise to the "Machiavellian Intelligence Hypothesis" which posits that "the advanced cognitive processes of primates [and humans] are primarily adaptations to the *special complexities of their social lives* rather than only to nonsocial environmental problems such as finding food."[7] Such a "politicizing" of human social organization is, nevertheless, a sociohistorical reality observable from the beginnings of human history. In this presentation, I should like to turn from the kinship and, again, to illustrate this type of human social organization from the Hellenistic period.

Kingship in the Hellenistic Period

Since the publication in 1836 of J. G. Droysen's *Geschichte Alexanders des Großen*, the first volume of his monumental three-volume *Geschichte des Hellenismus* (1836–1843), historians have marked the beginnings of a Hellenistic period of history by the military conquests, the political consolidations, and the cultural coalescences wrought by Alexander the Great. The imperial ideal of cultural hegemony associated with his name perdured to the Roman empire and beyond into the mentality of Western civilization.[8]

The institution of kingship established by Alexander was an innovation for the Greek world, since "monarchy was not a natural feature of . . . [that] world before the Hellenistic age."[9] Whereas Alexander's father Philip II, was, for example, "king" of Macedonia, he was only the "leader" (ἡγεμών) of the Corinthian League.[10] The power of any "king," where the title survived, e.g., in Sparta, was restricted; as Pindar is reputed to have said, "the law," for the

4. Smith, *Religion of the Semites*, 29.
5. Bekoff, "Dominance."
6. Hirschfeld, "Naive Sociology," 580.
7. Whiten, "Machiavellian," 495; see Koukolík, *Machiavelianská*, 9.
8. Ternes, "Study of Roman Religion."
9. Bilde et al., "Introduction," 9; Murray, "Symposia," 15.
10. Tod, *Greek Historical Inscriptions*, No. 177, 224, 229.

Greek world generally, "is the king of everyone, man and god" (*Fragments* 169.1–2). With Alexander, however, power in all its forms became "radically centralized" into what has been characterized as "perhaps the most important single information in the Hellenistic period."[11]

Although "no single model" can fully account for the varieties and complexities of the institution of kingship during the Hellenistic period, any period may be characterized and analyzed in terms of the distribution of power, and the history of that distribution, which characterizes its sociopolitical organization. As Michel Foucault persuasively argued,

> power is not an institution, and not a structure; neither is it a certain strength we are endowed with: it is the name that one attributed to a complex strategical situation in a particular society.[12]

The distribution and consolidation of power, consequently, offers a way to understand and analyze relationships of dominance and submission between the various constituencies of any given sociopolitical system. The relationships between the dominator and the dominated are generally one of the tacit consent. Again, in the words of Foucault:

> What makes power hold good, what makes it accepted, is simply the fact that it doesn't only weigh on us as a force that says no, but that it traverses and produces things, it induces pleasure, forms knowledge, produces discourse. It needs to be considered as a productive network which runs through the whole social body, much more than as a negative instance whose function is repression.[13]

Power, in other words, is not always imposed—although it may take that form. As Eric Wolf concludes, for power to be maintained, it must spread "into an ever larger number of instrumental domains, while curtailing the ability of subaltern groups to advance viable alternatives." If such redundancy falters, "the deficit may be made up by force."[14] However established, when power becomes centralized in a particular place or consolidated in the hands of one or a few, we may speak of the institution of kingship.

---

11. Bilde et al., "Introduction," 12, cf. 9.
12. Foucault, *Sexuality*, 1:93; see the summary of Sheridan, *Michel Foucault*, 183–85.
13. Foucault, *Power/Knowledge*, 119.
14. Wolf, *Europe*, 390.

Consolidation of Power in the Hellenistic Period

By the time of Alexander's empire, a growing acceptance of the necessity, or even the desirability, of political alliances required a transfer of loyalty from local or regional allegiances to some centralized power and authority, and finally to the imposed reality of empire. In Greece, pre-imperial alliances already included, of course, the well-known *poleis*, the relatively well organized city-state organizations and their various federations, e.g., the Delian League, the Arcadian League, the Aetolian Confederacy, and so forth as well as the less well known ἔθνη, large populations (Aristotle, *Politica* 1326B) within which individual communities had transferred some, but not all, power to a cosmos assembly with, however, a varying and complex range of loyalties to their collective goals.[15] Whereas the πόλεις were highly centralized organizations of "tribes" (φυλαί) and smaller kinship groups such as φρατρίαι and δῆμοι, the ἔθνη preserved some measure of local autonomy an identity. Both of these types of sociopolitical organizations established a collective identity based upon an extended social homogeneity. Such extra-familial, regional identity is referred to by contemporary social scientists as "ethnicity."[16]

In a well-known passage, Herodotus defined ethnicity by the four criteria of "common blood [ὁμαιμος], common language [ὁμόγλωσσος], common religion [θεῶν ἱδρύματά τε κοινὰ καὶ θυσίαι], and common culture [ἤθεά τε ὁμότροπα] (8.144), in which he gave pride of place to ὁμαιμος.[17] Greek society and state had been founded on kin groups that claimed common blood through descent from a common ancestor. If for some reason a common ancestor was absent or unknown, one might be invented, especially if a heroic or divine progenitor was desired. This ancestor gave his name to the family, and the veneration of the ancestor gave religious sanction to these social entities.[18] This sense of kinship was one of the most common characteristics of Hellenic societies.[19]

Fictive kin ties, extended by adoption and marriage, were common Graeco-Roman practices of kin recruitment that ensured legitimate descendants in the face of high mortality. And Hellenization, in the sense of assimilating non-Greeks to Greek culture, often involved inventing for colonized or conquered peoples eponyms that were connected with figures from

---

15. Morgan, "Ethnicity," 559.
16. Patterson, "Context and Choice," 308.
17. Kluckhohn, *Anthropology*, 134.
18. Nilsson, *Cults*, 65.
19. Kloppenborg and Wilson, *Voluntary Associations*, 13, 18, 112, 132, 134–35, 180, 189.

Greek myths who had similar names.[20] It is upon such claims to inclusive kinship that extrafamilial policies were constructed and by which the early kinship organization became subordinated to larger political entities.

Monarchs typically attempted to appropriate the ideological values of kinship alliances in support of imperial allegiance and stability. Such values of universal kinship were attributed to Alexander himself. Arrian, for example, reported that Alexander sacrificed to the gods and offered prayers in behalf of the kinship of mankind (*Anabasis* 7.11), and Diodorus Siculus (18.4.4) wrote that among Alexander's "last plans" was his desire to bring the largest continents into a common harmony through intermarriage and ties of kinship. Similarly, Plutarch averred that Alexander "bade ... all consider as their fatherland the whole inhabited earth ..., as akin to them all good men ..., being blended together into one by ties of blood and children" (Plutarch, *Moralia* 329C–D). And Alexander did, in fact, confirm his own political alliances by marrying first of all the daughter of a Bactrian noble in 327 and again a daughter of Darius in 324.

The Hellenistic Emperor Cult

The traditional forms of sociopolitical organization that had served the Greeks with remarkable success for centuries proved inadequate for the functioning of international empire. With their breakdown, new, universal forms of legitimating imperial authority were required. In Persia, Alexander had encountered cult practices that attributed divine qualities to their king; in Egypt, too, he found an official cult devoted to the king as god[21] and, in both places, the young conqueror was himself so received. The ideas of "paying cult to a man in his lifetime" is, however, "essentially Greek, linked, since the early fourth century B.C., with the cult of heroes."[22] Accounts of Alexander's own heroic exploits told of his descent on his mother's side from Achilles, the bravest of Homeric heroes and on his father's side—despite tales of his virgin mother having been impregnated by a lightning bolt—from Heracles, the greatest of the Greek heroes (Plutarch, *Alexander* 22).[23] Both Achilles and Heracles had, according to Greek mythology, ascended from heroic to divine status; and Alexander was to follow suit. "If," in the words of Isocrates to Alexander's father, Philip of Macedon, "you make the barbarians helots of the Greeks and force the [Persian] king called great

20. Nilsson, *Cults*, 97–98, 105.
21. Taylor, *Divinity*, 6.
22. Fishwick, *Imperial Cult*, 4–5.
23. Nilsson, *Cults*, 108.

to do your command ... then nothing remains for you except to become a god" (Isocrates, *Epistle* 3; see *Philippus* 132). And, Alexander's teacher, Aristotle, concluded that a man of such political virtue and ability might well be considered "a god among men" (*Politica* 1284A). With Alexander's successful establishment of Greek hegemony over Persia, he realized his father's ambition, and in 324/323 BCE, Athens, followed by other Greek cities, voted Alexander to be Dionysus—if not in response to Alexander's demand, at least in recognition of his desires (Aelianus, *Varia Historia* 2.19; Plutarch, *Moralia* 219E).[24] Although accounts of this identification of Alexander with Dionysus have been challenged as originating in later tradition,[25] it does seem to be the case that Alexander was recognized at that time as "son of Zeus" (Hyperides, *Against Demosthenes* 31).[26] His distinctive image on coins, while recognizable, was influenced by representative clichés of heroes and gods, and was shown with divine attributes, the most common being the horns of Zeus Ammon.[27]

Although the "boundary between gods and men was narrower in Graeco-Roman belief than in ours and more fluid,"[28] and "cults of single rulers... spontaneously created by... individual *poleis*" were well known, Greek notions of divine incarnation—Euhemeristic myth aside—were not so common[29] and the emergence of a state cult of the monarch was even more of an innovation for the Greeks than was the establishment of the kingship itself.

With the precedent argued by Euhemerus,[30] and by claiming kinship with or "descent" (i.e., succession) from Alexander, the Hellenistic kings asserted their own heroic or divine status, or both.[31] The real heirs of Alexander, however, were Julius Caesar and Augustus, both in terms of their successful consolidation of political power, and in terms of the divine right to rule, which they claimed—a right subsequently claimed by monarchy in the West until the rise of the modern democratic state.

Divine right to rule, whether as divinity incarnate or by divine sanction, provided, in the observation of Arthur D. Nock, "an etiquette for the

---

24. Taylor, *Divinity*, 21–23; Fishwick, *Imperial Cult*, 9–10.
25. Nock, "Notes," 134–44.
26. Ibid., 135.
27. Fleischer, "Hellenistic Royal Iconography," 37.
28. Fishwick, *Imperial Cult*, 41.
29. Nock, "Notes," 152.
30. Actually Leon of Pella (Augustine, *De civitate Dei* 8.5; 12.11; Minucius Felix, *Octavius* 21.3); see Taylor, *Divinity*, 26–27.
31. Taylor, *Divinity*, 25; Fishwick, *Imperial Cult*, 11–20.

relation of monarch and dwellers within the sphere of influence: on their side homage, on his side a divine pose which admitted of a wide range of variation between moderate and exaggerated forms."[32] Whatever the source of the ruler cult in the West, however the details and history of this cult might finally be interpreted, and however different the situation might have been in different areas and in different times, there is no question that the Hellenistic period can be characterized as a period when a consolidation of religious as well as political power took place around the person and office of the emperor. Were ideas about a divine emperor simply a means to establish authority and to enforce his (or her, as in the case of Egypt) absolute rule—"more of a matter of personal politics than of religion," as an earlier generation of scholars concluded?[33] Or, as Simon Price suggested, was the imperial cult a socially effective way to articulate the overwhelming power of the emperor, who stood at the focal point between humans and gods but was, nevertheless, very much human?[34] Or might the situation have been a more subtle projection by the king of "himself as [the] principal agent in transmitting the favour of the gods [and their power] to the subjects of his realm," as Erich Gruen suggested?[35] The final evaluation of such questions depends, of course, on one's definition of *religion*.[36]

Consolidations of Religious Power in the Hellenistic Period

Religions and politics are both ways of organizing power as a variable social system.[37] Like any political system, religion may be understood as that social system that seeks to legitimate and to maintain itself by appealing to rituals of power, whether the exercise of those rituals is consensual or imposed. The sole difference between religious and political systems is that the nature of the power appealed to in legitimation of religious systems is superhuman.[38] This is, of course, a taxonomic definition that allows the

32. Nock, "Rules-Worship," 552–53; see also Fishwick, *Imperial Cult*, 11.

33. E.g., Taylor, *Divinity*, 35, 237.

34. Price, *Rituals and Power*, 233; see the similar position suggested in Nock, "Ruler-Worship," 552–53.

35. Gruen, "Hellenistic Kingship," 118.

36. Fishwick, *Imperial Cult*, 42–43.

37. Martin, "Religia."

38. Scholars of religion have traditionally focused all of their efforts on descriptions, taxonomies, etc. of this singular characteristic of religious systems. This focus on the dimension of superhuman power rather than on the social *claims* to superhuman

scholar to analyze religious systems in different cultural domains, whether or not such a system is actually differentiated from other effective systems in that domain. For example, the official religions of Greece and Rome, and the power distributions they represented, were not distinguished from their respective political systems and the distribution of power they represented; this is unlike modern Western ideas about the separation and autonomy of such systems. Consequently, we would generally expect the structures and transformations of a particular religious system would parallel those of the political system in a common cultural domain. For example, the Israelite deity received the title *malek* (king) only in the context of Israel's postexile construction of a royal epic first of all in the form of promise (Deut 17.14) that was only realized, according to the Deuteronomic narrative, when "all the tribes of Israel [were gathered] together," i.e., when they became consolidated as a singular political entity (33.5).

Consolidations of religious power in the first centuries of the Christian era have been termed, a "monotheistic trend." Such consolidations were not, however, the historical destiny claimed by theologians in explanation of the "triumph" of Christianity in the face of the imperial state and of the Hellenistic religious alternatives, but represented, rather, a systemic consolidation of religious power in parallel to the successive consolidations of political power from Alexander to Augustus. Parallel examples of the consolidation of religious power include the iconographic homogeneity of Mithraism (still not fully explained historically), and the reemergence of Platonic essentialism in face of Aristotelian taxonomies from the pseudo-Platonic dialogue of Axiochus in the first century BCE to its theopolitical apogee with Plotinus in the third century.[39] The culmination of the parallel consolidation of political and religious power during the Roman Empire was, of course, their convergence under Constantine's reunification of the empire and his reconsolidation and reassertion of Roman political power following the administrative division of the empire under Diocletian—a division that reflected a wider political discord on the one hand, and his embrace of an increasingly consolidated Christian monotheism on the other: a successful religiopolitical alliance of various strands of the early Christianities that received juridical confirmation by Theodosius at the end

---

power as a strategy of legitimation has led to conclusions about the *sui generis* nature of religion—discussions that neglect, thereby, the role played by this system in the context of its sociocultural domain. See Boyer, *Naturalness*, 116.

39. Martin, "Self and Power." On a general consolidation of knowledge characteristic of this period, see Greenwald, "*Canon*."

of the fourth century.[40] As history has shown, when religious and political powers become joined as one, that power is formidable indeed.

Religiopolitical consolidation of power may, of course, be challenged, as when Athens and Sparta purportedly ridiculed the deification of Alexander,[41] or when the Maccabees led the Jews of Palestine in armed revolt against the policies of Antiochus.[42] And, religious power can consolidate in ways parallel to but alternative to official consolidations of religiopolitical power, as in the construction on the basis of fictive kinship alliances of the ubiquitous clubs and cults that populated the Hellenistic world. Such local assertions of power threaten the perceptions of absolute sovereignty even as political consolidations challenge the identity and autonomy of local distributions of power. Such consolidations were viewed (often correctly) by Rome, for example, as a potential threat to the power of the state, and these threats, whether real or perceived, had to be controlled. The most well-known example of Rome's control of a religious movement was the suppression of the Bacchanalia by the senatorial decree in 186 BCE. According to this decree, cult officials and a common treasury were prohibited and any practice of the Bacchanalia required official permission—and then it was limited to five persons, no more than two men and three women at any celebration, measures that finally restricted any organized communities for this group (Livy 19.8–18). This action by the senate with respect to the Bacchanalia may have been part of the legal precedent employed by Rome against the early Christianities.

The kinship/kingship model of ideal types here proposed offers a theoretical rationale from the numerous religiopolitical entities of the Hellenistic world, for their relationship to one another and to empire at large. Actual distributions of power in the context of Hellenistic, as of any, culture represent, of course, a potentially infinitive number of historical variations between these ideal types of human sociopolitical organization.

---

40. Cameron, *Christianity*; Fowden, *Empire*.

41. Taylor, *Divinity*, 21–22.

42. For studies in the Near Eastern resistance to Hellenism, see Eddy, *The King Is Dead*.

References

Bekoff, Marc "Dominance in Animal Social Groups." In *The MIT Encyclopedia of the Cognitive Sciences*, edited by Robert A. Wilson and Frank C. Keil, 240–42. Cambridge: MIT Press, 1999.

Bilde, Per et al. "Introduction." In *Aspects of Hellenistic Kingship*, edited by Per Bilde et al., 9–14. SHC 7. Aarhus: Aarhus University Press, 1996.

Boyer, Pascal. *The Naturalness of Religious Ideas: A Cognitive Theory of Religion*. Berkeley: University of California Press, 1994.

Cameron, Averil. *Christianity and the Rhetoric of Empire: The Development of Christian Discourse*. Sather Classical Lectures 55. Berkeley: University of California Press, 1991.

Eddy, Samuel K. *The King Is Dead: Studies in the Near Eastern Resistance to Hellenism, 334–31 BC*. Lincoln: University of Nebraska Press, 1961.

Fishwick, Duncan. *The Imperial Cult in the Latin West*. 2 vols. EPRO 18. RGRW 148. Leiden: Brill, 1987.

Fleischer, Robert. "Hellenistic Royal Iconography on Coins." In *Aspects of Hellenistic Kingship*, edited by Per Bilde et al., 28–40. SHC 7. Aarhus: Aarhus University Press, 1996.

Foucault, Michel. *The History of Sexuality*. Translated by Robert Hurley. 3 vols. New York: Pantheon, 1978.

———. *Power/Knowledge: Selected Interviews & Other Writings, 1972–1977*. Edited and translated by Colin Gordon. New York: Pantheon, 1980.

Fowden, Garth. *Empire to Commonwealth: Consequences of Monotheism in Late Antiquity*. Princeton: Princeton University Press, 1993.

Greenwald, Michael R. "The New Testament Canon and the Mishnah: Consolidation of Knowledge in the Second Century CE." PhD diss., Boston University 1989.

Gruen, Erich. "Hellenistic Kingship: Puzzles, Problems, and Possibilities." In *Aspects of Hellenistic Kingship*, edited by Per Bilde et al., 116–25. SHC 7. Aarhus: Aarhus University Press, 1996.

Hirschfeld, Lawrence A. "Naive Sociology." In *The MIT Encyclopedia of the Cognitive Sciences*, edited by Robert A. Wilson and Frank C. Keil, 579–81. Cambridge: MIT Press, 1999.

Kloppenborg, John S., and Stephen G. Wilson, eds. *Voluntary Associations in the Graeco-Roman World*. London: Routledge, 1996.

Kluckhohn, Clyde. *Anthropology and the Classics*. The Colver Lectures in Brown University, 1960. Providence: Brown University Press, 1961.

Koukolík, František. *Machiavelianská inteligence: Eseje ze třetí kultury v roce 2000*. Prague: Makropulos, 1999.

Martin, Luther H. "Biology, Sociology and the Study of Religion: Two Lectures." Religio: *Revue pro Religionistiku* 5/1 (1997) 21–35 (chapter 6, this volume).

———. "Religia I wladza polityczna: Hipotezt krytyki wybranych wzorów zależności." *Przeglad Religioznawczy* 2/168 (1993) 67–74.

———. "Self and Power in the Thought of Plotinus." In *Czlowiek i wartości*, edited by Antoni Komendera et al., 91–99. Kraków: Wydawnictwo Naukowe WSP, 1997 (chapter 24, this volume).

Morgan, Catherine A. "Ethnicity." In *The Oxford Classical Dictionary*, edited by Simon Hornblower and Antony Spawforth, 558–59. 3rd ed. Oxford: Oxford University Press, 1996.

Murray, Oswyn. "Hellenistic Royal Symposia." In *Aspects of Hellenistic Kingship*, edited by Per Bilde et al., 15–27. SHC 7. Aarhus: Aarhus University Press, 1996.

Nilsson, Martin P. *Cults, Myths, Oracles, and Politics in Ancient Greece*. Skrifter utg. av Svenska institutet i Athen 8/I. Lund: Gleerup, 1951.

Nock, Arthur D. "Notes on Ruler-Cult I–IV." In *Arthur Darby Nock: Essays on Religion and the Ancient World*, edited by Zeph Stewart, 1:134–59. Cambridge: Harvard University Press, 1972.

———. "Ruler Worship and Syncretism." In *Arthur Darby Nock: Essays on Religion and the Ancient World*, edited by Zeph Stewart, 2:551–58. Cambridge: Harvard University Press, 1972.

Pattersen, Orlando. "Context and Choice in Ethnic Allegiance: A Theoretical Framework and Case Study." In *Ethnicity: Theory and Experience*, edited by Nathan Glazer and Daniel P. Moynihan, 305–49. Cambridge Harvard University Press, 1975.

Price, S. R. F. *Rituals and Power: The Roman Imperial Cult in Asia Minor*. Cambridge: Cambridge University Press, 1984.

Sheridan, Alan. *Michel Foucault: The Will to Truth*. London: Tavistock, 1980.

Smith, W. Robertson. *The Religion of the Semites: The Fundamental Institutions*. 1889. Reprint, New York: Schocken, 1972.

Taylor, Lily R. *The Divinity of the Roman Emperor*. Philological Monographs 1. Middletown, CT: Philological Monographs 1. American Philological Association, 1931.

Ternes, Charles M. "The Study of Roman Religion after World War II." In *The Academic Study of Religion during the Cold War: East and West*, edited by Iva Dolezalova et al., 3–17. Toronto Studies in Religion 27. New York: Lang, 2001.

Tod, Marcus Niebuhr. *A Selection of Greek Historical Inscriptions*. Vol. 2, *From 403 to 323 BC*. Oxford: Clarendon, 1948.

Whiten, Andrew. "Machiavellian Intelligence Hypothesis." In *The MIT Encyclopedia of the Cognitive Sciences*, edited by Robert A. Wilson and Frank C. Keil, 495–97. Cambridge: MIT Press, 1999.

Wolf, Eric R. *Europe and the People without History*. Berkeley: University of California Press, 1997.

6

Biology, Sociology, and the Study of Religion: Two Lectures[1]

IN THE FOLLOWING TWO lectures, I suggest (1) a thoroughly *natural* rather than *supernatural* (or metaphysical) basis for the study of religion and (2) illustrate this approach from the Hellenistic cults. In juxtaposing the natural with the social sciences and with the humanities, I do not intend to join the discussion about the relationship *between* science and religion, a discussion that has as its goal some sort of scientific validation for traditional religious claims. Rather than to conduct such an exercise in apologetics, my intent is to suggest a scientific explanation for religion and, consequently, for its study.

Biology, Sociology, and Religion

The study of religion has made remarkable progress since its nineteenth-century origins out of liberal Protestant theology, especially in those institutions unattached to divinity schools—state universities in the United States, for example. Nevertheless, metaphysical "survivals" still characterize our field. These are most evident in the various sui generis definitions of *religion*.

---

1. These lectures were first delivered in December 1996 at the Institute for the Study of Religions, Masaryk University, Brno, Czech Republic; the second lecture was sponsored also by the Czech Society for the Study of Religions. They are presented here in revised form. I am grateful to Dr. Dalibor Papoušek, Head of the Institute for the Study of Religions, for inviting me to deliver these lectures; to Dr. Iva Doležalová for her careful and tireless translations to my Czech audience; and to all members of the Institute for their warm hospitality. My stay at the Masaryk University was realized thanks to the kind support of the Open Society Fund (Higher Education Support Program, grant no. HC11/96), and to the Dean's Fund, College of Arts and Sciences, the University of Vermont.

If we are to take seriously an academic or scientific *study* of religion, however, we must distance our study from its discursive *practice*, viz. theology, and with it the metaphysical legitimation with which it has been so implicated in Western culture at least since Aristotle (*Metaphysica* 1026A.19; see 1064B.3).

The term *metaphysics* was not, of course, Aristotle's but was employed by his Hellenistic commentators in reference to the united group of texts he wrote "after those he wrote on nature" (μετὰ τὰ φυσικὰ βιβλία). Medieval philosophers, however, imputed to *meta* a philosophical rather than its simple prepositional meaning, transforming its temporal into a transcendental sense.[2] Since the Enlightenment, however, epistemology has been returning from the metaphysical to the physical sciences in the study of reality—including the study of the ubiquitous reality of religious practice. The most appropriate physical science with which to begin a study of human behavior is, of course, biology.

In his recent book *Creation of the Sacred*, the classicist and historian of ancient religions Walter Burkert has urged a merger of cultural studies "with general anthropology, which is ultimately integrated into biology."[3] One's "biological makeup," he suggests, "forms preconditions or 'attractors' to produce [cultural] phenomena in a consistent fashion." Consequently,

> the details and sequences in rituals, tales, works of art, and fantasies hark back to more original processes in the evolution of life; they become understandable not in isolation nor within their different cultural contexts, but in relation to this background.[4]

Though indeed produced by "cultural choice," "religion," Burkert concludes, "keeps to the tracks" of this biological "landscape."[5]

Burkert is working out of a naturalistic tradition that has its origins in the Enlightenment, with David Hume, for example (*Dialogues Concerning Natural Religion* [1779]), and has its immediate roots in the ethological research of Konrad Lorenz and the sociobiological theories of Edward O. Wilson.[6] Whereas Lorenz's research sought to extend observations about animal behavior to that of humans,[7] Wilson defines sociobiology more comprehensively "as the systematic study of the biological basis of all forms

---

2. Hancock, "Metaphysics," 289.
3. Burkert, *Creation*, 8.
4. Ibid., 22.
5. Ibid., 23, 28, 33.
6. Ibid., 8–12.
7. Konrad, *Aggression*.

of social behavior, in all kinds of organisms, including man."[8] Wilson considered the "redisposition to religious belief" to be "the most complex and powerful force in the human mind and in all probability an ineradicable part of human nature."[9]

Perhaps the most significant development for understanding a biological basis for religion has been the explosion of research since the mid-twentieth century among the cognitive sciences. Understood as the empirically based effort to explain the basis of knowledge (human as well as nonhuman),[10] the ultimate, and distant, goal of cognitive psychology is a global understanding of the physical structure of the human mental system and how it operates to produce intelligent, including religious, behavior. By paying attention to the role that human minds play in the production of cultural forms and expression, a cognitive "mapping" of the architecture of human thought and behavior promises not only to contribute to our knowledge of religion and its persistence in human history, but to suggest also a formal, species-specific framework for the comparative work that is so central to the academic study of religion.[11]

All of the approaches mentioned above—ethology, sociobiology, and cognitive science—share the perspective of contemporary evolutionary biology. This is not the social Darwinism of an earlier time, however, for one of its disconfirmed assumptions is the notion of survival based upon collective successes. Rather, focus has shifted to the survival of genes and not of groups or even individuals.[12] Rather, instances of human cultural diversity are understood by contemporary or neo-Darwinian theorists "as products of a single human nature responding to widely varying circumstances,"[13] "a generic specieswide development program that absorbs information from the social environment and adjusts the maturing mind accordingly."[14] Whereas these theorists trace differences among people to environment, they understand a "deeper unity within the species" to reside in genetically governed roles for mental development.[15] Nevertheless, Burkert presumes

---

8. Wilson, *On Human Nature*, 16.

9. Ibid., 169.

10. Gardner, *Mind's New Science*, 6.

11. See especially the work of Lawson and McCauley, *Rethinking Religion*; Boyer, *Naturalness*; Sperber, *Explaining Culture*.

12. Dawkins, *Selfish Gene*.

13. Wright, *Moral Animal*, 8.

14. Ibid., 9.

15. Ibid., 7–10.

that "a certain survival fitness of religion has to be granted," because, on the whole, the history of religions has been a story of success."[16]

In his review of Burkert's book, the cognitive theorist Daniel Dennett, following Richard Dawkins, poses the question: "survival fitness for whom?—an elite, the social group as a whole, certain so-called self genes?"[17] Dawkins has also suggested the possibility of "selfish vehicles of *cultural* transmission," which he termed "memes," units of culturally acquired information, which tend to replicate themselves even though they may not be of any benefit. Dennett suggests that religions might be just such memes, replicating themselves by "parasitically exploiting proclivities . . . in the human cognitive-immune system."[18] Thus, as Burkert concludes, "information survival asserts itself side by side with and even instead of genetic survival."[19]

The presence and persistence of human universals must, in Burkert's conclusion, "be presumed to fulfill basic functions for human social life in all its forms."[20] One such human universal is social life itself. Human beings are social beings and, apparently, innately so. It is not difficult to imagine the evolutionary benefit to humans of this trait. This recognition of a biological basis for human sociability undermines the conviction of much social science about the autonomy of social act and the determinate role of culture.[21] Rather, social fact and cultural determinates are themselves effects to be explained.

In his groundbreaking study of *The Religion of Semites*, William Robertson Smith recognized not only the ubiquity but the naturalness of human society. Smith averred that "every human being, without choice on his own part, but simply in virtue of his birth and upbringing, becomes a member of . . . a natural society."[22] Membership in these societies is modeled upon biological patterns of descent; they are, in other words, kinship societies.[23]

The sociological significance of kinship societies is heightened with the emergence of a second type of human social organization—kingships. In Smith's formulation:

---

16. Burkert, *Creation*, 13.
17. Dennett, "Appraising Grace."
18. Ibid., 41.
19. Burkert, *Creation*, 24.
20. Ibid., 4.
21. Wilson, *On Human Nature*, 33.
22. Smith, *Religion of the Semites*, 29.
23. Wilson, *On Human Nature*, 22 and Burkert, *Creation*, 4, also list "kin groups" among human universals.

> The primitive equality of the tribal system tends in progress of time to transform itself into an aristocracy of the more powerful kins, or of the more powerful families within one kin ... [with the consequence that] wealth begins to be unequally distributed.[24]

Initially, kinship alliances were established through marriage, as Lévi-Strauss has shown.[25] Subsequently, and alternatively, alliances were effected by agreement (treaty) or imposed by force.

All social relationships may be understood as relationships of power, as Michel Foucault has emphasized.[26] Consequently, the differences between "kinship" and "kingship" as types of social organization might be formulated in terms of differing distributions of power.[27] Whereas power in kinship groups is disseminated more or less equally throughout the society, kingships are consolidations of power. These consolidations of power present a threat to the autonomy of kinship organizations and their local distributions of power even as the continuing existence of local power challenges the pretensions of imperial sovereignty and their legitimating state religions.

The maintenance and persistence of kinship societies in the face of social tendencies to consolidation is not solely a matter of biology but of sociology. As Smith put it, "the idea that kinship is not purely an affair of birth, but may be acquired, has quite fallen out of our circle of ideas."[28] Although Smith largely neglects it, the preeminent technique for kinship recruitment apart from birth is adoption.[29] Such fictive kin status could be extended not only to sons (and daughters) but to ancestors and ancestral heroes and deities as well. It is these common and commemorated ancestors, linked to the present by narrative of descent, that provide collective identity for

---

24. Smith, *Religion of the Semites*, 73.

25. Lévi-Strauss, *Elementary Structures*.

26. See the helpful summary of Foucault's use of "power" by Sheridan, *Michel Foucault*, 183–85.

27. Independently of Foucault, Sagan, *Dawn*, 240 has offered this same distinction between "kinship" and "kingship."

28. Smith, *Religion of the Semites*, 273. Fustel de Coulanges, one of the influences on Smith, noted that agnation, from ancient Greece until imperial Rome, was cultic and not physiological (*City*, 51, 59).

29. See Smith, *Kinship*, 52–54.

any particular group;³⁰ and the transgenerational authority of these attested ancestors guarantees the stability and continuity of the putative descent group.³¹

Smith was perhaps the first scholar of religion to recognize that religion must be accounted for by its social nature.³² Although scholars of religion regularly acknowledge that religion is a social phenomenon, we have not developed any timely social theory of religion, relying instead still on the pioneering but dated theories of Marx, Weber, and Durkheim. Rather, religious studies have been sidetracked by

> a lingering fascination with a romantic individualism ... [which has been v]alorized by the Enlightenment, cultivated within the humanities, and moralized [especially] in American ideology.³³

Certainly such "individualistic" values have informed the study of the religions of antiquity, as I argued in my article on "The Anti-Individualistic Ideology of Hellenistic Culture."³⁴

I should like to suggest Smith's typology of "kinship" and "kingship" as "ideal types" or poles of a continuum that describe all human social organization and, consequently, their religious communities. In light of the above, we might redefine Smith's "natural" or kinship societies as cultural elaborations of biology in terms of varying power distributions. And, we might understand religion to be the effective means of legitimating this political power, in whatever manner that power might be distributed, by claims to superhuman power. Such superhuman powers may also be imagined as supernatural; and they might be imaged anthropomorphically, theriomorphically, dendromorphically, technomorphically, and so forth. The object of the history of religions, consequently, may be identified as the history of those sociocultural elaborations of biology that are legitimated by claims to superhuman power.

I have argued that sociability is a universal characteristic of the species, *Homo sapiens*, and thus programmed by evolution and biologically—i.e., genetically—transmitted. I have argued further that the kinship/kingship model of social organization, based upon the natural family, is a cultural elaboration of this innate characteristic of human existence shaped by social

---

30. Smith, *Religion of the Semites*, 40–41. See Hutton, "Collective Memory." Hutton builds upon the work of Maurice Halbwachs, (*Topographie*) one of Durkheim's students; see also, Smith, *To Take Place*, 115–17.

31. Burkert, *Creation*, 15.

32. Malinowski cited by Kardiner and Preble, *They Studied Man*, 73 n2.

33. Mack, "Caretakers."

34. Martin, "Anti-Individualist."

distributions of power. This universal typology of social organization is applicable also to an understanding of religious communities.

We can illustrate this thesis historically from Hellenistic religious communities. In my book on *Hellenistic Religions*, I identified three types of discourse and practice that are usually grouped together as "religious" in contrast to the "official" or state religion(s): piety, mystery, and gnosis. I should like to associate these discourses and practices with the sociology of different forms of kinship organization.

Pietistic practices are the most exemplary of kinship societies. Piety (Gk: εὐσέβεια, Lat: *pietas*) designates a traditional system of "right" relationships:

> conventional practices concerning home and family and, by extension, those practices which surround and are part of being at home in one's world under the rule of a family of gods ... [Such practices] are always in terms of a particular locale or place and are transmitted through local tradition. They represent the expression by a particular people of their local order of things.[35]

So defined, piety belongs to the sociology of kinship societies, the correctness of the relationships being defined by each society and legitimated by their local, or even kin-specific, deities.

Less noted are the claims by various gnostic traditions to kinship bonds established through descent from a common divine ancestor or deity. The clearest example is those claiming descent from Seth;[36] however, it is characteristic of all gnostic anthropology to claim consubstantiality with hypercosmic power and is elaborated, consequently, in myths of cosmogonic fall.[37]

Finally, the Hellenistic mystery cults may be understood as "fictive" kinships groups, as their frequent use of kinship terminology suggests. Their existence is legitimated by appeal to a universalized native deity and, concomitantly, nonnative membership in these alternative kin groups is established through initiation modeled upon the kin-recruitment process of adoption.

The family cults, mystery religions, and the gnostic traditions represented three different types of kinship groups, all of which stood in tension with the imperial power of Hellenistic kingships, both politically and, in the case of the emperor cult, religiously. Whereas "family cults" and gnostic claims are rather explicit in their claims to kinship identity, the Hellenistic

---

35. Martin, *Hellenistic Religions*, 11–12.
36. Martin, "Genealogy."
37. Jonas, *Gnostic*, 44.

mystery cults are much less obvious in this regard. Consequently, it is this sociohistorical example to which I should like to devote a more detailed analysis in my second lecture.

Sociology and the Study of Religion: The Case of Hellenistic Religious Communities[38]

The whole range of ideas in the philosophy and in the theory of development [of Christianity] had to date been treated as history of ideas, as with Hegel and Dilthey. It occupied the central place in every philosophy of religion ... Then I came under the spell of that overwhelming personality, Max Weber, who had long been well aware of wonders which for me were just dawning. At the same time, I was captivated by the Marxist doctrine of infrastructure and superstructures. Not that I simply considered it correct, but it does contain a mode of questioning which can never be evaded, even though each separate case must be examined individually. Its mode of questioning was how far the origin, development, change and modern plight of Christianity is sociologically conditioned, and how far it itself operates as a formative sociological principle. These are extraordinary difficult questions and scarcely any useful preparatory studies had been done on them. And yet, it was no longer possible to speak solely of a history of doctrine or a history of ideas approach to Christianity [or to other religions] once this problem had been grasped.

ERNST TROELTSCH[39]

In my first lecture, I responded to the challenge formulated by Troeltsch by suggesting a sociological view of religious communities based upon biology, that is, upon social elaborations of the "natural" family and organized according to cultural distributions of power. In this lecture, I should like to illustrate this view by example of the Hellenistic mystery religions understood as fictive kinship societies, that is, precisely as social elaborations of natural kin associations that were occasioned by new cultural conditions.

---

38. This lecture is a revised version of my paper, "Akin to the Gods."
39. Troeltsch, *Writings*, 46–47.

Autonomous associations, alternative to the public institutions of larger society, are documented in Greece as early as the sixth century BCE when Solon accepted their legality "provided they were not contrary to the laws of the state" (Gaius, *Iustiniani Digesta* 47.22.4). Such associations proliferated during the Hellenistic period, and sporadic attempts by the Romans to suppress or at least control them, they perdured well into the Christian period.[40] The Hellenistic groups seemed to function initially as associations whereby ethnic "brethren," separated from their natural kin by military service perhaps, or by commercial enterprise, might nevertheless commemorate some aspects of their native society and maintain, consequently, the cultural requisites of their traditional social identity in light of the cosmopolitan pressures of Hellenistic empire.[41] These requisites would include care of their ancestral dead and the patronage of some native deity. Over time, care for the ancestral dead would be replaced by care for the dead of the new diaspora community, and the native deity would either become universalized so that it might provide patronage for its internationally dispersed clients or be replaced altogether by a deity more appropriate to the new cosmopolitan context. Unless new members from the homeland continued to replenish these groups and their memories, their native character would eventually dissipate, as a consequence of continued mobility, for example, or of assimilation into the new and larger Hellenized context. Since the first priority of any social group is to maintain itself, new members would, in such cases, need be recruited from the surrounding nonethnic population. As successive kingships more or less successfully established an internationalized culture around the Mediterranean basin, such associations of disperse "ethnic" kin, many of which called themselves "mysteries," would become groups in which a local nonethnic membership might be made kin through initiation (μυεῖν, τελεῖν) and become, consequently, devotees of formerly native deities.

We can understand the development of the Hellenistic mystery cults as the transformation of associations of ethnic kin. Their Hellenistic development seems to have been modeled largely upon various interpretations of the Greek ideal of an initiatory cult exemplified by the ancient and prestigious mysteries of Demeter celebrated at Eleusis.

The fictive kin groups that developed into mystery cults—and of course not all of them did—seemingly went through a development from

---

40. Tod, *Sidelights*, 72. The classic work on Greek associations remains that of Poland, *Geschichte*. On the Latin associations, see Waltzing, *Corporations*. See now the studies in Kloppenborg and Wilson, eds., *Voluntary Associations*.

41. Nock, "Historical Importance," 105.

family cult to open membership analogous to that of the Eleusinian celebrations. As Erwin Rohde observed,

> Originally, this festival ... admitted only the citizens of Eleusis, perhaps only the members of certain noble Eleusinian families ... [Later, a]dmission to it was thrown open to all Greeks—not merely Athenians, but every Greek without distinction of race or country, whether man or woman, was welcomed at Eleusis. ... What a contrast to the exclusive cult-unions into which a man had to be born in order, as citizen of a state, member of a *phratria*, clan, or family, to participate in the advantages they offered![42]

Ernst Samter extended Rohde's argument to conclude that the mystery cults, generally, developed from such exclusivistic family cults.[43]

Conceived as fictive kinship groups, two types of mystery associations may be spoken of, both modeled upon interpretations of the Eleusinian mysteries: the first defined by associations of fictive siblings, and a second defined by claims of fictive descent from the cult deity—both types of relationships established through rites of initiation.

In the first type of mystery groups, the initiates, in the observation of Franz Cumont, "considered themselves brothers no matter where they came from." And, as Cumont recognized, these "communities of initiates" were replacements for the "ancient social groups."[44]

In the second type of mystery group, it was, as W. K. C. Guthrie concluded, "kinship with the gods [that] was the real qualification for a blessed immortality."[45] These communities were related to the later development of gnostic groups with their understanding of relation to deity through descent. This shared understanding of some form of kinship with deity seems to have been mediated by middle Platonism and Neoplatonic elaborations—from the *Axiochus* to Apuleius to Plotinus—on the Platonic ideal of ὁμοίωσις θεῷ, "likeness to God" (Plato, *Theaetetus* 176B).[46] Whereas a fraternal structure of fictive sibling relations established group solidarity, structures of descent ensured the transgenerational continuity of the group.

The sole Hellenistic text that clearly speaks of kinship to deity, again with reference to the Eleusinian Mysteries, is the second or the first

---

42. Rohde, *Psyche*, 221.
43. Samter, *Familienfeste*, 102.
44. Cumont, *Oriental Religions*, 27.
45. Guthrie, *Greeks*, 292.
46. Dillon, *Middle Platonists*, 44, 192; Hershbell, *Axiochus*, 18; Martin, "Self and Power."

century BCE pseudo-Platonic dialogue, *Axiochus*. In this dialogue, Axiochus is named as γεννητὴς τῶν θεῶν, "kin to the gods," as a consequence of his initiation (371D).[47] As a precedent, Guthrie cites the episode in the *Odyssey* where Menelaus is promised an afterlife on the Elysian Plain as a consequence of "his adoption into the family of the gods . . . through his marriage to Helen" (*Odyssey* 4.561f.). Like Samter, Guthrie thereby extends Rohde's argument about the Eleusinian rites as an expanded family cult to suggest that the privileges of Elysium were extended at Eleusis from kin by marriage (the example of Menelaus) to kin by initiation, modeled upon the legal practice of adoption.[48]

To the extent that the mysteries were in some sense fictive kinship groups, adoption, the juridical category of kinship recruitment, provided a natural model for the rites of initiation.[49] Coulanges had already suggested that such ceremonies as marriage, birth, adoption, and installation of a new slave were initiation rites through which new members were received into the cult of the house.[50] Subsequently, Albrecht Dieterich argued that initiation into cults such as Orphism and Mithraism was equivalent to a symbolic adoption by their respective deities,[51] a position that Hugo Hepding later argued for the cult of the Phrygian Mother.[52] And, as has been much discussed, Paul uses the juridical term for adoption, υἱοθεσίαν, to described those redeemed by God's son as themselves adopted sons of God (Gal 4:4-5; Rom 8:14, 23).[53]

The "real and original meaning of all adoption," according to Rohde, was that

> One who has no son to leave behind him will make haste to take a son from another family into his own house, who, together with his property will inherit also the duty of offering a regular

---

47. Hershbell, *Pseudo-Plato, Axiochus*, 68–69 n.76 (cf. 20 on the dating of the *Axiochus*); Rohde, *Psyche*, appendix 11, 601–603. As Burkert (*Mystery Cults*, 7–8 n33) has noted, *initia* is the Latin translation of μυστήρια.

48. Guthrie, *Greeks*, 291–92. But see Walton, "Kinsman."

49. La Piana, "Foreign Groups," 325.

50. Rather than adoption, Samter (*Familienfeste*, 100) suggests marriage as the analogy for mystery initiation. To the extent that the intent of initiation was to establish (fictive) kin relationships, (fictive) *affine* relationships established by marriage would not be to the point. In either case, however, kinship established through rites of initiation are derived from or modeled upon initiation into the family cult. See ibid., 9.

51. Dieterich, *Hymnis*, 38; but see Rohde, *Greeks*, 601–2; Dieterich, *Mithrasliturgie*, 136–37.

52. Hepding, *Attis*, 178 n4.

53. Dieterich, *Mithrasliturgie*, 152–53.

and enduring cult to his adopted father, and his new ancestors, and of caring for the needs of their souls.⁵⁴

An example of this kin reassignment is provided by early Christian developments, themselves a part of the larger Hellenistic religious tradition, and the Christian establishment of novel formation at the expense of their ancestral kin: "leave the dead to bury their own dead," Jesus says to a potential follower, and "follow me" (Matt 8:22; Luke 9:60). The subsequent institutionalization of an "orthodox" Christianity in the third and fourth centuries was accomplished not only by a condensation of religious power from the heterogeneous possibilities of its socially marginal predecessors—a consolidation not without political implications—but also by the adoption of new, distinctively Christian ancestors—i.e., the martyrs. Christians, like many of the Hellenistic societies before them, began to accept funerary responsibilities for their members (see, e.g., Tertullian, *Apology* 39), exemplifying a persistent, transgenerational pattern of relationship among their members. As part of this process, one of these "Christian special dead," as Peter Brown calls them,⁵⁵ became commonly accepted as the divine founder of Christianity. Citing Rohde's observation that adoption was represented as a rebirth from the womb of the new mother,⁵⁶ Guthrie notes that "rebirth was [for this reason] a category applied to initiates in certain mysteries."⁵⁷ Specifically, he cites Apuleius's *Metamorphoses*, in which Lucius's status in the Isis cult is not attained by his birth or inheritance (*Metamorphoses* 11.15) but by a rebirth (*renatus*) (11.16), a transformation explicitly identified with cult initiation (11.23; compare Plutarch, *De Isis et Osiride* 35 on the "rebirth" of Osiris).⁵⁸ What Guthrie does not note is that in the fifth book of the *Metamorphoses*, Venus, who later is identified with Isis in Lucius's famous prayer to the "Blessed Queen of Heaven" (11.2), castigates her son Eros for his disobedience and, despite her advanced age, threatens to "produce another son much better than" him through "adoption" (*adoptatio*) and to make over Eros's inheritance to this adopted son (5.29).⁵⁹

54. Rohde, *Greeks*, 172.

55. Brown, *Saints*.

56. Gernet, *Anthropology*, 196 notes that both "Greeks and Romans remembered the ancient custom of adoption in *cubiculo*, i.e., simulated childbirth by the mother of the new family." See Diodorus Siculus, 4.39.2; Pliny, *Panegyricus* 8.

57. Guthrie, *Greeks*, 292.

58. See on these passages, Griffiths, *Apuleius*, 258.

59. See Merkelbach, *Roman and Mysterium*, 28: "jeder Myste durch die Initiation Adoptivsohn der Isis wurde." Merkelbach also notes with respect to *The Story of Apollonius King of Tyre*, which he states "liegt ursprünglich ein griechischer Isis-roman zugrunde" (60), that "[d]ie Adoption und Weihe [of king Antiochus's daughter] als

In the face of the Hellenistic kingships, the threatened existence of perduring kin groups began to be expressed through a rhetoric of secrecy. The closed nature of such groups was not a sui generis characteristic of their "mystery" or religiosity but simply of their bounded identity: their nonexclusivity with respect to one another is well documented—one might be and often was initiated in any number of these groups.[60] Claims of secrecy were, in other words, a prophylactic against the homogenizing power of the inclusive state that characterized the Hellenistic world since Alexander, a political power increasingly reinforced by the cult of the emperor.[61] The repression of Roman power from Augustus to Theodosius increasingly vitiated the role of the "secret" or bounded societies and occasioned the possibility of social organizations with universalistic claims, societies such as the Isiac, the Mithraic, and the Christian. Only the latter consolidated itself into a viable alternative to the declining fortunes of Roman political power and to the ascendant claims of its religious rivals.

If this analysis rests indeed upon biology, it stands as a general biosocial hypothesis of religious groups to be tested by those with expertise in other cultural domains. By way of conclusion, therefore, I should like briefly to suggest two further examples where the kinship/ kingship model of social organization would seem to be relevant to the religious situation.

A first example is provided by the Chinese consolidation of power of independent warring states into a common cultural entity under the Han dynasty, a period that parallels the Hellenistic (206 BCE—220 CE). This political transformation was paralleled by a social relocation of the ancestors from their traditional habitation in a this-worldly, if transgenerational, realm of local kin relations to a common transcendental place shared by all.[62] In the emergent imperial context, as in the Hellenistic, secret societies provided those whose kinship bonds had been broken an alternative affiliation by which to promote their interests.[63]

For a second example, we might turn to the contemporary religious situation in Latin America. Similar to the Hellenistic and Chinese contexts, new religions have been occasioned by consolidations of power—in this case, largely economic—in and around major cities. The consequent rush to urbanization has undermined local, traditional lifestyles and uprooted much of the population. The religious formations that result are constructed

---

Priesterin [im Tempel der Diana] werden im Ritual identisch sein" (165).

60. Martin, "Secrecy."
61. Martin, "Genealogy," 35.
62. Needham, *Science and Civilization*, 77–82; Martin, "Manichean," 192–93.
63. Weckmann, "Secret Societies," 153.

by numerous newly constituted groups from various native practices but expressed in terms of a colonially imposed Christianity.[64] As in modern comparative studies generally, Latin American "syncretistic" formations have typically been explained as the consequence of similarities perceived between native religious practices and Catholic Christianity.[65] Most recent scholarship, however, has emphasized the "noncorrespondences and contradictions" preserved by these religious formations.[66] As in studies of Hellenistic religions, the employment of the category "syncretism" as explanatory has masked the emergence of novel social formations.

What I have tried to suggest is that the study of religion, if it is to avoid metaphysical musings on the one hand and ethnocentric excess on the other, might best proceed on the basis of inherent, species-specific characteristics. I have selected one of the most fundamental of these traits, our apparently innate social character. As William Roberson Smith already argued, human beings are necessarily social creatures engaged in social formation. Following Smith, anthropologists have agreed that there are but two types of social—and hence religious—formations: kinship and kingship, differing distributions of power subject, however, to an infinite number of social variations and cultural permutations. The study of such social formations, then, must lead to history, the study of the development of these formations over time and in terms of the contingent characteristics of different places. I am suggesting, in other words, a theoretical progression from biology to sociology to history and to the history of the stipulated object of historical investigation—in our case, religion.

References

Boyer, Pascal. *The Naturalness of Religious Ideas: A Cognitive Theory of Religion.* Berkeley: University of California Press, 1994.
Brown, Peter. *The Cult of the Saints: Its Rise and Function in Latin Christianity.* Haskell Lectures on History of Religions, n.s. 2. Chicago: University of Chicago Press, 1981.
Burkert, Walter. *Ancient Mystery Cults.* Cambridge: Harvard University Press, 1987.
———. *Creation of the Sacred: Tracks of Biology in Early Religions.* Cambridge: Harvard University Press, 1996.
Cumont, Franz. *Oriental Religions in Roman Paganism.* With an introductory essay by Grant Showerman. New York: Dover, 1956.
Dawkins, Richard. *The Selfish Gene.* Oxford: Oxford University Press, 1989.

---

64. Masferrer, "Religious Transformations."
65. Hedrick, *Religious Syncretism*, 3.
66. Torres, *Hegemony*, 105.

Dennett, Daniel. "Appraising Grace: What Evolutionary Good Is God?" *Sciences* 37/1 (1997) 39–45.
Dieterich, Albrecht. *De Hymnis Orphicis*. Marpugri Cattorum: Elwerti, 1891.
———. *Eine Mithrasliturgie*. Darmstadt: Wissenschaftliche Buchgeslleschaft, 1966.
Dillon, John. *The Middle Platonists, 80 BC to AD 220*. Ithaca, NY: Cornell University Press, 1977.
Fustel de Coulanges, Numa. *The Ancient City: A Study of the Religion, Laws, and Institutions of Greece and Rome*. Glousester, MA: Smith, 1979.
Gardner, Howard. *The Mind's New Science: A History of Cognitive Revolution*. New York: Basic Books, 1985.
Gernet, Louis. *The Anthropology of Ancient Greece*. Translated by John D. B. Hamilton and Blaise Nagy. Baltimore: John Hopkins University Press, 1981.
Griffiths, John Gwyn. *Apuleius of Madauros: The Isis Book (Metramorphoses, Book XI)*. EPRO 39. Leiden: Brill, 1975.
Guthrie, W. K. C. *The Greeks and Their Gods*. Boston: Beacon, 1950.
Halbwachs, Maurice. *La Topographie légendaire des évangiles en Terre Saint*. Bibliothèque de philosophie contemporaine. Paris: Presse Universitaire de France, 1941.
Hancock, Roger. "Metaphysics, History of." In *The Encyclopedia of Philosophy*, edited by Paul Edwards, 5:289–300. 8 vols. New York: Macmillan, 1967.
Hedrick, Basil C. *Religious Syncretism in Spanish America*. Museum of Anthropology Miscellaneous Series. Greeley: Colorado State College, Museum of Anthropology, 1967.
Hepding, Hugo. *Attis: Seine Mythen und sein Kult*. Religionsgeschichtliche Versuche und Vorarbeiten 1. Geissen: Ricjer, 1903.
Hershbell, J. P. *Pseudo-Plato: Axiochus*. Texts and Translations 21. Graeco-Roman Religion Series 6. Chico, CA: Scholars, 1981.
Hutton, Patrick H. "Collective Memory and Collective Mentalities: The Halbwachs-Aries Connection." *Historical Reflection/Réflexions Historiques* 15 (1988) 311–22.
Jonas, Hans. *The Gnostic Religion: The Message of the Alien God and the Beginnings of Christianity*. Boston: Beacon, 1958.
Kardiner, Abram, and Edward Preble. *They Studied Man*. New York: New American Library, 1961.
Kloppenborg, John S., and Stephen G. Wilson, eds. *Voluntary Associations in the Graeco-Roman World*. London: Routledge, 1996.
La Piana, George. "Foreign Groups in Rome during the First Centuries of the Empire." *Harvard Theological Review* 20/4 (1927) 183–403.
Lawson, E. Thomas, and Robert N. McCauley, eds. *Rethinking Religion: Connecting Cognition and Culture*. Cambridge: Cambridge University Press, 1990.
Lévi-Strauss, Claude. *The Elementary Structures of Kinship*. Translated by James H. Bell et al. Beacon Paperbacks. Boston: Beacon, 1969.
Lorenz, Konrad. *On Aggression*. Translated by Marjorie K. Wilson. Helen and Kurt Wolff Book. New York: Harcourt, 1966.
Mack, Burton L. "Caretakers and Critics: On the Social Role of Scholars Who Study Religion." *Council of Societies for the Study of Religion* 30 (2001) 32–38.
Martin, Luther H. "Akin to the Gods or Simply One to Another? Comparison with Respect to Religions in Antiquity." In *Vergleichen and Verstehen in der Religionswissenschaft: Vorträge des Jahrestagung der DVRG von 4 bis 6 October 1995*, edited by Hans-Joachim Klimkeit, 146–60. Studies in Oriental Religions 41. Wiesbaden: Harrasowitz, 1997.

———. "The Anti-Individualist Ideology of Hellenistic Culture." *Numen* 41/2 (1994) 117–40.

———. "Genealogy and Sociology in the Apocalypse of Adam." In *Gnosticism and the Early Christian World: In Honor of James M. Robinson*, edited by James E. Goehring et al., 25–36. Forum Fascicles 2. Sonoma, CA: Polebridge, 1990 (chapter 22, this volume).

———. *Hellenistic Religions: An Introduction*. New York: Oxford University Press, 1987.

———. "The Manichean Mission: Systemic or Syncretistic?" In *Religion and Modernization in China*, edited by D. Kangsheng et al., 187–96. Cambridge: Roots and Branches, 1995.

———. "Secrecy in Hellenistic Religious Communities." In *Secrecy and Concealment*, edited by Hans G. Kippenberg and Guy G. Stroumsa, 101–21. SHR 65. Leiden: Brill, 1995.

———. "Self and Power in the Thought of Plotinus." In *Czlowiek I Wartosci*, edited by Antoni Kommandera et al., 91–99. Kraków: Wydawnictwo Nankowe WPS, 1997 (chapter 24, this volume).

Masferrer, Kan. "Religious Transformations and Social Change in Latin America." In *Religious Transformations and Socio-Political Change: Eastern Europe and Latin America*, edited by Luther H. Martin, 207–19. Religion and Society 33. Berlin: de Gruyter, 1993.

Merkelbach, Reinhold. *Roman and Mysterium in der Antike*. Munich: Beck, 1962.

Needham, Joseph. *Science and Civilization in China*. Vol. 5, *Chemistry and Chemical Technology. Part 2: Spagyrical Discovery and Invention: Mysteries and Gold and Immortality*. Cambridge: Cambridge University Press, 1974.

Nock, Arthur D. "The Historical Importance of Cult-Associations." *Classical Review* 37 (1924) 105–9.

Poland, Franz. *Geschichte des griechischen Vereinswesens*. Fürslich Jablonowskische gesellschaft der wissenschaften, Leipzig. Preisschriften 38. Leipzig: Teubner, 1909.

Rohde, Erwin. *Psyche: The Cult of the Souls and Belief in Immortality among the Greeks*. Translated by W. B. Hill. London: Kegan Paul, 1925.

Sagan, Elli. *At the Dawn of Tyranny: The Origins of Individualism, Political Oppression and the State*. New York: Knopf, 1985.

Samter, Ernst. *Familienfeste der Griechen und Römer*. Berlin: Reimer, 1901.

Sheridan, Alan. *Michel Foucault: The Will to Truth*. London: Tavistock, 1980.

Smith, Jonathan Z. *To Take Place: Toward Theory in Ritual*. Chicago Studies in the History of Judaism. Chicago: University of Chicago Press, 1987.

Smith, W. Robertson. *Kinship & Marriage in Early Arabia*. London: Black, 1903.

———. *The Religion of the Semites: The Fundamental Institutions*. New York: Schocken, 1972.

Sperber, Dan. *Explaining Culture: A Naturalistic Approach*. Oxford: Blackwell, 1996.

Tod, Marcus N. *Sidelights on Greek History*. Oxford: Blackwell, 1932.

Torres, Carlos Alberto. *The Church, Society, and Hegemony: A Critical Sociology of Religion in Latin America*. Translated by Richard A. Young. Westpoint, CT: Praeger, 1992.

Troeltsch, Ernst. *Writings on Theology and Religion*. Edited by Robert Morgan and Michael Pye. Atlanta: John Knox, 1977.

Walton F. R. "Kinsman of the Gods." *Classical Philology* 48/1 (1953) 24–28.

Waltzing, Jean Pierre. *Étude historique sur les corporations professionelles chez les Romains*. 4 vols. Louvain: Peeters, 1895–1900.

Weckmann, George. "Secret Societies." In *The Encyclopedia of Religion*, edited by Mircea Eliade, 13:151–54. 16 vols. New York: Macmillan, 1987.
Wilson, Edward O. *On Human Nature*. Cambridge: Harvard University Press, 1978.
Wright, Robert. *The Moral Animal: Evolutionary Psychology and Everyday Life*. New York: Pantheon, 1994.

PART 2

Oracular Dreaming

7

Religion and Dream Theory in Late Antiquity

We already have so many truths in our possession that if the day came when someone insisted on deriving a truth even from our dreams, then the day of the Antichrist would truly be at hand.

UMBERTO ECO[1]

I

THE ASSOCIATION OF RELIGIOUS language with the language of dreams has become commonplace in the modern study of religion, largely as the result of Freud's *Die Traumdeutung*, published in 1900. While it may be disputed to what extent Freud's interpretation of dreams heralded the day of the Antichrist, it did restore to the modern world the view that truths are to be derived from our dreams,[2] and anticipated the common view that "Freud, Jung, and others were not so much innovators as restorers, since they were reassigning to dreams and dreamreadings the importance that they had held in antiquity, and which they had lost in more recent centuries."[3] It seemed appropriate, therefore, that Freud began his scientific reflections upon dream interpretation with reference to the only complete work on dreams from antiquity, Artemidorus's *Oneirocritica*.[4]

---

1. Eco, *Name of the Rose*, 438.
2. For example, Carrington, Review of *Interpretation*, 43 concluded: "The 'truths contained in popular superstitions' have again been unearthed and vindicated, and dreams are found to have a value and a meaning after all."
3. White, trans., *Interpretation* (preface).
4. Freud, *Interpretation of Dreams* [*Traumdeutung*], 98 n1.

Artemidorus of Ephesus had written his dream book in the mid-second century CE as an apology for *mantik*, or divination, generally, with dreams as a case in point.⁵ Despite his continuing influence upon popular dream practice through the nineteenth century,⁶ and Freud's reference to him at the beginning of the twentieth, Artemidorus has not been much read in this century, "a well-deserved neglect," in the opinion of some who have judged his effort "laborious," or have dismissed it as "pseudo-scientific."⁷

Although Freud shared with Artemidorus a certainty about the truth of dreams, E. R. Dodds has cautioned that "the Greek and the modern attitude to dreams may reflect not only different ways of interpreting the same type of experience, but also variations in the character of the experience itself."⁸ An examination of Graeco-Roman dream practice as exemplified by Artemidorus suggests that Dodds's admonition might well be heeded by psychology's enthusiastic "rediscovery" of a historical precedent for its universalizing hypothesis concerning dreams.⁹

II

The Greeks, from whom we get our proverb, "seeing is believing,"¹⁰ differentiated two modes of vision: ὕπαρ, or "actual seeing while awake," and ὄναρ, a "seeing in sleep," or "dreaming."¹¹ As Dodds has emphasized, each of these modes of vision had "its own logic and its own limitations; . . . [but there was] no obvious reason for thinking one of them more significant than the other."¹² Dreams belonged in principle, therefore, to the veracity generally accorded vision by the Greeks, who differentiated, further, between three types of dreams: the ἐνύπνιον or "nonpredictive dream"; the ὄνειρος or "predictive dream"; and the χρηματισμός or oracular dream.¹³

---

5. 1, *praef.* (P 1.13–19). References are to White's English translation of Artemidorus; as chapters of the *Oneirocritica* are often several pages long, reference will also be made to page and line of Roger A. Pack's edition of the Greek text [P], *Artemidori Daldiani*.

6. Brelich, "Place of Dreams," 294.

7. Geer, "On Theories of Dreams," 663.

8. Dodds, *Greeks and the Irrational*, 103.

9. See in this regard the excellent study by Price, "Future of Dreams."

10. Aristophanes, *Ecclesiazusae* 1.772. See also Plautus, *Asinaria* 1.202; Cicero, *Epistulae ad Atticum* 16.1.

11. For a third, intermediate category of "waking vision," see Aristides, *Sacred Tales* 2.18.

12. Dodds, *Greeks and the Irrational*, 102.

13. Behr, *Aelius Aristides*, 174; on dream classification in antiquity, see 173–88; cf.

Unlike Freud, for whom no dream was insignificant, the Greeks were interested in ἐνύπνια only to cast into relief the truth of predictive and oracular dreams. Artemidorus, for example, considered ἐνύπνια to be completely ἀσήμαντος, "without significance" (1.2 [P 6.13–14]; 4, *praef.* [P 239.1–2]).

The Greek distinction between nonpredictive and predictive dreams was based upon the Homeric contrast between dreams that "find no fulfillment," and those that "bring true issues to pass" (*Odyssey* 19.560f.). A theoretical grounding for this Homeric association of predictive dream with truth was first suggested by Plato. In the *Republic*, he has Socrates suggest that since dreams generally reflect a bestial element in human nature, moderate living and justness of the mind would permit the soul in sleep to grasp the truth (9.571f.).

This Platonic argument was repeated for the Hellenistic world by Cicero in his well-known treatise *De Divinatione* (1.2.115; see also 1.57.129). Although Cicero inveighed against divination, his antagonist, Quintus, represented the argument for its efficacy. Like Socrates, Quintus was certain that moral purity of the soul was a necessary condition for oneiromancy as for all divinatory practice. "It is the healthy soul and not the sickly body," Quintus concluded, "that has the power of divination" (1.23.82; 1.53.121). Similarly, Artemidorus understood the predictive activity of ὀνείρατα, or "predictive dreams," as "a movement or condition of the soul" (1.2 [P 5.17]), predicated upon its moral purity (4, *praef.* [P 239.14–19]).

Artemidorus divided predictive dreams into either "theorematic" or literal dreams, and "allegorical" dreams. Whereas theorematic dreams "correspond exactly to their own dream-vision" (1.2 [P 4.23]) and come true in the way that it had been presented in sleep (1.2 [P 5.1–9]), most predictive dreams, he concluded, are allegorical in which "the soul is conveying something obscurely by physical means" (1.2 [P 5.10–11]). Artemidorus was primarily concerned with clarifying these allegorical dreams,[14] and it is in regard to these that the central principle of his work is most evident.[15]

Since, according to Artemidorus, allegorical dreams "signify one thing by means of another" (1.2 [P 5.9–10]), he assumed that their significance would be clear to the dreamer once their analogues were made.[16] Such dreams, he wrote, are "nothing other than the juxtaposition of similarities" (2.25 [P 145.11–12]). In addition, he employed a correlate "principle of

---

Kessels, "Ancient Systems."

14. Behr, *Aelius Aristides*, 186; Kessels, "Ancient Systems," 392.

15. For a summary of Artemidorus's classification of allegorical dreams, see Osley, "Notes," 68.

16. Dodds, *Greeks and the Irrational*, 33 n107.

opposites,"[17] or a "law of antithesis,"[18] in which an allegorical dream might signify something contrary to its content. For example:

> A man who brought his son to the Olympic games to compete as a wrestler dreamt that the child was slain in front of the chief judges of the Olympic games and was buried in the stadium. Naturally [!], his son became an Olympic victor. (5.76 [P 320.3–7])

Artemidorus, then, organized correspondences between dream content and dream signification in terms of a system of oneiromantic resemblances that included similarities and contraries.[19] "In judging a dream," he concluded, "one must imitate the diviners. For they know how each individual sign fits into the whole and base their judgments as much on the total sum of the signs as on each individual sign" (3.66 [P 235.3–7]). Dream signs, in other words, had no significance apart from a systemic corpus of oneiromantic knowledge. For Artemidorus, this knowledge consisted of an "objective" system of relationships having to do with the self, the cosmos, and society (1.2 [P 7.1–15]); as opposed to the introspective strategy of modern psychology, predictive dreams were expressions by the self of its participation in an external order of things.

Artemidorus affirms throughout his dream work that his oneiromantic knowledge was based upon experience (1, *praef.* [P 1.12 13]; 2.70 [P 202.11–21]; 4, *praef.* [P 236.13–14]; and 4.20 [P 253.20–21]). He received his experience not only from his own investigations and extensive travel but from his colleagues and the dream books of his precursors (1, *praef.* [P 2.11–14]). As Peter Brown has observed, "the *Dream Book* of Artemidorus … takes us into a Mediterranean world where the common meanings that can be attached to dream images are well rooted and exceedingly matter of fact."[20] And as Dodds has concluded, such "experiences reflect a pattern of belief which is accepted not only by the dreamer but usually by everyone in the environment; their form is determined by the belief, and in turn confirms it; hence they become increasingly stylized."[21]

---

17. Osley, "Notes," 69.

18. Brelich, "Place of Dreams," 295–97.

19. On the role of similarity and antipathy in Greek thought generally, see Lloyd, *Polarity and Analogy.*

20. Brown, *Late Antiquity*, 40–45; see also Behr, *Aelius Aristides*, appendix D (196–204) for a comparison of conventional dream symbols in Artemidorus and Aristides; "Commentaries," in White, trans., *Interpretation.*

21. Dodds, *Greeks and the Irrational*, 112.

The ancient system of dream significations, in other words, was constituted by historically and culturally specific relationships between oneiromantic signs and their conventional meanings—more like the relationships accorded signifier and signified by modern linguistic theory, than the universal claims made by Freudian theory. And ancient dream accounts, consequently, give no support to modern psychological theory—this is a modern project operating out of a different epistemological possibility—but to the circle of late antique knowledge,[22] an "encyclopedia" constructed upon the Greek taxonomy of seeing, strategies of purification, and the systemic play of resemblances.

Unlike his contemporary, Aelius Aristides, who was concerned solely with "religious dreams,"[23] Artemidorus was not concerned with specifying dream content as "religious." Rather, Artemidorus was as little interested in χρηματισμοί, "oracular dreams," as were the Greeks generally in nonpredictive dreams, but for the opposite reason: as nonpredictive dreams are completely nonsignificative, oracular dreams, according to Artemidorus, have a divine significance that is "immediately evident" (1.2 [P 6.13–14]; 4, *praef.* [P 239.1–2]); these dreams "come true just as they are seen" (4.1 [P 241.2–3]). Consequently, he omits any discussion of this type of dream from his considerations.[24] Rather, Artemidorus was a "professional" dream specialist concerned with "ordinary" dreams and with distinguishing between them as either predictive or nonpredictive. Whereas predictive dreams *may* have a divine content, there is, for Artemidorus, no necessary relationship between them, the gods, or religious practice, as many interpreters have assumed.[25]

III

In his inquiry into the mental world of those who remained unenlightened during the Enlightenment, the historian Robert Darnton turns to a consideration of folklore, a medium of expression often compared to that of dream and myth.[26] He shows how psychoanalysts, and those influenced by their work, have read these tales "as if they had no history . . . [as if they were]

---

22. Martin, "*Encyclopedia Hellenistica.*"

23. On the dream theory of Aelius Aristides, see Martin, "Aelius Aristides."

24. Despite Artemidorus's indication to the contrary, Kessels ("Ancient Systems," 396) nevertheless argues that oracular dreams "certainly formed part of the general cultural pattern of those times," and concludes, consequently, that they did occur in Artemidorus's practice and "were in need of interpretation."

25. E.g., Geer, "On Theories of Dreams," 663–70; Kee, *Miracle*, 103.

26. Darnton, *Great Cat Massacre*, 9–72.

flattened out, like patients on a couch, in a timeless contemporaneity."[27] Darnton gives the example of Erich Fromm's interpretation of "Little Red Riding Hood" as an adolescent's confrontation with adult sexuality. In Fromm's reading, the red riding hood is a symbol of menstruation; the bottle carried by the little girl is a symbol of her virginity, which her mother admonishes her to protect. The wolf is the ravishing male. The two stones that are placed in the wolf's belly after the hunter saves the girl and her grandmother represent sterility, the punishment for breaking a sexual taboo.[28] But, as Darnton's textual history demonstrates, none of the points upon which the psychoanalytic reading depends appear in the seventeenth- and eighteenth-century versions of the text, but only in nineteenth-century retellings. Darnton concludes that the psychoanalyst, "with an uncanny sensitivity to detail that did not occur in the original folktale ... takes us into a mental universe that never existed, at least not before the advent of psychoanalysis."[29]

In other words, psychological theory, from which a Fromm has interpreted the text, has contributed to the very telling of the tale; the history of the text is correlate to the history of theory. The common historical constitution of text and theoretical context establishes a mutual relationship between the two that gives an appearance of universal theoretical validity supported by historically prior data. This circular methodological principle may be illustrated by the title attributed to Artemidorus's dream book.

The traditional title of Artemidorus's work, the *Oneirocritica*, was borrowed from his introduction (1, *praef.* [P 2.3–4; 11–13] and elsewhere. See P Index, 343f.). *Oneirocritica*, however, does not mean "interpretation of dreams." Rather, the word is derived from κρίνω ("to distinguish," or "to separate") and signifies an arranging or ordering of or by dreams. A secondary meaning of κρίνω is "to distinguish between good and bad," which, according to Artemidorus, is precisely the function of predictive dreams (1.2 [P 5.17–18]).[30] *Oneirocritica* signifies, thus, an ordering or system of classification whereby those dreams that are true, that is, that are predictive, may be distinguished from those that are not. Consequently, Artemidorus's book may better be titled *A Taxonomy of Dreams*. As Artemidorus himself concluded, "in [the first three books of the *Oneirocritica*] I brought together all the dreams that one can have and which actually come true in an order

---

27. Ibid., 13.

28. Fromm, *Forgotten Language*, 235–41; Darnton, *Great Cat Massacre*, 10–11.

29. Darnton, *Great Cat Massacre*, 11.

30. Liddell and Scott, *Lexicon* attests a meaning of κριτικά as "interpretation" only with reference to Artemidorus.

[τάξις] and sequence that corresponded to human life" (4, *praef.* [P 236. 9-10]).

Oneirocritica only became translated into various European languages as "the interpretation of dreams" since the sixteenth century.[31] This modern understanding of Artemidorus's dream work as an ὀνειροερμηνεία derived from the Renaissance impulse to translate, or to interpret (ἑρμηνεύειν), the texts of antiquity. The premise for this modern "science" of hermeneutics is the hiddenness of truth, whether concealed by historical distance, by the limits of human knowing, or, since Freud, by the embodiment of psyche.

Artemidorus, however, was not concerned with uncovering some truth assumed to be hidden in dreams. On the contrary, he warned aspiring ὀνειροκρίτες that "those who attribute . . . too much hidden meaning to dreams should be treated with contempt since they have no insight into the structure of a dream" (4.63 [P 286.13–15]). The difference between Artemidorus's taxonomy of dreams and Freud's interpretation of dreams is that the late antique system of oneiromantic knowledge was understood as constructed upon culturally constituted signs of the external world to be discerned, whereas modern psychoanalytic theory is predicated upon the presumption of a universal but hidden subjective reality to be uncovered.

Too often, it seems, our theorizing about dreams, about religion, and about their relationship has fallen prey to the sort of ironic observation made by William of Baskerville, the fourteenth-century hero of Umberto Eco's novel, *The Name of the Rose*. In response to the disclosure of a troublesome dream by his assistant, Adso, William responds:

> The more I think of your dream, the more revealing it seems to me. Perhaps not to you, but to me. Forgive me if I use your dreams in order to work out my hypothesis.[32]

References

Behr, C. A. *Aelius Aristides and "The Sacred Tales."* Amsterdam: Hakkert, 1968.
Brelich, Angelo. "The Place of Dreams in the Religious World Concept of the Greeks." In *The Dream and Human Societies*, edited by G. E. von Grunebaum and Roger Caillois, 293–403. Berkeley: University of California Press, 1966.
Brown, Peter. *The Making of Late Antiquity*. Cambridge: Harvard University Press, 1978.
Carrington, Hereward. Review of *The Interpretation of Dreams*, translated by Abraham A. Brill. *The New York Times Book Review* 20 (March 1983) 43.

---

31. Pack, *Artemidori Daldiani*, xviii.
32. Eco, *Name*, 438.

Darnton, Robert. *The Great Cat Massacre and Other Episodes in French Cultural History.* New York: Basic Books, 1984.

Dodds, E. R. *The Greeks and the Irrational.* Sather Classical Lectures 25. Berkeley: University of California Press, 1951.

Eco, Umberto. *The Name of the Rose.* Translated by William Weaver. San Diego: Harcourt Brace Jovanovich, 1983.

Freud, Sigmund. *The Interpretation of Dreams* [*Die Traumdeutung*]. In *The Standard Edition of the Complete Psychological Works of Sigmund Freud*, edited by James Strachey, vol. 4. London: Hogarth, 1953.

Fromm, Erich. *The Forgotten Language: An Introduction to the Understanding of Dreams, Fairy Tales and Myths.* New York: Rinehart, 1951.

Geer, Russel M. "On the Theories of Dream Interpretation in Artemidorus." *Classical Journal* 22/9 (1927) 663–70.

Kee, Howard Clark. *Miracle in the Early Christian World: A Study in Sociohistorical Method.* New Haven: Yale University Press, 1983.

Kessels, A. H. M. "Ancient Systems of Dream Classification." *Mnemosyne* 22/4 (1969) 389–424.

Liddell, Henry G., and Robert S. Scott. *A Greek–English Lexicon.* 9th ed. Oxford: Oxford University Press, 1940.

Lloyd, G. E. R. *Polarity and Analogy: Two Types of Argumentation in Early Greek Thought.* Cambridge: Cambridge University Press, 1971.

Martin, Luther H. "Aelius Aristides and the Technology of Oracular Dreams." *Historical Reflections/Réflexions Historiques* 14 (1987) 65–72.

———. "The *Encyclopedia Hellenistica* and Christian Origins." *Biblical Theology Bulletin* 20/3 (1990) 123–127 (chapter 20, this volume).

Osley, Arthur S. "Notes on Artemidorus' *Oneirocritica.*" *Classical Journal* 59 (1963) 65–70.

Pack, Roger A. *Artemidori Daldiani: Onirocriticon Libri V.* Bibliotheca Scriptorum Graecorum et Romanorum Teubneriana. Leipzig: Teubner, 1963.

Price, S. R. F. "The Future of Dreams: From Freud to Artemidorus." *Past & Present* 113 (1986) 3–37.

White, Robert J., trans. *The Interpretation of Dreams: Oneirocritica by Artemidorus.* Noyes Classical Studies. Park Ridge, NJ: Noyes, 1975.

8

Prayer in Graeco-Roman Religions

PRAYER IS A PROMINENT feature of Graeco-Roman religious life as it is of any religious system in which superhuman power is imagined anthropomorphically in terms of agency. Most fundamentally, prayer is a request made of such divine agents. The significance of the prayer will vary, of course, according to the religious context and to the deity or deities addressed in this context, to the occasion of its utterance, and to the specific nature of the request and its formal character.

Form and Content of Prayer

The structure of Graeco-Roman prayers (Gk: εὐχαί; Lt: *vota, devotiones*) is typically tripartite: an invocation of deity; a narrative argument justifying the petition of the suppliant; and, finally, the request itself. This formal structure may be illustrated already from the early Greek tradition in the Homeric prayer of Achilles to Zeus:

[invocation]

High Zeus, lord of Dodona, Pelasgian, living afar off, brooding over wintry Dodona, your prophets about you living, the Selloi who sleep on the ground with feet unwashed. Hear me,

[justification]

As one time before when I prayed to you, you listened and did me honour, and smote strongly the host of the Achaians, so one more time bring to pass the wish that I pray for.

[request]

For see, I myself am staying where the ships are assembled, but I send out my companion and many Myrmidons with him to fight. Let glory, Zeus of the wide brows, go forth with him to fight. Let glory, Zeus of the wide brows, go forth with him. Make brave the heart inside his breast, so that even Hektor will find out whether our henchman knows how to fight his battles by himself, or whether his hands range invincible only those times when I myself go into the grind of the war god. But when he has beaten back from the ships their clamorous onset, then let him come back to me and the running ships, unwounded, with all his armour and with the companions who fight close beside him. (*Iliad* 16.233–248)

The invocation deals with a problem characteristic of polytheistic systems that is absent from monotheisms, namely, the choice of the deity to be addressed. In a monotheistic system, of course, the only available deity cannot be misidentified by confusing it with another; however, asking Mars for health or Isis for victory in war could be disastrous for a well-meaning but misinformed supplicant. Any misdirected request will result in failed communication. Hence the need for precision in naming the proper god is at least as deep a need as that expressed through the content of the prayers.

The invocation of Graeco-Roman prayers, consequently, may be quite elaborate. In addition to the identification of the deity by name, it may include alternative names for the deity, descriptive predicates of the deity, the sphere of activity, residence and cult-places associated with the deity, and references to mythic accomplishments; and even such inclusive precautions as "or whatever other name it is lawful to name you" (e.g., Aeschylus, *Agamemnon* 160; Apuleius, *Metamorphoses* 11.2; Macrobius, *Saturnalia* 3.9.10–11). This θεοκρασία, or fluidity of divine nomination, is often referred to as *syncretism* by those who privilege theological content over cultic practice in the religious systems of Graeco-Roman antiquity.

The narrative section might give justification for why this particular deity is considered the appropriate one to be called upon, and why just this deity should now respond. It may include the relationship of the suppliant to the deity, such as previous occasions on which the deity has given aid. In this section, praise and honor were usually offered to the deities rather than the expressions of gratitude more characteristic of Jewish and Christian prayer.

The final section will consist of some favor sought from the god. The specific content of the pagan prayers varies but several themes recur, such as the needs and fears of those praying together with their hopes for support and assistance. Ramsey McMullen points out that pagans generally prayed for health and beauty, for relief and protection, for safety and rescue, and for the needs of the household in addition, of course, for mastery of one's enemies.

In a system in which agency is hierarchically related, gods rank higher than humans, with the result that humans ask and gods grant. Consequently, prayer as a mode of communication in a polytheistic system not only involves identifying the proper recipient of a message, but also necessitates negotiation between the participants in the system. This sense of bargaining, clearly exemplified in the prayers of Cato, is expressed in the Roman distinction between *votum*, "vow" or promise by the suppliant to recognize the deity in an appropriate manner upon compliance with the suppliant's request, and *devotio*, a recompense by the suppliant in advance of the deity's response.

Behaviors and Attitudes Associated with Prayer

Proper behavior and attitude are required of those who pray. Greeks and Romans stood during prayer, facing and with arms outstretched towards the domain associated with the deity, i.e., towards the sky, the sea, or the underworld. Consequently, one of the Christian prayer postures, that of kneeling or prostration, was viewed as curiously "un-Greek" or "un-Roman."

And while there were exceptions, Greek and Roman prayers were almost always spoken aloud (as were Jewish prayers; see 1 Sam 1:12) and in a public context, especially that of sacrifice. By contrast, private or personal prayer, such as that recommended by some Christians (e.g., Matt 6:6), tended to be viewed by Greek and Romans as magic, especially when they were offered at night (e.g., Mark 1:35; Luke 6:12; 22:41, 55). Apuleius, for example, writes of magic as a "mysterious," "loathly and horrible" art that requires "night-watches and concealing darkness, solitude absolute and murmured incantations" (*Apologia* 47). But this denunciation of magic within the Latin tradition should not be seen as supporting the scholarly habit of distinguishing religion, in which worshipers revere and submit to their deity, from magic, in which performers seek to coerce their deity. Submission and coercion are less distinctions between religion and magic, and more differing strategies employed by suppliants in their conduct of communication in an asymmetrical religious framework. For example, the magical appeal to Selene contains both submission and coercion. The act of offering sacrifice does not so much "compel" Selene in the strict sense as display a certain submissiveness that makes the petitioner's dismissal difficult.[1]

1. Faraone, "Hymn to Selene."

While nondiscursive practices of religious ritual were prescribed and had to be performed absolutely correctly, what was actually spoken in the accompanying prayers was less fixed. Nevertheless, the words of prayer were carefully considered. The wrong word will be βλασφημία, an ill use of words, which brings harm. But on the other hand, the employment of good words, εὐφημία, is a proclamation of auspicious silence during religious rites. In Plato's *Timaeus*, we find the most general statement about addressing the gods: it is right to seek the aid of the gods and goddesses at the beginning of any undertaking in the hope that the words will be good for both suppliant and deity (27C).

The Place of Prayer

Important as is the form and practice of pagan prayer for our study, equally significant is their place in the religious life of the Graeco-Roman world. Most of the prayers display a combination of reserve and dignity, recognizing the qualities of both the god and the one praying, mentioning both the ability of the god and the need of the petitioner. As the two parties, humans and gods, participate in the exchange of information, the suppliants want good ends for their entire lives and the gods receive their wishes. Both humans and their superhuman agents must recognize their proper domains as well as the needs and abilities under negotiation; both parties must observe the proprieties befitting them. Thus, the pagan prayers require that humans know themselves as much as they know the gods. They operate within a framework of etiquette, in which piety and knowledge of these right relationships (Gk: εὐσέβεια; Lt: *pietas*), will enable the participants to play their proper roles. In the world of Graeco-Roman religions, then, imagination will be a primary requirement in composing and directing prayers. Humans must imagine many deities who can play multiple roles and grant diverse requests; in the face of multiple possible outcomes, prayer is simultaneously a move toward the self-knowledge involved in formulating the suppliant's situation and an act of imagining new and desirable alternatives.

References

Apuleius. *The Apologia and Florida of Apuleius of Madaura*. Translated by Harold E. Butler. Westport, CT: Greenwood, 1970.
Faraone, Christopher A. "Hymn to Selene-Hecate-Artemis from a Greek Magical Handbook (*PGM* IV 2714–83)." In *Prayer from Alexander to Constantine: A Critical Anthology*, edited by Mark Kiley, 195–99. London: Routledge, 1997.

Homer. *The Iliad of Homer*. Translated by Richmond Lattimore. Chicago: University of Chicago Press, 1951.
McMullen, Ramsay. *Paganism in the Roman Empire*. New Haven: Yale University Press, 1981.

9

Petitionary Prayer in the Graeco-Roman World: Comparison, Consequences, Cognition, and a Few Conclusions

> Prayer is a prominent feature of Greco-Roman religious life as it is of any religious system in which superhuman power is imagined anthropomorphically in terms of agency. More fundamentally, prayer is a request made of such divine agents.
>
> ALDERINK AND MARTIN[1]

> Prayer involves communication between a material being—a person—and an immaterial being—God.
>
> WOOLLEY AND PHELPS[2]

> Talking with God is called prayer;
> God talking with us is called schizophrenia.
>
> LILY TOMLIN[3]

Comparison

THE STUDY OF PRAYER in Graeco-Roman antiquity is not only a historical study but it is also a comparative study of religion, not only because of a

1. Alderink and Marting, "Prayer," 123.
2. Woolley and Phelps, "Development," 141.
3. Tomlin, "Anniversary."

comparison between past and present but also because of that between ancient cultures. The comparative study of religion raises questions, however, of generalizations, i.e., the construction of categories into which it is to be expected that more shared than nonshared data will be admitted. But how is the increased amount of nonshared data amassed through comparative study to be assessed? Comparisons of prayer within the shared context of the Graeco-Roman period have dealt with this issue by emphasizing similarities over differences and by explaining these similarities on the basis of a shared cultural context. More often than not, however, these explanations have exhibited a Christian bias, whereby similarities of Christian to Jewish prayer are explained as the consequence of a historically antecedent tradition, and those between Christian and pagan prayer are dismissed as superficial syncretisms rather than as examples of "substantial equivalence."[4] In fact, when the comparative net is cast cross-culturally to include, for example, requests made of ancestors by Confucians or by the Ashanti of West Africa,[5] prayers of ancient Vedic priests or those of the Vestal Virgins of Roman antiquity, the repetitive rotations of Buddhist prayer wheels and the aimless flutterings of Tibetan prayer flags,[6] the only substantial equivalence to be found among the distributed varieties of prayer seems to be that human beings everywhere pray.[7]

Consequences

Prayer, like any aspect of religion, "can be understood on the basis of exchange relations between human and supernatural beings."[8] But given the cost in terms of times and resources, what are the benefits of petitionary prayer? Does, in other words, petitionary prayer work?

One contemporary interpreter of religion begins with the premise that "religion . . . makes truth-claims; in fact, it makes no other kind; it is totally objectivist in its outlook; it repudiates the attachment of any subjectivity to its central claims."[9] Applied to prayer, this means that prayer is either efficacious or not; and if not, why then do people continue to pray?

Petitionary prayer can be viewed generally as a human request of some superhuman agent who receives and understands that request and from

4. Kiley, *Prayer*, 3 n9.
5. Goody, "Social Intelligence," 209–10.
6. Heiler, *Prayer*; van der Leeuw, *Essence*, ¶62.
7. For a recent typology of prayer, see Ladd and Spilka, "Inward."
8. Stark, "Micro Foundations," 264.
9. Faber, *Magic of Prayer*, 138, 5–6.

which a response is expected;[10] e.g., Mark 11:24: "Ask and you shall receive." Whereas the request is usually linguistic,[11] the anticipated response is not expected to be verbal (à la the insight of Lily Tomlin) but is to be an event—a hierophanous presence or a miraculous intervention—that is consequential upon an intentional act of agent to whom the request has been directed. That the specific response requested of the god was expected is instantiated by Aelius Aristides's thirteen-year pursuit of his health as a consequence of his continuing entreaties to Aesclepius (Aristides, *Sacred Tales*).

The absence of expected responses to prayer is often explained by having prayed to an incorrect or inappropriate deity (Horace, *Epistulae* 1.16.53-62)—or, in the case of monotheistic traditions, to a "false" deity (Plato, *Cratylus* 400C). This question of exactly which deity one should pray to had been debated in Graeco-Roman culture since at least the fifth century BCE. According to an oracle from Dodona, for example, the Corcyreans asked Zeus Naios and his spouse Dione "to which of the gods or heroes they must sacrifice and pray in order to succeed in obtaining concord."[12] And the passage from Xenophon's *Anabasis* in which the historian asks Apollo to which gods he should sacrifice is well known (3.1.5). The practical futility of prayer could, however, be generalized. As one anonymous complainant from the ancient world fumed, "just as the gods paid no heed (ἐφείσαντο) to me, I shall pay no heed (φείσομαι) to them."[13]

The question of the efficacy of prayer was strikingly raised for modernity in 1872 in an anonymously published article, "The 'Prayer for the Sick': Hints towards a Serious Attempt to Estimate its Value," generally attributed to the London surgeon Sir Henry Thompson.[14] The author of this article proposed a scientific study of the matter employing control groups having a statistically significant population.[15] The most well-known response to what became known as "the prayer-gauge debate"[16] was by Sir Francis Galton, a cousin of Charles Darwin and one of the founders of modern statistics.[17]

Premised on the regular and frequent offerings of prayer for the health of their sovereigns, Galton compared the mean age attained by members

---

10. Alderink and Martin, "Prayer," 123; Faber, *Magic of Prayer*, 69–70.

11. Hinde, *Why Gods Persist*, 133; Faber, *Magic of Prayer*, 60.

12. Parke, *Oracles of Zeus*, 260 n3, cited by Versnel, "Religious Mentality," 5.

13. Mitteis and Wilcken, *Grundzüge und Christomathie*, 1.2.149 n120 [third-century CE], translated by Versnel, "Religious Mentality," 37.

14. Means, *Prayer-Gauge Debate*, 7.

15. Thompson, "Prayer," 16–17.

16. Means, *Prayer-Gauge Debate*.

17. See David, "Galton."

of the British royal house with that of other well-to-do classes: e.g., clergy, lawyers, doctors, bankers, military officers, professors, and the like. He discovered, however, that the "sovereigns are literally the shortest lived of all who have the advantage of affluence."[18] He further noted such statistical evidence as that for missionaries who, Galton argued, "one after another, dies shortly after his arrival" in the field, despite the sacred goals of their careers and the wealth of prayer with which they are showered;[19] and he observed that insurance companies make absolutely no difference between the risks encountered by missionary vessels and those engaged in ordinary trade.[20] An explanation for these statistical anomalies concerning the efficacy of prayer had been offered several years earlier by John Tyndall in the challenge to which Galton was replying. No prayer, he reasoned, "could call one shower from heaven or deflect towards us a single beam of the sun" without a "disturbance of natural law, quite as serious as the stoppage of an eclipse."[21] Even if "the known physical and biological laws of the universe" *could* be suspended "with a prayer (or, for those who are less institutionalized, by crossing your fingers)," the "trick," Scott Atran writes, "is in knowing how and when to suspend factual belief without countermanding the facts and compromising survival." But why, he concludes, task such a risk at all?[22]

Contemporary research on the efficaciousness of prayer has confirmed the sovereignty of natural law. Such studies, which have continued the focus on healing, have—as in the pioneering statistical studies of healing in the mid-nineteenth century—been either negative or inconclusive, or have identified causal variables independent of prayer in observed cases of healing.[23] The probability of actually obtaining the desired outcome of prayer ranges, in other words, "between zero and chance."[24]

In the absence of statistical or scientific evidence for the efficacy of prayer, claims to positive results continue (as in the Asclepian tradition of antiquity) to rest on testimonials, i.e., on anecdotal evidence—a confusion of correlations with causes. This is, however, much like arguing against the enormous odds of winning the lottery that you must enter to win. It is true that someone generally, but not always, wins the lottery in the same way

18. Galton, "Statistical Inquiries," 91.
19. Ibid., 92–93.
20. Ibid., 99–101.
21. Tyndall, "Prayer," 36.
22. Atran, *Gods*, 5.
23. Wulff, *Psychology of Religion*, 167–72; Krymkowski and Martin, "Religion as Independent Variable."
24. Atran, *In Gods*, 5.

that it is true that events which have been the object of prayer sometimes, but not always, transpire. But recommendations to act on the basis of such anecdotal evidence do not seem to be, in either case, the result of generalizable evidence. As the cognitive psychologist Daniel Kahneman has shown, people are not very good at intuitively assessing probability, a critique of some aspects of rational choice theory for which Kahneman was awarded the Nobel Prize in economics (in 2002). When people are asked, for example, to value two wagers, one with a high probability of winning but having a moderate stake and one with a low probability of winning but having a larger stake, they consistently value the option with the lower probability of winning over that with higher, even though they may claim a preference for the former.[25] Such overweighting of low probability outcomes contributes, Kahneman argues, to the attractiveness of such pursuits as gambling and, we might add, of prayer.[26] As Janson Slone has noted, gamblers often seek to influence the outcome of their actions by talking to their games they play as though they had psychological agency.[27] Slone concludes that "when humans encounter circumstances in which they appear to have no control ... they will still tend to act as if they do," or, "they will try to figure out ways to gain control."[28] Such cognitive psychological insights into how people actually behave might offer further insights into the universal and curiously tenacious perception of the efficaciousness of prayer even though any generalizable basis for that efficaciousness remains unestablished.[29]

Cognition

The fundamental question explored by cognitive scientists is how the brain functions to produce the mental representations that it does on the basis of perceptual and conceptual input. The fundamental premise of the cognitive science of religion is that religious cognition is generated from such ordinary processes of human cognition.[30]

---

25. Slovic and Lichtenstein, "Performance Reversals."

26. Kahneman and Tversky, "Prospect Theory"; see also Kahneman et al., *Judgement*; Hogarth and Reder, eds., *Rational Choice*; Kahneman and Tversky, *Choices*; Gilovich, Griffin, and Kahneman, *Heuristics and Biases*.

27. Slone, "Luck Beliefs."

28. Ibid.

29. Goody, "Introduction," 28.

30. See Lawson and McCauley, *Rethinking*; McCauley and Lawson, *Bringing Ritual*; Boyer, *Religion Explained*; Barrett, "Exploring the Natural Foundations."

Developmental psychologists, for example, supporting the insights of R. R. Marett a century ago, have argued that the perennial question of the relationship between magical incantation and religious prayer, familiar from the Hellenistic as from other ages,[31] involves the same natural cognitive dynamic,[32] specifically that employed by children in their longings and desires.[33] Woolley and Phelps, for example, have argued, specifically with reference to wishing and praying, that such actions "involve internal mental processes aimed at bringing about external, often physical, changes in the absence of intervening physical action on the part of the person" performing them.[34] Building upon natural representations of causal relations, this inference of causality at a distance[35] is, according to Rosengren and Hickling, an innate exploitation of a person's ordinary causal-explanatory system that is documented already during the first year of life, which by four to five years of age is capable of specifying the intentional actions of agents.[36] It is, such researchers conclude, only the semantic inflections of culture that contrast wish with reality, magic with science, and that explain prayer through interpretations of faith.[37] Since, as Kahneman and Tversky discovered, "it is not natural to group events by their judged probability," it is not possible for an individual to discover the percentage of predictions

---

31. Alderink and Martin, "Prayer," 125; see, e.g., Leeuw, *Essence*, ¶62; Douglas, *Purity*, 28.

32. Marett, "Prayer."

33. Faber, *Magic of Prayer*, 18 offers a very interesting psychoanalytic explanation for this dynamic. Although, as one historian (Gaddis, *Landscape*, 57, 59) has recently observed: "Freudian psychology ["which seeks to account for the actions of individuals by invoking a set of unconscious impulses and inhibitions inherited—by everyone—from childhood"] offers a less than adequate explanation of human behavior, especially when it's projected across cultures and through time, or when it's compared with physiological explanations." In the critique of Ernest Gellner (*Psychoanalytic Movement*, 156–57; italics original), "The idea that certain types of infancy experiences lead to certain types of adult personality" is untestable. Such an idea "is testable if either of the two domains (early experiences or adult personalities) is subdivided, with some reasonable degree of precision and above all of *independence*, into sub-categories. Then, *and only then*, can one say that there is some kind of functional relation, as specified in the theory, linking members of the one domain to those of the other. In fact, of course, the sub-categorization in either domain is (1) extremely loose and wooly, and (2) entirely under the control of that very theory which is to be tested."

34. Woolley and Phelps, "Development," 158.

35. Rosengren and Hickling, "Metamorphosis and Magic," 79; Woolley, "Development," 118.

36. Rosengren and Hickling, "Metamorphosis and Magic," 78, 80.

37. Ibid., 80; Woolley and Phelps, "Development," 159.

to which he has assigned probability have actually come about.[38] Assessing the efficacy of prayer may shift, in other words, "from an early reliance on empirical observation (e.g., noticing how many times one actually got what one wished for) to a more faith-based method, in which 'failed' attempts [... can be] re-interpreted or explained away" by adjusting an initial expectation to the final answer.[39] Further, cognitivists argue, praying activates the mental system that handles intuitions about ordinary verbal communication with another agent who, like any agent with whom one communicates, is expected to hear and to answer.[40] Again, these ordinary intuitions are violated only by a single, cultural stipulation that the agent with whom one communicates in prayer is superhuman. Whereas any mode of action is, in theological principle, available to such divine agents, the actions of particular divine actors are nevertheless constrained by intuitions about human agents generally. As H. S. Versnel has concluded of Western antiquity, "the believer ... approached his god, in word and deed, as though he was a great and powerful human being."[41]

A minimal violation of such ordinary intuitive categories has been shown to be mnemonically salient,[42] and prayer as a technique for transmitting the particular cultural representations of superhuman agency may be a sufficient explanation for its retention in the absence of demonstrable results, especially in the case of formulaic prayers codified by a given religious tradition.[43]

Conclusion

The discriminatory effects of cultural inflection upon the universalistic tendencies offered by the growing field of the cognitive science of religion for why we (human beings) do what we do brings us back to prayer in the context of a particular historical tradition or cultural domain. From a cognitive perspective, "the differences among animistic, pantheistic, and monotheistic religions can be ascribed to differences" in the cultural postulation of superhuman agency. "These content differences concern the relative

38. Tversky and Kahneman, "Judgement," 19.

39. Woolley and Phelps, "Development," 159; Tversky and Kahneman, "Judgement," 14.

40. Marett, "Prayer," 217; Goody, "Social Intelligence"; Boyer, *Religion Explained*, 313.

41. Versnel, "Religious Mentality," 38.

42. Boyer, *Religion Explained*.

43. Whitehouse, *Arguments and Icons*; Faber, *Magic of Prayer*, 81.

psychological 'distance' between representations of society and representation of nature."[44] The cognitive psychologist Justin Barrett, for example, has argued that the cultural "characteristics attributed to the [... divine agent] being petitioned ... provide believers with intuitions about what to ask the god for, even in the absence of explicit instruction."[45] When a divine agent is imagined to be at a significant distance, Barrett predicts that petitionary prayer, in the absence of a pertinent theology to the contrary, will tend to ignore the superhuman powers attributed to that agent—omnipotence for example—and will consist instead of a disproportionate number of requests for that agent to act psychologically as opposed to through physical or biological mechanisms.[46] This is in accordance with the findings of a growing body of cognitive and developmental research (about folk psychology) that demonstrates that people know from infancy that what intentional agents do best from a distance is to influence psychological states: beliefs, opinions, desires, emotions, etc.[47] If, on the other hand, a divine agent is imagined in close proximity to the petitioner, then that agent is available to act also through causal mechanisms. This is in accordance with research showing that infants also know that physical contact (folk mechanics; folk biology) is required in order to move or alter a physical object.[48]

Prayer from the Graeco-Roman period seems to confirm Barrett's prediction. Because of the general "presence of the gods" in the Graeco-Roman world,[49] we might expect that Greek and Roman popular petitions included requests for physical and biological as well as psychological remedies—and they did: solutions to problems of human relationships such as theft, kidnapping, and family problems; petitions for financial well-being as well as for health and well-being for self, family, and the emperor as well as for one's crops and one's horse or donkey; for pregnancy or for relief from pregnancy; from all sorts of dangers, from storms at sea to mad dogs,[50] not to mention

44. Atran, *In Gods*, 9.
45. Barrett, "Dumb Gods," 94.
46. Barrett, "Petitionary Prayer,"; Barrett, "Dumb Gods."
47. Barrett, "Dumb Gods," 97.
48. Barrett, "Petitionary Prayer," 260; Barrett, "Dumb Gods," 97; see also Ladd and Spilka, "Inward," 482. There remains considerable debate about the exact ontological boundaries of the folk psychological domain and those of folk mechanics and folk biology. Barrett's suggestion notwithstanding, it is debated exactly "how people decide ... when it is appropriate to invoke psychological versus mechanical principles ..., or psychological versus biological principles ... to explain or predict regularities in the world" (Atran, *In Gods*, 58).
49. Hopkins, *World Full of Gods*.
50. Versnel, "Religious Mentality," 8–9.

prayers of revenge whereby misfortune was removed from one's own domain to that of one's enemy.[51] Greek and Roman prayers for the more noble virtues of friendship, concord, happiness, and peace are evinced only in literary and philosophical texts.[52] In the Hellenistic shifts towards utopian, cosmological deities—e.g., the reimagining of Isis, Queen of the Nile, i.e., consort of Osiris (Plutarch, *De Iside et Osiride* 32) as Isis, Universal Queen of Heaven (Apuleius, *Metamorphoses* 11.2)—we can increasingly document, however, a trend towards psychological petition: for example, the prayer of Apuleius's Lucius for "peace and rest" in the face of his "misfortune" (11.2), or those of the *Corpus Hermetica* in support of spiritual goals.[53] The numerous physical and biological consequences requested of the incarnate deity Jesus in the gospel tradition increasingly shifts, for example, to the psychological concerns of faith following accounts of his ascension, coming thereby into conformity with the central focus of the Pauline tradition with its representation from the beginning of a distant cosmic Christ.

On the one hand, then, it is such culturally informed factors as the characteristics posited of the superhuman agents to whom prayer is offered that differentiate expectations of prayer and that distinguish between the wishes of fantasy, the incantations of magic, and the petitions of prayer—if indeed that culture makes such distinctions at all. On the other hand, to the extent that certain predictions about religious practices can be made on the basis of "cognitive observations about how minds function," historians can, in these cases, be relieved from searching for cultural data that can explain or model similarities among such distributed religious practices as those categorized as "prayer";[54] at least historians can assess the utility of organizing the cultural data of their comparative and historical research according to certain predictable patterns of human cognition.

References

Alderink, Larry, and Luther H. Martin. "Prayer in Greco-Roman Religions." In *Prayer from Alexander to Constantine: A Critical Anthology*, edited by Mark Kiley, 123–27. London: Routledge, 1997 (chapter 8, this volume).

Atran, Scott. *In Gods We Trust: The Evolutionary Landscape of Religion*. Evolution and Cognition. Oxford: Oxford University Press, 2002.

51. Ibid., 20.
52. Ibid., 10.
53. E.g., Sellew, "Secret Hymn," 165.
54. Barrett, "Dumb Gods," 106.

Barrett, Justin L. "Dumb Gods, Petitionary Prayer and the Cognitive Science of Religion." In *Current Approaches in the Cognitive Science of Religion*, edited by Ilka Pyysiäinen and Veiko Anttonen, 93–109. London: Continuum, 2002.

———. "Exploring the Natural Foundations of Religion." *Trends in Cognitive Sciences* 4/1 (2000) 29–34.

———. "How Ordinary Cognition Informs Petitionary Prayer." *Journal of Cognition and Culture* 1/2 (2001) 259–69.

Boyer, Pascal. *Religion Explained: The Evolutionary Origins of Religious Thought*. New York: Basic Books, 2001.

David, F. N. "Galton, Francis." In *International Encyclopedia of the Social Sciences*, edited by David L. Sills, 6:48–53. 19 vols. New York: Macmillan, 1968.

Douglas, Mary. *Purity and Danger: An Analysis of the Concepts of Pollution and Taboo*. New York: Ark Paperbacks, 1984.

Faber, Mel D. *The Magic of Prayer: An Introduction to the Psychology of Faith*. Westport, CT: Praeger, 2002.

Gaddis, John L. *The Landscape of History: How Historians Map the Past*. Oxford: Oxford University Press, 2002.

Galton, Francis. "Statistical Inquiries Into the Efficacy of Prayer." *The Fortnightly Review* 12 (August 1872) 125–35.

Gellner, Ernest. *The Psychoanalytic Movement; or The Cunning of Unreason*. Paladin Movements and Ideas London: Paladin, 1985.

Gilovich, Thomas et al., eds. *Heuristics and Biases: The Psychology of Intuitive Judgment*. Cambridge: Cambridge University Press, 2002.

Goody, Esther N. "Introduction." In *Social Intelligence and Interaction: Expressions and Implications of the Social Bias in Human Interaction*, edited by Esther N. Goody, 1–33. Cambridge: Cambridge University Press, 1995.

———. "Social Intelligence and Prayer as Dialogue." In *Social Intelligence and Interaction: Expressions and Implications of the Social Bias in Human Interaction*, edited by Esther N. Goody, 206-20. Cambridge: Cambridge University Press, 1995.

Heiler, Friedrich. *Prayer: A Study in the History and Psychology of Religion*. Translated and edited by Samuel McComb. New York: Oxford University Press. 1958.

Hinde, Robert A. *Why Gods Persist: A Scientific Approach to Religion*. London: Routledge, 1999.

Hogarth, Robin M., and Melvin W. Reder, eds. *Rational Choice: The Contrast between Economics and Psychology*. Chicago: University of Chicago Press, 1994.

Hopkins, Keith. *A World Full of Gods: The Strange Triumph of Christianity*. New York: Penguin, 1999.

James, William. *The Varieties of Religious Experience*. New York: Library of America, 1987.

Kahneman, Daniel, and Amos Tversky, eds. *Choices, Values, and Frames*. Cambridge: Cambridge University Press, 2000.

———. "Prospect Theory: An Analysis of Decisions under Risk." *Econometrica* 47 (1979) 263–91.

Kahneman, Daniel et al., eds. *Judgement under Uncertainty: Heuristics and Biases*. Cambridge: Cambridge University Press, 1982.

Kiley, Mark, ed. *Prayer from Alexander to Constantine: A Critical Anthology*. London: Routledge, 1997.

Krymkowski, Daniel, and Luther H. Martin. "Religion as an Independent Variable: An Exploration of Theoretical Issues." *Method & Theory in the Study of Religion* 10/2 (1998) 187–98.

Ladd, Kevin L., and Bernard Spilka. "Inward, Outward, and Upward: Cognitive Aspects of Prayer." *Journal for the Scientific Study of Religion* 41/3 (2002) 475–84.

Lawson, E. Thomas, and Robert N. McCauley, eds. *Rethinking Religion: Connecting Cognition and Culture*. Cambridge: Cambridge University Press, 1990.

Leeuw, G. van der. *Religion in Essence & Manifestation: A Study in Phenomenology*. Translated by J. E. Turner. Sir Halley Stewart Publications 5. London: Allen & Unwin, 1938.

Marett, Robert R. "Prayer." In *The Encyclopaedia Britannica*, 22:256b–258b. 11th ed. Cambridge: Cambridge University Press, 1911.

McCauley, Robert, and E. Thomas Lawson. *Bringing Ritual to Mind: Psychological Foundations of Cultural Forms*. Cambridge: Cambridge University, 2002.

Means, John O., ed. *The Prayer-Gauge Debate*. Boston: Congregational Publishing Society, 1876.

Mitteis, Ludwig, and Ulrich Wilcken. *Grundzüge und Chrestomathie der Papyruskunde*. 2 vols. Leipzig: Teubner, 1912.

Parke, H. W. *The Oracles of Zeus*. Oxford: Blackwell, 1967.

Rosengren, Karl S., and Anne K. Hickling. "Metamorphosis and Magic: The Development of Children's Thinking about Possible Events and Plausible Mechanisms." In *Imagining the Impossible: Magical, Scientific, and Religious Thinking in Children*, edited by Karl Rosengren et al., 75–98. Cambridge: Cambridge University Press, 2000.

Sellew, Philip. "A Secret Hymn about Rebirth: *Corpus Hermeticum* XIII.17–20." In *Prayer from Alexander to Constantine: A Critical Anthology*, edited by Mark Kiley, 165–70. London: Routledge, 1997.

Slone, Jason. "Luck Beliefs: A Case of Theological Incorrectness." In *Religion as a Human Capacity: A Festschrift in Honor of E. Thomas Lawson*, edited by Timothy Light and Brian Wilson, 375–94. SHR 99. Leiden: Brill, 2004.

Slovic, Paul, and Sarah Lichtenstein. "Performance Reversals: A Broader Perspective." *American Economic Review* 73 (1983) 596–605.

Stark, Rodney. "Micro Foundations of Religion: A Revised Theory." *Sociological Theory* 17/3 (1999) 264–89.

[Thompson, Henry]. "The 'Prayer for the Sick': Hints towards a Serious Attempt to Estimate Its Value." *The Contemporary Review* 7 (July 1872) 205–10.

Tomlin, Lily. "40th Anniversary of the Improv." NBC Television, broadcast 3 September 2002.

Tversky, Amos, and Daniel Kahneman. "Judgment under Uncertainty: Heuristics and Biases." In *Judgement under Uncertainty: Heuristics and Biases*, edited by Daniel Kahneman et al., 3–20. Cambridge: Cambridge University Press, 1982.

Tyndall, John. "Prayer and Natural Law." In *Fragments of Science for Unscientific People*, 31–38. London: Longmans & Green, 1871.

Versnel, Henk S. "Religious Mentality in Ancient Prayer." In *Faith, Hope and Worship: Aspects of Religious Mentality in the Ancient World*, edited by H. S. Versnel, 1–64. Studies in Greek and Roman Religion 2. Leiden: Brill, 1981.

Whitehouse, Harvey. *Arguments and Icons: Divergent Modes of Religiosity*. Oxford: Oxford University Press, 2000.

Woolley, Jacqueline D. "The Development of Beliefs about Direct Mental-Physical Causality in Imagination, Magic, and Religion." In *Imagining the Impossible: Magical, Scientific, and Religious Thinking in Children*, edited by Karl Rosengren et al., 99–129. Cambridge: Cambridge University Press, 2000.

Woolley, Jacqueline D., and Katrina E. Phelps. "The Development of Children's Beliefs about Prayer." *Journal of Cognition and Culture* 1/2 (2001) 139–66.

Wulff, David M. *Psychology of Religion: Classic and Contemporary Views*. New York: Wiley, 1991.

PART 3

Graeco-Roman Mysteries

10

Imagistic Traditions in the Graeco-Roman World

IN HIS REVIEW OF a monograph in which the author advocates a study of religion informed by recent research in the cognitive sciences, the historian of religion Michael Stausberg concludes that "one of the (several) reasons why many scholars [especially historians] tend to be critical towards the cognitive paradigm is that they feel that it doesn't help them to do something with their data."[1] Apart from a tendentious appeal to apprehensive "feelings," identified by Stausberg as a basis for the criticisms from many scholars of religion, he is correct in noting that any new theoretical paradigm must stand or fall on the basis of its methodological utility for "doing something helpful" with relevant data.

Although several cognitive theories have increasingly been employed by historians of religion,[2] the theory of divergent modes of religiosity proposed by the British anthropologist Harvey Whitehouse has had particular appeal.[3] Whitehouse proposes a generalizable explanation for the dynamics and transmission of two religious movements he encountered during in his fieldwork among the Baining people in Papua New Guinea between 1987 and 1989, a relatively stable religious movement and a splinter group that separated from it.[4] The conservation and transmission of any religious knowledge, Whitehouse argues, necessarily involves the panhuman dynamics of human memory. The ways by which different systems of memory are activated in the transmission of knowledge, Whitehouse concludes, result in historical formations that conform to a predictable divergence of sociopo-

1. Stausberg, Review of *Incorrectness*, 151.

2. Vial, *Liturgy Wars*; Lisdorf, "Spread"; Martin, "Ritual Competence"; Martin, "Preface"; Martin, "Why Christianity"; Martin, "Amor and Psyche."

3. E.g., Whitehouse and Martin, eds., *Theorizing Religions Past*; Martin, "Performativity."

4. Whitehouse, *Inside the Cult*.

litical scale and structure. Drawing on the distinction between episodic and semantic memory,[5] Whitehouse proposes two different styles of religious codification, transmission, and political association, which should appear across all cultures and throughout the course of human history.[6]

The "imagistic traditions" of the title to this paper refers to one of the divergent modes of religiosity proposed by Whitehouse to describe the dynamics of small-scale societies such as those represented by the New Guinean splinter group that he studied. It should be emphasized at the outset that "imagistic" does not refer, in Whitehouse's hypotheses, to traditions that trade in images, as most religions do—although a textual, even narrative, minimalism *does* seem to characterize the Graeco-Roman mystery cults.[7] Rather, the imagistic mode of religiosity, as described by Whitehouse, refers to a convergence of precepts and practices that are transmitted through infrequently performed but high-arousal rituals among small-scale, face-to-face groups. The emotional salience of such rites functions to evoke an analogical or "revelatory" knowledge that is triggered by episodic recall among the ritual subjects and that provides, in turn, a focus for their individual exegetical reflections. The relatively detailed recollections concerning those who went through such rituals together reinforces, thereby, group cohesion while the personal meanings associated with the religious knowledge of this modality mitigate against their dissemination beyond the confines of that group.[8]

On the other hand, Whitehouse identifies a "doctrinal mode of religiosity" that is associated with a widespread transmission and affirmation of a commonly held set of cogently argued and narratively expressed beliefs that allow for the construction of large-scale, if anonymous, communities. In order to maintain some degree of coherence for the distributed sets of often-complex beliefs and teachings characteristic of this modality, some centralized or institutionalized authority must emerge or be established. Official representatives of such authorizing bodies or institutions may then transmit their doctrines to converts and followers through routinized instruction and regular review. Such pedagogical repetition encodes knowledge in the semantic memory system of subjects to be recalled as formalized and shared scripts by which their lives might be organized collectively and that might be widely disseminated.

---

5. See, e.g., Baddeley, "Memory," 516.

6. Whitehouse, *Inside the Cult*; Whitehouse, *Arguments and Icons*; Whitehouse, "Modes of Religiosity"; Whitehouse, *Modes of Religiosity*.

7. Martin "Reflections"; Martin, "Performativity"; Casadio, "Dionysus."

8. Whitehouse, *Arguments and Icons*, 73.

If confirmed, the modes theory would provide historians of religion a significant basis for explaining religious transmission and religious diversity generally. In 2002, Martin and Whitehouse assembled a number of archaeologists, classicists, historians, and historians of religion in order to assess the predictions of the modes theory in terms of their own historical specialization.[9] The theoretical focus of the conference successfully allowed this diverse group of historically oriented specialists constructively to dispute with one another the utility of this theory for explaining a diversity of topics—from prehistoric religiosity to Graeco-Roman religions to the beginnings of Christianity and its medieval and Reformation developments to instances of modern religion.[10] However, a number of questions have been raised concerning the adequacy of this theoretical generalizing for dealing accurately with issues of historical complexity and precisely with specificities of proximate cause. It might be instructive to cite a few of these questions as they have been raised with respect to Graeco-Roman religions.

One recurring question posed by historians of religion is whether or not the two modes of religiosity are "like oil and water" that "remain discernibly separate as domains of operation" even "if they occur within the same [broad historical] tradition,"[11] or whether elements of both might, in fact, mix or interact and, thus, appear together within the complexity of common historical formations. In his consideration of the Roman cult of Mithras, Roger Beck, for example, had argued that a number of "doctrinal" features seemed to characterize a cult, which, in other respects, seems to conform to predictions for an imagistic modality. He includes among these doctrinal features the rapid and efficient spread of the cult throughout the Roman Empire, its possible employment of semantic schemas and implicit scripts, the possibility of learned rather than internally generated ritual meanings, the presence of a dynamic leadership, and a high degree of uniformity among the individual Mithraic cells.[12]

Anita Leopold has argued not only for the presence of mixed modes within the early Christianities but for an active interaction among some of them. These heretical "syncretisms" either provoked an orthodox doctrinal reaction or provided a foundational basis upon which subsequent doctrinal developments might be constructed.[13] Similarly, Douglas Gragg

9. Whitehouse and Martin, eds., *Theorizing Religions Past*.
10. Martin, "Preface," x.
11. Whitehouse, "Theorizing Religions Past," 216.
12. Beck, "Four Men," 96–99; for Whitehouse's iteration of doctrinal features in contrast to those of the imagistic modality, see Whitehouse, *Inside the Cult*, 197; Whitehouse, "Modes of Religiosity," 309; Whitehouse, *Modes of Religiosity*, 65–70.
13. Leopold, "Syncretism."

has described Roman religion as a representing a pre- or protodoctrinal congregation of cognitively natural or optimal traits that could have developed into a full-blown doctrinal modality—but that did not.[14]

As might be anticipated in a consideration of any new theory, one of the reasons that some questions may have arisen about the modes theory may have been the very diversity of scholars engaged with its initial assessment and the extensive range of data considered.[15] Although Whitehouse himself has judged the modes theory generally to have survived questions raised by such specialized studies presented,[16] a panel to (re)assess the predictions of modes theory within a particular domain of historical data, in this case, Graeco-Roman religious traditions during the early period of Roman Empire, was organized for the XIXth Quinquennial Congress of the International Association for the History of Religions meeting in Tokyo, March 2005. From the perspective of a shared historical specialization, historians of religion, here, addressed two related issues. First, they assessed the *validity* of the modes theory by questioning the degree to which a particular set of historical data might support or contravene its theoretical predictions. Second, they assessed the *utility* of the modes theory by questioning the degree to which it can help in the organization of their data and in the reconstruction of their historiographical conclusions. While the utility of the theory is, in principle, dependent upon conclusions concerning its validity, these two concerns in historiographical practice overlap.

Fundamental to assessing the validity of the modes theory for historical research is the question of whether the divergent modes of religiosity it predicts are to be understood synchronically or diachronically. The answer to this question determines whether the two modalities are judged to be proto-, mixed, or interdependent, or whether they represent discrete attractors for diverging historical trajectories. Read synchronically, the two religious modalities would seem to offer a descriptive typology of historical and ethnographic data that is theoretically similar to a number of other social-scientific typologies.[17] Atemporal analyses of data in terms of such ideal types will normally freeze any given religious tradition at some intermediate point of its development with a consequent conclusion of apparently mixed or interdependent relationships. Read diachronically, however, the theory of religious modalities predicts a divergence of transmissive trajectories

---

14. Gragg, "Old and New," 75–76; see Whitehouse, *Modes of Religiosity*, 29–47.

15. See also Whitehouse and Laidlaw, eds., *Ritual and Memory*; Whitehouse and McCauley, eds., *Mind and Religion*.

16. Whitehouse, "Theorizing Religions Past," 216.

17. Whitehouse, *Inside the Cult*, 203–17; Whitehouse, *Arguments and Icons*, 3; "Modes of Religiosity," 63.

over time. Since the modes theory is not a theory of religion types but a theory about the transmission of religious knowledge, this latter, historical reading of the modes theory would seem to be fundamental.

The diachronic hypotheses of the modes theory predict that the transmission of any religious tradition will, over time, diverge into an imagistic or a doctrinal modality. Gragg's contention, therefore, that official Roman religion maintained a position of "cognitively optimal" stasis over the some five-hundred-year period of the Republican era[18] therefore seems problematic. Since, however, the crucial foundation of the modes theory is its acknowledgment of differential functions of the human memory system, a consideration of any particular religious tradition might best begin with an analysis of how these systems of memory are principally involved in the transmission of that tradition.[19] From this cognitive perspective, official Roman religion seems, indeed, to conform to the predictions of the doctrinal mode. It does so not because it maintains and transmits any coherent or organized set of orthodox "doctrines" but because it is characterized by a ritual orthopraxy controlled by centralized authorities and by encoding semantic memory through routinized and repetitious ritual practices.[20] If, in other words, semantic memory is encoded by a frequently repeated set of inputs, it would seem to be irrelevant whether that information becomes consolidated and transmitted as "schemata," cognitive templates for the organization of conceptual information (doctrine), or as "scripts," cognitive templates for sequences of action (ritual).[21]

Since official Roman religion, republican and imperial, was a ritual system inseparable from state interests and functions, it can be argued, further, that the concern with and transmission of orthopraxy was also concerned to transmit coherent sets of "doctrine," in the sense of state sanctioned and controlled values of "Romanness."[22] On the other hand, a divergent imagistic modality has not (yet) been fully documented for Roman religion during

18. Gragg, "Old and New," 76.

19. Whitehouse, *Inside the Cult*, 214.

20. Martin, "History, Cognitive Science," 92; Pachis, "Imagistic Modes of Religiosity"; Chalupa, "Religious Change"; Lisdorf, "Cybele and Attis"; Griffith, "'Modes Theory.'"

21. *Script* is a term generally used by cognitive scientists to designate cognitive templates for sequences of action; *schema* is a generic term for cognitive templates sometimes used to designate conceptual in contrast to action templates (Brewer, "Schemata," 720). Eric Kandel ("Biology," 508), the Nobel Prize recipient for his research on human memory, has concluded that the semantic and procedural "memory systems overlap and are commonly used together so that many . . . [repetitive] experiences recruit both of them."

22. Martin, "Why Christianity"; Martin, "Amor and Psyche."

the republican era. One candidate for this modality might be the common custom of divination by prodigies. On the one hand, are those prodigies that were evaluated as and accepted by Roman officials (preeminently by the Senate) as of significance for public welfare and, on the other hand, those dismissed by these officials as foreign, overly charismatic, or private. These latter traits of patronage by "foreign" deities, emotional rites, and enigmatic personal revelation are precisely variables that are predictors of an imagistic modality.[23] As the concern with divination by prodigies waned towards the end of the republican period, the Graeco-Roman mystery cults emerged as apparently unambiguous instances of the imagistic modality, clearly divergent from the official "doctrinal" system of Roman orthopraxy.[24]

With this (tentative) conclusion about the presence of increasingly divergent modes of religiosity over the religious history of Rome, concerns about other exceptions to the predictions of the modes' theory with respect to the Graeco-Roman mysteries can now be addressed. Whitehouse formulated his theory of religious transmission to offer hypotheses that might explain a specific set of data. Although Whitehouse claims that his theoretical predictions are universalizable, his theory nevertheless remains formulated largely in terms of the historical conditions and ethnographical variables characteristic of a contemporary New Guinean religious movement. Although the psychological and ethnographic/historical variables identified by Whitehouse *do* seem to be present within and significant to all human societies, they may well *function* differently in dissimilar environments and present, thereby, a problem for historians (and others) who seek to utilize the modes theory to understand the particularity of their historical objects.

The widespread dissemination of some of the mysteries, for example, can be accounted for by means other than the restricted dynamics of cult transmission predicted for that modality and does not indicate a doctrinal variable exceptionally present in an otherwise dominantly imagistic modality. Whereas Whitehouse predicts that those religious movements that conform to the predictions of the imagistic modality are not portable,[25] the empire-wide distribution of Mithraism, for example, can be explained simply by (re)deployments of the military personnel or by (re)assignments of the civil servants that accounted for much of its membership.[26] Similarly, the Isis cult was distributed—initially, at least—by the movements of

23. See Lisdorf, "Spread"; Griffith, "'Modes Theory.'"
24. Martin, "History, Cognitive Science"; Martin, "Performativity"; Berner, "Imagistic Tradition"; Lisdorf, "Cybele and Attis"; Griffith, "'Modes Theory'"; Pachis, "Imagistic Modes of Religiosity."
25. Whitehouse, *Arguments and Icons*, 73–74; 77; 224.
26. E.g., Clauss, *Roman Cult of Mithras*, 36–37.

Egyptian traders and immigrants.[27] The Eleusinian mysteries, by contrast, retained their locative character essentially because they never became "Hellenisticized," i.e., they never developed an expanded cosmic structure or an internationalized sociopolitical scale.[28] (Although Demeter was identified with Isis in the Isis diaspora, she never became identified with Isis in the Eleusinian cult—despite Greek precedent for such identification by Herodotus.)

Nor did the mysteries seem ever to develop the kind of dynamic leadership predicted by Whitehouse for the doctrinal modality. For the leadership predicted for this modality requires a hierarchical structure to control and manage a set of doctrines that might be widely disseminated through the orations of authorized agents or through writings associated with their authority.[29] Although each Graeco-Roman mystery association certainly had its leader, we have scant evidence for their actual functions. But whatever the role of such leaders among the various mystery traditions, their leadership was confined to their individual mystery cell. No wider, much less centralized, form of leadership ever developed among any of them. And any perception of knowledge shared among the mysteries would seem to reflect, rather, generalized points of common cultural reference upon which a "mysterious religious knowledge" might be built[30]—or, at least, constructed by modern scholars. The popular knowledge of astrology, which characterized virtually all religious concern at the beginning of the Roman imperial period, offers a case in point.[31]

The doctrinal ideal of a strong leader who might formulate, control, and disseminate a set of commonly held beliefs *did* develop from among the early Christianities. The dynamics of this "doctrinal" modality, initially envisioned by Paul, gave this Christian tradition, when developed, a selective advantage over the alternative imagistic modalities of Christianity.[32] It was no accident that this doctrinal tradition became a dominant form of Christianity, finally established as the official religion of the Roman state.[33]

Finally, Giovanni Casadio situates and evaluates the utility of the cognitive approach to the study of religion with his comprehensive survey of

27. Heyob, *Cult of Isis*, 10–12; Martin, "Performativity," 195–96.

28. Martin, *Hellenistic Religions*. The retention of its locative character by the Eleusinian Mysteries may have an explanation in the persistence of its political and economic ties to Athens (and Attica) (see, Martin, "Eleusinian Mysteries").

29. Whitehouse, *Inside the Cult*, 183.

30. Whitehouse, "Theorizing Religions Past," 219.

31. Cumont, *Astrology*, 51–52; Beck, "Four Men," 92–96.

32. Braun, "Theories of Persuasion."

33. Martin, "Why Christianity."

history-of-religions research, exemplified by that on Dionysus. Although he acknowledges his own "discomfort" with this approach, reflecting, perhaps, the negative "feelings" about cognitive theorizing that Stausberg attributes historians of religion generally, Casadio nevertheless concludes his assessment by conceding that the cognitive approach has allowed him to discern new aspects of a subject that has dominated his thoughts since his "first steps in the field of the history of religions."[34] Whether the general validity of the modes theory for history-of-religions research will ultimately prove to be as sound as its utility has proven productive remains to be demonstrated from further historical and comparative research. Its would seem, however, that the promise of the cognitive theory proposed by Whitehouse, and that of others as well, can no longer be neglected.

References

Baddeley, Alan. "Memory." In *The MIT Encyclopedia of the Cognitive Sciences*, edited by Robert A. Wilson and Frank C. Keil, 514–17. Cambridge: MIT Press, 1999.

Beck, Roger. "Four Men, Two Sticks, and a Whip: Image and Doctrine in a Mithraic Ritual." In *Theorizing Religions Past: Archaeology, History, Cognition*, edited by Harvey Whitehouse and Luther H. Martin, 87–103. Cognitive Science of Religion Series. Walnut Creek, CA: AltaMira, 2004.

Berner, Ulrich. "The Imagistic Tradition of Dionysos in the Graeco-Roman World." In *Imagistic Traditions in the Graeco-Roman World*, edited by Luther H. Martin and Panayotis Pachis, 35–54. Thessaloniki: Vanias, 2009.

Braun, Willi. "Theories of Persuasion and Modes of Religiosity in the Study of Emergent Christianities." In *Imagistic Traditions in the Graeco-Roman World*, edited by Luther H. Martin and Panayotis Pachis, 55–88. Thessaloniki: Vanias, 2009.

Brewer, William F. "Schemata." In *The MIT Encyclopedia of the Cognitive Sciences*, edited by Robert A. Wilson and Frank C. Keil, 729–30. Cambridge: MIT Press, 1999.

Casadio, Giovanni. "Dionysus' Image in the Post-Modern Age." In *Imagistic Traditions in the Graeco-Roman World: A Cognitive Modeling of History of Religious Research: Acts of the Panel Held during the XIX Congress of the International Association of History of Religions (IAHR), Tokyo, Japan, March 2005*, edited by Luther H. Martin and Panayotis Pachis, 89–112. Thessaloniki: Vanias, 2009.

Chalupa, Aleš. "Religious Change in Roman Religion from the Perspective of Whitehouse's Theory of the Two Modes of Religiosity." In *Imagistic Traditions in the Graeco-Roman World*, edited by Luther H. Martin and Panayotis Pachis, 113–36. Thessaloniki: Vanias, 2009.

Clauss, Manfred. *The Roman Cult of Mithras: The God and His Mysteries*. Translated by Richard Gordon. New York: Routledge, 2000.

Cumont, Franz. *Astrology and Religion among the Greeks and Romans*. 1912. Reprint, New York: Dover, 1960.

---

34. Casadio, "Dionysus," 106.

Gragg, Douglas L. "'Another People': Understanding the Roman Senate's Suppression of the Bacchanalia." In *Imagistic Traditions in the Graeco-Roman World*, edited by Luther H. Martin and Panayotis Pachis, 137–52. Thessaloniki: Vanias, 2009.

———. "Old and New in Roman Religions: A Cognitive Account." In *Theorizing Religions Past: Archaeology, History, Cognition*, edited by Harvey Whitehouse and Luther H. Martin, 69–86. Cognitive Science of Religion Series. Walnut Creek, CA: AltaMira, 2004.

Griffith, Alison B. "The 'Modes Theory' and Roman Religion: National Catastrophe and Religious Response in the Second Punic War." In *Imagistic Traditions in the Graeco-Roman World*, edited by Luther H. Martin and Panayotis Pachis, 153–78. Thessaloniki: Vanias, 2009.

Heyob, Sharon K. *The Cult of Isis among Women in the Graeco-Roman World*. EPRO 51. Leiden: Brill, 1975.

Kandel, Eric R. "Biology and the Future of Psychoanalysis: A New Intellectual Framework for Psychiatry Revisited." *American Journal of Psychiatry* 156/4 (1999) 505–24.

Leopold, Anita M. "Syncretism and the Interaction of Modes of Religiosity: A Formative Perspective on Gnostic-Christian Movements in Late Antiquity." In *Theorizing Religions Past: Archaeology, History, Cognition*, edited by Harvey Whitehouse and Luther H. Martin, 105–21. Cognitive Science of Religion Series. Walnut Creek, CA: AltaMira, 2004.

Lisdorf, Anders. "The Cybele and Attis Religion and the Theory of Modes of Religiosity." In *Imagistic Traditions in the Graeco-Roman World*, edited by Luther H. Martin and Panayotis Pachis, 179–202. Thessaloniki: Vanias, 2009.

———. "The Spread of Non-Natural Concepts: Evidence from the Roman Prodigy Lists." *Journal of Cognition and Culture* 4/1 (2004) 151–73.

Martin, Luther H. "The Amor and Psyche Relief in the Mithraeum of Capua Vetere: An Exceptional Case of Graeco-Roman Syncretism or an Ordinary Instance of Human Cognition?" In *The Mystic Cults in Magna Graecia*, edited by Giovanni Casadio and Patricia A. Johnston, 277–89. Austin: University of Texas Press, 2009.

———. *Hellenistic Religions: An Introduction*. New York: Oxford University Press, 1987.

———. "History, Cognitive Science, and the Problematic Study of Folk Religions: The Case of the Eleusinian Mysteries of Demeter." *Temenos: Nordic Journal of Comparative Religions* 39/40 (2003–2004) 81–99 (chapter 13, this volume).

———. "Performativity, Discourse and Cognition: 'Demythologizing' the Roman Cult of Mithras." In *Rhetoric and Reality in Early Christianities*, edited by Willi Braun, 187–217. Studies in Christianity and Judaism 16. Waterloo, ON: Wilfrid Laurier University Press, 2005.

———. "Preface." In *Theorizing Religions Past: Archaeology, History, Cognition*, edited by Harvey Whitehouse and Luther H. Martin, ix–x. Cognitive Science of Religion Series. Walnut Creek, CA: AltaMira, 2004.

———. "Those Elusive Eleusinian Mystery Shows." *Helios* 13/1 (1986) 17–31 (chapter 11, this volume).

———. "Reflections on the Mithraic Tauroctony as Cult Scene." In *Studies in Mithraism: Papers Associated with the Mithraic Panel Organized on the Occasion of the XVIth Congress of the International Association for the History of Religions, Rome 1990*, edited by John R. Hinnells, 217–24. Storia delle religioni 9. Rome: L'Erma" di Bretschneider, 1994.

———. "Ritual Competence and Mithraic Ritual." In *Religion as a Human Capacity: A Festschrift in Honor of E. Thomas Lawson*, edited by Timothy Light and Brian C. Wilson, 245–63. SHR 99. Leiden: Brill, 2004.

———. "Why Christianity Was Accepted by Romans but not by Rome." In *Religion und Kritik in der Antike*, edited by Ulrich Berner and Illinca Tanaseanu, 93–107. Religionen in der pluralen Welt 7. Münster: LIT, 2009.

Pachis, Panayotis. "Imagistic Modes of Religiosity in the Cult of Isis/Sarapis during the Graeco-Roman Age." In *Imagistic Traditions in the Graeco-Roman World*, edited by Luther H. Martin and Panayotis Pachis, 203–37. Thessaloniki: Vanias, 2009.

Slone, D. Jason. *Theological Incorrectness: Why Religious People Believe What They Shouldn't*. Oxford: Oxford University Press, 2004.

Stausberg, Michael. Review of *Theological Incorrectness: Why Religious People Believe What They Shouldn't*, by D. Jason Slone. *Numen* 52 (2005) 149–51.

Vial, Theodore M. *Liturgy Wars: Ritual Theory and Protestant Reform in Nineteenth-Century Zurich*. Religion in History, Society & Culture 4. New York: Routledge, 2004.

Whitehouse, Harvey. *Arguments and Icons: Divergent Modes of Religiosity*. Oxford: Oxford University Press, 2000.

———. *Inside the Cult: Religious Innovation and Transmission in Papua New Guinea*. Oxford: Oxford University Press, 1995.

———. *Modes of Religiosity: A Cognitive Theory of Religious Transmission*. Cognitive Science of Religion Series. Walnut Creek, CA: AltaMira, 2004.

———. "Modes of Religiosity: Towards a Cognitive Explanation of the Sociopolitical Dynamics of Religion." *Method & Theory in the Study of Religion* 14/3–4 (2002) 293–315.

———. "Theorizing Religions Past." In *Theorizing Religions Past: Archaeology, History, Cognition*, edited by Harvey Whitehouse and Luther H. Martin, 215–32. Cognitive Science of Religion Series. Walnut Creek, CA: AltaMira, 2004.

Whitehouse, Harvey, and Robert N. McCauley, eds. *Mind and Religion: Psychological and Cognitive Foundations of Religiosity*. Cognitive Science of Religion Series. Walnut Creek, CA: AltaMira, 2005.

Whitehouse, Harvey, and James Laidlaw, eds. *Ritual and Memory: Toward a Comparative Anthropology of Religion*. Cognitive Science of Religion Series. Walnut Creek, CA: AltaMira, 2004.

Whitehouse, Harvey, and Luther H. Martin, eds. *Theorizing Religions Past: Archaeology, History, Cognition*. Cognitive Science of Religion Series. Walnut Creek, CA: AltaMira, 2004.

11

Those Elusive Eleusinian Mystery Shows[1]

IN 1806, JAMES CHRISTIE privately published his *Disquisitions upon the Painted Greek Vases, and their probable connection with the Shows of the Eleusinian and Other Mysteries.*[2] Christie's premise was this: "What has hitherto been discovered of the Mysteries seems rather calculated to excite, than to satisfy curiosity." He followed this rather contemporary-sounding observation with his conviction that "it is scarcely to be expected, that many new hints on this subject will be collected from a further critical examination of the writers of antiquity."[3] However, Christie's early nineteenth-century judgement concerning the study of Greek Mysteries was soon challenged by two major works that reemphasized textual study and from which modern treatments of the Mysteries can be dated: G. F. Creuzer's comprehensive *Symbolik und Mythologie der alter Völker, besonders der Griechen* (1810–1823), and C. A. Lobeck's critical rejoinder, *Aglaophamus sive de Theologiae Mysticae Graecorum Causis* (1829). These works resulted in two enduring conventions concerning the Mysteries, grounded in the assumptions of nineteenth-century scholarship: the Romantic theory of the Mysteries as preserving well-kept secrets, and a positivistic emphasis on describing the contents of Mystery initiation in terms of what was said (λεγόμενα), what was done (δρώμενα), and what was shown (δεικνύμενα).

---

1. An earlier version of this paper was presented to the Section on Graeco-Roman Religions at the 1984 annual meeting of the Society of Biblical Literature.

2. In 1825 it was reprinted commercially. See Christie, *Disquisitions*.

3. Ibid., 43. Christie suggested that the Eleusinian shows, as he termed them, were effected by transparencies, scrims, or shadow shows lighted by fire and mirrors, and that these shows have been faithfully preserved by vase paintings (37). This curious thesis nevertheless calls attention to the neglected possibilities of "reading" Mystery iconography. See, for example, the provocative studies by R. L. Gordon of the almost exclusively iconographic evidence of Mithraism (Gordon, "Sacred Geography").

I

Creuzer, together with Friedrich Schelling, exemplified the nineteenth-century "symbolists," who argued that all mythology symbolically expressed underlying primordial truths or archetypal patterns.[4] However, Creuzer's "enthusiasm for parallels between East and West," in the words of Robert B. Palmer, "becloud[ed] his better judgement to the point where he began to ignore the uniqueness of his source materials."[5] Nevertheless, the comparative and evolutionary emphases of late nineteenth- and early twentieth-century anthropology reinforced earlier convictions about a hidden religious essence preserved by mythology, especially that of the Mysteries. With these emphases of anthropology, earlier theological concerns with primordial revelation were replaced with "scientific" concerns about nature or vegetative backgrounds comparable with other "primitive rites,"[6] and their more lately evolved "higher" analogues. This Romantic "essentialism" directly influenced the developing thought of the psychologist C. G. Jung,[7] and informed C. Kerényi's study of the Eleusinian Mysteries.[8]

The classicist Lobeck, on the other hand, insisted upon the careful philological and historical analysis of texts, which initiated the scholarly tradition followed by Ulrich von Wilamowitz-Moellendorff and Martin P. Nilsson.[9] Anticipating Leopold von Ranke's positivistic dictum that the historian's task is to show "wie es eigentlich gewesen"[10] Lobeck attacked what he considered to be the "fanciful speculations" of the Symbolists,[11] and set out to establish "everything that is really known about Greek mysteries."[12]

Contrary to the Symbolists, Lobeck concluded that since the Mysteries were open to all Greeks without distinction, including slaves and later even

---

4. See Sandys, *History*, 3:66–67; and Sandys, "Religionsgeschichte," 5.990.

5. Palmer, "Introduction," xvi–xvii.

6. Richardson, *Homeric Hymn*, 13.

7. "I came across Friedrich Creuzer's *Symbolik und Mythologie der alten Völker*— and that fired me! . . . It was as if I were in an imaginary madhouse and were beginning to treat and analyze all the centaurs, nymphs, gods, and goddesses in Creuzer's book as though they were my patients. While thus occupied I could not help but discover the close relationship between ancient mythology and the psychology of primitives, and this led me to an intensive study of the latter" (Jung, *Memories*, 162).

8. Kerényi, *Eleusis* despite his presentations otherwise in Kerényi, *Asklepios*, xxi–xxii.

9. Palmer, "Introduction," xvii. See especially Wilamowitz-Moellendorff, *Glaube*.

10. Carr, *What Is History?* 5–6.

11. Sandys, *History*, 3:104; Kristensen, *Meaning* 401–4.

12. Sandys, *History*, 3:104.

foreigners, they involved no revelations of profound religious secrets.[13] As W. Brede Kristensen has noted,

> The whole concept of a religious symbol was unknown to the Ancients . . . There is no Ancient instance to show that ideas or myths must be symbolically interpreted, and this fact has always been the strongest argument of classical philologians against such symbolic interpretations.[14]

Similarly, Creuzer's student, Erwin Rohde, whom J. E. Sandys judged to have written "the most important work on the Eleusinian Mysteries since Lobeck,"[15] broke with the tradition of this teacher and concluded:

> Since the labors of Lobeck . . . drastically reducing to order the confusion of opinions on that subject, no reasonable person believes that . . . the secret to be kept had taken the form of dogma expressed in concept and words and capable of being communicated verbally to others . . . It was difficult to let out the 'secret', for there was essentially no secret to let out.[16]

Rohde referred, by example, to the charges brought against the popular Greek general Alcibiades, which record one of the few breaches of silence concerning the Mysteries.[17] He understood that Alcibiades was not charged with revealing previously unknown Mystery secrets to noninitiates but with "mocking" the Eleusinian Mysteries by performing them in private houses (Thucydides 6.27f.), thereby profaning them (6.60f.; also Plutarch, *Alcibiades* 19). These charges against Alcibiades, for which he was convicted, suggests that the Eleusinian Mysteries had less to do with kept secrets[18] than with a sacred institution to be respected.[19] This respect would account for

---

13. See "μυστηριον," in Lidell and Scott, *Greek-English Lexicon*, 1156.
14. Kristensen, *Meaning*, 401.
15. Sandys, *History*, 3:186.
16. Rohde, *Psyche*, 222.
17. Ibid.
18 MacMullen, *Paganism*, 23 has argued that "[a] *mystērion* normally meant something more open and unexciting, essentially a lesson in a cult to be learned, perhaps by very large numbers at a time, as in the Eleusinian rites."
19. I am indebted to Professor C. Robert Phillips for calling my attention to the complexity of historical and political events in 415 BCE Athens and their possible implications with the charge of ἀσέβημα against Alcibiades. Towards this understanding, see Comme et al., *Historical Commentary*, 264–88; MacDowell, *On the Mysteries*; Bloedow, *Alcibiades*. On the relationship between piety and politics in antiquity generally, see Wilken, *Christians*, chapter 3; Price, *Rituals and Power*.

the reverence generally shown these Mysteries by initiate, uninitiate, and apostate alike. Even Ovid wrote:

> Who would dare to publish to the profane the rites of Ceres...? Keeping silence is but a small virtue, but to speak what should not be uttered is a heinous crime (*Ars Amatoria* 2.601–4).[20]

As F. B. Jevons argues,

> If participation in and knowledge of the mysteries were withheld from all who were not duly initiated, the object of such exclusion was not a desire to keep the mysteries a secret, but fear of the danger which contact between the holy and unclean would bring upon both.[21]

The romantic secrecy theory, nevertheless, became an accepted scholarly convention. George E. Mylonas, for example, concluded his standard study on the Eleusinian Mysteries with the lines:

> We cannot know, at least we still do not know, what was the full content and meaning of the Mysteries of Demeter held at Eleusis. The ancients kept their secret well. And Eleusis still lies under its heavy mantle of mystery.[22]

And Kerényi, like Creuzer, is convinced that he has penetrated the secret of the Eleusinian Mysteries with his archetypal analysis.[23]

Lewis R. Farnell's study of *The Cults of the Greek States* at the beginning of the twentieth century[24] was influenced by both the philological/historical and the anthropological traditions.[25] Although he rejected the evolutionary concern with origins that characterized both of these traditions, he acknowledged, in the traditions of Creuzer, the "signal aid" of "the science of

---

20. The translation is drawn from John Mozley's Loeb edition (1939). Phillips, "Augustan Poetry," 806 has argued that Ovid's "work contains a view of religion and its meaning which, while still religious, represents a veritable antithesis to everything Roman religion stood for."

21. Jevons, *Introduction*, 361.

22. Mylonas, *Eleusis*, 316.

23. Kerényi, *Eleusis*, 26. But see Kerényi, "Kabeiroi," 36–37, where he distinguishes between "secrets" and "mystery."

24. Farnell, *Cults*.

25. Farnell was educated in the German philological tradition, which he later rejected (*Cults*, 1:x, 1–12). He acknowledged also the work of Robertson Smith, James Frazer, and Andrew Lang, as, indeed, did most everyone else at the time. Cf. Farnell, *Cults*, 1:vii–viii; Farnell, *Oxonian*, 91; 114–15. By the time he published the third volume of *Cults* in 1907, however, Farnell was much more circumspect in acknowledging this debt (3:iv)!

anthropology," which "unlocks many of the mysteries of myth and reveals some strange secrets of early thought and life,"[26] and that set out, in the tradition of Lobeck, to assemble a comprehensive "statement of the facts" concerning Greek cult.[27]

In his monumental study, Farnell followed Clement of Alexandria in describing the Eleusinian Mysteries as a δράμα μυστικόν (*Protrepticus* 2.12.3).[28] He went on to characterize this Mystery ritual in terms of the five characteristics of Mysteries generally reported by the second-century Platonist Theon of Smyrna:[29] καθαρμός, or initial purification; τελετῆς παράδοσις, or mystic communication; an ἐποπτεία, or sacred vision; ἀνάδεσις or στεμμάτων ἐπίδεσις, or an honorary crowning with garlands; and finally, the εὐδαιμονία, or happiness that arises from friendship and communion with the deity.[30] Farnell's emphasis on ritual drama over content allied him with the concerns of the "Cambridge School,"[31] and anticipated the priority of cult to myth argued by the English "Myth and Ritual School" of the 1930s.[32]

Paul Foucart, in his *Les Grands Mystères d'Eleusis*, similarly described mystery initiation as "*un drame sacré*."[33] However, these nontechnical attempts by Farnell and Foucart to structure discussions of the Eleusinian initiation emerged in Foucart's later *Les Mystères d'Eleusis*, formalized as the well-known tripartite formula of Mystery content: the δρώμενα, the δεικνύμενα, and the λεγόμενα.[34]

Foucart's formulaic constellation, however, occurs nowhere in ancient literature, as he and later interpreters claimed.[35] Some interpreters have attempted to establish this formula on the basis of the passage in the

---

26. Ibid., 1:vii–viii.
27. Ibid., 1:ix.
28. Ibid., 3:130–31.
29. *On the Usefulness of Mathematics*; the translation is drawn from Angus, *Mystery*, 76–77.
30. Farnell, *Cults*, 3:131; see also Farnell, "Mystery."
31. Farnell, *Cults*, 3:192; see also Farnell, "Mystery," 121. In his Preface to *Cults* (1: vii), Farnell refers to the new interest in Greek ritual and myth, especially at Cambridge. The Cambridge School consisted of Jane Harrison, Arthur B. Cook, and Francis M. Cornford at Cambridge University, and Gilbert Murray, Farnell's colleague at Oxford. See Kirk, *Myth*, 3–5.
32. On the Myth and Ritual School, see Brandon, "Myth and Ritual." On the anthropological influence on the Cambridge School, also see Kirk, *Myth*, 3–5.
33. Foucart, *Grands Mystères*, 137.
34. Foucart, *Mystères d'Eleusis*, 356–57.
35. Ibid.

Homeric Hymn to Demeter (474–476) that states that the goddess "showed (δεῖξεν) the contents (δρησμοσύνην) of her rites and taught (ἐπέφραδεν) all the mysteries."[36] Apparently assuming the mystery formula, these interpreters infer from δρησμοσύνην, the δρώμενα, and from φράζω, the λεγόμενα. However, Lobeck, who did not know the formula, understood δεῖξεν, the only one of the so-called technical terms that actually appears in the text, to characterize the showing of the Mysteries as a whole.[37]

Other interpreters find support for the Mystery formula by referring to the etymology of cultic personnel. By this dubious method, the practice of "showing things" is derived from *Hierophant*, the title of the chief Eleusinian official, whose name means "the one who shows sacred things"; and a "sacred discourse" is inferred from *Eumolpidae*, the name of the Eleusinian family from which the Hierophant was chosen, and whose name means "those who sing beautifully."[38] The existence of ritual drama is based variously upon the account of Alcibiades's reenactment of the Eleusinian Mysteries, the incorrect supposition of a theatre-like construction of the Eleusinian Τελεστήριον,[39] or upon the trivial observation that the priests or the μύσται or both surely must have done *something*.[40]

Finally, appeal is made to relatively late classical references to the Mysteries. For example, Galen refers to Eleusinian Hierophant as both doing and saying things (δρώμενα τε καὶ λεγόμενα), but not to his "showing" anything (*De usu partium* 7.14.19–22).[41] However, Galen is simply alluding to the Mysteries in passing in order to command the serious attention of his readers. Similarly, Lucius in Apuleius's *Metamorphoses* refers to "what was said and done" (quod dictum, quid factum) during his initiation into the Mysteries of Isis (11.23). However, he too does not refer in this connection to the "showing" of anything. Rather than offering any insight into Mystery initiation, these passages establish rather a general, nontechnical convention for speaking about the Mysteries.

Despite the lack of evidence in classical literature for any technical use of this Mystery formula, it too became firmly ensconced in academic

---

36. The translation is drawn from Hugh G. Evelyn-White's Loeb edition (1936).

37. Lobeck, *Aglaophamus*, 49; followed by Kerényi, *Eleusis*, 96.

38. For example, Willoughby, *Pagan Regeneration*, 55–59 clearly worked with the tripartite Mystery formula although he did not use technical terms; cf. Nilsson, *Geschichte*, 1:661, and Nilsson, "Mysteries," 716.

39. Willoughby, *Pagan Regeneration*, 47–55.

40. Nilsson, "Mysteries," 716.

41. The translation is based upon Helmreich's Teubner edition (1907–1909). Cf. May, *Galen*.

convention by the second decade of the twentieth century.⁴² And modern scholars confidently assert it as describing the content of the Eleusinian Mysteries.⁴³

These two academic conventions characterizing the Eleusinian Mysteries as certainly consisting of δρώμενα, δεικνύμενα, and λεγόμενα on the one hand but as wondrously kept secret and finally unknowable on the other hand, became ironically conflated and continue to inform contemporary research. However, the understanding of the Eleusinian Mysteries in terms of mythology that preserves some primordial or archetypal truth is simply the expression of another, Romantic, mythologem, even as the understanding of the Mystery content on the basis of a philological/historical analysis belongs to the antithetical assumptions of positivism. In agreement with the sentiments of James Christie, it is scarcely to be expected that many new hints on the subject of the Mystery Shows will be gained from further inquiry based upon what has hitherto been discovered. It is time, rather, for a new return to the text, which situates it no longer in the conventions of earlier research but in relation to its own historical and cultural locus.

II

In what is perhaps its most oft-cited and well-known passage, the *Homeric Hymn to Demeter* (480–82) proclaims the initiate as ὄλβιος, "happy," a conventional distinction of Eleusinian initiation in the ancient world.⁴⁴ Traditionally, interpreters of this passage refer this happiness of initiates to the afterlife. In Homer, however, ὄλβιος refers always to worldly goods.⁴⁵ And as Farnell argued, Demeter's gift is more than simply corn; she is the giver of all good things that the earth nourishes.⁴⁶ Therefore, it would seem, the Eleusinian initiate's happiness embraced a this-worldly, earthly mode of life.⁴⁷

---

42. For example, Persson, "Der Ursprung," 305 cited by Bornkamm, "Mystērion," 814 n45. In the authoritative encyclopedia, *Religion in Geschichte und Gegenwart* (*RGG*), this formula first appears in the second edition (4:327) as a confident description of the mystery celebrations.

43. In addition to these cited above, see Mylonas, *Eleusis*, 261; Kerényi, *Eleusis*, 52, 96.

44. See Allen et al., eds., *Homeric Hymns*, 180; Nilsson, *Folk Religion*, 58–59.

45. Lidell and Scott, *Greek-English Lexicon* (9th ed. [1940]). In the *Homeric Hymn to Demeter* (303, 325, 345), ὄλβιος is opposed to μάκαρος, the comparable characteristic of the immortals.

46. Farnell, *Cults*, 3:32, 37–38; see also Zuntz, *Persephone*, 100–101.

47. The Greeks were more interested in this life than in an afterlife, the central concern with which is a Christian development and bias. See Cumont, *Afterlife*, 5–17.

Contrary to nineteenth-century evolutionary theories, the soteriological meaning of Eleusinian discourse was linked to agricultural imagery from its beginnings.[48] According to the *Homeric Hymn*, Demeter first showed her mysteries to "the kings who deal justice" immediately upon her restoration of fertility to the earth (470–79). In an analysis of the Hymn, Larry Alderink has shown that Eleusinian agriculture and the Mysteries are systemically linked in a common network of mythocosmological relations.[49] He argues that Demeter's actions following the abduction of her daughter not only transformed the antecedent relationships between the four major deities of the Eleusinian myth (Demeter, Persephone, Plouton, and Zeus)[50] but transformed agriculture as well, "from a natural process to a human activity surrounded by divine guarantees."[51] In this way, not only did gods and humans became linked through Demeter's identification with Eleusinian agrarian life, but the agrarian life itself became valued. Eleusinian discourse was a discourse of the land.

Traditionally, scholarship has concerned itself with the urban aspect of ancient cultures.[52] However, in his provocative work *The Class Struggle in the Ancient Greek World*, G. E. M. de Ste. Croix has emphasized the distinction between the land (χώρα) and the city (πόλις) in the ancient world,[53] and the central importance of the land to the economy of urban civilization:

> Wealth in the Greek world, in the Archaic, Classical and Hellenistic periods, as in the Roman empire throughout its history, was essentially wealth in land, upon which was conducted the cultivation of cereals (providing the main source of food) and of the other agricultural products.[54]

"A Greek (or Roman) city," de Ste. Croix continues, "normally expected to feed itself from corn grown in its own chōra (*territorium*) or at any rate grown nearby."[55] an increasingly difficult task given the growth in urban

---

Price, *Rituals and Power*, 191 has observed that "individual salvation from death was not the primary preoccupation of these [Mystery] cults"; see also Teixidor, *Pagan God*, 4–5; MacMullen, *Roman Social Relations*, 53.

48. Richardson, *Homeric Hymn*, 14.
49. Alderink, "Mythic and Cosmological Structure."
50. Ibid., 5.
51. Ibid., 8.
52. Price, *Rituals and Power*, 91. Nock, *Gentile Christianity*, 3, for example, disclaims any interest in "the life of the undeveloped countryside."
53. De Ste. Croix, *Origins*, 9–19.
54. De Ste. Croix, *Class Struggle*, 120; also MacMullen, *Roman Social Relations*, 49.
55. De Ste. Croix, *Origins*, 11.

population during the seventh and sixth centuries BCE.[56] Despite Attica's claim to be the original home of agriculture as well as of colonization and law,[57] and despite Plato's claim that Attica was the first to produce an abundance of grain and barley (*Menexenos* 7),[58] Attica was unable to feed its own population.[59] More than any other Greek city, Athens relied upon imported grain to feed its population.[60] Strategically, this was a dangerous situation "because it placed that city at the mercy of any power which was able to interrupt its supply."[61] This economic situation in Attica prompted Solon, in the early sixth century BCE, to ban the export of all agricultural products, except for the bounteous olives, and their oil (Plutarch, *Solon* 24),[62] for which the acidic soil of Attica was especially well suited.[63] As barley was grown in the relatively poorer soil of the nearby Marathon and Mesogeia plains, the domestic supply of wheat in Attica was grown almost entirely in the Eleusinian Thriasian Plain, some of the most fertile land in Attica.[64] This domestic source of wheat was surely one of the primary motivations for the annexation of Eleusis by Athens and provided the economic condition for a continuing Eleusinian prosperity and an autonomy represented by its retention of authority over the celebration of Mysteries.[65]

Exactly when Eleusis was incorporated by Athens into greater Attica is disputed. However, this ancient fortified city and the fecund plain it controlled was the last territory to be annexed, and was clearly the most independent. "The Sacred Way," the sole land route between Athens and Eleusis, not only united the two cities commercially and politically, but emphasized their separation, named as it was after the Eleusinian privilege over the Mysteries.[66] Whether the *Homeric Hymn to Demeter* is dated prior

56. Fine, *Ancient Greeks*, 94.
57. Mylonas, *Eleusis*, 21.
58. Cited in Mylonas, *Eleusis*, 21.
59. Boeckh, *Public Economy*, 109; Michel, *Economics*, 48.
60. De Ste. Croix, *Origins*, 46. Sicily, the major port city of which was Syracuse, was "one of the granaries of Greece . . . [which] continued to supply the Athenian market for centuries" (Humphrey, *Economics*, 322). It was also the site of a significant Demeter cult; see Zuntz, *Persephone*, part 3.
61. De Ste. Croix, *Origins*, 47.
62. Bury and Meiggs, *History*, 122.
63. Hammond, *History of Greece*, 12.
64. Pausanias (1.38.6) claimed that the Eleusinian Plains were the first to bear grain. See also Wason, *Class Struggles*, 77.
65. On the significance of grain, and especially of wheat, to the Athenian economy, see Boeckh, *Public Ecomomy*, chapter 15.
66. Price, *Rituals and Power*, 111. For a provocative analysis of spatial relations as a

to the Athenian domination of Eleusis, as most commentators maintain,[67] or in response to Athenian domination, as a few contend,[68] all agree that the Hymn is non-Athenian and of an Eleusinian provenance.[69]

While civilization in antiquity most often was identified with "citification," from which the word is derived,[70] the *Homeric Hymn to Demeter* implies an identification of civilization with cultivation (468–488f.), an identification made explicit with the introduction into Eleusinian discourse of Triptolemos's agrarian mission to the nations.[71]

Ὄλβιος, however, implies more than mere outward prosperity.[72] Thus, the *Homeric Hymn* distinguishes the initiate from uninitiate in another important way. Initiatory happiness also is the valuation by the Eleusinian goddess of the agrarian life through an initiatory participation in her share of τιμή, or "divine honor."

Τιμή, a major theme of the Hymn, is a cosmic characteristic of the immortals. Plouton's τιμή is his rule of a third share of the cosmos (85–87). It is his prerogative to distribute τιμή to others from his share (334–366), as it is that of his brother Zeus (441–447), and, indeed, that of "all the blessed and eternal gods" (325–328). In the Hymn, Demeter, as "the greatest help and cause of joy" for both immortals and mortals, claims for herself a share of τιμή (269–270). By withdrawing from the company of gods and subsequently devastating the earth through famine (301–13), she effectively robs the Olympians of their rightful τιμή (311–313, 351–354). In response, Zeus promises both Demeter and Persephone whatever τιμή they might choose among the immortals (441–47, 459–62).

Demophoōn is the only mortal in the *Homeric Hymn* who shares in τιμή. Accepting the hospitality of the Eleusinians during her quest for Persephone, Demeter attempts to show her gratitude, and at the same time adopt a substitute for her abducted daughter, by investing her charge, Demophoōn, with the quality of the company she had fled, immortality. However, as the realms of the immortal gods (ἀθάνατοι θεοί) and the mortals

---

socioeconomic "language," see Davis, "Sacred and the Body Social."

67. See Allen et al., eds., *Homeric Hymns*, 113; and Richardson, *Homeric Hymns*, 6–11.

68. Walton, "Athens, Eleusis," 114.

69. See especially Allen et al., eds., *Homeric Hymns*, 113.

70. White, *Middle Ages*, 144–45 cited by de Ste. Croix, *Class Struggle*, 10–11.

71. The legends of Triptolemos had entered Eleusinian discourse by the sixth century BCE (see, Mylonas, *Eleusis*, 20; Kerényi, *Eleusis*, 125). The linking of civilization and cultivation by Osiris as reported by Plutarch (*De Iside et Osiride* 13) and its relation to the mission of Triptolemos has not been fully explored. See Hopfner, *Isis und Osiris*, 1:35; Griffiths, *Iside et Osiride*.

72. Liddell and Scott, *Greek-English Lexicon* (9th ed. [1968]).

(θνητοὶ ἄνθρωποι) "represent two disparate and incommensurate levels of existence,"[73] this gift of the goddess was fated to fail:

> I would have made your dear son deathless [ἀθάνατος] and unaging all his days and would have bestowed on him everlasting honour [τιμή], but now he can in no way escape death and the fates. Yet shall unfailing honour [τιμή] always rest upon him, because he lay upon my knees and slept in my arms. (*Homeric Hymn to Demeter* 260-264)

While it was not possible in the Greek order of things for even a goddess to bestow upon a mortal immortality, she could bestow her honor (τιμή) upon Demophoōn—and upon all the children of Eleusis. It would seem, therefore, that Demophoōn, who had lain upon Demeter's knees and slept in her arms, was the first of Demeter's initiates at Eleusis, before her epiphany to the Eleusinians (268-83), and before she revealed her mysteries to their leaders.[74]

The Eleusinian Mysteries, then, established a we/they distinction between initiate and uninitiate.[75] Whereas the uninitiate is described as perishing (φθίμενος [482]), Demophoōn has been bestowed with an "unfailing honor" (τιμήν ἄφθιτον [263]). The initiate "we," as the adopted "children" of Demeter, participate in her honor (τιμή) and her rule over the gifts of the earth, and are happy (ὄλβιοι) in this agrarian way of life.

III

The *Homeric Hymn to Demeter*, understood as situated discourse, articulated an Eleusinian affirmation of the χῶρα as an alternative to the encroachment of Athenian civilization in Attica. This valuation of the rural life over the urban was expressed through ritual initiation into a share of the Eleusinian goddess's honor, and thus into a salvific or secure happiness sustained in the face of Athenian politicoeconomic domination.[76] De St. Croix cites

---

73. Alderink, "Mythic and Cosmological Structure," 10. While "disparate and incommensurate," these two realms are nevertheless cosmically bound into a systemic whole. See Richardson, *Homeric Hymn to Demeter* 11, 22, 43, 55, 62, 73.

74. Triptolemos replaces Demophoōn in the later legend. See Allen et al., eds., *Homeric Hymns*, 157; cf. Mylonas, *Eleusis*, 20-21.

75. Alderink, "Mythic and Cosmological Structure," 15-16 and n15.

76. Walton ("Athens, Eleusis," 105-6) has argued that the *Homeric Hymn* in fact was composed as an Eleusinian polemic against Athenian dominance. Gordon ("Reality, Evocation and Boundary," 63-64) has written in connection with his study of the Mithraic Mysteries that "honour was the means where men in the Graeco-Roman

the medievalist Lynn White, who estimates that ten people were required to work the land to support each one who lived in the *polis*.[77] Eleusinian discourse thus established the agrarian life as a value in itself over against urban exploitation. The well-known Eleusinian icon of wheat, then, can be understood as a religioeconomic emblem of agrarian identity and power, and its ritual display (Hippolytus, *Refutatio omnium haeresium* 5.38–41),[78] a religiopolitical gesture of defiance and independence. In the face of the later expanse of Hellenistic cosmopolitanism and then of the Roman Empire,[79] in the face of the Ptolemaic cosmological revolution and the religious systems of late antiquity which sought escape from this world altogether, the Eleusinians never relinquished their grasp upon the land and the values of the rural life.[80] It was this persistence of a locative structure over against an encroaching and exploitative urban utopianism that established Eleusis as a sacred center for so many throughout antiquity.[81]

References

Alderink, Larry, "Mythic and Cosmological Structure in the Homeric Hymn to Demeter." *Numen* 29/1 (1982) 1–16.
Allen, Tom W., et al., eds. *The Homeric Hymns*. 2nd ed. Oxford: Clarendon, 1936.
Angus, Samuel. *The Mystery Religions*. 2nd ed. New York: Dover, 1975.
Bloedow, Edmund F. *Alcibiades Reexamined*. Historia: Zeitschrift für alte Geschichte. Einzelschriften 21. Wiesbaden: Steiner, 1973.
Boeckh, Augustus. *The Public Economy of the Athenians*. Translated by Antony Lamb. 2nd ed. Boston: Little, Brown, 1857.
Bornkamm, Günther. "*Mystērion*." In *Theologisches Wörterbuch zum Neuen Testament*, edited by Gerhard Kittel, 4:823–26. 10 vols. Stuttgart: Kohlhammer, 1930.

---

world articulated the relationship between perceived rights and obligations and negotiated with their peers for status . . . Alternations of the rules [through social and economic change] . . . involved a revaluation, slight or intense, of the honour system."

77. See de Ste. Croix, *Class Struggle*, 10–11.

78. See Mylonas, *Eleusis*, 275–78.

79. The Roman emperors initiated into the Eleusinian Mysteries—Marcus Aurelius, Commodus, L. Verus—represented the late Stoic valuing of the rural retreat as technique whereby nature helps put one in contact with the self. For example, se Marcus Aurelius's *Meditations* 4.3.

80. Agrarian life, structured around the remains of the ancient Demeter sanctuary, persisted at Eleusis until modern industrialization. See Mylonas, *Eleusis*, chapters 1 and 2.

81. The important distinction between "locative," to signify religious structures bound to particular space, and "utopian," to signify religious structures bound to "no space," is Smith's (*Map*, 110–13).

Brandon, Samuel G. F. "The Myth and Ritual Position Critically Considered." In *Myth, Ritual, and Kingship*, edited by S. H. Hooke, 261–91. Oxford: Clarendon, 1958.
Bury, John B., and Russell Meiggs. *A History of Greece*. 4th ed. New York: St. Martin's, 1975.
Carr, Edward H. *What Is History?* New York: Vintage, 1961.
Christie, James. *Disquisitions upon the Painted Vases, and Their Probable Connection with the Shows of the Eleusinian and Other Mysteries*. London: Longman & Green, 1825.
Comme, Arnold W. et al. *A Historical Commentary on Thucydides*, 5 vols. Oxford: Clarendon, 1945–1981.
Creuzer, G. F. *Symbolik und Mythologie der alter Völker, besonders der Griechen*. Leipzig: Leske, 1810–1823.
Davis, Natalie Z. "The Sacred and the Body Social in Sixteenth-Century Lyon." *Past & Present* 90/1 (1981) 40–70.
De Ste. Croix, G. E. M. *The Class Struggle in the Ancient Greek World: From the Archaic Age to the Arab Conquests*. Ithaca: Cornell University Press, 1981.
———. *The Origins of the Peloponnesian War*. Ithaca: Cornell University Press, 1972.
Farnell, Lewis R. *The Cults of the Greek States*. 5 vols. New Rochelle, NY: Caratzas, 1977.
———. "Mystery." In *The Encyclopædia Britannica*, 19:117–23. 11th ed. Cambridge: Cambridge University Press, 1910–1911.
Farnell, Lewis R. *An Oxonian Looks Back*. London: Hopkinson, 1934.
Fine, John V. A. *The Ancient Greeks*. Cambridge: Harvard University Press, 1983.
Foucart, Paul. *Les Grands Mystères d'Eleusis*. Paris: Klincksieck, 1900.
———. *Les Mystères d' Eleusis*. Ancient Religion and Mythology. New York: Arno, 1975.
Gordon, Richard L. "Reality, Evocation and Boundary in the Mysteries of Mithras." In *Image and Value in the Graeco-Roman World: Studies in Mithraism and Religious Art*, chapter 5. Collected Studies Series. Aldershot: Variorum, 1996.
———. "The Sacred Geography of a Mithraeum: The Example of Sette Sfere." In *Image and Value in the Graeco-Roman World: Studies in Mithraism and Religious Art*, chapter 6. Collected Studies Series. Aldershot: Variorum, 1996.
Griffiths, J. Gwyn. *Plutarch's De Iside et Osiride*. Cardiff: University of Wales Press, 1970.
Hammond, N. G. L. *A History of Greece to 322 BC*. 2nd ed. Oxford: Clarendon, 1967.
Hopfner, Theodor. *Plutarch Über Isis und Osiris*. 2 vols. Monographien des Archiv Orientálni 9. Darmstadt: Wissenschaftliche Buchgesellschaft, 1967.
Humphrey, Michel. *The Economics of Ancient Greece*. 2nd ed. New York: Barnes & Noble, 1957.
Jevons, Frank B. *An Introduction to the History of Religion*. New York: Macmillan 1896.
Jung, Carl G. *Memories, Dreams, Reflections*. Recorded and edited by Anicia Jaffe; translated by Richard Winston and Clara Winston. New York: Vintage, 1961.
Kerényi, Carl. *Asklepios: Archetypal Image of the Physician's Existence*. Translated by Ralph Manheim. New York: Pantheon, 1959.
———. *Eleusis: Archetypal Images of Mother and Daughter*. Translated by Ralph Manheim. New York: Pantheon, 1967.
———. "The Mysteries of the Kabeiroi." In *The Mysteries: Papers from the Eranos Yearbooks*, edited by Joseph Campbell; translated by Ralph Mannheim and Richard F. C. Hull, 32–63. New York: Pantheon, 1955.

Kirk, G. S. *Myth: Its Meaning and Functions in Ancient and Other Cultures.* Sather Classical Lectures 40. Berkeley: University of California Press, 1970.
Kristensen, W. Brede *The Meaning of Religion: Lectures in the Phenomenology of Religion.* Translated by John B. Carman. The Hague: Nijhoff, 1960.
Liddell, Henry G., and Robert S. Scott. *A Greek-English Lexicon.* 3rd ed. Oxford: Oxford University Press, 1849.
———. *A Greek English Lexicon.* 9th ed. Oxford: Oxford University Press, 1968.
Lobeck, Christian A. *Aglaophamus sive de Theologie Mysticae Graecorum Causis libri tres.* 3 vols. Darmstadt: Wissenschaftliche Buchgesellschaft, 1968.
MacMullen, Ramsay. *Paganism in the Roman Empire.* New Haven: Yale University Press, 1981.
———. *Roman Social Relations.* New Haven: Yale University Press, 1974.
MacDowell, Douglas, ed. *On the Mysteries,* by Andocides. Oxford: Clarendon, 1962.
May, Margaret Tallmadge, trans. *Galen on the Usefulness of the Parts of the Body.* Cornell Publications in the History of Science. 2 vols. Ithaca: Cornell University Press, 1968.
Mylonas, George E. *Eleusis and the Eleusinian Mysteries.* Princeton: Princeton University Press, 1961.
Nilsson, Martin P. *Geschichte der Griechischen Religion.* Vol. 1, *Die Religion Griechenlands bis auf die griechische Weltherrschaft.* Handbuch der Altertumswissenschaft 5. 3rd ed. Munich: Beck, 1967.
———. *Greek Folk Religion.* Harper Torchbooks. The Cloister Library. New York: Harper, 1961.
———. "Mysteries." In *The Oxford Classical Dictionary,* edited by Nickolas G. L. Hammond and Howard H. Schullard, 716. 2nd ed. Oxford: Clarendon, 1970.
Nock, Arthur D. *Early Gentile Christianity and Its Hellenistic Background.* New York: Harper, 1964.
Palmer, Robert B. "Introduction." In *Dionysus: Myth and Cult,* by Walter F. Otto. Translated by Robert B. Palmer. Bloomington: Indiana University Press, 1965.
Persson, Axel W. "Der Ursprung der eleusinischen Mysterien." *Archiv für Religionswissenschaft* 21 (1922) 287–309.
Phillips, C. Robert. "Rethinking Augustean Poetry." *Latomus* 62 (1983) 780–818.
Price, S. R. F. *Rituals and Power: The Roman Imperial Cult in Asia Minor.* Cambridge: Cambridge University Press, 1984.
Richardson, N. J. *Homeric Hymn to Demeter.* Oxford: Clarendon, 1974.
Rohde, Erwin. *Psyche: The Cult of Souls and the Belief in Immortality among the Greeks.* Translated by W. B. Hillis. International Library of Psychology, Philosophy, and Scientific Method. London: Routledge & Kegan Paul, 1950.
Sandys, John E. *A History of Classical Scholarship.* 3 vols. Cambridge: Cambridge University Press, 1908.
———. "Religionsgeschichte." In *Die Religion in Geschichte und Gegenwart,* 5:990. 3rd ed. Tübingen: Mohr/Siebeck, 1957–1965.
Smith, Jonathan Z. *Map Is Not Territory: Studies in the History of Religions.* 1978. Reprint, Chicago: University of Chicago Press, 1993.
Teixidor, Javier. *The Pagan God: Popular Religion in the Greco-Roman Near East.* Princeton: Princeton University Press, 1977.
Walton, Francis R. "Athens, Eleusis and the Homeric Hymn to Demeter." *Harvard Theological Review* 45 (1952) 105–14.

Wason, Margaret O. *Class Struggles in Ancient Greece*. New York: Fertig, 1973.
White, Lynn T. "The Expansion of Technology 500–1500." In *The Middle Ages*, edited by Carlo M. Cipolla, 143–74. The Fontana Economic History of Europe 1. London: Collins/Fontana, 1972.
Wilamowitz–Moellendorf, Urlich von. *Der Glaube der Hellenen*. 2 vols. Munich: Beck, 1967.
Wilken, Robert L. *The Christians as the Romans Saw Them*. New Haven: Yale University Press, 1984.
Willoughby, Harold R. *Pagan Regeneration: A Study of Mystery Initiations in the Graeco-Roman World*. Midway Reprints. Chicago: University of Chicago Press, 1974.
Zuntz, Günther. *Persephone: Three Essays on Religion and Thought in Magna Graecia*. Oxford: Clarendon, 1971.

12

Greek Goddesses and Grain: The Sicilian Connection[1]

> Spread much more Knowledge and Civility, yea, Religion, through all parts of the Land, by communicating the natural heat of Government and Culture more distributively to all extreme parts, which now lie numb and neglected.
>
> JOHN MILTON[2]

THE ANCIENT GREEK STORY of Persephone's abduction from a flowery meadow by the Lord of the Underworld, of Demeter's distraught search by torchlight for her missing daughter, and of Demeter's gifts of culture—agrarian economy and sacred rites—to the Eleusinians upon reunion with her daughter is familiar to all historians of religion and antiquity through the *Homeric Hymn to Demeter*. The Mysteries celebrated annually at Eleusis, for which this *Hymn* preserved the official cult myth,[3] have been described as "the highest and finest bloom of Greek popular religion."[4]

Contrary to interpretations that seek to understand these Mysteries as evolved from an "old agrarian cult,"[5] the Eleusinian *Hymn* indicates that

---

1. A first draft of this paper was read at the Annual Meeting of the Society of Biblical Literature (1986).

2. Milton, *Readie*.

3. The *Homeric Hymn to Demeter* is generally considered the official myth of the famous Eleusinian Mysteries. See Mylonas, *Eleusis*, 3; see the discussion by Richardson, ed., *The Homeric Hymn*, 12–30.

4. Nilsson, *Folk Religion*, 42.

5. Ibid. Cf., for example, the view expressed at the end of the nineteenth century by John M. Robertson that "all religions run into and derive from some other religions,

soteriological imagery has always been linked to the agrarian economy of Eleusis *(Homeric Hymn to Demeter* 470–79). It also seems clear that the Eleusinian economy was the reason for its forcible incorporation by Athens, the only other well-fortified town in its proximity.[6] As all Greek cities were expected to be self-sufficient, the Eleusinian plains provided Athens its sole, if inadequate, supply of domestic wheat. Over against the encroaching requirements of Athenian urban civilization, the Eleusinian cult offered divine sanctions for the life of cultivation through ritual participation in the honor (τιμή) of Demeter, their charter goddess. The sheaf of wheat, prominently displayed in the architectural adornments of the Eleusinian sanctuary and, according to Hippolytus, at the height of the initiation ceremony itself (*Refutatio omnium haeresium* 5.38–41), remained a religioeconomic emblem of Eleusinian identity and power in the context of Athenian dominance.

The example of Eleusis confirms Milton's view that culture is a covert politics in validation of the state.[7] But Milton suggests further the role of this covert politics of culture in support of colonial distribution. The worldwide mission of the panhellenic hero, Triptolemos, seems to be an Athenian elaboration upon a figure described by the *Hymn* only as one of Demeter's first, albeit royal, initiates (474–76), in support of Athenian expansionist pretense.[8] Little note has been taken, however, of later Western accounts by Diodorus and Cicero of the mythic events narrated in the *Homeric Hymn* but situated now in the Greek colonial context of Sicily.[9] As Cicero reported,

> It is an ancient belief . . . established by the oldest Greek books and inscriptions, that the island of Sicily as a whole is sacred to Ceres and Libera whom they also call Proserpina. The Sicilians hold that these goddesses were born in Sicily: that corn was first brought to light in Sicilian soil; and that Libera . . . was carried off from a wood near Henna, a place which, lying in the midst

---

the creeds of all mankind being simply phases of a continuous evolution" (taken from his chapter titled "Mithraism" [here, 196] of a volume titled *Religious Systems*, and judged by Robertson to be the principle that unifies the fifty-eight contributions to the volume).

6. I have argued the points of this paragraph in Martin, "Elusive Eleusinian."

7. Lentricchia, *Critic*, 14.

8. Mylonas, *Eleusis*, 20–21.

9. Diodorus Siculus 5.2–5 and Cicero, *In Verrem* 2.4.48–49. Timaeus of Tauromenium (c. 356–260 BCE) is most likely the common source for both Cicero and Diodorus. See Zuntz, *Persephone*, 71 n1. On Timaeus, see Brown, *Timaeus*. Cf. Ovid who, in *Fasti* 4.419–560, also situates the Demeter/Persephone story in Sicily, but who knows additionally the Athenian version of the Demeter tradition with its legend of Triprolemus; see Mylonas, *Eleusis*, 20.

of the island, is known as the navel of Sicily. Ceres, the tale goes, in her eager search for traces of her lost daughter, lighted her torches at the fires that burst forth from the peak of Aetna, and roamed over all the earth carrying these in her hands (Cicero, *In Verrem* 2.4.48).[10]

Although classicists have given some notice to the Sicilian cult of Demeter, it has been neglected by historians of religion. Mircea Eliade's bibliographical survey of the Eleusinian mysteries, for example, nowhere alludes to this Sicilian cult,[11] although he emphasizes in this same work the importance for the historian of religion of *every* manifestation of the sacred.[12]

The accounts of the Sicilian cult of Demeter/Persephone by Cicero and Diodorus suggest three interrelated themes for consideration:

(1) the antiquity of the Demeter/Persephone tradition in colonial Sicily;

(2) the association, familiar from the Eleusinian example, of the Sicilian Demeter/Persephone cult with Sicily's agrarian economy; and

(3) the association of this cult with the political economy of Sicily.[13]

I

Sow then some seed of fame athwart the isle,
that Zeus, the lord of Olympus, gave to Persephone.

PINDAR, *NEMEAN ODES* 1.13-14

The earliest Greek colonists in Sicily, if Thucydides is to be believed (6.3–5), were Euboeans, who established a colony at Naxos in 734 BCE.[14] More certain is the founding of Syracuse by Corinthian settlers the following year.[15] These Corinthian colonists most certainly imported their own religious practices, preeminent of which was the worship of Demeter and Persephone.[16] The antiquity and popularity of the Demeter/Persephone cult in Corinth itself

10. Translation drawn from L. H. G. Greenwood's Loeb edition.
11. Eliade, *History*, 1:458–64; see also ibid., 1:290–301.
12. Ibid., 1:1–2.
13. See Freeman, *History of Sicily*, 1:530–42; Dunbabin, *Western Greeks*, 179–81; White, "'Demeter's Sicilian Cult."
14. Freeman, *History of Sicily*, 1:314–15, 570–72; Dunbabin, *Western Greeks*, 8–10.
15. Freeman, *History of Sicily*, 1:572–78.
16. Ibid.,1:532; Finley, *History of Sicily*, 27.

are now attested by the large number of votive offerings that have been discovered since 1964 in the sanctuary of the two goddesses at Acrocorinth that Pausanias mentions (2.4.6).[17] Early activity at this Corinthian site is suggested by late Mycenean, Protogeometric, and Early Geometric pottery finds, while architectural remains document continuous activity at this sanctuary from the beginning of the sixth century BCE until the fourth century CE.[18]

A cult, at least of Kore, is documented in Sicily by the so-called Langanello head, an early sixth-century statue in the Corinthian style,[19] which has been identified as the remains of Kore's cult statue.[20] A Sicilian Demeter/Persephone cult was also noted by Pindar in his sixth *Olympian Ode* in honor of Hagesias of Syracuse (6.95). Diodorus, citing the Syracusan tradition of fourth-century-BCE poet Carcinus, who set the Demeter/Persephone story in Sicily,[21] indicates the antiquity of the Demeter/Persephone cult in Corinthian Syracuse with his claim that it had been founded by Heracles (5.4.2).

Not only did Gelon's unopposed seizure of Syracuse and transfer there of his capital from Dorian Gela in 485 BCE consolidate Dorian dominance of eastern Sicily, but his construction of the twin temples of Demeter/Persephone in Neapolis, the new quarter of Syracuse,[22] consolidated the power of the goddesses for their eventual dominance of the entire island.[23] According to Thucydides (6.4), Gela had been founded in 688, forty-five years after the settlement of Syracuse, by Antiphemos of Rhodes and Entimos of Crete. Gelon (540–478) was the successor to Hippocrates of Gela (d. 480), the first of the great tyrants of Sicily. Gelon had fought and conquered on behalf of the gods of Greece, and his construction of the temples of Demeter/Persephone belonged to the foremost of his thank offerings.[24] His brother Hieron, a kinsman of Chromios, in honor of whom Pindar wrote his first *Nemean*

---

17. Stroud, "Sanctuary I," 1; Stroud, "Sanctuary II," 300.

18. Bookidis and Fisher, "Sanctuary of Demeter and Kore IV," 284; see also Bookidis, "Sanctuary of Demeter and Kore III," and Zuntz, *Persephone*, 72 n5.

19. Wallenstein, *Korinthische Plastik*, 54.

20. Orsi, "Daedalica Siciliae"; Zuntz, *Persephone*, 71–72; White, "Demeter's Sicilian Cult."

21. Carcinus was a member of the court of Dionysius II (from 367/6 until he surrendered to Timoleon in 345). Freeman, *History of Sicily*, 1:533–34.

22. Diodorus Siculus 11.26.7; Cicero, *In Verrem* 2.4.53, 119. Cf. Freeman, *History of Sicily*, 2:213.

23. Diodorus Siculus 11.26; Freeman, *History of Sicily*, 2:524–25; Finley, *History of Sicily*, 53.

24. Freeman, *History of Sicily*, 2:212.

Ode, retained the rule over Gela and succeeded Gelon (d. 467) as tyrant of Syracuse in 478 (Diodorus Siculus 9.38).

Gelon and Hieron both claimed to have inherited a hierophantic office of Demeter and Persephone from Telines, their great-grandfather (or some earlier ancestor).[25] Herodotus (7.153) reports that Telines had once settled a dispute in Gela, probably in the second half of the seventh century,[26] by using the ἱερά (*hiera*) of Demeter and Persephone. These ἱερά had been brought to Gela from the Demeter sanctuary in (Dorian?) Cnidos by one of Telines's ancestors—Deinomenes, according to Geloan tradition[27]—who was from Telos, an island off the Tropian distinct of Cnidos.[28] "Deinomenes's" descendants retained the title ἱεροφάνται τῶν χθονίων θεῶν (Herodotus 7.153)—referring presumably to Demeter and Persephone.[29] A Demeter sanctuary in Gela, built before the end of the seventh century,[30] belongs to this history, as does the possibility, suggested by the office of "Hierophant," that mysteries may have been celebrated in Sicily. The Sicilian hierophantic office thus belonged to the Deinomenid dynasty, even as the Eleusinian office remained the privilege of the Eumolpids.

The association of Demeter/Persephone with the whole of Sicily, first attested by Pindar around 477 (*Nemean* 1), was fully accomplished when Henna, an indigenous sacred center of Sicily, came under Syracusan influence. Introduction at Henna of a cult of Demeter/Persephone, or the identification of its indigenous Sicel deities with the Greek goddesses, is documented by coins from the middle of the fifth century and was possibly a result of Syracusan colonization.[31] Henna is first mentioned as the seat of the Greek goddesses in the source Livy used for his account of the Roman massacre there in 214 BCE (24.37–39).[32] The Sicel sanctuary itself finally became part of the Syracusan kingdom under Hieron II (c. 306–215).

---

25. Pindar, *Olympian Ode* 6.92–96; Dunbabin, *Western Greeks*, 64 and 483 on his genealogical table of the Deinomenids; Burkert, *Greek Religion*, 96.

26. See Dunbabin, *Western Greeks*, 64.

27. The name of Deinomenes, Gelon's father, later supplanted Antiphemos as the founder of Gela. See Freeman, *History of Sicily*, I, 400.

28. Farnell, *The Cults*, III, 65.

29. See A. D. Godley's Loeb edition of Herodotus's history, vol. III, 3:463 n2.

30. Woodhead, *The Greeks*, 51; Boardman, *Greeks Overseas*, 174–75; White, "Sicilian Cult," 264 n12.

31. Dunbabin, *Western Greeks*, 136, 180; Finley, *History of Sicily*, 141–42; Zuntz, *Persephone*, 70 n4.

32. Freeman, *History of Sicily*, 1:535–36.

Although the extent of Sicel influence on Greek religion in Sicily is argued,[33] indigenous influence on the Demeter/Persephone tradition seems to be primarily topographical.[34] The earliest colonial traditions of both Syracuse and Gela resituated the events of ancient myth, familiar from the *Homeric Hymn*, on the fertile isle.[35] Cicero, for example, locates the Sicilian version of the Demeter/Persephone myth at Henna:

> Henna . . . is built on a lofty eminence, the top of which is a table-land, watered by perennial springs, and bounded in every direction by precipitous cliffs, round which are numerous lakes and copses, and flowers in profusion at all seasons: one feels that the landscape itself confirms the story, familiar to us from childhood, of how the maiden was carried off. There is indeed in the neighborhood, facing north, a bottomless cave, from which, we are told, father Dis suddenly issued in his chariot; he seized the maiden, carried her away thence with him, and suddenly, not far from Syracuse, plunged underground; at this latter place, all in a moment, a lake appeared, near which the Syracusans to this very day hold an annual festival that is attended by crowds of men and women (*In Verrem* 2.4.48).

The Sicilian accounts depict the Eleusinians as offering hospitality to Demeter in her wanderings and thereby receiving the gifts of civilization next after Sicily (Cicero, *In Verrem* 2.4.49; Diodorus Siculus 5.4; Ovid, *Fasti* 4.502–60), a nice Dorian inversion of the Ionian tale.[36]

II

Throughout many . . . parts of Sicily the wheat men call "wild" grows even to this day.

DIODORUS SICULUS 5.2

The introduction by Greek immigrants of rites in honor of the corn goddesses is not surprising, given the remarkable fecundity of the Sicilian plains. Based upon the presumed realities of Scylla and Charybdis that defined the

---

33. Ibid., I, 78, 168–79; Zuntz, *Persephone*, part II.
34. Finley, *History of Sicily*, 14.
35. Ibid., 27.
36. Plato *(Menexenos* 7), followed by Pausanias (1.38.6), claimed that the Eleusinian Plains were the first to bear grain.

Straits of Messina, Sicily had become identified by some as the Homeric land in the West inhabited by sirens, monsters, and wonders.[37]

But the Homeric West, identified by Hesiod as an island *(Works and Days* 156–69; *Theogony* 215–16), also concealed the Elysian Plain. If the monstrous guardians of Elysium might be conquered, "the condition of men would be profoundly altered, for there nature's bounty was endless, happiness was certain, and death was banished forever."[38] Such mythological yearnings most certainly reinforced Greek colonization of Sicily, among the most fertile regions in the Mediterranean (Thucydides 6.20),[39] and Henna became the standard to which poets compared the Elysian fields.[40]

Immigrants to Sicily found "fertile plains on which wheat ... yielded almost miraculous crops,"[41] and colonial economics was based primarily on the production of wheat.[42] Although shipment of Sicilian wheat to Greece is documented only from the fifth century,[43] the Sicilian colonies must have shipped grain to their mother cities from their beginnings.[44] Corinthian Syracuse controlled the largest, if not the most fertile, territory of any Sicilian state, as well as Sicily's best harbor.[45]

Like Attica, Corinth did not produce enough grain to meet its needs. Although the small plain along the Corinthian Gulf was one of the most fertile areas in the Peloponnese (Livy 27.31), the Isthmus itself is rocky and unfertile, and the highlands to the south and east barren.[46] Corinth's economy was rather based upon the tolls leveled on the land trade it controlled into and out of the Peloponnese and upon its trade with both Asia and the West.[47] Grain was brought into Corinth's eastern harbor of Cenchreae from the Taurian peninsula, the Cimmerian Bosporus, Thrace, Syria, and Egypt, and into its western harbor of Lechaeum from Libya and, of course, Sicily.[48]

37. Freeman, *History of Sicily*, 1:106; Finley, *History of Sicily*, 16–17. But see Carpenter, *Folk Tale*, 109.

38. Baritz, "The Idea of the West," 618.

39. Toutain, *Economic Life*, 33.

40. Claudian, *Raptus Proserpinae* 2.289; 3.85, 220. See Freeman, *History of Sicily*, I, 539.

41. Toutain, *Economic Life*, 28.

42. Dunbabin, *Western Greeks*, 211.

43. Ibid., 214; Finley, *History of Sicily*, 35; De Ste. Croix, *Origins*, 217.

44. Dunbabin, *Western Greeks*, 214; Finley, *History of Sicily*, 35.

45. Dunbabin, *Western Greeks*, 215.

46. O'Neill, *Ancient Corinth*, 28; Salmon, *Wealthy Corinth*, 130.

47. Strabo 8.6.20; Thucydides 1.13.2–5. Cf. Salmon, *Wealthy Corinth*, 133.

48. Theophrastus, *Historia plantarum* 8.4; Boeckh, *Public Economy*, 109; de Ste. Croix, *Origins*, 216–18; de Ste. Croix, *Class Struggle*, 120, 132; Salmon, *Wealthy Corinth*,

A large part of Corinth's wealth derived from its control of this important Western trade.[49]

According to Herodotus (7.158), Sicily had such a surplus of wheat that Gelon could offer to feed the entire Greek army. When Egypt and the Dardanelles came under Persian control in 480, this Sicilian source of grain became of central importance to Greece.[50] Athens's break with Corinth around 460, its Egyptian expedition, and its early interest in Sicily were motivated by the desire to control the important overseas supplies of grain.[51] According to Thucydides (3.86.4), Athens "wished to prevent the importation of grain from Sicily into the Peloponnese [by Corinth], and also to make a preliminary test whether the affairs of Sicily could be brought under their own control."[52]

Under Timoleon (344–336) there was a revival of Sicilian economy based upon agricultural exports to Greece,[53] and again under Agathocles's rule (317–289).[54] The assassination of Agathocles in 289 set the stage for Carthaginian threats, Roman intervention, and the First Punic War (264–241), following which Sicily became a Roman province and, according to Cato, the "Republic's granary, the nurse at whose breast the Roman people is fed."[55]

Throughout its tumultuous colonial history, Sicily was sustained by the importance to others of its agrarian produce, a material reality given ideological sanction by its adopted cult of Demeter/Persephone. This economic ideology provided the basis for a Sicilian political identity.

III

> In the consulship of Publius Mucius and Lucius Calpurnius [143 BCE] a terrible political crisis had arisen: Tiberius Gracchus had been slain, and prodiges indicated that fearful dangers were threatening us. The Sibylline Books were consulted; and from them it was discovered that "the most ancient Ceres" must be

---

142, and 139–47 generally.

49. Dunbabin, *Western Greeks*, 214.
50. Ibid.
51. Ibid.
52. The translation is drawn from C. F. Smith's Loeb edition; cf. Finley, *History of Sicily*, 66.
53. Finley, *History of Sicily*, 100.
54. Ibid., 103.
55. Ibid., 123. See Rickman, *Corn*, 104–7; Casson, "Grain Trade."

placated. Therefore, although there was a splendid and beautiful temple of Ceres here in our own city, yet priests of the Roman state, members of the distinguished body of Decemvirs, left Rome to go all the way to Henna: so ancient, so awe-inspiring was that cult, that they were felt, in going thither, to be making their way not to a temple of Ceres but to the presence of Ceres herself. (Cicero, *In Verrem* 2.4.49)

Political crises in Rome might be addressed, according to Cicero, by placating Ceres, the corn goddess of Henna(!), for to offend Demeter was to risk famine *(Homeric Hymn to Demeter* 301–13). Offense against this goddess was one of the charges brought on behalf of the Sicilian people in 70 BCE against Gaius Verres, proconsul of Sicily from 73 to 71. Verres's exploitation of Sicily included removal of the central cult statue of Kore from Henna, which Cicero compared to the ancient abduction of Persephone by the Lord of the Underworld himself (*In Verrem* 2.4.49–50). The "sacrilege committed against Ceres," Cicero concludes, "is the chief reason why all the crops and fruits of Ceres in that part of the world have come to nothing" (2.4.51). This risk of economic disaster may have been the threat raised by Telines when he invoked the goddesses Demeter and Persephone to reconcile the quarrelling parties of Gela.[56]

Telines's reward for settling the dispute in Gela was the hierophantic office of Demeter and Persephone, a position retained by his descendants. Both Gelon and Hieron held the priesthood of Demeter and Persephone, and their construction of the Demeter/Persephone temples in Syracuse following their victory over Carthage in 480 established this cult as a continuing instrument of Deinomenid policy.[57] Another temple of Demeter planned by Gelon but completed by Hieron at the foot of Aetna suggests early Syracusan authority in that area as well.[58] Telines had established a publicly recognized divine legitimization for the Deinomenid dynasty, one reason for his ancestor's continued success in Gela.[59]

Even Sicilian military expeditions claimed the sanction of these deities, giving classical support to a famous premise of military theory that war is an extension of politics by other means.[60] When the aristocrats of Syracuse appealed in 345 for relief from the tyrannical rule of Dionysus II, Corinth

---

56. White, "Sicilian Cult," 262 n4.
57. Dunbabin, *Western Greeks*, 180.
58. Diodorus Siculus 11.26.7. Also see White, "Sicilian Cult," 266 n18.
59. Dunbabin, *Western Greeks*, 64, 66.
60. Clausewitz, *On War*, chapter 1.

responded by sending the expedition of Timoleon. When Timoleon's fleet was ready, according to Plutarch,

> and the soldiers provided with what they needed, the priestesses of Persephone fancied they saw in their dreams that goddess and her mother making ready for a journey, and heard them say that they were going to sail with Timoleon to Sicily. Therefore the Corinthians equipped a sacred trireme besides, and named it after the two goddesses.

On the sea journey to Sicily,

> the heavens seemed to burst open on a sudden above his ship, and to pour forth an abundant and conspicuous fire. From this a torch lifted itself on high, like those which the mystics bear, and running along with them on their course, darted down upon precisely that part of Italy towards which the pilots were steering. The soothsayers declared that the apparition bore witness to the dreams of the priestesses, and that the goddesses were taking part in the expedition and showing forth the light from heaven (Plutarch, *Timoleon* 8; cf. Diodorus Siculus 16.66.3–5).

And in 310, the Syracusan general Agathocles sacrificed to Demeter/Kore at the beginning of his African campaign (Diodorus Siculus 20.7).

Even as Demeter was one of the deities invoked in Athenian oaths,[61] a "Great Oath," sworn in the τέμενος (*temenos*) of the Syracusan Demeter/Persephone temples, was concerned directly with the preservation of the established state.[62] The oath, the Athenian statesman Lycurgus had proclaimed, was "what holds democracy together" (*Against Leocrates* 79).[63] The swearer of the Syracusan "Great Oath" was wrapped in the purple robe of the goddesses and held aloft the flaming torch of Demeter.[64] In the two cases documenting the practice—Agathocles's declaration that he had no evil intentions against the democracy (Diodorus Siculus 19.5.4), and Kallippos's that he was not plotting against Dion (Plutarch, *Dion* 57)—the "Great Oath" was considered binding, even on tyrants. For Greeks, the oath established the "very organization of [their] society,"[65] indissolubly linking

---

61. Burkert, *Greek Religion*, 251.
62. White, "Sicilian Cult," 265–66.
63. Cited in Burkert, *Greek Religion*, 250.
64. Diodorus Siculus 19.5; Plutarch, *Dion* 56; Freeman, *History of Sicily*, 2:213; Farnell, *Cults*, 3:74.
65. Burkert, *Greek Religion*, 250.

religion with "the entire organization of state, law, and commercial life."[66] The political economy of agrarian Sicily was joined thereby with its ancient cult of Demeter.

IV

Politics and Religion: both are ways of systematically constructing power.

S. R. F. PRICE[67]

The Sicilian cult of Demeter/Persephone paralleled the Eleusinian cult not only mythologically, topographically, and, with its inherited priesthood, administratively, but also economically and politically.[68] In both instances, Sicilian and Eleusinian, the Demeter cult articulated an analogous sociopolitical discourse.[69] The identity of the Eleusinian *populus*, challenged by the economic requirements of Athenian expansion, was paralleled in Sicily by a colonial people seeking identity in a new land settled primarily to meet the economic requirements of Corinth. The privilege of the mysteries that was retained by the Eumolpids of Eleusis preserved an Eleusinian autonomy and identity officially recognized by Athens and the world, as well as rural values of cultivation in the face of Athenian political domination and the urban life of civilization. Similarly, the official Sicilian Demeter cult of the Deinomenids maintained Greek values and identity for Dorian colonists in the face of Sicel, and competing Greek, Carthaginian, and finally Roman foes. However, the Eleusinian formation of the cult as a "religion of resistance" to Athenian incursion became, in its Sicilian transformation, a "religion of the status quo" in validation of the colonial state.[70]

The Sicilian cult of Demeter has been described as a "political instrument."[71] However, this functionalist view of cult formations assumes

66. Ibid., 254.
67. Price, *Rituals and Power*, 247.
68. The much analyzed Athenian-Sicilian expedition under Alcibiades in 415 offers yet a third fascinating example of an intricate web of events involving military adventurism, political intrigue, and the Demeter cult (Thucydides 6.27–29, 60–61). See Comme et al., *Commentary*, 4:264–88; MacDowell, *Andokides*; Bloedow, *Alcibiades*; Price, *Rituals and Power*, 247 (following Michel Foucault, *Archaeology*; see also Price, *Rituals and Power*, 241–42 and n24.
69. See Burkert, *Greek Religion*, 258.
70. See the helpful typology suggested by Lincoln, "Notes," 266–92.
71. So White, "Demeter's Sicilian Cult."

a sui generis nature for "religious" phenomena vis-a-vis their nonreligious political or economic functions.[72] Both the Sicilian and Eleusinian cults of Demeter and Persephone challenge this nineteenth-century essentialist theory.[73] They exemplify, rather, the insight that there was, in antiquity, no "ideology other than what we call 'religion.'"[74] The discourse and practices that we understand as "religious" articulated, in other words, those sacral processes that we differentiate as economic and political. Rather, such discursive formations as economics, politics, and religion may better be understood as differing, similar, or identical manifestations or explanations of power, depending upon the reflexive specificities of their historical and cultural situation,[75] and, as in the case of Demeter/Persephone, as ways of systematically organizing power as the "effective rallying point" for collective identity.[76]

References

Baritz, Loren. "The Idea of the West." *American Historical Review* 66/3 (1961) 618-40.
Bloedow, Edmund F. *Alcibiades Reexamined*. Historia; Zeitschrift für alte Geschichte. Einzelschriften 21. Wiesbaden: Steiner, 1973.
Boardman, John. *The Greeks Overseas*. Pelican Books. 2nd ed. Baltimore: Penguin, 1973.
Boeckh, Augustus. *The Public Economy of the Athenians*. Translated by Anthony Lamb. Boston: Little, Brown, 1857.
Bookidis, Nancy. "The Sanctuary of Demeter and Kore on Acrocorinth, Preliminary Report III: 1968." *Hesperia* 38/3 (1969) 297-310.
Bookidis, Nancy, and Joan E. Fisher. "The Sanctuary of Demeter and Kore on Acrocorinth, Preliminary Report IV: 1969-1970." *Hesperia* 41/3 (1972) 283-331.
Brown, Truesdell S. *Timaeus of Tauromenium*. Berkeley: University of California Press, 1958.
Burkert, Walter. *Greek Religion: Archaic and Classical*. Translated by John Raffan. Ancient World. Oxford: Blackwell, 1985.
Carpenter, Rhys. *Folk Tale, Fiction and Saga in the Homeric Epics*. Berkeley: University of California Press, 1946.
Casson, Lionel. "The Grain Trade of the Hellenistic World." *Transactions and Proceedings of the American Philological Association* 85 (1954) 168-87.
Clausewitz, Carl von. *On War*. Translated by Michael Howard and Peter Paret. Princeton: Princeton University Press, 1976.

72. Ibid., 278; cf. Penner, "Poverty"; but see McCauley and Lawson, "Functionalism."

73. For example, the Romantic essentialism of Creuzer, *Symbolik*; cf. Martin, "Elusive Eleusinian," 17-22.

74. Grottanelli, "Rebellion," 15.

75. Foucault, *Archaeology*, 22.

76. Lincoln, "Notes," 267.

Comme, Arnold et al. *A Historical Commentary on Thucydides.* 5 vols. Oxford: Clarendon, 1970.
Creuzer, F. G. *Symbolik und Mythologie der alten Völker, besonders der Griechen.* Leipzig: Leske, 1810–1823.
De Ste. Croix, G. E. M. *The Class Struggle in the Ancient Greek World: From the Archaic Age to the Arab Conquests.* Ithaca: Cornell University Press, 1981.
———. *The Origins of the Peloponnesian War.* Ithaca: Cornell University Press, 1972.
Dunbabin, Thomas J. *The Western Greeks.* Oxford: Clarendon, 1948.
Eliade, Mircea. *A History of Religious Ideas.* Translated by Willard R. Trask. Chicago: University of Chicago Press, 1978.
Farnell, Lewis R. *The Cults of the Greek States.* Oxford: Clarendon, 1907.
Finley, M. I. *A History of Sicily.* Vol. 1, *Ancient Sicily to the Arab Conquest.* New York: Viking, 1968.
Foucault, Michel. *The Archaeology of Knowledge.* Translated by A. M. Sheridan Smith. New York: Pantheon, 1972.
Freeman, Edward A. *The History of Sicily from the Earliest Times.* 4 vols. Oxford: Clarendon, 1891–1894.
Grottanelli, Christiano. "Archaic Forms of Rebellion and their Religious Background." In *Religion, Rebellion, Revolution: An Interdisciplinary and Cross-Cultural Collection of Essays,* edited by Bruce Lincoln, 15–45. New York: Palgrave MacMillan, 1985.
Lentricchia, Frank. *Criticism and Social Change.* Chicago: University of Chicago Press, 1983.
Lincoln, Bruce. "Notes toward a Theory of Religion and Revolution." In *Religion, Rebellion, Revolution: An Interdisciplinary and Cross-Cultural Collection of Essays,* edited by Bruce Lincoln, 266–92. New York: Palgrave MacMillan, 1985.
MacDowell, Douglas. *On the Mysteries,* by *Andokides.* Oxford: Clarendon, 1962.
Martin, Luther H. "Those Elusive Eleusinian Mystery Shows." *Helios* 13/1 (1986) 17–31 (chapter 11, this volume).
McCauley, Robert N., and E. Thomas Lawson. "Functionalism Reconsidered." *History of Religions* 23/4 (1984) 372–81.
Milton, John. *The Readie and Easie Way to Establish a Free Commonwealth.* London: Liverwell Chapman, 1660.
Mylonas, George E. *Eleusis and the Eleusinian Mysteries.* Princeton: Princeton University Press, 1961.
Nilsson, Martin P. *Greek Folk Religion.* Harper Torchbooks. The Cloister Library. New York: Harper, 1961.
O'Neill, John G. *Ancient Corinth.* The Johns Hopkins University Studies in Archaeology Baltimore: Johns Hopkins University Press, 1930.
Orsi, P. "Daedalica Siciliae." *Monuments Piot* 22/2 (1916) 131–62.
Penner, Hans. "The Poverty of Functionalism." *History of Religions* 11/1 (1971) 91–97.
Price, S. R. F. *Rituals and Power: The Roman Imperial Cult in Asia Minor.* Cambridge: Cambridge University Press, 1984.
Richardson, N. J., ed. *The Homeric Hymn to Demeter.* Oxford: Clarnedon, 1974.
Rickman, Geoffrey. *The Corn Supply of Ancient Rome.* Oxford: Clarendon, 1980.
Robertson, John M. *Religious Systems of the World.* London: Sonnenschein, 1889.
Salmon, J. B. *Wealthy Corinth: A History of the City to 338 B.C.* Oxford: Clarendon, 1984.

Stroud, Ronald S. "The Sanctuary of Demeter and Kore on Acrocorinth, Preliminary Report 1: 1961–1962." *Hesperia* 34 (1965) 1–24.

———. "The Sanctuary of Demeter and Kore on Acrocorinth, Preliminary Report II: 1964–1965." *Hesperia* 37 (1968) 299–330.

Toutain, Jules. *The Economic Life of the Ancient World*. Translated by M. R. Dobie. The History of Civilization. New York: Barnes & Noble, 1951.

Wallenstein, Klaus. *Korinthische Plastik des 7. und 6. Jahrhunderts vor Christus*. Abhandlungen zur Kunst-, Musik- und Literaturwissenschaft 113. Bonn: Bouvier Verlag Herbert Grundmann, 1971.

White, Donald. "Demeter's Sicilian Cult as a Political Instrument." *Greek, Roman, and Byzantine* Studies 5 (1964) 261–79.

Woodhead, A. G. *The Greeks in the West*. Ancient Peoples and Places 28. New York: Praeger, 1962.

Zuntz, Günther. *Persephone: Three Essays on Religion and Thought in Magna Graecia*. Oxford: Clarendon, 1971.

13

History, Cognitive Science, and the Problematic Study of Folk Religions: The Case of the Eleusinian Mysteries of Demeter

nihil humani a me alienum puto
TERENCE (*HAUTONTIMORUMENOS* 1.1)

Introduction

FOLKLORE STUDIES ARE DEFINED in the *HarperCollins Dictionary of Religion* as the recognition of a "common human ground" with newly encountered peoples.[1] I should like here to explore this methodological presumption of a "common human ground," presumably, by this definition, that common ground between modern scholars and "encountered" peoples, whether these peoples are those encountered in modern ethnographic fieldwork or whether they are those who have been the object of a more long-standing encounter through historical research. And in light of Ruth Benedict's suspicion, expressed some seventy-five years ago, that folklore may well be "a dead trait in the modern world,"[2] historical examples might provide at least as sound a basis for modeling for the study of folk religion as do the ethnographic. Consequently, I should like to focus my comments with reference to my own historical field of research, the religions of the Graeco-Roman world, and specifically on that example judged by the great Swedish scholar Martin P. Nilsson to be "the highest and finest bloom" of folk religion in

1. Smith, "Folklore," 365.
2. Benedict, "Folklore," 292.

Western antiquity, the Eleusinian Mysteries of Demeter.[3] And, although the "common human ground" presumed by folklore studies still tends to reflect the romantic view of a "spiritual" kinship among all people that is characteristic of this study's nineteenth-century beginnings,[4] I should like to explore my historical example from the perspective of contemporary researches in the cognitive sciences that are currently documenting the commonality of mental capacities and constraints for the species *Homo sapiens*. For, in the words of one reviewer of this perspective, "if . . . cultural universals are hard-wired, nothing human can be made alien to us"[5]—including, we might presume, those res gestae or human doings of the past that constitute the object of historiographical inquiry.

The Eleusinian Mysteries as Folk Religion

The Greek tale of the abduction of Persephone by Plouton, god of wealth and of the underworld, with whom the maiden subsequently dwells a third of the year, and of her reunion at the agrarian town of Eleusis with her mother, Demeter, with whom she subsequently dwells in the upper world two-thirds of the year, is familiar to all students of religion from the *Homeric Hymn to Demeter*. The "essential point" of this story, according to Nilsson, is its manifest connection to vegetation.[6] In the Mediterranean agrarian cycle, crops are threshed in June and stored in subterranean silos, the realm of Plouton. In October, the silos are opened and seed corn is brought up for the autumn planting. This meeting of the old crop with the new, the reunion of the Corn Maiden, Persephone, with the Corn Mother, Demeter, was, for Nilsson, the "kernel of the myth" and "must likewise have been the kernel of the . . . Mysteries."[7] In the view of Nilsson, an old myth from the agrarian "foundation of human civilization" became elevated "into the human sphere,"[8] in which the sprouting of the new crop became "a symbol of the eternity of life."[9] Consequently, he concluded, the Mysteries gave thereby

---

3. Nilsson, *Folk Religion*, 42.
4. Wilson, "Herder"; Bîrlea, "Folklore."
5. Turner, Review of *The Blank State*.
6. Nilsson, *Folk Religion*, 50.
7. Ibid., 52, 54.
8. Ibid., 54, 63–64.
9. Ibid., 53.

new expression to "the deepest longings of the human soul"[10]—which, according to Nilsson, is the essence of all folk-religion.[11]

A number of problems emerge from viewing the Eleusinian Mysteries as a model for folk religion. First, Nilsson supported his conclusions about the Eleusinian Mysteries largely from the seventh-century-BCE *Homeric Hymn to Demeter*.[12] Although many scholars have considered the Hymn the "official" story upon which the Eleusinian rites of Demeter were based,[13] Nilsson maintained that it contains "the ideas which were at the bottom of the belief of the initiated in the bliss conferred upon them in the Mysteries."[14] However, the relationship of this Hymn to the Eleusinian Mysteries has been questioned by contemporary scholars. The classicist Kevin Clinton, for example, has concluded—ironically in his 1990 Martin P. Nilsson Lectures on Greek Religion—that the *Homeric Hymn* is only "superficially" related to the Eleusinian Mysteries.[15] Absent from the *Hymn*, for example, are such important features of the Mysteries—documented from topographical, iconographic, and monumental evidence—as the ἀγέλαστος πέτρα, or "Mirthless Rock," upon which the grieving Demeter sat at the very gate of Hades—the shallow cave just inside the entrance to the sanctuary—and whose suffering was confronted there by initiates as they made their way to the initiatory precinct of the Telesterion.[16] This Mirthless Rock, according to Clinton, "was an essential part of the sacred landscape of the Eleusinian sanctuary and fundamental to the myth of the Mysteries."[17] Further, there is only passing mention in the Hymn of the important role in the Mysteries of the deity Triptolemos[18] and no mention at all of the role accorded by the Mysteries to Eubouleus, an enigmatic deity that was at least as important for the Mysteries as was Triptolemos.[19]

While the Mysteries of Demeter were unique to Eleusis,[20] there were a number of more ancient rites of Demeter celebrated throughout the Greek

10. Ibid., 63, 21.
11. Ibid., 64.
12. Ibid., 43, 49–51, 54.
13. Mylonas, *Eleusis*, 3.
14. Nilsson, *Folk Religion*, 45.
15. Clinton, *Myth and Cult*, 13, 30 n79, 35.
16. Ibid., 85.
17. Ibid., 97.
18. Richardson, ed., *Homeric Hymn to Demeter* 153, 474–77; see Clinton, *Myth and Cult*, 38–59, 77–84, 100–102, 111–13.
19. Clinton, *Myth and Cult*, 71–73, 97.
20. Ibid., 29, 61.

world, including at Eleusis. These local Demeteria were associated with the Thesmophoria, an ancient agrarian festival celebrated by women in honor of the goddess.²¹ Clinton concludes that the *Homeric Hymn to Demeter* is largely an αἴτιον of the Eleusinian Thesmophoria that, in his judgment, has "exercised an undeserved tyranny over historians of religion and archaeologists" concerned with the Eleusinian Mysteries.²²

Nilsson and Clinton both analyze the relationship between the *Homeric Hymn to Demeter* and the mystery rites celebrated at Eleusis in terms of finding elements or persons common to both. Neither, however, explores the much more interesting question of the relationship between cult myth and ritual practice in terms of how cult and narrative representations might mutate as they shift between different media and contexts.²³

Second, Nilsson's reliance upon the *Homeric Hymn to Demeter* for his understanding of the Eleusinian Mysteries raises further the question of the relationship of folklore and literature. Lauri Honko, for example, like a number of other folklorists, has argued that epic literature—to which the *Homeric Hymn* seems to be related²⁴—embodies a prior oral tradition and can be studied, therefore, as a repository of at least some folk religion.²⁵ On the other hand, others, such as Robert Redfield, have proposed something like a "folk-urban continuum," by which folklore is associated solely with "oral tradition" transmitted by "small communities of illiterate agriculturalists, carrying on a homogeneous culture" in contrast to "the towns and cities of . . . literate civilization."²⁶ Similarly, Nilsson argued that folk religions, such as the Eleusinian Mysteries, were religions of "simple and unlettered peasants,"²⁷ which represented a "lower level" of religious ideas than did those of "eminent literary men."²⁸ This view is reminiscent of those of an earlier generation of scholars in which "folklore" was understood generally as the "traditional learning of the uncultured classes of civilized nations."²⁹

The Eleusinian Mysteries originated, however, as a family cult of the Eumolpidae, one of the royal families of Eleusis that claimed descent from

21. Ibid., 13.
22. Ibid., 14.
23. Roger Beck, personal communication.
24. Evelyn-White, "Introduction," xxxiv; Richardson, ed., *Hymn to Demeter*, 3–4, 30–56; Richardson, "Introduction," vii.
25. Honko, *Religion*, 1.
26. Redfield, *Cham Kom*, 1.
27. Nilsson, *Folk Religion*, 21.
28. Ibid., 3–4; Nilsson, *Geschichte*, 784; see also Mikalson, *Athenian Popular Religion*, ix.
29. Thomas, "Letter," 601; Thomas, "Folklore," 601.

the legendary Eumolpos, to whom Demeter, according to the *Homeric Hymn* (154, 475), first revealed her mysteries, and "to which," Nilsson acknowledged, its aristocratic head "admitted whom he pleased."[30] It was the promise of immortality, the transgenerational authority of this family and the continuity of those adopted—or initiated—into it that the Mysteries guaranteed.[31] This account of the origins of the Mysteries, which may be legendary, nevertheless casts doubts on Nilsson's view that the Eleusinian Mysteries were based on the agrarian lore of illiterate masses.

Third, for Gustav Mensching, "folk religion" is a local matter, "limited to ethnic groups, or tribes . . . or at least to natural communities."[32] Folk deities, he concludes, "are exclusively related to a particular people and limited in their power and domain to that people."[33] Because of their expansive appeal to the Graeco-Roman world, an appeal that "transcends ethnic and territorial boundaries,"[34] Mensching concluded, contrary to Nilsson, that the Hellenistic Mysteries (including those of Eleusis) were not a form of folk religion at all but were "pronouncedly" a form of universal religion.[35]

Although both Nilsson and Mensching would agree with J. G. Herder's characterization of folklore as "imprints of the soul," the "living voice" of all mankind,[36] Nilsson nevertheless rejected the earlier view of "folk religion" as "survivals" from "primitive ages."[37] Mensching, on the other hand, understood "every universal religion" to retain a folk or "primitive" substratum. Although the "institution always seeks to preserve its organizational unity against . . . [these] upsetting [primitive] influences . . . [by maintaining] unity, concord, harmony, agreement, and integratedness,"[38] "the nature, the inclinations, and the desires" of that folk stratum, Mensching argued, [remain] "the same throughout the ages."[39]

---

30. Nilsson, *Folk Religion*, 46, 81; see also Mikalson, *Popular Religion*, 85. On the Eleusinian rites of initiation as adoption into kinship with the goddess, see Nilsson, *Folk Religion*, 44; Martin, "Akin to the Gods."

31. Nilsson, *Folk Religion*, 60, 63; Mikalson, *Athenian Popular Religion*, 81–82.

32. Mensching, *Tolerance and Truth*, 14, 101; Mensching, *Structures and Patterns*, 45.

33. Mensching, *Structures and Patterns*, 46; Mensching, *Tolerance and Truth*, 15.

34. Mensching, *Tolerance and Truth*, 18; Mensching, *Structures and Patterns*, 46, 51.

35. Mensching, *Structures and Patterns*, 48–49, 101–2.

36. Herder, *Werke*: 18:137, 9:530, 532, 3:29, 24:266; cited in Wilson, "Herder," 825–26.

37. Nilsson, *Folk Religion*, 3, 5; on the view of folklore as survivals, see Freund, "Cultural Evolution."

38. Mensching, *Tolerance and Truth*, 113.

39. Ibid., 112.

"Folk Religion" as an Analytic Category for the History of Religions?

If the case of the Eleusinian Mysteries is any indication, ambiguities and contradictions in the scholarly understanding and usage of the category "folk religion" seriously compromises its usefulness. Is "folklore"—and with it, "folk religion"—to be defined economically in terms of agrarian in contrast to technological modes of production? Or sociologically, in terms of illiterate rural in contrast to literate urban populations? Or politically, in terms of peasant "masses" in contrast to an empowered elite? Or theologically, as *low* in contrast to *high* forms of religion? Is folk religion to be understood as constrained by locality, or might it be universalizable? Is folk religion preserved solely by oral transmission, or might some literature, such as national epics, serve as its repositories?

It would seem that "folk religion" is less of an analytic category than it is itself a folk category that has little or no theoretical efficacy for the task of academic inquiry. This is the conclusion also reached by Bruce Jackson and Michael Taft while preparing an Index of "A Century of Folklore" for the centennial edition of the *Journal of American Folklore*, one hundred years after the founding of the American Folklore Society. Jackson and Taft reported that "there is still no single theoretical model, or even a small group of theoretical models that encapsulates the field"[40] and, consequently, "folklorists as a group are not of one mind when it comes to the definition of their discipline."[41]

The sentiment that gave rise to intuitions about "folklore" may have a religious bias originating in Reformation theologizing about spiritually pure Protestant folk in contrast to a syncretistic Catholic elite, as Jonathan Z. Smith suggested,[42] or even in the emergence of a Christian orthodoxy itself, as Nilsson suggested.[43] But the category itself was created in the nineteenth century by William Thoms, who intended his new category to differentiate "lore of the people" from "literature."[44] This concern with *the people* reflected the romantic nationalism of the period, "especially in [those northern European and Scandinavian] nations that were young or otherwise in need of support for their cultural identity."[45] So, for example, Nilsson's scholarly

---

40. Jackson and Taft, "Century of Folklore," 5.

41. Ibid., 11.

42. Smith, *Drudgery Divine*, 1–35.

43. Nilsson, *Folk Religion*, 16, 40; see also Butterworth, "Introduction," xv–xvii; Bîrlea, "Folklore," 363.

44. Thomas, "Letter," 362–63.

45. Honko, *Religion*, 7–8; Wilson, "Herder," 830–32; Christian, "Folk Religion," 373.

conclusions about the Eleusinian Mysteries based upon his reading of the *Homeric Hymn to Demeter* were shaped by a romanticization of his own agrarian background in southern Sweden. "I come from an old line of peasants who occupied the same farm for two hundred years," he reminisced, and

> I still know something of how the people thought seventy years ago ... I know something of the sanctity of bread. When I set about writing a history of Greek religion, I want to find out what it was in which the peasant on the farm, the shepherd on the mountains, and the town-dweller believed.[46]

And he explicitly evokes this agrarian background in his interpretation of the Eleusinian planting cycle.[47]

The rather widespread—if imprecise—use this category has achieved in scholarship since the nineteenth century suggests an important corpus of ethnographic and historical data—however intuitively and anecdotally educed—that might better be clarified from the perspective of and in the categories of the cognitive science of religion, a perspective that largely overcomes the kinds of ideologically and theologically constructed dichotomies iterated above.[48]

A Cognitive Perspective on the Eleusinian Mysteries

In his comprehensive *Geschichte der griechischen Religion*, Nilsson defined folk religion as simply "die Rolle der Religion im Volk und im öffentlichen Leben."[49] There is in this definition little (if any) theoretical distinction made between *religion* and *folk religion* apart from the context of its practice—much less any distinction between *folk* and *nonfolk*. For Nilsson, in other words, "folk religion" was not so much an analytical distinction in kind as it was as a functional stipulation of the general category of religion that referred to the actual (öffentliche) religious practices of real people (das Volk). Some fifty years ago, the sociologist of religion Will Herberg argued that people's operative beliefs—those beliefs upon which they actually act—are often very different from their formal beliefs, what these same people believe they believe (i.e., what they tell you they believe when asked

---

46. Cited in Nock, "Preface," vi–vii.
47. Ibid., 51.
48. Pyysiäinen, "Theory of Ideology."
49. Nilsson, *Geschichte*, 791.

about their beliefs).⁵⁰ It is this "formal" or "reflective" belief—what Justin Barrett has termed "theologically correct" belief—that is captured in most ethnographic reports and social science surveys, in the classic epics and canons, and upon which anthropologists and historians—despite their best intentions—continue to rely. Barrett has concluded, therefore, that scholars of religion must get beyond the reflective reports of their informants, including their extant texts, and "systematically observe how [people's operative] religious concepts are used to shape action, generate predictions, and undergird explanations"⁵¹—a somewhat more difficult task for historians. However, since cognitivists have shown that both formal and operative beliefs are constructed and constrained by the same domain-specific mental mechanisms,⁵² we might suggest that those religious beliefs which are operative may not be so far removed from analyses of historical remains as might first appear.

All religious concepts, Pascal Boyer has argued, are characterized by at least a minimal violation of cognitively intuitive assumptions about "reality."⁵³ These violations, however minor, nevertheless place a strain on the cognitive processing systems. "Increasing the cognitive burden of conceptualizing a thing by violating intuitive assumptions," Barrett has concluded, "is especially serious when a situation demands quick and efficient interpretation, information gathering, or prediction."⁵⁴ Barrett gives the example of the Christian god who is "simultaneously [thought of as] non-physical, formless, and omnipresent" but, in "real-time problem solving," is represented and related to anthropomorphically, i.e., as an intentional being located in time and space.⁵⁵

At least two strategies have been selected by religious traditions for relieving the cognitive dissonance between theologically correct affirmations and those cognitive demands requiring rapid and rich inferences that are often required of real-life situations—an intuitive form of processing sometimes termed "online." To modern scholars of religion, the more obvious of these strategies for narrowing the gap between the processing of counterintuitive and intuitive options is to inculcate theologically correct beliefs into the explicit, even the implicit, memory system through catechetical instruction

50. Herberg, *Protestant, Catholic, Jew*, 72.

51. Barrett, "Theological Correctness," 332; see Christian, "Folk Religion," 372.

52. Barrett, "Theological Correctness," 328; Lawson and McCauley, eds., *Rethinking Religion*.

53. Boyer, *Naturalness*; Boyer, *Religion Explained*; Barrett, "Theological Correctness," 331.

54. Barrett, "Theological Correctness," 331.

55. Ibid., 325–27.

and frequent repetition. The ready, even unconscious, recall characteristic of these memory systems increases the likelihood that this resource will be available to online processing. A paradoxical rationale for any remaining violation of theological correctness is well expressed in that influential affirmation of faith, attributed to Tertullian: *credo quia absurdum*.[56]

A second strategy for reconciling counterintuitive knowledge with online processing, more familiar to anthropologists than to scholars of religion, avoids developing any explicit corpus of theologically correct notions at all. It is this latter strategy that is represented by the Eleusinian Mysteries, as by the Hellenistic mysteries generally. As Nilsson concluded, the Eleusinian Mysteries had "no doctrines . . . but only some simple fundamental ideas about life and death as symbolized in the springing up of the new crop from the old,"[57] ideas that "every age might interpret . . . according to its own propensities."[58] This facility for relevant interpretation was not transmitted by catechetical instruction but by attention arresting rituals, especially those of initiation, whose salient, even violent, character impressed the episodic or autobiographical memory system of initiates with what the Greeks termed νοήματα, occluded mental apprehensions that provided initiates collective resources for individual reflection and interpretation.[59]

The fourth-century philosopher Themistius describes the rites at Eleusis as a wandering at first by initiates "through the dark . . . : then come all the terrors before the final initiation, shuddering, trembling, sweating,

56. Tertullian, *De Carne Christi* 5.4; see Sider, "Credo."

57. Nilsson, *Folk Religion*, 63.

58. Ibid., 63. Beck ("Ritual, Myth, Doctrine," 172) has similarly argued for the transmission of interpretative "norms" rather than of any corpus of doctrine by the Mithraic Mysteries.

59. For example, the late second- and early third-century Christian apologist Clement of Alexandria, who was familiar with the mysteries (Clement, *Protrepticus* 2.10–22) and may in his pre-Christian days have been initiated into several of them (Butterworth, "Introduction," xi), writes that

> Every question is solved from pre-existing knowledge . . . for it is after forming conceptions . . . in our mind, that we proceed to the question . . . Often the form of the expression deceives and confuses and disturbs the mind, so that it is not easy to discover [the answer] . . . [for it] is incorporeal, and may be called a thing and a notion, and everything. . . [The] grounds from which the point in question is to be established, must be admitted and known by the learner (Clement, *Stromateis* 8.4). See http://www.earlychristianwritings.com/text/clement-stromata-book8.html/ for the translation by Alexander Roberts and James Donaldson.

Of relevance to this discussion is the social cognitive neuroscience distinction drawn between "reflexion" and "reflection" in the important paper by Lieberman et al., "Reflexion and Reflection." (I am indebted to Ilkka Pyysiäninen for bringing this paper to my attention.)

amazement."[60] Whether or not any physical violence was actually inflicted, it was, according to Aristotle, the psychological effects consequent upon their anticipation that characterized initiation into the mysteries (Aristotle, *frag.* 15, in Synesius, *Oratio de regno* 48). These effects were heightened by the use of blindfolds, which would have further contributed to the nocturnal disorientation of the initiates,[61] by acoustic anomalies such as the sudden sounding of a gong from the midst of the darkness by the Eleusinian hierophant in summons of Kore from the underworld,[62] by a preparatory period of fasting,[63] by a somatic deprivation that would have heightened all the sensory effects of the initiation and contributed to its salient character, and possibly by the effects of a hallucinogenic beverage, the κυκεών, the preparatory ritual drink of the mysteries.[64]

The initiatory "night of the mysteries" at Eleusis culminated, according to Plutarch, with an abrupt burst of brilliant light that accompanied the sudden emergence of the hierophant from the Anaktoron and that astonished the disoriented initiates (Plutarch, *Moralia* 81E; also Hippolytus, *Refutatio omnium haeresium* 5.8.40). When the initiates emerged from their initiatory ordeals of darkness into revelatory light, they were, in the words of Themistius, "received into pure regions and meadows, with voices and dances and the majesty of holy sounds and shapes."[65]

Modes of Religiosity and the Eleusinian Mysteries

The suggestion of two selective strategies for relieving the cognitive burden which the processing of counterintuitive ideas occasion and for rendering them more accessible to online processing accords with, and were in part inspired by, a theory of two modes of religious transmission, a "doctrinal" and an "imagistic," proposed by the British anthropologist Harvey Whitehouse.[66] In brief, Whitehouse contends that a clustering of variables characterizes the doctrinal tendency, including a digital or discursive style of codification, which may be found in nonliterate contexts, but that is most often charac-

---

60. Stobaeus 4, cited by Mylonas, *Eleusis*, 264–65.
61. Bianchi, *Greek Mysteries*, 47, 49–50; Martin, "Performativity," 204–5 n21.
62. Clinton, *Myth and Cult*, 86 n128.
63. Mylonas, *Eleusis*, 258–59.
64. Wasson et al., *Road*.
65. Stobaeus 4, cited by Mylonas, *Eleusis*, 264–65; compare Apuleius, *Metamorphoses* 11.23 on Isiac initiation.
66. Whitehouse, *Inside the Cult*; Whitehouse, *Arguments and Icons*; Whitehouse, *Modes of Religiosity*.

teristic of literate societies or of those influenced by them; a transmission of beliefs by means of repetitive ritual and routinized instruction; and a wide dissemination of tradition as constitutive of large, imagined communities in which group affinities are largely anonymous. By contrast, the variables characteristic of an imagistic mode of religiosity, according to Whitehouse, include an analogic or imagistic style of codification; transmission through infrequently performed rituals rendered memorable through intense sensory pageantry and heightened emotionality; and an enduring cohesion of small, face-to-face communities of participants.[67]

According to Whitehouse, the two modes of religiosity he proposes rely on and are constrained by different memory systems. The catechetical instruction in and repetitive reinforcement of beliefs, which are characteristic of the doctrinal mode, become encoded as generalized schemas in the explicit memory system and rely upon this system for their transmission. The unique and personalized experiences characteristic of the imagistic mode are, on the other hand, encoded in the episodic, or autobiographical, memory system and rely upon this system for meaningful cohesion.

A particularly salient type of episodic memory, often referred to as "flashbulb" memory, is consequential upon participation in some particularly traumatic or vivid event,[68] and especially with the abrupt and overwhelming sentience characteristic of many initiation rites. The elaborate, costly, and vivid initiatory rites of the Eleusinian Mysteries, complete with ritualized flashbulb-like effects, and a consonant absence of any formal or authoritative doctrine seem to support a conclusion about these Mysteries that is consonant with Whitehouse's predictions about an imagistic mode of religiosity.

Mensching's characterization of "universal religion," on the other hand, accords well with Whitehouse's predictions concerning a doctrinal mode of religiosity. Central to universal religion, according to Mensching, is the preservation of right doctrine,[69] which "demands utmost formal rigidity in teaching, cult, and jurisdiction, [and] which, in turn, implies closure to new insights and experiences."[70] Such a "religious institution" is, for Mensching, the only authority capable of controlling the masses in matters of faith, cult, and ethical behavior.[71] Consequently, "universal religion" is, ac-

---

67. See Whitehouse, *Inside the Cult*, 197, table 5.

68. Brown and Kulik, "Flashbulb Memory"; Whitehouse, *Arguments and Icons*, 119–21.

69. Mensching, *Tolerance and Truth*, 104.

70. Ibid., 105.

71. Ibid., 106–7.

cording to Mensching, "always supra-ethnic... [and] strives for geographic universality or global expansion."[72] Mensching's conclusion that the Hellenistic Mysteries, including those celebrated at Eleusis, represent examples of universal religion does not agree, however, with my analysis of these Mysteries as instantiations of Whitehouse's imagistic modality. But if these Mystery religions are not universalistic in Mensching's sense and are best understood as instantiations of the imagistic modality—which, Whitehouse predicts, resists extensive dissemination—how might we explain their empirewide attraction and distribution?[73]

The Widespread Appeal of the Hellenistic Mystery Cults

Although rites in celebration of Demeter were widespread, her Eleusinian Mysteries, it might be argued, never lost their local character; rival Mysteries of Demeter, those performed in Sicily for example, never realized the appeal of those held at Eleusis, where participants from throughout the empire traveled to be initiated. This attraction of participants to the Eleusinian rites of Demeter begs the question, however, of their locative character. Although other of the Hellenistic deities retained their ethnic character—Dionysus like Demeter was a Greek deity, Isis was Egyptian, Mithras was Persian, and so forth—their Mysteries, which modeled themselves, at least in part, on the Eleusinian Mysteries, were transported throughout the Roman empire.

Douglas Gragg has recently suggested a most interesting thesis regarding the general attraction of the mystery religions by employing the predictions of the McCauley-Lawson "ritual form hypothesis"[74]—predictions based on a common feature of human cognition universally deployed in the representation of agents and actions.[75] Gragg notes an absence from the official Roman ritual system of any special agent rituals—rituals defined by McCauley and Lawson as those in which the role of the current ritual's actor

---

72. Ibid.

73. Whereas religions operating in the imagistic mode may become distributed across a wide area, often leading observers to conclude they are part of a unified tradition, they are nevertheless still characterized by a localism which may be quite different from groups in neighboring regions, or even from groups within a particular region (Whitehouse, *Arguments*, 72, 77). Whitehouse gives the example of the Taro Cult in Papua New Guinea (ibid., 72, 77–80); I have suggested that this is the case also with the Hellenistic mysteries, especially with reference to the Mysteries of Mithras (Martin, "Performativity").

74. Gragg, "Old and New"; McCauley and Lawson, *Bringing Ritual*.

75. Lawson and McCauley, eds., *Rethinking Religion*, ii, 9.

is represented as the deity or as the direct agent of the deity.[76] Rather, Roman religion was dominated by what McCauley and Lawson term special patient rituals—rituals in which the deity is not the actor but is the recipient of the ritual action.[77] Such special patient rituals are exemplified for McCauley and Lawson by sacrifice,[78] and Gragg affirms the scholarly consensus that rites of sacrifice were central to Roman religion[79]—as they were to that of the Greeks before them.[80]

Since the ritually mediated connection to the gods in special patient rituals is, in McCauley's and Lawson's theoretical scheme, less intimate in comparison with special agent rituals, they also carry less finality and are (indeed must be) repeatable.[81] Such religious systems as the Roman, they conclude,

> in which special patient rituals receive the overwhelming (if not exclusive) emphasis involve the uninterrupted repetition of rituals that have [comparatively] unremarkable levels of sensory pageantry and involve participants doing things to satisfy the . . . [deities] time and time again. Although they may enjoy long periods of . . . stability, . . . tedium is inevitable. If current cultural arrangements do not permit creative responses and the generation of new cultural representations, that tedium will gradually diminish the popularity of the prevailing cultural representations. Religious systems will not last in which such tedium goes forever unrelieved.[82]

We might suggest that the attraction of the mysteries was that their dramatic special agent rites of initiation provided relief from the dominant Roman system of repetitive and routinized special patient rituals, a system that had, in any case, fallen into neglect by the end of the republican period.[83] This neglect was exacerbated by a perception that the traditional gods no longer responded to sacrificial entreaty, a perception based (at least in part) in the political and moral crises surrounding the Punic wars (Livy 25.1). The new mysteries, on the other hand, provided many, if not all, citizens of Rome the creative possibility for generating "new cultural representations" by means

76. McCauley and Lawson, *Bringing Ritual*, 26, 35.
77. Ibid., 13, 26, 30–31.
78. Ibid., 26, 32, 147.
79. Turcan, *Gods*, 103.
80. Burkert, *Lore and Science*, 182.
81. McCauley and Lawson, *Bringing Ritual*, 31.
82. Ibid., 193.
83. Ferguson, *Religions*, 74.

of the "spontaneous exegetical reflections," which tended to follow upon their emotionally heightened initiation rites.[84] The nonexclusivistic initiations into one or more of these cults, Gragg concludes, were not competitive with but supplemental to traditional Roman religion. McCauley and Lawson term such a "complement of rituals" a "balanced ritual system."[85] While such balanced systems are not necessarily any more stable than "unbalanced" ones, they are nevertheless a characteristic of "virtually all of the world's most successful religions."[86]

"One of the factors that *is* critical to any stability that balanced systems might achieve," McCauley and Lawson argue, is the capacity of these systems to maintain conceptual control over "the interpretations of the special agent rituals that periodically inject . . . [their] stimulating experiences."[87] The conceptual resources transmitted by official Roman religion have, however, been overlooked by modern scholars of religion because of their embeddedness in the political system.[88] In the conventional view of the celebrated classicist and historian of religion Arthur Darby Nock, for example, "Roman religion was made up of traditional practice . . . animated by a patriotic spirit."[89] But the classicist C. Robert Phillips has questioned Nock's conclusion that Roman religion was, consequently, "not a matter of belief."[90] "Roman religion," Phillips demurs, "by its very postulation of superhuman beings and rituals for dealing with them cannot be mere actions."[91] I would like to suggest that the *beliefs* transmitted by the Roman ritual systems were not the sui generis kinds of beliefs familiar from post-Renaissance views of religion as representing a domain distinct from that of the state but were, in fact, concerns about "the meaning of Roman life and history"[92]—a civic canon legitimated, not only by claims to the authority of superhuman agen-

84. Whitehouse, "Modes of Religiosity," 305–6.
85. McCauley and Lawson, *Bringing Ritual*, 181.
86. Ibid.
87. Ibid. Whereas the Mysteries of Mithras, for example, had also developed their own complement of both special agent and special patient rituals (Martin, "Ritual Competence"), the Roman cults of Mithras, like the other Hellenistic mysteries, never developed any centralized mechanism for widespread conceptual control.
88. Malina, *Christian Origins*, 85–86. The complex relationship between the religious and the political, especially with respect to the introduction of new cults, was as characteristic of the Greek as of the Roman world (Garland, *Introducing*).
89. Nock, "Religious Developments," 469; see Beard et al., *Religions of Rome*, 117–18.
90. Nock, "Religious Developments," 469.
91. Phillips, "Sociology," 2710.
92. Beard et al., *Religions of Rome*, 75, 113.

cy, but also by that of state authority exercised through the Roman Senate by the religious functionaries it legitimated. Whereas Gragg argues that the rituals of the Roman religious system represented a minimalist, "cognitively optimum" position,[93] I should like to suggest that their religiopolitical conceptual load, their authoritative structure and control, their complexity, and their often costly performances indicate a social commitment far in excess of that dedicated to the minimally counterintuitive manifestations, and exhibit rather characteristics of Whitehouse's doctrinal mode of religiosity.[94]

The official religion of Rome maintained its conceptual control over any new interpretations occasioned by the special agent rituals of the mysteries in two ways. First, official Rome might proscribe outright any religious innovations perceived to be a threat to Roman values, as did the Senate in 186 BCE with respect to the celebrations of the Bacchanalia, for example, or as did certain of the emperors three centuries later with respect to some of the early Christianities. Second, those new religions deemed to be of no threat to the state were tacitly accepted (for example, the Mysteries of Mithras[95]), while others judged to be of actual benefit to the state received official sanction—for example, the importation of the Cybele cult by Senatorial decree in 205–204 BCE, and since the Antonine period, even her bloody mystery of the *taurobolium*, or of the Mysteries of Isis by Caligula.[96] And, of course, Romans traveled, since late republican times, to Eleusis to be initiated into the Mysteries of Demeter (Plutarch, *Sulla* 26.1). Subsequently, a number of Roman emperors, from Augustus to Aurelius, gave official sanction to

---

93. Boyer first used "cognitive optimum" to refer to those counterintuitive claims that combine a rich intuitive base with a limited series of violations in ways that are attention-demanding and are, thus, both learnable and nonnatural (Boyer, *Naturalness*, 121, 122). "Cognitive optimum" is, however, a designation employed variously by different cognitivists and begs therefore greater precision from those who evoke it. Does this description refer, for example, to particular claims or concepts, or might it refer to (or be the explanation for) entire sets or systems of concepts? E.g., "traditional Roman religion," as apparently suggested by Gragg—and for which there is some experimental support (Atran and Norenzayan, "Evolutionary Landscape," 32–39).

94. Ander Lisdorf, working at Aarhus University, has arrived at much the same conclusion (personal communication, 26 September and 2 October 2003).

95. Even as traditional Roman religion was concerned with maintaining "the meaning of Roman life and history," the Mysteries of Mithras, seem, in connection with the Roman military and civil service from which a number of its initiates were drawn, to have contributed to the introduction, legitimization, and maintenance of "Romanness," especially in the liminal regions of the empire (Martin, "Mithraic Tauroctony," 222; Turcan, *Gods*, 195). Similarly, the Eleusinian Mysteries, with their fundamental requirement that initiates be able to speak Greek; see, Mylonas, *Eleusis*, 248.

96. Turcan, *Gods*, 189–90.

the Eleusinian Mysteries by their visits there, their own initiations,[97] and by their financial support of the sanctuary; even Constantine excepted the Eleusinian celebrations from his proscription of nocturnal rites.[98]

Conclusions

I have concluded on the basis of antithetical analyses of the Eleusinian Mysteries by prominent historians of religion, that the category "folklore" has no theoretical basis and, consequently, no analytic usefulness for the academic study of religion (*Religionswissenschaft*). Rather, I have suggested that "folklore" is itself a folk category, intuitively employed by folklorists (and others) to identify—on the basis of their own politically and religiously reflective biases—the products of what were often termed by others a "primitive" folk. Like most intuitions, however, those concerning folklore can, as Pascal Boyer has argued, be "valuable as a starting point in a more serious investigation."[99] Employing the insights of the cognitive science of religion for such an investigation, I have suggested that the kinds of data adduced by folklorists might better be organized from such a cognitive perspective.

The cognitive psychologist Justin Barrett, for example, has differentiated data expressed in the absence of reflective belief systems from those remembered and transmitted by a reflective systematization and institutionalized recording of such data.[100] That is to say, what religion ought to be in the views of religious specialists can be differentiated from how religious people—including the religious specialist—*actually* behave and think in those quotidian situations that require rapid and efficient cognitive responses. Some might be tempted, consequently, to stipulate that "folk religion" might be an appropriate designation for such actual, online notions and behaviors. However, this differentiation between the "ought" and the "actual" is best understood as a differentiation of degree and not of kind. As I argued some years ago with reference to Hellenistic religions, "folk piety belonged . . . to the same world as the so-called 'higher' forms of spirituality and knowledge."[101] Following the cognitive anthropologist Harvey Whitehouse, I have argued further that those notions and behaviors we designate religious must not only be those having to do with superhuman agency—a characteristic of religion to be sure and of much folklore

97. Mylonas, *Eleusis*, 129, 161, 176, 231–33.
98. Beard et al., *Religions of Rome*, 223, 374.
99. Boyer, *Religion Explained*, 54.
100. Barrett, "Theological Correctness."
101. Martin, *Hellenistic Religions*, 35.

as well—but also consists of comparatively costly techniques for rendering offline, reflective notions and practices more available to online demand—a necessary condition for religion but not for folklore. Because of the costliness associated with the systematic transmission of beliefs and practices usually considered religious, whether doctrinal or imagistic, it might not be too venturesome to suggest simply doing away with the category of "folk religion" as a non-analytic oxymoron indistinguishable, in any case, from the relatively costless—cognitively and economically—notions and practices of "folklore," and to reserve the category of "religion" to refer to costly commitments to notions and practices legitimated by claims to superhuman agency.

I have suggested, finally, that cognitive theories, such as those employed here, can help historians of religion recognize that "different kinds of epistemological structures require different kinds of historical descriptions,"[102] and that such descriptive and functional categories can be explained in terms of predictable patterns of human expression shared by all peoples. The historical case of the Eleusinian Mysteries, I have argued, conforms to many cognitivist predictions, a conformation, it would seem, that indeed recommends the cognitive science of religion as a theoretical approach that can provide new and more useful analytic models and methods for the further study of the res gestae of religious folk everywhere.

References

Atran, Scott, and Ara Norenzayan. "Religion's Evolutionary Landscape: Counterintuition, Commitment, Compassion, Communion." *Behavioral and Brain Sciences* 27 (2004) 713–70.

Barrett, Justin L. "Theological Correctness: Cognitive Constraint and the Study of Religion." *Method & Theory in the Study of Religion* 11 (1999) 325–39.

Beard, Mary, et al. *Religions of Rome*. Vol. 1, *A History*. Cambridge: Cambridge University Press, 1998.

Beck, Roger. "Ritual, Myth, Doctrine, and Initiation in the Mysteries of Mithras: New Evidence from a Cult Vessel." *Journal of Roman Studies* 90 (2000) 145–80.

Benedict, Ruth. "Folklore." In *Encyclopaedia of the Social Sciences*, edited by Edwin R. A. Seligman and Alwin Johnson, 6:288–93. New York: Macmillan, 1931.

Bîrlea, Ovidiu. "Folklore." In *Encyclopedia of Religion*, edited by Mircea Eliade, 5:363–70. New York: Macmillan, 1987.

Bianchi, Ugo. *The Greek Mysteries*. Iconography of Religions, Section XVII, Greece and Rome, fasc. 3. Leiden: Brill, 1976.

Boyer, Pascal. *The Naturalness of Religious Ideas: A Cognitive Theory of Religion*. Berkeley: University of California Press, 1994.

———. *Religion Explained: The Evolutionary Origins of Religious Thought*. New York: Basic Books, 2001.

---

102. Malley, *How the Bible Works*, 271.

Brown, Roger, and James Kulik. "Flashbulb Memory." In *Memory Observed: Remembering in Natural Contexts*, edited by Ulric Neisser, 23–40. San Francisco: Freeman, 1982.
Burkert, Walter. *Lore and Science and Ancient Pythagoreanism*. Translated by Edwin L. Minar Jr. Cambridge: Harvard University Press, 1972.
Butterworth, G. W. "Introduction." In *Clement of Alexandria*. Translated by George W. Butterworth, xi–xviii. LCL 92. Cambridge: Harvard University Press, 1960.
Christian, William A., Jr. "Folk Religion: An Overview." In *Encyclopedia of Religion*, edited by Mircea Eliade, 5:370–74. New York: Macmillan, 1987.
Clinton, Kevin. *Myth and Cult: The Iconography of the Eleusinian Mysteries*. Skrifter-Svenska institut i Athen 11. Stockholm: Swedish Institute at Athens, 1992.
Evelyn-White, Hugh G. "Introduction." In *Hesiod: The Homeric Hymns and Homerica*. Translated by Hugh G. Evelyn-White, ix–xlii. LCL 57. Cambridge: Harvard University Press, 1936.
Ferguson, John. *The Religions of the Roman Empire*. Aspects of Greek and Roman Life. London: Thames & Hudson, 1970.
Frazer, James. *The Golden Bough*. London: Macmillan, 1914.
Freund, Hugo A. "Cultural Evolution, Survivals, and Immersion: The Implications for Nineteenth-Century Folklore Studies." In *100 Years of American Folklore Studies: A Conceptual History*, edited by William M. Clements, 12–15. Washington DC: The American Folklore Society, 1988.
Garland, Robert. *Introducing New Gods: The Politics of Athenian Religion*. Ithaca: Cornell University Press, 1992.
Gennep, Arnold van. *The Rites of Passage*. Translated by Monika B. Vizedom and Gabrielle L. Caffee. Phoenix Books. Chicago: University of Chicago Press, 1960.
Gragg, Douglas L. "Old and New in Roman Religion: A Cognitive Account." In *Theorizing Religions Past: Archaeology, History, and Cognition*, edited by Luther H. Martin and Harvey Whitehouse, 69–86. Cognitive Science of Religion Series. Walnut Creek, CA: AltaMira, 2004.
Herder, Johann G. *Sämmtliche Werke*. Edited by Berhard L. Suphan. 33 vols. Hildesheim: Olms, 1967–1968.
Honko, Lauri. "The Kalevala and the World's Epics: An Introduction." In *Religion, Myth, and Folklore in the World's Epics*, edited by Lauri Honko, 1–26. Religion and Society 30. Berlin: de Gruyter, 1990.
Herberg, Will. *Protestant-Catholic-Jew: An Essay in American Religious Sociology*. Garden City, NY: Doubleday, 1960.
Jackson, Bruce, and Michael Taft. "A Century of Folklore." *Journal of American Folklore* 101/402 (1988) 5–10.
Lawson, E. Thomas, and Robert N. McCauley, eds. *Rethinking Religion: Connecting Cognition and Culture*. Cambridge: Cambridge University Press, 1990.
Lieberman, Matthew D. et al. "Reflexion and Reflection: A Social Cognitive Neuroscience Approach to Attributional Inference." *Advances in Experimental Psychology* 34 (2002) 200–250.
Malina, Bruce J. *Christian Origins and Cultural Anthropology*. 1986. Reprint, Eugene, OR: Wipf & Stock, 2010.
Malley, Brian. *How the Bible Works: An Anthropological Study of Evangelical Biblicism*. Cognitive Science of Religion Series. Walnut Creek, CA: AltaMira, 2004.
Mannhardt, Wilhelm. *Antike Wald- und Feldkulte*. Berlin: Borntraeger. 1875–1877.

Martin, Luther H. "Akin to the Gods or Simply One to Another: Comparisons with Respect to Religion in Antiquity." In *Vergleichen und Verstehen in der Religionswissenschaft*, edited by Hans-Joachim Klimkeit, 147–59. Studies in Oriental Religions 41. Wiesbaden: Harrassowitz, 1997.

———. *Hellenistic Religions: An Introduction.* New York: Oxford University Press, 1987.

———. "Performativity, Narrativity and Cognition: 'Demythologizing' the Roman Cult of Mithras." In *Rhetoric and Reality in Early Christianities*, edited by Willi Braun, 187–217. Studies in Christianity and Judaism 16. Waterloo, ON: Wilfrid Laurier University Press, 2005.

———. "Reflections on the Mithraic Tauroctony as Cult Scene." In *Studies in Mithraism: Papers Associated with the Mithraic Panel Organized on the Occasion of the XVIth Congress of the International Association for the History of Religions, Rome 1990*, edited by John Hinnells, 217–24. Storia delle religioni 9. Rome: "L' Erma" di Bretschneider, 1994.

———. "Ritual Competence and Mithraic Ritual." In *Religion as a Human Capacity: A Festschrift in Honor of E. Thomas Lawson*, edited by Timothy Light and Brian C. Wilson, 245–63. SHR 99. Leiden: Brill, 2003.

McCauley, Robert N., and E. Thomas Lawson. *Bringing Ritual to Mind: Psychological Foundations of Cultural Forms.* Cambridge: Cambridge University Press, 2002.

Mensching, Gustav. *Structures and Patterns of Religion.* Translated by H.-J. Klimkeit and Sarma V. Srinivasa. Delhi: Motilal Banarsidass, 1976.

———. *Tolerance and Truth in Religion.* Translated by H.-J. Klimkeit. Tuscaloosa: University of Alabama Press, 1971.

Mikalson, Jon D. *Athenian Popular Religion.* Chapel Hill: University of North Carolina Press, 1983.

Mylonas, George E. *Eleusis and the Eleusinian Mysteries.* Princeton: Princeton University Press, 1961.

Nilsson, Martin P. *Geschichte der Griechischen Religion.* Vol. 1, *Die Religion Griechenlands bis auf die griechische Weltherrschaft.* 2 vols. Handbuch der Altertumswissenschaft. Munich: Beck, 1955.

———. *Greek Folk Religion.* Harper Torchbooks. The Cloister Library. New York: Harper, 1961.

Nock, Arthur D. "Forward." In *Greek Folk Religion*, v–vii. Harper Torchbooks. The Cloister Library. New York: Harper, 1961.

———. "Religious Developments from the Close of the Republic to the Reign of Nero." In *The Augustan Empire 44 BC—AD 70*, edited by Stanley A. Cook et al., 465–511. The Cambridge Ancient History 10. Cambridge: Cambridge University Press, 1934.

Phillips, Charles R. "The Sociology of Religious Knowledge in the Roman Empire to A.D. 284." *ANRW* II 16.3 (1986) 2677–773.

Pyysiäinen, Ilkka. "A Theory of Ideology: Implications for Religion and Science." *Method & Theory in the Study of Religion* 14.3/4 (2002) 316–33.

Redfield, Robert. *Cham Kom, a Maya Village.* Carnegie Institution of Washington. Publication 448. Washington DC: Carnegie Institution, 1934.

Richardson, N. J., ed. *The Homeric Hymn to Demeter.* Oxford: Clarendon, 1974.

———. "Introduction." In *The Homeric Hymns.* Translated by Jules Cashford, vii–xxxv. Penguin Classics. London: Penguin, 2003.

Sider, Robert D. "*Credo Quia Absurdum?*" *Classical World* 73/7 (1980) 417–19.

Smith Jonathan Z. *Drudgery Divine: On the Comparison of Early Christianities and the Religions of Late Antiquity.* Jordan Lectures in Comparative Religion 14. Chicago Studies in the History of Judaism. Chicago: University of Chicago Press, 1990.

——. "Folklore." In *The HarperCollins Dictionary of Religion*, edited by Jonathan Z. Smith, 365. San Francisco: HarperCollins, 1995.

——, ed. *The HarperCollins Dictionary of Religion.* San Francisco: HarperCollins, 1995.

Thoms, William J. [Letter, published under the pseudonym Ambrose Merton]. *Athenaeum* (22 August 1846) 362–63.

Thomas, Northcote Whitbridge. "Folklore." In *Encyclopædia Britannica*, 10:601. 11th ed. Cambridge: Cambridge University Press, 1911.

Turcan, Robert. *The Gods of Ancient Rome: Religion in Everyday Life from Archaic to Imperial Times.* Translated by Antonia Nevil. New York: Routledge, 2000.

Turner, John R. G. Review of *The Blank Slate*, by Steven Pinker. *Times Literary Supplement* (September 27 2002), 6–7.

Wasson, R. Gordon, et al. *The Road to Eleusis: Unveiling the Secret of the Mysteries.* Harvest/HBJ Book. Ethno-mycological Studies 4. New York: Harcourt Brace Javonovich, 1978.

Whitehouse, Harvey. *Arguments and Icons: Divergent Modes of Religiosity.* Oxford: Oxford University Press, 2000.

——. *Inside the Cult: Religious Innovation and Transmission in Papua New Guinea.* Oxford: Oxford University Press, 1995.

——. *Modes of Religiosity: A Cognitive Theory of Religious Transmission.* Cognitive Science of Religion Series. Walnut Creek, CA: AltaMira, 2004.

——. "Modes of Religiosity: Towards a Cognitive Explanation of the Sociopolitical Dynamics of Religion." *Method & Theory in the Study of Religion* 14/3–4 (2002) 293–315.

Wilson, William A. *Folklore and Nationalism in Modern Finland.* Bloomington: Indiana University Press, 1976.

——. "Herder, Folklore, and Romantic Nationalism." *Journal of Popular Culture* 6/4 (1973) 819–35.

14

Mithras, *Milites*, and Bovine Legs

A Response to Aleš Chalupa and Tomáš Glomb, "The Third Symbol of the *Miles* Grade on the Floor Mosaic of the Felicissimus Mithraeum in Ostia: A New Interpretation"

IN THEIR ARTICLE "THE Third Symbol of the *Miles* Grade on the Floor Mosaic of the Felicissimus Mithraeum in Ostia: A New Interpretation," Aleš Chalupa and Tomáš Glomb argue that one of the three symbols associated with the Mithraic initiatory grade of *Miles* on the floor mosaic in the Felicissimus Mithraeum has been misinterpreted. In addition to an image of a helmet and a spear, clear references to accessories appropriate to a *soldier*, there is a third no less distinct but nevertheless equivocal image that has most often been interpreted as a *sarcena* or soldier's sling bag or, less often, as a Phrygian cap. This understanding groups the sling bag with the helmet and spear as images appropriate for an initiatory grade that is named by and associated with the military service.

Chalupa and Glomb correctly question the identification of the ambivalent image of the third Mithraic initiatory grade as a Phrygian cap, since this image appears in another grade from the same mosaic (that of the Father) in an unambiguous and characteristic form and would be, therefore, the only image to be employed twice in the Felicissimus mosaic. The authors also question the identification of this ambivalent image as a *sarcena* (a) because it is a poor visual representation since the shape of a sling bag depends upon its contents; and, more convincingly, (b) because confirmation of this identification rests upon a circular argument whereby a similar image, carried by a Mithraic Soldier portrayed on a fresco in the Santa Prisca mithraeum in Rome, is identified with reference to the image from the Felicissimus mithraeum and vice versa.

Contrary to previous interpretations of the ambiguous image associated with the Mithraic grade of *Miles* represented on the Felicissimus mosaic, Chalupa and Glomb argue that this figure represents, rather, a bovine limb. They argue this interpretation resourcefully by consulting two specialists in animal anatomy who confirm that this image strikingly represents the shape and muscular structure either of a bovine pelvic or of a thoracic limb. And, the authors confirm this identification with reference to other Mithraic monuments, especially the Altar of Flavius Aper from ancient Poetovio. Although other scholars have also identified the image on this altar as a bull's leg, in my opinion, its interpretation is as equivocal as is that of the Felicissimus Mithraeum. While it certainly conforms to the anatomical characteristics of a bull's limb, as Chalupa and Glomb argue, it could also represent the ambiguous shape of a *sarcena*, depending upon the penchant of the viewer. Nevertheless, Chalupa and Glomb have, in my opinion, presented a credible new interpretation of the third symbol of the *Miles* grade as represented on the floor mosaic of the Felicissimus Mithraeum, an interpretation that will need to be carefully attended to in future research.

If the identification of the third symbol of the *Miles* grade as a bull's limb is correct, the question remains why a bull's leg should have military associations. Here Chalupa and Glomb's arguments become less convincing. They suggest this relationship by citing the "Mithras Liturgy," a text from a fifth-century Greek magical papyrus from Egypt that describes a "god," the characteristics of which are "consistent with some known figural monuments of Mithras." The figure is portrayed as holding in his right hand the "golden shoulder of a young calf," which is identified in the text as "the Bear which moves and turns the heavenly vault around." Chalupa and Glomb then refer to Egyptian mythology and astrology in which "a bull's limb could be used as a powerful symbol of the Northern Pole."

Although most scholars reject the "Mithras Liturgy" as reflecting the practices or beliefs of any actual Mithraic community, Chalupa and Glomb nevertheless suppose that this association of Mithras with the bovine limb might "have found its way to some Mithraic communities interested in astrology." Since there was but one documented Mithraic cell in all of Roman-occupied Egypt, this is, without further evidence, a rather weak supposition.[1] However, the authors refer to a zodiac on the stuccoed ceiling of the mithraeum on the island of Ponza that represents the constellations of the Great and Little Bear in its center (i.e., in the pole position). However,

---

1. There is anecdotal and some archaeological evidence for the existence of a mithraeum in Memphis. The later Christian apologetic reference to a mithraeum in Alexandria has not been confirmed by any archaeological evidence. See Martin, "Absence"; Martin, "Cognitive Science."

these somewhat tenuous associations of Mithras with the Northern Pole and again with Egyptian representations of that pole by a bull's limb fails to offer any convincing explanation for why this image would become associated with Mithras's *Milites*.

I find Chalupa and Glomb's arguments in the third section of their paper, in which they attempt to locate the bull's limb in "a Mithraic context," to be the most problematic. Although they fully acknowledge that their arguments in the section are only a "preliminary explorations of possibilities," I find their attempt problematic because of their methodological *essentialization* of that context (whether intentional or not).[2] Essentialization is the assumed view that certain categories—such as "the Mithraic context"—represent an underlying unity that gives them a distinctive identity.[3] Thus the authors speak of "episodes from Mithras' life" generally (twice), of "Mithras' sacred story," of "mythical episodes appearing in the Mithraic sacred narrative," and of "scenes from Mithras' sacred narrative," as though there was some unified story or sacred narrative of Mithras's life that was commonly shared among all Mithraic cells. They then attempt to locate the image of a bull's leg in this universal Mithraic context, which *they* suppose to have existed but for which there is little to no historical documentation, even at a regional level.[4]

In their discussion of a scene on the recently discovered cup from a mithraeum in Mainz, Chalupa and Glomb provide an example of how unrelated Mithraic images might become incorrectly associated by locating them in a synoptically supposed common Mithraic context. The Mainz cup portrays an image of an initiating Father drawing a bow and aiming an arrow at an initiate. The authors (following other scholars) associate this image with those portraying "Mithras shooting an arrow into a rock from which water is spurting." The only thing these two images seem to have in common is a bow, from which, however, the initiating Father threatens to shoot an initiate, but from which Mithras shoots an arrow into a rock. By this bowcentric methodology, the authors might also have referenced the hunting scene from the Dura-Europos mithraeum, in which Mithras is portrayed, astride his horse, aiming an arrow from his drawn bow at his prey in a typical Roman representation of a hunt (*CIMRM* 52). Given that Chalupa

---

2. I have previously noted that the essentialization of categories is a cognitive proclivity of *Homo sapiens* that must be explicitly guarded against by historians in their historiographical reconstructions. See Martin, "Devil."

3. Gelman, *Essential Child*, 3.

4. The authors correctly reject, for example any endeavor "to reconstruct any 'Myth of Mithras from the side scenes flanking' the various tauroctonies of Germania."

and Glomb employ a methodology emphasizing contextual significance, their disregard of the differing local contexts of these images is puzzling.

Rather, the scene on the Mainz cup has more accurately been compared with the initiation panels from the mithraeum in Capua Vetere. Although the initiating Father in this latter context threatens the initiate with a stick-like object, a spear or sword (?), rather than with a bow and arrow, the scenes are comparable in portraying a dominant initiator threatening a submissive initiate, who is represented in both scenes as smaller than the initiator, blindfolded and naked and, therefore, vulnerable. Of course, this tells us nothing about a specifically Mithraic initiatory context since this dominant-submissive relationship between initiator and initiate, together with similar motifs of threat, and of blindfolded and nude initiates are common representations of initiation into the Graeco-Roman mysteries.[5]

Rather than supposing any comprehensive Mithraic context in which to locate seemingly common but the widely distributed finds of decentralized Mithraic cells, I suggest that it might be more profitable to speak of a Mithraic network, a model of relationships that has already been productively employed in historical studies of the ancient Mediterranean world, that has been suggested as the model for early Greek religion and for the successes of early Christianity.[6]

Most succinctly, network theory is part of complexity theory, which explains the internal organization of decentralized patterns where none previously existed.[7] Network models attempt to map specific patterns of social ties between related nodes (which may be delimited as individuals, groups, or clusters of groups). These nodes are not necessarily contingent but are measured by "degrees of separation," that is, by the number of nodes that must be traversed in order to reach a target node rather than by physical distance. There can be a relatively small number of connections; in fact, the minimum requirement to stay connected is but one link per node.[8] For example, we know there was but a single link between the Mithraic cell at the Roman garrison of the Praetorian Guard and that on the Greek island of Andros to which members of the guard had been dispatched (*CIMRM* 2350). Rather than seeking a generalized Mithraic context in which to locate Mithraic finds, in other words, distributed finds, such as the image of the bull's leg, might provide clues to the "short links" (in terms of degree of

---

5. Martin, "Religious Experience."

6. Stark, *Rise*, 20–22, 55–57, 61–68, 115, 193; Barabási, *Linked*, 3–5, 7, 19, 129, 136.

7. Gribbin, *Deep Simplicity*, 125.

8. Barabási, *Linked*, 18.

separation) between nodes by which a Mithraic network might be defined. For example, we know that at each of the sites where legio V Macedonica was stationed, from 167 until the second half of the third century, Mithraic dedications and finds are attested. In fact, L. Valerius Fuscus, who dedicated the Altar of Flavius Aper, to which Chalupa and Glomb refer, served in the legio V Macedonica (*CIMRM* 2286),[9] the emblem of which was the bull—as it was of most of the Roman legions claiming their origin from Caesar![10] Of course, the emblem of an intact bull as an emblem of strength, and power is something other than that of a detached bovine limb. However, detached limbs of bulls, conforming precisely to the anatomical features identified by Chalupa and Glomb, were often used in the carved legs of Roman furniture, as they had been in Assyria, Egypt, and Greece, as representations of strength.[11] Perhaps it is such an emblem of bovine strength that is associated with and displayed by the Mithraic *Milites*?

Of course, assuming a Mithraic network is as tentative as assuming a Mithraic context. However, by mapping what we know of the empirical evidence (i.e., dates and geographic sites of Mithraic finds and of their epidemiology) and by, e.g., military redeployments, it may be possible to reconstruct something of a Mithraic network with more confidence than it takes simply to assume a Mithraic context. Nevertheless, Chalupa and Glomb are to be commended for their credible identification of the ambiguous image associated with the grade of *Miles* in the Felicissimus Mithraeum as a bovine leg and reopening, thereby, a larger discussion about explanations for the diffusion of (supposedly) analogous Mithraic images throughout the Roman Empire.

References

Barabási, Albert-László. *Linked: How Everything Is Connected to Everything Else and What It Means for Business, Science, and Everyday Life*. New York: Plume, 2003.

Daniels, C. M. "The Role of the Roman Army in the Spread and Practice of Mithraism." In *Mithraic Studies: Proceedings of the First International Congress of Mithraic Studies*, edited by John R. Hinnells, 2:249–74. 2 vols. Manchester: Manchester University Press, 1975.

Eidinow, Esther. "Networks and Narratives: A Model for Ancient Greek Religion." *Kernos* 24/1 (2011) 9–38.

Gelman, Susan A. *The Essential Child: Origins of Essentialism in Everyday Thought*. Oxford Series in Cognitive Development. Oxford: Oxford University Press, 2003.

9. Daniels, ""Role," 251.
10. Keppie, *Making*, 120.
11. E.g., "Met Museum: Bull's Leg."

Gribbin, John. *Deep Simplicity: Bringing Order to Chaos and Complexity*. New York: Random House, 2004.

Keppie, Lawrence. *The Making of the Roman Army: From Republic to Empire*. London: Routledge, 1998.

Malkin, Irad. *A Small Greek World: Networks in the Ancient Mediterranean*. Oxford: Oxford University Press, 2011.

Malkin, Irad, et al., eds. *Greek and Roman Networks in the Mediterranean*. London: Routledge, 2011.

Martin, Luther H. "Aspects of 'Religious Experience' among the Graeco-Roman Mystery Religions." *Religion & Theology* 12 (2005) 349–69.

———. "Cognitive Science, Ritual, and the Hellenistic Mystery Religions." *Religion & Theology* 13 (2006) 383–95.

———. "'The Devil Is in the Details': Hellenistic Mystery Initiation Rites; Bridge-Burning or Bridge-Building?" In *Conversion and Initiation in Antiquity: Shifting Identities, Creating Change*, edited by Birgitte S. Bøgh et al., 153–68. Early Christianity in the Context of Antiquity 16. Frankfurt: Lang, 2014.

———. "The Surprising Absence of Mithras Cult in Roman Egypt." In *Alternative Voices: A Plurality Approach for Religious Studies; Essays in Honor of Ulrich Berner*, edited by Afe Adogame et al., 100–15. Critical Studies in Religion, Religionswissenschaft 4. Göttingen: Vandenhoeck & Ruprecht, 2013.

The Met Museum: Bull's Leg. http://www.metmuseum.org/collections/search-the-collections/100004096/.

Stark, Rodney. *The Rise of Christianity: A Sociologist Reconsiders History*. Princeton: Princeton University Press, 1996.

15

"Star Talk": Native Competence; Initiatory Comprehension

In his impressive and important study of *The Religion of the Mithras Cult in the Roman Empire* (2006), Roger Beck works as a historical anthropologist doing fieldwork in that "foreign country," famously identified by the novelist L. P. Hartley as *the past*, "where," Hartley avers, "they do things differently."[1] The foreign country in which Beck conducts his "fieldwork" is that of Graeco-Roman antiquity, and one of the things he finds that they do differently there is to speak another language, not just the Greek and Latin we learn today in school but, Beck argues, also a Graeco-Roman astral language that he calls "star-talk."

"Star-talk," Beck proposes, is "both an actually existing language spoken [and] written by ancient astronomers and astrologers [as] ... a specialist discourse in Greek and Latin [but is also] ... an imagined language thought to be spoken by its own signs";[2] that is, star-talk is a language understood to be spoken both by the stars and by humans who replicate "this celestial language in various discourses of their own."[3] According to Beck, this star-talk "has a set grammar and a set semantics transparent to all users and accessible to anyone who wants to learn it"[4]—including our intrepid historical anthropologist. There are, he concludes, no arcana in this language, "though the grammar and semantics generally operate below the level of conscious manipulation. (If you have to think about them while speaking, you have not yet acquired full competence to the standard of a native speaker)"[5]—a

1. Hartley, *Go-Between*, 1.
2. Beck, *Religion of the Mithras Cult*, 160.
3. Ibid., 7, 188.
4. Ibid., 160.
5. Ibid., 161.

characteristic, of course, of any natural language. Finally the grammar of star-talk, like that of any language "offers the limitless potential for generating new utterances within the set grammar,"[6] which, as Beck notes, the output of Graeco-Roman horoscopal astrology clearly confirms.[7] Beck argues that Mithraists (and others) communicated in a specifically identifiable idiom or jargon of standard star-talk discourse,[8] even as, for example, African Americans will sometimes converse in Ebonics, a vernacular dialect of American English that is distinctively different from standard usage.[9]

Symbols as Evocative

Mithraic remains are notable for an absence of written texts but for an abundance of material imagery. Students of Mithraism have long presumed that these images are symbols that "mean" in the sense of language signs that are "paired with their interpretations in a code structure,"[10] and that this meaning constitutes a hermeneutical object of study. However, the cognitive anthropologist Dan Sperber, in his seminal monograph, *Rethinking Symbolism* (1975), has persuasively argued that symbols do not mean in this sense of language signs; rather, they evoke—a position argued for Mithraic symbolism by Richard Gordon (1980).[11] For Sperber, *evocation* refers, most simply, to individuals' search of long-term memory for relevant recollections,[12] whenever attention is *focused* upon new information.[13] Beck is theoretically more venturesome. He argues that in addition to their evocative utility,[14] Mithraic symbols also function as language signs in precisely the way that Sperber contests.[15]

6. Ibid., 160.
7. Ibid., 162.
8. Ibid., 7.
9. Rickford, "Ebonics."
10. Sperber, *Rethinking Symbolism*, 85.
11. Gordon, "Reality, Evocation."
12. Ibid., 118–20.
13. Ibid., 119, 136–37.
14. Beck, *Religion of the Mithras Cult*, 163.
15. Ibid., 157.

Symbols as Linguistic Signs

The model of language as sign derives, of course, from Ferdinand de Saussure's structural analysis of language as an arbitrary relationship between signifier and signified;[16] the model of this structure as code derives from telecommunications technology as inspired by the work of Claude Shannon (and others) in the late 1930s and 1940s by which communication is achieved by a more or less accurate encoding and decoding of messages.[17]

Beck proposes that the code structure of star-talk is the strict geometry—or, as he prefers, uranometry—of basic Hellenistic astronomy, a system extremely rich in necessary relationships[18]—a number of which Beck fully explicates.[19] As he explains, "once the decision had been taken to deploy certain star-talk signs rather than others, what the signs mean and say in collaboration with each other at the literal level is fixed and unalterable."[20] It is this astronomical logic of relationships that Beck identifies as the grammar of star-talk.[21]

Assuming that Beck is correct in his analysis of Mithraic imagery as a set of signs functioning in a code system—and his elucidation of this hypothesis is far more sophisticated than I am able to represent here—the problem of *communication* still remains. In *Relevance*, a work published subsequent to Sperber's earlier *Rethinking Symbolism* that is followed by Beck, Sperber in collaboration with the linguist Deidre Wilson argue that a code-model for language is insufficient to fully explain communication[22]—and, surely, the capacity of star-talk to communicate is central to Beck's linguistic thesis.[23]

Sperber and Wilson argue that "cultural phenomena," such as the imagery associated with Mithraism, "do not, in general, serve to convey [the] precise and predictable messages [the code model supposes]. [Rather] they focus the attention of the audience in certain directions; they help to impose some structure on experience. To that extent, some similarity of representations between the . . . [source and the receiver of a message], and hence some degree of communication, is achieved. However, this is a long

---

16. Saussure, *Linguistics*.
17. Shannon, "Symbolic Analysis"; Shannon, "Mathematical Theory."
18. Beck, *Religion of the Mithras Cult*, 162.
19. Ibid., chapters 7 and 9.
20. Ibid., 162.
21. Ibid., 161.
22. Sperber and Wilson, *Relevance*, 21.
23. Beck, *Religion of the Mithras Cult*, 66, 163, 258.

way from the identity of representations which coded communication is designed to guarantee."[24] While, "it is true," they conclude, "that a language is a code which pairs phonetic and semantic representations of sentences," there nevertheless remains a gap between semantic representations "and the thoughts actually communicated by utterances."[25] They propose to fill this gap with what they term "the mutual-knowledge hypothesis."[26]

In formulating their "mutual-knowledge hypothesis," Sperber and Wilson follow the philosopher of language Paul Grice[27] in recognizing that any "speaker who intends an utterance to be interpreted in a particular way must also expect the hearers to be able to supply a context which allows that interpretation to be received."[28] As they argue, the "only way to make sure that misunderstandings . . . could not arise would be to make sure that the context actually used by the hearer was always identical to the one envisaged by the speaker."[29]

The Mithraeum as Contextual Field

More recently, the evolutionary anthropologist Michael Tomasello, in his study of the *Origins of Human Communication* (2008), follows both Grice and Sperber and Wilson in similarly emphasizing the centrality of context for communication. "Most fundamentally," he writes, "communicator and recipients interact cooperatively to get the message across . . . which is their joint goal."[30] "It is important to note," he elaborates, "that the comprehension of iconic gestures [like that of any communication] depends fundamentally on an understanding of the intention to communicate behind the gesture; without a recognition of my intention to communicate the proprietor will see my [gesture] . . . as some kind of strangely misplaced instrumental action, rather than an action designed to inform him of something."[31] Without this contextual field, in other words, "conventional communication using 'arbitrary' linguistic symbols" can function neither as performative

---

24. Sperber and Wilson, *Relevance*, 8.
25. Ibid., 9.
26. Ibid., 15–21; see already Sperber, *Rethinking Symbolism*, 137.
27. Grice, "Logic and Conversation."
28. Sperber and Wilson, *Relevance*, 16.
29. Ibid., 17.
30. Tomasello, *Origins*, 82.
31. Ibid., 69.

utterance,[32] which Beck claims for star-talk,[33] nor as a faithful conveyance of thought,[34] but rather, as Tomasello concludes, "simply noise."[35] "The ability to create common conceptual ground—joint attention, shared experience, common cultural knowledge—," Tomasello insists, "is an absolutely critical dimension of all human communication"[36]—a point already emphasized by Sperber in 1975.

"Since any two people are sure to share at least a few assumptions about the world," Sperber and Wilson continue, "they should use only these shared assumptions"—such as those assumptions shared by inhabitants of the Graeco-Roman antiquity about their world. "However," Sperber and Wilson conclude, "this cannot be the whole answer, since it immediately raises a new question: how are the speaker and hearer to distinguish assumptions they share from those they do not share?"[37] For the Mithraists, it is their initiation into the symbolic structure of the mithraeum itself that ensures their shared assumptions.

Initiatory Relevance

Sperber and Wilson argue that communication, like any human cognitive process, is "geared to achieving the greatest possible cognitive effect for the smallest possible processing effort." To realize this cognitive efficiency, "individuals must focus their attention on what seems to them to be the most relevant information available."[38] By "information," Sperber and Wilson include "not only facts, but also dubious and false assumptions presented as factual."[39] By "assumptions," they mean thoughts or conceptual representations "treated by the individual as representations of the actual world,"[40] whether those representations are mistaken or genuine.[41] "Relevance" is a more complex notion. By it Sperber and Wilson seek to describe "an important psychological property—a property of mental processes" whereby individuals can intuitively and consistently "distinguish relevant from ir-

32. Austin, *Words*.
33. Beck, *Religion of the Mithras Cult*, 161.
34. Sperber and Wilson, *Relevance*, 9.
35. Tomasello, *Origins*, 73–74.
36. Ibid., 5, 6.
37. Sperber and Wilson, *Relevance*, 17.
38. Ibid., vii.
39. Ibid., 2.
40. Ibid., 2.
41. Ibid., 39.

relevant information."[42] They identify two conditions whereby relevance might be recognized. First, "an assumption is relevant in a context to the extent that its contextual effects in this context are large."[43] This condition is an elaboration upon Sperber's earlier notion of *focalization*. When, for example, an assumption contributes new information that connects with some information already present in that context,[44] or that affects the strength of an assumption already in that context,[45] then that assumption is relevant. In other words, features that are relevant are those that are shared in comparable contexts.[46] Second, "an assumption is relevant in a context to the extent that the effort required to process it in this context is small."[47] As a psychological property, then, relevance is sought and achieved through certain mental processes,[48] for example, through the cognitive and contextual focusing effected by religious ritual.[49]

Elsewhere I have argued that Mithraic initiation is into and within the mithraeum, a simplified and structured Mithraic re-representation of a complex and perplexing Hellenistic cosmos.[50] The initiatory deployment of the distinctive Mithraic vernacular of star-talk, which the mithraeum embodies, would prompt a cognitive remapping for the initiate of the Mithraic contextual world, which ensures that shared Mithraic assumptions about the world are optimally relevant and—I now add in light of Beck's work—which ensures a context within which star-talk might be maximally communicative.[51]

Conclusion

Mithraic star-talk, Beck emphasizes, is not a key to any encrypted secrets of the mysteries; it simply lets us read the language in which Mithraism is *written* by correctly apprehending its signs in context.[52] However, Beck's

42. Ibid., 119, cf. 15.
43. Ibid., 125.
44. Ibid., 121.
45. Ibid., 120.
46. Watts, *Everything*, 44.
47. Sperber and Wilson, *Relevance*, 125.
48. Ibid., 132.
49. Martin, "What Do Religious Rituals Do?"
50. Martin, "Ecology."
51. Sperber and Wilson, *Relevance*, 158.
52. Beck, *Religion of the Mithras Cult*, 163, 188.

emphasis on "reading a language in which Mithraism is written,"[53] suggests the existence of Mithraic texts and that he has discovered the proper astral code by which the contents of these texts might be "exegeted."[54] Although it is clear that for Beck these texts are not written in Latin on papyrus or parchment but are inscribed in star-talk on the material monuments of the Mithraists, it might be asked whether he, nevertheless, opens himself to the charge that his project is but a more sophisticated but little different version, *in principle*, of the previous two-thousand-year history of Mithraic interpretation, whereby attempts have been made to understand the synoptic assembly of Mithraic imagery as a standardized text to be properly decoded—a task that, indeed, he promises at the conclusion of his book to pursue.[55] Rather than emphasizing metaphors of reading and exegeting texts, might Beck, in the tradition of Grice, Sperber and Wilson, and Tomasello, better elaborate upon star-talk as a contextually contingent *medium of communication*, presumably the central function of any language, which Beck, in fact, alludes to but does not develop.[56]

Nevertheless, Beck's hypothesis about Mithraic symbols as star-talk addresses, I believe, one of the more difficult problems for understanding this cult, namely, how can the kind of technical astrological system attributed to the Roman cult of Mithras by historical anthropologists like Beck have been relevant to the numerous quotidian initiates who, according to Mithraic dedicatory inscriptions, were drawn largely from the lower ranks of the military and from the cadre of the petty bureaucracy? The answer often given to this question, first proposed by Origen, is that there was a distinction between the wise (οἱ σοφοί) and the vulgar (οἱ ἰδιῶται) (Origen, *Contra Celsum* 1.12)—a distinction rejected by Beck and, in my opinion, rightly so. Rather than the Origenian distinction between the "wise and the vulgar," however, or the somewhat vague Beckian invocation of a cognitive egalitarianism,[57] we might rather suggest Mithraic levels of augmented communicative competency, which are, nevertheless, mutually comprehensible.

a) Already in 1912, Franz Cumont noted that astrological conceptions permeated the entire Latin world,[58] especially in religious discourse from the beginning of the imperial period.[59] Although Cumont

53. Ibid., 189.
54. Ibid., 190–215.
55. Ibid., 260.
56. Ibid., 66, 163.
57. Ibid., 96.
58. Cumont, *Astrology*, xv, 56.
59. Ibid., 32, 51–52.

steadfastly maintained an Origenian distinction between what he termed the understandings of "the *savants*" and that of "irrational" manifestations among the common populace.[60] We can nevertheless assume with him a degree of native competency among inhabitants of the Graeco-Roman world in what Beck has now identified as star-talk.

b) As Beck notes, there also existed a formal level of star-talk spoken by educated astronomical and astrological "specialists,"[61] (as well as by modern anthropological "linguists" who, like Beck, have reconstructed the scope of its semantic and generative possibilities). Clearly, the founder(s) of Mithraism and, presumably, the subsequent leaders of the various Mithraic communities, drew upon this learned discourse in their construction and maintenance of a specifically Mithraic idiom.[62]

c) Quotidian initiates into the cult, who, we must assume, were significantly less erudite than the Fathers, even formally unschooled, would have learned to communicate in the specifically Mithraic idiom of star-talk. In contrast to standard discourse, such vernaculars are typically associated with nonstandard linguistic constructions, often spoken, like Ebonics, within countercultural groups as markers of in-group status and associated with an experiential "street-smarts."[63]

Beck's star-talk hypothesis, then, allows us to propose that Mithraic insiders (initiates) shared with outsiders (noninitiates) a certain native competency in an astral discourse that was common to inhabitants of the

---

60. Ibid., xii, 53.

61. Beck, *Religion of the Mithras Cult*, 160.

62. Ibid., 242, 253.

63. Tomasello, *Origins*, 210; Martin, "Cult Migration," 101–2. In contrast to one who acquires knowledge through formal education, one who has "street smarts," according to the online *Urban Dictionary*, refers to (among other things): "A person who has lots of common sense and knows what's going on in the world. This person knows what every type of person has to deal with daily and understands all groups of people and how to act around them. This person also knows all the current things going on in the streets and in the ghetto [Mithraic cell!] and everywhere else and knows how to make the right decisions, knows how to deal with different situations and has his own independent state of mind" (*Urban Dictionary* #1); someone with "street smarts" "knows the workings of the mind inside people who are less educated, and knows how to make the correct choices while in their presence" (*Urban Dictionary* #7). "Street Smarts" (plural) is defined by the online *Urban Dictionary* as referring (among other things) to "Intelligence gained outside of school. Just as useful as book smarts, and in many cases more so" (*Urban Dictionary* #1); also, and of interest with reference to the military population of Mithraic initiates, "the ability to survive in dangerous situations, fighting skills" (*Urban Dictionary* #4).

Graeco-Roman world. The specifically Mithraic idiom of this star-talk, whether formal or vernacular, differentiated Mithraic initiates from noninitiates. Differentiated grades of Mithraic initiation, presumably seven, and presided over by a *Pater* or, perhaps, by a lower ranking surrogate—a *Heliodromus* or a *Leo*—would have marked levels of communicative competence and comprehension within the cult. These Mithraic levels of communicative facility mirrored, in turn, the pedagogical tiers of the Roman system of formal education with its pedagogical hierarchy of *litterator, grammaticus,* and ῥήτωρ (*rhetor*)—all of whom spoke a common Latin but with increasing erudition, with the ῥήτωρ achieving competence in *controversia*, the most specialized form of Latin discourse and the culminating stage of Roman higher education.[64] Thus, whether as accomplished Mithraic *Pater* or newly recruited *Corvus*, Mithraists of all grades were able to achieve an increasing comprehension of Mithraic star-talk communication, a fundamental competence that was nevertheless guaranteed to all initiates within the shared context of their local mithraeum.[65] As Beck concludes, Mithraism, like religion in general, persisted as a work "in progress re-created"—and, we now emphasize, *communicated*—"across the generations as their members, leaders and led alike, fashion[ed] their mental representations by interaction both with each others and with the religion's external memory archived in text, ritual, [and in its] symbolic iconography."[66]

References

Austin, John L. *How to Do Things with Words*. Oxford: Clarendon, 1962.
Beck, Roger. *The Religion of the Mithras Cult in the Roman Empire: Mysteries of the Unconquered Sun*. Oxford: Oxford University Press, 2006.
Cumont, Franz. *Astrology and Religion among the Greeks and Romans*. Translated by J. B. Baker. 1912. Eugene, OR: Wipf & Stock, 2005.
Gordon, Richard. "Reality, Evocation and Boundary in the Mysteries of Mithras." *Journal of Mithraic Studies* 3/1 (1980) 19–99.
Grice, Paul. "Logic and Conversation." In *Speech Acts*, edited by Peter Cole and Jerry Morgan, 43–58. Syntax and Semantics 3. New York: Academic Press, 1975.
Hartley, L. P. *The Go-Between*. Penguin Twentieth-Century Classics. Harmondsworth: Penguin, 1997.
Martin, Luther H. "Cult Migration, Social Formation, and Religious Identity in Graeco-Roman Antiquity: The Curious Case of Roman Mithraism." In *The Mind of*

---

64. A Roman student might, of course, pursue "postgraduate" study, as it were, in "philosophy," but pursuit of this reputedly "Greek" subject usually required travel to study with a particular philosopher, especially, in Greece.

65. Beck, *Religion of the Mithras Cult*, 66.

66. Ibid., 98.

Mithraists: Historical and Cognitive Studies in the Roman Cult of Mithras, 89–106. Scientific Studies of Religion: Inquiry and Explanation. London: Bloomsbury, 2015.

———. "The Ecology of Threat Detection and Precautionary Response from the Perspectives of Evolutionary Psychology, Cognitive Science and Historiography: The Case of the Roman Cults of Mithras." *Method & Theory in the Study of Religion* 25/4–5 (2013) 431–50.

———. "What Do Religious Rituals Do? (And How Do They Do It?): Cognition and the Study of Religion." In *Introducing Religion: Essays in Honor of Jonathan Z. Smith*, edited by and Willi Braun and Russell T. McCutcheon, 325–39. London: Equinox, 2008.

Rickford, John R. "What Is Ebonics (African American Vernacular English)?" Washington DC: Linguistic Society of America. https://www.lsadc.org/info/ling-faqs-ebonics.cfm/.

Saussure, Ferdinand de. *Course in General Linguistics*. Translated by Wade Baskin. New York: Philosophical Library, 1959.

Shannon, Claude E. "A Mathematical Theory of Communication." *Bell System Technical Journal* 27/3 (1948) 379–423.

———. "A Symbolic Analysis of Relay and Switching Circuits." *Transactions of the American Institute of Electrical Engineers* 57/12 (1938) 1–11.

Sperber, Dan. *Rethinking Symbolism*. Translated by Alice L. Morton. Cambridge Studies in Social Anthropology 11. Cambridge: Cambridge University Press, 1975.

Sperber, Dan, and Deirdre Wilson. *Relevance: Communication and Cognition*. 2nd ed. Oxford: Blackwell, 1995.

Tomasello, Michael. *Origins of Human Communication*. Jean Nicod Lectures 2008. Cambridge: MIT Press, 2008.

Urban Dictionary. "Street Smart." www.urbandictionary.com/define.php?term=street smart/.

Watts, Duncan J. *Everything Is Obvious: How Common Sense Fails*. New York: Crown Business, 2011.

16

When Size Matters: Social Formations in the Early Roman Empire

From 1995 to 1997, a consultation to "redescribe Christian origins" was organized in the context of the annual meetings of the Society of Biblical Literature (SBL).[1] The aim of this discussion was to map the diversity of Christian beginnings by adopting "the standards, perspectives, and questions of a thorough-going social anthropology,"[2] and to understand this diversity as "junctures of mythmaking and social formation."[3] Despite the groundbreaking work of these discussions, Stanley Stowers concluded, in a selection of "meta-reflections" on the work of the consultation, that "the Seminar is at a point where it needs to sharpen its social theory with more detail and some choices about what kind of social theory it wants."[4]

In a subsequent publication, Stowers noted "that the basic social formation in the movement that would become Christianity was communities."[5] However, he rightly concluded that such claims "are usually unreflective and almost always untheorized."[6] Rather, "the social complexity hidden by [this notion of] community needs to be described and explained." He emphasized that

> The task of the historian ought to be inquiry into which of the vast number of possible social formations . . . were involved in

---

1. Cameron and Miller, *Redescribing*.
2. Cameron and Miller, "Introduction," 28.
3. Ibid., 4.
4. Stowers, "Mythmaking," 490.
5. Stowers, "Concept," 241.
6. Ibid., 245.

the beginnings of what came to be known as Christianity and the roles of these formations in those historical processes.[7]

In other words, in the Roman world there was already a plurality of social groups, which (pre-)Christian groups "exapted" for their own purposes.[8]

But what exactly was the character of Roman social formations generally, especially those social formations that might have proven amenable to exaptation by the emerging (pre-)Christian movements? We might begin such a historical investigation by heeding Stower's call to sharpen social theory with more attention to detail. And, since the structures and functions of a group are correlate with its scale, one neglected detail to which we might attend is a size inventory for social formations in the Roman world.

Social Formations: Scale

The fundamental scale of social formations in the Roman world was essentially that of any era of human history. This is because social formations are limited by regularities in human cognition.[9] Evolutionary anthropologist Robin Dunbar has shown that differential levels of group size are constrained by the information processing capacity of the neocortex, a capacity that has remained essentially constant for *Homo sapiens* since the emergence of anatomically modern humans some 160,000 years ago.[10] Based upon correlations between neocortex volume and social-group size among non-human primates, Dunbar extrapolated a numerical limit for stable human groups at a mean of 150. This number corresponds to the maximum "number of people we know individually with whom we have a relationship based on personal trust and obligation."[11] He supported his formulaic calculations with historical and ethnographic correlations, e.g., the size of contemporary hunter-gatherer groups, of Neolithic Mesopotamian villages, of American Hutterite and Amish farming communities, of academic research circles, of Christmas card lists, of optimal working groups in large businesses, of the basic units of armies throughout military history, etc.[12] So accepted is this argument that "150" is now widely referred to as "Dunbar's number."[13]

7. Ibid., 249.
8. Stowers, "Mythmaking," 493–94.
9. Stiller et al., "Small World," 406.
10. Dunbar, "Coevolution."
11. Dunbar et al., *Evolutionary Psychology*, 97.
12. Dunbar, "Coevolution," 685–86; Dunbar, *How Many Friends*, 224–28.
13. E.g., "Dunbar's Number." 16 November 2011. Online: http://en.wikipedia.org/

Subsequently, Dunbar identified three sub-groups, differentiated by relations of intimacy. First, informal conversation groups that number no more than four; if a fifth person shows up, the group will inevitably split into two groups of three and two.[14] Second, circles of close friends or efficiently working colleagues—e.g., juries, inner cabinets of governments, most sports teams—will typically number twelve to fifteen.[15] Finally, there are groups, which number approximately thirty-five, and correspond in size to temporary overnight camps of many hunter-gatherers and to clubs and cliques.[16] Social alliances larger than approximately 150, Dunbar concluded, require permanent leadership that commands sufficient power to overcome in-group/out-group conflict, whether that power is consensual or imposed—although he notes that cohesion in such large-scale societies has proven, throughout history, to be less than stable.[17]

Social Formations: Roman

Scholars now routinely speak about the plurality—and relative autonomy—of various small-scale religious associations in the Roman world, of mystery cults, of Judaisms, of early Christianities (though they still often essentialize them by treating them synoptically in the singular as, for example, "Mithraism," or "post-Temple Judaism," or "early Christianity"). It is now possible to use Dunbar's formulaic scale as a theoretical heuristic for estimating the sizes of known social formations during the Roman period and to assess these size estimates in light of comparative, archaeological and literary evidence.

Roman Army

One of the examples that Dunbar educes for his reference number of 150 is basic units of armies throughout military history. We might then begin our

---

wiki/Dunbar%27s_number/. Despite the proliferation of contacts in modern social media, a preliminary study of the number of friends on Facebook has confirmed the validity of Dunbar's numerical limit. Dunbar himself is conducting a study of Facebook friending.

14. Dunbar, *Grooming*, 121.

15. Ibid., 76.

16. Dunbar et al., *Evolutionary Psychology*, 98; Dunbar, *Grooming*, 118–20.

17. Dunbar, "Coevolution," 693; Turchin, *War and Peace*. The Eleusinian Mysteries, with its dynastic hierarchical leadership and its annual large-scale initiations (estimated to be up to three thousand) but with its minimal, even negligible, enduring social cohesion among initiates, provides a good example of a large-scale religious associations in the Hellenistic world.

inquiry into social formations in the Roman Imperial period with a brief look at the organization of the Roman army.

The basic tactical unit of the Roman army during the republic was the *centuria*, under the command of a *centurion*, and originally made of up 100, but later, of 80 men. These *centuriae* were generally grouped in pairs or *manipuli* of 160 men, corroborating Dunbar's number.[18]

As might be expected with expansionist aspirations and imperial successes, the size of Roman military units also grew. Following the military reforms of the Roman general Gaius Marius in 107 BCE, the *manipuli* were replaced by *cohortes* of 480 men, three groups of *manipuli* (or six *centuriae* of 80 men each) (Polybius 3.24; Vegetius, *De re military* 2.3.1). In accordance with Dunbar's predictions, this larger military unit required an increasingly complex and hierarchical command structure, typically a senior centurion (*centurio primi pili*) overseeing the other five in addition to an increasing number of junior officers.[19] Although the organization of the Roman legions varied, the *centuria* endured as the fundamental unit of the Roman army throughout the imperial period.

Roman Clubs (θίασοι, *collegia, sodales*)

Of more interest to scholars of religion than military units are the club-sized groups. Although documented from ancient Greece, these clubs proliferated in the Hellenistic world following the conquests of Alexander and the subsequent establishment of imperial rule.[20] Although the size of these associations ranged from between fifteen or twenty to 1,200 members,[21] their average size has been estimated at between thirty to thirty-five,[22] a number that conforms nicely to the mean size of club membership predicted by Dunbar's scale.

Roman Mithraism

Whereas most scholars agree that nonofficial religions of the Roman Empire were organized, like the clubs, as small, face-to-face associations, specific membership numbers for these groups are difficult to ascertain. The best

18. Adkins and Adkins, *Handbook*, 63.
19. Ibid.
20. Tod, *Sidelights*, 73; Tarn, *Hellenistic Civilization*, 93.
21. Scheid, "Community," 373; Kloppenborg, "Collegia and *Thiasoi*," 25.
22. Tod, *Sidelights*, 83; citing Poland, *Vereinswesen*.

evidence is material, i.e., an estimate of the number of participants who might reasonably fit space delimited by archaeological remains. An exemplary model in this regard is Roman Mithraism, for which numerous *mithraea* or Mithraic temples have been discovered. Although the space defined by these *mithraea* varies from small to large, the average *mithraeum* measures less than 10x10 meters,[23] an area that could accommodate between twenty and forty people.[24] Although the number of available "seats" in a mithraeum does not necessarily correlate with the size of an individual Mithraic community, it would seem that the membership of the average community correlates well with the mean number of approximately thirty-five predicted for clubs by Dunbar.

Christian Associations

The single pre-Constantinian edifice that can be identified as Christian is a third-century building at Dura-Europos, converted from an earlier private residence.[25] Although the assembly hall of this relatively late structure could accommodate sixty-five to seventy-five people,[26] the earlier house structure from which it was modified would have accommodated fewer. Most early Christians met in members' homes (Acts 2:46; 5:42; 12:12; Rom 16:5; 1 Cor 16:19; Col 4:15; Phlm 2) in groups estimated to number between twenty to forty.[27] However, since the earliest meetings most certainly included an ἀγάπη or fellowship meal (Acts 20:7–8),[28] that number must have been somewhat smaller. According to the second-century-CE Latin author Aulus Gellius, the first-century-BCE Roman writer Marcus Varro counseled that the proper number of guests at a dinner ought not be less than that of the Graces (i.e., three) or more than that of the Muses (i.e., nine) (*Noctes Atticae* 13.11). Compliant with Varro's ideal dining size, the usual Roman dining room, or *triclinium*, had three couches upon which guests reclined while eating, typically three to a couch (Vitruvius, *De architectura* 6.5.6). Depending upon the wealth of a householder and the size of his house, however, up to twenty might be accommodated, an indication of wealth and status unlikely to be associated with many early Christian groups. According to the Synoptic Gospels, Jesus reclined (ἀνάκειμαι) at the Last Supper with

23. Clauss, *Roman Cult of Mithras*, 43.
24. Liebeschuetz, "Expansion," 197; Meiggs, *Ostia*, 372.
25. Snyder, *Ante Pacem*, 128.
26. Ibid., 132.
27. Liebeschuetz, "Expansion," 196–97.
28. White, *Building God's House*, 107.

twelve followers (Matt 26:20; Mark 14:18; [Luke 22:27]), which, whether fictive or historical, conforms to Dunbar's predicted number for intimate social groups whose members are in regular association with one another.

A second location where early Christians assembled was burial places, especially in covered cemeteries and, later, in the second century, in the *cubicula* or family burial rooms in catacombs, where ἀγάπη meals were eaten with the dead.[29] The size of these rooms varied with the wealth of the family but, for the most part, are quite modest, large enough only for family and close friends. Although most burials within a *cubiculum* would have been in *loculi* or graves carved in the tufa walls and covered with marble or terracotta plates (*tituli*), *cubicula* also had to accommodate the *sarcophagi* of the more prominent ancestors.[30] Given the typical size of *cubicula*, the space required for one or more *sarcophagi*, and the benches sometimes carved into the tufa, the typical *cubiculum* would seem to be limited to an intimate number of approximately twelve.

The literary constructions of the New Testament attest not only Dunbar's estimate of twelve members for an intimate group but also to conversation groups of fewer than five. In a preliminary study of the New Testament gospels, Justin Lane has shown that there are no more than four persons portrayed as speaking at any one time.[31] The total number of characters with whom people are portrayed as having recurring social contact in any of the gospels (e.g., Pharisees) or significant, i.e., plot-altering, contact (e.g., centurions) is fewer than the thirty to forty with whom people have social contacts in any society. As Stiller et al. concluded in their analysis of ten Shakespearean plays, "fictional social networks . . . have the same properties as those typical of human beings across ages and cultures" and those "properties" are those of "small world" networks.[32]

Social Formations: Networks

Among the social formations that Stowers commends historians to consider are the various networks established in the Roman world, e.g., those of merchants or artisans, those between entrepreneurs and consumers, and so forth.[33] As network theorists emphasize, "humans don't just live in groups,"

---

29. Snyder, *Ante Pacem*, 155–57, 301.
30. Ibid., 156.
31. Lane, "Brains and the Bible."
32. Stiller et al., "Small World," 397.
33. Stowers, "Mythmaking," 249.

they "live in [social] networks."[34] Two general models have been employed to describe (and to explain) such networks: the genealogical or tree model of serial continuity and the "small world" model of social interaction and relationship.[35]

The Tree Model

The tree model has been used productively to represent instances of historical diffusion, e.g., the development of Indo-European languages, or of scientific change, e.g., biological evolution. This model is ultimately derived, however, from the Genesis story of singular origination that dominated Western views of history until the nineteenth century, and that more often models mythological origins than historical change.[36] Early Christianity, for example, is typically presented in terms of this arboreal myth, whereby the historical diversities of Christianity are represented as forking branches of a tree rooted in the founding actions and teachings of Jesus of Nazareth.

Skepticism about the historical validity of the tree model for early Christianity was, of course, a fundamental premise of the SBL consultation on "Redescribing Christianity Origins."[37] When this mythological tree was felled, however, there was little agreement upon, or even attention to alternative views of how a pluralistic dispersion of (pre-)Christian associations interacted historically in a way or ways that eventually became institutionalized as an empirewide "imagined" community with centralized hierarchical control.[38]

The Small World Model

Unlike the tree model, the "small world" model of networks is not based in myth but in mathematics and experimentation.[39] It has already been

---

34. Christakis and Fowler, *Connected*, 214.
35. Shryock and Smail, "Introduction."
36. Ibid., 6–17; Shryock et al., "Imagining."
37. Cameron and Miller, *Redescribing*, 1–4.
38. On "imagined communities," see Anderson, *Imagined Communities*.
39. Watts and Strogatz, "Collective Dynamics"; and the pioneering experiments of Milgram, "Small World Problem"; Travers and Milgram, "Experimental Study."

productively employed in historical studies of the ancient Mediterranean world[40] and suggested as the model for the successes of Pauline Christianity.[41]

Network theory is part of complexity theory; its principles are considered to be universal, from the organization of neural networks to that of modern power grids. Most succinctly, in the small world model, nodes (individuals, groups or clusters of groups), which are not contingent, can nevertheless be linked by a relatively small number of connections that are measured by their degree of separation rather than by physical distance[42]—a proposal that originated in Stanley Milgram's demonstration that all people are connected to one another by no more than "six degrees of separation."[43]

In contrast to degrees of *connection*, however, recent research documents that networks of *influence* are characterized by no more than three degrees of separation or less, i.e., from one's friend, to one's friend's friend, to one's friend's friend's friend.[44] Three degrees of influence is simply the extent that evolution has favored people who have so recently lived in large groups.[45]

Networks of influence constitute clusters of at least three nodes, which may themselves function as network nodes.[46] As the degree of separation between nodes in a social network increases, however, the network tends to become more fragmented; this trend establishes upper boundaries of thirty to forty connections for a stable network: interestingly, the number associated by Dunbar with the upper limits of individual club membership.[47]

Network theory represents a decentralized model that requires a "release from proximity"[48] that may be accomplished by a replication and distribution of identical objects that are shared,[49] or by a process of "kinshipping,"[50] which represents a replication of social claims to common ancestry. The Mithraic network, for example, shared a central cult scene, the

40. Malkin, *Small World*; Malkin et al., *Greek and Roman Networks*.
41. Barabási, *Linked*, 3–5, 7, 19, 129, 136.
42. Malkin, *Small World*, 9.
43. Actually, for Milgram, "Small World Problem," 5.5 degrees. The idea for tracking degrees of connectedness goes back to "Chain-Links," a 1929 short story by Frigyes Karinthy (English translation 2006). The actual phrase "six degrees of separation" seems to go back to a play by that name; see Guare, *Six Degrees*.
44. Malkin, *Small World*, 9.
45. Christakis and Fowler, *Connected*, 29.
46. Malkin, *Small World*, 27.
47. Stiller et al., "Small World," 403–4.
48. Worthman, "Urban Networks."
49. Smail et al., "Goods," 236.
50. Shryock and Smail, "Introduction," 31–34; Trautman et al., "Deep Kinship."

tauroctony, which was faithfully reproduced in all mithraea throughout the empire. In addition, every Mithraic association was organized as a fictive kinship group of *fratres* under the leadership of a local (but never translocal) *pater*.

Recent research by Dunbar et al. confirms that associations organized as (fictive) kinship groups have special status in terms of bonds of intimacy,[51] e.g., the κοινωνίαν relationships among some of the early Christians (Acts 2:44; 1 John 1:3). Such claims to kinship resonate well with *Homo sapiens* as a rationale for the transmutation of local networks into large-scale imagined communities where "houses become worlds."[52] For example, claims to kinship among Greeks were explicitly exploited by Alexander the Great to solidify the first Western empire (Arrian, *Anabasis* 7.11; Diodorus Siculus 18.4.4; Plutarch, *De fortuna Alexandri* 1.329C-D). However, the *collegia*, the Mithraists, and other religious groups of the Roman imperial period never seem to have developed their kinship claims into a universal ideology supported by centralized control, as did some of the early Christian groups.

Early Christian Networks

The kinship claims of the early Christian associations exemplify two types of networks: those characterized by relatively loose or "weak" ties between acquaintances that encourage a shared if nebulous relationships and those defined by "strong" or "dense" ties that bind individuals into clearly defined groups at the expense of the larger world.[53] Both the Palestinian "Jesus people" and the Pauline associations come to exemplify strong claims to kinship; as later portrayed in the tree-representation in the book of Acts and, subsequently, in that of "orthodox" Christianity, both claim Jesus as the founding ancestor.

Networking tendencies among Palestinian Jesus groups must initially have been based upon at least some "weak" social exchanges among the Palestinian Jesus groups, whereby those with similar interests would undoubtedly be in some form of contact, especially in the literally "small world" of Palestine. If this is the case for networking globally, it is reasonable to assume it could be the case during the first and second centuries of the Roman Empire for the (pre-)Christian Jesus groups, as well as for the various ethnically defined groups of posttemple Judaism. Some of the early Jesus

---

51. Dunbar et al., *Evolutionary Psychology*, 99.

52. Trautman et al., "Deep Kinship," 181; Martin, "Very Idea of Globalization," 129–30.

53. Christakis and Fowler, *Connected*, 157.

associations, however, made notably strong claims to fictive kinship ties that involved the rejection of their biological (ethnic) kin in favor of socially constructed kin ties, at least in their early ideological representation (Matt 8:22; Luke 9:60), a view subsequently shared by an expanding community (Matt 12:50 and Luke 8:21; Mark 3:35).

The network of associations Paul established represents another example of what became a "strong" network, with an authoritative leader who articulated a robust strategy for a centralized organization. Like the Palestinian Jesus associations, Paul claimed a spiritual, i.e., fictive, kinship with Jesus as the basis for his authority. He used the Greek juridical term for adoption (υἱοθεσία) to described those redeemed by God's son as themselves adopted sons of God (Rom 8:14, 23; Gal 4:4–5).[54] However, Paul declared his own teachings to be the measure of this "spirituality" (Gal 1:12). *His* teachings, Paul asserted, are "a command of the Lord" (1 Cor 1:14, 37). "If any one does not recognize this," Paul asserted, "he is not recognized" (1 Cor 14:38) and can, as he bluntly puts it, simply "go to hell" (ἀνάθεμα ἔστω) (Gal 1:6–9). When, however, a link is removed from a strong network, e.g., when Paul left one of his communities to visit another, interactions among components of the network become vulnerable (e.g., 1 Cor 1:14–17).[55] Paul's idea for a network of associations centrally controlled by his own teachings, consequently, initially failed (e.g., 1 Cor 1:10–12; Gal 1:8–9). Nevertheless, subsequent acceptance of the Pauline idea of a centralized network of Christian ἐκκλησία (church), with a concomitant hierarchical and increasingly complex administrative structure became, like that of the Roman military, progressively documented, as exemplified by the Marcionite consolidation, the Valentinian church, and, of course, by the deutero-Pauline trajectory itself.

Social Formations: Practices

The social-processing capacity of human brains delimits not only social scale but also a shared "theory of mind," by which "the embodied simulation of others' actions, rather than an abstract, representational theory of behavior, underpins understanding of the actions, sensations and emotions of others."[56] Such "embodied simulations" rather than "abstract, representational theories" are especially exemplified by rites of initiation.[57] The Roman

54. Dieterich, *Mithrasliturgie*, 152.
55. Christakis and Fowler, *Connected*, 104.
56. Coward and Gamble, "Big Brains," 1969.
57. Whitehouse, *Modes of Religiosity*, 105–15.

mystery cults are, of course, defined by such embodied rites, as are the early Christianities' rite of baptism.[58] The priority of these practices of inclusion and their concomitant mythmaking justifications for that behavior over any codified beliefs characterized the small-scale societies of Palestinian "Jesus people" and possibly the pre-Pauline "Christ" groups, which initially resisted the Pauline initiative, as well.

Whereas the mystery traditions, like the Roman *collegia*, remained local organizations throughout their history, the transformation of the Christianities into larger-scale societies involved a deflation of baptism as the central rite among early Christian groups, especially as birth increasingly replaced conversion as a recruitment strategy. Increasingly, the Christians' fellowship meal was elevated to a collective, sacramental rite performed by a surrogate of central authority, which united participants into their large-scale imagined community. That is to say, there was a concomitant shift from the ritual incorporation of individual bodies into small, face-to-face societies based on claims to what the founder, Jesus, *performed*, to a communal participation through ritual in a corporate body based on the increasingly codified claims to what Jesus *commanded*.

Conclusion

As I noted at the beginning of this chapter, Stowers rightly contends that references to "community" in the Roman world are "usually unreflective and almost always untheorized." Further, he emphasizes that the numerous social formations that inhabited the Roman world also need to be described and explained.[59] To this project of further theorizing Roman communities, I have attempted to estimate the size of differing Roman communities by employing Robin Dunbar's formulaic scale and, like Dunbar, I have measured these estimates against the available historical evidence. Following Dunbar, I have identified small, intimate groups of approximately twelve to fourteen members, such as the Mithraic cells, the Palestinian "Jesus People," and, perhaps, the pre-Pauline "Christ" groups. Second, there seem to be larger communities of approximately thirty to thirty-five members, such as some of the *collegia* and the more stable of the communities established by Paul.

I have argued that the differing sizes of Roman social formations matter for the following reasons:

---

58. Thomassen, "Becoming a Different Person"; Martin, "Why Christianity," 98–100.

59. Stowers, "Mythmaking," 245, 249.

1. There is a relationship between size and organization. Smaller, face-to-face social groups, such as those portrayed in the Gospels, are able to function efficiently without permanent leadership. Was Jesus really the leader of all, or of any, of the Palestinian Jesus groups? Or, was he a distant, even fictive, founder, represented as leader by a subsequent literary tradition? Or, perhaps, was Peter the leader of (some of) the Jesus People, as is also represented by subsequent literary tradition? In any case, such small face-to-face groups *require* no *permanent* leadership until they begin to exceed Dunbar's mean number of approximately 150, a fact with which Paul had to contend.

2. There is a relationship between group size and network affiliation. I suggested that there was initially a "weak" network of loose or informal contacts among various groups of "Jesus People." The possibility of such informal contacts is supported by "small world" theory. Similarly, we know that there were such informal contacts among Mithraists as its military and bureaucratic members were redeployed and reassigned throughout the "small world" of the Roman Empire, which, by contrast with the Palestinian, was literally quite expansive. "Strong" networks, characterized by formal contacts, central leadership, shared beliefs, and exclusive practices were essentially unknown in the Roman world apart from despoiled (but still remembered) Second Temple Judaism and, of course, from the exclusivist Jesus People and from the coalescence of "Pauline" traditions in the second century.

3. Finally, there is a correlation between group size and ritual practice. For small, face-to-face communities, initiation, supporting group cohesion, is their most important rite, however elaborate their ritual system might otherwise be. For large-scale imagined communities, on the other hand, initiation rites become deflated in favor of collective rites supporting large-group identity.

The fundamental problem raised by the previous analysis is, of course, the reliability of any formulaic scale for estimating the size of historical groups in the absence of hard data. However, historians need begin paying attention to recent methodological advances that facilitate estimations and understandings of such otherwise undocumented historical details. For, as I have attempted to show, such details as the size of a group do indeed matter.

References

Adkins, Lesley, and Roy A. Adkins. *Handbook to Life in Ancient Rome.* New York: Oxford University Press, 1998.
Anderson, Benedict. *Imagined Communities: Reflections on the Origin and Spread of Nationalism.* Rev. and extended ed. London: Verso, 1991.
Barabási, Albert-László. *Linked: How Everything Is Connected to Everything Else and What It Means for Business, Science, and Everyday Life.* New York: Plume, 2003.
Cameron, Ron, and Merrill P. Miller. "Introduction: Ancient Myths and Modern Theories of Christian Origins." In *Redescribing Christian Origins*, edited by Ron Cameron and Merill P. Miller, 1–30. Society of Biblical Literature Symposium Series 28. Atlanta: Society of Biblical Literature, 2004.
———, eds. *Redescribing Christian Origins.* Society of Biblical Literature Symposium Series 28. Atlanta: Society of Biblical Literature, 2004.
Christakis, Nicholas A., and James H. Fowler. *Connected: The Surprising Power of Our Social Networks and How They Shape Our Lives.* New York: Little, Brown, 2011.
Clauss, Manfred. *The Roman Cult of Mithras.* Translated by Richard Gordon. London: Routledge, 2001.
Coward, Fiona, and Clive Gamble. "Big Brains, Small Worlds: Material Culture and the Evolution of the Mind." *Philosophical Transactions of the Royal Society* B 363 (2008) 1969–79.
Dietrerich, Albrecht. *Eine Mithrasliturgie.* 1923. Reprint, Darmstadt: Wissenschaftliche Buchgesellschaft, 1966.
Dunbar, R. I. M. "Coevolution of Neocortical Size, Group Size and Language in Humans." *Behavioral and Brain Sciences* 16/4 (1993) 681–735.
———. *Grooming, Gossip, and the Evolution of Language.* Cambridge: Harvard University Press, 1996.
———. *How Many Friends Does One Person Need? Dunbar's Number and Other Evolutionary Quirks.* London: Faber & Faber, 2010.
Dunbar, R. I. M. et al. *Evolutionary Psychology: A Beginner's Guide; Human Behaviour, Evolution and the Mind.* Oneworld Beginner's Guides. Oxford: OneWorld, 2005.
Guare, John. *Six Degrees of Separation.* 2nd ed. New York: Vintage, 1994.
Karinthy, Frigyes. "Chain-Links." In *The Structure and Dynamics of Networks*, edited by Mark Newman et al., 21–26. Princeton Studies in Complexity. Princeton: Princeton University Press, 2006.
Kloppenborg, John. "Collegia and *Thiasoi*: Issues in Function, Taxonomy and Membership." In *Voluntary Associations in the Roman World*, edited by John S. Kloppenborg and Stephen G. Wilson, 16–39. London: Routledge, 1996.
Lane, Justin. "Brains and the Bible: How Neuroscience Can Help to Illuminate Early Christian Texts." Paper presented to the Cognitive Science Society of Masaryk University, Brno, Czech Republic, November, 2010.
Liebeschuetz, Wolf. "The Expansion of Mithraism among the Religious Cults of the Second Century." In *Studies in Mithraism: Papers Associated with the Mithraic Panel Organized on the Occasion of the XVIth Congress of the International Association for the History of Religions, Rome 1990*, edited by John R. Hinnells, 195–216. Storia delle religioni 9. Rome: "L'Erma" di Bretschneider, 1994.
Malkin, Irad. *A Small Greek World: Networks in the Ancient Mediterranean.* Oxford: Oxford University Press, 2011.

Malkin, Irad et al, eds. *Greek and Roman Networks in the Mediterranean*. London: Routledge, 2011.
Martin, Luther H. "Why Christianity Was Accepted by Romans but Not by Rome." In *Religionskritik in der Antike*, edited by Ulrich Berner and Illinca D. Tanaseanu, 92–107. Religionen in der pluralen Welt 7. Münster: LIT, 2009.
———. "The Very Idea of Globalization: The Case of Hellenistic Empire." In *Hellenisation, Empire and Globalisation: Lessons from Antiquity*, edited by Luther H. Martin and Panayotis Pachis, 123–39. Thessaloniki: Vanias, 2004 (chapter 2, this volume).
Meiggs, Russell. *Roman Ostia*. Oxford: Clarendon, 1973.
Milgram, Stanley. "The Small World Problem." *Psychology Today* 2/1 (1967) 60–67.
Poland, Franz. *Geschichte des griechischen Vereinswesens*. Fürslich Jablonowskische gesellschaft der wissenschaften, Leipzig. Preisschriften 38. Leipzig: Teubner, 1909.
Scheid, John. "Community and Community: Reflections on Some Ambiguities Based on the *Thiasoi* of Roman Egypt." In *The Religious History of the Roman Empire: Pagans, Jews, and Christians*, edited by J. A. North and S. R. F. Price, 366–82. Oxford: Oxford University Press, 2011.
Shryock, Andrew et al. "Imagining the Human in Deep Time." In *Deep History: The Architecture of Past and Present*, edited by Andrew Shryock and Daniel Lord Smail, 33–38. Berkeley: University of California Press, 2011.
Shryock, Andrew, and Daniel Lord Smail. "Introduction." In *Deep History: The Architecture of Past and Present*, edited by Andrew Shryock and Daniel Lord Smail, 3–20. Berkeley: University of California Press, 2011.
Smail, Daniel Lord et al. "Goods." In *Deep History: The Architecture of Past and Present*, edited by Andrew Shryock and Daniel Lord Smail, 219–41. Berkeley: University of California Press, 2011.
Snyder, Graydon F. *Ante Pacem: Archaeological Evidence of Church Life before Constantine*. Rev. ed. Macon: Mercer University Press, 2003.
Stiller, James, et al. "The Small World of Shakespeare's Plays." *Human Nature* 14/4 (2003) 397–408.
Stowers, Stanley K. "The Concept of 'Community' and the History of Early Christianity." *Method & Theory in the Study of Religion* 23/3–4 (2011) 238–56.
———. "Mythmaking, Social Formation, and Varieties of Social Theory." In *Redescribing Christian Origins*, edited by Ron Cameron and Merill P. Miller, 489–95. Society of Biblical Literature Symposium Series 28. Atlanta: Society of Biblical Literature, 2004.
Tarn, W. W. *Hellenistic Civilization*. Rev. ed. by the author and G. T. Griffith. Meridian Books. Cleveland: Meridian 1961.
Thomassen, Einar. "Becoming a Different Person: Baptism as an Initiation Ritual." In *Theoretical Frameworks for the Study of Graeco-Roman Religions*, edited by Luther H. Martin and Panayotis Pachis, 209–22. Thessaloniki: University Studio Press, 2003.
Tod, Marcus N. *Sidelights on Greek History*. Oxford: Blackwell, 1932.
Trautman, Thomas R. et al. "Deep Kinship." In *Deep History: The Architecture of Past and Present*, edited by Andrew Shryock and Daniel Lord Smail, 160–88. Berkeley: University of California Press, 2011.
Travers, Jeffrey, and Stanley Milgram. "An Experimental Study in the Small World Problem." *Sociometry* 32/4 (1969) 425–43.

Turchin, Peter. *War and Peace and War: The Rise and Fall of Empires*. New York: Penguin, 2007.

Watts, Duncan J., and Steven H. Strogatz. "Collective Dynamics of 'Small World' Networks." *Nature* 393/6684 (1998) 440–42.

White, Michael L. *Building God's House in the Roman World: Architectural Adaptation among Pagans, Jews, and Christians*. Baltimore: Johns Hopkins University Press, 1990.

Whitehouse, Harvey. *Modes of Religiosity: A Cognitive Theory of Religious Transmission*. Cognitive Science of Religion Series. Walnut Creek, CA: AltaMira, 2004.

Worthman, Robert A. "Urban Networks, Deregulated Religious Markets, Cultural Continuity and the Diffusion of the Isis Cult." *Method & Theory in the Study of Religion* 18/2 (2006) 103–23.

PART 4

Hellenistic Judaism and Christianity

17

Josephus's Use of *Heimarmenē* in the *Jewish Antiquities* 8.171–173

JOSEPHUS USES THE WORD εἱμαρμένη ("fate" or "destiny") in but four passages in his *Jewish Antiquities* (8.171–73; 15.397; 18.12–22; and 19.347).[1] In two of these passages, in *The Jewish War* 2.162–66, he uses the use of determinism to distinguish between the three Jewish "philosophies": the Pharisees, the Sadducees, and the Essenes.[2]

The Pharisees, according to Josephus in *Antiquities* 18.13,

> postulate that everything is brought about by fate [εἱμαρμένη], still they do not deprive the human will of the pursuit of what is in man's power, since it was God's good pleasure that there should be a fusion and that the will of man with his virtue and vice should be admitted to the council-chamber of fate.

Later, in the same passage, he characterizes the position of the Sadducees and the Essenes by contrasting them with this Pharisaic position on εἱμαρμένη. The Sadducees, he writes, "own no observance of any sort apart from the laws," while the Essenes "leave everything in the hands of God" (18.16). Josephus also refers here (18.11) to a parallel account in the second book of his earlier *The Jewish War* (2.162–64), in which he described both the Pharisees and the Sadducees, in part, in terms of their contrasting attitudes toward εἱμαρμένη:

---

1. In *Antiquities* 16.397, Josephus speaks abstractly of the inevitability of Fate. In 19.347, he describes the death of Agrippa as fated.

2. In *Antiquities* 18.11, Josephus refers to φιλοσοφίαι τρεῖς (so also in *The Jewish War* 2.119). This seems to be an attempt by Josephus to cast the varieties of Judaism into the Hellenistic category of philosophical schools. In *Antiquities* 13.171, however, he speaks of τρεῖς αἱρέσεις τῶν Ἰουδαίων. I will speak conventionally of the three Jewish "philosophies" in referring to all passages.

> The Pharisees ... attribute everything to Fate [εἱμαρμένη] and to God; they hold that to act rightly or otherwise rests, indeed, for the most part with men, but that in each action Fate [εἱμαρμένη] cooperates ... The Sadducees ... do away with Fate [εἱμαρμένη] altogether.

This passage from *The Jewish War* seems to clarify the description of the Sadducees that Josephus gives in the *Antiquities* 18.16: In owning "no observance of any apart from the laws," "the Sadducees ... do away with Fate."

In the brief passage on the three philosophies in *Antiquities* 8.171–73, Josephus presents the attitude towards εἱμαρμένη as the single issue which distinguishes the three philosophies:

> Now at this time there were three schools of thought among the Jews, which held different opinions concerning human affairs: the first being that of the Pharisees, the second that of the Sadducees, and the third that of the Essenes. As for the Pharisees, they say that certain events are the work of Fate [εἱμαρμένη], but not all; as to other events, it depends upon ourselves whether they shall take place or not. The sect of Essenes, however, declares that Fate [εἱμαρμένη] is mistress of all things, and that nothing befalls men unless it be in accordance with her decree. But the Sadducees do away with Fate [εἱμαρμένη], holding that there is no such thing and that human actions are not achieved in accordance with her decree, but that all things lie within our own power, so that we ourselves are responsible for our well-being, while we suffer misfortune through our own thoughtlessness.

This is the only passage in which Josephus presents the opinion of all three philosophies explicitly toward εἱμαρμένη. Given the singularity and centrality of his use of this term in 18.171–73, an examination of Josephus's use of this term in the *Antiquities* best might be focused upon his use of εἱμαρμένη in this passage.

The problem that can be focused upon this passage is essentially twofold. First, what does Josephus mean by εἱμαρμένη? And, why does he use so centrally a concept for which as George Foot Moore has observed, "there was no equivalent word in Hebrew—and no corresponding conception?"[3] Second, as εἱμαρμένη means "fate" or "destiny," in some sense, its meaning must be discussed in relation to the determinism/free will issue Josephus raises in this passage and that is implied in any discussion of fate. What then

---

3. Moore, "Free Will," 379. Many interpreters, e.g., Stählin ("Das Schicksal") have assumed an identity between Josephus's use of πρόνοια and εἱμαρμένη, or have translated these and other" fate" terms both similarly and variously, thus adding to the confusion.

is the relationship of any kind of determinism to a God in whose hands, according to Josephus, is a universe, a God who is "perfect and blessed, self-sufficing and sufficing for all" and who "is the beginning, the middle, and the end of all things" (*Contra Apionem* 2.190)?

Josephus's use of εἱμαρμένη in the historical and theological context of his description of the three Jewish "philosophies" is a problematic question, not only in studies of Josephus and Hellenistic Judaism, but in the study of Hellenistic religion as a whole. The satirical writings of Lucian of Samosata, for instance, in the following century point to these issues:

> This Zeus—and I beg you by the Fates and the Destiny not to hear me with exasperation or anger when I speak the truth boldly. If . . . the Fates rule everything and nobody can ever change anything that they have once decreed, why do we men sacrifice to you gods and make you great offerings of cattle, praying to receive blessings from you? I really do not see what benefit we can derive from this precaution. If it is impossible for us through our prayers either to get what is bad averted or to secure any blessing whatever by the gift of the gods. (*Zeus Catechized* 5)

Satirization of such issues suggests their widespread and popular currency.

The problem of Josephus's use of εἱμαρμένη, therefore, can be placed in the context of two more overriding concerns. First, does (and to what extent does) Josephus's description of the Jewish philosophies reflect the broader concerns of Hellenistic religiosity? For, as W. C. van Unnik has reemphasized with respect to Josephus, "every historian . . . is a child of his time, and as such Josephus is a typical example of a man living in Hellenistic culture."[4] The second, related, problem is to what extent Josephus is correct in the use of εἱμαρμένη to characterize and distinguish the Jewish philosophies—that is, the larger problem of the reliability of Josephus as a historian.

Ludwig Wächter has argued the essential correctness of Josephus's characterization of the three Jewish philosophies.[5] He begins with Josephus's description of the Sadducees, who, in their strict and total adherence to the written law, completely denied εἱμαρμένη. It is the Sadducees' strict observance of the written Torah alone distinguishes them from the Pharisees, who observe not only the written Torah but also God's continuing plan in the oral tradition.

The Pharisees are described by Josephus in *Antiquities* 8.172 as attributing certain events to the work of Fate, but not all. These latter events depend upon human actions, but under God in obedience to Torah. This

---

4. Unnik, "Josephus," 247.
5. Wächter, "Haltung."

relationship between Fate and God is concisely stated in *The Jewish War* 2.162, where Josephus reports that the Pharisees attribute everything to the parallel reality of Fate *and* God. As Wächter notes, however, this parallelism between Fate and God does not appear explicitly in the *Antiquities*. Nevertheless, he concludes that the relationship of determinism and free will was paradoxical for the Pharisees, and that this Pharisaic paradox continued to be distinctive of later Judaism.[6]

The Essenes, according to Wächter, followed not only the Torah but also the rules of their community. Consequently, they were distinguished from the Sadducees and the Pharisees by their practical religion. Josephus describes the Essenes variously as leaving "everything in the hands of God" (*Antiquities* 18.18), perhaps reflecting their own understanding, and as declaring that "Fate is the mistress of all things" (13.172)—perhaps Josephus's perception of their strict adherence to community rule.[7] In any case, a synopsis of these passages does not result in the identification of Fate with God, but, as Josephus concludes of the Pharisees, in the paradoxical attribution of everything to Fate and God.

Wächter accepts the influence of the Stoic identification of εἱμαρμένη with God, or with the will of God, upon Josephus.[8] He refers to *Antiquities* 19.347, where Josephus seemingly had Agrippa conclude that fate is identical with God's will:

> I [Agrippa], a god in your eyes am now bidden to lay down my life, for fate [εἱμαρμένη] brings immediate refutation of the lying words lately addressed to me. I, who was called immortal by you, am now under the sentence of death. But I must accept my lot [πεπρωμένη] as God wills it.

---

6. Rabbi Akiba is quoted this way: "All is foreseen and free will is given, and the world is judged by goodness; and all is according to the amount." *Abot* 3, 19 in Herford, trans., *Pirke Aboth*, 88.

7. In *Vita* 10–12, Josephus tells us he studied first hand all three of the Jewish philosophies. Although he finally identified with the Pharisees, it seems fair to conclude from the amount of space he devotes to a description of the Essenes (*Jewish War* 2.119–61; and *Antiquities* 18.18–22) in comparison with that devoted to the Pharisees and the Sadducees that his affinities may lie with them. However, for some reason, perhaps whatever he means by their position on εἱμαρμένη, Josephus rejected their community for the Pharisees.

8. Wächter, "Haltung," 113. So also Nötscher, "Schicksal"; Flusser, "Josephus," 63; Nikiprowetzky, *Commentaire*, 46 among others. Moore, "Free Will," 383–84, attributes the use of εἱμαρμένη by Josephus to his dependence upon Nicolaus of Damascus.

Although Josephus greatly admired Agrippa,[9] are we to accept his version of Agrippa's view towards the role of εἱμαρμένη and God as Josephus's own position? And even if we do, this text identifies the will of God with πεπρωμένη and not with εἱμαρμένη, which is associated in this passage with Agrippa's immortality. More convincingly, Wächter notes that in 13.172, Josephus describes the Essenes as accepting Fate as the "mistress of all things," while in 18.18, he describes this same group as "wont to leave everything in the hands of God." This apparent identity of εἱμαρμένη with the will of god, at least for the Essenes, would be more convincing had it appeared in the same passage, especially in light of Josephus's reference in his description of the Essenes in *Antiquities* 18 to his earlier description in *The Jewish War* 2, but with no mention of this supposedly parallel passage in *Antiquities* 13. Nevertheless, Wächter concludes that the Essenes recognized God as Lord over all because His will and Fate are one and the same. Josephus used εἱμαρμένη, he believes, with its overtones of the determinism/free will issue current in Stoic debate, to clarify the differences between the Jewish philosophies for his Hellenistic readers, who would have little comprehension of the subtleties of Jewish theological debate.[10]

The understanding of certain language and concepts as borrowing from, or the influences of, Hellenistic philosophy, especially Stoicism, is an accepted tenet of much Josephus scholarship. Louis Feldman represents this position when he writes, in connection with another passage of the Antiquities, that "Josephus consciously colors his narrative with Stoic phraseology to make it more intelligible and attractive to his readers."[11] And, from the same article: "Since much of Josephus' projected audience was sympathetic to Stoicism, it is not surprising that there are a number of Stoic touches in his narrative."[12] Of course, we have Josephus's own account of his decision to govern his life "by the rules of the Pharisees," a sect, which, he informs his audience, has "points of resemblance to that which the Greeks call the Stoic School" (*Vita* 12). Since εἱμαρμένη is a *terminus technicus* of the Stoic philosophical tradition,[13] can we assume the influence of this widespread philosophy in *Antiquities* 13.171–73, or in the parallel passages?[14]

---

9. See *Antiquities* 19.328–31.

10. For a discussion of the determinism/free will issue in Stoicism, see Long, "Freedom and Determinism."

11. Feldman, "Josephus," 71.

12. Ibid., 90.

13. Moore, "Free Will," 376–79; see Pohlenz, *Stoa*, 101–6.

14. Flusser, "Josephus," 61–67. On the other hand, see Pines, "Platonic Model."

Unlike the Epicureans, who similar to Josephus's depiction of the Sadducees, rejected any view of existence which was determined (cf. Plutarch, *Antonius* 10.277), the Stoics harmoniously embraced the rule of Fate as the orderly principle of the universe.[15] This supreme power, as Cleanthes writes in his *Hymn to Zeus*, was called by various names, whether that principle was imagined theologically as the great god Zeus, or philosophically as the central Fire evoked by Heraclitus, or the more abstract *Logos*, or cosmologically as the World-soul, as Φύσις, or as Εἱμαρμένη. Thus, from the perspective of Stoic thought, Wächter's identification of εἱμαρμένη with God, or with πρόνοια, the will of God, in Josephus is fully justified.

However, while the central cosmic principle of Stoicism offered Hellenistic existence an understanding of a theophilosophical order, it did so at the price of determinism. As this problem has been summarized by J. Mansfeld: "In the domain of ethics, the Stoic conception of god's fatal rule gave rise to famous perplexities regarding the evaluation of human responsibility . . . As a matter of fact, the Stoics were constrained to either leave some openings for human freedom at the cost of a loss in consistency in so far their general theory was concerned . . . or to restrict human freedom to the sphere of our mental dispositions."[16] This Stoic constraint indeed would seem to parallel Josephus's description of the Pharisees as believing in Fate and God.

However, as Wächter points out, Josephus was not a philosophical thinker but an educated storyteller.[17] Further, H. Attridge suggests that Josephus does not employ the themes that generally accompany philosophical discussions of fate, e.g., a strong emphasis on teleology, the regularity of nature, and the harmony of the universe.[18] Consequently, we must conclude that if Josephus was influenced by Stoicism in his use of εἱμαρμένη, he did not use his philosophical borrowings technically but in an extremely casual manner. If such a nontechnical usage of influence were the case, it is of little value to modern interpreters to delve into the "orthodox" Stoic usages of this word. Rather, we might look to the more popular currency of this word by the first century CE.

Εἱμαρμένη was not only a Stoic technical term, but was also a central designation of the widespread and influential Hellenistic popular

---

15. Theiler, "Tacitus," 38–40 presents a survey of τύχη and εἱμαρμένη in Josephus in relation to Stoic and Epicureans views of fate.

16. Mansfeld, "Providence," 131–32.

17. Wächter, "Haltung," 101.

18. Attridge, *Interpretation*, 155–56.

astrology.[19] In the cosmogony of the *Poimandres*, we have the locus classicus of the astrological identity of εἱμαρμένη:

> God ... created seven Rulers [i.e., the planets] which encircle the world perceived through the senses. Their government is called Εἱμαρμένη. (*CH* 1.9)

This tractate later identifies this rule of εἱμαρμένη with the deterministic oppression characteristic of the anticosmism common to later Hellenistic gnostic and Hermetic literature. As in Stoicism, the comforting order of celestial causation had evolved in astrology to an oppressing determinism that actively disallowed human free will. However, whereas Stoicism had composed its deterministic view to leave openings for human freedom, the more mechanistic understandings of astrological celestial causality resulted in the dominant late Hellenistic anticosmism which was designated generally by the term εἱμαρμένη.

It is certain that Josephus was familiar with and influenced by the astrological tradition. He presents Abraham as a knowledgeable teacher of astrology to the Egyptians (*Antiquities* 1.167; see also 156). This association of Abraham with astrology was widespread.[20] As L. Feldman observes: "The picture in the Bible (Gen. 15:5) of Abraham being told by God to look at the heaven and to count the stars, since his offspring will be as numerous as they, together with the general view (Josephus I 168) that the Chaldeans, among whom Abraham was born, were the originators of the science of astronomy and astrology, gives rise to the picture of Abraham as the astronomer [astrologer] par excellence."[21]

Moreover, in *Antiquities* 3.179–87, Josephus himself employs astrological symbolism to interpret the symbolism of the Jewish tabernacle and of the vestments of the high priest. Thus, for example, he equates the twelve stones of the priest's breastplate with the twelve months and the signs of the zodiac.[22]

However, Josephus never uses εἱμαρμένη in any astrological context; but it was not necessary for him to have done so. For by his time, anticosmism was increasingly characteristic of popular piety, whether as a nontechnical casual Stoicism, as a popular astrologism, or as a theologism to designate existence after the fall.

---

19. So also Moore, "Free Will," 385; See also Cumont, *Astrology*, 84–85.
20. Baron, *Religious History*, 16–17.
21. Feldman, "Abraham," 155.
22. Patai, *Man and Temple*, 170–73.

Paul, for example, the first-century contemporary of Josephus, seems to refer to a similar negative understanding of the world when he counsels the Galatians to renounce the weak and beggarly στοιχεῖα τοῦ κόσμου which formerly determined their lives (Gal 4:8–9; 4.3; see also Col 2:8). The reverence for the "days, and months, and seasons, and years" alluded to in this passage suggests that the deterministic στοιχεῖα refer to the astrological powers of the celestial realm, which were associated with the calendar and that ruled the religious observance of this worldly existence (see Col 2:16).[23] In other words, the common understanding of the world by the first century was negative, whether expressed through such images as slavery under the στοιχεῖα τοῦ κόσμου, or the astrological images of εἱμαρμένη, or otherwise.[24]

It is this more popular sense of εἱμαρμένη as a generally negative designation of existence that we find in Josephus's *Antiquities*. In his discussion of Herod's domestic tragedy (16.395–398) Josephus writes:

> We are persuaded that human actions are dedicated by her [Fortune] beforehand to the necessity of taking place inevitably, and we call her Fate [εἱμαρμένη] on the ground that there is nothing that is not brought about by her. (16.397)

It is clear from this passage that Josephus accepts the popular usage of εἱμαρμένη as the determined governance of the human condition. However, he immediately qualifies this statement with an observation about man's responsibility for his own actions:

> Now it will, I think, suffice to compare this doctrine with that according to which we attribute some part of the cause to ourselves and hold ourselves not unaccountable for the difference in our behavior, as has been philosophically discussed before our time in the Law. (16.398)

In this passage, similar to Paul's view of freedom from the deterministic powers of the cosmos in Christ (e.g., Col 5:1), Josephus speaks of man's responsibility for his own actions, that is, of his freedom from εἱμαρμένη, in his obedience to Torah.

In *Antiquities* 13.171, Josephus further distinguishes those under the law, the three Jewish philosophies, according to their attitude towards fate, περὶ τῶν ἀνθρωπίνων πραγμάτων (concerning human affairs). By referring comprehensively to human as opposed to Jewish affairs (under the law), Josephus makes a universal statement that reflects the general Hellenistic

---

23. Betz, *Galatians*, 204–5.

24. Gnostic literature, for example, is replete with imagery of this type. See Jonas, *Gnostic*, 48–97.

"heimarmenic" view of human existence, and then gives, by contrast, the Jewish alternative of life in obedience to Torah in its various interpretations. In other words, a life of obedience to Torah offers man an alternative to the otherwise universal determinism of εἱμαρμένη, together with the subsequent freedom for directing, within the requirements of Torah, his own life.

Εἱμαρμένη, then, in Josephus's writings names a particular sense of human existence prior to and apart from Torah. It views human existence as deterministic, in the usual Hellenistic manner. For Josephus, freedom from this determinism, and thus human responsibility, is possible only in obedience to the will of God. His use of the term can be understood as a semantic ploy that sets up an apologetic contrast: life under and life apart from Torah. Contrasted with the universal givenness of human existence under the rule of εἱμαρμένη is the human will under divine law, designated by Josephus as the rule of πρόνοια, or divine providence.[25] Josephus strikingly summarizes his view of divine providence in the conclusion to his discussion of the fulfillment of Daniel's prophecy (*Antiquities* 10.276–281). In this passage he contrasts God's revelations to Daniel with the Epicurean, "who excludes Providence from human life and refuse to believe that God governs its affairs [πράγματα] or that the universe is directed by a blessed and immortal Being" (10.278).

This understanding of the use of εἱμαρμένη suggests a reevaluation of Georg Foot Moore's judgement that *Antiquities* 13.171–173 "has no connection with the preceding (Jonathan's letter to the Lacedaemonians and the reception of his overtures) nor with the following narrative (the plans and movements of Demetrius' generals)."[26] The discussion in 13.171–173 about the rule of εἱμαρμένη over all human affairs would seem to present a parallel contrast to the affairs of Jonathan, directed by the πρόνοια θεοῦ (providence of God, in 13.163). Jonathan, then, exemplifying life under God and thus freedom from εἱμαρμένη, presents a model for Jewish initiative and freedom from εἱμαρμένη under Torah. *Antiquities* 13.163–164, further, narrates how Jonathan, when he saw that by God's providence his affairs were going well, sent envoys to Rome and to Sparta. Josephus's description of the Jewish parties in 13.171–173 not only locates the Jews nicely in the international world of Romans and Greeks, but comments further upon the uniqueness

---

25. As Attridge, *Interpretation*, 157 has pointed out, "in later stages of Greek philosophy, primarily as a result of the critique of Stoic fatalism by Carnaedes and the skeptical middle Academy, εἱμαρμένη and πρόνοια regularly designated two separated spheres of causation, and πρόνοια was seen to be the more proper term for God's activity." See also ibid., 71–76. Sandmel, *Philo*, 101, concludes that Philo makes this same distinction.

26. Moore, "Free Will," 371–72.

of the Jews from the perspective of the various Jewish philosophies and their relation to Hellenistic thought. *Antiquities* 13.174 then returns to an account of the actions of Demetrius's generals.

Thus, in *Antiquities* 13.171–173, Josephus not only distinguishes between the various Jewish parties in terms of their attitude towards the law, which he presents to his Hellenistic audience through the more comprehensible terminology of εἱμαρμένη, but he locates also the Jewish people in an international setting with a universal problem: the relation of the Jews to the universal rule of εἱμαρμένη, which is over all human affairs. He presents the Jews as the people who are freed from εἱμαρμένη by the providence of God, and who consequently exercise free will and human responsibility in and through their obedience to Torah.

References

Attridge, Harold, W. *The Interpretation of Biblical History in the Antiquitates Judaicae of Flavius Josephus*. Harvard Dissertations in Religion 7. Missoula: Scholars, 1976.

Baron, Salo Wittmeyer. *A Social and Religious History of the Jews*. Vol. II, part II, *Ancient Times*. New York: Columbia University Press, 1952.

Betz, Hans Dieter. *Galatians: A Commentary on Paul's Letter to the Churches in Galatia*. Hermeneia. Philadelphia: Fortress, 1979.

Borst, Arno. *Der Turmbau von Babel*. Vol. 1, *Fundamente und Aufbau*. Stuttgart: Hiersemann, 1957.

Cumont, Franz. *Astrology and Religion among the Greeks and Romans*. 1912. Reprint, Eugene, OR: Wipf & Stock, 2005.

Feldman, Louis H. "Abraham the Greek Philosopher in Josephus." *Transactions of the American Philological Association* 99 (1968) 143–56.

———. "Josephus as an Apologist to the Graeco-Roman World: His Portrait of Solomon." In *Aspects of Religious Propaganda in Judaism and Early Christianity*, edited by Elisabeth Schüssler Fiorenza, 68–98. Studies in Judaism and Christianity in Antiquity 2. Notre Dame: University of Notre Dame Press, 1976.

Flusser, David. "Josephus on the Sadducees and Menander." *Immanuel* 7 (1977) 61–67.

Herford, Travers R., trans. *Pirke Aboth*. New York: Schocken, 1962.

Jonas, Hans. *The Gnostic Religion*. 2nd rev. ed. Boston: Beacon, 1963.

Long, Anthony A. "Freedom and Determinism in the Stoic Theory of Human Action." In *Problems in Stoicism*, edited by Anthony A. Long, 173–99. London: Athline, 1971.

Mansfeld, Jörg. "Providence and the Destruction of the Universe in Early Stoic Thought." In *Studies in Hellenistic Religions*, edited by Maarten J. Vermaseren, 129–88. EPRO 78. Leiden: Brill, 1979.

Moore, George Foot. "Fate and Free Will in the Jewish Philosophers according to Josephus." *Harvard Theological Review* 22 (1929) 371–89.

Nikiprowetzky, Valentin. *Le Commentaire de l'ecriture chez Philon d'Alexandrie*. Arbeiten zur Literatur und Geschichte des Hellenistichen Judentums 11. Leiden: Brill, 1977.

Nötscher, Friedrich. "Schicksal und Freiheit." *Biblica* 40/2 (1959) 446–62.
Patai, Raphael. *Man and Temple in Ancient Jewish Myth and Ritual*. 2nd ed. New York: Ktav, 1967.
Pies, Shlomo. "A Platonic Model for Two of Josephus's Accounts of the Doctrine of the Pharisees Concerning Providence and Man's Freedom of Action." *Immanuel* 7 (1977) 38–43.
Pohlenz, Max. *Die Stoa: Geschichte einer geistigen Bewegung*. 3rd ed. Göttingen: Vandenhoeck und Ruprecht, 1964.
Sandmel, Samuel. *Philo of Alexandria*. New York: Oxford University Press, 1979.
Stählin, Gustav. "Das Schicksal im Neuen Testament und bei Jospehus." In *Josephus Studien: Untersuchungen zu Jospehus, den Antiken Judentum und den Neuen Testaments. Otto Michel zum 70. Geburtstag gewidmet*, edited by Otto Betz et. al., 319–43. Göttingen: Vandenhoeck & Ruprecht, 1974.
Theiler, Willy. "Tacitus und die antike Schicksalslehre." In *Phyllobolia: Für Peter von der Mühll*, edited by Olaff A. Gigon, 35–90. Basel: Schwabe, 1946.
Unnik, W. C. van. "Flavious Josephus and the Mysteries." In *Studies in Hellenistic Religions*, edited by Maarten J. Vermaseren, 244–79. EPRO 78. Leiden: Brill, 1979.
Wächter, Ludwig. "Die unterschiedliche Haltung der Pharisäer, Saddizäer und Essener zur Heimarnene nach dem Bericht des Josephus." *Zeitschrift für Religions- und Geistesgeschichte* 21/2 (1969) 94–114.

18

Gods or Ambassadors of God? Barnabas and Paul in Lystra

ON WHAT IS CONVENTIONALLY characterized as Paul's "first missionary journey," the apostle, accompanied by Joseph Barnabas and John Mark, ventured into Asia Minor where they encountered a mixed reception. According to the familiar account in Acts 13–14, the delegation came first to Cyprus, Barnabas's native land (Acts 4:36), and then through Perga in Pamphylia, where Mark unaccountably left the delegation and returned to Jerusalem, and on to Antioch of Pisidia, a Roman colony known as Caesarea (Pliny, *Naturalis historia* 5.94). Despite initial successes, the apostles were expelled from the city by the leaders of the synagogue there.[1] They then traveled on to Iconium in neighboring Lycaonia, also a Roman colony (5.95),[2] where, as in Antioch, initial success was also met with persecution organized by Jewish leaders. These two stylized accounts of the apostles' missionary successes among both Jews and Gentiles (Acts 13:46; 14:1) and their subsequent rejection by local Jewish leaders provide a narrative transition to the account of their mission in the Roman colony of Lystra,[3] the next city to which they fled and, according to the narrative construction of Acts, their first entirely non-Jewish audience.[4] Although they are eventually chased from Lystra as well, but this time at the instigation of outside Jewish agitators from Antioch and Iconium (Acts 14:19), the positive reception ac-

---

1. The appearance of the Hebrew name Deborah in a Greek inscription from Antioch suggests the presence of a Jewish community in Pisidian Antioch. Legrand and Chamonard, "Inscriptions," 257; Ramsay, *Cities*, 255–59.

2. Ramsay, *Cities*, 317–82.

3. Ibid., 407–18. On the colonies of Antioch of Pisidia, Iconium, and Lystra, see Levick, *Roman Colonies*.

4. Stokes, *Acts*, 2:212; Conzelmann, *Acts*, 110.

corded Paul and Barnabas by the Lystran Gentile audience was dramatic indeed!

> Barnabas they called Zeus, and Paul . . . they called Hermes. And the priest of Zeus, whose temple was in front of the city, brought oxen and garlands to the gates and wanted to offer sacrifice with the people. (Acts 14:12–13)

The identification of Barnabas and Paul with deities was, from their ascribed Christian perspective, scandalous (Acts 14:14); apparently not, however, for the purpose of the author of Acts, who preserves also an account of Paul being taken for a deity by the inhabitants of Malta (28:6). What might be the intent of the author of Acts for including in his account of the Lystran gentile mission the identification of the two apostles with Zeus and Hermes?

Commentators generally note that early in the first century, Ovid had told a similar story set in nearby Phrygia,[5] in which Jupiter (Zeus) and Mercury (Hermes) also appear together disguised as mortals (*Metamorphoses* 8.611–725), a motif of deity or other superhuman being wandering about on earth in disguise that was as familiar in the Hellenistic world as it is in folk tales generally.[6] The difference between Ovid and Acts, of course, is that in the *Metamorphoses*, the strangers were deities mistaken for mortals while in Acts they were mortals taken for deities. And yet, both mistakes involve the divine pair, Zeus and Hermes, whose association in the region is documented by inscription and statuary.[7] It has been argued most recently that the association between Zeus and Hermes and their appearance together in human form reflects a local tradition in which Zeus and Hermes had been identified with Hittite-Luwan weather deities in the Hellenistic period, and that this tradition was not only taken up by Ovid but also by the author of Acts 14:12–13, who has shaped it in accordance with the mission

---

5. See the discussion of possible geographical settings in Fontenrose, *Philemon*, 93–120.

6. Ibid., 97. See also the Genesis story of Lot, alluded to by the author of Acts (Luke 17:28–32), in which two angels disguised as mortals (Gen 19:1) are received by Lot (19:3) before revealing themselves to be messengers of Yahweh (19:13). Fontenrose argues that the "Lot and Philemon stories are variants of the same story type, which is a subtype of the Babylonian flood myth" (ibid., 119).

7. Foakes-Jackson and Lake, *Acts*, IV, 164; Conzelmann, *Acts*, 10. See also Calder, "The 'Priest'"; Swoboda et al., *Denkmäler*; Breytenbach, "Zeus," 400 n31. Although this documentation is from the third century CE, an earlier association of Zeus and Hermes is documented from the late third century BCE in statuary: on a later-third-century to early-second-century marble relief cylinder from Alexander, for example, or on a mid-second-century to mid-first-century-BCE marble base from Rome (Long, *Twelve Gods*, 3–4, 34–35).

terminology of Greek-speaking Judaism.[8] An earlier commentator had concluded, however, that, given the author's "classical" perspective, "it need not be asked whether we have here a Greek interpretation of . . . native gods. For the author . . . they are recognized simply as Zeus and Hermes."[9] To the extent that any religious expression reflects its cultural context, it would seem that this latter conclusion, situating the intent of the author of Acts in a larger Greek context, better elucidates this enigmatic passage than do attempts to situate it largely in localized histories of religion or in light of the missionary efforts of Jews who are, in any case, clearly portrayed in Acts as antithetical to the Christian mission. This conclusion does not, however, address the intent of the author of the Acts narrative for the misidentification of the missionaries Barnabas and Paul with Zeus and Hermes.

What biblical commentators on Acts 14 seem not to have noticed is the thoroughly Greek description of Zeus and Hermes precisely as the guarantors of emissaries and missions. As Plato summarized in his *Laws* 941A,

> If anyone, while acting as ambassador [πρεσβευτής] or herald, conveys false messages from his State to another State, or fails to deliver the actual message he was sent to deliver, or is proved to have brought back, as ambassador or herald, either from a friendly or hostile nature, their reply in a false form,—against

---

8. Breytenbach, "Zeus," 403. On Jewish missions, see Bultmann, *Theology*, 1:65–92. Focusing on facticity rather than narrativity, many commentators fret over the problems of communication between the Greek-speaking apostles and the Lycaonian speaking Lystrans reported in Acts 14:11 (see, for example, Foakes-Jackson and Lake, *Acts*, 4:164; Haenchen, *Apostelgeschichte*, 367), and this presumption has led to convoluted semantic discussions about whether or not Ovid's story of Baucis and Philemon constitutes a parallel to the account of the identification of Barnabas and Paul with Zeus and Hermes by the Lystrans. Foakes-Jackson and Lake (*Acts*, 4:164), for example, conclude that "if the populace had been talking Greek a conscious reference to this [Latin?] story would be probable, but since they were talking Lycaonian it is very unlikely that they used the names Zeus or Hermes." [Ovid, of course, used the names Jupiter and Mercury]. Those designated "Hellenes" in Lystra, however, were so by education and were restricted to the upper classes (Ramsay, *Cities*, 417–18), and despite the large number of Latin inscriptions at Lystra (ibid., 412), its Roman element was "scanty and unimportant" (ibid., 417). The population of Lystra seems rather to have been dominated by uneducated Lycaonian natives (ibid., 418). Breytenbach, "Zeus," 399 correctly points out that it was this indigenous, Lycaonian population of Lystra and not the Roman colonists that are presented by the author of Acts as having identified the apostles with Zeus and Hermes. Conzelmann, *Acts*, 110 correctly understands the reference to native language in Acts as the author's "development of a literary motif." On the native deities of southern Asia Minor and their Greek identities, see Houwink ten Cate, *Luwian Population*, 190–92, 194, 210–13.

9. Conzelmann, *Acts*, 110; on the use of classical style and language by the author of Acts, see also Harnack, *Acts*, xxxvi–xxxvii; Plummer, *Critical and Exegetical*, xxxiii–lxvii; Cadbury, *Luke-Acts*, 337–50; Plümacher, *Lukas*.

all such there shall be laid an indictment for breaking the law by sinning against [ἀσεβησάντων] the sacred messages and injunctions of Hermes and Zeus.

Since the time of Homer, who pointed out that "gods in the guise of strangers from afar put on all manner of shapes, and visit the cities" (*Odyssey* 17.485-87),[10] Greeks had known Zeus, as he was known to the Plato of the *Laws*, as Ξένιος, the patron of strangers who accompanied certain "revered" travelers on their journeys and who, as their "avenger," supported and defended their rights in foreign places (9.270-72; Plato, *Sophist* 216A-B; *Laws* 729E-730A; 843A; 879D-E).[11] Further, Zeus is portrayed in the *Laws*, as is Hermes in Greek mythology generally, as ὅριος, the god of boundaries (842E), "extending his protection . . . to foreigners on the frontier."[12] Diodorus Siculus confirms that this tradition of ambassadorial patronage and protection, at least by Zeus's son, Hermes, was still recognized during the reign of Augustus (5.75.1).

As most commentators have further noted, the Lystrans associated Paul specifically with Hermes "because he was the chief speaker" (Acts 14:12: ὁ ἡγούμενος τοῦ λόγου), certainly a requisite qualification for any ambassador. This characterization accords well with mythological portrayals of Hermes since Homer and almost exactly with the description of Hermes by Iamblichus, the third-century-CE Neoplatonist, who described the god as he "who is the leader in speaking" (*De mysteriis* 1.1: ὁ τῶν λόγων ἡγεμών). Although Zeus does not speak, both deities guarantee that what is to be spoken are not "false messages" (Plato, *Laws* 941A) but "good news." As the representative or messenger of his father, Zeus, one of whose epitaphs was εὐαγγέλιος, "giver of glad tidings" (Aristides, *Orationes* 53), Hermes was himself εὐαγγέλος, "bringer of glad tidings" (Hesychius *s.v.*),[13] an association of the messenger with his good news recognized also in the first century CE (Philo, *Legatio ad Gaium* 99) and explicitly attributed to Paul by the author of Acts (14:15).[14] It was this symbiotic warranting of

---

10. This passage, conflated with *Odyssey* 9.270-272 (considered below), is cited by Plato in *Sophist*, 216A-B.

11. Nock, "Emperor's Divine," II, 2:160.

12. Morrow, *Plato's Cretan City*, 437.

13. For documentation of this title in the first century BCE, see Rubensohn, "Paros II," 221; for Hermes as ἄγγελος, see *Odyssey* 5.29; *Homeric Hymn to Demeter* 407; *Homeric Hymn to Pan* 29; for Paul's own account of being taken by the "Galatians" for an ἄγγελος θεοῦ, see Gal 4:14; compare the *Acts of Paul and Thecla* 3, which describes Paul as having the ἀγγέλου πρόσωπον.

14. Breytenbach, "Zeus," 397, notes that εὐαγγελίζεσθαι is also characteristic of LXX usage.

both the source and bearer of messages that associated Zeus and Hermes in their traditional Greek role as guarantors of the veracity of missions and, by a narrative implication by misidentification, legitimated the Christian mission of Barnabas and Paul to their Hellenistic audience—as to that of the author of Acts.

The stories of Zeus and Hermes in Acts and in Ovid's *Metamorphoses* share further the theme of hospitality extended to strangers, a right also under the protection of Zeus Xenios (*Odyssey* 9.271; *Iliad* 13.625; Plato, *Laws* 718A; 879A). Although the disguised deities of Ovid's story came to a thousand houses seeking a place for rest, they were received in but one: the home of Baucis and Philemon (628–632). When the elderly couple offered the "travelers" what little refreshment they could provide, the "strangers" revealed their true nature as gods. Similarly, the Lystrans offered their hospitality to Barnabas and Paul following earlier rejections of the itinerant missionaries in Antioch and Iconium.

Lystran hospitality is represented in Acts by the apparently extravagant gesture of sacrifice by the priests of Lystra. This offer might better be understood as an invitation to honor Barnabas and Paul by including these foreign dignitaries in the local civic ceremonies of the Lystrans, perhaps in reference to the legal requirement, also recorded in Plato's *Laws*, that sacrifice always be public (909E–910A), but most certainly including the customary table fellowship attendant on it.[15] As with the inverse themes of human-deity identification in Ovid's *Metamorphoses* and Acts, the apostles proclaimed their own true nature while rejecting the Lystran manner of hospitality (Acts 14:15).

Whatever local traditions the author of Acts may have employed in constructing his narrative, it seems clear that he firmly situated it, as did Ovid, in the context of classical Greek tradition. We might conclude, therefore, that the account in Acts about Barnabas and Paul being mistaken by the Lystrans for Zeus and Hermes reflects a Greek juridical trope,[16] employed by the author of Acts from his "classical perspective," to remind his Hellenistic readers of customary ambassadorial prerogatives and to recommend to them traditional Hellenic obligations of hospitality upon the occasion of such a well-intentioned ambassadorial initiative. The apostles' rejection of Lystran hospitality establishes, in the narrative construction of Acts, a sharp contrast between the Greek view of deities, their sometimes disguised presence and their prescribed worship, on the one hand, and the "living God"

---

15. Kane, "Mithraic Cult Meal," 321–29; Detienne, "Culinary."

16. Πρεσβευτής, as is the verb πρεσβεύω, was a juridical term of Greek foreign relations (Deissmann, *Light*, 379), as well as a self-designation of Paul (2 Cor 5:20; Phlm 9) continued in the deutero-Pauline tradition (Eph 6:20).

of the biblical tradition, on the other (Acts 14:15),[17] even as a distinction between the "unbelieving Jews" and the Christians is made in the passages that precede and follow the account of the Lystran mission (Acts 14:1–7; 19–23). The author of Acts represents, thereby, not only the legitimacy and veracity of the Christian mission to the Gentiles but its uniqueness.

References

Breytenbach, Celliers. "Zeus und der lebendige Gott: Anmerkungen zu Apostelgeschichte 14.11–17." *New Testament Studies* 39/3 (1993) 396–413.
Bultmann, Rudolf. *Theology of the New Testament*. 2 vols. Translated by Kendrick Grobel. 1951–1955. Reprint, Waco, TX: Baylor University Press, 2007.
Cadbury, Henry J. *The Making of Luke-Acts*. New York: Macmillan, 1927.
Calder, W. M. "The 'Priest' of Zeus at Lystra." *Expositor* 7/10 (1910) 148–55.
Conzelmann, Hans. *The Acts of the Apostles*. Translated by James Limburg et al. Hermeneia. Philadelphia: Fortress, 1987.
Deissmann, Adolf. *Light from the Ancient East: The New Testament Illustrated by Recently Discovered Texts of the Graeco-Roman World*. Translated by Lionel R. M. Strachen. 1927. Reprint, Eugene, OR: Wipf & Stock, 2004.
Detienne, Marcel. "Culinary Practices and the Spirit of Sacrifice." In *The Cuisine of Sacrifice among the Greeks*, edited by Marcel Detienne and Jean-Pierre Vernant, 1–20. Translated by Paula Wissing. Chicago: University of Chicago Press, 1989.
Foakes-Jackson, F. J., and Kirsopp Lake. *The Acts of the Apostles*. 5 vols. Beginnings of Christianity, part 1. Grand Rapids: Baker, 1979.
Fontenrose, Joseph. *Philemon, Lot, and Lycaon*. University of California Publications in Classical Philology 13/4. Berkeley: University of California Press, 1945.
Harnack, Adolf. *The Acts of the Apostles*. Translated by J. R. Wilkinson. 1909. Reprint, Eugene, OR: Wipf & Stock, 2000.
Haenchen, Ernst. *Die Apostelgeschichte*. Kritisch-exegetischer Kommentar über das Neue Testament 3. Göttingen: Vandenhoeck & Ruprecht, 1961.
Houwink ten Cate, Philip H. J. *The Luwian Population Groups of Lycia and Cilicia Aspera during the Hellenistic Period*. Documenta et monumenta Orientis antiqui 10. Leiden: Brill, 1961.
Kane, J. P. "The Mithraic Cult Meal in its Greek and Roman Environment." In *Mithraic Studies: Proceedings of the First International Congress of Mithraic Studies*, edited by John R. Hinnells, 2:33–51. 2 vols. Manchester: Manchester University Press, 1975.
Legrand, E., and J. Chamonard. "Inscriptions de Phrygie (1)." *Bulletin de Correspondance Hellénique* 17 (1893) 241–93.
Levick, Barbara. *Roman Colonies in Southern Asia Minor*. Oxford: Oxford University Press, 1967.
Long, Charlotte R. *The Twelve Gods of Greece and Rome*. EPRO 107. Leiden: Brill, 1987.
Morrow, Glenn R. *Plato's Cretan City: A Historical Interpretation of the Laws*. Princeton: Princeton University Press, 1960.

---

17. Breytenbach, "Zeus," 397, notes that ὁ θεός ζῶον is a characteristic of LXX usage.

Nock, Arthur D. "The Emperor's Divine *Comes.*" In *Arthur Darby Nock: Essays on Religion and the Ancient World*, edited by Zeph Stewart, 2:653–81. 2 vols. Cambridge: Harvard University Press, 1972.

Plümacher, Eckhard. *Lukas als hellenistischer Schriftsteller*. Studien zur Umwelt des Neuen Testaments 9. Göttingen: Vandenhoeck & Ruprecht, 1972.

Plummer, Alfred. *A Critical and Exegetical Commentary on the Gospel according to S. Luke*. The International Critical Commentary. Edinburgh: T. & T. Clark, 1922.

Ramsay, W. M. *The Cities of St. Paul: Their Influence on His Life and Thought*. The Dale Memorial Lectures 1907. London: Hodder & Stoughton, 1907.

Rubensohn, O. "Paros II." *Mitteilungen des Kaiserlich Deutschen Archäologischen Instituts. Athenische Abteilung* 26 (1901) 157–222.

Stokes, G. T. *The Acts of the Apostles*. Expositor's Bible. 2 vols. New York: Armstrong, 1905.

Swoboda, H. et al., eds. *Denkmäler aus Lykaonien, Pamphylien und Isaurien*. Brno: Rohrer, 1935.

19

The Hellenisation of Judaeo-Christian Faith or the Christianisation of Hellenic Thought?

> The transition from pagan to Christian is the point at which the ancient world still touches ours directly. We are heirs to its conclusion...
>
> ROBIN LANE FOX[1]

THE THEME "THE HELLENIZATION of Judaeo-Christian thought" focuses our attention on the ambiguous relationship between faith and reason that has characterized Western culture from the origins of Christianity until modernity. This theme is usually approached from the perspective of the history of ideas whereby some understanding of Christian origins in the context of Jewish religiosity becomes transformed into a rational, philosophical theology under the influence of Greek thought. So, for example, a Jewish, and then a Judaeo-Christian, belief in a personal god becomes transformed into the totalizing monotheistic theologies of an Augustine or an Aquinas.

As Bernhard Lang has so profitably instructed us, however, monotheism, in the biblical tradition, is not a matter of faith but is a matter of power. And as Max Weber has taught us and Michel Foucault reminded us, power is the fundamental characteristic of all social relationships and their formation.

Consequently, I should like to approach my theme not from the perspective of the history of ideas but from that of social history—a history in which claims to a universal and absolute monotheism represent the ideological aspirations of an increasingly successful consolidation of power by

---

1. Fox, *Pagans*, 11.

alliances between some of the early Christianities. In this sense, my thesis is that rather than understanding a Hellenization of Judaeo-Christian thought, we might better speak of the Christianization of Hellenic thought.

The Conventional View

The conventional view of the Hellenization of Judaeo-Christian thought was given scholarly establishment by Edwin Hatch in his 1888 Hibbert Lectures, *The Influence of Greek Ideas and Usages on Christianity*.[2] In this study, Hatch contrasts the ethical simplicity of the Sermon on the Mount with fourth-century creedal doctrine as exemplified by the Nicene Creed; the former, he observed, "belongs to a world of Syrian peasants, the other to a world of Greek philosophers."[3] The "change in the centre of gravity from conduct to belief is coincident with the transference of Christianity from a Semitic to a Greek soil."[4] Jonathan Z. Smith has argued persuasively that Hatch's view of "the rapid hellenization of Christianity from its primitive simplicity to the decadent complexity of its later 'Catholic' forms" is essentially a Protestant theological paradigm of Christian origins.[5] As formulated by Adolf von Harnack, "the most important premises of the Catholic doctrine of faith belong [. . . to] an element which we cannot recognize as dominant in the New Testament, viz., the Hellenic spirit."[6]

Harnack went a step further than Hatch to argue that the Hellenization that produced the "Catholic system" was analogous to that which produced heresy.[7] Harnack distinguished "the Catholic embodiment of Christianity" from Gnosticism only in that the latter represents an "*acute* . . . hellenising of Christianity,"[8] a position still widely held.[9] For Harnack, "Gnosticism" was "just Hellenism"[10]—"Greek society with a Christian name."[11] The Gnostics, Harnack concluded,

---

2. Hatch, *Influence*, 2.
3. Ibid., 1.
4. Ibid., 2.
5. Smith, *Drudgery Divine*, 60; Hatch, *Influence*, 121–22.
6. Harnack, *Lehrbuch*, 1:48–49.
7. Ibid., 1:226.
8. Ibid.
9. E.g., Frend, *Rise*, chapter 6.
10. Harnack, *Lehrbuch*, 1:227.
11. Ibid., 1:227 n1.

were the theologians of the first century. They were the first to transform Christianity into a system of doctrines (dogmas). They were the first to work up tradition systematically. They undertook to present Christianity as the absolute religion, and therefore placed it in definite opposition to the other religions, even to Judaism. But to them the absolute religion, viewed in its contents, was identical with the result of the philosophy of religion for which the support of a revelation was to be sought. They are therefore those Christians who, in a swift advance, attempted to capture Christianity for Hellenic culture, and Hellenic culture for Christianity.[12]

In contrast to a Hellenized Christianity, Harnack characterized the original or simple form of Christianity, in part, by its "enthusiastic character . . . : the Charismatic teachers and the appeal to the Spirit."[13] Harnack's invocation of "charisma" as characteristic of Christian origins was borrowed, of course, from Paul's First Letter to the Corinthians but also from Max Weber, who introduced the term as a sociological category.[14]

According to Weber, "charismatic" individuals are often understood as the "founders" of religious traditions. "The holder of charisma," Weber wrote,

> seizes the task that is adequate for him and demands obedience and a following by virtue of his mission. His success determines whether he finds them. His charismatic claim breaks down if his mission is not recognized by those to whom he feels he has been sent. If they recognize them, he is their master.[15]

The originating "charismatic impulse" is then succeeded, more or less rapidly, by the dynamics of a proceduralized rationality, a dynamics Weber termed the "castration of charisma."[16]

A "Protestant" reading of Weber's theoretical model emphasizes the simple but charismatic personality of the founder, Jesus, for example, which lends authority to his ideas. This understanding of charismatic authority gives charter to the central Protestant principle of salvation by faith alone as confirmed in an *experience* of grace. The paradigm of this Reformation

---

12. Ibid., 1:227.
13. Ibid., 1:141.
14. Weber, "Sociology," 246. Weber, Harnack, and Ernst Troeltsch were involved in mutual discussions in the context of the "Protestant-oriented 'approach to the history of religion.'" See Schluchter, *Rise*, 219.
15. Weber, "Sociology," 246.
16. Weber, *Economy*, 1132; Diggins, *Max Weber*, 82.

attribution of centrality to personal experience is mysticism, often understood in Weberian terms of charismatic possession exemplified and legitimized by the Lucan ecclesiastical mythology of Pentecost.[17] For Weber, however, charisma is only that "which is recognized, by believers and followers, as 'charismatic' in the behaviour of those they treat as charismatic."[18] It is that "to which the governed submit because of their belief in the extraordinary quality of the specific person."[19] In this sense, charisma describes a "social relationship, not an attribute of individual personality or a mystical quality"; it is "a datum not a confirmation," an ascription not an achievement.[20] It was, in fact, not Jesus but the Jesus movement that served as the "material" out of which Weber developed his "ideal type" of charismatic authority.[21] That is to say, Weber was not describing a personal attribute of leaders in the founding of religions, or any other social group, but was characterizing rather a typical sociological strategy employed by new movements to legitimize themselves by imputing—either contemporaneously or retrospectively—"charismatic" authority to their founders—whether real or fictive.[22]

It is such a social view of the early Christianities which I should like to explore. This agenda was already formulated by Ernst Troeltsch in 1922:

> The whole range of ideas in the philosophy of history and theory of development [of Christianity] had to date been treated onesidedly as history of ideas, as with Hegel and Dilthey. It had to play a large part in every philosophy of religion. Now it was changing. New problems emerged out of all the existing solutions. At the same time I came under the spell of that overwhelming personality Max Weber who had long been well aware of these wonders which for me were just dawning. And at the point I was captivated by the Marxist doctrine of infrastructures and superstructures. Not that I simply considered it correct, but it does contain a mode of question which can never be evaded, even though each separate case must be examined individually. Its mode of questioning was how far the origin, development, change and modern plight of Christianity is sociologically conditioned, and how far it itself operates as a

---

17. Martin, "Anti-Individualistic," 138 n53.
18. Weber, "Social Psychology," 295; Weber, *Economy*, 242; Worsley, *Trumpet*, xii.
19. Weber, "Social Psychology," 295.
20. Weber, "Sociology," 246; Worsley, *Trumpet*, ix–xxi.
21. Schluchter, *Rise*, 205; Gerth-Mills, "Introduction," 55: "Not Julius Caesar, but Caesarism; not Calvin, but Calvinism is Weber's concern."
22. Stark, *Rise*, 24.

formative sociological principle. These are extraordinarily difficult questions and scarcely any useful preparatory studies had been done on them. And yet it was no longer possible to speak of a purely history of doctrine or history of ideas approach to Christianity, once this problem had been grasped.[23]

Troeltsch's realization of sociological import should at least problematize the conventional history of ideas approach to the Hellenization of Judaeo-Christian thought. And as Troeltsch suggested, Weber might well help us, for Weber pursued his study of Judaism and Christianity, which he judged had given shape to the "unique character of Western civilization"[24] through a combination of concrete historical research and systematic sociological analysis.[25]

The Weberian View

Weber never wrote the monograph on early Christianity that he had envisioned.[26] Nevertheless, he did discuss early Christianity in various places throughout his other writings. I am indebted in the following to Wolfgang Schluchter's reconstruction of Weber's view of Christian origins.[27]

For Weber, it was, indeed, the early Christian encounter with Hellenistic philosophy that produced Christian theological thought. However, the theology it produced was, according to Weber, inherently and finally anti-intellectual.

Clement of Alexandria and Origen had followed the early second-century apologist, Justin Martyr, in harmonizing Christianity with Greek philosophy. "Reason," Justin wrote, "directs those who are truly pious and philosophical to honor and to love only what is true" (1 *Apology* 2; see also 1 *Apology* 12; 2 *Apology* 4.15). He reflected, thereby, the philosophical tradition that claimed piety as one of its own fruits (e.g., Seneca, *Epistulae* 90.3). "We say things similar to the Greeks," Justin conceded (1 *Apology* 24); and Clement even defended the divine origin of philosophy (Clement *Stromateis* 7.6.4). As Henry Chadwick noted, the learned among the Christians found in Greek philosophy "a partial apprehension of truths

---

23. Troeltsch, "Meiner Bücher (1922)," 11.
24. Schluchter, *Rise*, xv.
25. Ibid., xiii.
26. Ibid., xv.
27. See also Kippenberg, *Erlösungsreligionen*.

more completely found in Christianity."[28] Consequently, the philosophers, in Origen's view, might even been converted to that Christianity for which they had long been preparatory (Origen, *Contra Celsum* 75; Justin, *Dialogue with Trypho* 2; 1 *Apology* 24, 46; Clement, *Stromateis* 1.1, 5, 7, 20, 80; 6.17; 7.3). Despite the rejection of philosophy in favor of "revelation" by many of the first Christians (e.g., Gal 1:12; 2 Tim 2:14; Nag Hammadi Codex 1.4.46.3–13; 11.3.67.20–38), philosophical argument was readily adopted by second-century Christians.

By the end of the second century, however, the intellectualist stance of many of the earlier Christian thinkers was challenged by Tertullian, whose thundering anti-intellectualism still resounds in contemporary religious expression: Christian doctrine "is absolutely worthy of belief because it is absurd" (*de Carne Christi* 5).[29] And, although Athanasius excused Origen's earlier philosophical zeal on the grounds that many of his arguments were for the sake of practice and investigation (*De decretis* 27),[30] he castigated the fourth-century Origenists and their Arianist followers by defending the position of faith over intellect.[31] Weber followed Harnack's judgement that it was Athanasius who finally saved the church from philosophy.[32] As Weber concluded, "Athanasius won out with his [anti-Arian] formula—completely absurd when viewed rationally—in his struggle against the majority of the Hellenic philosophers of the time."[33]

Weber identified two other intellectual movements against which the early Christianities defined themselves. The first were the Pharisees, who established in their own dispute with the Sadducees the principle of education over the principle of birth. This principle was followed in Talmudic Judaism in which salvation was achieved through knowledge of the law.[34]

The second intellectual movement against which Christianity defined itself was, according to Weber, Gnosticism, in which *gnosis* was opposed to faith. Gnosticism shared generally with philosophy the premise that salvation was based upon cognition.[35] For Weber, then, the Christian gospel "was

28. Chadwick, *Early Christian*, 22.

29. Ibid., 1–2. The phrase *Credo quia absurdum*, often attributed to Tertullian, is not his; rather, his formulation in this passage is: *Prorsus credibile est, quia ineptum est.*

30. Cited in Harnack, *History*, 3:183.

31. Harnack, *Lehrbuch*, 3:141–44; 4:26 n2.

32. Ibid., 3:144; 4:46.

33. Weber, "Religious Rejections," 351.

34. Weber, *Judaism*, 391; Weber, *Economy*, 631; Schluchter, *Rise*, 206.

35. Schluchter, *Rationalism*, 243. One of the Nag Hammadi gnostic documents, "The Treatise on the Resurrection" (*De Res.* 46.3–13) apparently opposes philosophy in favor of faith. Bentley Layton notes, however, that the "ordinary Christian" reference to

conceived in opposition to Rabbinical and Hellenic Wisdom" as a "nonintellectual's proclamation directed to nonintellectuals."[36]

Paul represented, for Weber, the second generation of the Christian movement, i.e., that which developed relatively independently of the Jesus movement out of the milieu of urban intellectualism.[37] In contrast to Pharisaic congregations, Paul, in Weber's view, organized charismatic communities that subordinated law to spirit,[38] transforming thereby the charismatic congregation into an "institutional carrier of a charismatic community."[39] While Paul was interested in the possibilities of the mind, he was also concerned with constraining rationality within the framework of a religiosity of faith. Paul's accomplishment, according to Weber, was to temper the charismatic character of the Jesus movement with an intellectual supplementation while not eliminating its pneumatic nature.[40] It was this Pauline transformation of charisma from the personal to the institutional that represented, for Weber, one of the "turning point[s] for the entire cultural tradition of the West."[41]

The charismatic congregations established by Paul soon gave way, in Weber's view, to the rational bureaucratization of Catholicism. However, "encapsulations" of the Pauline congregations maintained themselves in sectarian movements as, in the words of Wolfgang Schluchter, a revolutionary "potential that finally explosively unfolded in the Reformation."[42] Protestantism thus "concluded the process of disenchantment in the history of religions that had begun, in Weber's scheme, with ancient Jewish prophecy."[43]

"faith," "actually means [in this context] acquaintance with the truth, i.e., *gnosis*" (Layton, *Gnostic Scriptures*, 321 n46.d). This treatise may be closer to Pauline thought than to what is usually characterized as "gnostic," at least, Paul is authoritatively invoked by this tractate (45.24), cf. Layton, *Gnostic Scriptures*, 321 n45.i.

36. Schluchter, *Rise*, 158; Weber, *Economy*, 631–32.
37. Schluchter, *Rationalism*, 212.
38. Ibid., 219.
39. Ibid., 216.
40. Schluchter, *Rationalism*, 212. In the similar view of Harnack, *Lehrbuch*, 1:131, Christian dogma "did not spring from the eschatological, but from the spiritual mode of thought."
41. Schluchter, *Rationalism*, 227; Weber, *Judaism*, 5; so Harnack, *Lehrbuch*, 1:136.
42. Schluchter, *Rationalism*, 243.
43. Ibid., 240; Weber, *Protestant Ethic*, 105.

The Weberian View: A Critique

Weber's recourse to the heritage of Judaism underlines the attraction of Jewish imagery for Protestant theology and the more recent American-mythic evocations of a common "Judaeo-Christian" tradition.[44] Such retrospective legitimizations are an inherent characteristic of the collective genealogical claims made by all successful social formations. By contrast, however, such claims also pose the historical question of the sociocultural location of these claims. Despite Weber's central contribution to understanding the early Christianities from a sociological point of view, I should like to suggest two Reformation characteristics attributed to Weber that I believe have been inappropriately situated in Mediterranean antiquity: the "absolute religious individualism" often attributed to early Christianity and a consequent asocial/apolitical character attributed to the early Christian groups.

In his reconstruction of Weber's view of ancient Christianity, Schluchter speaks of the centrality of the "two-fold sociological character" of early Christianity: its "absolute religious individualism" and its "absolute religious universalism."[45] This twofold sociology of early Christianity is not Weber's, however, but that of Troeltsch, which, Schluchter believes, "can be applied—without doing violence—to Weber's view of Christianity."[46] I believe that the application of Troeltsch's view to that of Weber's does, on this point, do violence, for Troeltsch's point here is neither sociological nor historical but theological. The "basis and ... justification" for the "standard of individualism in the gospel ethic," Troeltsch wrote,

> lies in the fact that man is called to fellowship with God, or, as it is here expressed, to be the child of God, and in the eternal value of the soul which this filial relation confers. The individual ... reaches this goal only through self-abnegation in unconditional obedience to the Holy Will of God ... It is ... clear that such an individualism is only possible at all upon this religious basis.[47]

As Hatch similarly summarized this conventional view, "the first age of Christianity ... was profoundly individual. It assumed for the first time in history the infinite worth of the individual soul."[48] Many modern scholars are still concerned with the question of "how the charismatic [that is, indi-

---

44. On the construction of American myths of inclusion based upon claims of common heritage, see Kammen, *Mystic Chords*, especially 3–39, 531–38.
45. Schluchter, *Rationalism*, 240–41; Schluchter, *Rise*, 166–67.
46. Schuchter, *Rationalism*, 241.
47. Troeltsch, *Social Teaching*, 1:55.
48. Hatch, *Influence*, 334.

vidualistic] fellowship of the apostolic Church," that *original* Christianity *rediscovered* by the Protestant reformers, "gave rise to the bureaucracy of Roman Catholicism."[49]

Weber himself never wrote much about individualism, and when he did, it was in connection with the Protestant ethic.[50] His own concern with individualism only arose out of his disillusionment with the "German organic vision of the nation-state." Instead, he "adopted a vision of politics closer to Anglo-American traditions, in which the purposes of individuals take precedence over the universal claims of the state."[51] Perhaps Weber's turn to an individualistic politics together with his interest in the Reformation as another "turning point in Western cultural development" has led some of his interpreters to project this modern value into their own studies of antiquity, especially, as we have seen, with erroneous reference to the individual character of charisma.

In an article on "The Anti-Individualistic Ideology of Hellenistic Culture,"[52] I argued that the indisputably modern Western value of individualism (that is, a valuing of the individual over society as the carrier of permanent values)[53] has come to shape historical generalizations about antiquity by historians who tend to claim the origins of individualism for their own domains of research—a historical conceit already recognized by Weber.[54] Examples extend from sixth-century-BCE Greece through modern Europe.[55] Whenever an "ideal" of the individual self first became valued differently from that of the society of which it is a member, any concept approaching that of modern Western individualism was irrelevant, I concluded, for the Hellenistic world.[56] I tend to agree with Jacob Burckhardt that the emergence of individualism is sometime around the Renaissance,[57] as apparently does Weber.[58]

Although it was the case that the sociopolitical transformations that characterized Hellenistic imperial culture challenged the traditional

49. Nelson, "Weber, Troeltsch," 232.
50. Weber, *Protestant Ethic*, 105–6.
51. Diggins, *Max Weber*, 69; see Weber, "Vocation."
52. Martin, "Anti-Individualistic."
53. Dumont, *Essays*, 25; for further literature, see Martin, "Anti-Individualistic," 135 n11.
54. Weber, *Protestant Ethic*, 222 n22.
55. Martin, "Anti-Individualistic," 117; Kippenberg, *Erlösungsreligionen*, 67.
56. Martin, "Anti-Individualistic," 134.
57. Burckhardt, *Civilization*.
58. Weber, *Protestant Ethic*, 105, 222 n22.

localized cultural bases for identity, the consequence of this challenge was not the emergence of individualism but rather of a proliferation of alternative social strategies of identity: philosophical groups, religious and social clubs, and mystery cults.[59]

Although Weber accepted the historically evident proliferation of diverse social groups during the Hellenistic era, and especially during the first period of the Roman Empire, he emphasized the absence of any "social consciousness" among them.[60] "Because of the belief in the permanence of Roman rule until the end of time," he wrote that

> men felt it was hopeless to strive for social reform and therefore rejected all class struggles; and this was the source from which flowed Christian love—purely ethical, charitable and transcendental.[61]

However, most of the alternative associations of the Hellenistic period can be seen as fictive kinship societies organized in contrast with the power of imperial kingship.[62] I should like to illustrate this political concern from the thought of Plotinus, a philosopher usually associated with the spiritual paradigm of bodily transcendence and otherworldliness that forms the basis for many popular as well as scholarly models of mysticism.[63]

Although it might be assumed that a thoroughgoing metaphysical position, such as that of Plotinus, accords best with the apolitical stance Weber attributes to groups in this period, Plotinus was quite aware of the vulnerability of Roman rule, which he understood to be the illusory attraction of sensory existence (*Enneades* 4.4.43–44). His goal was nothing less than the establishment of his own ideal community. Whether intentionally or not, Plotinus transferred into his vision a model of hierarchical social stratification with its inherent privilege of power that not only characterized the philosophy of India to which he had initially been attracted (Porphyry, *Vita Plotini* 3.15–17) but also the third-century Roman aristocracy among whom he moved so comfortably (7). Plotinus considered the aristocracy to be the best of all political systems; effective, though less desirable, was the control exercised by cities through their democratic constitutions; the worst condition, by far, was for Plotinus the "common gathering" (τὸ κοινόν . . .

---

59. Martin, "Anti-Individualistic," 117. Weber recognized that Paul was not the only representation of Christian developments but simply the best documented. See Schluchter, *Rationalism*, 211.

60. Weber, *Agrarian*, 258–59.

61. Ibid., with reference to Troeltsch.

62. Martin, "Akin to the Gods."

63. Martin, "Self and Power."

κατὰ πολιτείαν) (*Enneades* 4.4.17). In contrast to gnostic complaints about the inequalities that, in their view also, characterized the imperfections of this world, Plotinus responded that there are two kinds of this-worldly life: one for the "good and wise" and one for the "common crowd" (οἱ πολλοί). These "simple masses" (ὁ φαῦλος ὄχλος) who, in Plotinus's Strangelovean diagnosis, are ruled by their "bodily fluids" (ὑγροὶ σώματι) (*Enneades* 6.8.3; see also 1.1.5), exist solely to do "manual labor" for the "better sort" (2.9.9).

In practical pursuit of his social ideal, Plotinus actually petitioned the emperor Gallienus to consign him a deserted city in Campania, which he and his companions might resettle under the name of Πλατονόπολις (*Platonopolis*) (Porphyry, *Vita Plotini* 12). The inhabitants of this alternative community would be those intellectual elite who had realized their "natural kinship with the One" (*Enneades* 2.3.9; 2.9.18; 3.3.1; 3.5.1; 4.4.45; 5.1.1). The emperor refused Plotinus's request and his transcendental "city above," upon which his utopian Πλατονόπολις was modeled, awaited Christian recognition by Augustine.

The Roman senate had already established legal precedent for controlling the "common gatherings" so despised by Plotinus by restricting, in 186 BCE, the celebration of the Bacchanalia in Rome, precisely because they suspected its subversive nature (Livy 39). Thus, in addition to rebellions against Hellenistic imperialism, such as the series of Egyptian anti-Hellenic revolts from as early as 245 BCE or the Jewish insurrections against the Hellenizing zeal of Seleucid rule in the second century BCE, attempts at internal social reform (or at least Roman perceptions of such) from the second century BCE through the third century, clearly gainsay Weber's (and Troeltsch's) view of sociopolitical indifference to imperial power by social groups during this period. Rather, alternative social formations endowed with idealistic goals attributed to charismatic leaders, characterized the social situation of the Roman world generally—including the Christians. Indeed, in contrast to Weber's conclusion that "it is absolute nonsense" to attribute sociopolitical concerns to early Christian groups,[64] Burton Mack attributed the attractiveness of these groups precisely to their being among the more ambitious and practical social experiments during this period.[65]

Despite his Protestant proclivities, Weber has nevertheless shown us, historically as well as theoretically, that social formations, such as the early Christianities, are contingent upon the cultural conditions and constraints of their development. Their differential identity is won through reason, not

---

64. Weber, *Agrarian*, 258.
65. Mack, *Christian Myth*, 19.

reason as critical reflection but reason as rationalization,[66] the systematic unification of all that is calculable and controllable[67]—including the imputation of charisma. Michel Foucault, with whom Weber has been compared,[68] has more recently emphasized that the rationalized authority of such groups constitutes a consolidation of power that, as in the case of Plotinus, is always analyzing, measuring, and calculating external events for purposes of control.[69] It is this consolidation of power that enfranchises a distinctive identity for new groups in contrast to their constituting social matrix.

A Social View

The early Christianities must be seen as a specific type of Hellenistic social formation that attributed their legitimacy to the name of Jesus but, in other ways, stood in cultural continuity with the welter of alternative groups in the Graeco-Roman world. The story of the social and political negotiations between them and the non-Christian religious world, of the alliances made among some of the Christian groups and their ascendancy and eventual religiopolitical dominance in the fourth century, cannot be told in terms of Reformation ideas about the uniqueness of Christian "faith," its ethic of "love," or of the infinite worth accorded individual souls.

A view of the early Christianities in cultural continuity with their Hellenistic neighbors presents a challenge to the conventional idea of a novel Christian charter that only later borrowed from "pagan" religious practice and was rationalized through the employment of "alien" Hellenic thought. Rather, we might view Hellenistic cult practices together with Hellenic thought as characteristic of the early Christian movements from their inception.

In a collection of the archaeological evidence for Christian cults prior to Constantine—mostly to be found in Rome—Graydon Snyder concluded that the remains of Christian people "simply cannot be distinguished from the remains of the non-Christian culture" during the first two centuries of this era.[70] In other words, early Christian culture, in its material reality, existed in an indistinguishable continuity with its non-Christian social matrix.

Further, when a discernible Christian culture did begin to emerge, at the end of the second century, the evidence suggests that Christians

---

66. Diggins, *Max Weber*, 67.
67. Ibid., 11.
68. Ibid., 273.
69. Ibid., 108–9.
70. Snyder, *Ante Pacem*, 2.

maintained continuity with Roman cultic practice, albeit under Christianized forms. So, for example, Snyder showed that the ritual meal of early Christians was not the eschatological meal attached to the Passover meal portrayed in the Synoptic Gospels and taught in early church doctrine but, rather, was "a continuation of the non-Christian meal for the dead in light of the New Testament paradigm of the Feeding of the Five Thousand."[71] Pre-Constantinian Christian practices and images, Synder concluded, "consist primarily of symbols, normally with a long history in the social matrix, placed in the context of the revelation—or Scripture—of the new religion"[72]—surely a more interesting view of religion than the dismissive notion of "syncretism" by which the Hellenization of Christianity is often explained.[73] Similarly, I should like to suggest that Christian rationality, like its cult practices, also stood in continuity with their cultural matrix from the inception of the various movements and that this shared intellectual world became Christianized only with the emergence of a distinctively Christian identity.

There is, of course, the matter of a common linguistic matrix. "When Alexander was taming Asia," Plutarch wrote, "Homer became widely read" (*De fortuna Alexandri* 1.328C–329D). By this Hellenistic account, Plutarch understood that the basis for Alexander's imperial ideal had been the Greek language, and with it Greek culture and the Greek thought world.

The language of the early Christians, insofar as we know, was Greek; their writings were in Greek and the majority of these were transmitted in this language.[74] Despite the Hellenic provenance of Q, the earliest possible evidence for a Christian written expression, attempts persist to establish an Aramaic *Vorlage* for one or more of the New Testament writings and/or to locate early Christian expression and practice in some variant of a Jewish religious world, insulating Christianity, thereby, from any contextualization within the Hellenistic thought world.

The Jews, of course, were not immune to the influence of Greek language and culture. In a hyperbolic but nevertheless instructive passage from Talmud, Rabbi Gamaliel, the putative teacher of Paul (Acts 22:3), is reported as saying that his father headed an academy in Jerusalem in which five hundred pupils studied the wisdom of the Jews while another five hundred

---

71. Ibid., 65.
72. Ibid., 45.
73. Harnack, *History*, 1:223.
74. The following section is adapted from Martin, "New Testament Writings," 210–11.

studied that of the Greeks (*Sotah* 49b).⁷⁵ And, the well-known legend of the origin of the Septuagint, reported in the *Letter of Aristeas to Philocrates*, is to the point. Aristeas concludes that the translation of Hebrew Scriptures into Greek should "delight" Philocrates "more than the books of the mythologists, for . . . [his] inclination lies in the direction of concern for things that benefit the mind." (*Letter of Aristeas* 322). And, of course, analogies between Christian and other Hellenistic literary expression and rhetoric have been well documented since at least since Bultmann's famous study of the influence of Cynic-Stoic diatribe style on Paul in 1910.⁷⁶

What, in other words, distinguished the early Christianities from other Hellenistic religious cults, on the one hand, but allies them with their intellectual context, on the other, is a transition from an oral or parochial culture to a more public—and thus political—one based on written texts.⁷⁷ A general Hellenistic tendency toward such a literary "consolidation of knowledge" began in the mid-first century with Pliny's *encyclopaedia* (*Naturalis historia*, *praef.* 14), and intensified in the second with such literary compilations as the Egyptian compendia of magical formulae, the astronomical syllabus of Claudius Ptolemy, the religious propaganda of the various mystery traditions, the oneiromantic taxonomy of Artemidorus of Ephesus, the Jewish anthology of Mishnah, and the first Christian testament of Marcion.⁷⁸

Hellenic thought belonged to this "Hellenistic encyclopedia." Thus, even Hatch conceded that

> Christianity came into a ground which was already prepared for it. Education was widely diffused over the Greek world, and among all classes of the community. It had not merely aroused the habit of inquiry which is the foundation of philosophy, but had also taught certain philosophical methods. Certain elements of the philosophical temper had come into existence on a large scale, penetrating all classes of society and inwrought into the general intellectual fibre of the time . . . [This] habit of mind which had preceded [Christianity] remained and dominated.⁷⁹

And Henry Chadwick noted that in addition to the rationalistic arguments of the skeptical and empirical philosophers, "a blend of Stoicism

75. Cited in Knox, *Hellenistic Elements*, 30.
76. Bultmann, *Predigt*.
77. Fox, *Pagans*, 304.
78. Martin, Martin, "Encyclopedia Hennelistica," 300 (Chapter 20, this volume). Greenwald, *New Testament Canon*.
79. Hatch, *Influence*, 134–35; see also the classical study by Knox, *Hellenistic Elements*.

and Platonism" was "taken by granted by ordinary educated folk."[80] These popular philosophies, Robin Lane Fox concluded, "did more to supplement religious cult than to undermine it."[81]

It will perhaps be enough simply to note here that no one with a modicum of education in the Greek-speaking world could possibly hear the opening to the Gospel of John, whatever its allusion to the opening of Genesis and/or its sapiential elaborations, without supposing the central logos teachings of Greek philosophy from Heraclitus to the Stoics.[82] Given the "Protestant paradigm" outlined earlier, it is not surprising that interpretations of the opening of John have emphasized the Jewish in contrast to the Hellenic character of the Johannine usage and resisted the temptation of seeing this usage as anything but a hint of the later Hellenization of Christian faith to come. Whether or not historians of ideas can establish an intellectual continuity between the Gospel of John and Justin, a tradition of logos-theology was central to the development of Christian thought from Justin to Augustine (*Confessions* 7.13) and exemplifies the Christianization of Hellenistic thought. It is under this banner of an increasingly monomorphic Christology that not only Hellenistic thought but the *mentalité* of world at-large became largely Christianized.

Conclusion

At least since Tertullian, "thought" in Western culture has been associated with (a Christianized) Athens while "religion" has been traced from Jerusalem (*De praescriptione haereticorum* 7)—as though the Greeks had no cults and the Jews were deficient in intellect. Since the second century BCE, however, Athens and Jerusalem contended with a common Hellenistic culture. Other cultural traditions shared this same context, the Egyptian, for example, for which protestations of a discrete integrity and influence have only recently emerged in the ideological apologetics of Afrocentrism. Those first-century groups that began to define their social boundaries with reference to the name of Jesus shared fully in this complex matrix which provided the possibilities for social identities generally. Rather than tracing their development in history-of-ideas terms about the influence of Hellenic thought on some privileged view of religious origins, we might better view it sociologically in terms of the establishment, through rationalization, of

---

80. Chadwick, *Early Christian*, 5; see also Bevan, "Popular Philosophy," 81 ("Philosophers were to be seen everywhere...").

81. Fox, *Pagans*, 30.

82. Marrou, *History of Education*, 312.

alternative social identities and the concomitant Christianization of their Hellenic matrix of diverse social identities, an alliance and consolidation of power between some of these, together with a concomitant construction of a rationalized theological orthodoxy totalizing in its claims to absolute truth and legitimated by its singular deity. Only in a Protestantized genealogy, however, is this Christianization of thought attributed to a secondary Hellenization of religious faith and subsumed to the priority of individual experience. It is this anti-intellectual but no less totalizing claim that like its Catholic forebears, appeals to Jerusalem over Athens and continues to inform the theological cultures of Western modernity.

References

Bevan, Edwyn. "Hellenistic Popular Philosophy." In *The Hellenistic Age: Aspects of Hellenistic Civilization*, edited by John B. Bury et al., 79–107. SHC 7. Cambridge: Cambridge University Press. 1925.

Bultmann, Rudolf. *Der Stil der paulinischen Predigt und die kynish-stoisch Diatribe*. Forschungen zur Religion und Literatur des Alten und Neuen Testaments 13. Göttingen: Vandenhoeck & Ruprecht, 1910.

Burckhardt, Jacob. *The Civilization of the Renaissance in Italy*. London: Allen & Unwin, 1928.

Chadwick, Henry. *Early Christian Thought and the Classical Tradition*. Oxford: Oxford University Press, 1966.

Diggins, John P. *Max Weber: Politics and the Spirit of Tragedy*. New York: Basic Books, 1996.

Dumont, Louis. *Essays on Individualism: Modern Ideology in Anthropological Perspective*. Chicago: University of Chicago Press, 1986.

Frend, W. H. C. *The Rise of Christianity*. Philadelphia: Fortress, 1984.

Fox, Robin Lane. *Pagans and Christians*. New York: Knopf, 1987.

Gerth, Hans H., and Charles Wright Mills. "Introduction: The Man and His Work." In *From Max Weber: Essays in Sociology*, edited and translated by Hans H. Gerth and Charles Wright Mills, 3–74. New York: Oxford University Press, 1946.

Greenwald, Michael. "The New Testament Canon and Mishnah: Consolidation of Knowledge in the Second Century C.E." PhD diss., Boston University, 1989.

Harnack, Adolf von. *History of Dogma*. Translated and edited by Neil Buchanan. 7 vols. Theological Translation Library. New York: Russell & Russell, 1958.

———. *Lehrbuch der Dogmengeschichte*. 3 vols. in 2. 2nd ed. Sammlung theologischer Lehrbücher. Freiburg: Mohr/Siebeck, 1886–1890.

Hatch, Edwin. *The Influence of Greek Ideas and Usages upon the Christian Church*. Edited by Andrew M. Fairbairn. London: Williams & Norgate, 1890.

Kammen, Michael. *Mystic Chords of Memory: The Transformation of Tradition in American Culture*. New York: Knopf, 1991.

Kippenberg, Hans G. *Die vorderasiatischen Erlösungsreligionen in ihrem Zusammenhang mit der antiken Stadtherrschaft*. Suhrkamp Taschenbuch Wissenschaft 917. Frankfurt: Suhrkamp, 1991.

Knox, Wilfred Lawrence. *Some Hellenistic Elements in Primitive Christianity*. Oxford: Oxford University Press, 1944.

Layton, Bentley. *The Gnostic Scriptures: A New Translation with Annotations and Introductions*. Garden City, NY: Doubleday, 1987.

Mack, Burton L. *Who Wrote the New Testament? The Making of a Christian Myth*. San Francisco: HarperSanFrancisco, 1995.

Marrou, Henri. *A History of Education in Antiquity*. Translated by George Lamb. New York: Sheed & Ward, 1956.

Martin, Luther H. "Akin to the Gods or Simply One to Another? Comparison with Respect to Religions in Antiquity." In *Vergleichen und Verstehen in der Religionswissenschaft*, edited by Hans-Joachim Klimkeit, 147–59. Studies in Oriental Religions 41. Wiesbaden: Harrassowitz, 1997.

———. "The Anti-Individualistic Ideology of Hellenistic Culture." *Numen* 41/2 (1994) 117–40.

———. "The *Encyclopedia Hellenistica* and Christian Origins." *Biblical Theology Bulletin* 20/3 (1990) 123–27 (chapter 20, this volume).

———. "The New Testament Writings as Hellenistic Religious Texts." In *The Bible in Cultural Context*, edited by Helana Pavlincová et al., 209–13. Brno: Czech Society for the Study of Religion, 1994.

———. "Self and Power in the Thought of Plotinus." In *Czlowiek i Wartosci*, edited by Antoni Komendera, 91–99. Kraków: Wydawnictwo Naukowe WSP, 1997 (chapter 24, this volume).

Nelson, Benjamin. "Weber, Troeltsch, Jellinek as Comparative Historical Sociologists." *Sociological Analysis* 36/3 (1975) 229–40.

Schluchter, Wolfgang. *Rationalism, Religion and Domination: A Weberian Perspective*. Translated by Neil Solomon. Berkeley: University of California Press, 1989.

———. *The Rise of Western Rationalism: Max Weber's Developmental History*. Translated by Günter Roth. Berkeley: University of California Press, 1981.

Smith, Jonathan Z. *Drudgery Divine: On the Comparison of Early Christianities and the Religions of Late Antiquity*. Jordan Lectures in Comparative Religion 14. Chicago Studies in the History of Judaism. Chicago: University of Chicago Press, 1990.

Snyder, Graydon F. *Ante Pacem: Archaeological Evidence of Church Life Before Constantine*. Macon: Mercer University Press, 1985.

Stark, Rodney. *The Rise of Christianity: A Sociologist Reconsiders History*. Princeton: Princeton University Press, 1996.

Troeltsch, Ernst. "Meiner Bücher (1922)." In *Gesammelte Schriften*, 4:3–18. Tübingen: Mohr/Siebeck, 1925. Translated and cited in *Ernst Troeltsch: Writings on Theology and Religion*, edited by Robert Morgan and Michael Pye, 46–47. Atlanta: John Knox, 1977.

———. *The Social Teaching of the Christian Churches*. Translated by Olive Wyon. 2 vols. Halley Stewart Publications 1. New York: Macmillan, 1931.

Weber, Max. *The Agrarian Sociology of Ancient Civilizations*. Translated by Richard I. Frank. Foundations of History Library. London: NLB, 1976.

———. *Ancient Judaism*. Social Theory. Glencoe, IL: Free Press, 1952.

———. *Economy and Society: An Outline and Interpretative Sociology*. Edited by Günther Roth and Claus Wittich. 3 vols. New York: Bedminster, 1968.

———. "Politics as a Vocation." In *From Max Weber: Essays in Sociology*, edited by Hans H. Gerth and C. Wright Mills, 77–128. Oxford: Oxford University Press, 1946.

———. *The Protestant Ethic and the Spirit of Capitalism*. Translated by Talcott Parsons. New York: Scribner, 1958.

———. "Religious Rejections of the World and their Directions." In *From Max Weber: Essays in Sociology*, edited by Hans H. Gerth and C. Wright Mills, 323–59. New York: Oxford University Press, 1946.

———. "The Social Psychology of the World Religions." In *From Max Weber: Essays in Sociology*, edited by Hans H. Gerth and C. Wright Mills, 267–301. New York: Oxford University Press, 1946.

———. "The Sociology of Charismatic Authority." In *From Max Weber: Essays in Sociology*, edited by Hans H. Gerth and C. Wright Mills, 245–64. New York: Oxford University Press, 1946.

Worsley, Peter. *The Trumpet Shall Sound: A Study of "Cargo" Cults in Melanesia*. 2nd, augmented ed. New York: Schocken, 1968.

20

The *Encyclopedia Hellenistica* and Christian Origins

ONE OF THE MOST well-known passages from the works of Michel Foucault is his citation of a passage from J. Borges quoting "a certain Chinese encyclopedia." In this encyclopedia, animals are classified as

> (a) belonging to the emperor; (b) embalmed; (c) tamed; (d) sucking pigs; (e) sirens; (f) fabulous; (g) stray dogs; (h) included in the present classification; (i) frenzied; (j) innumerable; (k) drawn with a very camelhair brush; (l) *et cetera*; (m) having just broke the water pitcher; (n) that from a long way off look like flies. (xv)

For Foucault, this taxonomy shattered the familiar landmarks of our thought, "the thought that bears the stamp of our age and our geography" (xv). It forces upon him the realization that any system of knowledge must be "envisaged apart from all criteria reference to its rational value or to its objective forms" (xxii). In contrast to a view of knowledge as metaphysical positivity, Foucault concluded that knowledge is a system of thought constituted out of the epistemological possibilities of its own time and place. It "thereby manifests a history which is not that of its growing perfection, but rather that of its conditions of possibility" (xxii).

Foucault's history of "discourses," those "verbal expressions of mental structures through which man organizes his activities and classifies his perceptions of the world,"[1] is theoretically equivalent to the historian Lucien Febvre's inventory of the "possibilities of thought" as they are delimited by the "mental horizons of an age."[2] It is these historically specific possibilities

---

1. Foucault, *Order*, xiv.
2. Hutton, "History of Mentalities," 242, 252.

of thought that organize what is knowable in a given age and make up its metaphorical "encyclopedia."

The Encyclopedia Hellenistica

The designation ἐγκύκλιος παιδεία—"instruction in the circle of knowledge"—was first used during the Hellenistic period by Pliny the elder (23/24–79 CE) to describe his *Natural History* (*praef.* 14). This first Western attempt to compile a complete system of knowledge was followed by other, more specialized, compilations of knowledge: the Egyptian compendia of magical formulae (from the second century BCE to the fifth century CE); the astronomical syllabus of Claudius Ptolemy (c. 140 CE); the religious propaganda of the various mystery traditions (e.g., the second-century-CE romance of Apuleius, popularly known as *The Golden Ass*); the oneiromantic taxonomy of Artemidorus of Ephesos (late second century CE); the second-century-CE Jewish anthology of Mishna, and that of the Christian Second Testament; the second- and third-century CE texts collected as the *Corpus Hermeticum*; the alchemical reflections of Zosimos of Panopolis (late third–early fourth century CE). This consolidation of knowledge that began with Pliny and intensified in a second-century-CE concentration was a characteristic trait of the Hellenistic period.[3] Together, these compilations gave expression to the Hellenistic "circle of knowledge" and, collectively may be termed the "Encyclopedia Hellenistica."

The Invention of a Hellenistic Age

A Hellenistic period of history is itself a category of recent historical knowledge that has subtly directed our own inquiry into the epistemological products of the age. No historian from antiquity to the Enlightenment recognized such a discrete historical period. It was first "invented" by J. G. Droysen in the nineteenth century and exhibited the "great man" and political criteria for historical periodization especially characteristic of romantic historiography.[4] "The name Alexander marks the end of one world epoch, the beginning of a new,"[5] Droysen wrote in his *Geschichte Alexanders des Grossen*, published in 1836, the first of his three-volume *Geschichte des Hellenismus* (1836–1843). Droysen's work gave currency to the view that Al-

---

3. Greenwald, "New Testament."
4. Stover, "Great Man."
5. Droysen, *Geschichte*, 1:3.

exander's heroic transformation of the world into his Graeco-Macedonian empire at the end of the fourth century BCE inaugurated a Hellenistic era of political history that endured until the consolidation of Roman power by Caesar Augustus in 31 BCE. This historical periodization, defined by the political exploits of two men judged to be "great," provided the paradigm for a religious periodization, in which an era of Hellenistic paganism, shaped by the new conditions for knowledge established by Alexander's political revolution, was supplanted by a Christian era, inaugurated by its "great teacher" during the Augustan era.

The newly defined Hellenistic era was generally neglected by classicists, who focused on the language, history, and culture of classical Greece and on the Latin "high" culture of republican and imperial Rome. George Grote, for example, author of an influential twelve-volume *History of Greece*, published between 1846 and 1856, pronounced the period after Alexander to be "of no interest in itself and it is only so far of value as it helps us to understand the preceding centuries."[6] The new field of Hellenistic studies became populated primarily by biblical theologians who were concerned with the religions of this period as a background for their understanding of a subsequent origin for Christianity.

Creating a Hellenistic Religious Period

The German "history of religions school" at the beginning of the twentieth century, was the first to locate Christian origins systematically within, rather than over against, a Hellenistic field of religious knowledge. At the same time, however, French historians were challenging conventional historiographical theory itself. This challenge was directed precisely at the political criterion exemplified by Droysen's definition of a Hellenistic era. Since the 1920s, these French historians, associated with the journal *Annales d'histoire sociale*, have persistently questioned political events as the sole foundation for historical study. Fernand Braudel has argued, for example, that a second level of social time, modulated by the slower pace of everyday life, underlies a view of history structured by the episodic flux of political events.[7] Rather than evincing the discontinuities characteristic of political history, this view of social history is characterized by signs of

---

6. Grote, *History*, 1.10.
7. Braudel, *Mediterranean*, 20–21.

continuity;[8] rather than emphasizing the individual contributions of great men, it stresses enduring collective attitudes.[9]

From the perspective of the *Annales* historians, the appropriateness of Droysen's definition of a Hellenistic period for religious history must be questioned, whatever its merits for political history. Ironically, this point had already been anticipated by Droysen. While he had marked the conclusion of a period of Hellenistic political history with the consolidation of Roman power by Augustus, Droysen warned that religious history must include the enduring influence of Hellenistic culture throughout the centuries of the empire.[10]

Transformations in collective religious attitudes during the fourth century CE, bracketed by Constantine's conversion (313) and Theodosius's religious legislation that formally established a Christian culture (391), effectively establish a suitable conclusion to what Braudel would term "the long duration" of a Hellenistic religious history and the beginning of a Christian era. According to this longer periodization from a Hellenistic religious history, enduring some 750 years from Alexander's political revolution to Christian catholicity, Christian origins must be understood as a Hellenistic religious alternative rather than a unique religious formation cast against a Hellenistic backdrop.

A reevaluation of Hellenistic religious periodization must not be attributed solely to recent theoretical development in the historiographical evaluation of the already remarkable and rich data—literary, artistic, and archeological—documenting the religions of this period. New contributions to the Hellenistic circle of knowledge also support the fourth century as the conclusion of one religious era and the beginning of a new.

The continuing discovery of Mithraic sites in Italy, especially around Rome,[11] has challenged an earlier understanding of the Persian origins for the Roman Mysteries of Mithras[12] by suggesting an origin for Western Mithraism out of specifically Hellenistic conditions for knowledge.[13] New understandings of these Mithraic mysteries have challenged, in addition, conventional understandings of the religious environment in Rome in the first four centuries CE and may finally produce results as significant for

---

8. Hutton, "History of Mentalities," 240.
9. Burke, "Strengths," 499.
10. Bayer in Droysen, *Geschichte*, 3:474–75.
11. Beck, "Mithraism."
12. Cumont, *Mysteries of Mithra*.
13. Ulansey, "Mithraic Studies."

understanding Christian origins as has research on the better known Nag Hammadi gnostic library.

The discovery of the Nag Hammadi texts in 1946 resulted in a veritable army of researchers turning their attention to Gnosticism.[14] Although these researchers have been predominantly New Testament scholars, whose investigations generally privilege the question of Christian origins, the dating of these texts from the first century BCE through the third century CE has redirected attention to Gnosticism as a context for rather than as a consequence of these origins.

The Structure of Hellenistic Knowledge

Braudel proposed a third, "constant and stable" time-scale underlying both political history and even the enduring continuities of social history.[15] He termed this scale-time, which may perdure for millennia, a geographical time that "governs certain areas of the world and certain realities depending on period and place."[16] The Hellenistic image of physical cosmology may be taken as an empirical exemplum of Braudel's geographic time-scale and as the governing field for religious formations in this period.[17]

The Hellenistic image of the cosmos, named for Claudius Ptolemy, the mid-second-century-CE astronomer and mathematician who systematically codified it, shared with Alexander's empire a protracted conquest of space. In contrast to the traditional trilevel cosmology, its expanded but still contained cosmic image depicted the earth as a flat cylinder, or as a ball, suspended in space, and surrounded by seven planetary spheres—the whole enclosed within a spherical realm of fixed stars. Arguably more significant for religious history than were Alexander's political exploits, this new Ptolemaic architecture of the cosmos circumscribed the possibilities of collective thought throughout the Hellenistic age and gave objective structure to the emergence of its distinctively religious knowledge.

As is well known, the historian of religion Mircea Eliade[18] and the New Testament scholar Rudolf Bultmann[19] based many of their insights into the nature of religious expression upon the horizons of religious knowledge afforded by the closed three-storied cosmic image of antiquity in contrast

14. Scholer, *Nag Hammadi*.
15. Braudel, *Mediterranean*, 21; Braudel, *Civilization*, 1:20, 352.
16. Braudel, *Civilization*, 3:17–18.
17. Martin, *Hellenistic Religions*, 6–8.
18. Eliade, *Cosmos*.
19. Bultmann, "New Testament."

to that of a Copernican/historical modernity. Curiously, both ignored the import of Ptolemaic cosmology.

The significance of the Prolemaic cosmology for structuring Hellenistic religious formations was most vividly expressed by the pervasiveness of astrological influence.[20] This dominance of astral structures in Hellenistic expression has been reemphasized in recent Mithraic studies.

The central icon of Mithras slaying a bull, common to virtually every Mithraic find, has been decoded as a cosmic image rather than the scene from Persian mythic narrative perceived by an earlier religious historiography.[21] According to this new research, the collage of conventional Graeco-Roman imagery that constitutes the bull-slaying is organized by the structural relationships of astral constellations familiar from Hellenistic star-maps.[22] Paganism generally shared this cosmic paradigm for terrestrial life with Mithraism and gave counterpoint to the formulations of religious meaning in terms of historical development by Christian thinkers from Paul (Gal 1:3–11) to Ambrose (*Epistula* 18.28).[23]

The Sovereignty of Fate

The expanded cultural and mental horizons of the Hellenistic age, exemplified by imperial and cosmic increase, were organized in philosophical and religious thought by a "grammar of fate," that is, by a structure of natural and universal relationships perceived within the comic order of things. Already at the end of the nineteenth century, Wilhelm Anz had argued that Gnosticism might be understood as contending with the sovereignty of an astrological formulated εἱμαρμένη, the view of fate as deterministic and oppressive.[24] But perceptions of fate during the Hellenistic period were not limited to this late antique notion of εἱμαρμένη. The structures of fate had been in transformation during the Hellenistic period: from μοῖρα, a continuation of the classical view of fate as the expression of an assumed natural order of things,[25] to a concern with τύχη/*fortuna* (luck or fortune, both good and evil), or fate as an expression of the contingency of existence,[26] a view that came to dominance in the Hellenistic period and that is exemplified

20. Cumont, *Astrology*; Cramer, *Astrology in Roman Law*.
21. Cumont, *Mysteries of Mithra*, 20–32.
22. Beck, "Mithraism," 2079–84; Ulansey, "Mithraic Studies."
23. Martin, "Roman Mithraism."
24. Anz, *Frage*.
25. Greene, *Moira*.
26. Nussbaum, *Fragility*, 3–7.

in Apuleius's *The Golden Ass*, to the late antique view of a deterministic εἱμαρμένη, documented from the first century CE (e.g., Josephus, *Antiquities* 13.171–73; 18.12–22; and *Jewish War* 2.263–64).

The transformed and revalued inflections in the grammar of fate generated a coherent if shifting paradigm underlying and shaping the mental structures of Hellenistic culture. These possibilities of knowledge shaped the understanding of shifts in the sociopolitical fortune of the imperial idea from Alexander to Augustus, and the increasing philosophical concern with ethics following the death in 322 BCE of Aristotle, Alexander's teacher. The emergence of universalized mystery cults and gnostic tendencies out of traditional localized practices of piety were expressions of the democratized play of fate. Rather than representing a "failure of nerve"[27] resulting in an "age of anxiety"[28] or in "cosmic paranoia"[29] as they are generally characterized, the pagan religious expressions of the Hellenistic age can be understood, along with Christianity, as formulating, within the perspective of this systemic condition for knowledge, a bold view of human existence that endured to the foundations of Renaissance thought.

Gnostic thought, for example, far from representing the nihilism by which it is usually characterized,[30] challenged a view of human existence mastered by the material world and its universal claim of fate, anticipating thereby the Renaissance humanistic ideal of mastery over the physical world through knowledge of its universal natural laws. And the radical dualism of Gnosticism, its systematic removal of sanctity from any human reference, its apocalyptic expectations of the dissolution of the present world, so anticipated such themes associated with the German Reformation that Calvin could accuse the Lutherans of raising "Marcion from Hell" (*Institutes* 4.17).[31]

The Encyclopedic Irony

To affirm that Hellenistic religious thought—including Christian origins—was generated from the epistemological possibilities of its age is to affirm that our own interpretative concerns and efforts are subject to the same irony of historical constitution. For example, the last of the great Western encyclopedias, the eleventh edition of the *Encyclopædia Britannica* (1910–1911),

27. Murray, *Five Stages*, 119–20.
28. Dodds, *Pagans and Christians*.
29. Smith, *Map*, 161.
30. E.g., Jonas, *Gnostic*, 32–40.
31. Rothkrug, "German Holiness," 206.

published in the same era in which the study of Hellenistic culture was receiving its historical definition, organizes knowledge in categories as antithetical to contemporary sensibilities as those of Borges's Chinese encyclopedia. Antisemitism for example, is presented as "a passing phase in the history of culture";[32] statistics showing four or five times as many Negroes as whites (in proposition of population) imprisoned in the southern United States demonstrate only the prominent criminal tendencies of the Negro race;[33] and the inability of converted New England Indians to maintain their new Christian faith is similarly attributed to their "racial traits."[34]

These observations express a prevailing assumption, summarized in the article on "Civilization," that important lines of progress will include "the important lines of the race through wise application of the law of heredity,"[35] an evolutionary and mechanistic assumption that within a generation would become associated with a sinister nationalistic agenda. The conditions of knowledge governing such a nineteenth-century "common rationality" have been summarized by Hans Konig in his perceptive reflections on the *Britannica*:

> Darwin had explained our origin, Schliemann ... had revealed our history; Lister had announced a coming end of disease. Science ... was there to level all stumbling blocks put up by nature. The mystery of far places still existed, but steam was beginning to make them accessible to all—and with dry feet and a Scotch-and-Soda at hand.[36]

While those of us engaged in historical and comparative studies have paid lip-service to the "mystery of far places," the historical locating of knowledge within its own encyclopedic system of epistemological possibility discloses the familiarity presumed of our past to be as "alien" as the "otherness" assumed of geographical remove—for example, that of Chinese knowledge.

The value of locating Hellenistic religious formations in their own historically constituted "circle of knowledge" has been demonstrated by R. L. Gordon's preliminary work on the grades of Mithraic initiation,[37] and by Bruce Malina's use of anthropological theory to imagine Pauline religion in

---

32. Konig, "Onwards and Upwards," 72; *Britannica* 15:410a.
33. Konig, "Onwards and Upwards," 73–44; *Britannica* 19:348–498a.
34. Konig, "Onwards and Upwards," 44; *Britannica* 9:278a.
35. Konig, "Onwards and Upwards," 73; *Britannica* 6:410a.
36. Konig, "Onwards and Upwards," 71.
37. Gordon, "Reality," 58–61.

the first-century Mediterranean world.[38] It is to the epistemological conditions expressed by this "encyclopedia" that Christian origins belong. The historical issue for understanding these origins is not the triumph of early Christians over rival pagans and "heretical" expressions, but their participation in the shared possibilities of Hellenistic religious knowledge. Although biblical scholars are increasingly knowledgeable of and sensitive to the Hellenistic field of knowledge as a result of the renaissance of research in this area, Christian origins are still largely cast against a background of that culture—and from the concerns of our own—rather than as an entry in their own "Encyclopedia Hellenistica."

References

Anz, Wilhelm. *Zur Frage nach dem Ursprung des Gnostizismus*. Texte und Untersuchungen zur Geschichte der altchristlichen Literatur 15/4. ATLA monograph preservation program ATLA fiche 1987-1624. Leipzig: Hinrich, 1897.

Beck, Roger. "Mithraism since Franz Cumont." *ANRW* II 17.4 (1984) 2002–115.

Braudel, Fernand. *Civilization and Capitalism, 15th–18th Century*. Vol. 1, *The Structures of Everyday Life*. Translated by Sian Reynolds. New York: Harper & Row, 1981.

———. *Civilization and Capitalism, 15th–18th Century*. Vol. 3, *The Perspective of the World*. Translated by Sian Reynolds. New York: Harper & Row, 1984.

———. *The Mediterranean and the Mediterranean World in the Age of Philipp II*. Translated by Sian Reynolds. New York: Harper & Row, 1972.

Bultmann, Rudolf. "New Testament and Mythology." In *New Testament and Mythology, and Other Basic Writings*. Translated by Schubert M. Ogden. Edited by Rudolf Bultmann. Philadelphia: Fortress, 1984.

Burke, Peter. "Strengths and Weaknesses of the History of Mentalities." *History of European Ideas* 7/5 (1986) 439–51.

Cramer, Frederick H. *Astrology in Roman Law and Politics*. Memoirs of the American Philosophical Society 37. Philadelphia: American Philological Society, 1954.

Cumont, Franz. *Astrology and Religion among the Greeks and Romans*. New York: Dover, 1960.

———. *The Mysteries of Mithra*. Edited and translated by Thomas J. McCormack. 2nd ed. New York: Dover, 1903.

Dodds, E. R. *Pagans and Christians in an Age of Anxiety: Some Aspects of Religious Experience from Marcus Aurelius to Constantine*. Wiles Lectures 1963. New York: Norton, 1970.

Droysen Johann G. *Geschichte der Hellenismus*. 3 vols. New Edition by Erich Bayer. Munich: Deutsche Taschenbuch, 1952–1953.

Eliade, Mircea. *Cosmos and History*. Translated by Willard R. Trask. Harper Torchbooks, The Bollingen Library. New York: Harper & Row, 1959.

Encyclopædia Britannica. 11th ed. Cambridge: Cambridge University Press, 1910–1911.

Febvre, Lucien. "Psychologie et histoire." In *La Vie Mentale*, 3–7. *Encyclopédie Française*, 8. Paris: Ste de l'Encyclopédie Française, 1938.

---

38. Malina, "'Religion.'"

Foucault, Michel. *The Order of Things: The Archaeology of the Human Sciences*. 1970. Reprint, New York: Vintage, 1973.
Gordon, Richard L. "Reality, Evocation and Boundary in the Mysteries of Mithras." *Journal of Mithraic Studies* 3/1 (1980) 19–99.
Greene, William C. *Moira: Fate, Good and Evil in Greek Thought*. Glousester, MA: Smith, 1944.
Greenwald, Michael R. "The New Testament Canon and the Mishnah: Consolidation of Knowledge in the Second Century CE." PhD diss., Boston University 1989.
Grote, George. *History of Greece*. 2nd ed. Boston: Jewett, 1851.
Hutton, Patrick H. "The History of Mentalities: The New Map of Cultural History." *History and Theory* 20/3 (1981) 237–59.
Jonas, Hans. *The Gnostic Religion*. 2nd rev. ed. Boston: Beacon, 1963.
Konig, Hans. "Onward and Upward with the Arts: The Eleventh Edition." *The New Yorker* 2 (March 1981) 67–83.
Malina, Bruce J. "'Religion' in the World of Paul." *Biblical Theology Bulletin* 16/3 (1986) 92–101.
Martin, Luther H. *Hellenistic Religions: An Introduction*. New York: Oxford University Press, 1987.
———. "Roman Mithraism and Christianity." *Numen* 36/1 (1989) 2–15.
Murray, Gilbert. *Five Stages of Greek Religion*. Garden City, NY: Doubleday, 1955.
Nussbaum, Martha C. *The Fragility of Goodness: Luck and Ethics in Greek Tragedy and Philosophy*. Cambridge: Cambridge University Press, 1986.
Rothkrug, Lionel. "German Holiness and Western Sanctity in Medieval and modern History." *Historical Reflections/Réflexions Historiques* 15/1 (1980) 161–249.
Scholer, David M. *Nag Hammadi Bibliography: 1948–1969*. NHS 1. Leiden: Brill, 1971.
Smith, Jonathan Z. *Map Is not Territory: Studies in the History of Religions*. 1978. Reprint, Chicago: University of Chicago Press, 1993.
Stover, Robert. "Great Man Theory of History." In *Encyclopedia of Philosophy*, edited by Paul Edwards, 3:378–82. 8 vols. New York: Macmillan, 1967.
Ulansey, David. "Mithraic Studies: A Paradigm Shift?" *Religious Studies Review* 13/2 (1987) 104–10.
———. *The Origins of the Mithraic Mysteries: Cosmology and Salvation in the Ancient World*. New York: Oxford University Press, 1989.

21

Past Minds: Evolution, Cognition, and Biblical Studies

The purpose of a man's mind is like deep water,
but a man of understanding will draw it out.

(PROV 20:5)

OVER THE YEARS, CONSIDERABLE effort has been devoted by philosophers, psychologists, and by ordinary peoples in their everyday lives, to an understanding of human minds—their own as well as those of others. For the ancient Israelites, as in the passage from Prov 20, the seat of the "mind" was considered to be the heart—as it was for many Greeks (Gk: κῆρ or θυμός).[1] Although the physiology was off, the sense of the Hebrew *lêb* (LXX: καρδία) quite accurately captures those functions associated with mind by contemporary cognitive scientists—"affect" or "emotion," "thought" and "reflection," "will" or "intentionality," and, of course, "memory."[2] Since the fifth century BCE work of the Greek physician Alcmaeon of Croton, who discovered, by dissection, that "passages" led from the eyes to the brain (ἐγκέφαλος), that organ became increasingly viewed the seat of mental functions, which in contemporary biocognitive research finally became identified with mind itself.

As the Proverbalist suggested, human minds may be "drawn out" (*dālâh*), i.e., inferred, from their output—from gesture or glance, from touch or speech, from ideas expressed to others or, sometimes, inscribed into material form—a drawing, a pot, a text. An understanding of past minds is more difficult. While the ephemeral gesture, glance, touch, or speech is

---

1. See Kittel, *Wörterbuch*; Liddell and Scott, *Lexicon*, s.v.
2. Brown et al., *Lexicon*, s.v.

now faded into time, the material inscription of some of those minds has nevertheless survived as the basis for historiographical investigation.

Historians have always been concerned with the minds of their subjects. Chester Starr, for example, writes in his 1965 *History of the Ancient World* that if one is to understand "any era of the past one must be able to penetrate into the minds of its inhabitants."[3] Their psychological assumptions, however, have generally been implicit and, for the most part, decades out of date. Attention to recent advances in evolutionary psychology and the cognitive sciences can help correct this deficiency.

I

Historians—like philosophers and psychologists generally—have traditionally viewed the human mind as a tabula rasa, a "blank slate," upon which social and cultural input is inscribed.[4] An understanding of past minds, consequently, has been conceived as a project of situating their historical productions in a context of plausible sociocultural inputs. More nuanced historians have even attempted to plot trajectories of these seminal contexts over time by stratifying the historical data. But if contexts are so determinative of minds, why then are widely differing mental representations found in the same sociocultural contexts—or similar ones in disparate contexts? For the most part, descriptions—even "thick descriptions"—of cultural contexts have failed to offer any satisfactory explanation (*explanans*) either for the diversity of minds in common contexts or for cross-cultural similarities among them (the *explananda*). Rather, historiographical understandings of cultural contexts are all too often but descriptive generalizations about the productions of these same past minds.[5] This epistemological redundancy undermines the hermeneutical principle that understanding arises simply by situating mental products in their context.

Further, recent findings from the cognitive sciences have now disputed traditional views of the mind as simply a blank slate. Since Noam Chomsky's challenge to behaviorism in the 1950s, it has been accepted—and experimentally confirmed—that while input into human brains is certainly necessary for a particular output, that input underdetermines mental output. While linguistic ability, for example, requires exposure to language, this input is, as Chomsky argued, insufficient to explain the robust character of linguistic

---

3. Starr, *History*, 27.
4. Pinker, *Blank Slate*.
5. Tooby and Cosmides, "Foundations"; Sperber, *Explaining Culture*.

competency.[6] Mental output is, in other words, structured, constrained, transformed, and contributed to by innate and developmentally precocious cognitive capacities that have been established as shared products of our evolutionary history, as have all other biological functions of our somatic system. Given the scale of evolutionary time and change, it is reasonable to conclude that our cognitive capacities, like our behavioral biases, have remained significantly unaltered since the emergence of modern humans by the late Pleistocene Era, some sixty thousand to fifty thousand years ago. Whatever the date for that emergence—and it seems regularly to retreat in light of new paleontological discoveries—and however strenuously it might be argued that culture subsequently influenced a continuing evolution of human cognition (though I would prefer the language of historical development over biological evolution), I think it safe to conclude that human brains and their fundamental mental functions have changed little, if at all, over the last three thousand to four thousand years with which most historians are concerned, even though these mental capacities and functions will be expressed differently in different environments.

II

Biblical scholars are, of course, but historians who focus upon a particular body of data from a certain period of time. Like the best historians, most are interested in, somewhat knowledgeable about, and generally work rather explicitly on the basis of theory; and they know what counts as evidence. Because of their theoretical foundations, biblical scholars already in the nineteenth century had discovered that the biblical texts represent productions of different minds from different times and places. Recent evidential finds of entire libraries of texts, for example, have dramatically broadened the scope of biblical scholarship to include considerations of representations by past minds that had previously been marginalized or even ignored. It is increasingly apparent that these minds emerged from no single context, religious movement, or tradition but, at best, constitute a spectrum of small, semiautonomous social movements that have been named by scholars on the basis of texts that were produced by some. Collectively, these minds and the movements associated with them are now referred to in the plural, the biblical or Hellenistic Judaisms, for example, or the early Christianities. It cannot be assumed, of course, that all texts produced by participants in such groups survived or, indeed, that texts were even produced by all such groups. Consequently, if biblical scholars are to shift their attention from

---

6. See, e.g., Chomsky, Review of *Verbal.*

a narrow preoccupation with canonical texts toward a broader historical understanding of religious representations—whatever their relation to contemporaneous social groups or to subsequent institutionalized norms—they must also pay closer attention to the evidence for such groups preserved in material culture.

Although archaeological evidence has long been held significant for interpretations of Hebrew Scripture, these interpretations have generally been read in light of—and, thus, as supportive of—the accounts of canonical texts. Nils Peter Lemche has rightly concluded, however, that the question of which historical remains should be read in light of the other—whether archaeological evidence should be read in light of texts, or vice versa, or neither—is itself a methodological conclusion "to be demonstrated and not accepted in advance of the historical analysis."[7]

New Testament scholars, on the other hand, continue to neglect the evidence of Christian material culture, even though that archaeological evidence was collected and published over thirty years ago.[8] Since, however, this evidence challenges many representations found in the canonical texts—representations subsequently preserved by "orthodox" institutions, and even some of those preserved in the noncanonical, writings, most biblical scholars seem simply to have ignored this evidence, even while acknowledging its existence. Nevertheless, these remains all confirm a historical view of varying productions by different minds, all of which represent themselves as being, in some sense or other, "Christian." This variety of the early Christianities is, indeed, what we might expect when we relinquish the outmoded notion of minds as blank slates upon which are inscribed the common patterns and processes of a dominant cultural context.

But human minds are not operationally idiosyncratic; not everything is possible to think or even to imagine.[9] Perhaps the universal capacities of and constraints upon the workings of the human brain, the processes and patterns of its productions, can aid the biblical scholar in organizing and assessing the relationships among the broad range of data that survives from the biblical traditions, the textual as well as the material. Historians generally, however, have been reluctant to extend their explorations to the naturalistic level of the brain functions. Two recent exceptions are the recent study of *Human Nature in Rural Tuscany* by Gregory Hanlon (2007) and *On Deep History and the Brain* by Daniel Lord Smail (2008). Hanlon organizes and interprets detailed archival evidence from a seventeenth-century

7. Lemche, *Israelites*, 30.
8. Snyder, *Ante Pacem*.
9. Lawson, "Constraints."

Tuscan village in the theoretical context of evolutionary psychology and cognitive science whereas Smail, who explicitly rejects a biblically biased view of history that began in Sumeria some four thousand years ago for a view of human history that began in Africa fifty thousand years ago, tracks that history in terms of alterations in and modifications of brain chemistry—both natural and induced: their discoveries, manipulations, commodifications, and so forth.[10] The larger theoretical context for both, as proposed by Hanlon, "sets the limits of what can and cannot occur or endure beyond the short term."[11] The evolutionary and cognitive themes employed by Hanlon and Smail also recur throughout the history of literature as well[12] and, unsurprisingly, characterize the biblical narratives as well. I should like here to suggest but one example.

III

The Hebrew epic, which may be dated as late as the early Hellenistic period,[13] preserves the account of a sociopolitical formation that is remarkable for its theoretical insights whatever one concludes about its historicity.[14] Most succinctly, this epic recounts the formation of a confederated group by a number of late Bronze Age Middle Eastern Bedouin tribes. The success and stability of such large(r)-scale federations, then as now, remains problematic since the cognitive capacities of *Homo sapiens*' social cognition evolved for life in small-scale societies of roughly 150—a constraint that characterizes units of military organization throughout history, for example, or of contemporary hunter-gatherer groups.[15] The basis for the organization of these small-scale societies was kinship, which *Homo sapiens* not only defined by biology—a modern science in any case—but also extended to nonkin through socially legitimated strategies like marriage and adoption. While the basis often given for the Israelite federation and for its "solidarity" was its foundation on their collective faith in a single deity, much more fundamental to its success was their construction of a fictive genealogy that posited for this alliance of nonkin a common ancestral descendant (Genesis 12–25). This claim to an inclusive fictive kinship for the cooperating tribes exploited evolved kin biases of *Homo sapiens* and allowed for a trust

10. On such long-term views of the past, see also Renfrew, *Prehistory*.
11. Hanlon, *Human Nature*, 8.
12. Carroll, *Evolution*; Gottwald and Wilson, *Literary Animal*.
13. Lemche, *Israelites*, 159.
14. Martin, "Introduction."
15. Dunbar, "Coevolution."

to be extended among them that previously would have been restricted to members of one's own group. Such claims for defining large-scale inclusivity were, for example, similarly attributed to attempts by Alexander the Great to unify his Graeco-Macedonian empire.[16] It was the Israelite view of a large(r)-scale society established on the basis of (fictive) claims to kinship that allowed the autonomous deities of the individual tribes to become re-represented by members of the new federation as aspects of a single god in the first place. Nevertheless, in-group competition among members of the new and still fragile alliance required regulation as well.

According to our epic, the nascent Israelite federation adopted a set of governing rules, the so-called Ten Commandments (Exod 20:1–17), and legitimated this code by appeal to the authority of their still tenuously accepted leader, Moses, and, of course, to that of their now common deity (4:1). To a great extent, any society is defined by its governing rules. These codes, however, have their roots in certain universal behavioral and cognitive biases that are displayed already by primates. These evolved biases include such behaviors as mutual altruism (familiar from moral codes around the world as some version of "love your neighbor as yourself"), and those apparent recognitions of fairness that become elaborated as codes of justice.[17] Social elaborations upon such universal moral instincts also include a set of socially contingent overrides for evolved behavioral biases considered to be antisocial, individualistic behaviors of competition, for example. In the so-called environment of evolutionary adaptation, in ancient historical contexts, and in much of the contemporary world, such moral precepts and overrides extend only to fellow members of the in-group, ensuring, thereby, the sociality and solidarity of its alliance. Certainly, prohibitions against stealing from or against killing members of one's own group is a fundamental requirement for any successful social maintenance, as are exhortations to honor one's mother and father, i.e., one's ancestral genealogy. Such in-group morality often, but not always, provides an occasion for the establishment of religion, i.e., as appeals to the authority of superhuman agents as a possible legitimization for social coherence, in which case, exhortations to honor the authority of the deity that has come to legitimate and, thus, to represent, the federation are considered to be fundamental, if exclusive. Universalized, hegemonic, and even secularized understandings of the contingent particularities of the Israelite federation's social code have provided the charter myth for most of Western morality.

16. Martin, "Very Idea of Globalization."
17. Hauser, *Moral Minds*.

Presumably, the motivation for large(r)-scale cooperation by the federated Israelite tribes in the first place was a view of enhanced competition with their neighbors for the scarce resources of their rather barren environment, the storied "milk and honey" (Exod 3:8, 17; 13:5; 33:3), and to satisfy, thereby, the Darwinian imperative of survival. According to the Hebrew epic, they engaged in some rather nasty behavior in competition with those who remained outside of the federation: the Canaanites, the Hittites, the Amorites, the Perizzites, the Hivites, and the Jebusites. They were expected not only to expel these non-Israelite tribes from their land (Exod 34:11) but to "blot them out" (23:23)—a genocidal stance toward the enemies of the federation that recurs throughout their history (e.g., 1 Sam 15:3; 2 Kgs 8:12; Ps 137:9; Isa 13:16; Nah 3:10).

Further, in conflict with the Midianites, the warriors of the federation are described by the epic as killing all enemy adults and their children, except for the young virgins, which they kept for themselves (Num 31:7–18). This account is consistent with the second Darwinian imperative of surviving for a time sufficient to secure a reproductive advantage in which "none [of the Israelites] will be barren in . . . [their newly conquered land]" (Exod 23:26), remedying, presumably, a remembered state of underpopulation among the tribes.[18] If, after all, we accept—for our theoretical model—the traditional claim of twelve for the affiliated tribes and a cognitively optimal population of roughly 150 people for each tribe, then the total Hebrew population would have been only around two thousand, of which roughly half would have been males—hardly the overwhelming number of twelve thousand imagined in the Hebrew epic for their armies (Num 31:5). And an estimated 20 to 60 percent of these males would, of course, have fallen in battle.[19]

By contrast, early Christians initially seemed to neglect reproductive concerns—to abandon family in order to follow Jesus (Mark 3:31–35; Luke 9:59–62), for example, or to refrain from marriage and practice abstinence (1 Cor 7:27, 38; 1 Tim 4:3), presumably because of a fervor and focus that characterized these new movements. Subsequently, however, Christians began to embrace practices that gave them a reproductive advantage over non-Christians—according greater status to women than was the case in many contemporaneous social groups: for example, their rejection of infanticide, abortion, birth control, and so forth. Rodney Stark has argued that the embrace of such reproductive strategies contributed to the successful

---

18. Chang et al., "Face."
19. Keeley, *War*.

rise of Christianity during the second and third centuries.[20] These later "moral practices" were, of course, legitimated by claims to the same divine authority initially invoked for their rejection.

In addition to legitimating social formation and governance, claims to the authority of deities contribute as well to the continuing transmission of such formations. The presumed presence of such superhuman agents is a product of breaches in what cognitivists refer to as the "intuitive ontologies" of *Homo sapiens*, that is to say, to violations of ordinary human expectations about the world.[21] One such ontology is that of agency, from which, consequently, a great deal of information may be inferred on the basis of ordinary expectations apart from any learned knowledge. Because of the capacity of the human mind to entertain the realm of possibility in addition to representing actuality, the boundaries of these categories may, in the absence of complete information, sometimes become "blurred." A common example of the category of agent or person being violated to generate a superhuman agent is that of ghosts. Ghosts are ordinary agents in most expectations. They are, for example, intentional beings who have minds, which act and react in terms of expected sensory information (e.g., sight, sound, smell, touch); they exist in time and hold memories of the past; they communicate and can be communicated with; and the like. However, they also manifest a few unexpected characteristics, such as transparency or the ability to walk through walls. Whereas such counterintuitive beliefs and claims about ghosts violate ordinary expectations about agents, they are not so excessive as to be judged bizarre (like the unleashed power represented by the Godzilla of Japanese film or the technologically superior beings who observe us from alien spaceships) and dismissed, thereby, as fantasy or as popular diversion (at least, not by many). Rather, minimally violated ontologies are attention-grabbing and, consequently, highly memorable and readily transmissible while being, at the same time, *ordinary* enough to be easily accepted and readily understood.[22] Such attention-focusing and memorable representations support the transmission of socially contingent information associated with them. The Bible, for example, contains a collection of rather mundane, some might even say insignificant, stories—genealogies, family squabbles, accounts of petty warlords and their skirmishes, insightful but unexceptional teachings—which are, however, associated with counterintuitive acts and events attributed to superhuman agents (i.e., to God, or to his Son, or to Satan) and that violate normal expectations: ordinary bushes

---

20. Stark, *Rise*, 98–128.
21. Boyer, *Religion Explained*, 51–71.
22. Ibid.

that burn without being consumed, for example; village maidens who give birth virginally; very human sentiments mythologized (rationalized) as temptations by nonhuman agents. It is such counterintuitive events and superhuman acts that attract and focus attention on the social information associated with them and render them memorable for believers—many of whom admit to never having read the "ordinary" portions of the Bible at all, including, nonincidentally, the Hebrew charter epic itself.

The Hebrew epic and the knowledge it transmits is further characterized by an emphasis on certain ritual practices, especially with that of keeping the Sabbath (Exod 16.23–29; 20.8–11; 31.14–16; 35.2–3). This practice of the federated people to rest one day out of seven was unique among the peoples of Middle Eastern antiquity as, indeed, was the concept of a seven-day week itself. Unlike days, months, seasons or years, a seven-day week does not correspond to any natural cycle but is an artificial measure of time that must be created by them—the social definition that is, of course, the point of Genesis 1—and, of course, legitimated by claims to the authority of their now common god (Gen 1; Exod 20.11; 31.17).

Cognitive scientists distinguish between frequently and infrequently performed rituals, how their performance is associated with the encoding of different systems of human memory, and, thereby, with how memory further supports the transmission of religious knowledge.[23] Keeping the Sabbath was a regularly repeated rite that—along with the other rites prescribed by the federation—constituted a highly controlled and regulated system of ritual orthopraxy—not unlike that of official Roman religion during the period of Empire.[24] This ritual system of orthopraxy remained central to the distinctive identity of the federation and to its transmission over time until it began to be replaced by a doctrinal system of *orthodoxy* in the postbiblical period, a process of religious transformation sealed with the Roman destruction of the Jerusalem temple in 74 CE, and with it, the defining centrality of the priestly (ritual) practices of Judaism.

By contrast, the initial identifying ritual for early Christians was baptism, a rite performed but once for each participant. By the fourth century, however, the repetitive rite of the Eucharist replaced baptism as the central ritual of Christianity. This process of ritual substitution is predicted by (i.e., explainable by) cognitive theories of ritual.[25]

23. Whitehouse, *Modes*; McCauley and Lawson, *Bringing Ritual*.
24. Martin, "Conclusion."
25. Martin, "Why Christianity."

Conclusion

The social anthropologist Jerome Barkow has recently edited a volume titled *Missing the Revolution*.[26] In it, he and his contributors argue that many social scientists have, for various historical, disciplinary, and political reasons, missed the evolutionary and cognitive revolution that has so impacted the natural sciences—and even literary criticism, the foundations for which have rightly been attributed to biblical scholarship. I would add to Barkow's list of those who have missed the revolution historians of religions, including biblical scholars.[27]

Whether or not the evolutionary and cognitive sciences will finally become established as a shared paradigm for research in the study of religion remains to be seen. The possibility that it will is suggested, however, by an increase in the number of research programs devoted to cognitive science, including the cognitive science of religion at, for example, Queen's University Belfast; the Universities of Aarhus, Helsinki, and Oxford; the University of California, Santa Barbara; and Emory University. Further, the number of panels devoted to discussions of this paradigm has increased significantly at meetings of various professional associations. In addition to the Society of Biblical Literature, other organizations also have hosted panels on the cognitive science of religion at recent meetings: for example, the American Academy of Religion, the North American Association for the Study of Religion, the Society for the Scientific Study of Religion, the American Anthropological Association, and the International Association for the History of Religions. And ethnographic, experimental, and historical dissertations and monographs on religious behaviors and traditions from an evolutionary and cognitive approach have begun to appear. Perhaps most telling, because most public, was a recent cover story in the *New York Times Magazine* that presented an overview of evolutionary and cognitive explanations for "Why We Believe."[28] I invite you, therefore, to engage this new scientific paradigm in your own work, to assess its utility, evaluate its validity, and then to draw your own conclusions.

---

26. Barkow, *Revolution*.
27. See, however, Luomanen et al., *Origins*.
28. Henig, "God."

References

Barkow, Jerome H., ed. *Missing the Revolution: Darwinism for Social Scientists*. Oxford: Oxford University Press, 2006.

Brown, Francis et al., eds. *A Hebrew and English Lexicon of the Old Testament*. Oxford: Oxford University Press, 1959.

Boyer, Pascal. *Religion Explained: The Evolutionary Origins of Religious Thought*. New York: Basic Books, 2001.

Carroll, Joseph. *Literary Darwinism: Evolution, Human Nature, and Literature*. New York: Routledge, 2004.

Chang, Lei, et al. "The Face That Launched a Thousand Ships: The Mating-Warring Association in Men." *Personality and Social Psychology Bulletin* 37/7 (2011) 976–84.

Chomsky, Noam. A Review of *Verbal Behavior*, by B. F. Skinner. *Language* 35/1 (1959) 26–58.

Dunbar, R. I. M. "Coevolution of Neocortical Size, Group Size and Language in Humans." *Behavioral and Brain Sciences* 16 (1993) 681–735.

Gottwald, Jonathan, and David Slone Wilson, eds. *The Literary Animal: Evolution and the Nature of Narrative*. Rethinking Theory. Evanston: Northwestern University Press, 2005.

Hanlon, Gregory. *Human Nature in Rural Tuscany: An Early Modern History*. Italian and Italian American Studies. New York: Palgrave Macmillan, 2007.

Hauser, Marc D. *Moral Minds: How Nature Designed Our Universal Sense of Right and Wrong*. New York: HarperCollins, 2006.

Henig, Robin M. "Darwin's God." *New York Times Magazine* (March 4, 2007).

Keeley, Lawrence H. *War before Civilization: The Myth of the Peaceful Savage*. New York: Oxford University Press, 1996.

Kittel, Gerhard, ed. *Theologische Wörterbuch zum Neuen Testament*. Vol. 3. Stuttgart: Kohlhammer, 1938.

Lawson, E. Thomas. "Cognitive Constraints on Imagining Other Worlds." In *Sci-fi in the Mind's Eye*, edited by Margret Grebowicz et al., 263–74. Chicago: Open Court, 2007.

Lemche, Niels P. *The Israelites in History and Tradition*. Library of Ancient Israel. Louisville: Westminster John Knox, 1998.

Liddell, Henry G., and Robert Scott. *A Greek-English Lexicon*. Oxford: Oxford University Press, 1968.

Luomanen, Petri et al., eds. *Explaining Christian Origins and Early Judaism: Contributions from Cognitive and Social Science*. Biblical Interpretation Series 89. Leiden: Brill, 2007.

McCauley, Robert N., and E. Thomas Lawson. *Bringing Ritual to Mind: Psychological Foundations of Cultural Forms*. Cambridge: Cambridge University Press, 2002.

Martin, Luther H. "Conclusion: Imagistic Traditions in the Graeco-Roman World." In *Imagistic Traditions in the Graeco-Roman World*, edited by Luther H. Martin and Panayotis Pachis, 237–47. Thessaloniki: Vanias, 2009 (chapter 10, this volume).

———. "Introduction." In *Religious Transformations and Socio-Political Change: Eastern Europe and Latin America*, edited by Luther H. Martin, 1–5. Religion and Society 33. Berlin: de Gruyter, 1993.

———. "The Very Idea of Globalization: The Case of Hellenistic Empire." In *Hellenisation, Empire and Globalisation: Lessons from Antiquity*, edited by Luther H. Martin and Panayotis Pachis, 123–39. Thessaloniki: Vanias, 2004 (chapter 2, this volume).

———. "Why Christianity Was Accepted by Romans but Not by Rome." In *Religionskritik in Der Antike*, edited by Ulrich Berner and Ilinca Tanaseanu-Döbler, 93–107. Religionen in der pluralen Welt 7. Mümster: LIT, 2009.

Pinker, Steven. *The Blank Slate: The Modern Denial of Human Nature.* New York: Viking, 2002.

Renfrew, Colin. *Prehistory: The Making of the Human Mind.* New York: Modern Library, 2008.

Smail, Daniel Lord. *On Deep History and the Brain.* Berkeley: University of California Press, 2008.

Snyder, Graydon F. *Ante Pacem: Archaeological Evidence of Church Life before Constantine.* 2nd ed. Macon: Mercer University Press, 2003.

Sperber, Dan. *Explaining Culture: A Naturalistic Approach.* Oxford: Blackwell, 1996.

Stark, Rodney. *The Rise of Christianity: A Sociologist Reconsiders History.* Princeton: Princeton University Press, 1996.

Starr, Chester G. *A History of the Ancient World.* Oxford: Oxford University Press, 1965.

Tooby, John, and Leda Cosmides. "The Psychological Foundations of Culture." In *The Adapted Mind: Evolutionary Psychology and the Generation of Culture*, edited by Jerome H. Barkow et al., 3–136. New York: Oxford University Press, 1992.

Whitehouse, Harvey. *Modes of Religiosity: A Cognitive Theory of Religious Transmission.* Cognitive Science of Religion Series. Walnut Creek, CA: AltaMira, 2004.

PART 5

Gnosticism

22

Genealogy and Sociology in the Apocalypse of Adam

At either end of the earth and at both extremes of time, the Sumerian myth of the golden age and the Andaman myth of the future life correspond, the former placing the end of primitive happiness at a time when the confusion of languages made words into common property, the latter describing the bliss of the hearafter as a heaven where women will no longer be exchanged, i.e., removing to an equally unattainable past or future the joys, eternally denied to social man, of a world in which one might *keep to oneself.*

LÉVI-STRAUSS[1]

ALTHOUGH GNOSTICISM HAS PROVIDED a rich trove for psychological analyses,[2] it offers meagre data for sociological inquiry, unless a parallel between mythological metaphysics and social situation is assumed. Such social analyses of gnostic traditions most often employ a general sociology of individualism (for example, that of Marx or Weber) or a sociology of context (Green)[3] that simply reformulates the orthodox judgements

---

1. Lévi-Strauss, *Elementary Structures*, 497.

2. See especially the insightful inquiries of Gilles Quispel informed by the analytical psychology of C. G. Jung, after whom Codex I from Nag Hammadi was named; but see Darnton, *Cat Massacre*, 9–72; Martin, "Artemidorus"; and Martin, "Religion and Dream Theory," who question the historical adequacy of interpreting prepsychological-era texts psychologically, a hermeneutic that assumes the universal as opposed to the contingent validity of psychological theory.

3. Green provides a helpful overview of sociological interpretations of Gnosticism in *Economic and Social*, chapter 1.

of early heresiological literature in terms of social scientific categories of alienation or marginality. Yet the prominence in gnostic myth of kinship categories of relationship, especially that of father and son,[4] and of those based upon claims to a common ancestry suggests an unexplored possibility of social insight. Accounts of descent from a common ancestor represent a conventional strategy of collective identity among people of antiquity. The discourse of such inclusion is that of kin relationship, which anthropologists consider "the most central of social processes."[5] Kinship systems tell us how *people themselves* see their world of kin, from whom they distinguish themselves, and on what basis.[6]

Kinship nomenclature systems are social inventions. The criteria for assigning persons to the role of kin vary from culture to culture in ways having little or nothing to do with biology.[7] Rather, systems of kinship represent implicit classifications of an ideal kinship universe.[8] This distinction between idealized kinship systems and actual kin relationship corresponds to the distinction between "culture" and "society," whereby "culture" designates shard patterns of expectations, evaluations, and symbolic meanings, and "society" designates a group of people who share these cultural attributes with some measure of regularity.[9] As J. A. Barnes summarized,

> it is obvious that many people can think alike without having anything to do with one another, and that many people who come into contact with each other every day [may] hold radically different views.[10]

While ideal kin classification systems may or may not correspond to real groups or strategies, they do give an accurate picture of significant categories of social relationship in a kinship universe. Bruce J. Malina has shown the value of anthropological theory for addressing the meaning of social realities in the world of early Christianity, and Robert A. Oden has demonstrated the usefulness of theoretical kinship for understanding the conventionalized biblical genealogies of Genesis.[11]

---

4. The father-son relationship in gnostic myth is usually treated as "an expression of spiritual or didactic filiation." See, e.g., Peel, "Treatise," 137.

5. Fox, *Kinship and Marriage*, 3, 13: an excellent introduction and overview of this difficult and often confused subject.

6. Ibid., 243.

7. White, *Anatomy*, 6; Fox, *Kinship and Marriage*, 34.

8. Fox, *Kinship and Marriage*, 245.

9. Barnes, *Three Styles*, 25.

10. Ibid.

11. Malina, *New Testament World*; Oden, "Jacob." See also Leach, *Genesis as Myth*; and Donaldson, "Kinship Theory."

In the spirit of Hans Jonas's "experimental vein" of gnostic studies,[12] it might be asked what an analysis of gnostic claims to kin inclusion determined by eponymous descent might disclose about gnostic society, if indeed there be any gnostic societies,[13] and/or about the culture that has produced such a kin system. "Sethian Gnosticism," the fixed point of which has been described as "the idea that Gnostics constitute a special 'race' descended from Seth,"[14] provides the ideal case study for an anthropological "demythologization" of a gnostic kinship universe.[15] Because of the relatively early date of the Apocalypse of Adam (Nag Hammadi Codex 5.5), hypothesized on the basis of an absence of distinctively Christian imagery,[16] and because that document belongs to a general class of "charter myths," in which privilege is established through a genealogy that the descendent comes "to know in contrast to others who are excluded,"[17] it will be the focus of the following analysis.[18]

Kinship in the Apocalypse of Adam

Any cultural system defines two patterns of kin relationship: descent and alliance. Descent groups are defined by a real, putative, or fictive descent from a common ancestor through either the male line (patrilineally) or the female line (matrilineally), or through both sexes (cognatically).[19] Such groups may share common property, ritual, some activity, or, as in the Apocalypse of Adam, a name.[20]

---

12. Jonas, *Gnostic Religion*, 320.

13. Wisse ("Elusive Sethians," 575) concludes that the Sethian tractates "must not be seen as the teaching of a sect or sects, but as the inspired creations of individuals who did not feel bound by the opinions of a religious community."

14. Epiphanius, *Against Heresies*, 39.2.3, in Layton, *Gnostic Scriptures*, 188; MacRae, "Seth," 21; Pearson, "Figure of Seth," 489; Stroumsa, *Another Seed*, 125.

15. As with Gnosticism generally, there is no information about the social makeup or practices of any Sethian group; see Wisse, "Elusive Sethians," 564.

16. Klijn, *Seth*, 90 n42; Rudolph, *Gnosis*, 135; Turner, "Sethian Gnosticism"; but compare Stroumsa, *Another Seed*, 103.

17. Burkert, *Ancient Mystery Cults*, 76; on "charter myths," see Kirk, *Myth*, 256–57.

18. See the translations by MacRae and Parrott in Robinson, *Nag Hammadi Library*, 256–64; by MacRae in Parrott, ed., *Nag Hammadi Codices*, 151–95 (includes Coptic text), and in Charlesworth, *Pseudepigrapha*, 1:707–19; and by Layton in Layton, *Gnostic Scriptures*, 52–64.

19. Fox, *Kinship and Marriage*, 34.

20. Ibid., 49.

According to the *Apocalypse of Adam*, Seth is the descendent of Adam and Eve (64.26; 65.2–3, 12–13; 66.7–8), while Cain (although the same name is absent from the corrupt text) is the offspring of Eve and Sakla, the demiurgic deity of this world (66.25–27).[21] The descendants of this primordial *menage à trois* constitute two patrilineally defined descent groups (γενεαί) (68.8; 71.19, 23; 82.19; 83.1), in which the typical father-son-bother constellation dominates:[22] the Sethites and the Cainites. Descent is traced from Adam to Seth and his seed, on the one hand (64.1–3; 67.14–21; 69. 9–17; 85.19–24), and from Saklas through Seth's half-brother, Cain, to Noah and to his sons Japheth, Ham, and Shem, on the other (70.10–11).[23] The name of Shem does not recur in the text, but Shem is most certainly the covenanter with Sakla (72.31—73.12). Shem's descendants are the Israelites (73, 1–12) who have "done all [Sakla's] will" (74.17–18).[24] By contrast, the descendants of Japheth and Ham form twelve kingdoms of Gentiles (73.25–27). Four hundred thousand (Gentile) men, who have departed from the descendants of Japeth and Ham, "enter into another land and sojourn with those men who came forth from the great eternal knowledge" (73.13–24; 74.8–16), that is, with the descendants of Seth (73.13–20; cf. 65.5–9).

The *Apocalypse of Adam* employs two kin terms in dealing with descent: "son" and "seed." The Coptic *shēre*, or "son" (equivalent to Greek υἱός) is used to refer both to Seth (67.15; 85.21) and to the (Cainite) sons of Noah (70.10, 21; 71.2, 4; 72.16, 18; 74.18), including their sons (76.13). As a man gains complete rights over the possession of his own children in patrilineal systems,[25] so Seth dominates his line as their forefather, even as Cain dominates his.

The kin category "son" is further qualified in the *Apocalypse of Adam* by the use of "seed," for which three words are employed: the Greek loanwords σπορά and σπέρμα and the Coptic word *grog*. L. Schottroff has pointed out

21. Abel, who according to Epiphanius was replaced by Seth after Cain killed him (39.2.4), is not mentioned in the *Apocalypse of Adam*.

22. Fox, *Kinship and Marriage*, 121.

23. The text has it that Sakla gives "power to his [Sakla's] sons and their wives by means of the ark," thus making Noah a Cainite by descent in contradiction to the account in Genesis, where Noah is a Sethite. MacRae and Stroumsa suggest that the text suffers from a haplography and restore it to read, "and he will give power to *Noah, his wife*, his sons and their wives" (Stroumsa, *Another Seed*, 83 n11). By betraying the requirements of descent through his covenant with Sakla and the Cainites, however, Noah becomes a "sinful Sethite" (Stroumsa, *Another Seed,* 86), allied thereby with the Cainites. From the perspective represented by the *Apocalypse of Adam*, the question seems to be not whether Noah is a Cainite, but whether he is considered to be a Cainite by birth or by alliance.

24. Klijn, *Seth*, 94; Stroumsa, *Another Seed,* 85.

25. Fox, *Kinship and Marriage*, 121.

that σπορά is always used positively in the *Apocalypse of Adam* and refers to the line of Adam/Seth, whereas σπέρμα refers to the descendants of Sakla/Cain.[26]

Σπορά characterizes authentic descent from Seth, the sole legitimate offspring of Adam and Eve. His legitimacy is based upon his parents' union in *knowledge* (γνῶσις), which had been taught Adam by Eve (64.12–13), and which is inherited by Seth (65.3–5; 69.11–17). It is into the *seed* (σπορά) of the great aeons that *knowledge* (γνῶσις) entered (65.4) to become the *seed* (σπορά) of the great generation who is Seth (65.8). Σπορά is the equivalent, therefore, of γνῶσις, and three revealers tell Adam that this *seed* (σπορά) of knowledge has passed to Seth (66.3–8). Like angels, those men who work in the imperishable *seed* (σπορά, 65.7) will receive the gnosis that passed from Adam through Seth to that *seed* (σπορά, 85.22).

Cain's illegitimacy, on the other hand, is based on his father's position being lower than that of Eve (64.16–19). This low "rank" is characterized by his lack of gnosis and by his acting on the basis of an antithetical "desire" (ἐπιθυμία) that he introduced into the world through his union with Eve (67.1–4). This primordial opposition between knowledge and desire defines the separate races of Seth and Cain.

Σπέρμα is used to describe the seed of Noah and his sons (72.24; 73.14, 25, 28; 74.17; 76.12) and that of the four hundred thousand men who are from the seed of Japeth and Ham (74.11). Although the Coptic *grog* can translate both σπορά and σπέρμα,[27] it is used in the *Apocalypse of Adam* to refer to the descendants of Noah (73.2, 6) and thus in the sense of σπέρμα.

There are no further genealogical connections established in the *Apocalypse of Adam* between any of the ancestors and the gnostic Ego. This "telescoping" tendency, whereby "those ancestors whose presence in the genealogy is inessential for the reckoning of contemporary relationships" have disappeared,[28] establishes an ancestral ordering for classes of human identity.[29] The genealogical taxonomy defined by the *Apocalypse of Adam* establishes three such classes: (1) the descendants of Seth; (2) the descendants of Cain, including Noah and his descendants (Jews through Shem and twelve kingdoms of Gentiles through Ham and Japheth); (3) the four hundred thousand apostate Gentiles.[30] The kinship universe articulated by

26. Schottroff, "*Animae naturaliter salvandae*," 79 (cited in Stroumsa, *Another Seed*, 125 n2).

27. Crum, *Coptic Dictionary*, 831b.

28. Goody, "Kinship," 403.

29. Geertz, *Interpretation*, 373 n12; Sagan, *Dawn*, 146.

30. Layton, *Gnostic Scriptures*, 52.

the *Apocalypse of Adam* provides authority for this proper order of nature because its genealogy from mythical time can be stated.[31]

The paradigm of identity established by the *Apocalypse of Adam* for the contemporary gnostic Ego, is, of course, Sethian descent. Comparative sociologists distinguish descent (the transmission of kinship membership rights) from inheritance (the transmission of property) and from succession (the transmission of office), neither of which necessarily requires a kin relationship.[32] Whereas, succession, which validates right to an exclusive office,[33] is not an issue in the *Apocalypse of Adam*, the tractate does link inheritance to descent. Descent systems establish the procedure for transmitting inheritance not only of property and position but also of values and knowledge.[34] The inheritance of γνῶσις (*gnosis*) belongs to the race of Seth (65.4-9) and no other race (71.16-26). The tractate legitimates as heirs of γνῶσις those "sons" who claim Seth as their ascendant.

Although the Sethites and Cainites are differentiated by separate patrilineal ascendants, they share a common matrilineal ancestor. This shared relationship in the Sethian kinship universe gives rise to an overlapping grouping of descendent kin with membership rights dependent upon additional criteria of eligibility, involving choice among such alternatives as marriage or adoption.[35] Since intercourse is renounced by the Sethites (72.12-13; 73.23-24; 75.1-4) and by the four hundred thousand (73.20-24), the joining of the four hundred thousand with the Sethites may be understood in terms of the kin category of adoption.

Kinship in Roman Society

Adoption is a legal fiction that permits a family tie to be artificially created.[36] The frequency of this practice in Roman society shows that biology was of little concern in the Roman conception of the family.[37] As adoption involved also the ascent of the adoptee,[38] it may be considered a practice of kinship recruitment upon which the religious notion of conversion was modeled in genealogically articulated systems.[39] The Greek technical tem

---

31. Kirk, *Myth*, 256-57.
32. Goody, "Kinship," 401-2, following Rivers, *Social Organization*.
33. Ibid., 403.
34. Barnes, *Three Styles,* 139.
35. Goody, "Kinship," 406.
36. Maine, *Ancient Law*, 22.
37. Ibid., 107; Veyne, "Roman Empire," 17.
38. Maine, *Ancient Law,* 114-15.
39. *Contra* Stroumsa, *Another Seed*, 86.

for legal adoption, υἱοθεσία ("sonship"), is used in this metaphorical sense of conversion most notably by Paul (see Gal 4:5).[40]

Adoption in Roman society was not by legal document but by will or testament,[41] the instrument by which the devolution of an inheritance was prescribed in antiquity.[42] Following the lead of G. MacRae,[43] Stroumsa notes that the *Apocalypse of Adam* "is actually a 'testament' of Adam, for the revelation took place at the time of his death."[44]

Sir Henry Maine, founder of the contemporary study of jurisprudence and one of the founders of modern kinship analysis, understood ancient law to be based upon the problem of legitimate inheritance.[45] Because such discursive formations as the canon of law have their own histories—viz., when they emerged, the conditions of their emergence, from which discourse they diverged or merged, and so forth[46]—and because "insistence on abiding by shared values and norms was an expression of commitment to the existing social structure,"[47] it is useful to review some of Maine's conclusions concerning inheritance and law as exemplars of the historical boundaries of kinship discourse within which the *Apocalypse of Adam* might have been articulated.

"The original Will or Testament," Maine writes, "was . . . an instrument . . . by which the devolution of the *Family* was regulated."[48] "In the old Roman Law of Inheritance the notion of a will or testament is inextricably mixed up . . . with the theory of a man's posthumous existence in the person of his heir."[49] The Roman law of inheritance is that "though the physical person of the deceased had perished, his legal personality survived and descended unimpaired on his Heir or Co-Heirs, in whom his identity (so far as the law was concerned) was continued"[50]—the elimination, Maine concludes, "of the fact of death."[51]

40. Betz, *Galatians*, 208–9, also ibid., 185–86.
41. Veyne, "Roman Empire," 17.
42. Maine, *Ancient Law*, 147.
43. MacRae, "Seth," 18; and in Parrott, ed., *Nag Hammadi Codices*, 152.
44. Stroumsa, *Another Seed*, 82.
45. Maine, *Ancient Law*, 1. Maine's work not only remains a classic of comparative jurisprudence but is one of the foundations of modern kinship studies. See, for example, Fox, *Kinship and Marriage*, 18; and Fortes, *Social Order*, 11–12. Morgan, *Consanguinity* is the undisputed foundation for kin term systems.
46. Foucault, *Archaeology*, 22.
47. Malina, "'Religion' in the World of Paul," 99.
48. Maine, *Ancient Law*, 158.
49. Ibid., 157.
50. Ibid., 151, 156.
51. Ibid., 157–58.

"The prolongation of a man's legal existence in his heir, or in a group of co-heirs, is neither more nor less than a characteristic of the *family* transferred by a fiction to *the individual*."[52] Ancient history "has for its units, not individuals, but groups of men united by the reality or the fiction of blood-relationships."[53] "All ancient societies regarded themselves as having proceed from one original stock, and even labored under an incapacity for comprehending any reason except this for their holding together in political union."[54] All ancient witnesses to testaments in Rome "indicate that what passed from the Testator to the Heir was the *family*, that is, the aggregate of rights and duties contained in the *Patria Potestas* and growing out of it."[55] Under Roman law, *patria potestas* was the basis of family life.[56] "The life of each citizen is not regarded as limited by birth and death; it is but a continuation of the existence of his forefathers, and it will prolonged in the existence of his descendants,"[57] whether through agnatic descent or through adoption.[58]

Under Roman law, the line of inheritance was as follows:

1. The *sui*, or direct descendants, equivalent in the *Apocalypse of Adam* to Seth.

2. The nearest agnate. Agnatic descent refers to cognates who trace their connection exclusively through males, as does the Apocalypse of Adam. Whereas "Paternal Powers proper are extinguished by the death of the Parent . . . Agnation is as it were a mould which retains their imprint after they have ceased to exist."[59] Agnation is not based upon the marriage of Father and Mother, but only upon the "authority of the Father" (*patria potestas*), including for those brought under this authority through adoption.[60]

3. The *Gentiles*, i.e., the collective members of the dead man's *gens* or *house*, who, on the ground of bearing the same name, were supposed to be descended from a common ancestor.[61] The four hundred thousand

---

52. Ibid., 154.
53. Ibid, 152, see also 104, 213–14.
54. Ibid., 106.
55. Ibid., 158.
56. Ibid., 32.
57. Ibid., 214.
58. Ibid., 32.
59. Ibid., 124.
60. Ibid., 123.
61. Ibid., 165–66.

descendants of Japheth and Ham adopted by the house or race of Seth establish the primordial model of those who will inherit *gnosis*. Under Roman law, "the only purpose of *adoptio* is to bring *patria potestas* into existence."[62] Even as Jesus requires those who will do "the will of my Father in heaven" to reject their natural family (Matt 12:46–50; Mark 3:31–35; Luke 8:21), adoption into the *patria potestas* of Seth requires the rejection of the adoptee's Cainite origin.

Kinship Rationales in the *Apocalypse of Adam*

"Whatever else kinship systems do," Robin Fox summarized, "they divide people into categories of kin and then define marriageability in terms of these categories."[63] Marriage was equivalent in status to adoption under Roman law,[64] and, like adoption, has been treated by kinship analysis largely in the context of recruitment to kinship groups.[65] Lévi-Strauss, however, has emphasized the importance of marriage alliance over descent as the basis for the social state. For Lévi-Strauss, kinship groups are "units in a system of 'alliance' made or 'expressed' by marriage."[66] In the *Apocalypse of Adam* alliance, based upon desire, is the identifying mark of the Cainites.

Adam/Eve, an androgynous pair who are divided by Sakla (64.20–23), are as much brother/sister as husband/wife. Sakla, the God who created them, created fom himself a son (Cain) with Eve (65.25–28), thus establishing exogamous marriage. Exogamy is regarded as equivalent to the prohibition of incest, which, according to Lévi-Strauss, is not so much the prohibition of marriage with mother, sister, or daughter as it is an obligation to give mother, sister, or daughter to others.[67] It "provides the only means of maintaining the group as group, of avoiding infinite fission and segmentation which the practice of consanguineous marriages would bring about."[68] This exogamous bond of alliance with another family represents a tendency to social cohesion[69] and "ensures the dominance of the social over the biological."[70]

62. Schutz, *Roman Law*, 144.
63. Fox, *Kinship and Marriage*, 2.
64. Veyne, "Roman Empire," 17.
65. Fox, *Kinship and Marriage*, 22.
66. Ibid.
67. Lévi-Strauss, *Elementary Structures*, 481.
68. Ibid., 479.
69. Ibid., 480.
70. Ibid., 479. Similarly, in Roman society marriage was understood primarily as a

Because of the *gnosis* that the Sethian seed contains, Sakla enjoins Noah against mixing his σπέρμα with the alien σπορά ("no seed will come from you [Noah] of the man who will not stand in my presence in another glory [Seth]" [71.4–8]).[71] In exchange for Noah's pledge not to mingle with the race of gnostics, Sakla offers "power to Noah, his sons and their wives" (70.10–11).[72] Authority over his newly established exogamous alliance is granted by Saklas to Noah and his sons as a kingly rule over the earth. The gnostic sons of Seth, by contrast, are described as a "race without a king over it" (92.19–20).[73] Thus a Sethite kinship based upon an agamous kin model of adoption is contrasted with a Cainite kinship system based upon exogamous marriage alliances.

Anthropologists regularly disitnguish between "kinship" and "kingship" systems as types of social organization.[74] Whereas kinship systems are characterized by a genealogically defined communal authority and a "self-consciousness about their superior place in the world,"[75] kingship systems represent the tendency towards centralized leadership and power.[76]

Whereas sexual licence is universally reputed of kings,[77] it is related to the breakdown of kinship systems.[78] In the *Apocalypse of Adam*, marriage alliances, mandated by the rule of exogamy, are viewed negatively. They are based upon *lust* (ἐπιθυμία, 67.3) which results in pregnancy (80.3; 81.9, 17) and the transmission of σπέρμα. And in the hymnic section of the *Apocalypse of Adam* (77.27—83.3), spokesmen of the twelve kingdoms enumarate various views of the incarnation of the savior "in their own language of lustful beginnings and carnal births,"[79] which had been "imparted to them by their god Sakla" (73.3–4).[80]

---

civic duty rather than as a matter of establishing a family. See Veyne, "Roman Empire," 37–38.

71. Stroumsa, *Another Seed,* 83.
72. See n23 above.
73. See Fallon, "Gnostics."
74. Sagan, *Dawn*, 225–42.
75. Ibid., 236, 240.
76. Ibid., 236.
77. Ibid., 320–21.
78. Ibid., 72.
79. Stroumsa, *Another Seed,* 91.
80. Ibid., 90. It is tempting to explore the relation of this section of the *Apocalypse of Adam* to the Matthean genealogy of Jesus, in which all the women named "conceived Jesus's forebears in illicit sexual encounters," culminating in the virgin birth (Rothkrug, "German Holiness," 218–19). Matthew borrows the phase, βίβλος γενέσεως, "book of origin," with which he begins his gospel from Gen 2:4a (LXX), which introduces the "J" narrative covering the genealogy of mankind from Adam to Seth (Gen 2:4a—4:26).

The gnostics, on the other hand, having no such desire (83.16) are underfiled (Coptic *atdjōʰᵐ* 75.3–4; 75.6; 82.23), and are protected, therefore, from such ἐπιθυμία (73.24; 75.4). By avoiding ἐπιθυμία, *djōʰᵐ*, and the transmission of σπέρμα, which are characteristic of marriage alliances, the Sethites avoid the social state itself.

The Sethites' inverse reading of Genesis emphasizes the asocial implications of its Sumerian prototype. According to the citation of Lévi-Strauss, which concludes his study of kinship and opened this essay, the Sumerian myth places a golden age of primitive happiness prior to the time when a confusion of languages made words into common property and established the possibility of alliances between people. This possibility is represented in the *Apocalypse of Adam* by the dispersion of Noah's sons and their descendants, who constitute the twelve kingdoms. Before this confusion of tongues, words were the property of each particular group. A privilege of *gnosis* is still claimed by the Sethites (as by "orthodox" Christians following the miracle of tongues reported in Acts 2).

Lévi-Strauss compares the Sumerian denial of happiness to social man with the Andaman myth of the future life, which

> will be but a repetition of the present, but all will then remain in the prime of life, sickness and death will be unknown, and there will be no more marrying or giving in marriage.[81]

Kinship and Society in the *Apocalypse of Adam*

Contrary to those who would find within gnostic myth a cultural paradigm for the positive evaluation of women in ancient society, I find the idealized kinship universe articulated in the *Apocalypse of Adam* to be a staunchly patriarchal cultural system.[82] It defines gnostics as those who claim patrilineal descent from Seth.

In the "racial theology" of the *Apocalypse of Adam*,[83] membership in the Sethian descent system is defined as a potential of the descendants of Japheth and Ham, the Gentiles; Jews, the descendants of Shem, are considered unregenerate Cainites. Such "antisemitic" Gentiles,[84] who nevertheless

---

See Allen, *Matthew*, 1.

81. Man, *Aboriginal*, 94–95, cited in Lévi-Strauss, *Elementary Structures*, 457.

82. Malina, "'Religion' in the World of Paul," 94, makes this same point with respect to theological studies of the Bible.

83. Stroumsa, *Another Seed*, 86.

84. Ibid., 85; on "anti-semitism" in the Nag Hammadi documents, see Gager, *Anti-Semitism*, 167–73.

read the book of Genesis as their "charter myth," could only be a "class" of Christians,[85] the thirteenth kingdom referred to in the *Apocalypse of Adam* (82.10–19).[86]

Membership in this Sethite-Christian descent group is not understood biologically but rather is based upon the paradigm of the four hundred thousand descendants of Japheth and Ham who join with the Sethians, and with whom the primordial genealogical drama of the *Apocalypse of Adam* concludes. Sethites are Sethites not through some literal claim to consanguinity but by choice: "adoption" in the discourse of kinship, "conversion" in that of religion.

The four hundred thousand converts are a heterogenous people who renounce all alliances, whether based upon desire, which has characterized the Cainites ever since the union of Sakla with Eve; or upon power, which has characterized the Cainites ever since the covenant of Sakla with Noah and his sons. From the anthropological perspective of this study, their rejection of marriage should be taken less as evidence for an ascetic lifestyle than as a rejection of alliances—that is, as a rejection of any definition of identity. Such "keeping to oneself" should not be understood as recommending individuality, a modern notion, but as the embodiment of sacrality. Since birth and death are part of a single process of corruption (70.3–5; 76.15–17), this embodiment of sacrality is not in the corporeal body produced through sexual relations but in an angelic or resurrected body (76.6, 23–24; 83.14) that "will not perish" (76.21–23). "For," as "orthodox" Christians well knew, "in the resurrection they neither marry nor are given in mariage, but are like angels in heaven" (Matt 22:30; Mark 12:25; Luke 20:35–36).

The rejection of kingship, or political alliances, by the Sethites in favor of a kinship model suggests a form of social relations characteristic primarily of peoples defined by place. "The first century world," writes Malina, "was marked by geographical and social immobility which resulted in the heightened support of a closed social network."[87] With the newly bureaucratic urbanization characteristic of Hellenistic civilization,[88] new inhabitants came to cities from the coutryside where their ancestors had lived for centuries. Such a move provides the conditions for the creation of alternative social systems. The question then arises of the basis for nonkinship forms of social cohesion or identity inclusion. One option is adherence to the centralized leadership or authority characteristic of kingship systems; another is the formation of quasi-family associations to replace the kinship

---

85. Layton, *Gnostic Scriptures*, 20–21.
86. Stroumsa, *Another Seed*, 94–100.
87. Malina, *New Testament World*, 101.
88. See de Ste. Croix, *Class Struggle*, 10–11; Martin, *Hellenistic Religions*, 26.

networks left behind.[89] The Sethite emphasis on kinship suggests a conservative (and "orthodox" [Matt 22:21; Mark 12:17; Luke 20:57]) evaluation of Hellenistic urban life, favoring a previous status quo[90] rather than the radical posture conventionally attributed to an urbane Gnosticism from the interpretative orientation of normative Christianity.[91] Such kin associations do not represent powerlessness, but the absence or rejection of a centralized locus of power in favor of a diffused embodiment of power.

When the four hundred thousand renounced their Cainite alliances, they joined the "kingless race" (82.19–20) and settled in "another place" with the Sethites (73.13–25), who had already rejected such alliances. This "other place" is no geographical place but "heaven," the placeless place of angels (72.10–11; 73.16–20). Here they may "reflect upon the knowledge of the eternal God" embodied in their hearts and attributed to their redeemer, the heavenly Seth (76.24–30), with whom they are now identified by name. A placeless people who no longer bury because they have lost contact with their natural kin,[92] the Sethites are linked through their fictive kinship relations and are "already resurrected" into their legitimate inheritance of gnosis, a cultural system that defines an asocial reality.

References

Allen, Willoughby C. *A Critical and Exegetical Commentary on the Gospel according to St. Matthew*. International Critical Commentary 17. 3rd ed. Edinburgh: T. & T. Clark, 1912.

Barnes, John A. *Three Styles in the Study of Kinship*. London: Tavistock, 1971.

Betz, Hans D. *Galatians: A Commentary on Paul's Letter to the Churches in Galatia*. Hermeneia. Philadelphia: Fortress, 1979.

Burkert, Walter. *Ancient Mystery Cults*. Cambridge: Harvard University Press, 1987.

Charlesworth, James H. *The Odes of Solomon*. Pseudepigrapha Series 7. Texts and Translations 13. Missoula: Scholars, 1977.

———. *The Old Testament Pseudepigrapha*. Vol. 1, *Apocalyptic Literature and Testaments*. 2 vols. The Anchor Bible Reference Library. Garden City, NY: Doubleday, 1983:

Crum, W. E. *A Coptic Dictionary*. 1939. Reprint, Ancient Language Resources. Eugene, OR: Wipf & Stock, 2005.

Darnton, Robert. *The Great Cat Massacre and Other Episodes in French Cultural History*. New York: Basic Books, 1984.

De Ste. Croix, G. E. M. *The Class Struggle in the Ancient Greek World: From the Archaic Age to the Arab Conquests*. Ithaca: Cornell University Press, 1981.

---

89. Sagan, *Dawn*, 72. See also Little, *African*; and Mitchell, *Mishpokhe*.

90. Malina, "'Religion' in the World of Paul," 96.

91. On Gnosticism as a "city religion," see Rudolph, *Gnosis*, 291. See also Kippenberg, "Verländlichung."

92. Rothkrug, "German Holiness," 215–41; Johannesen, "Sunset Park."

Donaldson, Mara. "Kinship Theory in the Patriarchal Narratives: The Case of the Barren Wife." *Journal of the American Academy of Religion* 49/1 (1981) 77–87.

Fallon, Francit T. "The Gnostics: The Undominated Race." *Novum Testamentum* 21/3 (1979) 271–88.

Fortes, Meyer. *Kinship and the Social Order: The Legacy of Lewis Henry Morgan*. Lewis Henry Morgan Lectures, 1963. Chicago: Aldine, 1969.

Foucault, Michel. *The Archaeology of Knowledge*. Translated by A. M. Sheridan Smith. New York, Pantheon, 1972.

Fox, Robin. *Kinship and Marriage: An Anthropological Perspective*. Pelican Anthropology Library Harmondsworth: Penguin, 1967.

Gager, John G. *The Origins of Anti-Semitism: Attitudes toward Judaism in Pagan and Christian Antiquity*. New York: Oxford University Press, 1983.

Geertz, Clifford. *The Interpretation of Cultures: Selected Essays*. New York: Basic Books, 1973.

Goody, Jack. "Kinship: Descent Groups." In *International Encyclopedia of Social Sciences* 8 (1968) 401–8.

Green, Henry A. *The Economic and Social Origins of Gnosticism*. Society of Biblical Literature Dissertation Series 77. Atlanta: Scholars, 1985.

Johannesen, Stanley. "The Holy Ghost in Sunset Park." *Historical Reflections/Réflexions Historiques* 15/3 (1988) 543–77.

Jonas, Hans. *The Gnostic Religion: The Message of the Alien God and the Beginnings of Christianity*. Boston: Beacon, 1958.

Kippenberg, Hans. "Verländlichung des Gnosticismus als Forge siner staatlichen Unterdrückung." In *Geisteshaltung und Umwelt. Festschrift zum 65. Geburtstag von Manfred Büttner*, edited by Kreise Werner, 309–20. Abhandlungen zur Geschichte der Geowissenschaften und Religion/Umwelt-Forschung 1. Aachen: Alano, 1988.

Kirk, G. S. *Myth: Its Meaning and Functions in Ancient and Other Cultures*. Sather Classical Lectures 40. Berkeley: University of California Press, 1970.

Klijn, Albertus F. J. *Seth in Jewish, Christian and Gnostic Literature*. Supplements to Novum Testamentum 46. Leiden: Brill, 1977.

Layton, Bentley. *The Gnostic Scriptures: A New Translation with Annotations and Introductions*. Garden City, NY: Doubleday, 1987.

Leach, Edmund. *Genesis as Myth, and Other Essays*. Cape Editions 39. London: Cape, 1969.

Lévi-Strauss, Claude. *The Elementary Structures of Kinship*. Translated by James Harle Bell et al. Rev. ed. Beacon Paperbacks. Boston: Beacon, 1969.

Little, Kenneth. *West African Urbanization: A Study of Voluntary Associations in Social Change*. Cambridge: Cambridge University Press, 1965.

MacRae, George. "Seth in Gnostic Texts and Traditions." In *Society of Biblical Literature 1977, Seminar Papers*, edited by Paul J. Achtemeier, 17–24. Missoula: Scholars, 1977.

MacRae, George, and Douglas M. Parrott. "The Thunder, Perfect Mind (VI 2)." In *The Nag Hammadi Library*, edited by James M. Robinson, 287–94. 3rd rev. ed. San Francisco: Harper & Row, 1988.

Maine, Henry S. *Ancient Law: Its Connection with the Early History of Society, and Its Relation to Modern Ideas*. Classics of Anthropology. Tucson: University of Arizona Press, 1986.

Malina, Bruce J. *The New Testament World: Insights from Cultural Anthropology*. Atlanta: John Knox, 1981.

———. "'Religion' in the World of Paul." *Biblical Theology Bulletin* 16/3 (1986) 92–101.
Man, Edward H. *Aboriginal Inhabitants of the Andaman Islands*. Delhi: Sanskaran Prakashak, 1975.
Martin, Luther H. "Artemidorus: Dream Theory in Late Antiquity." *Second Century* 8 (1991) 97–108.
———. *Hellenistic Religions: An Introduction*. New York: Oxford University Press, 1987.
———. "Religion and Dream Theory in Late Antiquity." In *The Notion of "Religion" in Comparative Research*, edited by Ugo Bianchi, 369–74. Storia delle religioni 8. Rome: L' "Erma" di Bretschneider, 1994 (chapter 7, this volume).
Mitchell, William E. *Mishpokhe: A Study of New York City Jewish Family Clubs*. New Babylon, Studies in the Social Sciences 30. The Hague: Mouton, 1978.
Morgan, Lewis H. *Systems of Consanguinity and Affinity of the Human Family*. Washington DC: Smithsonian Institute, 1871.
Oden, Robert A. "Jacob as Father, Husband and Nephew: Kinship Studies and the Patriarchal Narratives." *Journal of Biblical Literature* 102/2 (1983) 189–205.
Parrott, Douglas M., ed. *Nag Hammadi Codices V, 2–5 and VI, with Papyrus Berolinensis 8502, 1 and 4*. The Coptic Gnostic Library. NHS 11. Leiden: Brill, 1979.
Pearson, Birger A. "The Figure of Seth in the Gnostic Literature." In *The Rediscovery of Gnosticism*, edited by Bentley Layton, 2:472–504. 2 vols. SHR 41. Leiden: Brill, 1981.
Peel, Malcolm L. "The Treatise on the Resurrection (I,4)." In *The Nag Hammadi Library*, edited by James M. Robinson, 52–57. 3rd rev. ed. San Francisco: Harper & Row, 1988.
Quispel, Gilles. "C. G. Jung und die Gnosis." *Eranos-Jahrbuch* 37 (1968) 277–98.
Rivers, William H. R. *Social Organization*. New York: Knopf, 1924.
Rothkrug, Lionel. "German Holiness and Western Sanctity in Medieval and Modern History." *Historical Reflections/Réflexions Historiques* 15/1 (1988) 161–249.
Rudolph, Kurt. *Gnosis: The Nature and History of Gnosticism*. Translated and edited by Robert McLachlan Wilson. 2nd ed. San Francisco: Harper & Row, 1983.
Sagan, Eli. *At the Dawn of Tyranny: The Origins of Individualism, Political Oppression, and the State*. New York: Knopf, 1985.
Schottroff, Luise. "*Animae naturaliter salvandae*." In *Christentum und Gnosis: Zum Problem der himmlischen Herkunft des Gnostikers*, edited by Walter Eltester, 65–97. Beihefte zur Zeitschrift für die neutestamentliche Wissenschaft und die Kunde der älteren Kirche 37. Berlin: Töperlmann, 1969.
Schutz, Fritz. *Classical Roman Law*. Oxford: Clarendon, 1951.
Stroumsa, Gedaliahu A. G. *Another Seed: Studies in Gnostic Mythology*. NHS 24. Leiden: Brill, 1984.
Turner, John D. "Sethian Gnosticism: A Literary History." In *Nag Hammadi, Gnosticism, and Early Christianity*, edited by Charles W. Hendrick and Robert Hodgson Jr., 55–89. 1986. Reprint, Eugene, OR: Wipf & Stock, 2005.
Veyne, Paul. "The Roman Empire." Translated by Arthur Goldhammer. In *A History of Private Life*. Vol. 1, *From Pagan Rome to Byzantium*, edited by Paul Veyne, 5–233. Cambridge: Harvard University Press, 1987.
White, Harrison C. *An Anatomy of Kinship: Mathematical Models for Structures of Cumulated Roles*. Prentice-Hall Series in Mathematical Analysis of Social Behavior. Englewood Cliffs, NJ: Prentice-Hall, 1963.
Wisse, Frederick. "Stalking Those Elusive Sethians." In *The Rediscovery of Gnosticism*, edited by Bentley Layton, 2:563–78. 2 vols. SHR 41. Leiden: Brill, 1981.

23

Technologies of the Self and Self-Knowledge in the Syrian Tradition

> In studying both the most admired and the most detested figures in any society, we can see, as seldom through other evidence, the nature of the average man's expectations and hopes for himself.
>
> PETER BROWN[1]

THE UNDERSTANDING OF A Hellenistic period of history, since its first delineation by Johann G. Droysen in the mid-nineteenth century as the result of Alexander's challenge to Persian hegemony, has resulted in a tendency to understand Hellenistic culture as a syncretistic homology. Although common systemic structures are indeed identifiable as defining a Hellenistic culture,[2] we must take care not to lose sight of such cultural differences as exist, for example, between views of self-identity, within this system.

The emergence of individualism in the Hellenistic world did not signal the promise of potential that characterized Renaissance humanism but presented rather a problematic to be solved in response to those transformations that characterized the Hellenistic period. A locative image of the cosmos had been replaced by the exploded topography of what came to be termed the Ptolemaic system. The ascent of Alexander's Graeco-Macedonian empire had challenged the traditional social conventions of political identity with its imposed but often unrealized cosmopolitan ideals. The collective piety of political allegiance or that of antiestablishment Dionysian ὄργια (*orgia*) as portrayed in Euripides's *Bacchae* gave way to the labyrinthian wanderings

---

1. Brown, "Rise and Function," 106.
2. Martin, "Why Cecropian Minerva?"

of Apuleius's Lucius. And the classical speculations of Plato and Aristotle about a metaphysical and cosmological order of things were replaced by the ethical concerns of Hellenistic philosophy. These Hellenistic transformations all generated the question asked of Jesus by the anonymous everyman: "What must I do?" (Mark 10:17).

Stoic and Gnostic ethics represented alternative responses to the new exigencies of existence represented by the Hellenistic world. Both accepted εἱμαρμένη, or a natural fate, as the normalizing principle of the cosmos, more than the power of any sovereign, whether emperor or god. And both knew the disastrous effects of the passions, of the sensuous world, for self-knowledge. Neither responded, however, in terms of fixed systems of thought; they represented, rather, antithetical strategics of existence within a contiguous cultural and historical context.

The Stoics applied traditional philosophical values to the new individualism and taught the taming of human passions by self-examination in order to effect a harmonious relation with the external order of things. True freedom was the moral freedom of a philosophical self-knowledge that recognized and conformed to an assumed orderly principle of the cosmos.

Gnostics, on the other hand, represented a Hellenistic strategy of individual existence par excellence. They were rarely, if ever, organized into autonomous institutional forms but articulated their perspective through existing religious and philosophical alternatives.[3] They repudiated this world, along with its ruling powers, altogether. This anticosmic rebellion was based upon their absolute certainty of a knowledge that they believed was revealed from beyond the normalizing cosmic limits of what, hitherto, had been considered possible.[4]

To the new exigencies of existence represented by the Hellenistic world, Gnostic thought responded, "Know yourself, and you will possess," in the well-known words of the second-century Valentinian gnostic Theodotus: "knowledge of who we were, and what we have become, where we were or where we were placed, whither we hasten, from what we are redeemed, what birth is and what rebirth" (*Excerpta ex Theodoto* 78.2). Or, again, in the words of his contemporary, the gnostic Christian theologian Clement of

---

3. Rudolph, *Gnosis*, 54–55.

4. The ascetic rejection of the ethical in its conventional sense suggests the basis for representing its Gnostic ethic as "licentious." Based upon accusations by Christian apologists, it has been argued, at least since the end of the nineteenth century, that the ascetic renunciation of the sensuous nature of the self had a counterpart in a libertine indifference toward the sensuous (see Harnack, *Dogma*, 1:263), and even a "positive obligation" to violate this-worldly ethical standards (see Jonas, *Gnostic*, 273).

Alexandria: "It is then ... the greatest of all lessons to know one's self. For if one knows himself, he will know God" (*Paedagogus* 3.1).

The Delphic maxim concerning self-knowledge was widely cited in Greek and Hellenistic literature generally,[5] and in gnostic literature specifically.[6] Since the *Alcibiades I*, attributed to Plato, self-knowledge had been at the center of Western ethical thought. When the young Alcibiades wishes to begin his public life (123D), Socrates intervenes and, with reference to the Delphic inscription, seeks to lead Alcibiades to a knowledge of himself (124A–124B), for, by knowing oneself, the political leader knows the proper affairs of others and thereby the affairs of state (133D–134A).

To Alcibiades's query about how he might achieve this self-knowledge (124B) Socrates responds that he would come to know himself if he takes care of himself (ἐπιμελεῖσθαι σεαυτοῦ; 127E, 132C). Thus, for the Western tradition, self-knowledge was the function of certain obligations associated with taking care of the self.[7] An Eastern "gnostic" tradition, probably centered in Edessa, presents Thomas, contrary to the Western canonical tradition of a "doubting" Thomas (John 20:24–29), as the exemplum of individual self-knowledge.[8] This tradition can be traced from the *Gospel of Thomas* through a *Book of Thomas*, both from the second codex of the Nag Hammadi library, to the *Acts of Thomas*.[9] The association of taking care of oneself with the Delphic maxim and Self-knowledge concerning self-knowledge, which was characteristic of Graeco-Roman ethical literature since Plato, is characteristic of this Eastern Thomas tradition as well, but as an interdiction rather than as an obligation.

The Syrian *Acts of Thomas*, dated in the early third century CE,[10] belongs to an Eastern collection of apocryphal *Acts of the Apostles* attributed, since the fifth century, to Leucius Charinus, a supposed companion of the apostle John.[11] The *Acts of Thomas* is generally considered to belong to a genre of Hellenistic-Oriental romances, a somewhat loosely defined genre of literature characterized primarily by the adventurous travels of a hero

---

5. Wilkins "*Know Thyself,*" 100–104.

6. Rudolph, *Gnosis*, 113; Betz, "Delphic Maxim."

7. Foucault, *History of Sexuality*, 3:37–68; Foucault, "Technologies"; Wilkins, "*Know Thyself,*" 60–61.

8. On the identity of the Eastern with the Western Thomas, see Koester, "GNOMAI," 127–28, 133–34. On the origins of Christianity in Syria, see Klijn, *Acts of Thomas*, 30–33; Voobus, *Asceticism*; Drijvers, "Facts and Problems."

9. Robinson and Koester, *Trajectories*, 126–43; see also Turner, *Book of Thomas*, 233–39; and Drijvers, "Facts and Problems."

10. For the translation of the Syriac text, see Bornkamm, *Acts of Thomas*, 2:442–531.

11. Bornkamm, *Acts of Thomas*, 2:427; Schäferdiek, *Acts of John*, 2:178–88.

to exotic foreign places and by his erotic encounters.[12] This "romance" of Thomas elaborates earlier themes of the Thomas tradition in terms of the apostle's supposed missionary activities in India.

The *Acts of Thomas* begins with the disciples of Jesus conducting a lottery to determine which region of the world each would evangelize. Thomas draws India but, as an Israelite, is reluctant to travel to so foreign a region. Jesus forces the issue by selling him as a slave to the Indian merchant Abban, who soon sets sail with Thomas in tow. They arrive first in Andrapolis during a citywide festival celebrating the marriage of the local king's only daughter.

During the celebrations, a cupbearer unexpectedly slaps Thomas, presumably because of the attention shown him by one of the entertainers, an Israelite flute girl. Responding to this unwarranted attack, Thomas promises that "my God will forgive this injury in the world to come, but in this world he will show forth his wonders, and I shall even now see that hand that smote me dragged by dogs" (*Acts of Thomas* 6)—a somewhat uncharitable response by canonical standards. And indeed, according to the Acts, when the cupbearer goes out to the well for water, he is slain and dismembered by a lion, and a black dog picks up the right hand, which had struck Thomas, and carries it back to the party.

Having now attracted the attention not only of the flute girl but of the entire gathering, Thomas is conscripted by the anxious king to pray for the marriage of his daughter. After praying that Jesus might do "the things that help and are useful and profitable" for these newlyweds, Thomas blesses the couple and departs.

When everyone finally leaves, the bridegroom anxiously approaches his bride but is amazed to find Jesus, in the likeness of his twin, Thomas, chatting with his new wife in the bedroom. As the three of them sit down together to discuss the situation, Jesus counsels the newlyweds to abandon the 'filthy intercourse' they obviously had been anticipating and

> become holy temples, pure and free from afflictions and pains both manifest and hidden, and you will not be girt about with care for life [φροντίδας βίου] and children, the end of which is destruction . . . But if you obey and keep your souls pure unto God, you shall have living children . . . and shall be without care [ἀμέριμνοι]. (*Acts of Thomas* 12)

Unexpectedly for the modern reader, and likely for Thomas's non-Christian contemporary as well, the bridegroom thanks Jesus for this unsolicited but

---

12. Lesky, *History of Greek Literature*, 857–79; Perry, *Ancient Romances*; Walsh, *Roman Novel*.

timely advice and for revealing his corrupt and morally sick condition by directing him to seek himself and to know (γνῶναι) who he was and who and how he now is (15).

The *Acts of Thomas* presents a self-knowledge constituted by secret teachings (γνῶσις), which Thomas has received from Jesus (39), and which are now recorded in this account of his missionary activities. Contrary to the Western ethical tradition, this self-knowledge results in a freedom from care (ἄφροντις, ἀμέριμνος; 12; 35). This antithetical relationship between self-knowledge and taking care of oneself is soteriological. In her rejection of "filthy intercourse" (cf. 43), the bride did not become yoked to a "short-lived" husband but was wedded to the "true man" (14); the bridegroom came to know his true self (15; see also 43 and 144); and even the flute girl found soteriological rest (ἀνάπαυσις) as a result of these events.[13] Similarly, in the third act of Thomas, a young man who had been killed by a giant serpent but resuscitated through Thomas's intercession concludes that "I have become free from care [φροντίδος] . . . from the care [φροντίδος] of night, and I am at rest [ἀναπαύειν] from the toil of day" (34).

In the Socratic obligation to take care of oneself, two points of view intersect, the political and the erotic. When the young Alcibiades wishes to enter political life, he submits to Socrates, the first of his lovers (*Alcibiades* 1.103A; 104E). According to Socrates, to know oneself one must know one's body, one's sexuality, and how to participate in the sociopolitical world. This positive relationship between techniques of self and that which is not self—teachers, the city (or the sociopolitical realm), and the cosmos—is a persistent theme of Western philosophizing.

Similarly, in the *Acts of Thomas*, a political context is established when Thomas attends the wedding celebration of the princess at the court of the king and then participates in this royal celebration by blessing the union. However, this participation in public life is required of Thomas against his will, whereas Alcibiades aspired to political life. An erotic context is also established in the *Acts of Thomas* when the groom approaches his new bride for the first time. However, the new wife submits not physically to her husband but spiritually to the "true man," Jesus.

Jesus shows the bride and groom, even as Socrates taught Alcibiades, that self-knowledge is not of the body but of the soul (*Alcibiades* 1.130E, 132B–C). However—and here the two traditions diverge—in the Platonic and later Stoic traditions, self-knowledge requires practices of taking care of oneself characterized by a network of obligations and services, whereas

---

13. See Bornkamm, *Acts of Thomas*, where "carefreeness" [ἄφροντις] is equated with "rest."

in the Eastern Thomas tradition, self-knowledge results in a carefreeness characterized by a network of interdictions.

The Coptic *Book of Thomas*, from the same Nag Hammadi codex as the *Gospel of Thomas*, is dated earlier in the second century CE than the *Acts of Thomas*.[14] It introduces the same interdiction as does the *Acts*, but in the context of a revelatory dialogue. This form is revealed as pseudodialogical, however, when Thomas tells Jesus that "It is you Lord whom it benefits to speak, and me to listen" (*Book of Thomas* 142.9). Although Jesus points out that the secret teachings are already known to and have been pondered by Thomas, he invites Thomas to examine himself in order to know who he is in light of this revelation. Jesus does not consider it seemly that his twin brother should be ignorant of himself (138.10–12): "For he who has not known himself has known nothing, but he who has known himself has at the same time already achieved knowledge about the Depth of the All" (138.16–18).

The relation between self-knowledge and rejection of the world is clearly summarized by Jesus in a concluding section of the *Book of Thomas*.[15] Those who have not received the revealed doctrine are ignorant and, thus, are renounced. Their soul has been corrupted by the body and by the world. The blessed, on the other hand, are those who, like Thomas, have prior knowledge of these things.

The general rejection of the world by the *Book of Thomas* (143.13–14) does not explicitly refer to political involvement as does the *Acts of Thomas*, but it is explicit concerning rejection of the body. The body is transitory (139.4); it decays and perishes (139.5). This cycle of fleshly life derives finally from "intimacy with women and polluted intercourse" (144.9f.; cf. 139.8–10), the fire of lust "that scorches the spirits of men" (140.3–4), "the bitterness of the bondage of lust for those visible things that will decay and change" (140.33).

The rejection of world by Jesus is summarized in the *Book of Thomas* by the interdiction against *prooush* βίος (*bios*) (141.12–14, 38–39). The Coptic word *rooush* translates not only φροντίς and μέριμνα, the words for "care" used in the Greek version of the *Acts of Thomas*, but also ἐπιμέλεια, the technical term for "care" in the Western ethical tradition.[16] This interdiction against any concern or care for this life seems to include the practice of care itself. When Thomas shows care (μέριμνα) for those deprived of the

14. Turner, *Book of Thomas*, 188–94.

15. This section may originally have been a separate work. See Turner, *Book of Thomas*, 164–99; 215–25.

16. Crum, *Coptic Dictionary*, 307b.

kingdom (142.3–5), he is persuaded by the Savior not to care for them, for their deprivation is the lot of the ignorant (142.11–19).

The obligation to know oneself is central also to the teachings of the *Gospel of Thomas*. One of the first things Jesus tells his disciples in this gospel is that "when you come to know yourselves, then you will become known, and you will realize that it is you who are the sons of the living Father. But if you will not know yourselves, you dwell in poverty and it is you who are that poverty" (*Gospel of Thomas* 3). Consequently, they are repeatedly exhorted to seek this knowledge until it is found (2; 92; 94). This is a difficult task, however, for the knowledge that is to be sought has already come, and the disciples have not recognized it (51). As Jesus says in another passage, "That which you have will save you if you bring it forth from yourselves" (70).

Dated from the second half of the first century CE to the first half of the second century CE,[17] the opening lines of the *Gospel of Thomas* differ significantly from the *Book of Thomas* only in that Thomas himself is represented as recording "the secret sayings which the living [or resurrected] Jesus spoke" (*Gospel of Thomas*, incip.), rather than the secretary Mathias (*Book of Thomas* 138.1–3). Thomas, however, is not simply the secretary for Jesus and the other disciples in the gospel, for Jesus takes him aside and reveals to him knowledge not shared with the other disciples (*Gospel of Thomas* 13). In other words, the knowledge that saves and is revealed by Jesus only to Thomas (13) is an inner knowledge (108), which Thomas has written down (*incip.*) for whoever has ears to hear (8; 21; 63; 65; 96) or, for his readers, eyes to see.

For the *Gospel of Thomas*, self-knowledge seems to result in a negative stance toward the external world: "Whoever finds himself is superior to the world" (111). However, this priority of knowledge to action is not so clear as it comes to be in the *Book of Thomas*. Other sayings of Jesus in the *Gospel of Thomas* seem to suggest that self-knowledge is the result of certain practices of world rejection: "Be on your guard against the world," Jesus warns (21), for "If you do not fast as regards the world, you will not find the Kingdom" (27). In either case, the self-knowledge is clearly understood by the *Gospel of Thomas* to be inner, apart from, and other than the external world: "Whoever has come to understand the world has found [only] a corpse" (56).

Although a specific interdiction against care does not appear in the *Gospel of Thomas*, the earliest of the Thomas texts, its sense is clearly present. Like the *Acts of Thomas*, the Gospel rejects not only the external "world" generally but also the sexual and political activities of this world specifically. "Blessed is the womb which has not conceived and the breasts which have

---

17. But see Drijvers, "Facts and Problems," 173.

not given milk," Jesus tells an adoring woman (*Gospel of Thomas* 79), for only those who "make the male and the female one and the same, so that the male not be male nor the female female," will enter the Kingdom (22). And again Jesus commands his disciples: "Give Caesar what belongs to Caesar, give God what belongs to God, and give Me what is Mine" (100; see also 81, 100). Self-knowledge for the *Gospel of Thomas*, therefore, is other than the social relationships required by sexual and political activity. "Many are standing at the door," Jesus says, "but it is the solitary who will enter the bridal chamber" (75).[18]

The rejection of sociopolitical obligations in the Eastern Thomas tradition stands in marked contrast to their necessary inclusion within practices of self-identity in the Western tradition. In the Platonic and later Stoic traditions, self-knowledge is the result of a "caring for the self," characterized by a network of external obligations and practices, whereas in the Thomas tradition self-knowledge is a revealed or prior knowledge, resulting in a carefreeness characterized by inner discipline within a network of interdictions. This revealed "prior" knowledge is the subject of the "gnostic" Thomas literature.

The Thomas tradition consists of the secret teachings of Jesus "received" by "listening" to the revelations of Jesus (*Gospel of Thomas*, incip.; *Book of Thomas* 138.1–4; 142.9–10; *Acts of Thomas* 39),[19] which, according to the *Gospel of Thomas*, Thomas wrote down, whereas according to the *Book of Thomas* they were written down by a secretary. Whatever the historical origin of these pseudodialogues, they claim to reveal a prior γνῶσις in writing. They do not recommend dialogic activity, for which the questioning Thomas of the Western canon might have served as model, but instead record a particular content to be read and known. This self-emphasis by the Thomas tradition on the writing of revelation suggests a solitary, inner technique of reading the self.

The practice of reading as a technique for knowing self is described in the *Acts of Thomas* itself, in the "Hymn of the Pearl," which was sung by Thomas while in prison to encourage his fellow inmates (*Acts of Thomas* 108–13). In this famous hymn, a king's son, the first-person author of the song, is sent forth to seek a precious pearl, an allegorical designation for his true self,[20] which is guarded by a ferocious serpent in Egypt. But the son soon forgets his task, and himself, as he takes up a foreign way of life.

18. See also ibid., 49; for "solitary," the Coptic text uses the Greek word μοναχός, "monk."

19. In the *Acts of Thomas*, the Greek word used for "receive" (δέχομαι) also means "to listen."

20. Reitzenstein, *Mystery-Religions*, 58; Jonas, *Gnostic*, 125–26.

The royal parents write their lost son a letter, identical to what is already "written" in his heart, recalling him to its contents so that he might know who he really is. When the son reads this letter, he is awakened to his true self and is able successfully to complete his quest for the pearl and return home. In this hymn, the son's knowledge of himself is arrived at by reading a text. This text reveals a prior knowledge of his true self, already written within, but forgotten. In other words, this Eastern tradition represents a practice of reading the self in which the reader is disclosed to himself.

This technique of "reading of the self" recalls the thesis advanced by Richard Reitzenstein early in this century of a genre of *Lese-Mysteria*, or literary mysteries.[21] This genre, he argued, preserved the outward form of a Hellenistic mystery religion through a series of discursive and doctrinal writings. If the reader of such a literary mystery were one who had turned away from the world, the literary presentation would affect him just as if he had actually participated in a mystery ritual.[22] A.-J. Festugière has described the enigmatic Orphic literature as such a literary mystery,[23] following the lead of Pausanias, who equated a reading of Orphic writings with the witnessing of initiation at the Eleusinian Mysteries (1.37.4).

Reinhold Merkelbach also has argued that the Hellenistic romances were written in the service of the Hellenistic mystery cults;[24] though his view has been challenged,[25] it is generally agreed to hold true for two late romances, Apuleius's *Golden Ass* and the *Acts of Thomas*.[26] Apuleius's romance is clearly propaganda for the Hellenistic cult of Isis, whereas the *Acts of Thomas* presents a Christian-gnostic mystery of redemption.[27] Therefore, their point is not to recommend dialogic—or social—activity but, like the *Gospel* and the *Book of Thomas*, to present a particular content through the written word. The reading of such texts constituted a hermeneutics of the self.

In conclusion, two differently situated technologies of the Hellenistic self may be identified. The first, characteristic of the Western ethical tradition, might be termed an epistemological technology of self. This tradition emphasizes the activity of self-disclosure always in terms of an other. By disclosing oneself in dialogue, self was constituted. The second, exemplified by

21. Reitzenstein, *Hellenistic Mystery Religions*, 51–52; 62.
22. Ibid., 51–52.
23. Festugière, *L'Ideal Religieux*; Festugière, "Dionysos."
24. Merkelbach, *Mysterium*, 27.
25. E.g., Perry, *Ancient Romances*.
26. Koester, *Introduction*, 1:139.
27. Bornkamm, *Acts of Thomas*, 2:429.

the Eastern Thomas tradition, might be termed an ontological technology of self. This tradition emphasizes the discernment or deciphering of what the self already is. This knowledge is reclaimed by passive listening and, later, through the solitary activity of reading. The first, dialogic activity, is social. The second, contemplative activity was more conducive to the Syrian Encratitic technology of self generally considered to have been introduced to Western Christianity by John Cassian only at the end of the Hellenistic period in the early fourth century.[28]

References

Betz, Hans Dieter. "The Delphic Maxim ΓΝΩΘΙ ΣΑΥΤΟΝ in Hermetic Interpretation." *Harvard Theological Review* 63 (1970) 465–84.
Bornkamm, Gunther. *The Acts of Thomas*. In *New Testament Apocrypha*, edited by Wilhelm Schneemelcher, 2:442–531. Translated by Robert McLachlan Wilson. 2 vols. Philadelphia: Westminster, 1965.
Brown, Peter. "The Rise and Function of the Holy Man in Late Antiquity." In *Society and the Holy in Late Antiquity*, 103–52. Berkeley: University of California Press, 1982.
Casey, Robert P. *The Excerpta ex Theodoto of Clement of Alexandria*. Studies and Documents 1. London: Christophers, 1934.
Chadwick, Owen. *John Cassian: A Study in Primitive Monasticism*. 2nd ed. Cambridge: Cambridge University Press, 1968.
Cross, Frank L., ed. *Oxford Dictionary of the Christian Church*. London: Oxford University Press, 1958.
Crum, W. E. *A Coptic Dictionary*. 1939. Reprint, Ancient Language Resources. Eugene, OR: Wipf & Stock, 2005.
Drijvers, H. J. W. "Facts and Problems in Early Syriac-Speaking Christianity." *Second Century* 2 (1982) 157–75.
Festugière, A. J. *L'Ideal Religieux des Grecs et L'Evangile*. Etudes bibliques. Paris: Lecoffre, 1932.
———. "Les mystères de Dionysos." *Revue Biblique* 44 (1935) 192–211 and 366–96.
Foucault, Michel. *The History of Sexuality*. Vol. 3, *The Care of the Self*. Translated by Robert Hurley. New York: Pantheon, 1986.
———. "Technologies of the Self." In *Technologies of the Self: A Seminar with Michel Foucault*, edited by Luther H. Martin et al., 16–49. Amherst: University of Massachusetts Press, 1988.
Harnack, Adolf von. *History of Dogma*. Translated and edited by Neil Buchanan. 7 vols. Theological Translation Library. New York: Russell & Russell, 1958.
Hennecke, Edgar, and Wilhelm Schneemelcher, eds. *New Testament Apocrypha*. Translated by Robert McLachlan Wilson. 2 vols. Philadelphia: Westminster, 1963–1966.
Jonas, Hans. *The Gnostic Religion*. 2nd rev. ed. Boston: Beacon, 1963.
Klijn, Albertus F. J. *The Acts of Thomas*. Supplements to Novum Testamentum 5. Leiden: Brill, 1962.

---

28. Cross, *Oxford Dictionary*, 243; on Cassian, see Chadwick, *John Cassian*.

Koester, Helmut. "GNOMAI DIAPHOROI: The Origin and Nature of Diversification in the History of Early Christianity." In *Trajectories through Early Christianity*, by James M. Robinson and Helmut Koester, 114–57. 1971. Reprint, Eugene, OR: Wipf & Stock, 2006.

———. *Introduction to the New Testament*. Vol. 1, *History, Culture, and Religion of the Hellenistic Age*. Foundations and Facets: New Testament. Philadelphia: Fortress, 1982.

Lesky, Albin. *A History of Greek Literature*. Translated by James Willis and Cornelis de Heer. New York: Crowell, 1966.

Martin, Luther H. "Why Cecropian Minerva? Hellenistic Religions Syncretism as System." *Numen* 30 (1983) 131–45 (chapter 4, this volume).

Merkelbach, Reinhold. *Roman und Mysterium in der Antike*. Munich: Beck, 1972.

Perry, Ben E. *The Ancient Romances: A Literary-Historical Account of Their Origins*. Sather Classical Lectures 37. Berkeley: University of California Press, 1967.

Reitzenstein, Richard. *Hellenistic Mystery-Religions: Their Basic Ideas and Significance*. Translated by John E. Steely. Pittsburgh Theological Monograph Series 15. Pittsburgh: Pickwick Publications, 1978.

Robinson, James M., and Helmut Koester. *Introduction to the New Testament*. Vol. 1, *History, Culture, and Religion of the Hellenistic Age*. Foundations and Facets. New Testament. Philadelphia: Fortress, 1982.

———. *Trajectories through Early Christianity*. 1971. Reprint, Eugene, OR: Wipf & Stock, 2006.

Rudolph, Kurt. *Gnosis: The Nature and History of Gnosticism*. Translated and edited by Robert McLachlan Wilson. 2nd ed. San Francisco: Harper & Row, 1983.

Schäferdiek, Knut. *The Acts of John*. In *New Testament Apocrypha*, edited by Edgar Hennecke and Wilhelm Schneemelcher, 2:152–209. Translated by Robert McWilson. 2 vols. Philadelphia: Westminster, 1965.

Turner, John D. *The Book of Thomas the Contender*. Society of Biblical Literature Dissertation Series 23. Missoula: Scholars, 1975.

———. "The Book of Thomas the Contender." In *The Nag Hammadi Library in English*, edited by James M. Robinson, 199–207. 3rd rev. ed. San Francisco: Harper & Row, 1988.

Voobus, Arthur. *History of Asceticism in the Syrian Orient*. Corpus scriptorum Christianorum Orientalium 184, 197. Subsidia 14, 17, 81. 2 vols. Louvain: CSCO, 1958–1960.

Walsh, Peter G. *The Roman Novel: The "Satyricon" of Petronius and the "Metamorphoses" of Apuleius*. Cambridge: Cambridge University Press, 1970.

Wilkins, Eliza G. *Know Thy*. Chicago: Ares, 1980.

24

Self and Power in the Thought of Plotinus

> It is perhaps correct to say that the soul acts unthinkingly according to destiny . . . ; but the best actions come from ourselves; for this is the nature we are of, when we are alone; good and wise men do act, and do noble actions by their own will.
>
> PLOTINUS (*ENNEADS* 3.1.10)

PLOTINUS, THIS "MOST METAPHYSICAL of all philosophers," has also presented, in the judgement of John Rist, "perhaps the most powerful affirmation of one way of thinking about man, his nature and his place in the cosmos."[1] Although Porphyry (232/3—c. 305 CE) judged the writings on ethics by this third-century Neoplatonist to deal with the "less difficult questions" (Porphyry, *Vita Plotini* 24.15–18), he nevertheless gave them first place in his organization of Plotinus's *Enneads*. Modern commentators on Plotinus have focused, however, almost exclusively on the metaphysical aspects of his thought; they do so largely because of the subsequent influence of Plotinus's metaphysics on the history of theology.[2] The question that might be asked of metaphysics, however, as of its theological offspring, is that posed by Lévi-Strauss of myth: "What's it good for?" Lévi-Strauss later modified his initial answer that myths are "good to think" with, to suggest that they often "operate in men's minds without their being aware of the fact."[3] What is operating in Plotinus's mind beyond the relationships

---

1. Rist, *Plotinus*, 247.

2. Henry, "Introduction," xxxiv–xxxv; O'Meara, *Plotinus*, 113, 117.

3. Lévi-Strauss did not ask this question of myth explicitly. It is, rather, an extension of the question he asked of totems in *Totemism* (Lévi-Strauss, *Totemism*, 89); the modified answer is in *The Raw and the Cooked* (Lévi-Strauss, *Raw*, 12). The notion of

he imagined to exist between the manifest world and the unmanifest One, which provided the overt subject of all his writings? Although this aspect of Plotinian discourse has not been entirely neglected,[4] such expositions have remained thoroughly situated in the metaphysical context established by Plotinus himself.[5] The question that remains unasked is not that of Plotinus's metaphysics of the self, but of his view of the self's real "presence in the world."[6]

I

Plotinus's reflections on his own "presence in the world" seem to have been occasioned by some sort of disorienting experience of Unreason sustained, according to Porphyry, on four separate occasions during the time he was Plotinus's student (Porphyry, *Vita Plotini* 23). "Often," Plotinus observed in one of his earlier writings, "I have woken up out of the body [ἐξ τοῦ σώματος] ... [and] I am puzzled" (*Enneads* 4.8.1, no. 6 chronologically). He spoke of this experience directly only by claiming that "anyone who has seen it knows what I mean when I say that it is beautiful" (1.6.7; 6.9.9)— thereby presaging both Rudolf Otto's idiosyncratic approach to his definition of the *numinous*,[7] as well as that of U.S. Supreme Court Justice Potter Stewart concerning obscenity.[8] While such "out-of-body" experiences may have been unintelligible to Plotinus, they conformed to certain Hellenistic epistemic expectations with respect to "reality," or "the things that are" (περὶ τῶν ὄντων), well exemplified by the famous opening passage of the early second-century Hermetic text, *Poimandres* (*CH* 1.1):

> Once, when thought came to me of the things that are and my thinking soared high and my bodily senses were restrained, like someone heavy with sleep from too much eating or toil of the body ... [*Nous* called out] and in an instant everything was

---

"myth" as "thought" is essentially the thesis of *The Savage Mind*.

4. E.g., Blumenthal, *Psychology*; O'Daly, *Plotinus' Philosophy*.

5. Armstrong, trans., *Plotinus*. This point is exemplified by the title of Rist's article "Metaphysics and Psychology."

6. "Presence in the world" is Michel Foucault's apt translation of Heidegger's notion of *Dasein*; see Macey, *Lives*, 59.

7. Otto, *Idea of the Holy*, 8: "The reader is invited to direct his mind to a moment of deeply-felt religious experience ... Whoever cannot do this, whoever knows no such moments in his experience, is requested to read no farther; for it is no easy to discuss questions of religious psychology with one who ... cannot recall any intrinsically religious feelings."

8. Justice Potter Stewart concurring in *Jacobellis*, 197: "I know it when I see it."

immediately opened to me. I saw an endless vision in which everything became light—clear and joyful—and in seeing the vision I came to love it (*CH* 1.1–4).⁹

Plotinus interpreted his experience of "going out of the body," similarly, as coming to an identity with the divine Νοῦς—Intellect or Reason (*Enneads* 4.8.1)—an experience he termed "ecstatic" (6.9.11), the first such use of this word in a strictly "mystical" sense.¹⁰ However, because of the priority he assigned to "the self as an agent of rational activity" (1.1.7; 1.1.10),¹¹ Plotinus apparently feared that such externalizations of the self-constituted madness (6.9.7: ἑαυτοῦ ἔχω ἐν μανίᾳ; 6.8.2: ἐξεστήκοσιν = μαινομένοις), a state he later attributed to his gnostic opponents (2.9.8: ἔκφρων; see 2.9.18 for their στόματι μαινομένῳ).¹² For, as Lloyd Gerson has argued, the transitory nature of Plotinus's experiences "distinguish them from the experience of an individual self in communion with the Intellect."¹³ But, Plotinus concludes, it is unlikely that a "really good man" (σπουδαῖος), that is, one who has reasoning and true intelligence (1.4.4: λογισμὸς καὶ νοῦς ἀληθινός), will become mad (= ληρεῖν) (1.9.1). Since his own journey to the edge of madness had effectively threatened any reflexive locus of self-identity, he argued that all external things (πάντων τῶν ἔχω) must be abandoned, and one must turn entirely to what is internal (πρὸς τὸ εἴσω πάντες) (6.9.7; see 6.8.18), that is, to reason (Νοῦς) (1.1.9; 5.9.5), for any thought that is of the outside (τοῦ ἔχω) is deficient (5.3.13). Rather than any "mystical" conventional about fleeing the body, Plotinus's noetic internalization of the self anchors the self in an "embodied self-awareness" (see 5.5.7; 5.8.11; 6.8.18; 6.9.7).¹⁴

Upon returning to his body, to the level of "discursive reasoning" (λογισμός) with its heightened awareness of external things (5.3.1), Plotinus attempted to make intelligible sense of his experience (4.8.1).¹⁵ Employing

---

9. Copenhaver, *Hermetica*, 93–97.

10. Dodds, *Pagan and Christian*, 72.

11. Gerson, *Plotinus*, 147.

12. Plotinus does not identify the particular gnostic tradition(s) he opposes; for an examination of the views they held, or were believed by Plotinus to hold, see Puech, *Plotin*, 161–90, and Runia, *Plotinus*. I refer, in the following characterization, to those broad themes of religiophilosophy of late antiquity conventionally referred to as gnostic. This generalizing approach to the complex phenomenon of Gnosticism was, in the judgment of Porphyry, also that of Plotinus (*Vita Plotini* 16).

13. Gerson, *Plotinus*, 219.

14. Kristeva, *Tales*, 109; Gerson, *Plotinus*, 210.

15. For the reasons stated above, Gerson, *Plotinus*, 220, discounts any positive significance of Plotinus's experiences for his philosophy.

the third-century understanding of Platonic philosophy (4.8.2),[16] which undoubtedly gave shape to his experience as to that of the Hermetist in the first place,[17] he articulated the embodiment of the self as a metaphysical devolution. This image of the soul's descent into the particularity of matter and the singularity of the body represents for Plotinus, as for hermetic and gnostic myth generally, a fall—in comparison with the One and the Good "experienced" by Plotinus, this fall represents a corruption of reason and a corrosion of the soul.[18]

However, the image of the soul's descent, for Plotinus, also complies with the law of the universe and the plan of Universal Soul (4.8.5).[19] Error is the granting of reality to the accretions necessarily acquired by the soul on its downward journey (1.6.8).[20] Plotinus articulates the soul's return to itself, as in the *Poimandres*, as a distancing of oneself from such externalia (*CH* 1.24–26; *Enneads* 5.3.17; cf. 1.1.13), which establishes the conditions for examining one's "own intimacy."[21] In the words of Plotinus, one must

> strip off what we put on in our descent; (just as for those who go up to the celebrations of sacred rites there are purifications, and stripping off of the clothes they wore before, and going up naked) until, passing in the ascent all that is alien to the God, one sees with one's self alone. (*Enneads* 1.6.7; see also 5.3.17).[22]

E. R. Dodds notes that this same image is employed also by Philo (*Legum allegoriae* 2.56) and by a Valentinian writer cited by Clement of Alexandria as an image of "mystical return" (Clement, *Excerpta ex Theodoto* 27).[23] This

---

16. "Perhaps it is a characteristic of certain great philosophers of originality and power to associate themselves closely with a great predecessor whose work they can recapture without merely reproducing it and can transcend while never abandoning it" (Henry, "Introduction," xxxiv–xxxv).

17. Wayne Proudfoot (*Religious Experience*) has argued, with respect to religion, against any "core" experience that might be prior to and supportive of thought. Rather, all so-called experience emerges from prior cultural interpretations of what is held to be important or significant. From this "pretense to antiquity" (Jonas, *Gnostic*, 25), Plotinus nevertheless makes bold to attack the gnostics for their alleged lack of respect for truths sanctified by the ancients (*Enneads* 2.9.6)—even as Celsus had attacked the Christians for their lack of ancestry (*Contra Celsum* 5.25). See Dillon, "Self-Definition," 70.

18. Kristeva, *Tales*, 105.

19. Armstrong, trans., *Plotinus*, xxiii.

20. Merlan, "Plotinus," 354A; Kristeva, *Tales*, 106.

21. Merlan, "Plotinus," 358A; Kristeva, *Tales*, 106.

22. See similar language in O'Neill, trans., *Alcibiadem* 138.16–18 and the discussion by Rist, *Plotinus*, chapter 14.

23. Dodds, *Pagans and Christians*, 94–96.

"way of return" was, according to Porphry, "Plotinus's main object in living, writing, and teaching" (*Vita Plotini* 2.26–27).[24]

The beginning of the soul's return is, in the view of Plotinus, its recognition of the higher reality with which it is kin (*Enneads* 1.6.2). Consequently, according to the report of Porphryry, Plotinus not only felt shame about being in his body, but "could . . . never bear to talk about his race [γένους] or his parents [γονέων] or his native country [πατρίδος]" (*Vita Plotini* 1.1–5; cf. *Enneads* 6.6.8). Rather, Plotinus characterized the "returned" soul in terms of its "natural kinship with the One."[25] Although he repudiates gnostic claims to be "children of God" (παῖδες θεοῦ) (*Enneads* 2.9.9), and complains about their willingness to call even the lowest of men brothers (2.9.18), Plotinus nevertheless argues that "every soul is a child of That Father" (2.9.16, 9–10). In even the youngest son, one can see the greatness of the father and of the brothers who have remained with the father (5.8.12). Further, he talks about souls as children (παῖδες) who are torn from "their father, God" and "brought up far away," not knowing "who they themselves or their parents are" (5.1.1). And the "World-Soul," by whom "we are begotten [γεννήματα] inside the universe" is, he writes, our "elder sister" (4.3.7).[26] It is this metaphysical genealogy of descent that finally provides Plotinus the therapeutic rationalization for his ecstatic episodes. "A child . . . who is outside himself in madness," he writes, "will not know his father; but he who has learnt to know himself will know from whence he comes" (6.9.7). In occupying ourselves with our soul, consequently, "we should be obeying the command of the god who urged us to know ourselves" (4.3.1; see 5.3.1; 6.8.5).

II

Because of its central theme, γνῶθι σαυτόν, the Neoplatonists were fond of characterizing (Ps-)Plato's *1 Alcibiades* as the ἀρχή (beginning) of all philosophy (Proclus, *in Alcibiadem* 11).[27] It has long been recognized that this

24. Armstrong, trans., *Plotinus*, xv, xxv.

25. Rist, *Plotinus*, 230; Jonas, *Gnostic*, 263; See *Enneads* 2.3.9; 2.9.18; 3.3.1; 3.5.1; 4.4.45; 5.1.1 and Sleeman and Pollet, *Lexicon Plotinianum*, s.v. γένος, συγγενεία.

26. Armstrong, trans., *Plotinus*.

27. See Westerink, *Diadochus*, and O'Neill, trans., *Alcibiades* was following the lead of Iamblichus (*in Alcibiadem* 11); see also Westerink, *Anonymous*, 219.24–29: "We relate what the divine Iamblichus did. Now he divided all [of Plato's dialogues] . . . Ten [of the] dialogues are then given in the following order: first the *Alcibiades* (because therein we learn the knowledge of ourselves)"; also Westerink, ed., *Commentary on the First Alcibiades*. The *Alcibiades* was also used as the introduction to philosophy in

Delphic command to "know yourself" was understood in the Hellenistic period in primarily an ethical sense,[28] but it was Michel Foucault who emphasized that this injunction to self-knowledge was associated in the *Alcibiades* with the practical imperative to "take care of yourself" (ἐπιμελεῖσθαι σαυτόν), an imperative that requires also the care of others (see, e.g., Luke 10:30–37). In addition to the Platonist tradition, these mutual obligations were central to Epictetus and his followers, to the Cynics, and to the Stoics.[29]

For Plotinus, however, ἐπιμελεῖσθαι does not have the practical sense of "taking care of oneself" and of "others" that it has in the *Alcibiades* but designates, rather, the obverse: the care of the universal soul for all that is souless (*Enneads* 2.9.18; 3.3.1; 3.4.2; 4.3.1; 4.3.7; cf. 3.2.7; 4.8.8, primarily with reference to Plato, *Phaedus* 246B) (An exception is the metaphorical usage in *Enneads* 3.2.8). Plotinus's inversion of this central Hellenistic ethical injunction approaches the gnostic prohibition against such social "care" most familiar from the Syrian Thomas tradition[30]—his interdiction of marriage, for example, as an enticement that gives pleasure to carnal desires (ἐπιθυμία) or of care for children (τέκνων ἐπιμέλειαι) (4.4.44). Though Plotinus can speak of the "desire" of the soul/body mixture (1.1.1), or even of the soul, ἐπιθυμία is primarily a carnal characteristic (2.9.5; 3.2.4; 4.4.20–21), mastery by which is Plotinus's definition of evil (1.1.9). The ethical imperative, for Plotinus, consequently, is to purify the embodied soul from its base concerns (1.1.12). "We can exist," he concludes, "without loving the body, and be pure" (2.9.18).[31]

III

The self's way to itself and to God had led, from Plato to Plotinus, to the moralistic self-perfection by which a social elite characterized itself. Those held to be most "pure" were to be the rulers. Whereas most of these visionaries, in the opinion of Plotinus, were likely to consider civic life unworthy and remain above it all (ἄνω), some might elect to exercise their divine right (τοῦ θεοῦ ἐπαφή) to rule (*Enneads* 6.9.7). For, "things here below depend on the world above, the things in this world on divine beings" (4.4.39). "The rational formative principle of the All," he concluded, "is more like

---

fifth- and sixth-century Platonic studies in Athens and Alexandria (Festugière, "L'ordre de lecture.")

28. Theiler, *Schriften*, 5:368–69, cited by O'Daly, *Plotinus' Philosophy*, 11 n16.
29. Martin, "Technologies."
30. Ibid.
31. Merlan, "Plotinus," 358B.

the formative thought which establishes the order and law of a state, which knows already what the citizens are going to do and why they are going to do it, and legislates with regard to all this" (4.4.39). Consequently, the soul in its particularity exists for Plotinus as an act of "illegitimate self-assertion" (see 3.7.11).[32] "One must not look at what is agreeable to the individual," Plotinus concludes, "but at the All" (2.9.9). He seems to consign the individual self to the subhuman status by which Aristotle characterized those who stood apart from properly constituted social relationships (Aristotle, *Politica* 1253A).[33]

Like the body and its sexual relations that define the vitality of social life together with its familial mode of organization, the prevailing corporate body and its political relations were, for Plotinus, an illusory attraction of sensory existence (*Enneads* 4.4.43–44).[34] He understands the "common gathering" (τὸ κοινόν . . . κατὰ πολιτείαν) to be the worst condition of life; better is the control exercised by cities through their democratic constitutions; the best condition of this life, however, is the aristocracy, within which Plotinus and his senatorial friends moved, far removed from the common masses (4.4.17). In contrast to gnostic complaints about such inequalities that characterized, in their view, the imperfection of this world, Plotinus responds that there are two kinds of this-worldly life: one for the "good and wise" and one for the "common crowd" (οἱ πολλοί); these "simple masses" (ὁ φαῦλος ὄχλος) who, in the "Strangelovean" diagnosis of Plotinus, are ruled by their "bodily fluids" (ὑγροὶ σώματι) (6.8.3; cf. 1.1.5), exist to do "manual labor" for the "better sort" (2.9.9)—in which χειροτεχνία, "manual labor," the opposite of φιλοσοφία (philosophy) in the usage of Plato (*Respublica* 405A), is, in that of Aristotle, "the work of slaves" (*Metaphysica* 981A.31). As Plotinus concludes, "the good man's pleasure that his country is saved will be there even if someone else saves it" (*Enneads* 1.5.10); "if the world is like a sports-ground, where some win and others lose, what's wrong with that?" (2.9.9). The higher soul, in the view of Plotinus, should "be detached" from such "human concerns," and should, consequently, forget country along with wife, children, and friends (4.3.32).

Although it might be assumed that a thoroughgoing metaphysical position, such as that of Plotinus, accords best with an apolitical stance, Plotinus's goal was nothing less than the establishment of a new, alternative community of those who have realized their spiritual kinship with one another as descendants of the metaphysical One and who have, thereby,

---

32. Armstrong, trans., *Plotinus*, xiii.
33. Martin, "Anti-Individualistic."
34. Armstrong, trans., *Plotinus*.

internalized the "laws of Plato" into their corporate body (Porphyry, *Vita Plotini* 12; see *Enneads* 5.5.4; 5.9.5).[35] Whether intentional or not, Plotinus transferred into his utopian vision the social stratification with its privilege of power that not only characterized the philosophy of India to which he had initially been so attracted (Porphyry, *Vita Plotini* 3.15–17) but the third-century Roman aristocracy within whom he moved so comfortably (7).[36] Born, perhaps, of the decay that characterized Roman sociopolitical relations as a consequence of continual invasions and internal revolts during his lifetime,[37] as much as it was of his circumspect contempt for the common folk, Plotinus's hierarchical figuration of metaphysical Otherness situated the "realized" self in a "city above," far removed from the "city below" with its sociopolitical contingencies of historical reality (*Enneads* 4.4.17). To this end, Plotinus actually petitioned the emperor Gallienus to consign him a deserted city in Campania, which he and his companions might resettle under the name of Πλατανόπολις (*Platonopolis*) (Porphyry, *Vita Plotini.* 12).

Given Plotinus's emphasis on the kinship of realized souls, it is perhaps not too venturesome to suggest that this Plotinian society would be constituted as a fictive kinship group on the model of those communities that proliferated in the Hellenistic period generally: the clubs, the mystery religions, the gnosticizing groups, associations that provided a substitute or alternative status to that ascribed by birth and that, we might conclude, likely provided the model for his alternative vision.[38] Whereas the Hellenistic clubs and cults constructed their fictive kinship alliances by means of an initiation modeled on the juridical procedure of adoption,[39] the gnostics typically claimed kinship on the basis of descent from a common divine ancestor[40]—as did Plotinus with his appeal to kinship with the metaphysical One.

35. See, e.g., Weber, *Religion of India*, 331. Apoliticism is attributed to Plotinus by both Armstrong, trans., *Plotinus*; and Gerson. Gerson (*Plotinus*, 287–88 n2) does suggest, however, that the situation might have been quite different had Plotinus realized his plan to establish a Platonic utopia.

36. On the relationship between myth, social stratification, and power in India, see Dumont, *Homo Hierarchicus*.

37. "Gallienus" in Hammond and Scullard, eds., *Oxford Classical Dictionary*, 456.

38. The classic work on the Greek associations remains Poland, *Vereinswesens*. Poland builds upon the work of Foucart, *Des associations*. See the brief but helpful summary of Poland's work by Tod, *Sidelights*; and Tod, "Clubs, Greek," 254–55. On the Latin associations, see Waltzing, *Corporations*. The investigations of Foucart, Poland, and Waltzing were made possible by the pioneering work Mommsen, *De Collegiis*.

39. On initiation as adoption by the god, see Rohde, *Psyche*, appendix 11; and Paul in Gal 4:5 and Rom 8:23.

40. Martin, "Genealogy and Sociology."

Although Plotinus and the gnostics belonged to the same late Hellenistic world of sociophilosophical thought,[41] Plotinus's claim to an optimistic view of the world ironically masks an even more elitist position than that conventionally attributed gnostic groups. Unlike Plotinus's proposal to establish an alternative Platonic commune to which the elite might retreat, the self-despair of the "gnostic principle" resulted in a democratized realization of human worthlessness. To "know oneself" in this latter context is, in the earlier conclusion of the Jewish Platonist Philo, "to know the nothingness of the mortal race" (*De mutatione nominum* 54); then, Philo concludes, "is the time for the creature to encounter the Creator" (*Quis rerum divinarum haeres sit* 30).[42] The gnostic rejection of the given world resulted, similarly, in the discovery of the self in its ordinariness and solitude, and a consequent recognition and acknowledgment that the actual realm of human kinship is social existence, not united by myths of common origin but by the historical exigencies of community situated in the real world. The gnostics recognized, in other words, that the fallen and imperfect world they inhabited might be redeemed through ethical and political action, an aspiration that Plotinus's contemporary Mani was shortly to pursue with notable success in the East, and as the Roman Christians, under the tutelage of Augustine, successor of both Plotinus and Mani, were later to attempt in the West.

IV

The transcendental "city above," proposed by Plotinus as the model for his Πλατανόπολις, was finally given Christian articulation by Augustine as the ideal City of God. Its political articulation of the metaphysical hypothesis, like the Western theological tradition it has been so instrumental in shaping, remains a legitimating discourse for hierarchical distributions of power;[43] Augustine's "hope for a Christian public order . . . [became the] dream of many Christian centuries."[44] Despite Nietzsche's attempted disposition of metaphysics, together with John Stuart Mill's challenge to the concomitant view of human nature as corrupt over fourteen hundred years later,[45] this totalizing discipline of determination and domination remains for many, in the academy as in everyday life, the sole bulwark of the self against the

---

41. Jonas, *Gnosis*, 171–75.
42. The argument of this paragraph follows that of Jonas, *Gnostic*, 280.
43. Hardy notes that Augustine's vision of a "Christian Commonwealth" provided the inspiration for imperial goals ("City," 257). See also Williams, "St. Augustine," 9–10.
44. Hardy, "City," 264.
45. Mill, *Liberty*.

limits of reason. Even those who embrace the anarchy of experience as epistemological persist in advocating its normalization, which, as in the case of Plotinus, remains rationally grounded upon moralistic legitimizations of power. The history of the self and of its embodied nature that has been engendered by this Western metaphysic of power is only now being written.

References

Armstrong, A. H., trans. *Plotinus*. 7 vols. Cambridge: Harvard University Press, 1966–1988.
Blumenthal, H. J. *Plotinus' Psychology: His Doctrines of the Embodied Soul*. The Hague: Nijhoff, 1971.
Copenhaver, Brian P., trans. *Hermetica*. Cambridge: Cambridge University Press, 1992.
Dillon, J. "Self-Definition in Later Platonism." In *Self-Definition in the Greco-Roman World*, edited by Ben F. Meyer and E. P. Sanders, 60–75. Jewish and Christian Self-Definition 3. Philadelphia: Fortress, 1982.
Dodds, E. R. *Pagan and Christian in an Age of Anxiety*. New York: Norton, 1970.
Dumont, Louis. *Homo Hierarchicus: The Caste System and Its Implications*. Rev. ed. and trans. by Mark Sainsbury et al. Chicago: University of Chicago Press, 1980.
Festugière, A.-J. "L'ordre de lecture des dialogues de Platon au Ve/VIe siècles." *Museum Helveticum* 26 (1969) 281–96.
Foucart, P. *Des associations religieuses chez les Grecs*. New York: Arno, 1975.
Gerson, Lloyd P. *Plotinus*. The Arguments of the Philosophers. London: Routledge, 1994.
Hammond, Nicholas, G. L., and Howard H. Scullard, eds. *Oxford Classical Dictionary*. 2nd ed. Oxford: Oxford University Press, 1970.
Hardy, Edward R. "The City of God." In *A Companion to the Study of St. Augustine*, edited by Roy W. Battenhouse, 257–86. Oxford: Oxford University Press, 1955.
Henry, Paul. "Introduction." In *Plotinus: The Enneads*. Translated by Stephen Mackenna. London: Faber & Faber, 1956.
Jonas, Hans. *Gnosis und spätantiker Geist*. Vol. 2, 1: *Von der Mythologie zur mystischen Philosophie*. 2nd ed. Göttingen: Vandenhoeck & Ruprecht, 1966.
———. *The Gnostic Religion*. 2nd ed. Boston: Beacon, 1958.
Kristeva, Julia. *Tales of Love*. Translated by Leon S. Roudiez. New York: Columbia University Press, 1987.
Lévi-Strauss, Claude. *The Raw and the Cooked*. Translated by John and Doreen Weightman. Introduction to a Science of Mythology. New York: Harper, 1969.
———. *The Savage Mind*. The Nature of Human Society Series. Chicago: University of Chicago Press, 1966.
———. *Totemism*. Translated by Rodney Needham. Beacon Paperbacks. Boston: Beacon, 1963.
Macey, David. *The Lives of Michel Foucault*. New York: Pantheon, 1993.
Martin, Luther H. "The Anti-Individualistic Ideology of Hellenistic Culture." *Numen* 41/2 (1994) 117–40.

———. "Genealogy and Sociology in the *Apocalypse of Adam*." In *Gnosticism & the Early Christian World*, edited by James Goehring et al., 25–36. Forum Fascicles 2. Sonoma, CA: Polebridge, 1990 (chapter 22, this volume).

———. "Technologies of the Self and Self-Knowledge in the Syrian Thomas Tradition." In *Technologies of the Self: A Seminar with Michel Foucault*, edited by Luther H. Martin et al., 50–63. Amherst: University of Massachusetts Press, 1988 (chapter 23, this volume).

Merlan, Philip. "Plotinus." In *Encyclopedia of Philosophy*, edited by Paul Edwards, 6: 351–59. 8 vols. New York: Macmillan, 1967.

Mill, John S. *On Liberty*. In *On Liberty and Other Writings*, 1–116. Edited by Stefan Collini. Cambridge Texts in the History of Political Thought. Cambridge: Cambridge University Press, 1989.

Mommsen, Theodor. *De Collegiis et Sodaliciis*. Kiel: Schwersiana, 1843.

O'Daly, G. J. P. *Plotinus' Philosophy of the Self*. New York: Barnes & Noble, 1973.

O'Meara, Dominic J. *Plotinus: An Introduction to the "Enneads."* Oxford: Clarendon, 1993.

O'Neill, William. *Proclus: Alcibiades I. A Translation and Commentary*. The Hague: Nijhoff, 1965.

Otto, Rudolf. *The Idea of the Holy*. Translated by John W. Harvey. Oxford: Oxford University Press, 1958.

Poland, Franz. *Geschichte des griechischen Vereinswesens*. Fürstlich Jablonowskische Gesellschaft der Wissenschaften, Leipzig. Preisschriften 38. Leipzig: Teubner, 1909.

Proudfoot, Wayne. *Religious Experience*. Berkeley: University of California Press, 1985.

Puech, H.-C. *Les sources de Plotin: dix exposés et discussions, Vandoeuvres-Genève, 21–29 août 1957*. Entretiens sur l'antiquité classique 5. Geneva: Vandoeuvres, 1960.

Rist, John M. "Metaphysics and Psychology in Plotinus' Treatment of the Soul." In *Graceful Reason: Essays Presented to Joseph Owens*, edited by Lloyd P. Gerson, 135–51. Papers in Mediaeval Studies 4. Toronto: Pontifical Institute of Mediaeval Studies, 1983.

———. *Plotinus: The Road to Reality*. Cambridge: Cambridge University Press, 1967.

Rohde, Erwin. *Psyche: The Cult of Souls and Belief in Immortality among the Greeks*. Translated by W. B. Hillis. New York: Harcourt, Brace, 1925.

Runia, David T., ed. *Plotinus amid Gnostics and Christians*. Amsterdam: Free University Press, 1984.

Sleeman, J. H., and Gilbert Pollet, eds. *Lexicon Plotinianum*. Ancient and Medieval Philosophy Series 1, 2 Leiden: Brill, 1980.

Stewart, Potter. *Jacobellis v. Ohio. Oyez*. Chicago-Kent College of Law at Illinois Tech, n.d. June 23, 2016. https://www.oyez.org/cases/1963/11/.

Theiler, Wilhelm. *Plotins Schriften*. Translated by Richard Harder et al. 6 vols. in 12. Philosophische Bibliothek. Hamburg: Meiner, 1956–1971.

Tod, Marcus N. "Clubs, Greek." In *The Oxford Classical Dictionary*, edited by Nicholas G. L. Hammond and Howard H. Scullard, 351–52. 2nd ed. Oxford: Oxford University Press, 1970.

———. *Sidelights on Greek History*. Oxford: Blackwell, 1932.

Waltzing, Jean Pierre. *Étude historique sur les corporations professionelles chez les Romains*. 4 vols. Louvain: Peeters, 1895–1900.

Weber, Max. *The Religion of India: The Sociology of Hinduism and Buddhism.* Translated by Hans H. Gerth and Don Martindale. New York: Free Press, 1958.

Westerink, Leendert G. *Anonymous Prolegomena to Platonic Philosophy: Introduction, Text, Translations and Indices.* Amsterdam: North-Holland, 1962.

———, ed. *Commentary on the First Alcibiades of Plato,* by Alexandrinus Olympidorus. Amsterdam: North-Holland, 1956.

———. *Commentary on the First Alcibiades of Plato,* by Proclus Diadochus. *Critical Text and Indices.* Amsterdam: North-Holland, 1954.

Williams, Daniel D. "The Significance of St. Augustine Today." In *A Companion to the Study of St. Augustine,* edited by Roy W. Battenhouse, 3–14. Oxford: Oxford University Press, 1955.

INDEX

A. Names/Subjects

Aarhus University, 25, 122, 123, 224, n. 94
Abban, 341
Abraham, 85, 88, 149, 269, 272
absolute religious individualism, 288
universalism, 288
abstinence, 315
academic research circles, 247
study of religion, x, 78, 123, 126, 225
acculturation, 7
Achaians, 151
Achilles, 40, 117, 151
Acrocorinth, 199, 207, 209
Activity, 10, 12, 41, 145, 152, 188, 199, 271, 325, 345–47, 351
Acts, 30, 43, 244, 250, 254, 274–80, 293, 316–17, 333, 340–48
Adam vi, xv, 59, 139, 323, 325–35, 337, 359
Adam/Seth, 327
Adonis, 16
Adoption, x, 6, 18, 20, 42,53, 55–56, 58, 66, 101, 116, 130, 134–35, 214, 255, 313, 328, 332, 334, 356
aeon(s), 59, 327
Aelianus, 118
Aelius Aristides, 144–47, 149–50, 158
Aeschylus, 152
Aetna, 198, 204

Aetolian Confederacy, 116
Africa(n), 30, 36, 84–85, 102, 110, 157, 205, 237, 245, 313, 335–36
agamous kin model of adoption, 332
Agathocles, 203, 205
Agathodaimon, 14
age of anxiety, 305, 307, 358
agency, ix–x, 74, 91–92, 94, 151, 153, 156, 160, 162, 225–26, 316
agents, 17, 151, 154, 156, 161–64, 177, 221, 314, 316–17
agnate, 330
agnatic descent, 330
agrarian economy, 196, 197–98
agrarian lore of illiterate masses, 214
Agrippa, 263 n.1, 266–67
Ai-Khanoum (Alexandria Oxeiana), 7
Alcibiades, 183, 186, 192, 206–7, 340, 342, 353n. 27
Alcmaeon of Croton, 302
Alderink, Larry, xiv, 156, 158 n. 10, 161 n. 31, 164, 188, 192
Alexander of Abonoteichos, 56
Alexander the Great, vii, 1, 6, 8–9, 12–13, 30, 35, 44, 63, 65, 70, 96, 114, 254, 314
Alexander's political revolution, 301–302
Alexandria, 7, 9–10, 28, 32, 37, 49, 62, 185, 218, 227, 231, 273, 285, 340, 347, 352, 353–54 n. 27

alien, 41, 69, 138, 211, 218, 292, 306, 316, 332, 336, 352
Allah, 97
alliance(s), 11, 66, 71, 83, 87, 116–17, 120–21, 128, 248, 282, 292, 296, 313–14, 325, 326 n.23, 331–35, 356
Allogenes, 59
Almagest, 38
Altar of Flavius Aper, 231, 234
Altar-priest, 52
alternative kin groups, 130
  social systems, 334
amazement, 219
ambassador(s), vi, xiv, 274–77, 279
ambassadorial patronage, 277
American Academy of Religion, 318, 336
  Anthropological Association, 318
  Folklore Society, 215, 227
  Hutterite communities, 247
  mythic evocations, 288
Amish farming communities, 247
Amorites, 315
Anaktoron, 219
anatomical features, 234
ancestors, 52–53, 58, 71, 128–29, 135–36, 157, 200, 251, 327, 334
ancestry, 41, 253, 324, 352 n.17
Anaximander, 84
Andaman myth of the future life, 323, 333
Anderson, Benedict, 69, 70, 73, 76, 80 n. 9, 83 nn. 21–22, 88 n. 49, 95, 252 n. 38, 258
Andrapolis, 341
Andros, 233
Annales d'histoire sociale, 301
  historians, 302
anti-Arian formula, 286
Antichrist, 143
Antioch, 9, 278
  of Pisidia, 274
Antiochus, 49, 121, 135 n. 59
  of Ascolon, 49
Antiphemos of Rhodes, 199

antisemitic Gentiles, 333
antithetical, 58, 113, 276, 306
  analyses, 225
  assumptions, 187
  desire, 327
  relationship, 342
  strategics of existence, 339
Antonine period, 224
Anz, Wilhelm, 109–10, 304, 307
Apollonius of Perga, 44
  of Tyana, 56
Apuleius, 3, 19, 27–29, 55–56, 97, 104–8, 110–11, 133, 135, 138, 152–54, 164, 186, 219 n. 65, 300, 305, 339, 346, 348
Aquinas, 281
arabian mullahs, 97
aramaic *Vorlage*, 293
Arcadian League, 116
Archimedes, 44
Arianist followers, 286
Aristarchus of Samos, 38, 44
Aristeas, 294
Aristomenes, 105
Aristotelian Peripatetics, 45
Aristotle, 4, 6, 13, 21, 44–46, 66, 80, 116, 118, 125, 219, 305, 339, 355
Aristotle's superlunar and superhuman cosmos, 46
Arrian(us), 36, 42 n. 22, 70, 254
Artemidorus of Ephesus, 144, 294
artisans, 251
ascetic lifestyle, 334
Asclepius, 16, 56, 61
Ashoka, empire of, 73
Ashurbanipal, 83
Asia, 30, 46, 84, 90, 202, 293
  Minor, 27–28, 31,46, 84,123, 194, 208, 274, 276, 279
associations, 24, 28–29, 41–43, 45–46, 51–55, 60, 62–63, 67–68, 107 n.60, 116 n.19, 122, 131–33, 138–39, 231–32, 248–50, 252, 254–55, 258, 290, 318, 334–36, 356, 358
  of Zeus in Philadelphia, 42
  of classical Athens, religious, 42

INDEX   363

astral structures in Hellenistic
   expression, 304
astrologers, viii, 236
astrological celestial causality, 269
   conceptions, 242
   identity, 269
   influence, 304
   powers, 270
astrology, 15, 24, 27, 177–78, 231,
   237, 242 n.58, 244, 269, 272,
   304 n. 20, 307
astronomer(s), viii, 38, 44, 236, 269,
   303
astronomical and astrological,
   observations, 38
astronomical and astrological
   "specialists, 243
   Babylonian, 15, 38
   Persian, 15, 38
   Egyptian, 15
astronomical and astrological
   "specialists, 243
   ecumenism, 16
   knowledge, 38
   logic of relationships, 238
   syllabus, 3, 294, 300
astronomy, 38, 45, 238, 269
Astyages, 83, 90
Atargatis, Syrian Goddess, 61, 107–8
Atemporal analyses of data, 174
Athanasius, 286
Athens, 6, 16, 21, 24, 27, 30–31, 40,
   42, 46, 48, 52–54, 57, 80 n.5,
   108 n.66, 118, 121, 177 n.
   28, 183 n. 19, 189–91, 194,
   197, 203, 206, 227, 295–96,
   353–54 n. 27
atdjō^{hm}, 333
Atran, Scott, 65, 68, 70, 74 n. 62, 76,
   159, 163–64, 224, n. 93, 226
Attica Eleusinian Thriasian Plain,
   189
Attis, 16–17, 20, 29, 134 n.52, 138,
   175–76, 179
Attridge, Harold W., 268, 271–72
*Aufstieg und Niedergang der
   Römischen Welt*, 2

Augustine, 30, 50, 59, 62–63, 73,
   89, 118 n. 30, 281, 291, 295,
   357–58, 360
Augustus, 1, 8, 10, 12, 16, 17, 36, 41,
   62, 99–100, 118, 120, 136,
   192, 224, 277, 301–2, 305
Aulus Gellius, 250
Aurelius, 48–49, 57, 192, 224, 307
authoritative doctrine, 220
authority, 12, 18, 43–44, 49,55,
   70, 73–74, 80, 87, 92–93,
   116–17, 119, 129, 172, 177,
   189, 204, 214, 220, 223–24,
   255–56, 283–84, 292, 298,
   314, 316–17, 328, 330, 332,
   334
authority, central, 74, 256
autobiographical memory, 74, 218,
   220
   system, 220
Autogenes, 59

Babylon, 83, 337
Babylonian(s), 15, 38, 83–85, 88,
   91–92, 111, 275 n. 6
Bacchanalia, 121, 178, 224, 291
Baining people in Papua New
   Guinea, 171
balanced ritual system, 223
baptism, 39, 256, 259, 317
barley, 189
Barkow, Jerome, 76, 318–20
Barr, James, 81, 95
Barrett, Caitlin, 24
Barrett, Justin, 160, 163–65, 217,
   225–26
Baths of Caracalla, Mithraeum, 58
Baucis, 276 n.8, 278
Beck, Roger, 24, 26, 31, 75–76, 173,
   177–78, 213 n. 23, 218 n. 58,
   226, 236–238, 240–244, 302
   n. 11, 304 n. 22, 307
Beckian invocation, 242
beginnings, 35, 38, 44,61, 63, 99–
   100, 114,136, 173, 188, 202,
   211, 246–47, 279, 332, 336

behavior(s), viii, x, 68, 125–26, 153, 161 n.33, 220, 225, 255–56, 270, 314–15, 318–19, 337
behavioral, 76, 226, 258, 311, 314, 319
behaviorism, 310
Benedict, Ruth, 210, 226
Bethlehem, 39
Bianchi, Ugo, xiii, 2, 24, 25, 219 n. 61, 226, 337
Bible, iv, xv, 51, 82, 95–96, 226–27, 251, 258, 269, 280, 297, 316–17, 333 n.82, 335
biblical scholars, 81, 307, 311–12, 318
biblical
  studies, vi, xv, 80, 309
  tradition(s), 44, 82, 279, 281, 312
biocognitive biases, 69
  dynamics of mutual altruism, 72
  optimum, 67
  research, 309
  theories, 75
biological evolution, 252, 311
  functions, 311
  landscape, 125
biology, v, xiii, 66 n.11, 77, 113 n.2, 122, 124–29, 131, 133, 135–37, 139, 163, 175 n.21, 179, 313, 324, 328
blank slate, 229, 310, 312, 320
Blessed Queen of Heaven, 135
blind *Fortune*, 14, 106
blood-relationships, 330
Boman, Thorleif, 81, 95
bonds of intimacy, 254
book of Acts, 254
Borges, Jorge, 299, 306
bovine leg, vi, xiv, 230, 234
Boyer, Pascal, ix–x, 66–67, 74 n. 60, 76, 119–20 n. 38, 122, 126 n. 11, 137, 160 n. 30, 162 nos 40; 42, 165, 217, 224–26, 316 n. 21, 319
Brahma, 97
brain chemistry, 313
Braudel, Fernand, 301–3, 307

Brown, Peter, 26, 39 n. 10, 135, 137, 146, 149, 338, 347
Buddha, 97
Buddhism, 73, 76, 360
Bull, xv, 26, 28, 58, 231–35, 304
Bultmann, Rudolf, 276 n .8, 279, 294, 296, 303, 307
bureaucratic urbanization, 334
Burckhardt, Jacob, 289, 296
Burkert, Walter, vii, x, 2, 26, 45 n. 31, 62, 125–27, 129 n. 31, 134 n. 47, 137, 200 n. 25, 205–7, 222 n. 80, 227, 325, 335

Cain, 326–27, 331
Caligula, 224
Calvin, John, 284 n. 21, 305
Cambridge School, 185
Cambyses, 83, 85–86
Campania, 50, 291, 356
Canaite(s), 326, 328, 331–35
Capua Vetere, mithraeum in, 179, 233
Carcinus, 199
Carthage, 204
Casadio, Giovanni, 172 n.7, 177–79
Castration, charisma of, 283
catacombs, 251
catechetical instruction, 217–18, 220
Catholic doctrine of faith, 282
Catholic embodiment of Christianity, 282
Cato, 48, 153, 203, 239, 242
Cecropian Minerva, v, xiii, 97, 99, 101, 103, 105, 107–9, 111, 338 n. 2, 348
celestial equator, 58
  realm, 270
cemeteries, covered, 251
Cenchreae, 202
center(s), 5, 7–9, 17, 21, 53–54, 84, 192, 200, 231, 340
centralized hierarchical control, 252
  leadership, 332, 334
centrifugal, 7
centripetal, 7

INDEX 365

centurion(s), 43, 249, 251
Ceres, 107 n. 60, 184, 197–98, 203–4
Chadwick, Henry, 285–86, 294–96, 347
Chaldeans, 269
Chalupa, Aleš, vi, xiv, 26, 175 n. 20, 178, 230–232, 234
Chance, 39, 45, 47, 56, 105–6, 159
charisma, 283–84, 287, 289, 292
charismatic authority, 283–284, 298
  communities, 287
  congregations, 287
  impulse, 283
  individuals, 283
  possession, 284
charter myths, 325
China, 71 n. 39, 73, 77, 139
chinese encyclopaedia, 299, 306
  knowledge, 306
Chomsky, Noam, 310–11, 319
Christakis, Nicholas A., 252–55, 258
Christian associations, 250, 252, 254
  beginnings, 35, 44, 61, 246
  catholicity, 100, 302
  communities, 19, 21
  culture, 36, 292, 302
  groups, 40, 43, 247, 250, 254, 256, 288, 291–92
  mission, 276, 278–79
  origins, vi, xv, 63, 150, 223 n. 88, 227, 246, 258–59, 261, 282–83, 285, 297, 299, 301–3, 305, 307, 319
  orthodoxy, 215
  Second Testament, 3, 300
  gnostic mystery of redemption, 346
Christie, James, 181, 187, 193
Chrysippus, 48
Christianities, early, vii, 32, 35, 37, 43, 61, 63, 77, 113, 120–21, 173, 177–79, 224, 228–29, 248, 256, 282, 284, 286, 288, 291–92, 294, 297, 311–12
Christianity, vi, 1, 4, 36, 60, 73, 77, 93, 96, 98, 100, 103, 109, 120, 121 n. 40, 122, 131, 135, 137–38, 165, 171, 173, 175 n. 22, 177, 179–80, 188 n. 52, 194, 228, 233, 235, 246–48, 252–54, 256 n. 58, 259, 261, 272, 279, 281–86, 288–89, 293–94, 296–97, 301, 305, 308, 316–17, 320, 324, 335–37, 340, 347–48
Christianization of Hellenic thought, 282
Christmas card lists, 247
Chromios, 199
Cicero, 48–49, 81, 90, 144–45, 197–99, 201, 204
Cimmerian Bosporus, 202
City of God 50, 62, 357–58
city-state, 4, 6, 11, 15, 72, 116
civilization, 26, 61, 71, 73, 99 n. 10, 101, 111, 114, 136 n. 62, 139, 188, 190–91, 197, 201, 206, 209, 211, 213, 249 n. 20, 259, 285, 289 n. 57, 296–97, 303 nn. 15–16, 306–7, 319, 334
classifications of an ideal kinship universe, 324
Claudius Ptolemy, 3, 15, 38, 294, 300, 303
Cleanthes, 48, 268
Cleisthenes, 21
Clement of Alexandria, 62, 185, 218 n. 59, 227, 285, 347, 352
Clinton, Kevin, 27, 52 n. 45, 62, 212–13, 219 n. 62, 227
club-sized groups, 249
clubs viii, 41–42, 67, 113, 121, 248–50, 290, 337, 356, 359
clusters of groups, 233, 253
Cnidos, 200
Cocconas, 56
codes of justice, 314
coercion, 153
cognatically, 325
cognition, v–vi, ix–x, xv, 32, 76–77, 138, 156, 160, 164–67, 178–80, 221, 227–28, 239, 245, 247, 286, 291, 309, 311, 313
cognition, human, ix, 160, 164, 179, 221, 237, 311

cognitive approach, ix, 31, 177–78, 318
    capacities of *Homo sapiens*, 313
    constraint, ix, 67, 226, 319
    efficiency, 240
    egalitarianism, 242
    history, 66
    perspective, 74, 162, 175, 216, 225
    processing systems, 217
    psychology, 126
    mapping, 126, 241
    science of religion, 32, 76–77, 160, 162, 165, 178–80, 216, 225–27, 229, 260, 318, 320
    sciences, x, 30, 122–23, 126, 165, 171, 178, 211, 310, 318
    scientists, ix, 69, 160, 175 n. 21, 309, 317
    theories of ritual, 317
cognitively natural or optimal traits, 174
    optimal, 175, 315
cognitively optimum position, 224
cohesion, 4, 172, 220, 248, 257, 331, 334
collective genealogical claims, 288
    memory, 86–88, 93, 95–96, 129 n. 30, 136
    mentality, 82, 86
    rites, 257
Coleridge, Samuel Taylor, 79 n. 2, 95
collegia, viii, 41, 42 n. 20, 56 n. 50, 62, 249, 254, 256, 258
commercial centers, 21
    mobility, 51
common ancestry, 253, 324
    divine ancestor, 130, 356
    Hellenistic language, 18
    human ground, 210–11
    language, 71–72, 116
    matrilineal ancestor, 328
    sense, 69, 243 n. 43, 245
communication, 4–6, 9, 18, 65, 71, 81, 152–53, 156, 162, 185, 238–40, 242, 244–45, 276
communicative competency, 242
communicator, 239

communities, 18–19, 21, 50, 66–70, 73, 75–76, 113, 116, 121, 129–31, 133, 139, 172, 213–14, 220, 231, 243, 246–47, 252 n. 38, 254–58, 287, 356
community rule, 266
complement of rituals, 223
complexity theory, 233, 253
conceptual integration, 75
concomitant mythmaking-justifications, 256
Concord, concord, 12, 158, 164, 214
conformism, 18
confusion of languages, 323, 333
consolidation
    of knowledge, 3, 120 n. 39, 122, 294, 296, 300, 308
    of power, 40, 115–16, 121, 136, 281, 292, 296
Constantine, xiv, 28, 98, 120, 154, 164–65, 225, 259, 292, 297, 302, 307
constraints, biological, ix
consumers, 251
contemporary hunter-gatherer groups, 247, 313
contingency of existence, 304
conventional historiographical theory, 301
    strategy of collective identity, 324
Copernican cosmological revolution, 38
Copernican / historical modernity, 304
Corinth, 114, 198, 202–6, 208
Corinthian(s), 198–99, 202, 283
Corinthian League, 114
Corn Maiden, 211
    Mother, 211
Corpus Hermeticum, 3, 166, 300
corruption, 334, 352
corvus (Mithraic grade), 244
cosmic firmament, 12, 22
    paranoia, 22, 305
cosmological revolution,
    Copernican, 38, 108
    Ptolemaic, 99, 192

cosmology
    Ptolemaic, vii, ix, 6, 15, 38, 99 n.
        14, 108, 304
    Hellenistic, 38
cosmopolitan city, 6
cosmos, ix, 37–38, 40, 45–48, 58,
    92–93, 105, 116, 146, 190,
    241, 270, 303, 307, 338–39,
    342, 349
counterintuitive beliefs, 316
    claims, 224 n. 93
    events, 317
    ideas, 74, 219
Crates, 47–48
Creator, 59, 357
Creuzer, George Friedrich, 181–84,
    193, 207–8
credo quia absurdum, 218, 226, 286
    n. 29
creedal doctrine, fourth-century,
    282
criteria of eligibility, 328
Croix, G. E. M. de Ste., 188–93, 202
    n. 43, 208, 334–35
cult of Mithras, ix, xi, 18, 20, 27,
    29, 57, 77, 173, 176 n. 26,
    178–79, 228, 242, 245, 250
    n. 23, 258
cult of the Phrygian Mother, 134
cults of "eastern origin", 12, 16
cultural fusion, 101
    -transmission, 127
culture(s), viii, x, 4–5, 7–8, 19, 26,
    29, 31–32, 36–38, 41–42,
    51, 60–61, 67–69, 76–78, 80,
    83–84, 92–93, 97, 100–102,
    108, 116, 121, 125–27, 129,
    132, 138–39, 157–58, 161,
    164–67, 172, 179–80, 188,
    194, 196–97, 213, 227, 229,
    251, 258, 265, 281, 283, 289,
    292–97, 301–2, 305–7, 310
    n. 5, 311–12, 320, 324–25,
    336, 338, 348, 58
Cumont, Franz, 25, 27, 97–98, 100,
    103, 110, 133, 137, 177–78,
    187 n. 47, 242, 244, 269 n.

19, 272, 302 n. 12, 304 n.
    20, 307
cup, 58, 232–33
Cybele, 16–17, 20, 25, 27, 29, 31,
    175–76, 179, 224
Cynic thought, 5
    Stoic diatribe style, 294
Cynicism, 47
Cynics, 6, 13–14, 17, 47, 354
Cyprus, 274
Cyrus Cylinder, 83
Cyrus of Persia, 82

dālâh, 309
Daduch, 52
Daniel's prophecy, 271
Darnton, Robert, 147–48, 150, 323
    n. 2, 335
Dardanelles, 203
Darius, 86, 117
Darwinian imperative of survival,
    315
Darwinism, 66 n. 12, 68 n. 22, 70
    nn. 32, 34, 36, 76, 126, 319
    social, 126
daughter(s), 90, 117, 126, 135 n. 59,
    188, 190, 193, 196, 198, 331,
    341
dead, 28, 30, 51 n. 44, 62, 72–73, 76,
    121 n. 42, 122, 132, 135, 210,
    251, 293, 330
death, 1, 8, 14, 40, 44, 56, 83, 98–99,
    187–88 n. 47, 191, 202, 218,
    263 n. 1, 266, 305, 329–30,
    333–34
Dawkins, Richard, 126–27, 137
Decemvirs, 204
decentralized patterns, 233
degrees of connection, 253
Deinomenes, 200
Deinomenid dynasty, 200, 204
    policy, 204
Delian League, 116
Delos, 24, 31, 41, 63
Delphi, 42, 80, 87, 354
Delphic oracle, 80

Demeter, v, xi, xiv, 15, 30–31, 51–56, 72, 78, 107, 132, 177, 179, 184, 186–92, 194, 196–97, 201, 203–14, 216, 221, 224, 228, 277
Demeter's gifts of culture, 196
Demetrius Falireas, 10, 13
Democritus, 46
demonic elements, 12
Demophoôn, 190–91
Demosthenes, 5, 118
demythologization, of a gnostic kinship universe, 325
descent, 41, 50, 52–53, 58, 85–86, 116–18, 127–30, 133, 213, 324–328, 330–31, 333–34, 336, 352–53, 356
Dennet, Daniel, 127, 138
descent groups, 325–26, 336
descriptive typology, 174
destiny, 47, 60, 120, 263–65, 349
determinism, 79, 89, 92, 263–69, 271
deterministic powers of the cosmos, 270
Deutero-Isaiah, 82–89, 91–94
  Pauline trajectory, 255
Deuteronomic narrative, 120
Diaspora, 51, 132, 177
Dieterich, Albrecht, 134, 138, 255 n. 54
Dilthey, Wilhem, 131, 284
Diocletian, 120
Dionysus, 32, 40, 51, 104, 118, 172 n. 7, 178, 194, 204, 221
  II, 204
Diodorus Siculus, 30, 42, 54, 70, 80, 83, 117, 135 n. 56, 197 n. 9, 199 nos. 22–23, 200–201, 204–205, 254, 277
Diogenes Laertius, 46–50
  of Sinope, 47
Dis, 201
discourse(s), 3, 30, 49, 56, 64–65, 86, 89, 91, 105, 108, 110, 115, 122, 130, 179, 186, 188, 190–92, 206–7, 236–37, 242–44, 299, 324, 329, 334, 350, 357
discursive and doctrinal writings, 346
  formations, 207, 329
distribution of power, 84, 115, 120
divergent modes of religiosity, 78, 166, 171–72, 174, 176, 180, 229
divination, 89–91, 93–94, 144–45, 176
divine nomination, 152
divine right, 41, 118, 354
djōhm, 333
doctrinal features, 173
  modality, 74, 174–75, 177
  mode of religiosity, 73, 172, 220, 224
doctrinal system of orthodoxy, 317
doctrine(s), 35, 49, 55, 58, 76, 95, 131, 172, 175, 177–78, 218, 220, 226, 270, 273, 282, 283–85, 286, 293, 343, 358
Dodds, Eric R., 99 n. 13, 110, 144–46, 150, 305 n. 28, 307, 351–52, 358
Dodona, 151,158
dog (Mithraic cult), 58
dogs, 81, 183, 299, 341
downward journey, 352
drame sacré, 185
Dream Theory, v, xiii, 143, 145, 147, 149, 323 n. 2, 337
dream, professional, 147
dreams, 146, 149
  allegorical, 145–46
  oracular, 144–45, 147, 150
  ordinary, 147
  (non)predictive, 144–48
  theorematic, 145
Droysen, Johann Gustav, 1, 7, 27, 37 n. 5, 62, 98–101, 105, 108–10, 114, 300–302, 307, 338
dualism, 22, 24, 60, 305
Dunbar, Robin, 66–67, 72 nn. 43–44, 76, 247–51, 253–54, 256–58, 313 n. 15, 319

Dura-Europos, 250
  mithraeum, 232
Durkheim, Émile, 68, 73 n. 54, 76, 86, 129
dynamic leadership, 173, 177

early Christian groups, 40, 250, 254, 256, 288, 291
  Christian networks, 254
  Christianities, vii, 32, 35, 37, 43, 61, 63, 77, 113, 120–21, 173, 177, 179, 224, 228–29, 248, 256, 282, 284, 286, 288, 291–92, 294, 297, 311–12
eastern "gnostic" tradition, 340
Ebonics, 237, 243, 245
Eco, Umberto, 143, 149–50
economic ideology, 203
  situation in Attica, 189
economy of urban civilization, 188
Edessa, 340
Egalitarianism, 13, 21, 86, 242
Egypt, 1, 10, 15–16, 24, 26–29, 36–37, 40, 46, 54–55, 57, 77, 83–85, 88, 99, 102, 108, 117, 119, 202–3, 231, 234–35, 259, 345
Egyptian compendia of magical formulae, 3, 294, 300
  mythology, 231
Egyptians, 54, 83, 269
Eleusinian agrarian life, 188
  celebrations, 57, 133, 225
  Demeter, 51
  economy, 197
  initiation, 185, 187
  mystery (-ies), v, xi, xiv, 20, 27, 30, 52–54, 56–57, 62–63, 72 n. 50, 77–78, 133, 177, 179, 181–87, 191–92, 194, 196 n. 3, 198, 208, 210–16, 218–21, 224–28, 248 n. 17, 346
  myth, 188
  plains, 189 n. 64, 197, 201 n. 36
  planting cycle, 216
  populus, 206
  sanctuary, 197, 212

Eleusinians, 190–92, 196, 201
Eleusinion, in Athens, 53
Eleusis, 20, 30, 52–55, 62–63, 72, 78, 132–34, 182 n. 8, 184–87, 189–94, 196–97, 206, 208, 211–14, 218–19, 221, 224–25, 228–29
Eliade, Mircea, 140, 198, 208, 226–27, 303, 307
Elysian fields, 202
  plain, 53, 134, 202
Elysium, 134, 202
embeddedness, 223
embodied rites 256
  -simulations, 255
embodiment of power, 335
emigration, 37, 51, 67
emotionality, 220
emotionally heightened initiation rites, 223
emotions, 27, 67, 163, 255
emperor cult, 117, 130
emperor Gallienus, 50, 291, 356
encyclopaedia, 32, 111, 166, 193, 226, 229, 294, 305, 307
  Hellenistica, vi, xv, 3, 27, 147 n. 22, 150, 297, 299–301, 303, 305, 307
enkyklios paideia, 3
Enlightenment, 37, 125, 129, 147, 300
Entimos of Crete, 199
entrepreneurs, 251
Epictetus, 48–49, 354
Epicurean Garden, 45
Epicureans, 13, 29, 46–49, 57, 63, 268
Epicurus, 46–47
"epidemiological" explanation for culture, 69
Epidemiology, 234
episodic memory, 220
epistemological products of the age, 300
equator, 38, 58, 84
Erathosthenes, 44
Eros, 135

eschatological pattern, Christian, 80
  Jewish, 80
eschatology, 81
essentialist theory, 207
eternity of life, 211
ethic(s), 27, 44–45, 48, 111, 268, 287–89, 292, 298, 305, 308, 339, 349
ethical, 3, 48, 102, 220, 282, 290, 339–40, 342–43, 346, 354, 357
ethnic groups, 5, 214
ethology, 126
Études Preliminaires aux Religions Orientales dans l'Empire Romain, 2
Euboeans, 198
Euclid, 44
Eudorus of Alexandria, 49
Eudoxus of Cnidus, 15, 38
Euhemerus of Messene, 13, 118
Eumolpid(s), Eumolpidae, Eumolpos, 52, 55, 57, 186, 200, 206, 213–14
Eve, 327, 331, 334
everyman, anonymous, 339
evocation(s), 191n.76, 193, 237, 244, 288, 308
evocative, 237
evolution, vi, xv, 66 n. 10, 76–77, 90, 98, 125, 129, 164, 197, 214, 227, 252–53, 258, 309, 311, 313 n. 12, 319
evolutionary biology, contemporary, 126
  history, 72, 311
  psychology, 76, 140, 245, 247–48, 254 n. 51, 258, 310, 313, 320
exogamous marriage alliances, 332
exogamy, 331–32
experience(s), 16, 37, 88, 94, 102 n. 34, 123, 144, 146, 161 n. 33, 165, 175 n. 21, 220, 223, 233 n. 5, 235, 238, 240, 283–84, 296, 307, 350–52, 358–59
experimental vein of gnostic studies, 325
explicit memory system, 220

face-to-face communities of participants, 220
factors, ecological, 65
  institutional, 65
  physical, 65
  psychological, 65
failure of nerve, 45, 305
faith, vi, xiv, 15–17, 45, 102 n. 34, 161–62, 164–66, 181 n. 3, 218, 220, 281–83, 286–87, 292, 295–96, 306, 313
fall, 59, 70, 83, 130, 171, 260, 269, 352, 357
family burial rooms, 251
  cults, 130, 133
  resemblance, 52
fantasy, 164, 316
Farnell, Lewis R., 184–85, 187, 193, 200 n. 28, 205 n. 64, 208
fatal rule, 268
Fate, v, xiii, 14, 22, 39, 48, 60, 79–80, 90–91, 92–94, 107 n. 65, 191, 263–68, 270, 272, 304–5, 308, 339
father, 28, 40, 50, 56, 58, 79, 81–82, 85–86, 94, 114, 117–18, 135, 200 n. 27, 201, 277, 293, 314, 324, 326, 327, 330–31, 337, 344, 353
father (mithraic grade), 230, 232–33, 243
father-son-bother constellation, 326
Febvre, Lucien, 3, 299, 307
Feldman, Louis, 267, 269, 272
Felicissimus Mithraeum in Ostia, vi, xiv, 230
fellowship meal, 250
Festugière, André-Jean, 346–47, 353–54 n. 27, 358
fictive descent, 133, 325
  genealogy, 58, 313
  kin associations, 67
  kinship group, 133–34, 254, 356
  kinship, viii, 21, 56, 121, 130–31, 133–34, 254–55, 290, 313, 335, 356
  kin societies, 55, 66
Figulus, 49

Finley, Moses I., 93–95, 99–101, 110, 198–203, 208
first Punic war, 203
fixed stars, 38, 303
flashbulb memory, 220, 227
focalization, 241
folk deities, 214
　religion, v, xi, xiv, 179, 187 n. 44, 194, 196 n. 4, 208, 210–18, 225–28
　urban continuum, 213
folklore, 147, 210–11, 213–15, 225–27, 229
folklorists, 213, 215, 225
foreign cults, 17–18
Foucault, Michel, xv, 3, 61–62, 64–65, 76, 97, 104 n. 46, 110, 115, 122–23, 128, 139, 206–8, 281, 292, 299, 308, 329 n. 46, 336, 340 n. 7, 347, 350 n. 6, 354, 358–59
Fortune, x, 8, 13–14, 17, 39, 56, 92, 105–7, 136, 270, 304–5
Fox, Robin Lane, vii, xi, 28, 281, 294–96, 324–26, 329 n. 45, 331, 336
fraternity, 8, 70
free will, 264, 266–67, 269, 271–72
freedom, 11, 92, 268–73, 339, 342
French historians, 301
Freud, Sigmund, 143–45, 149, 150, 161 n. 33
Freudian theory, 147
friendship, 13, 46, 164, 185
Fromm, Erich, 148, 150
funerary legislations, Greek and Roman, 71
Fuscus L. Valerius, 234
Fustel de Coulanges, Numa Denis, 128 n. 28, 134, 138
Futurity, v, xiii, 79

Gaius, 132, 204, 249
　Verres, 204
Galatians, 92 n. 66, 95, 270, 272, 277 n. 13, 329 n. 40, 335
Galen, 186, 194

Gela, 199–201, 204
Gelon, 199–200, 203–4
genealogy, vi, xv, 50, 52, 58–59, 86, 130 n. 36, 136 n. 61, 139, 296, 313–14, 323, 325, 327–28, 332 n. 80, 353, 356 n. 40, 359
genes, 126–27
gentiles, 274, 279, 326–27, 330, 333
gentleness, 13
geocentric system, 15, 38
Gehrke, Hans.-J., 7, 28
geocentricity, of Hellenistic science, 38
German "history of religions school", 301
　organic vision of the nation-state, 289
ghosts, 316
globalization, v, xiii, 30, 64–69, 71–73, 75–77, 254, 259, 314 n. 16, 320
Glomb, Tomáš, vi, xiv, 230–34
gnosis, 31, 55 n. 44, 63, 130, 286–87, 110, 325, 327–28, 331–33, 335, 337, 339–40, 348, 357–58
Gnostic and Hermetic traditions, 58
　communities, 19, 21
　Ego, 327–28
　groups, 133, 357
　myth of kinship, 324
gnostic society, 325
Gnosticism, vi, xv, 14, 24, 31–32, 59, 63, 109, 139, 282, 286, 303–5, 321, 323, 325, 335–37, 348, 351 n. 12, 359
gnosticizing groups, 356
gnostics, 59–60, 282, 325, 332–33, 336, 339, 352 n. 17, 356–57, 359
God(s), vi, ix, xiv, 7, 13–17, 20, 24, 27–28, 30–32, 39–40, 43–44, 46–50, 53, 60–62, 66 n. 11, 68 n. 23, 70–71, 74 n. 62, 76–78, 80, 82, 90–91, 101–2, 104, 106, 111, 115, 117–19, 130–31, 133–34, 138–39,

372   INDEX

God(s) (continued)
    147, 152–56, 158–59,
    162–65, 178, 182 n. 7, 186,
    187–88 n. 47, 190, 194, 199,
    211, 214 n. 30, 217, 222,
    224, 227–29, 231, 250 n. 28,
    255, 260, 263–69, 271–72,
    274–79, 281, 288, 290 n. 62,
    297, 314, 316–19, 331–32,
    335–36, 339–41, 345, 352–
    54, 356–58
Good Fortune, 56, 106–7
Gordon, Richard L., 27–28, 77, 122,
    178, 181 n. 3, 191 n. 76, 193,
    237, 244, 258, 306, 308
Grace, 1, 27 n. 17, 138, 250, 283
Graeco-Macedonian empire, 35, 71,
    83, 99, 301, 314, 338
Graeco-Roman antiquity, 89, 152,
    156, 236, 240, 244
    ethical literature, 340
    horoscopal astrology, 237
    imagery, 304
    mystery cults, 172, 176
    world, v–vi, xiv, 4–5, 16, 20,
    28–30, 32, 35, 40, 61–63,
    78–79, 122, 138, 154,
    156–57, 159, 161, 163, 165,
    167, 171, 178–80, 193, 195,
    210, 214, 243–44, 272, 279,
    292, 319
Gragg, Douglas, 75 n. 65, 77, 173–
    75, 179, 221–24, 227
grain, v, xiv, 72, 189, 196–97, 199,
    201–3, 205, 207, 209
grammar, 79, 236–38, 304–5
    of fate, 79, 304–5
grammaticus, 244
gratitude, xiii, 52, 152, 190
Great and Little Bear, 231
Great Church, 43
great man, 99, 111, 300, 308
    view of history, 99
Great Mother of the Gods, 61
great teacher, 301
Greek collectivity and identity, 87
Greek cult(s), 42, 185

culture, 4, 7–8, 19, 37, 51, 116,
    293
heroes, 40, 117
historians, 80, 83, 87–89
language, 4–5, 8, 16, 18, 51, 72,
    76, 86, 101, 293
mysteries, 24, 181–82, 219 n.
    61, 226
philosophers, 282
popular and philosophical
    conceptions, 80
popular religion, 196
society, 41, 116, 282
thought, 81, 111, 146 n. 19, 150,
    281, 293, 308
Greekness, 42, 54
Green, Henry A., 323 n. 3, 336
Green, Peter, 28
grids, 37, 253
Grice, Paul, 239, 242, 244
Griffiths, Gwyn J., 28, 105, 110, 135
    n. 58, 138, 190 n. 71, 193
grog, 326–27
Grote, George, 36 n. 4, 62, 301, 308
Gruen, Erich, 28, 119, 122
group cohesion, 172, 257
guilds of astrologers/astronomers,
    viii
Gunkel, Hermann, 103, 110
Guthrie, William Keith C., 102 n.
    35, 111, 133–35, 138

Hades, 212
Hagesias, 199
Halbwachs, Maurich, 86–88, 96, 129
    n. 30, 138
Halicarnassus, 80 n. 5, 84
hallucinogenic beverage, 219
Halpern, David, 81–82, 95
Ham, 326–27, 331, 333–34
Hanlon, Gregory, 312–13, 319
happiness, 14, 18, 46, 164, 185, 187,
    190–91, 202, 323–33
harmony of the universe, 268
Harnack, Adolf von, 276 n. 9, 279,
    282–83, 286–87, 293, 296,
    339, 347

INDEX   373

Hartley, Leslie. Poles, 236, 244
Hartog, François, 81–82, 84–86, 95
Hatch, Edwin, 282, 288, 294, 296
hearafter, 323
hearing gods, 16
heaven(s), 39–40, 56, 58, 80, 91, 105,
    135, 159, 164, 205, 269, 323,
    331, 334–35
Hebrew Bible, 51, 95
    charter epic, 317
    epic, 313, 315, 317
    scripture(s), 294, 312
Hecataeus, 84
Hegel, G. W. F., 131, 284
Heidegger, Martin, 89, 91 n.61, 95,
    350 n. 6
Hektor, 152
Helen, 53, 134, 138
heliocentric model, 38
heliodromus (Mithraic grade), 244
hellenic character of the Johannine
        usage, 295
    matrix of diverse social
        identities, 296
    spirit, 282
    thought, vi, xiv, 281–83, 285,
        287, 289, 291–95, 297
    Wisdom, 287
hellenistic, "heimarmenic" view of
        human existence, 271
    associations, 41, 51
    astronomy, 238
    circle of knowledge, 302
    clubs, 356
    commentators, 125
    communities, 113
    cosmopolitanism, 4, 192
    culture, x, 29, 37–38, 51, 60,
        77,100–101,129, 139, 265,
        289, 295, 297, 302, 305–6,
        338, 358
    East, 5, 7
    Empire, v, xiii, 64, 132, 259, 320
    Gnostic and Hermetic literature,
        269
    imperial culture, 289
    imperialism, 291
    Judaism(s), vi, 261, 265, 311

kings, 41, 43, 118
kinship groups, 42
kinships, 25, 42, 119 n. 35,
    122–23, 130, 136
monarchies, 7, 9
mysteries, 51, 54, 214, 218, 221,
    223 n. 87
mystery religion(s), 75, 131, 235,
    346, 348
paganism, 301
philosophy, 29, 37, 44–46, 60–
    61, 63, 267, 285, 339
political history, 99–100, 302
Religions, vii–viii, 2, 19 n. 4,
    28–29, 37 n. 8, 48–49,
    51–52, 61–63, 74 n. 61, 77,
    79, 96, 100–101, 104, 110,
    114, 130, 137, 139, 177 n. 28,
    179, 225, 228, 232, 272–73,
    300, 303 n. 17, 308, 324, 334
    n. 88, 337, 348
religiosity, ix, 51, 74, 265
religious formations, 304, 306
religious groups, 44, 55
religious syncretism, v, xiii, 19,
    97, 104–5, 108
rulers, 40
star-maps, 304
strategy of individual existence,
    339
transformations, 339
world, 2–3, 6, 11, 13, 15–16, 21,
    23–28, 32, 35, 38, 40–42, 46,
    51, 55, 61, 96, 101 n. 27, 105,
    108, 110, 121, 136, 145, 207,
    248–49, 275, 289, 338–39,
    357
oriental romances, 340
hellenization, 30, 42, 51, 54, 71–72,
    77, 101, 116, 281–82, 285,
    293, 295–96
hellenizing Jews, 71
helmet, 230
Henna, 197, 200–202, 204
Hepding, Hugo, 134, 138
Heracles, 40, 117,199
Heraclitus, 48, 88, 268, 295
Herberg, Will, 216–17, 227

374 INDEX

Hermes, 28, 32, 50, 52, 60, 62, 275–78
    Thoth, 60
Hermetist(s), 60, 352
Herodotus, 54, 60, 71, 80–88, 90–96, 101, 118, 177, 200, 203
Herder, Johan Gottfried, 211 n. 4, 214–15, 227, 229
heroes, 40, 117–18, 128, 158
hierarchical distributions of power, 86, 357
Hieron II, 200
Hierophant, 52, 55, 57–58, 186, 200, 204, 219
Hindu pundits, 97
Hipparchus, 38, 44
Hippocrates of Gela, 199
Hippolytus, 192, 197, 219
historians of religion, vii, x, 100, 171, 173–74, 178, 196, 198, 213, 225–26, 318
historical and ethnographic correlations, 247
    data, 174
historical anthropologist, 236, 242
    consciousness, v, xiii, 79–80, 82, 89, 94–95
    diffusion, 252
    periodization, 99–100, 300–301
    comparative methodology, 2
    inquiry, 211
historiographical issues, ix
    understandings
    of cultural contexts, 310
historiography, xi, 26, 28, 30–31, 81–82, 86 n. 40, 89, 92, 94, 96, 245, 300, 304
Hittite-Luwan weather deities, 275
Hittites, 315
Hivites, 315
Homer, 53, 155, 187, 277, 293
Homeric prayer of Achilles to Zeus, 151
Homo sapiens, x, 66–67, 70, 129, 211, 232, 247, 254, 313, 316
Honko, Lauri, 213, 215 n. 45, 227
humanism, 111, 338
Hume, David, 125

Hutton, Patrick H., 86–87, 96, 129 n. 30, 138, 299 n. 2, 302 n. 8, 308
Hyperides, 118

Iamblichus, 277, 353 n. 27
Iconium, 274, 278
ideal types, of social organization, viii
identity inclusion, 334
ideological apologetics of Afrocentrism, 295
    aspirations, 281
    representation, 255
ideologically constructed dichotomies, 216
illiterate, 213–15
imagined community (- ies), 69, 70, 73 nos. 52–55, 74, 76, 220, 252, 254, 256–58
imagined language, 236
imagistic modality (-ies), 173, 175–77, 221
    mode of religiosity, 74, 172, 220
    traditions, v, xiv, 30, 171–72, 178–80, 319
Immerwahr, Herny R., 80 n. 8, 82–84, 87–88, 90 n. 56, 92 n. 64, 96
immigrants, 41, 54, 177, 201–2
immigration, 37, 67
immortality, 133, 139, 190–91, 194, 214, 267, 359
imperial age, 5, 12, 16
    era, 4
    period, 17, 177, 242, 249, 254
    Rome, 83, 98, 128 n. 28, 301
    rule, 42, 73, 249
imputation of charisma, 292
incantations, 153, 164
inclusivistic values, 46
India, 36, 290, 341, 356, 360
individualism, 20–21, 129, 139, 288–90, 296, 323, 337–39
    romantic, 129
Indo-European languages, 252
indoctrination, 69

influence(s), x, 7, 10, 12–14, 16, 22, 36, 60–61, 80 n. 5, 92, 100–101, 103 n. 37, 119, 144, 160, 163, 184–85, 200–201, 214, 253, 266–67, 280–82, 288 n. 48, 293–96, 302, 304, 349
inheritance, 53, 56, 66, 135, 328–30, 335
initiation (s), viii, 20, 24–26, 45, 52–56, 58, 72, 107 n. 58, 74, 130, 132–135, 181, 185–87, 191, 195, 197, 214 n. 30, 218–20, 222–23, 225–26, 233, 235, 240–41, 244, 248 n.17, 255, 257, 259, 306, 346, 356
initiatory comprehension, vi, xiv, 236
Isocrates, 5, 52–53, 117–18
Isiac, societies, 136
  initiation, 219 n. 65
Isis, 14, 16–17, 19–20, 26–32, 51, 54–56, 62, 78, 97, 101 n. 23, 104, 106–7, 110–12, 135, 138, 152, 164, 176–77, 179, 180, 186, 190 n. 71, 193, 221, 224, 260, 346
  diaspora, 177
  Regina, 30, 97
  Queen of Nile, 164
  Universal Queen of Heaven, 164
Israelites, 80, 82–85, 309, 312–13, 315, 319, 326
Ister, river (Danube), 84
Isthmus, 202
Italian School, 2

Jackson, Bruce, 215, 227
Japheth, 326–27, 331, 333–34
Jebusites, 315
Jerusalem, 51, 83–85, 87–88, 96, 274, 293, 295–96, 317
  temple, 39
Jesus, 36, 39–40, 43, 47, 56, 135, 164, 250, 252–57, 283–84, 287, 292, 295, 315, 331–32, 339, 341–45
Jesus movement, 284, 287

Jevons, Frank B., 184, 193
Jewish "philosophies", 263, 265
  anthology of Mishnah, 3, 294, 300
  leaders, 274
  prophecy, 287
Jewish religious world, 293
Jewish revolts, against Seleucid, 51
Jewish tabernacle, 269
Jewish theological debate, 267
John, 39, 59 n. 53, 254, 274, 295, 340
  Cassian, 347
  Mark, 274
Jonas, Hans, 130 n. 37, 138, 270 n. 24, 272, 305 n. 30, 308, 325, 336, 339 n. 4, 345 n. 20, 347, 352–53, 357 nn. 41–42, 358
Joseph Barnabas, 274
Josephus, vi, xiv, 39, 263–73, 305
Joyce, James, 75, 77
Judaism(s), vi, 32, 51, 60, 63, 63, 77, 96, 139, 179, 228–29, 248, 254, 257, 261, 263 n. 2, 265–66, 272, 276, 283, 285–88, 297, 311, 317, 319, 336
Judeo-Christian faith, vi, xiv, 281
  thought, 281–82, 285
Julius, 41, 118, 284 n. 21
Jung, Carl Gustav, 143, 182, 193, 323 n. 2, 337
Jupiter (planet), 15, 17, 38
Jupiter Dolichenus, 17, 61
Justin Martyr, 285

Kabeiroi, 20, 184 n. 23, 193
Kallippos, 205
Kant, Immanuel, 37, 62
Kerényi, Carl, 182, 184, 186–87, 190 n. 71, 193
Keryx, 52
kin(s), 40, 42, 44, 49–50, 53–55, 58, 66–67, 69–72, 113, 116, 127 n. 23, 128, 130, 132, 134–36, 255, 313, 324–26, 328–29, 331–32, 335, 353

kin classification systems, 324
  fictive, 42, 55, 66–67, 116, 128, 132, 134 n. 50
kingship(s), v, viii, xi, xiii, 11 n. 3, 25, 29, 40, 71 n. 39, 73, 77, 85, 113–15, 118–19, 121–123, 127–30, 132, 136–37, 193, 290, 332, 334
  associations, 42
  groups, 10, 42, 66, 116, 128, 130, 331
  groups, biologically based, 66
  universe, 324–25, 327–28, 333
know oneself, 342, 344, 357
koinē, 5
Konig, Hans, 306, 308
Kore, 199, 204–5, 207, 209, 219
Kristensen, Brede W., 182–83, 194

Lampsacus, 46
Lane, Justin, 251, 258
Lane, Eugen N., 29
Lang, Andrew, 102, 111, 184 n. 25
Langanello, 199
Last Supper, 250
Late Antiquity, v, xiii, 4, 11, 14, 18–19, 22, 24, 26, 32, 37, 48–49, 58, 61, 63, 77, 122, 143, 146 n. 20, 149, 179, 192, 229, 297, 337, 347, 351 n. 12
late Bronze Age Middle-Eastern Bedouin tribes, 313
  Hellenistic anti-cosmism, 269
  Pleistocene Era, 311
law of antithesis, 146
Lawson, E. Thomas, xi, 78, 126 n. 11, 138, 160 n. 30, 166, 180, 207–8, 217 n. 52, 221–23, 227–28, 312 n. 9, 317 n. 23, 319
lêb, 309
Lechaeum, 202
legio V Macedonica, 234
legitimacy, 13, 53, 73, 279, 292, 327
Lemche, Nils Peter, 312–13, 319
leo (Mithraic, grade), 244
Leopold, Anita M., 173, 179

Lese-Mysteria, 346
Lesser Mysteries, 53
Leucius Charinus, 340
Libera, 40, 197
Libya, 64, 84, 202
literary mysteries, 346
  tradition, 257
literate urban populations, 215
litterator, 244
Livy, 80, 121, 200, 202, 222, 291
Lobeck, Christian A., 181–83, 185–86, 194
Logos, 48, 60, 268, 295
Lord of the Underworld, 196, 204
Lorenz, Konrad, 125, 138
Lucian of Samosata, 265
Lucius, 105–7, 135, 164, 186, 203, 339
  Calpurnius, 203
Lycaonia, 274, 276
Lucretius, 46–47
Lycurgus, 16, 205
Luke, 36, 39, 43, 62, 135, 153, 251, 255, 275–76, 279–80, 315, 331, 334–35, 354
Lystra, vi, xiv, 274–78

Maccabeean revolts, 71
Maccabees, 51, 71, 121
Macedonia, 8, 29, 105
Machiavellian Intelligence Hypothesis, 114, 123
Mack, Burton, 43 n. 24, 47 n. 34, 63, 129 n. 33, 138, 291, 297
MacRae, George, 325–26, 329, 336
Macrobius, 152
macrocosm, 14
Magi, from the East, 39
Magic, xv, 28, 45, 153, 157–58, 161–62, 164–67
magical formulae, 3, 294, 300
  incantation, 161, 164
  papyrus, 231
magician(s), 17, 92 n. 65
Maine, Henry S., 328–29, 336
Mainz cup, 232–33
malek (king), 120

INDEX   377

Malina, Bruce, J., 223 n. 88, 227,
    306–8, 324, 329 n. 47,
    333–36
Malta, 275
Mandane, 90
Mani, 357
Manichaean communities, 19, 21
    mission, 73 n. 54, 77, 136 n. 62,
    139
    gnostic tradition, 59
Manichaeism, 73, 76
Mansfeld, Jörg, 268, 272
Marathon, 189
Marcion, 294, 305
Marcus Aurelius, 48–49, 57, 192 n.
    79, 307
Mark, 39–40, 43, 63, 153, 158, 251,
    255, 274, 315, 331, 334–35,
    339
Mars, 152
Mars (planet), 15, 38
Martin, Luther H., viii n. 4, ix nos
    5–6, xi, xiii, xiv–xv, 2–3, 10–
    11, 19, 23, 29, 30, 32, 37 n.8,
    61 n. 59, 63, 66 n. 11, 67 nn.
    17–18, 69 n. 29, 70–79, 92
    n. 67, 95–96, 113 n. 2, 119
    n. 37, 120 n. 39, 122, 129–30,
    133 n. 46, 136 nn. 60–62,
    138–39, 147 nn. 22–23, 150,
    156, 158–59, 161 n. 31, 164,
    166, 171–73, 175–80, 182,
    197 n. 6, 207–8, 214 n. 30,
    219 n. 61, 221 n. 73, 223–25,
    227–28, 231–33, 235, 241
    nn. 49–50, 243–44, 254 n.
    52, 256 n. 58, 259, 284 n. 17,
    289–90, 293–94, 297, 303–4,
    308, 313–14, 317 nn. 24–25,
    319–20, 323 n. 2, 334 n. 88,
    337–38, 347–48, 354–56,
    358–59
Marx, Karl, 129, 323
Mathias, 344
matrilineally, 325
McMullen, Ramsey, 152, 155
McNeill, William, 69, 78

Mediterranean, 16, 24, 28, 31,
    57, 84–85, 132, 202, 235,
    258–59, 288, 301 n. 7, 303 n.
    15, 307
Mediterranean agrarian cycle, 211
    goddesses, 97
    world, xi, 28, 146, 233, 253, 307
    antiquity, 288
    religion(s), vii, 28
memes, 127
memories of the past, 316
memory, 28–29, 74, 79, 82, 88–89,
    174 n.15, 178, 180, 217, 296,
    309, 317
memory, collective, 86–88, 93,
    95–96, 129, 138
    constitutive, 94
    systems, 175 n. 21, 218, 220
    episodic, 220
    external, 244
    flashbulb, 220 n. 68, 227
    human, 171, 175, 317
    long-term, 237
    semantic, 172, 175
    systems of, 171, 218, 220
Menelao(u)s, 53, 134
Mensching, Gustav, 214, 220–21,
    228
mental flexibility, 13
    functions, 309, 311
    horizons of an age, 299
    mechanisms, ix, 74, 217
    output, 310–11
Merkelbach, Reinhold, 18, 30, 73 n.
    57, 78, 105 n. 51, 107 n. 58,
    111, 135 n. 59, 139, 346, 348
merchants, 17, 251
Mercury (planet), 15, 38
Mercury (Hermes), 275–76
Meroe, 105
Mesogeia plains, 189
Messos, 59
meta-reflections, 246
metaphors, 23, 242
metaphysical devolution, 352
metaphysical legitimation, 125
metaphysical One, 355–56
microcosm, 14

378 INDEX

Middle Eastern antiquity, 317
Midianites, 315
miles (Mithraic grade), vi, xiv, 230–31, 234
military history, 247–48
milites, vi, xiv, 230, 232, 234
Mill, John Stuart, 357, 359
Milton, John, 196–97, 208
mind(s), vi, viii–xi, xv, 23, 28–31, 47, 62, 66, 68–71, 76, 81, 126, 138, 145, 164, 166, 174, 180, 215, 218 n. 59, 228, 243 n. 63, 244, 255, 258, 287, 294, 309, 310–17, 319–20, 336, 349, 350, 358
minimally counterintuitive manifestations, 224
Mirthless Rock, 212
Mithraea /*Mithraia*, 20, 57–58, 250, 254
mithraic association, 254
　cells, 57, 173, 232–33, 256
　idiom, 243–44
　imagery, 238, 242
　images, 232, 234
　initiation, 58, 241, 244, 306
　initiatory context, 233
　initiatory grade, 230
　monuments, 231
　mysteries, 63, 191, 218, 302, 308
　network, 233–34, 253
　sites, 302
　Soldier, 230
　star-talk communication, 244
Mithraism, 24, 28, 57–58, 73, 120, 134, 176, 179, 181 n. 3, 193, 196–97 n. 5, 228, 234, 237–38, 241–44, 248, 258, 302, 304, 307
Mithraism, Roman, 57, 92 n. 67, 96, 249–50, 308
Mithras Liturgy, 231
model of hierarchical social stratification, 290
modern ethnographic fieldwork, 210
　kinship analysis, 329

modes of religiosity, 74 n. 59, 78, 166, 171–76, 178–80, 219–20, 223, 229, 255 n. 57, 260, 320
modes of religious transmission, 219
Momigliano, Arnaldo, 81, 83 n.22, 89, 96
monarchs, 10, 117
monotheism(s), 24, 102 n. 35, 120, 122, 152, 281
monotheistic theologies, 281
　trend, 120
moon (planet), 15, 38, 40, 91, 106
Moore, George Foot, 264, 266–67, 269 n. 19, 271–72
Muilenburg, James, 83 nn. 21–23, 87, 89 n.54, 95–96
multidimensionality, 2
mundane fortune, x
Murdock, George Peter, 68, 78
mutual altruism, 72, 314
mutual-knowledge hypothesis, 239
Mylonas, George E., 30, 52 n. 45, 63, 72 n. 47, 78, 184, 187 n. 43, 189–92, 194, 196–97, 208, 212 n. 13, 219 nn. 60; 63; 65, 224–26
Myrmidons, 152
mysteries, v, vii, xi, xiv, 20, 24, 26–27, 30, 51, 52–54, 57, 62–63, 78, 100 n. 18, 112, 132–35, 139, 169, 176–79, 181–89, 191–94, 196, 198, 200, 206, 208, 211–16, 218–21, 222–29, 233, 241, 244, 248, 273, 304 n. 21, 307–8, 346
　of Demeter, xi, xiv, 52, 54, 56, 72, 132, 210–12, 221, 224
　of Glycon, 56
　of Isis, 54–56
　of Mithras, 57, 302
mysterious religious knowledge, 177
mystery cults, vii, x, 2, 20, 25–26, 55, 113, 130–34, 137, 172, 176, 187–88 n. 47, 221, 248, 256, 290, 305, 325 n.17, 335, 346
　formula, 186

initiation, 134 n. 50, 181, 185–86, 195, 235
traditions, 3, 177, 256, 294, 300
mystic beatitude, 20
mysticism, 284, 290
myth(s), 9, 25, 27, 30, 40–43, 47 n. 34, 53 n. 47, 55, 63, 87, 102 n. 34, 110–11, 117–18, 123, 130, 147, 150, 183, 185, 188, 193–94, 196, 201, 211–13, 218–19, 226–28, 232 n. 4, 252, 258, 273, 275 n. 6, 288 n. 44, 291 n. 65, 297, 314, 319, 323–25, 328 n. 31, 333–34, 336, 349–50, 352, 356–57
Myth and Ritual School, 185
myth, Euhemeristic, 118
mythological (or theological) discourse, 89
mythological metaphysics, 323
mythology, 61, 63, 68 n. 22, 78, 117, 182, 187, 193 231, 277, 284, 307, 337, 358
mythology, Greek, 41
myths of cosmogonic fall, 130
Mytilene, 46

Nabonidus, 83
Nag Hammadi Codex, 286, 325, 343
  gnostic library, 303
  texts, 303
nationalism, 69, 72, 76, 215, 229, 258
natural communities, 214
  order, 39, 48, 90, 304
  sciences, 318
naturalistic tradition, 44, 125
nature, human, 86 n. 34, 95, 126–27, 140, 145, 259, 312, 319–20, 357
Naxos, 198
Neapolis, 199
Nebuchadnezzar, 83, 92 n. 65
Necessity, 14, 116, 270
neo-Darwinian theorists, 126
Neoplatonist, 49–50, 96

neocortex volume, 247
Neolithic Mesopotamian villages, 247
network affiliation, 257
  nodes, 253
  of mythocosmological relations, 188
  of obligations and services, 342
network(s), 27, 72–73, 234, 235, 251–54, 257–60, 335
  of trade, 72
  neural, 253
New Testament, xiv, 63, 103 n. 37, 110, 122, 251, 279, 282, 293–94, 296–97, 300 n. 3, 303, 307–8, 312, 324 n. 11, 334 n. 87, 336, 347–48
  scholars, vii, 303, 312
Nicene Creed, 282
Nicotheus, 59
Nietzsche, Friedrich, 357
Nigidius Figulus, 49
Nile, 26, 84, 164
Nilsson, Martin P., 27, 40–42, 51 n. 43, 53 n. 47, 63, 99 n. 14, 102 n. 35, 111, 116–17, 123, 182, 186–87, 194, 196 n. 4, 208, 210–16, 218, 228
Noah, 88, 326–27, 332–34
Nock, Arthur Darby, 30, 44 n. 25, 63, 107 n. 59, 111, 118–19, 123, 132 n. 41, 139, 188 n. 52, 194, 216 n. 46, 223, 228, 277 n. 11, 280
nocturnal rites, 225
nomos, 37
Norenzayan, Ara, 65, 76, 224 n. 73, 226
North American Association for the Study of Religion, 318
northern Pole, 231–32
Nous, 350
numinous, 350

oaths, 205
Octavian Augustus, 1, 10, 16
Oden, Robert A., 324, 337

380 INDEX

oecumene, 4–6, 16
Olympia, 87
Olympian pantheon, 15
Olympians, 190
Olympic games, 146
Olympus, 198
oneiromancy, 145
oneiromantic knowledge, 146, 149
    resemblances, 146
    signs, 147
    taxonomy, 3, 294, 300
orgia, Dionysian, 338
Orwell, George, 94
Origen, 58 n. 52, 242, 285–86
Ovid, 184, 197 n. 9, 201, 275–76, 278, 295
Orphism, 134
orthodox "doctrines", 175
orthodoxy, 55, 103, 215, 296, 317
Osiris, 107 n.58, 135, 164, 190 n. 71, 193
Ostia, vi, xiv, 17, 25, 230, 250 n. 24, 259
Otto, Rudolf, 350, 350
Otto, Walter F., 194

Pachis, Panayotis, v, x, xiii–xiv, 1, 30, 69 n. 29, 76–78, 175–76, 178–80, 259, 319–20
Paganism, 24, 54, 97–98, 100, 103, 109–10, 137, 155, 183 n. 18, 194, 301, 304
Palestinian Jesus groups, 254, 257
Palmer, Robert B., 182, 194
Pamphylia, 274
Panaetius of Rhodes, 13
Panchaea, 13
Panaetius of Rhodes, 13
Passover meal, 293
pater (Mithraic grade), 58, 244, 254
paternal powers, 330
patriarchal cultural system, 333
patrilineal ascendants, 328
patrilineal systems, 326
Paul, vi, xiv, 40, 42–43, 53, 92, 95, 134, 177, 255–57, 270, 272, 274–80, 283, 287, 290 n. 59, 293–94, 304, 308, 329, 333 n. 82, 335, 337, 356 n. 39
Pauline Christianity, 253
    congregations, 287
    religion, 306
    traditions, 257
Pausanias, 17, 52, 189 n. 64, 199, 201 n. 36, 346
Peace, peace, 12–13, 64, 164, 248 n. 17, 260
peasant(s), 213, 215–16, 282
Pentecost, 284
Pindar, 114, 198–200
Perizzites, 315
Persephone, 187 n. 46, 188–90, 195–201, 203–7, 209, 211
Persephone's abduction, 196
Persia, 40, 57, 73, 82, 85, 117–18
Persian control, 203
    Empire, 72, 82–83
    hegemony, 35, 98, 338
Peter, 257
petition of the suppliant, 151
Pharisaic congregations, 287
Pharisees, 251, 263–68, 273, 286
Philemon, 275–76, 278–79
Philip II, 114
Phillips, C. Robert, 183–84, 194, 223, 228
Philocrates, 294
philosophical borrowings, 268
    discussions of fate, 268
    groups, 290
    schools, 6, 12, 14, 43, 45–46, 50, 113, 263 n. 2
    theology, 281
    thought, 357
    values, 339
philosophy of religion, 131, 283–84
Phrygia(n), 61, 134, 230, 275
physical violence, 219
pietistic practices, 130
piety, 89–90, 93, 102, 130, 154, 183 n. 19, 225, 269, 285, 305, 338
    popular, 93, 269
Piraeus, 7
pirates, Cilician, 57

Plato, 13, 45–46, 49, 53, 59, 80, 89,
  91, 95, 133–34, 138, 145,
  154, 158, 189, 201 n. 36,
  276–79, 339–40, 353–56,
  358, 360
Plato's Good, 46
platonic Academy, 45
  essentialism, 120
  philosophy, 352, 360
  tradition, 10, 44
  transcendentalism, 59
Platonism, 46, 49, 58, 60, 62, 133,
  295, 358
Platonism, Hellenistic, 49–50, 61
Platonopolis, 50, 291, 356
Pliny the Elder, 3, 39, 300
Plotinian
  discourse, 350
  society, 356
Plotinus, vi, viii, xi, xv, 50, 59–60,
  120, 122, 133, 139, 290–92,
  297, 349–59
Plouton, 188, 190, 211
pluralism, 2
Plutarch, 8, 19, 28, 40 n. 14, 42,
  55, 57, 70, 80, 104, 108,
  111, 117–18, 135, 164, 183,
  189–90, 193, 205, 219, 224,
  254, 268, 293
poleis, 116, 118
Polybius, 83, 249
polytheistic systems, 152
Ponza, 231
Porphyry, 50, 58–59, 290–91, 349–
  51, 356
Posidonius, 13–14, 80, 83
possibilities of thought, 3–4, 299
post-Renaissance views of religion,
  223
    Temple Judaism, 243
posthumous salvation, 20
power(s), v-vi, viii, xi, xiii, xv, 6,
  9–13, 16–18, 23, 26, 29, 31,
  40–46, 50, 62, 64–66, 70–71,
  73–78, 83–85, 92, 99–100,
  104–6, 108, 113–23, 128–31,
  133 n. 46, 135–37, 139, 145,
  151, 156, 163, 183 n. 19,
  187–88 n. 47, 188 n. 52, 189,
    192, 194, 197, 199, 206–8,
    214, 234, 248, 253, 258, 263–
    64, 268, 270, 281, 290–92,
    296–97, 301–2, 316, 326 n.
    23, 330, 332, 334–35, 339,
    349, 351–52, 353, 355–59
  grids, 253
  of imperial kingship, 290
practical religion, 266
practice of consanguineous
    marriages, 331
Praetorian Guard, 233
prayer(s), v, xiv, 42 n. 22, 117, 135,
    151–67, 265
prayer, Christian, 153
prayer, Jewish, 153, 157
pre-Constantinian Christian
    practices and images, 293
preindustrial society, 1
preparatory period of fasting, 219
    ritual, 219
Price, Simon. R. F., 30–31, 119, 123,
    144 n. 9, 150, 183 n. 19,
    187–89, 194, 206, 208, 259,
    268
prodigies, 176
Prolemy I Soter of Egypt, 55, 108
prooush, 343
propaganda, 3, 9, 17, 28, 272, 346
  Jewish anti-Seleucid, 72
  political, 9, 294, 300
Proserpina, 197, 202 n. 40
Prostration, 153
Protestant ethic, 287 n. 43, 289, 298
  folk, 215
  reformers, 289
  Syncretists, 103
Providence, xiv, 14, 60, 122, 268 n.
    16, 271–73
Psyche, 133–34, 139, 149, 171 n.
    2, 175 n. 22, 179,183 n. 16,
    194, 356 n.19, 359
psychoanalytic theory, 149
ptolemaic architecture of the
    cosmos, 303
  cosmological map, 49

ptolemaic architecture of the cosmos (*continued*)
  cosmology, vii, ix, 6, 15, 38, 99 n. 14, 108, 304
  Egypt, 10, 29
Ptolemais, 9
Ptolemy I Soter (Savior) of Egypt, 9–10, 55
Publius Mucius, 203
Punic wars, 222
Puteoli, 17
Pythagoras, 43, 45–46, 49–50, 57
Pythagoreanism, 45, 49, 60, 227

Q, 43, 63, 293
Quintus, 90, 145

racial theology, 333
Ranke, Leopold von, 94, 182
rebirth, 135, 166, 339
  initiatory, 56
redemption, 61, 85, 346
Redfield, Robert, 103 n. 42, 111, 213, 228
Reformation, 173, 215, 283, 287–89, 292, 305
Reitzenstein, Richard, 345–46, 348
religions of loyalty, 73
religionsgeschichtliche Schule, 2, 103
Religionswissenschaft, 77, 138, 194, 225, 228, 235, 297
religious and social clubs, 290
  associations, 42–43, 45, 53, 248
  communities, 113, 129–31, 139
  cults, 16, 55, 67, 258, 294
  discourse, 105, 108, 242
  diversity, 173
  formations, vii–viii, 136–37, 303–4, 306
  institution, 220
  knowledge, 92 n. 68, 96, 171–72, 175, 177, 228, 301, 303, 307, 317
  periodization, 301–2
  propaganda, 3, 272, 294, 300
  ritual, 154, 241, 245
  secrets, 183
  symbol, 183
  thought, ix–x, 76, 165, 226, 304–5, 319
  traditions, 43, 48, 50, 73, 174, 217, 283
  transformations, 26, 137 n. 64, 139, 319
    codification, 172
    transmission, 73, 176, 180, 219, 229, 260, 320
repetition, pedagogical, 172
repetitive reinforcement of beliefs, 220
  ritual, 220
reproductive strategies, 315
republican, era, 175–76
  period, 176, 222
  Rome, 175, 301
  times, 224
res gestae, 87, 211, 226
Réville, Jean, 102–3, 111
ritual(s), x, 16, 18, 20, 22, 31, 53, 74–76, 78, 87–88, 96, 102 n. 34, 107 n.65, 110, 111, 119, 123, 125, 136, 139, 154, 160 n. 30, 166, 171–76, 180, 183 n. 19, 185–86, 187–88 n. 47, 188–89, 191–94, 197, 206 n. 67, 208, 213, 218–24, 226, 228, 235, 241, 244–45, 256–57, 259, 273, 293, 317, 319, 325, 346
ritual commemorations, 87
  orthopraxy, 175, 317
  practice(s), 88, 175, 213, 257, 317
rituals of power, 119
Rohde, Erwin, 72 n. 46, 78, 133–35, 139, 183, 194, 356 n. 19, 359
roman aristocracy, 290, 356
  army, 18, 234–35, 248–49
Roman Catholicism, 103, 289
  conception of the family, 328
  emperors, 11, 16, 102, 192 n. 79, 224
  Empire, 1, 8, 10, 12, 17, 20, 24, 26–27, 30, 32, 36, 66,

INDEX   383

77, 96, 110, 114, 120, 156,
  173–74, 188, 192, 194, 221,
  227–28, 234, 236, 244, 246,
  249, 254, 257, 259, 290,
  328–29, 331–32, 337
legions, 234, 249
religion, 31–32, 65 n. 5, 77–78,
  102, 114 n. 8, 123, 166, 174–
  75, 178–79, 184, 222–24,
  227, 317
religion, official, 175, 317
senate, 179, 224, 291
state, 18, 20, 73, 177, 204
values, 224
Romanness, 175, 224 n. 75
romantic "essentialism", 182
  historiography, 300
  secrecy theory, 184
  theory of the Mysteries, 181
Rome, xiii, 11, 17–18, 24, 26, 28,
  36–37, 40, 45, 49, 54, 57–59,
  61, 63, 73, 83, 92 n. 67, 95,
  98, 111, 120–21, 128 n. 28,
  138, 176, 180, 204, 208,
  222–26, 229–30, 258–59,
  271, 275 n.7, 279, 291–92,
  301–2, 320, 330, 337
rural life, 191–92

Said, Edward, 35, 63
Seneca the Younger, 48
S(e)arapis, Sarapis, 14, 30, 32, 16–
  17, 20, 55, 108, 180
Sabbath, 317
sacred herald, 52
  rites, 196, 352
sacrifice(s), 54, 153, 158, 205, 222,
  265, 275, 278, 279
sacrilege, 204
Sadducees, Essenes , 263–66, 268,
  272, 286
Sakla, 326, 331–32, 334
Sakla/Cain, 327
Salvation, 9, 20, 22, 27, 60–61, 63,
  188, 283, 286, 308
Samter, Ernst, 133–34, 139

San Clemente in Rome, Mithraeum,
  58
Sandys, John E., 182–83, 194
sarcena, 230–31
Satan, 316
satirization, 265
Saturn (planet), 15, 38
Saussure, Ferdinand de, 238, 245
Schelling, Friedrich, 182
Schluchter, Wolfgang, 283–88, 290
  n. 59, 297
Schottroff, Luise, 326–27, 337
science of astronomy and astrology,
  269
scientific paradigm, 318
  / astronomical universalism, 51
scorpion (Mithraic cult), 58
Scylla and Charybdis, 201
Scythians, 85
Second Sophistic, 4, 18
secret sayings, 344
selective strategies, 219
Selene, 153–54
Seleucid rule, 71, 291
self-knowledge, vi, xv, 154, 338–45,
  347, 354, 359
Selloi, 151
Senate, 121, 176, 179, 224, 291
sensory existence, 290, 355
  information, 316
  pageantry, 220, 222
sensuous world, 339
separation, 7, 45, 88, 120, 189,
  233–34, 253, 258
Septuagint (LXX), 51, 294
Sermon on the Mount, 282
Seth, 59, 107 n. 58, 130, 325–33,
  335–37
Sethian gnostic tradition, 59
Sethian Gnosticism, 325, 337
Sethite kinship, 332
Sethites, 326, 328, 333–35
seven grades
  of Mithraic initiation, 58
  of planetary spheres, 22, 303
sexual and political activities of this
  world, 344

sexuality, 61 n. 58, 62, 64 n.2, 76, 115 n. 12, 122, 148, 340 n. 7, 342, 347
Sfameni Gasparro Giulia, 30, 32
Shannon, Claude, 238, 245
shēre, 326
sheaf of wheat, 197
Shem, 326–27, 333
Showerman, Grant, 98, 104, 109–10, 137
Sibylline Books, 203
Sicel deities, 200
Sicilian
    cult, 198–200, 204–6, 209
    wheat, 202
Sicily, 189 n. 60, 197–206, 208, 221
Sicily's agrarian economy, 198
signs of the zodiac, 58, 269
six degrees of separation, 253, 258
Smail, Daniel Lord, 252–53, 259, 312–13, 320
"small world" model, 252–53
Smith, Jonathan Z., 2, 22, 25, 30, 32, 43 n. 24, 63, 82 n. 19, 85–88, 96, 100 n. 19, 111, 129, 139, 192 n. 81, 194, 210, 215, 229, 245, 282, 297, 305 n. 29, 308
Smith, William Robertson, 113, 123, 127, 139, 184 n. 25
Snyder, Graydon, 250–51, 259, 292–93, 297, 312 n. 8, 320
social alliances, 248
    aspects, 37
    clubs, 41, 67, 290
    cognition, 313
    cohesion, 248 n. 17, 331, 334
    consciousness, 290
    dominance, 114
    formations, vi, viii, ix, xiv, 137, 246–49, 251, 255–56, 288, 291
    groupings, 40, 67
    groups, viii, 20–21, 44, 59, 122, 133, 247, 251, 257, 290–91, 312, 315
    history, 281, 301, 303
    immobility, 334
    inventions, 324
    mapping, 87
    nature, 129
    network(s), 251–53, 258, 334
    organization, viii, 10, 40–42, 60, 66, 75, 113–14, 127–30, 136, 328 n. 32, 332, 337
    phenomenon, 129
    relationships, 37, 66, 128, 281, 345, 355
    scientific categories of alienation or marginality, 324
    state, 331, 333
    stratification, 290, 356
    structure, 329
    theory, 129, 246–47, 259, 297
    theory of religion, 129
    scientific typologies, 174
    society, 1, 4, 12, 18–19, 21, 27–28, 31, 41, 43, 50, 62, 68, 78, 86, 88, 90, 93, 96, 113, 115–16, 124 n. 1, 127–28, 130, 132, 139, 146, 163, 166, 180–81, 196 n.1, 205, 215, 227, 245–46, 251, 258–59, 282, 289, 294, 297, 307, 314, 318–19, 324–25, 328–29, 331 n. 70, 333, 336, 338, 347–48, 356, 358
Society for the Scientific Study of Religion, 318
Society of Biblical Literature (SBL), 246
socio-historical methodology, 2
sociobiology, 125–26
sociology
    of context, 323
    of individualism, general, 323
Socrates, 5, 44, 49, 105, 145, 340, 342
Socratic obligation, 342
solidarity-based groups, 67
Solon, 132, 189
Sophia, 43
soul's descent, 352
soul's return, 50, 352–53
Sparta, 114, 121, 271
special patient rituals, 222–23

Sperber, Dan, 68–69, 78, 126 n.11, 139, 237–42, 245, 310 n. 5, 320
spontaneous exegetical reflections, 223
stable network, 253
star-map(s), 58, 304
star-talk, 30–31, 236–38, 240–44
Stark, Rodney, 157 n. 8, 166, 233 n. 6, 235, 284 n. 22, 297, 315–16, 320
Starr, Chester, 310, 320
Stausberg, Michael, 171, 178, 180
Stewart, Potter, 350, 359
Stiller, James, 247 n. 9, 251, 253, 259
Stoa, 48, 267 n. 13, 273
Stoic
    pantheistic allegory, 101
    philosophical tradition, 267
    phraseology, 267
    School, 267
    thought, 268, 272
    traditions, 46, 342, 345
Stoics, 6, 13–14, 29, 46–49, 63, 80, 268, 295, 339, 354
Stowers, Stanley K., xiv, 246–47, 251, 256, 259
Strangelovean diagnosis, 291, 355
study
    of folk religions, v, xiv, 179, 210
    of religion(s), v, x, xiii-xiv, 23, 29–30, 32, 63, 77–78, 113 n. 1, 122–27, 129, 131, 133, 135, 137–38, 143, 156–57, 166, 171, 177, 180, 225–26, 228–29, 245, 259–60, 297, 318
Stroumsa, Gedaliahu, A., 139, 325–29, 332–34, 337
sub-groups, 248
successors, 4, 6, 8–9, 11, 16, 36–37, 40–41, 43, 54
sui generis definitions, of religion, 124
Sumeria, 313
Sumerian myth, 323–33
    of the golden age, 323
    prototype, 333

sun, 15, 24, 38, 40, 159, 244
superhuman
    acts, 317
    agency, 162, 225–26
    agents, 154, 164, 314, 316
    being(s), 39, 223, 275
    power, 23, 44, 50, 119 n. 38, 129, 151, 156, 163
supernatural (or metaphysical) basis for the study of religion, 124
supraindividual concepts, 68
surveyor of otherness, 85
Symbolists, 182
symbols, 97, 146 n. 20, 230, 237–39, 242, 293
sympathy, 20, 107
    /antipathy, 104, 106 ,108
    cosmic, 14
synagogue(s), 28, 274
syncretism(s), v, xiii, 2, 19, 25, 62, 69, 78, 97, 101–5, 107–11, 123, 137–38, 152, 157, 173, 179, 293, 348
syncretistic
    Catholic elite, 215
    character, of the Hellenistic world, 3
    formations, 137
Synesius, 219
Synoptic Gospels, 250, 293
Syracusan
    "Great Oath", 205
    colonization, 200
    tradition, 199
Syracuse, 189 n. 60, 198–202, 204
Syria, 107 n. 62, 111, 202, 340 n. 8
Syrian
    Encratitic technology of self, 347
    goddess, 17, 61, 107, 111
    Jupiter, 61
    peasants, 282
    Thomas tradition, vi, xv, 354, 359
    tradition, 338

Talmudic Judaism, 286
Taurian peninsula, 202

taurobolium, 224
tauroctony, 31, 58, 179, 224, 228, 254
technologies of the Self, vi, xv, 61, 338, 347, 359
Taft, Michael, 215, 227
teleology, 268
Telesterion of Eleusis,the, 20, 53, 212
Telines, 200, 204
Telos, 200
Ten Commandments, 314
Terence, 210
Tertullian, 135, 218, 286, 295
Thales, 43, 46
Themistius, 218–19
Theodotus, Valentinian Gnostic, 59–60, 339
Theodosius, vii, 1, 36, 92 n. 67, 100, 120, 136
  Theodosius's religious legislation, 302
theory of mind, 255
Theon of Smyrna, 185
Theophrastus, 44, 208 n. 48
Thesmophoria, 213
Thomas tradition, vi, xv, 340–41, 343, 345, 347, 354, 359
Thoms, William, 215, 229
Thoth, 60
Thrace, 29, 202
three degrees of separation, 253
three-storied cosmic image of antiquity, 303
Thucydides, 41–42, 72, 80 n. 8, 89, 94–95, 183, 193, 198–99, 202–3, 206 n. 68, 208
Tiberius Gracchus, 203
time(s), viii, 1–2, 5–11, 13–22, 24, 43, 45–46, 49, 66, 71–73, 78, 80–81, 83 n. 22, 85–86, 88–96, 98, 103, 106, 113, 116–19, 126, 128, 131–32, 137, 147–48, 151–52, 157, 161–62, 175, 183–84, 187, 190, 208, 217, 222, 224, 229, 251, 259, 264–65, 269–70, 272, 274, 277, 284, 286, 288, 290, 294, 299, 301, 303, 306, 310–11, 315–18, 323, 328–29, 333, 342–43, 350, 357
time-scale, 303
Timoleon, 199, 203, 205
Timotheus, 55
Tocqueville, Alexis de, 67
Tomasello, Michael, 239–40, 242–43, 245
Torah, 92, 265–266, 270–72
traders, Egyptian, 177
trajectories, historical, 174
transmission, 75, 127, 171–73, 175–76, 180, 215, 218–20, 229, 260, 316–17, 320, 328, 332–33
  of beliefs, 220, 226
  of knowledge, 171
  of orthropraxy, 175
  of religious knowledge, 175, 317
tree model, 252
Triptolemos, 190–91, 197, 212
Troeltsch, Ernst, 131, 139, 283–85, 288–91, 297
Turcan, Robert, 32, 222 n. 79, 224 n. 95–96, 229
twelve kingdoms, 332–33
twelve kingdoms of Gentiles, 326–27
twelve months, 269
twelve stones of the Priests' breastplate, 269
Tychē, 13–15, 19

U.S. Supreme Court Justice, 350
underworld, 107 n. 60, 153, 196, 204, 211, 219
universal queen of heaven, 56, 164 soul, 352, 354
universalism, 48–49, 51, 84, 105, 288
Unnik, W. C. van, 265, 273
unreason, 165, 350
uranometry, 238
urban centers, 5, 8–9
utility, of the modes theory, 174
utopian vision, 50, 356

utopianism, 192

Valentinian, 59, 255, 339, 352
Valentinian church, 255
Van Seters, John, 81, 86 n. 30, 96
Varro, 250
Vegetius, 249
Venus (planet), 15, 38
Venus, 56, 107 n. 60, 135
Vermaseren, Maarten J., 2, 25, 29, 272–73
Vernant, Jean-Pierre, 93, 96, 279
Verschmelzung, 101
vestments of the High Priest, 269
Vico, Giambattista, 35, 63, 69, 78
victory, 1, 4, 12, 88, 152, 204
Victory, 13
virginity, 107 n. 60, 148
Vitruvius, 250

Wächter, Ludwig, 265–68, 273
wandering(s), 11, 30, 55, 201, 218, 275, 338
wandering priests, 12
Weber, Max, 32, 129, 131, 281, 283–92, 296–98, 323, 356 n. 35, 360
weak social exchanges, 254
Wealth,wealth, 13–14, 114, 128, 159, 188, 203, 211, 250–51
Wells, Herbert George, 94
Wells, Joseph, 80 n. 5, 95
Weltanschauung, 37
Western canonical tradition, 340
wheat, 189, 192, 197, 201–3
Whitehouse, Harvey, 32, 67, 71 n. 41, 73–74, 76–78, 162 n. 43, 166, 171–80, 219–221, 223–25, 227, 229, 255 n. 57, 260, 317 n. 23, 320
Wilamowitz-Moellendorff, Ulrich von, 182
William of Baskerville, 149
Wilson, Brian C., xi, 78, 166, 180, 211 n. 4, 214–15, 228

Wilson, Deidre, 238–42, 238–39, 240–42, 245
Wilson, Edward O., 125–27, 140
Wilson, David Slone, 313 n. 12, 319
Wilson, Robert A., 122–23, 178
Wilson, Robert McLachlan, 31, 63, 337, 347–48
Wilson, Stephen G., 29, 42, 62–63, 78, 116, 122, 132, 138, 258
Wilson, William A., 229
Wolf, Eric, 115, 123
women, 42, 46, 62, 107 n. 60, 121, 179, 201, 213, 315, 323, 332–33, 343

Xerxes, 85

Zeno of Citium, 6, 47
Zeitgeist, 4
Zeus, 30, 42, 48, 112, 151–52, 158, 166, 188, 190, 198, 265, 268, 275–79
  Ammon, 118
  Sarapis, 30
  Xenios, 278
Zoroaster, 59
Zosimos of Panopolis, 3, 300
Zostrianus, 59

B. Ancient Greek Words

Ἀγαθὴ Τύχη, 106
ἀγάπη, 250–51
ἀγέλαστος πέτρα, 212
ἀθάνατοι θεοί, 190
ἀθάνατος, 191
αἴτιον, 213
ἀμέριμνος, 342
ἀνάδεσις, 185
ἀνάθεμα ἔστω, 255
ἀνάκειμαι, 250
ἀναπαύειν, 342
ἀνάπαυσις, 342
ἄνω, 354
ἄπολις, 11

ἀρχή, 353
ἀσεβησάντων, 277
ἄφροντις, 342

βίος, 343
βλασφημία, 154

γεννήματα, 353
γεννῆται, 52–53
γεννητὴς τῶν θεῶν, 134
γένος, 52–53, 58, 353 n. 25
γένους, 353
γνῶθι σαυτόν, 21, 347, 353
γνῶθι τοὺς ἄλλους, 21
γνῶναι, 342
γνῶσις, 327–328, 342, 345
γονέων, 353

δεικνύμενα, 181, 185, 187
δεῖξεν, 187
δῆμοι, 10, 116
δρᾶμα μυστικόν, 185
δρησμοσύνην, 186
δρώμενα, 181, 185–87

ἑαυτοῦ ἔχω ἐν μανίᾳ, 351
ἐγκέφαλος, 309
ἐγκοίμησις, 16
ἐγκύκλιος παιδεία, 300
ἔθνη, 116
Εἱμαρμένη, ix, 14–15, 48, 109, 263–72, 304–5, 339
Εἰρήνη, 12
ἐκκλησία, 255
ἔκφρων, 351
ἐνύπνιον, 144
ἐξ τοῦ σώματος, 350
ἐξεστήκοσιν, 351
ἐπέφραδεν, 186
ἐπήκοος, 14
ἐπιθυμεῖν, 11
ἐπιθυμία, 327, 332–33, 354
ἐπιμέλεια(ι), 343, 354
ἐπιμελεῖσθαι, 340, 354
ἐπιμελεῖσθαι σαυτόν, 354
ἐπιμελεῖσθαι σεαυτοῦ, 340
ἐποπτεία, 20, 185

ἔρανοι, 21
ἑρμηνεύειν, 149
εὐάγγελος, 277
εὐαγγέλιος, 277
εὐδαιμονία, 185
εὐσέβεια, 89, 130, 154
εὐφημία, 154
εὐχαί, 151

ἡγεμών, 114, 277
ἤθεά τε ὁμότροπα, 116

θεοκρασία, 152
θεῶν ἱδρύματα τε κοινὰ καὶ θυσίαι, 116
θεωρία, 45
θίασοι, 21, 249
θνητοὶ ἄνθρωποι, 191
θυμός, 309

ἰδιῶται, οἱ, 242
ἱερά, 200
ἱεροφάνται τῶν χθονίων θεῶν, 200
Ἶσις Τύχη Ἀγαθή, ix

καθαρμός, 185
καρδία, 309
κῆρ, 309
κοινή, 72
κοινωνίαν, 254
κοινωνικὸν ἄνθρωπος (ἐστὶ) ζῷον, 21
κρίνω, 148
κυκεών, 219

λεγόμενα, 181, 185–87
ληρεῖν, 351
λογισμὸς καὶ νοῦς ἀληθινός, 351
λόγος, 48

μαινομένοις, 351
μέριμνα, 343
μετὰ τὰ φυσικὰ βιβλία, 125
μοῖρα, ix, 304
μυεῖν, 132
μύσται, 186
μυστήρια, 52, 134 n. 47

νοήματα, 218

Ξένιος, 277
ὁ ἡγούμενος τοῦ λόγου, 277
ὁ φαῦλος ὄχλος, 291, 355
οἱ πολλοί, 291, 355
ὄλβιος (-οι), 187, 190–91
ὁμόαιμος, 116
ὁμόγλωσσος, 116
ὁμοίωσις θεῷ, 133
Ὁμόνοια, 12
ὄναρ, 144
ὀνειροερμηνεία, 149
ὀνειροκρίτες, 149
ὄνειρος, 144
ὄργια, 338
ὅριος, 277

παῖδες, 353
παῖδες θεοῦ, 353
Πανθέα, 14
πάντων τῶν ἔχω, 351
παρεπιδημοῦντες, 21
πατρίδος, 353
πεπρωμένη, 266–67
περὶ τῶν ἀνθρωπίνων πραγμάτων, 270
περὶ τῶν ὄντων, 350
Πλατανόπολις, 291, 356–57
ποθεῖν, 11
πόλις (-εις), 10, 116, 188
πράγματα, 271
πρᾶξις, 45
πρεσβευτής, 276, 278 n. 16
πρόγνωσις, 89
πρόνοια, 264 n. 3, 268, 271
πρόνοια θεοῦ, 271
πρὸς τὸ εἴσω πάντες, 351

ῥήτωρ, 244

σοφοί, οἱ, 242
σπέρμα, 326–27, 332–33
σπορά, 326–27, 332
σπουδαῖος, 351
στεμμάτων ἐπίδεσις, 185
στενάζειν, 11

στοιχεῖα τοῦ κόσμου, 92, 270
στόματι μαινομένῳ, 351
συγκρητίζω, 104
συγκρητισμός, 103
σύλλογοι, 21
συνκεράννυμι, 103
σχίζω, 39
Σώτειρα Τύχη, 13

τάξις, 149
τέκνων ἐπιμέλειαι, 354
Τελεστήριον, 186
τελετῆς παράδοσις, 185
τέμενος, 205
τιμή, 190–91, 197
τιμὴν ἄφθιτον, 191
τὸ κοινόν . . . κατὰ πολιτείαν, 355
τοῦ ἔχω, 351
τοῦ θεοῦ ἐπαφή, 354
Τύχη, 13, 39
τύχη, ix, 106, 268 n. 15, 304
Τύχη Ἀγαθή, ix
Τύχη Πόλεως, 14

ὑγροὶ σώματι, 291, 355
υἱοθεσία(ν), 134, 255, 329
υἱός, 326
ὕπαρ, 144

φθίμενος, 191
φιλοσοφία, 263 n. 2, 355
φράζω, 186
φρατρίαι, 116
φρατρίες, 10
φροντίδας βίου, 341
φροντίδος, 342
φροντίς, 343
φυλαί, 10, 116
Φύσις, 268

χειροτεχνία, 355
χρηματισμός (-οί), 144
χρῆσθαι θεοῖς κατὰ τὰ πάτρια, 15
χῶρα, 188, 191

C. Latin Words

adoptatio, 135
adoptio, 331

centuria(e), 249
centurio primi pili, 249
cohortes, 249
collegia, viii, 41–42, 55 n. 50, 62, 249, 254, 256, 258
confusio, 103
cubicula, 251

devotio(nes), 151, 153
dividuus, 22

explananda, 310
explanans, 310

fortuna, ix, 42, 70, 254, 293, 304
Fortuna, 13, 39, 106
fratres, 254

gens, 52, 58, 330
gentiles, 330

Homo sapiens, x, 66–67, 70, 129, 211, 232 n. 2, 247, 254, 313, 316

imperium, 21, 36, 40, 73
incubatio, 16
individuus, 22
initia, 52, 134 n. 47
interpretatio, 16
interpretatio graeca, 16, 101

loculi, 251

manipuli, 249
mos maiorum, 12
mutatis mutandis, 1, 21

Orbis, 17

pater, 58, 244, 254
patria potestas, 330–31
pax romana, 1, 8, 12, 18, 73
pietas, 89, 130, 154

religio, 17
renatus, 135
res gestae populi Romani, 87

sacra peregrina, 17, 31
sacra publica, 17, 31
sarcophagi, 251
sodales, 249
sui generis, 35, 119–20 n. 38, 124, 136, 207, 223
superstitions, 17
tabula rasa, 310

tituli, 251

Urbs, 17

votum, vota, 151, 153

www.ingramcontent.com/pod-product-compliance
Lightning Source LLC
Chambersburg PA
CBHW051204300426
44116CB00006B/432